Powers of the Presidency

Powers of the
Presidency

CQ

Washington, D.C.

Congressional Quarterly Inc.

Congressional Quarterly Inc., an editorial research service and publishing company, serves clients in the fields of news, education, business, and government. It combines Congressional Quarterly's specific coverage of Congress, government, and politics with the more general subject range of an affiliated service, Editorial Research Reports.

Congressional Quarterly publishes the *Congressional Quarterly Weekly Report* and a variety of books, including college political science textbooks under the CQ Press imprint and public affairs paperbacks on developing issues and events. CQ also publishes information directories and reference books on the federal government, national elections, and politics, including the *Guide to the Presidency*, the *Guide to Congress*, the *Guide to the U.S. Supreme Court*, the *Guide to U.S. Elections*, *Politics in America*, and *Congress A to Z: CQ's Ready Reference Encyclopedia*. The *CQ Almanac*, a compendium of legislation for one session of Congress, is published each year. *Congress and the Nation*, a record of government for a presidential term, is published every four years.

CQ publishes *The Congressional Monitor*, a daily report on current and future activities of congressional committees, and several newsletters including *Congressional Insight*, a weekly analysis of congressional action, and *Campaign Practices Reports*, a semimonthly update on campaign laws.

An electronic online information system, Washington Alert, provides immediate access to CQ's databases of legislative action, votes, schedules, profiles, and analyses.

JK
511
.P75
1989

Copyright © 1989 Congressional Quarterly Inc.
1414 22nd Street N.W., Washington, D.C. 20037

Printed in the United States of America

Library of Congress Cataloging-in-Publication Data
Powers of the presidency.
    p.   cm.
    Includes bibliographical references.
    ISBN 0-87187-520-9:
    1. Executive power--United States--History. 2. Presidents--United States--History. I. Congressional Quarterly, inc.
JK511.P75 1989
353.03--dc20   89-17369
                                      CIP

Authors: Harold F. Bass, Jr.; W. Craig Bledsoe; Christopher J. Bosso; Daniel C. Diller; Dean J. Peterson; James Brian Watts
Editors: Margaret Seawell Benjaminson, Michael Nelson, John L. Moore
Production Assistant: Jamie R. Holland
Indexer: Patricia R. Ruggiero
Cover Designer: Ed Zelinsky

Congressional Quarterly Inc.

Andrew Barnes *Chairman and President*
Wayne P. Kelley *Publisher*
Neil Skene *Executive Editor*
John J. Coyle *General Manager*
Robert E. Cuthriell *Director of Development*

Book Division

Book Editorial

David R. Tarr *Director, Book Department*
John L. Moore *Assistant Director*
Joanne D. Daniels *Director, CQ Press*
Nancy A. Lammers *Managing Editor*
Carolyn Goldinger *Senior Editor*
Margaret Seawell Benjaminson *Project Editor*
Ann Davies *Project Editor*
Colleen McGuiness *Project Editor*
Kerry V. Kern *Production Editor*
Nancy Kervin *Production Editor*
Ann F. O'Malley *Production Editor*
Noell H. Sottile *Production Editor*
Jamie R. Holland *Editorial Assistant*
Linda White *Administrative Assistant*

Book Marketing

Kathryn C. Suárez *Director, Book Sales and Marketing*
Jacqueline A. Davey *Library Marketing Manager*
Ellen Loerke *Assistant College Marketing Manager*
Leslie Brenowitz *Administrative Assistant*

Production

I. D. Fuller *Production Manager*
Michael Emanuel *Assistant Production Manager*
Jhonnie G. Bailey *Assistant to the Production Manager*

Table of Contents

Chief Executive

The powers of the president can be divided into two categories, *formal powers* and *inherent powers*. The president's formal powers originate in the Constitution, in acts of Congress, and in judicial interpretations. The Constitution, for example, empowers presidents to appoint members of their administrations and some federal judges. Congressional acts instruct presidents to submit annual budget requests. Supreme Court decisions authorize them to desegregate public school systems.

Inherent powers reside in the office of president and come from the job itself rather than through constitutional or statutory law. Most inherent powers derive from the loosely worded statements in the Constitution that "the executive Power shall be vested in a President" (Article II, section 1) and that the president "shall take Care that the Laws be faithfully executed" (Article II, section 3). Emergency powers invoked by presidents during wartime are examples of inherent powers. When the Japanese bombed Pearl Harbor, Franklin D. Roosevelt used his inherent powers to relocate the Japanese living in the United States.

Even though all presidents have the same formal and inherent powers, different chief executives use these powers in different ways depending on their skills, their personalities, the people who serve them, and, often, circumstances that are beyond their control. Most presidential scholars classify presidential powers according to the categories devised by presidential scholar Clinton Rossiter in *The American Presidency.* Rossiter divided the presidency into several presidential jobs, entailing both formal and inherent powers. These are the administration of government, domestic policy development and leadership, foreign policy development and leadership, the promotion of national unity, and party leadership.[1]

Over the years, presidential scholars have changed greatly in their understanding of the use of presidential power. In 1884, long before he became president, Woodrow Wilson wrote *Congressional Government,* a study of U.S. politics. Wilson described the president's business as "usually not much above routine" and "mere administration." Placing most of the burden for directing the government squarely on the shoulders of Congress, Wilson saw the president as little more than a civil servant.[2]

Presidents have always had considerable power at their disposal, however. Wilson underestimated the significance of the powerful administration of Abraham Lincoln,

who took the reins of the federal government firmly in hand during the Civil War. He also overlooked the ambiguities present in the constitutional grants of power to the presidency. The Constitution's designation of the president as commander in chief means much more in the twentieth century than simply directing U.S. military forces. It also means directing the nation's economy and foreign policy.

One hundred years after *Congressional Government* was published, political analysts' perceptions of presidential power have changed drastically to accommodate a more realistic approach. As president, Wilson himself quickly changed his view of the demands of the job. In fact, Rossiter was so impressed with the demands of the presidency that he introduced his study with a quotation from Shakespeare's *Macbeth:* "Methought I heard a voice cry 'Sleep no more!'" A few days before he was assassinated on November 22, 1963, President John F. Kennedy wrote Rossiter to comment on the use of the quote from *Macbeth.* Kennedy believed the quote to be apt but thought an even more appropriate one could be found in Shakespeare's *King Henry IV, Part I*: Glendower boasts, "I can call spirits from the vasty deep," and Hotspur replies, "Why so can I, or so can any man; but will they come when you do call for them?" Kennedy pointed to the difference between presidents' calling for action and actually accomplishing their desired goals. After almost three years in office, he understood the paradoxical nature of presidential power and its limitations.

Article II of the Constitution lists the president's powers. Although it grants far fewer explicit powers to the president than it does to Congress in Article I, the ambiguity and vagueness of the article have made it possible for presidents to expand their powers. Article II, section 1, clearly grants executive power to the president. Section 3 makes the president responsible for the execution of federal law.

In theory, these directives make the president responsible for carrying out or executing the laws of the federal government. In practice, however, the ambiguity of this mandate often has increased the power of the presidency. For example, by broadly interpreting the authority to execute the law, Grover Cleveland used federal troops to break a labor strike in the 1890s and Dwight D. Eisenhower sent troops to help integrate a public school in Little Rock, Arkansas, in 1957.

From the beginning the Framers of the Constitution expressed a great deal of uncertainty over the exact nature

By W. Craig Bledsoe and James Brian Watts

1

> The executive Power shall be vested in the President of the United States of America.
> —from Article II, section 1

of the executive. They derived many of their political ideals from seventeenth- and eighteenth-century European writers such as John Locke, Jean Jacques Rousseau and Montesquieu, whose theories emphasized both popular sovereignty and individual liberty. If the political beliefs of these writers were adopted, the chief executive would not come from a ruling class or hereditary base but instead would represent the popular will. The presidency would not be set up as a monarchy, not even a limited one. The president would be an elected public official responsible only to the people.

Still, Framers feared the effects of an unrestrained democracy. They were afraid that the chief executive might be too inclined to appeal to popular demands in ways harmful to minority rights. Consequently, they attempted to insulate the office of president by having the public participate in presidential selection only indirectly through the electoral college.

This debate on the strength of the executive spilled over into the effort to define the exact nature of the president's administrative duties. Influenced by classical liberal writers, such as Montesquieu, the Framers dispersed power by structuring an executive branch separate and independent from the legislature. In doing so, they gave the presidency sweeping administrative responsibilities to "faithfully execute" the law. But to keep the presidency from becoming too powerful, they subjected it to certain constraints by giving Congress immense powers of its own. The president has the power to appoint officials of the executive branch, but the Senate must confirm many of the appointments. And the president is in charge of administering the federal laws and programs, but Congress creates them, and it may change them at any time. Specifically, Congress can create and destroy agencies, and it determines whether they are going to be located in the executive branch or outside it. In other words, if it chooses, Congress can make an agency completely independent of the president.

The legislature also has the power of appropriation, which gives it ultimate control over federal agencies. Congress can define exactly what an agency has the power to do and not do. Consequently, as political scientist Peter Woll has observed, "Congress has virtually complete authority to structure the administrative branch and determine where formal lines of accountability shall be placed. It may or may not decide to let the President exercise various types of control." [3]

In *The Federalist Papers,* Alexander Hamilton defined the presidents' administrative activities as "mere execution" of "executive details." His was a narrow interpretation, for he in no way understood what would develop later. Hamilton, however, saw the president as the person solely responsible for administrative action. In *Federalist* No. 72 he wrote,

> The persons, therefore to whose immediate management these different [administrative] matters are committed, ought to be considered as the assistants or deputies of the chief magistrate, and on this account they ought to derive

their offices from his appointment, at least from his nomination, and ought to be subject to his superintendence. This view of the subject will at once suggest to us the intimate connection between the duration of the executive magistrate in office and the stability of the system of administration. [4]

Since the 1930s Congress has delegated to the president the broad authority to achieve several general goals. Congress will often pass laws, leaving to the president and the executive branch the discretion to define the regulations and programs to be put into effect. This practice has come into being through political events, not by design. Americans increasingly look to the president for leadership in times of crisis and in everyday affairs, making the chief executive responsible for a growing portion of the nation's successes and failures. Consequently, the administrative responsibilities of the presidency have grown tremendously. As the presidency evolved, presidents found themselves serving as chief administrators, chief personnel officers, chief financial officers, and chief law enforcers—all part of the job of "chief executive."

The President as Chief Administrator

Although the Founders placed a high priority on the presidency's executive duties, the Constitution provides very few instructions about the president's tasks as head of the executive branch. Specific presidential administrative powers have evolved as the presidency has matured.

The Constitution does not make direct provisions for the vast administrative structure that the president must oversee. It does, however, authorize the president to demand written reports from the "principal Officer in each of the executive Departments, upon any Subject, relating to the Duties of their respective Offices" (Article II, section 2). This clause implies a division of labor within the executive branch and clearly establishes an administrative hierarchy with the president as the chief administrative officer.

Similar to chief executives in private corporations, the chief executive in the White House tries to persuade subordinates in government to conform to presidential objectives. The chief executive tries to give direction to the administration. Presidents do not have time to follow through on every action taken by the bureaucratic departments and agencies directly under their control. They sit atop a federal executive structure that has 2.7 million civilian employees. They must develop techniques that give them control over this vast administrative organization. Because this organization has grown tremendously since the early days of the Republic, analysis of the president's power as chief executive entails discussion of the structure of the executive branch.

> [H]e shall take Care that the Laws be faithfully executed.
> —from Article II, section 3

Structure of the Executive Branch

Often the term *bureaucracy* is considered pejorative, for to many it suggests red tape, inflexibility, and confusion. Opposition to "big government" has become almost synonymous with opposition to bureaucracy. Political candidates from both major political parties usually decry the evils of the burgeoning U.S. bureaucracy, denouncing it for removing Americans from the decision-making process of their federal government.

Those who work in the federal bureaucratic structure—"bureaucrats"—are often criticized for being unproductive and obstinate. Political scientist Charles Goodsell has written that "the employee of bureaucracy, that 'lowly bureaucrat,' is seen as lazy or snarling, or both. The office occupied by this pariah is viewed as bungling or inhuman, or both. The overall edifice of bureaucracy is pictured as overstaffed, inflexible, unresponsive, and power-hungry, all at once." [5]

Bureaucracy, however, has a technical meaning. The German sociologist Max Weber saw the bureaucratic model of organization as one distinguished by its large size, its formulation of rules and procedures, the presence of a clear hierarchy, the systematic maintenance of records, and the employment of a full-time appointed staff who performed specific duties using technical knowledge.[6]

By this definition, a large corporation or university is a bureaucracy, and so is a government. The departments, agencies, bureaus, commissions, and offices of the executive branch make up most of the federal bureaucracy. Although not as large and usually not as visible as the executive branch, Congress and the courts have their own bureaucracies.

Despite the negative connotations of the term, a bureaucrat is simply an administrator who carries out the policies of the elected officials of government. The structure of the federal bureaucracy under the president's control can be broken down into the Executive Office of the President (EOP), the cabinet departments, the executive agencies, and the regulatory commissions.

Executive Office of the President

In 1939 Executive Order 8248 created the Executive Office of the President to advise the president and to help manage the growing bureaucracy. The EOP includes the White House Office, the Council of Economic Advisers, the National Security Council (NSC), and the Office of Management and Budget (OMB)—agencies conceived to help the president more effectively control the expanding executive branch.

Since then the EOP has grown tremendously, employing approximately eighteen hundred people in the late 1980s. Its most important components are the White House Office, the NSC, and the OMB.

The White House Office consists of the president's closest assistants. Their actual titles vary from one administration to another, but under each new president it is this group who oversees the political and policy interests of the administration. Serving as a direct extension of the president, they do not require Senate confirmation. The creation of the White House Office has allowed the president to centralize executive power within the White House at the expense of the cabinet secretaries. Henry A. Kissinger, for example, Richard Nixon's assistant for national security

affairs, forged such a strong power base in foreign affairs that his authority eventually eclipsed that of the secretary of state.

In 1947, early in the cold war, Congress passed the National Security Act, which created the NSC to help coordinate military and foreign policies. Responsible for organizing activities between the State Department and the Defense Department, the NSC has four statutory members: the president, the vice president (added in 1949), the secretary of state, and the secretary of defense. The act further names the chairman of the Joint Chiefs of Staff and the director of the Central Intelligence Agency (CIA) as advisers to the NSC.

In addition to the National Security Council but distinct from its formal members is the NSC staff. Made up of foreign policy advisers and headed by the national security adviser, the NSC staff has evolved into an apparatus used by many presidents to implement their own foreign policy goals. Since the role of the NSC and its staff is purely advisory, presidents have used it to varying degrees. President Kennedy, preferring his own close advisers, used the NSC infrequently. President Nixon, however, gave the NSC formal authority in formulating and executing foreign policy.

In 1970 President Nixon created the Office of Management and Budget to replace the Bureau of the Budget (BOB), established in 1927. As the largest of the agencies that make up the Executive Office of the President, its six hundred staff members help presidents achieve their political objectives by formulating and administering the federal budget. Departments and agencies of the executive branch must submit annual budget requests to OMB.

Besides preparing the budget, OMB serves as an important managerial tool of the president by reviewing the organizational structure and management procedures of the executive branch, assessing program objectives, and developing reform proposals. OMB has tremendous power within the federal government. President Ronald Reagan relied heavily on OMB Director David Stockman for the technical expertise necessary to implement his political objective of cutting the budget.

Cabinet Departments

The cabinet is made up of the heads—or "secretaries"—of the major departments of the government. Originally, there were only three cabinet departments—State, War, and the Treasury. By 1989, the number had grown to fourteen. Lacking any constitutional or statutory base, the cabinet is primarily an advisory group. Although presidents may work closely with individual cabinet officers, they rarely use the collective cabinet for advice. Once President Lincoln, opposed by his entire cabinet on an issue, remarked, "Seven nays, one aye; the ayes have it." President Eisenhower, holding regular cabinet meetings and listening to opinions of others, came closer than any modern president to making the cabinet a truly deliberative body.

Each cabinet secretary is appointed to head a specific department with a specific constituency. Although presidents makes their own appointments, with Senate confirmation, the power they have over a specific department is limited. One reason is that the president can appoint only a limited number of a department's employees. When President Reagan came into office in 1981, for example, he could appoint only about one hundred people to positions in the Department of Transportation, less than 1 percent of its employees.

Executive Agencies

Executive agencies are agencies or commissions that are not considered a part of the cabinet and that by law often have quasi-independent status. Examples of these executive agencies include the National Aeronautics and Space Administration (NASA), the Peace Corps, and the CIA.

The difference between a "presidential" agency and an "independent" agency is often vague. Generally, heads of presidential agencies and commissioners serve at the discretion of, and may be removed by, the president. Independent agency heads and commissioners are appointed for fixed terms of office and have some independence from the president in their operations.

Government corporations, such as the Tennessee Valley Authority (TVA), also fall under the category of executive agencies. Similar to private corporations, these organizations perform business activities such as operating a transportation system (Amtrak) or selling electricity (TVA).

Government corporations are primarily controlled by a board of directors, allowing them to be run more like a business. Since the president appoints these boards and their chairs, they have come increasingly under the control of the presidency.

Regulatory Commissions

Regulatory commissions are responsible for regulating certain segments of the economy. Many of them, such as the Food and Drug Administration (FDA) and the Occupational Safety and Health Administration (OSHA) are located within the regular departments. FDA is a part of the Department of Health and Human Services, and OSHA is in the Labor Department. Other regulatory agencies, such as the Interstate Commerce Commission, are independent in their relationship to the executive branch and so are insulated from regular presidential control and policy direction.

By statutory law each regulatory agency is governed by a bipartisan board of commissioners, who serve overlapping terms of five years or more. Although presidents have the power to appoint board members, they do not have the power to remove these appointees from office unless they can prove reasons of incompetence. This regulation ensures a certain amount of independence from executive control. Presidents cannot fire commission members simply because they do not like the policy direction of the agency, nor can they veto agency actions.

Still, presidents are able to influence the policies of regulatory commissions by choosing the commissioners and the chairs. Bipartisanship rarely means much in the composition of these boards, for presidents always have been able to name board members who share their views regardless of political party affiliation. Many conservative Democrats share the same policy beliefs as Republicans, and many liberal Republicans share the same policy beliefs as Democrats. Although commissioners serve long, overlapping terms, presidents still have the opportunity to place a majority of their appointees in any given agency.

Bureaucratic Growth and Reform

In 1789 President George Washington's administration consisted primarily of his three cabinet departments (State, Treasury, and War) and employed only a few hundred people. By 1816 the number of federal civilian employees had grown to only a little over 4,800. Only about 500 of these worked in Washington. Most of the rest were scattered throughout the country providing mail service as employees of the Post Office Department. By 1931, however, the number of federal civilian employees had reached slightly more than 600,000, and by 1953 the number had expanded to approximately 2.5 million.

Although the number of federal employees has remained relatively constant since the 1950s, federal expenditures have continued to increase. Between 1965 and 1984, federal expenditures jumped from $118 billion to $850 billion. This period also saw an increase in the number of people working for the federal government as either contractors or consultants or through grant-in-aid programs administered by state or local governments. Federal employment figures usually overlook the large and growing number of people who work indirectly for the federal government as employees of private firms and state and local governments that are largely, or entirely, funded by U.S. taxpayers. In 1978 Secretary of Health, Education and Welfare Joseph Califano observed that although his department employed almost 144,000 people, it indirectly paid the salaries of about 980,000 more in state and local governments through numerous grant-in-aid programs.[7]

Every president, eventually frustrated by the large and often unresponsive bureaucracy, talks of bureaucratic reform. When Carter came into office, he vowed to make a wholesale overhaul of the ninety-five-year-old Civil Service system, but the Civil Service Reform Act (1978) that finally passed Congress in Carter's second year in office had little effect. Campaigning for office, Carter promised to reduce the nineteen hundred existing federal agencies to two hundred. After he took office, however, the campaign promise was quickly forgotten and never appeared in the civil service reform law. In fact, in attempting to win their support for the reform measure, Carter promised Civil Service employees, "No one will be demoted, have their salaries decreased, or be fired as a result of reorganization. You need not fear that."[8]

Even the most reform-minded presidents move slowly. They must convince key members of the bureaucracy that proposed changes are worth making for the country as a whole and that they will not hurt individual bureaucrats. Thus, presidents cautiously try to persuade bureaucracies to favor their reforms. In addition, and far more important, presidents are subject to the same clientelism that afflicts an individual agency. By the time they reach office, presidents have become indebted to people who have contributed to their campaigns and helped them achieve their political stature. Rarely do they bite the hand that feeds them. Presidents are very reluctant to undermine an agency that might serve one of their clientele groups.

This is not to say that presidents have never attempted to reform the bureaucracy, however. In fact, the evolution of the federal bureaucracy has been largely a history of attempts at reform. Although these efforts were aimed at reducing the power of the bureaucracy, instead they gradually increased it. In examining these recurring efforts, presidency scholar Michael Nelson has pointed out the irony in bureaucratic reform: the disparity that existed between what the reform intended and the actual result led not to a reduction in the power and scope of bureaucracy but an increase.[9]

The Founders were ambivalent about the exact nature of the government's administrative structure and about who was to control it. The subject was not mentioned in convention debates; consequently, it was not mentioned in the Constitution. Nelson has argued that this ambivalence helped create the rapid growth that later characterized the American bureaucracy. By not specifically spelling out the exact nature of the government's administrative structure, the Founders created a situation that allowed the bureaucracy to come under the simultaneous control of both the president and Congress in the nineteenth century. As a result, the system of dual control allowed administrators to increase their own independence by playing one institution off the other. Nelson observed:

> The Constitutional Convention, in loosing the agencies from their old legislative moorings (politically necessary if the support of executive power adherents was to be won) without tying them securely to the presidency (equally politic if anti-federalist support was to be kept) forced agencies to find and exercise relatively independent power. Agencies began to learn to play one branch off another; if neither president nor Congress was supreme, then law was, and the agencies interpreted and implemented the law.[10]

Nelson concluded that the power of bureaucracy has grown in part because of the attempts to control it. For example, reformers, intent on controlling the bureaucracy by making it less susceptible to corruption, actually made it less efficient and responsible. To make it harder for public employees to defraud the government, agencies developed elaborate systems of internal checks and balances. These checks and balances took time. Efficiency, responsiveness, or some other value often was sacrificed for the sake of preventing official cheating. The cause of this irony is that administrative institutions were scarcely mentioned in the Constitution and have remained somewhat illegitimate in U.S. political culture ever since. This has forced bureaucratic agencies to rely on independent bases of political support, such as their constituent groups, for their organizational goals, coincidentally freeing them from political control.

This historical account of bureaucratic reform points out that bureaucratic power endures even throughout the most challenging of reforms. Although the historical record indicates that reformers have unintentionally increased the power and scope of bureaucracy, attempts at reform will undoubtedly continue. Future presidents, like their predecessors, will become frustrated with the sluggishness and unresponsiveness of their administrations. Efforts at deregulation, civil service reform, and cutbacks in government expenditures that aim at removing the financial support for various bureaucratic agencies therefore will continue. Political scientist Robert Sherrill has outlined the problem: "Because so many portions of the bureaucracy are no longer responsive to the needs of the general public, and because they do their narrowly selfish work without fear of reprisal from the public, it may seem useless to talk of reform. But it isn't useless to talk of reform; it is only naive to expect much."[11]

Control of the Bureaucracy

Presidents often complain that they lack sufficient control over the executive branch bureaucracy. They are quick to blame the bureaucracy for the many problems that hinder the implementation of presidential programs. Franklin Roosevelt provided one of the best-known illustrations of a president's lack of control over the bureaucracy. He is reported to have told one of his aides:

> "When I woke up this morning, the first thing I saw was a headline in the *New York Times* to the effect that our Navy was going to spend two billion dollars on a ship-building program. Here I am, the Commander in Chief of the Navy having to read about that for the first time in the press. Do you know what I said to that?"
> "No, Mr. President."
> "I said: 'Jesus Chr-rist!' "[12]

Other presidents faced similar frustrations later. Contemplating what it would be like for Eisenhower to be president rather than a general, Harry S Truman once said, "He will sit here and he will say, 'Do this! Do that!' And nothing will happen. Poor Ike—it won't be at all like the Army! He'll find it very frustrating."[13]

Chief executives expect to have their orders obeyed and their programs set in motion. Yet upon assuming office, they often find that their programs rarely are implemented as promptly or as efficiently as they would like. They must face, and learn how to manage, an obstinate and unruly bureaucracy. Frank Carlucci, President Nixon's chief assistant for bureaucratic reorganization, stated that it takes "from six to eight months for a presidential directive to be translated into agency guidelines and reach the action level." In some cases, Carlucci maintained, it could take the policy two to three years to be put into action.[14]

Controlling the bureaucracy has become a major priority for most presidents. All presidents after Franklin Roosevelt, whether liberal or conservative, have shared the desire to make the bureaucracy more responsive to their program objectives. Historian Arthur M. Schlesinger, Jr., commented, "As any sensible person should have known, the permanent government has turned out to be, at least against innovating presidents, a conservatizing rather than a liberalizing force."[15]

Presidents face a tremendous task when they try to manage the bureaucracy and make it work for them. To control a specific agency, the chief executive must know what the agency does and what it did in the past. The president must know the preferences and inclinations of its members and the pressures being put on the agency from clientele groups. In addition, the president must anticipate the political implications of the agency's actions. Ideally, the chief executive should be able to do this for the hundreds of departments, bureaus, boards, commissions, independent commissions, and pubic corporations under White House supervision. But even with the help of the Executive Office of the President, it is an almost impossible task. Presidential scholar Richard Pious wrote, "It takes a few weeks for a new administration to learn how to intervene in the affairs of a bureau; it may take a few years for the president to know enough to stay out of them."[16]

Instead of being intimately involved in every little detail of an agency's affairs, a president must learn to delegate; that is, the president must be a manager. Presidential scholar Thomas E. Cronin wrote:

He must constantly delegate, he must be most precise about what he is delegating, and he must know whether and for what reasons the agencies to which he is delegating share his general outlook. He must be sensitive to bureaucratic politics, to the incentives that motivate bureaucrats, and to the intricacies of their standard operating procedures. He must have some assurance (and hence an adequate intelligence system) that what he is delegating will be carried out properly.[17]

Unfortunately, most presidents have not done well in this respect. They often have misunderstood the bureaucracy and have concentrated on the choice rather than the implementation of policy. Political scientist Richard Rose has argued that "once in office, a president is much more concerned with choosing what to do than he is with how these decisions are implemented (that is, how choices are turned into routine government activities) or the conduct of program activities on a continuing basis."[18]

In addition to the problems of understanding the exact nature of the bureaucracy, presidents must face problems inherent in the political process itself that make it difficult to control their administrations. Upon entering office, presidents find that most bureaucratic institutions are already fixed. If they want to reorganize, as did Nixon, they run the risk of a confrontation with Congress. Consequently, few presidents attempt to risk an outcry of disapproval from a Congress that tries to protect the interests of its constituencies, who are often the clients of the existing bureaucratic agencies. Instead, newly elected presidents attempt to do the best they can with the bureaucratic structures already at their disposal.

Constitutional inhibitions also make it difficult for the chief executive to fashion the bureaucracy into a more responsive institution. Presidential programs require legislative approval and appropriations, and they are subject to review, and possible nullification, by the courts. Even with statutory and constitutional authority, the president often faces untold difficulty in making the bureaucracy more responsive. Although the Constitution charges presidents with the execution of the laws, the formal authority to take that action is often statutorily vested in a cabinet secretary or the head of a specific agency. In theory, such presidential appointees will carry out the president's objectives. In practice, however, heads of departments and agencies often operate independently of the president and are more attuned to their clientele groups than to the administration's goals.

Instruments of Presidential Control

Although the obstacles to effective management of the bureaucracy are great, presidents do have two tools that afford them at least a small measure of influence: their authority to appoint top officials and their own centralized management staff—the Executive Office of the President.

Appointments. Presidents appoint fourteen cabinet heads and some 5,200 other executive officials, including all members of the independent and regulatory agencies. In other words, presidents may hire or fire almost all of their top officials at will, except the heads of independent regulatory commissions. This authority gives them great control over their immediate aides and department and agency heads, but not over the vast majority of the executive branch.

In addition to the power of removal, presidents may

also attempt to make appointments that are ideologically compatible with their policies. President Reagan attempted to transform departments and agencies by appointing officials who shared his desire to curb the size and influence of the federal establishment. For example, Reagan appointed Thorne Auchter, an opponent of "unnecessary" federal rules, to head the Occupational Safety and Health Administration and Robert F. Burford, who helped lead a movement to return greater control of federal lands to the states, as director of the Interior Department's Bureau of Land Management. Largely successful in his efforts, Reagan proved that the federal bureaucracy can be controlled by appointing officials whose political ideology is similar to the president's. By placing loyal appointees in bureaucratic leadership positions, the chief executive can ensure that the policies bureaucracies carry out are those of the White House.

Centralized Executive Power. In 1933, Franklin Roosevelt found himself facing a bureaucracy staffed by holdovers from preceding conservative Republican administrations. He feared that his New Deal programs, if left to the discretion of these bureaucrats, would never be put into effect, at least not in the way they were intended. To ensure compliance with the intent of the New Deal legislation, he established numerous new agencies, such as the short-lived National Emergency Council, to coordinate directives through new and old agencies committed to his liberal programs. By adding on to the existing bureaucracy, Roosevelt created an organizational monster.

Roosevelt found it difficult to get the information he needed to implement his policies. Frustrated by the bureaucratic mess of his administration, he asked Congress to expand his supervisory staff. Congress agreed, and on September 8, 1939, Roosevelt issued Executive Order 8248, which established the Executive Office of the President. In so doing, Roosevelt created a miniature bureaucracy to help him control the vast executive apparatus and thus expanded the modern presidency. Rossiter described the creation of the EOP as a "nearly unnoticed but nonetheless epoch-making event in the history of American institutions."[19]

Roosevelt maintained that only a strong, well-staffed presidency could provide unity and direction to the federal government. Later presidents agreed and continued trying to centralize power within the White House to control the bureaucracy. More often than not, however, such attempts overloaded the White House staff and undermined the effectiveness of the presidency. By the early 1970s, the presidency was attempting to centralize all policy at the White House by using White House staff to oversee programs of high presidential priority.[20] In attempting to centralize power within the White House, Nixon structured his staff in a way that limited his associates to those over whom he had the most control. This attempt at centralization isolated him and put him out of touch with the rest of the government.

However interested presidents might have been in centralizing power, it did not work. The White House staff was simply not large enough to control the massive executive branch, which in the early 1970s comprised nearly 5 million military and civilian employees and spent over $300 billion annually. This points to the reality that no presidential mechanism has ever been large enough or powerful enough to control the bureaucracy.

Some scholars maintain that presidents should not be

in complete control of the bureaucracy.[21] They contend that the president's role in overseeing the success or failure of federal programs should be relinquished to the executive departments. Most federal laws, they argue, deliberately provide for discretion to be given to top departmental and agency officials.

Presidential scholar Richard Rose has pointed out that the work of the executive branch is carried out by operating departments granted specific powers and responsibilities by acts of Congress, and not by presidential delegation.[22] Therefore, both appointed and career executives should have the liberty to apply standards, revise regulations, and interpret legislative intent to fit specific situations. The president and the EOP should not be involved in most situations. These scholars hold the view that Congress is as much in charge of administration as the president, for it is Congress that creates the laws, funds the programs, and confirms the appointments.

Most presidents oppose this view. They argue that only the presidency can provide the coordination necessary to master the complexity of the federal bureaucracy. Cronin summarized the presidential perspective: "Only the president should have discretion over budget choices and the administration of federal policies. He is the one charged with faithfully executing the laws. . . . a strong presidency makes a major difference in the way government works, and . . . this difference will be in the direction of a more constructive (desirable) set of policy outcomes."[23]

This is the position that Hamilton advocated in *Federalist* No. 70: "A feeble Executive implies a feeble execution of the government. A feeble execution is but another phrase for a bad execution; and a government ill-executed, whatever it may be in theory, must be, in practice, bad government."[24]

At the heart of this argument is the idea that the government bureaucracy has become so large and diverse that the White House itself spends more time reacting to the whims of the bureaucracy than controlling it. Former presidential adviser McGeorge Bundy maintained that the executive branch often "more nearly resembles a collection of badly separated principalities than a single instrument of executive action."[25] The answer, according to this logic, is more hierarchy. An accountable president must be able to control the bureaucracy.

Information Management

Part of the problem of management is the control of information. The maxim "Knowledge is power" is never more true than in the executive branch.

Obtaining Information. Presidents must deal with a highly specialized and expert bureaucracy. How does a president gather information necessary to make informed decisions? One way is to rely on information supplied by bureaucratic agencies themselves. But if this is the chief executive's only source of information, then the presidency runs the risk of being dominated by, or dependent upon, the bureaucracy itself.

To a large extent this dependence on the bureaucracy is unavoidable. Compared with the rest of the executive branch, the president's management staff—the Executive Office of the President—is quite small, usually comprising fewer than one thousand employees.

Thus the president and the EOP must make decisions on the facts and opinions supplied by the agencies themselves, a dependence that puts the president at an obvious disadvantage. But even if the EOP were enlarged to give the presidency greater information-gathering capability, it could never become large enough to provide the president with relevant information for *all* policy decisions for every agency. As Woll has written, "The scope and technical complexity of administrative legislation and adjudication alone precludes this, even if there were no legal and political obstacles to presidential control. What is of greater importance is the fact that the president alone cannot personally comprehend these areas."[26]

Those who insist upon expansion of the EOP argue that presidents need larger staffs to channel information from the multitude of agencies for which they are responsible. Since the offices within the EOP, such as the Office of Management and Budget, are not dependent upon any clientele or constituency group but serve as the president's staff, they are viewed as being independent of the political pressures that other agencies endure. But the EOP suffers from political tensions just like any other executive bureaucracy. In examining the effects of information within the EOP, Woll described the need for presidents to be sensitive also to other major departments and agencies, such as the OMB, which have powerful support from Congress. He has observed, "Such political support has a way of showing up in the White House sooner or later, and if OMB were continually at odds with the agencies it supposedly supervises, its job would be made impossible both politically and practically."[27]

Not only do agencies outside the EOP constantly seek to channel their points of view to the White House, but EOP offices inevitably become advocates of particular viewpoints of their own. Such advocacy within the president's own management staff poses a serious problem for chief executives who attempt to remain detached from many of their top advisers in the EOP. On the one hand, such detachment allows key EOP staffers to make decisions based on their own particular interests and without presidential supervision. On the other hand, it becomes increasingly difficult for presidents to maintain the type of information surveillance necessary to remain knowledgeable and up-to-date. According to the *Report of the President's Special Review Board (Tower Commission Report)*, the involvement of Oliver North and John Poindexter in the Iran-contra scandal was the result of detachment from their key advisers. Their strong advocacy of the pro-contra position coupled with the president's lack of direction in the activities of his aides resulted in a policy disaster for the Reagan administration.[28]

Transmitting Information. Not only gathering information but transmitting information can be a big obstacle for presidents. Transmitting information from one level of the administrative hierarchy to another provides the opportunity for a portion of the information to be screened out by those who receive it and in turn send it on. Screening out information may be deliberate by those who wish to frustrate the efforts of a president, or it may be unintentional. Economist Anthony Downs estimated that as much as 98 percent of information can be lost or distorted this way.[29] With as large a bureaucratic structure as the president must attempt to control, the task of disseminating information is particularly formidable. Presidents cannot simply assume that their instructions, statements of policy, or program directives are traveling down the bureaucratic hierarchy as they intended.

To ensure that presidential communications from the EOP have been received and accurately understood, presidents must do follow-ups, that is, check for agency compliance and require regular feedback. Since administrative agencies resist supplying feedback in the same way that they resist sending information through regular channels, presidents must conscientiously monitor bureaucratic activity to maintain control at the top of the bureaucracy. The extra personnel that this requires is one reason most presidents have called for a larger EOP.

Permanent versus Presidential Government

Beneath this desire to manage the transmission of information throughout the federal bureaucracy more deliberately is an equally important motivation for greater presidential control of the bureaucracy—an antipathy and a contempt for the bureaucracy's ability to frustrate presidential policy. Most presidents never completely trust civil servants and are not completely at ease with their own political appointees. They fear that bureaucrats and department appointees develop loyalties that would obstruct presidential policy objectives. With this view comes a widely accepted belief among presidential scholars that an administration's failures result from ineffective management of the bureaucracy. Or, more specifically, an administration's failures result from the attempts of careerists (career civil servants who have made their careers in a particular department or agency) to supplant the policies of the president with those of their own agencies.

Arthur M. Schlesinger, Jr., a former Kennedy staffer, said of the Kennedy administration:

> Our real trouble was that we had capitulated too much to the existing bureaucracy. Wherever we have gone wrong ... has been because we have not had sufficient confidence in the New Frontier approach to impose it on the government. Every important mistake has been the consequence of excessive deference to the permanent government.... The problem of moving forward seemed in great part the problem of making the permanent government responsive to the policies of the presidential government.[30]

Consequently, many presidents have sought to reform the executive branch to make the bureaucracy more responsive to their policy initiatives. They want to provide the EOP with a larger staff and greater resources for coordination of the various departments and agencies and their programs. According to Cronin, these presidents see themselves as "the recipients of endless special-interest pleas and narrow-minded agitation, even from many of their own cabinet members. In its crudest form, their goal is to presidentialize the executive branch."[31] To gain control over what they perceive to be hostile environments, they push for strong bureaucratic reform measures.

Presidential scholar Louis Koenig has argued for reforms that would give presidents powerful administrative control over the bureaucracy:

> The strong presidency will depend on the chief executive's capacity to control and direct the vast bureaucracy of national administration. Ideally, the president should possess administrative powers comparable to those of business executives. What the president needs most can be simply formulated: a power over personnel policy, planning, accounting, and the administration of the executive branch that approaches his power over the executive budget.[32]

Nixon stands out among recent presidents for the depth of his animosity toward the bureaucracy and his suspicion that it sought to sabotage his administration. In line with his view of a hostile bureaucracy, he attempted to adopt strategies of governance designed to decrease the role of bureaucracy and increase the power of the White House staff. After abandoning a legislative strategy to put his stamp on domestic policy, Nixon turned to an administrative strategy that would take over the bureaucracy and concentrate on achieving policy objectives through administrative action.

Public administration scholar Richard P. Nathan referred to the Nixon administration as the "anti-bureaucracy administration." He noted that over the course of Nixon's tenure in office "there was no reduction in mistrust of the bureaucracy. On the contrary, these attitudes hardened to the point where unprecedented reorganizational steps were planned for the second term to take control of the machinery of domestic government."[33]

Hostility toward the bureaucracy could be found in several statements of Nixon's aides. One staff member referred to the "White House surrounded"—apparently by a bureaucracy more attuned to the policies of interest groups than those of the president. Another Nixon aide, former White House staff assistant Michael P. Balzano, described the federal bureaucracy in June 1972 in the following terms: "President Nixon doesn't run the bureaucracy; the civil service and the unions do. It took him three years to find out what was going on in the bureaucracy. And God forbid if any president is defeated after the first term, because then the bureaucracy has another three years to play games with the next president."[34] This view of a hostile bureaucracy probably contributed greatly to some of Nixon's later difficulties in the Watergate affair.

Nathan pointed out that Nixon's 1973 decision to develop an administrative strategy for his second term brings up an important question. What should be the role of the elected chief executive in influencing the career professionals of the executive branch agencies? Should Congress, the courts, interest groups, the press, and the public be as powerful in controlling the executive branch, or even more so? Nathan argued that the president "should have the most important role in this area of modern government. Purely as a practical matter, the chief executive is in a much better position than a large group of people in a legislative body or the courts to give cohesive policy direction and guidance to the work of large public bureaucracies."[35]

The President's Administrative Style

How the chief executive organizes the EOP affects the success of any administration. Eisenhower, pointing to the necessity of a president giving considerable thought to administrative organization, wrote, "Organization cannot make a genius out of an incompetent. On the other hand, disorganization can scarcely fail to result in inefficiency and can easily lead to disaster."[36]

Presidents have used different styles in running their administrations. Some are more comfortable with a system that is tidy and neat; others prefer a chaotic system that allows them to be innovative. In choosing their administrative style, they determine how much advice and information they want to receive from within government and how much they want to receive from outside. Their decisions on administrative style determine whether they will give competing assignments and have overlapping jurisdictions or rely on aides with specific and narrowly defined responsibilities.

The Circular System

Some presidents, such as Franklin Roosevelt and John Kennedy, did not adopt a system with rigid lines of responsibility. They gave staffers different jobs over time and nurtured a competitive spirit. In this way they hoped to find the best person for any given task. Political scientist Stephen Hess described this style of staff organization as "circular," with the president at the hub of the wheel.[37] With no chief of staff to filter out less important information or decide who can and cannot see the president, this system permits large numbers of people—staffers, cabinet secretaries, members of Congress—to have relatively easy access to the Oval Office. Top staffers report directly to the chief executive.

Roosevelt is the clearest example of a hub-of-the-wheel president. Choosing a wide-open, free-wheeling, conflict-loaded system, Roosevelt delighted in encouraging and cultivating chaos in his staff. Although it was seldom clear either to outsiders or insiders where the lines of authority ran, there was never the slightest doubt that Roosevelt was in charge.

It was not unusual for Roosevelt to assign two of his top assistants to work on the same problem without informing either of them that the other had the same task. For example, Roosevelt pitted Secretary of State Cordell Hull against Assistant Secretary of State Raymond Moley at the International Monetary and Economic Conference held in London in 1933. Assigned the responsibility of working out a policy on protective tariffs, the two men had widely differing views. Hull considered protective tariffs a terrible mistake, and Moley was convinced that they were indispensable to industrial recovery at home during the New Deal. Hull, who was chairing the U.S. delegation at the conference, was surprised when Roosevelt sent Moley

as his personal liaison when the conference stalled. Who had the most authority? Which view was closer to Roosevelt's? No one knew until Roosevelt sided with Hull. Infuriated by the whole episode, Moley resigned.

At whatever cost, Roosevelt had no intention of being isolated in the White House. He was determined to get as much information from as many people as he could, even if doing so meant duplicating assignments or bruising egos. Political scientist Frank Kessler described the Roosevelt system:

> One hundred or so persons could get to him directly by telephone without being diverted by a secretary. He employed no chief of staff and permitted few of his staffers to become subject matter specialists. Except for Harry Hopkins, to whom he turned almost exclusively for foreign policy assignments, staffers were assigned problems in a variety of areas. He wanted to be sure that no staffer would become so steeped in an issue area that he would be forced to lean on that person for advice. Everyone but FDR had to be expendable. [38]

The Hierarchical System

Other presidents, such as Dwight Eisenhower and Richard Nixon, valued formal, hierarchical relationships. They felt more comfortable with an arrangement that placed greater coordinating and integrating responsibilities upon a chief of staff. According to Hess, these presidents designed a highly structured pyramidal system with themselves at the pinnacle.[39]

Leaning heavily on his experience in the army, Eisenhower set up a pyramid with himself at the top and delegated as much responsibility to his staff as possible. The key to the operation was Chief of Staff Sherman Adams, who served, in effect, as a deputy president. Adams, a former member of Congress and governor of New Hampshire, came to the Eisenhower administration with a great deal of government experience. Eisenhower placed much confidence in Adams and would not read memos or reports coming across his desk unless his chief of staff had seen them first. Adams wrote, "Eisenhower simply expected me

The White House

Chief of Staff H. R. Haldeman, left, was called the "Berlin Wall" because he jealously guarded the entrance to the Oval Office. He is shown here meeting with President Nixon and aide C. Stanley Blair.

to man a staff that would boil down, simplify and expedite the urgent business that had to be brought to his attention and keep . . . work of secondary importance off of his desk." [40]

The Nixon administration epitomized the pyramid staffing pattern. Similar to the Eisenhower system, Nixon constructed a highly stratified organization with himself at the top and a chief of staff standing between him and the rest of the executive branch. Preferring to make decisions from option papers rather than through face-to-face communications, Nixon allowed papers to get through to him more easily than people. Nixon's chief of staff (before the Watergate scandal forced his resignation), H. R. Haldeman, became known as the "Berlin Wall" because he jealously guarded the entrance to the Oval Office. Few staff members could get around Haldeman to see the president. Kessler has told the following story: "Once Federal Reserve Board Chairman Arthur Burns met Nixon for his allotted ten minutes but, on his way out, he remembered something else he wanted to tell the president. Haldeman reportedly thrust his arm across the doorway telling Burns to make another appointment." [41]

While Nixon's operation was successful in freeing the president to think out broad policy initiatives, Haldeman often was criticized for keeping too tight a reign on who got in to see the president. Critics argued that Haldeman took too much responsibility upon himself. But two other chief Nixon aides, speechwriter William Safire and National Security Adviser Henry A. Kissinger, contend that Haldeman was performing the very role that the president assigned him. They maintain that Nixon wanted to be protected from the "unnecessary" intrusions of his lower staff. [42] Haldeman himself reportedly once insisted, "Every president needs an S.O.B., and I'm Nixon's."

Hybrid Systems of Carter and Reagan

Jimmy Carter and Ronald Reagan provide an interesting contrast in presidential leadership styles. Neither fits neatly into either the hub-of-the-wheel or the pyramid administrative system; rather, they adopted hybrids of each style. Carter is an example of a president devoted to details and involved in the minutiae of office. Reagan, more in line with the traditional pyramid style of management, is an example of a president who values delegation, one who prefers to be free from all the small details of the presidency.

When Carter entered office, he professed to be a proponent of cabinet government and promised a decentralized system of administration, one in which great amounts of authority would be delegated to the department secretaries. He proclaimed, "I believe in cabinet administration. There will never be an instance while I am president where members of the White House staff dominate or act in a superior position to the Cabinet." [43] Yet, just two and one-half years after his inauguration, power within his administration had concentrated in the office of presidential assistant Hamilton Jordan. As Carter's term progressed, the role of the White House staff increased at the expense of the various departments and agencies in the executive branch.

Part of the reason Carter's commitment to cabinet government did not last can be found in a personal work style that proved cumbersome in the White House. Because of his predilection for immersing himself in detail,

Carter spent much time consuming large amounts of factual information. Early in his administration, senior career civil servants from OMB were astounded to learn that they were to brief Carter personally rather than his top aides on the defense budget. Once, in a meeting that lasted from 3:00 p.m. to 11:00 p.m., the president devoured every piece of information that OMB could feed him. This commitment to detail pushed the administration away from a hub-of-the-wheel approach to a more structured one. Political scientist Colin Campbell has suggested, "Every fiber of Carter's personal makeup had actually been conspiring all along to run a highly centralized administration. Here the president's tendency to engross himself in details served as the fifth column." [44]

Carter originally organized his staff along functional lines rather than strict lines of command. He devised three administrative levels: the president at the top, nine key aides on the next level, and the rest of the bureaucracy below. He planned no pecking order. All of his aides, especially those on the level right below him, would have equal access to the president. Yet, despite Carter's commitment to cabinet government, a natural hierarchy developed

Jimmy Carter Library

Even though President Jimmy Carter organized his White House staff with no formal pecking order, Hamilton Jordan, right, and Jody Powell became his closest advisers. By Carter's third year in office, Jordan had become his official chief of staff.

Treasury Department   Sue Klemens   Roger Sandler

In the early years of Ronald Reagan's White House, authority was divided among these advisers: from the left, James A. Baker III, chief of staff; Edwin Meese III, counselor to the president; and Michael K. Deaver, who scheduled appointments.

within the presidential staff. By the end of the second year of the Carter administration, two long-time campaign aides, Hamilton Jordan and Jody Powell, became Carter's closest advisers. By July 1979 Jordan had moved from the second level of equals in Carter's initial staff structure to his de facto chief of staff.

Thirty-one months into his administration, Carter finally appointed Jordan as his formal chief of staff. The addition of a chief of staff should have freed Carter from the minutiae of the presidency, but his passion for details continued throughout his tenure in office. Kessler wrote, "Often he overlooked the big picture because he was bogged down in particulars. Memos that crossed his desk in the Oval Office were often returned to the sender with Carter's comments penciled in the margin. He went so far as to correct his young staffer's grammar." [45]

Under Jordan's direction, the White House began to solidify its control over bureaucratic operations. In the first few months of the Carter administration, cabinet secretaries and the heads of many other agencies had enjoyed great latitude in appointing people to fill vacancies. Personnel officers in each of the departments eventually were told, however, that the White House wanted to be consulted on all appointments to high government positions—a major blow since the departments had been promised great flexibility and control over their own affairs.

In contrast to Carter, Reagan cared little for the details of the presidency. Throughout his administration, he conveyed almost a nonchalance about such specifics. Preferring one page mini-memos that boiled down even the most complex issues to the bare essentials, Reagan operated largely through massive delegation of duties. He maintained a "nine-to-five" schedule characteristic of pyramid presidents who prefer delegation to detail.

During the 1980 campaign, however, Reagan, like Carter, had stated his intention to establish a cabinet government. And, like Carter, he gradually discarded the idea. He chose instead a modified pyramid form of staffing in which authority was divided between Chief of Staff James A. Baker III and Edwin Meese III, who served as counsellor to the president. Baker was charged with handling political matters and selling the president's programs to the public, the press, Congress, and interests groups. Meese was charged with policy formulation. In addition, Michael K. Deaver became part of the inner circle of advisers who had easy access to Reagan. Deaver's responsibilities included scheduling, appointments, and travel.

Reagan's modified pyramid incorporated some important aspects of the hub-of-a-wheel approach to organizing the presidency. By dividing power among Baker, Meese, and Deaver, he gave these three aides almost unlimited access in his first term. This arrangement kept him from becoming completely isolated, as Nixon had become by having only a single chief of staff in Haldeman. Meese served as Reagan's political conscience, keeping him true to his conservative policy goals. And Baker and Deaver helped him undertake the practical aspects of policy implementation. It was a system that suited Reagan's personality and one with which he was quite comfortable.

Once in office Reagan exercised great control over the appointment process in the departments and agencies, thereby imposing exceptional discipline on his administration. By ensuring the ideological compatibility of his nominees, Reagan could delegate and not worry about subordinates sabotaging his programs. Reagan's most effective source of discipline early in his administration, however, was the OMB under the direction of David Stockman (1981-1985). By mastering the intricacies of the budget process and controlling the budgets of the various departments and agencies, Stockman was able to impose a stringent regimen on the departments and agencies and bring them under the policy directions of the Reagan administration.

How successful was Reagan's tight discipline and modified pyramid in formulating and implementing presidential initiatives? Many who served in the Reagan administration give the president credit for energetically involving himself in important issues such as tax reform and contra funding. One aide stated:

> One thing that Reagan does is, when push comes to shove, he'll stay up all night. I mean he will get involved at the important moment.... Reagan is usually above the fray except where he thinks the president's getting involved will make a difference.... But he has a ruthless sense of priorities. He really knows that he can accomplish a few things. He's going to pick some good people and let them handle the rest. [46]

The success of the kind of system Reagan used depends on the president's knowing when to become involved in details and which issues merit concentrated attention. Yet the president must have a certain amount of knowledge even to decide which issues not to concentrate on. In several instances Reagan lacked the depth of knowledge in a specific policy area to make this determination. In 1982 a member of the NSC staff made the following statement about Reagan's lack of background in national security policy:

David Stockman, Reagan's first director of the Office of Management and Budget, imposed strict budgetary discipline on the administration's departments and agencies.

Karen Ruckman

We really operate a bottom-up system. The president has a good overall idea of where he wants to go. When specific decisions are brought to him, I think he makes them with enormous good sense and skill. But, there's not really much push coming from him in the form of initiatives or unifying policies at an early stage. It's more waiting for the issues to come up when they get critical. [47]

In 1987 the *Tower Commission Report* confirmed this assessment of Reagan's delegation of power. Charging that President Reagan delegated too much authority to the NSC without following up on its activities, the report noted that Reagan did not give enough attention to important details of security policy. His inattention resulted in the secret sale of military equipment to Iran and the diversion of funds to assist U.S.-backed forces in Nicaragua during 1985 and 1986. This undertaking, which came to be known as the Iran-contra affair, became the subject of much public attention and embarrassment to the Reagan administration. The *Tower Commission Report* concluded that Reagan's management style put too much responsibility for policy review and implementation on the shoulders of his advisers. It stated, "The president should have ensured that the NSC system did not fail him. He did not force his policy to undergo the most critical review of which the NSC participants and the process were capable.... Had the president chosen to drive the NSC system, the outcome could well have been different." [48]

Congressional Oversight

Article I, section 1, of the Constitution states that "all legislative powers herein granted shall be vested in a Congress of the United States, which shall consist of a Senate and a House of Representatives." Section 8 lists specific congressional powers and gives Congress all powers "necessary and proper" to implement them. Over the years these provisions have been used to establish administrative agencies such as the General Accounting Office to implement congressional policies. The constitutional grants of authority have given Congress the power of life and death over these administrative agencies.

Since Congress has the power to enact laws and create and abolish executive branch agencies without presidential consent, members of Congress have significant opportunities to tell the bureaucracy what to do and how to do it. Most programs enacted into law by Congress are technical and complex, however. As a result, Congress usually states general goals to be achieved by programs administered through bureaucratic agencies.

The Economic Opportunity Act of 1964, for example, states that the poor should have "maximum feasible participation" in the administration of the programs of the Office of Economic Opportunity (OEO). The interpretation of the act was left entirely to OEO and its local branches. Congress occasionally specifies very precise standards that eliminate bureaucratic discretionary power, as it did in the Securities Act of 1933, but not often.

The very size of the *Federal Register,* a journal published each weekday in which agencies announce and publicize all the new rules and regulations used in administering programs, indicates the amount of freedom agencies have in interpreting congressional intent. Delegating this authority to the bureaucracy allows Congress to keep its workload manageable. Otherwise, the volume and complexity of its work would allow Congress to accomplish little.

By giving agencies considerable leeway in realizing their objectives, however, Congress abrogates a certain amount of control over the bureaucracy. Thus, a great deal of public policy is made by the bureaucracy, without any direct input from Congress. Since administrative agencies have wide latitude in promulgating regulations and establishing policies, the burden of reconciling conflicts among competing interest groups often falls on the bureaucracy rather than on Congress. Woll has written, "Theoretically, Congress still retains the primary legislative power, and is merely appointing an agent to act for it; in fact, however, virtually complete legislative discretion is given to the designated agency or to the President." [49]

Although Congress delegates to executive branch agencies much of its authority to make and implement policy, it retains considerable influence through a variety of activities known collectively as *congressional oversight.*

Through laws and precedents, Congress has developed procedures that allow it to monitor the way the bureaucracy exercises its delegated authority.

The Legislative Reorganization Act of 1946 requires congressional committees continuously to oversee those agencies that they created or that fall under their jurisdiction. For many years after passage of this act, members of Congress were more interested in creating new laws than in monitoring ones they had already made; oversight, therefore, was not a major concern of the committees. With the growth of grant-in-aid programs in the 1960s and 1970s, which gave state and local governments federal funds to administer specific programs in areas such as highways, hospitals, and welfare services, interest groups and state and local officials encouraged legislative oversight of agencies providing goods and services to constituents.

The Legislative Reorganization Act of 1970 increased the capability of Congress to oversee federal programs by giving committees additional staffing and funds to retain outside experts. In addition, the 1970 legislation increased the resources of the General Accounting Office (GAO)—created by Congress in 1921 to oversee the expenditures of the executive branch—and gave it power to review and analyze government programs whenever a congressional committee ordered it to do so. As a consequence GAO hired economists, systems analysts, engineers, and management consultants to help monitor and analyze programs requested by Congress. Despite the Pentagon's objections, during the 1970s approximately twelve hundred of GAO's twenty-seven hundred professional staff spent their time auditing and evaluating Department of Defense programs.[50]

Since legislation can allow considerable latitude in an agency's interpretation of congressional intent, the tools provided by GAO go a long way in giving committees a better capacity to monitor agency actions. In addition to GAO monitoring, committees can hold either regular hearings or special investigations on specific aspects of a program. They also can monitor an agency's actions through informal means, such as phone calls and visits with bureaucrats, lobbyists, and constituents. Program evaluations, done by either the committee's staff or GAO, often provide ways in which the agency's actions can be changed to bring it into line with what Congress intended.

The Legislative Veto

Congressional committees increasingly require bureaucratic agencies to meet specifications for their programs set forth by the committees themselves. These requirements provide committees a formal veto over executive actions and give them authority to approve or disapprove specific actions of the agency. In recent years the Armed Services committees have controlled the openings and closing of military bases; the public works committees have controlled contracts for capital expenditures; the House Interior and Insular Affairs Committee has controlled locations of regional offices; and the House Post Office and Civil Service Committee has located postal buildings, all through the legislative veto system. Describing the effects of legislative control over the bureaucracy, political scientist Allen Schick had noted that by 1983 "Congress had adopted more than 250 veto provisions; of these, more than half were enacted during the 1970s."[51]

The legislative veto was first written into legislation used by President Herbert C. Hoover in his attempt to reorganize the executive branch. In 1932 Congress passed a joint resolution that allowed Hoover to reorganize executive agencies but specified that his changes would not take effect for ninety days. During this time either house of Congress by a simple resolution could veto his reorganizations, but they did not.

Perhaps the best example of the use of a legislative veto comes from the Joint Committee on Atomic Energy (JCAE) in the 1950s. In setting up the Atomic Energy Commission, Congress required that agency to keep the JCAE informed on the development of its nuclear reactor programs. As Pious concluded, "In effect that provision made the committee a 'board of directors' that supervised the peaceful development of atomic energy. The committee determined what technology would be advanced, the location of experimental facilities, and policies relating to the private development of commercial power plants."[52]

Congress argues that the legislative veto is the most effective tool possible to ensure that the president and the bureaucracy conform to the intent of legislation. Many presidents, however, view the legislative veto as a violation of the doctrine of the separation of powers and as an unconstitutional encroachment into the powers of the presidency. Although the legislative veto has been challenged by various presidents and their attorneys general, not until 1983 did the Supreme Court rule on this congressional power, finding it unconstitutional.

Critics of congressional oversight and the legislative veto also argue that rather than allowing committees to oversee agencies effectively, the legislative veto gives too much influence to interest groups. They contend that "alliances" between the agency, its constituent group, and its congressional committee supersede the ability of the committee to monitor agency activities objectively. According to this theory, because the congressional committee is "captured" by the interest groups it serves, its oversight of agencies and programs will be biased to benefit the constituent groups.

Problems of Presidential Control

Congressional oversight and the legislative veto make it much more difficult for the president to control the bureaucracy. Through a variety of oversight techniques, Congress has made significant gains in controlling both foreign and domestic bureaucratic agencies. Congressional oversight helped thwart the efforts of the executive branch in its bombing of Cambodia in 1973 and inhibited various other covert intelligence activities during the Nixon years. In fact, political scientists Thomas Franck and Edward Weisband argued that executive dominance in foreign policy has been replaced by a system of policy codetermination in which power is shared by the president and Congress.[53]

As a result, presidents have learned to live with congressional efforts at bureaucratic control, often signing bills that include oversight and veto provisions not completely to their liking. Franklin Roosevelt signed the lend lease bill under which he lent American destroyers to Great Britain before the United States officially entered World War II, and other wartime measures that gave him extensive war powers, despite the constraints that Congress put on him. Nixon signed the 1974 Impoundment Control Act granting him authority to defer the spending of funds already appropriated by Congress, although either house could veto his actions. Almost any provision that delegates congressional authority to the executive branch will contain provisions for legislative review.

Presidential control of the bureaucracy, however, has not been replaced by congressional control. Congress is much too large and much too overworked to provide effective control over the bureaucracy. According to Pious, "Although Congress' oversight role has increased in recent years, it should not be exaggerated. It is still intermittent, especially in the Senate, where members are spread too thin, serving on too many committees and subcommittees to develop expertise in agency operations."[54]

In June 1983, *Immigration and Naturalization Service v. Chadha*, the Supreme Court held the legislative veto to be unconstitutional. It found that the Constitution positively requires in Article I that "every order, resolution, or vote to which the concurrence of the Senate and House of Representatives may be necessary . . . shall be presented to the president of the United States" who must either approve it or veto it.[55] In other words, the president must concur in any action that Congress takes that has the force of law, including the legislative veto. Yet, since the *Chadha* decision, Congress has passed several laws containing legislative vetoes. And these laws have yet to be challenged in court.

Reorganization Power

Because the president and Congress often find themselves opposing each other for control of the bureaucracy, presidents frequently look to reorganization as a means of gaining the upper hand and increasing their ability to manage their administrations. Presidents have attempted countless reorganization plans, however, only to find that the affected agencies are strongly protected by their sponsoring congressional committees. Without the cooperation of Congress, it is extremely difficult for presidents to effect any reorganization plan for making the bureaucracy more efficient.

Every president wants to coordinate policy-making efforts as much as possible, but because the number of federal programs has increased rapidly, coordination of the the many agencies and departments is difficult. In the area of transportation policy alone, the president must work not only with the Department of Transportation but also with the Interstate Commerce Commission, the National Transportation Safety Board, and the Federal Maritime Administration, and other agencies involved in transportation policy. This overlap among the agencies means that the executive branch often wastes time and effort trying to manage the development and implementation of public policy.

Brownlow Commission

The first real effort at administrative reorganization recognized these problems of inefficiency in the executive branch. Franklin Roosevelt wanted to establish a line of command that ran directly from the White House through the department secretaries to their subordinates. In March 1936 he created the Committee on Administrative Management and gave it the task of planning the overhaul of the executive branch. With Louis D. Brownlow as its chairman and political scientists Charles E. Merriam and Luther Gulick as the other members, the Brownlow Commission concluded in 1937 that the executive branch under Roosevelt had become so complex that "the president needs help." [56]

The Brownlow Commission specifically recommended that the president receive increased administrative support. It proposed the creation of six new presidential assistants, "possessed of high competence, great physical vigor, and a passion for anonymity," who would be assigned at presidential discretion. In addition, it recommended that discretionary funds be put at the presidency's disposal to allow him to acquire more help as needed. Finally, the commission proposed a major organizational addition to the presidency, consisting of the Executive Office of the President with the Bureau of the Budget as its centerpiece.[57]

With the exception of placing the Civil Service Commission under the control of the White House, Roosevelt won approval from Congress in 1939 for most of the Brownlow Commission's recommendations. He was given reorganization authority for a two-year period. In addition, Roosevelt was permitted to hire the six assistants that the Brownlow Commisison recommended.

In Reorganization Plan No. 1, the president moved three EOP offices—the Bureau of the Budget, the Central Statistical Board, and the National Resources Planning Committee—into the State, War, and Navy Building next-door to the White House. Soon after Reorganization Plan

No. 1, Roosevelt issued an executive order that delineated the organization and responsibilities of the newly expanded presidency. This order detailed the formal relationships in the EOP between the White House Office, the BOB, and the remaining agencies of the executive branch.

Although Roosevelt got much of what the Brownlow Commission had recommended, the reorganization bill that finally passed Congress in 1939 was less than what he had hoped. The original bill was introduced in 1937 and became embroiled in Roosevelt's attempt to modify the composition of the Supreme Court. The final bill was a compromise and lacked most of Roosevelt's initial proposals. Peri E. Arnold has written, "It [the Reorganization Act of 1939] was on its face a congressional product, drafted under the guidance of Representative Lindsay Warren (Dem., N.C.) as a way of short-circuiting the intense, negative connection between presidential strength and the reorganization program." [58]

Even so, the main thrust of the Brownlow Commission recommendations were preserved, not only in the commission's structural recommendations but also in its desire to strengthen the president's control over the administration. Although Congress has been reluctant to go along completely with presidential recommendations to extend top-level management, it has allowed presidents gradually to centralize control over the bureaucracy in the EOP.

First Hoover Commission

The next major effort at centralizing presidential control occurred during the Truman administration. After large gains in the congressional elections of 1946, Republicans anticipated the end of the Truman presidency in 1948. The Republican-controlled Congress approved legislation to help a new president grapple with the problems of executive branch organization by setting up the Commission on the Organization of the Executive Branch of the Government. In 1947 Truman appointed former president Herbert Hoover as chairman.

Hoover set about the task of evaluating the effectiveness of executive branch organization with much enthusiasm. Truman, who could have viewed the commission as a means of criticizing his administration, also was enthusiastic about the project and gave it his full cooperation. It is one of the ironies of the U.S. presidency that Truman would be the one to benefit from the Hoover Commission's efforts when the Republicans failed to capture the presidency in 1948.

The Hoover Commission report recommended 277 specific measures that would institute "a clear line of control from the president to these departments and agency heads and from them to their subordinates ... cutting through the barriers that have in many cases made bureaus and agencies practically independent of the chief executive." [59] The commission's report charged that the executive branch was unmanageable; its lines of communication and authority were confusing, and there were too few tools at the top for the development of effective policy.

The commission suggested three major areas of reform. First, department heads should assume the major authority within their departments rather than allowing it to reside in the bureau chiefs. This recommendation was aimed at overcoming the congressional practice of vesting statutory powers directly in agency chiefs. With department heads more easily held responsible to the president, the lines of authority and responsibility would be more distinct. Second, the commission wanted to achieve greater clarity of direction and greater control by grouping the executive branch agencies into departments "as nearly as possible by major purposes in order to give a coherent mission to each department." [60] Third, the commission recommended that the EOP be strengthened by giving the president a stronger staff, including a staff secretariat in the White House. The president should have absolute freedom in dealing with this staff, giving it shape and appointing its members.

Truman enthusiastically supported the commission's recommendations. In addition, both Congress and the public gave their support to most of the report's proposals. The most important recommendations were realized. Recommendations for increased presidential staff and discretion in the use and organization of the EOP were implemented. And, following the commission's proposals, the Post Office, and the Departments of Interior, Commerce, and Labor were reorganized. The NSC and a number of independent agencies, including the Civil Service Commission and the Federal Trade Commission, also were reorganized.

By and large, the success of the reforms reflected the depoliticized nature of the report. Hoover and his commission approached the presidency solely in managerial terms without engaging in political ideology. Arnold has observed, "At one and the same time, reorganization planning aimed at strengthening the presidency while presenting the issue of enhanced presidential capacity as merely managerial and irrelevant to politics. Herbert Hoover and his commission of 1947-1948 present perhaps the most successful application of that logic within reorganization planning's history." [61]

Second Hoover Commission

When Dwight Eisenhower came to office in 1952, he faced a bureaucracy that had grown tremendously since Hoover, the last Republican president. After twenty years of Democratic control of the presidency, few Republicans had experience in running the federal government. In fact, after years of opposing big government and big spending, Republicans now found themselves in charge of the same bloated government they had criticized. Further complicating things for Eisenhower was a bureaucracy composed mostly of Democrats appointed under Democratic presidents. Searching for a way to make the executive branch more responsive to his leadership, Eisenhower in 1953 called once more on Hoover—at that time seventy-nine years old—to head the second Commission on the Organization of the Executive Branch of Government (the Second Hoover Commission).

The First Hoover Commission had been interested primarily in improving the administrative management of the executive branch; the Second Hoover Commission centered on issues of policy and function. At the heart of its recommendations was the idea that the executive branch should reduce its scope, saving money, reducing taxes, and eliminating competition with the private sector. The Second Hoover Commission had a specific conservative ideological agenda that aimed at reducing the growth of the government since the time of the New Deal. It argued that many of the Roosevelt era programs and agencies had become counterproductive.[62] The commission was more concerned with prescribing what government should do rather than how it should be organized and managed.

Most of the commission's recommendations were of only indirect value to the Eisenhower administration as it wrestled with the problems of a massive executive bureaucracy. For the first time, however, a major reorganization report dealt with the relations between political appointees and career public servants. Among its specific recommendations was the creation of a "Senior Civil Service" comprising approximately three thousand upper-level career executives serving in administrative positions. The commission proposed that these senior civil servants be able to transfer from one agency to another, if their particular skills and competencies suited those agencies. These senior civil servants would constitute a personnel pool that would be rotated regularly to improve management quality. The idea finally became incorporated into general personnel practices in the executive branch with the establishment of the Senior Executive Service in 1978.

Ash Council

In April 1969, Richard Nixon sought to simplify the domestic side of policy making in the executive branch by creating the Advisory Council on Executive Organization. Intending to use private sector reform in reorganization planning for his administration, Nixon appointed industrialist Roy Ash, president of Litton Industries, as chairman and four other private citizens to the council. Known as the Ash Council, the reorganization group set out to address three problems. First, it examined the executive branch's response to increasing demands on the federal government. Second, it gave attention to the organization problems that occurred among the more than 150 departments, offices, and agencies in the executive branch. Third, the council evaluated the organizational complications resulting from intergovernmental relations.[63]

The Ash Council recommended that the executive branch's domestic programs should be directed by a small number of major purpose super-departments. The council believed that this reorganization not only would save the government money but also would increase the effectiveness of executive branch management. Specifically, the council proposed that departments be set up in which the secretary would be assisted by a small number of secretarial officers who held department-wide responsibilities. Secretarial officers would include a deputy secretary who would serve as an alter-ego and department manager for the secretary, two under secretaries, several assistant secretaries, and a general counsel. The recommendations pointed to a desire to "facilitate decentralized management while simultaneously providing for effective secretarial control and department cohesion." [64]

President Nixon sent four departmental reorganization proposals to Congress on March 25, 1971. These proposals would have abolished seven existing departments and replaced them with four new super-departments. The new Department of Natural Resources would have merged the Interior Department with parts of Agriculture, Defense, and Commerce. The Department of Health, Education, and Welfare would have become the Department of Human Resources. The Department of Community Development would have combined Housing and Urban Development with some of the remaining parts of the Agriculture. The Department of Economic Affairs would have combined Labor with parts of Commerce. None of the departmental bills ever got out of their congressional committees, and Nixon eventually lost interest in the super-departments.

Some of the Ash Council's recommendations did become important to executive branch reorganization, however. In its recommendations on the EOP, the council proposed the creation of a Domestic Council and the conversion of the Bureau of the Budget into the Office of Management and Budget. Nixon incorporated these proposals into his Reorganization Plan No. 2, which he submitted to Congress on March 12, 1970.

The Ash Council intended for the Domestic Council to serve as a domestic counterpart to the NSC. It would be a cabinet-level advisory group composed of the president, vice president, attorney general, and the secretaries of Treasury, Interior, Agriculture, Commerce, Labor, Transportation, Housing and Urban Development, and Health, Education, and Welfare. The important changes to the Bureau of the Budget included expanding its managerial, policy coordination, and program information functions in its reincarnation in OMB. Both President Nixon's reorganization efforts and the Ash Council's recommendations sought through reorganization to centralize executive branch policy formation in the EOP.

Under the authority granted by Congress through the periodic extension of the Reorganization Act of 1949, presidents could reorganize executive branch entities as they pleased. Congress retained oversight of such reorganizations through a legislative veto provision in the reorganization act.

President Carter used this method several times while in office. In 1978, for example, he ordered four thousand workers involved in border inspection to move their operations from the Justice Department to the Treasury Department. He also shifted thirty-five hundred people from the firearms and explosives division of the Treasury Department to the Justice Department. In 1977 Carter exerted his reorganization powers to their fullest when he established a whole new Energy Department, absorbing two independent agencies—the Federal Power Commission and the Atomic Energy Commission. In 1979, he divided the Department of Health, Education, and Welfare into two new departments, the Department of Education and the Department of Health and Human Services.

Congress, however, refused to renew the reorganization act after the Supreme Court declared legislative vetoes unconstitutional in 1983. As a result, executive branch reorganizations must now be achieved through normal legislative procedures.

The Appointment Power

As the size of the federal government has grown, presidents have been forced to delegate more and more of their administrative responsibilities to a growing number of political executives. No single chief executive can make all the important policy and administrative decisions necessary to carry out the functions of the U.S. government. Consequently, one of the most important administrative powers that presidents have at their disposal is their ability to recruit and appoint people to fill high-level positions in their administrations.[65]

Article II, section 2, of the Constitution gives the president the power to appoint top political executives. *(See box, this page.)*

The language of the Constitution separates the appointment process of major executive officers into a two-step procedure shared by the president and the Senate. The president recruits and nominates potential appointees, and the Senate either confirms or rejects the president's appointments.

The Constitution also gives Congress the ability to place other appointments within the prerogative of the president (such as the White House staff), of the courts (such as special independent counsels), or of the department heads without Senate confirmation.

Although the Constitution gives the chief executive the responsibility for selecting the approximately 2.7 million civilian employees (as of 1987) of the executive branch, over the years the chief executive has given up much direct participation in the process to the federal civil service system. Until the 1880s most executive branch jobs were apportioned through *patronage,* the system of granting favors and filling jobs as political rewards to the president's supporters. Nineteenth-century presidents placed their friends and allies in federal government positions. With the passage of the Pendleton Act in 1883, which created the Civil Service Commission, most agencies must now choose their employees according to their qualifications and ability to do the job.

Because over 90 precent of executive branch positions are covered by the Civil Service, only the most senior executive positions are filled by presidential appointees. By choosing personnel for these positions, presidents send their political goals to the bureaucracy.

At the beginning of a new administration, Congress publishes *Policy and Supporting Positions*—known as the "plum book"—which lists the top executive branch positions available for direct presidential appointment, many of which require Senate confirmation. Each new presidential administration must appoint approximately 200 members of the White House staff, 14 department heads, 400-500 members of the subcabinet, and approximately 150 ambassadors. In addition, agency and department heads appoint 600-800 members of the Senior Executive Service and about 1,800 special aides in Schedule C positions, which are exempted from the testing and qualification requirements of the civil service merit system. Altogether, presidents and their subordinates must appoint about 5,200 people to the executive branch.[66] Political scientist Hugh Heclo estimates that presidents are most interested in approximately 300 top political executive posts—cabinet secretaries, undersecretaries, assistant secretaries, and bureau chiefs.[67]

Since executive appointees link the president to the vast organizational components of the executive branch, the right to recruit and appoint these people is extremely

---

...he shall nominate, and by and with the Advice and Consent of the Senate shall appoint Ambassadors, other public Ministers and Consuls, Judges of the supreme Court, and all other Officers of the United States, whose Appointments are not herein otherwise provided for and which shall be established by Law; but the Congress may by Law vest the Appointment of such inferior Officers as they think proper in the President alone, in the Courts of Law, or in the Heads of Departments.

—from Article II, section 2

important to the chief executive's ability to control the disparate components of the federal government. To ensure effective leadership, presidents look for quality and loyalty in their appointees.

The sixteenth-century political theorist Niccolo Machiavelli observed, "The first opinion that is formed of a ruler's intelligence is based on the quality of men he has around him." [68] This observation suggests that an administration is only as good as the people the president appoints to fill it. The immense size of the executive branch makes it impossible, however, for presidents to know most of the people they appoint, much less to make personal assessments of their quality. Upon winning the presidency after several months of campaigning, John F. Kennedy complained about trying to fill many of his top positions: "People, people, people! I don't know any people. All I know is voters! How am I going to fill these 1,200 jobs?" [69] Kennedy knew fewer than half of his final cabinet appointments.

Some new appointees come to their positions well qualified, but others do not. What occupational and educational characteristics do presidential appointees have? Between 1982 and 1985 a National Academy of Public Administration survey found that 40 percent of federal appointees are transferred or promoted from other positions in the government. Sixty percent, however, come from occupations outside the federal government: 24 percent from business, 16 percent from academic and research communities, 12 percent from the legal profession, 7 percent from state and local governments, and 1 percent from other organizations. The education level of presidential appointees is relatively high: 19 percent hold bachelor's degrees, 21 percent hold master's degrees, 17 percent hold Ph.D.s, and 34 percent hold law degrees.[70]

In addition to quality and loyalty, presidents consider other factors as well when they make their selections. Most presidents have accumulated quite a few political debts on their way to the White House. Numerous groups and individuals have contributed both money and votes to their victories, and presidents look for ways to reward their chief supporters with major political appointments. Although these selections usually do not constitute the majority of a president's appointments, they are an important consideration. President Harry S Truman, for example, appointed banker John Snyder and Democratic National Chairman Robert Hannegan, both old friends from Missouri, to the positions of Treasury secretary and postmaster general, respectively. Hannegan also served as chairman of the Democratic National Committee. Early in his administration, President Ronald Reagan appointed political advisers Lyn Nofziger, Michael K. Deaver, and Edwin Meese III, all friends and longtime supporters.

Presidents also make many appointments for purely political reasons. The very first presidential personnel selections are the most important politically. In fact, the appointments that presidents make as they establish their administrations generally set the tone and priorities of their presidencies. These selections are important for symbolic reasons and are subject to very close public scrutiny. In his study of presidential cabinets, political scientist Richard Fenno commented: "The presidential decisions leading to the composition of a new 'official family' are taken during the peak period of public interest which attends the national election campaign. As executive decisions go, they are pre-eminently concrete and visible. Among the earliest of presidential moves, they are treated

Table 1 Number of Employees and Political Appointments in Cabinet Departments, 1989

Department	Total number of employees	Schedule C appts.	Total number of appts.[a]
Agriculture	124,706	226	308
Commerce	44,347	107	190
Defense	1,057,842[b]	119	248
Education	4,602	125	348
Energy	17,316	68	108
Health and Human Services	125,331	79	152
Housing and Urban Development	13,436	91	135
Interior	77,994	54	111
Justice	75,605	59	281
Labor	18,480	72	107
State	26,272	162	1,053
Transportation	63,386	73	136
Treasury	164,541	43	93
Veterans Affairs	246,529	9	190
Total	2,060,387	1,287	3,460

Sources: Office of Personnel Management; Center for Excellence in Government.

a. Includes noncareer employees in the Senior Executive Service and public law positions, such as State Department Foreign Service officers.
b. Total civilian employees.

as symbolic acts of considerable significance." [71]

In addition, presidents consider in what ways future political relationships will be affected by their early choices. An administration's success often depends on the ability of the president to forge political allies and broaden the presidency's base of support. Expanding political allies frequently can be accomplished through the appointment process. In addition to rewarding those who have supported them in the past, presidents often use appointments to get on the good side of members of their own political party, interest groups whose support they seek, and, often, members of Congress.

This strategy can backfire, however. William Howard Taft, quoting Thomas Jefferson, used to lament, "Every time I make an appointment I create nine enemies and one ingrate." As political scientist Calvin Mackenzie wrote: "The selection process, particularly in the early stages of a new administration, is governed by scarce resources and multiple, competing demands. Opportunities exist for gaining some political advantage from these early personnel choices, but, if used unwisely, those opportunities are easily squandered." [72]

Another important consideration in presidential appointments is the presidency's managerial needs. As the bureaucracy has become more technologically complex, presidents have had to choose appointees that bring with them managerial and administrative capabilities. The larger the department or agency, the greater the need for management expertise. Departments such as Defense and Health and Human Services and agencies such as the U.S. Postal Service are examples of large government organizations requiring consideration of administrative competence as a standard for appointment.

Although many presidents desperately seek better

management, rarely are appointments made on the basis of such an objective consideration as management ability. Most jobs are filled immediately after the presidential election, when presidents have the largest number of appointments to make and the least amount of time to consider them. Ironically, at this point in their administrations, when they are best able to lure potential appointees, presidents are unable to take full advantage of one their greatest administrative powers. More often than not, the ability to manage becomes one of the last considerations given a potential appointee. Political considerations, as well as an administration's inability to judge its management needs, often outweigh managerial skill. Characteristics such as an appointee's geographic or ethnic background are often much more obvious and easy to consider than administrative ability.

Constraints on the Appointment Process

The postelection rush to fill vacancies in the new administration places a number of constraints on the appointment process. Between the election and the inauguration, the president works to establish the policy objectives of the administration. While still forming their policy objectives, presidents or their subordinates must make the vast majority of their most important appointments. Cronin has noted: "Too frequently appointees are not carefully related to policy. Many subcabinet appointments, for example, are made by subordinates, with the president hardly aware of whether the appointee is matched with the position...." [73] Once in office many appointees adopt new attitudes as a result of new institutionalized responsibilities; or some, perhaps ill-suited for institutional management, may become rigidly wedded to the views of the interest groups with which they most frequently interact.

Presidents often find it difficult to persuade their potential nominees to give up high-paying positions in the private sector and move to Washington, D.C. In 1980 the Commission on Executive, Legislative, and Judicial Salaries concluded: "There is growing evidence that low salaries are a major reason for highly talented people declining appointment to key positions in the federal government." [74]

Other presidents have found it difficult to persuade potential nominees to disclose their financial background and income. Because the American public expects executive branch officials to perform their duties without undue regard for special interests, Congress passed strict financial disclosure laws in 1965. Certain top executive branch employees were required to report information about their personal finances to the head of the Civil Service Commission, who could report this information to the president if there seemed to be a conflict of interest. Title II of the Ethics in Government Act of 1978 broadened disclosure provisions by requiring all presidential appointees to complete the Executive Personal Financial Disclosure Report, which publicly discloses their personal financial information. These provisions have been a source of great concern for many potential appointees. E. Pendleton James, President Reagan's assistant for personnel, stated that "literally hundreds" of potential presidential nominees lost interest as a result of demanding disclosure provisions. [75]

Similarly, presidents must sometimes pass up potential nominees because of the person's involvement with a past administration, a scandal, or even the appearance of wrongdoing. For example, Peter Flanigan, a former Nixon aide, was nominated by President Gerald Ford as ambassador to Spain, but he had to withdraw under opposition from Congress over his relationship with the Watergate-plagued Nixon administration. In short, presidents face enormous difficulties in finding appropriate candidates in a shrinking pool of potential nominees who are willing to go to Washington and face public scrutiny and who have avoided any conflict of interest.

The Role of the Senate

The Senate is an integral part of the appointment process and serves as one of the most important limits to the presidential appointment privilege. Constitutionally, presidents share the appointment of many political executives with the Senate, and the Senate must confirm most of the president's major appointments. As a result, the Senate has come to view the appointment procedure as a process in which its members should have a considerable say. As Mackenzie has observed, "For Senators and Senate committees, the confirmation process is both a responsibility and an opportunity." [76] It is a constitutional responsibility and a political opportunity. Senators view the appointment process as a way to influence government policy. Cronin has noted that senators even try to influence presidential policy by getting the president to nominate their choices: "They ... often have candidates of their own. This is especially the case in recent years, for as the staffs of Congress have expanded ... there are more and more aides to Congress who seek top executive branch appointments." [77]

The number of presidential nominations sent to the Senate for confirmation is staggering. The Senate must process between 90,000 and 170,000 nominations each session (two-year period). Usually, the vast majority of these nominations are routine military commissions and promotions that require very little of the Senate's time. Although the number of civilian appointments is much lower, the Senate must still spend a great deal of time and energy processing them. For example. the Ninety-eighth Congress in 1983-1985 processed 7,581 civilian nominations. This figure includes routine nominations to such civilian organizations as the Foreign Service, the Public Health Service, and the National Oceanic and Atmospheric Administration. However, more highly scrutinized nominations to top-level policy-making positions in the executive branch—averaging only about 700 per session—require much attention from the Senate.

Like most other matters before Congress, the nomination process is handled mostly by standing committees. Although each committee has different sets of procedures for managing appointments referred to them, most committees have developed their own standard sets of structured proceedings. Usually, these procedures require additional background checks and financial disclosures, other than those already required by the president's personnel director and the Ethics in Government Act of 1978, and extensive hearings. The average length of time required by the Senate to confirm presidential nominees during the Reagan administration was 14.6 weeks. The result of this rigorous and lengthy investigative process has been an increase in demands on potential appointees. In his study of the Senate's role in the presidential appointment process, political scientist Christopher J. Deering pointed out that this demanding investigatory process has made the Senate's role in the nomination process not only more thorough but also more demanding: "Unfortunately, the process has . . . become more tedious, time-consuming, and intrusive for the nominees. For some the price is too high. . . ." [78]

The Founders intended the Senate's constitutional role in the presidential appointment process to serve as a check on executive power. To what extent has the Senate checked presidential power through its confirmation power? All presidents have been successful in getting the majority of their nominees confirmed. Over 92 percent of all civilian presidential nominations were confirmed by the 98th Congress. Most nominations are defeated in committees. Since 1960 only six nominees have been defeated on the floor of the Senate. Many, however, have had a few of their potential appointees rejected. The Senate regularly thwarted the efforts of James Madison and Ulysses S. Grant to nominate their choices for executive branch positions freely. John Tyler perhaps had the most difficulty with the Senate in attempting to fill vacancies. His appointees were frequently rejected by the Senate, including four cabinet and four Supreme Court appointees. In one day in 1843, the Senate rejected Tyler's nomination of Caleb Cushing as secretary of the Treasury three times. In 1984 President Reagan's nominee for associate attorney general, William Bradford Reynolds, was turned down by the Senate Judiciary Committee. His opponents argued that Reynolds had been negligent in enforcing antidiscrimination laws during his tenure as chief of the Justice Department's Civil Rights Division. Although the Senate does not often reject a presidential nominee, the occasions on which it has done so, and the thoroughness of its investigations of those who are confirmed, indicate that the Senate does exert some control over the president's prerogative to appoint key members to the administration.

In some cases, however, the Senate may use its confirmation power more as a political bargaining chip than anything else. It will often "hold" the nominee in limbo until the president agrees to support a political position. For example, President Reagan's nomination of Edwin Meese as attorney general was used by the majority leader as leverage to exact a promise to support farm aid legislation. During the 1980s Sen. Jesse Helms (R-N.C.) repeatedly held up nominations because he found them politically unacceptable or he wished to force political opponents to compromise on policy issues. Deering has written, "On numerous occasions in recent years, members of the Senate of both parties have placed holds on particular individuals. In some cases, the nominee is the target, in other cases merely a pawn, but in either case the use of nominees as, in effect, hostages has undermined the integrity of the system." [79]

The Presidential Personnel System

The presidential appointment process remained relatively unchanged throughout the first 150 years of U.S. history. Presidents had little, if any, staff to help them make their appointments; political parties usually controlled personnel selection for the president. *(See "Presidential Party Leadership within the Executive," p. 218, in Chief of Party chapter.)* Even when chief executives did

become actively involved in the selection process, they often used the existing political party structure. Other nominees were usually suggested to the president by party leaders or members of Congress from the president's party. Too often this dependence on the party resulted in administrations filled with top-level appointees with little loyalty to presidential objectives.

Roosevelt and Truman Administrations

Since Franklin D. Roosevelt entered the White House, however, newly elected presidents have needed significant staff support and a centralized procedure for choosing personnel because of the vast number of appointments that must be made in a short period of time. Perhaps more important, a centralized appointment process under the president's control ensures faithfulness to White House policies and objectives.

Until the 1960s, the selection of presidential appointments was haphazard and unfocused. Presidential personnel operations relied heavily on chance to place the right people in the right positions. During the 1940s, however, President Roosevelt attempted to alleviate much of the problem by introducing a number of governmental reforms that removed presidential patronage from the national political parties. For example, he appointed an assistant to handle personnel matters in an effort to improve presidential control over the appointment process. In the following decades the presidency experienced an increase in its administrative powers, allowing it more discretion in personnel selection.

Journalist Dom Bonafede has attributed the growth of a more centralized selection procedure within the White House after 1940 to three factors. First, political reforms that increased the number of state primaries and emphasized grass-roots politics "hastened the decline of the national parties and minimized their brokerage role as conduit and clearinghouse for appointments." Presidents were no longer obligated to party leaders for their election and, therefore, had less need to reward them with government jobs. Second, the movement toward a strong administrative presidency, which centralized power in the White House, further strengthened the president's hand vis-à-vis Congress and the bureaucracy. Third, "the complexity of domestic and foreign issues, such as arms control, tax reform, federal deficits and trade imbalances, necessitated elaborate institutional support, placing a premium on substantive knowledge and managerial competence." [80]

Specific recommendations by the Committee on Administrative Management, headed by Louis D. Brownlow, and the two Hoover Commissions helped centralize more power into the presidency. *(See "Reorganization Power," p. 14, in this chapter.)* In 1939, acting on Brownlow Commission recommendations, Congress created the Executive Office of the President (EOP) and brought the Bureau of the Budget under the control of the president within the EOP. These measures began what has become known as the "institutional presidency." The first and second Hoover Commissions further increased the administrative power of the presidency by giving it more control over the vast federal bureaucracy and substantial authority over the appointment process.

President Truman appointed the first full-time staff member responsible only for personnel matters. Although this aide, Donald Dawson, addressed mostly routine concerns and spent a good deal of time in contact with the

Democratic National Committee, the new position signaled the growing importance of staffing issues.

Eisenhower Administration

Dwight D. Eisenhower came to office in 1953 with a strong desire to improve the management of the executive branch but with a dislike for personnel matters. He frequently wrote in his diary that patronage was one of the great banes of his administration and one of the things most likely to cause him to lose his temper. Consequently, he delegated personnel concerns to members of his staff, primarily to Sherman Adams, his chief of staff. Adams, however, soon found the job of personnel director too demanding when added to his other responsibilities. The president then approved the position of special assistant for executive appointments, which several people held during the eight years Eisenhower was in office. These special assistants did not choose the president's appointees. Rather, they managed the appointment process by narrowing the president's choices to candidates with the best qualifications and the fewest political liabilities. More than anything else, Eisenhower sought appointees who were loyal to his political philosophy and his programs.

Kennedy and Johnson Administrations

Shortly after his election, president-elect Kennedy put together a personnel selection staff called "Talent Hunt." Comprising some of the best people from the campaign, Talent Hunt was a loosely organized operation with two objectives. First, it tried to determine the president-elect's political obligations—supporters who helped him win the election—and find appropriate jobs to pay off those debts. Second, it attempted to identify the most important jobs the president would have to fill and to find the best people for those positions. After the inauguration, Talent Hunt broke up, and its members went to their own jobs in the administration.

In mid-1961 Kennedy appointed Dan Fenn of the Harvard Business School faculty to take over the day-to-day personnel responsibilities of the White House. Asked to recommend changes in the traditional method of filling executive positions, Fenn concluded that the procedure was too limited. The most important jobs in the federal government were being filled by a very unsophisticated "Whom do you know?" system—a process he called "BOGSAT," that is, a "bunch of guys sitting around a table."

Dan Fenn, President John F. Kennedy's personnel aide, created a White House appointment process that gave the president recruiting ability independent of the political parties.

John F. Kennedy Library

Fenn attempted to correct this problem by creating a systematic White House appointment operation consisting of three major stages. First, he and his staff developed reliable job descriptions that allowed them to match candidates with positions, something most administrations had not been able to do. Second, Fenn offered the president a wider selection of candidates from which to choose. He believed that the range of people with whom presidents normally come into contact was too narrow to provide the talent necessary for a successful administration. Third, since he could offer a wider range of choices only by reaching beyond traditional political sources for appointments, Fenn established a network of well-positioned people throughout the country whose opinions the president trusted and who could provide Kennedy with candid information about potential nominees. Although the system Fenn established never worked quite as well as it might have, it nonetheless marked the first time a president had significant independent recruiting ability, separate and apart from the influence of the political parties.

During Lyndon B. Johnson's administration, the centralization of presidential personnel selection took a giant leap forward. Although Kennedy had put together a significant staff for selecting nominees, he would often bypass the process by selecting appointees without using the system Fenn had established. Johnson, too, would sometimes circumvent his personnel staff, but he always maintained the appearance that the selection had been made through the White House personnel system. The authors of one study of the presidential selection process concluded:

> Those who wanted to influence [Johnson's] appointment decisions quickly got the message that their contact point for this was the personnel staff and that efforts to evade the established personnel selection procedures would be difficult to pull off. This focused more attention on the White House and significantly strengthened its role at the hub of the appointment process.[81]

The Kennedy and Johnson presidencies effected three important long-term changes in presidential personnel management. First, a full-time personnel staff became a regular component of the White House Office. Second, presidents have attempted to maintain their independence from traditional political party pressures by recruiting their own candidates. Third, each administration has developed and followed routine procedures for scrutinizing the background, competence, integrity, and political loyalty of each potential appointee.

Nixon Administration

When Richard Nixon took office in 1969, he at first failed to incorporate in his presidency many of the advances made in personnel selection in preceding administrations. He had little interest in personnel matters and delegated most of the responsibility for filling offices to his staff. His initial appointment process was slow and cumbersome, and too many times the White House appointed people who had little loyalty to the president's programs. As a result, in 1970 Nixon appointed Frederic V. Malek to study the personnel staff and recommend improvements. His recommendations called for a personnel system similar to those of Nixon's predecessors: centralization of the recruiting process in the White House, recruitment outreach beyond traditional political party sources of potential nominees, and a more rigorous clearance process.

In 1971 Nixon appointed Malek director of his personnel operation. Malek, acting on his own recommendations, set up the White House Personnel Office (WHPO). Following the examples of the organizations set up by Fenn and John W. Macy, personnel assistant to President Johnson, Malek made the WHPO a tightly organized operation that employed a highly professional staff. The WHPO employed professional headhunters whose sole responsibility was to find the right person for the right job in the administration. In addition, the WHPO developed a much more sophisticated evaluation system than had ever been used before in the White House. After two years of haphazard personnel selection, the Nixon White House emerged with a firm commitment to centralized personnel decision making for almost all noncareer positions in the federal government. Eventually, the WHPO lost much of its intensity, and some of its members went beyond the limits of propriety in attempting to control the appointment process. The WHPO outlined ways in which the civil service could be manipulated by the administration. One way was to write job descriptions to fit specific applicants loyal to Nixon. Those unsympathetic were to become transfers to undesirable locations or assignments requiring a great deal of travel. The press and Congress finally intervened, forcing the WHPO to retreat from its continued efforts at centralization.

Frederic V. Malek, President Richard Nixon's personnel director, established the White House Personnel Office in 1971.

Nixon Project, National Archives

Ford and Carter Administrations

Gerald R. Ford's personnel staff spent much of its time trying to clean up the image of the aggressive WHPO under Nixon. The first thing that Ford changed was the name. The WHPO became the Presidential Personnel Office. In addition, Ford reduced the size of the personnel operation and narrowed the focus of its activities to positions traditionally viewed as presidential appointments rather than most noncareer appointments.

Jimmy Carter was the first president who began planning for his presidency while still running for election. In the summer of 1976, he set up a small staff in Atlanta to begin working on the staffing of his administration. Carter chose Jack Watson to head up the operation, which became known as Talent Inventory Program (TIP). After Carter won the election, Watson moved his operation to Washington. Once there he became locked in a power struggle with Carter's campaign manager, Hamilton Jordan, over who would control the appointment process. As a result of this struggle, the Presidential Personnel Office floundered for almost two years. Although a personnel staff was established in the White House, its ability to manage the appointment process effectively was hampered by the rivalry between Watson and Jordan. Throughout the Carter administration, there was no central coordination of appointments in the White House, and much of the early work of TIP was ignored.

Carter contributed to the disorder in the appointment process by insisting that cabinet heads be given almost total discretion in choosing their subordinates. At various times in the campaign, he had proclaimed: "There will never be an instance while I am president where members of the White House staff dominate or act in a superior position to the members of our Cabinet." [82] This promise made good campaign rhetoric, but it diminished Carter's ability to control his administration by decentralizing the decision-making process. Some departments made appointments after a rigorous search procedure. Others resorted to "politics as usual" and used the insiders' network

to select potential nominees whose main qualifications were friendship and loyalty to department secretaries. As Bonafede described the results, "In an unseemly brief period it became clear to the president's top lieutenants—and only later to Carter himself—that he had made a major mistake in giving secretaries carte blanche authority to hand-pick their assistants." [83]

Reagan Administration

Reagan viewed the appointment process as an integral part of his plans for changing the direction of the federal government. Determined to avoid the mistakes of the Carter administration, he centralized the appointment process squarely within the White House.

Reagan also made a determined effort to appoint only persons who shared his political philosophy. E. Pendleton James, Reagan's postelection talent search manager and eventual assistant to the president for personnel, declared, "You can't separate personnel from policy." [84] This outlook pervaded the administration's appointment efforts. From the "kitchen cabinet" made up of Reagan's elite, conservative California advisers who chose politically acceptable potential nominees before his election, to the personnel office, which managed appointments during the administration, the strategy was to choose nominees whose political philosophy matched the president's.

The Reagan appointment process benefited from some of Carter's mistakes. James gave the process a consistency it lacked under Carter. During the transition and throughout the first eighteen months of the Reagan administration, James presided over the day-to-day operation of the administration's personnel selection. As a result, there was very little confusion over the process itself or who was in charge. Also, Reagan visibly involved himself in the appointment process. He made the final decision on all of the important appointments during the transition and the first year. The authors of one study noted:

> This proved to be an effective deterrent to those in the departments and agencies and in Congress who might try and wrest control of appointment decisions away from the White House. It is one thing to attempt that when low-level White House staff members are making appointment decisions; it is quite another when those decisions are being made in the Oval Office. [85]

Since Franklin Roosevelt's administration, presidents have relied on increasingly sophisticated methods of cen-

Washington Star; courtesy Martin Luther King, Jr., Library

E. Pendleton James, Ronald Reagan's assistant to the president for personnel, saw to it that all appointees shared Reagan's political philosophy.

tralizing the appointment power in the White House in their attempts to strengthen control over their administrations. The personnel office is now a permanent part of the White House organizational structure. Succeeding presidents have significantly increased the number of staff assigned to find competent and loyal political executives. And presidential personnel operations have come to rely on professional recruiting techniques. Yet, as important as the office is to presidential control, it is not at the top of the executive branch hierarchy. Bonafede has concluded that, in most administrations, the presidential personnel office

> lacks institutional stability; the process varies from one presidency to another, and it even varies in the zeal and orderliness with which it is conducted within the same administration. Each incoming administration, distrustful of past personnel procedures, feels compelled to reinvent its own system. Few presidents have been willing to lend their prestige to the office.[86]

The Removal Power

The ability of presidents to control their administrations is often dependent on their authority to remove

subordinates from office. This issues lies at the very heart of the chief executive's power over the bureaucracy. The power of presidents to remove officials from office who are not doing their jobs properly or who disagree with presidential goals and programs is, however, controversial and has been significantly limited by the Supreme Court. Because the Constitution does not explicitly grant presidents power to remove officials from office, the legitimacy of the power often has rested on court interpretations of specific presidential removal actions.

Preferring to avoid the issue as long as possible, the Supreme Court refused to make a definitive ruling on the issue of presidential removal of public officeholders until 1926—just a few years before the growth of modern presidential power. In *Myers v. United States* the Court ruled that an 1876 law that limited the president's removal power over postmasters was unconstitutional. In 1917 President Woodrow Wilson had appointed Myers to be a postmaster in Portland, Oregon, for a term of four years. Attempting to make his administration responsive to his policy goals, Wilson removed Myers from office in 1920 without consent of the Senate, although the 1876 statute provided that postmasters should be appointed and removed by the president by and with the advice and consent of the Senate. Myers sued for his salary in the U.S. Court of Claims. When he received an adverse judgment, he took his case to the Supreme Court.

In delivering the opinion of the Court, Chief Justice William Howard Taft, a former president, strongly argued that presidents cannot effectively administer the executive branch unless they can control their subordinates with the threat of removal for political and other reasons. He stated that the power of removal was implied in the constitutional provision in Article II, which gave the presidency the responsibility to see that the laws be faithfully executed. Furthermore, Congress could not constitutionally restrain or limit that power. Taft contended that presidents cannot carry out their constitutional responsibilities if Congress interferes with their ability to control the executive branch.[87]

The *Myers* case arguably had given presidents sweeping authority to remove not only immediate executive subordinates but also members of independent regulatory commissions, such as the Interstate Commerce Commission and the Federal Trade Commission. Independent regulatory commissioners are appointed under the provisions of statutes that confer upon them a certain amount of independence and freedom from the political control of the president. In these agencies, Congress had carefully outlined the provisions by which a commissioner could be removed in an attempt to free these executives from political control. If the *Myers* case applied to all political executives, then the political independence of the regulatory commissions would no longer exist. Sooner or later the question of unlimited presidential power of removal would be challenged.

The question of the president's ability to remove independent regulatory commissioners quickly came up during Franklin Roosevelt's administration and was settled in 1935 by the Supreme Court in *Humphrey's Executor v. United States.* President Herbert C. Hoover had nominated William E. Humphrey to the Federal Trade Commission (FTC) in 1931. Under the terms outlined by Congress in the Federal Trade Commission Act of 1914, FTC commissioners were supposed to serve a term of seven years. The act stated that commissioners could be removed by the president only for "inefficiency, neglect of duty, or malfeasance in office." After his election to office, Roosevelt wrote Humphrey and requested his resignation from the FTC so that "the aims and purposes of the administration with respect to the work of the Commission can be carried out most effectively with personnel of my own selection." After Humphrey's initial reluctance to resign, Roosevelt again wrote him, this time stating: "You will, I know, realize that I do not feel that your mind and my mind go along together on either the policies or the administering of the Federal Trade Commission, and frankly, I think it is best for the people of the country that I should have full confidence." [88] When Humphrey refused to resign, Roosevelt notified him that he had been removed. Humphrey died in 1934, never having agreed to his removal. The executor of Humphrey's estate decided to sue for salary he believed was due Humphrey but never paid him.

The court of claims asked the Supreme Court to answer two questions before it could render a judgment. First, did the Federal Trade Commission Act limit the president's power to remove commissioners except for reasons stated in the act? Second, if the act did indeed limit the president's power to remove commissioners, was it constitutional?

Roosevelt had made clear that the removal of Humphrey was for political reasons. Justice George Sutherland delivered the Court's opinion that the *Myers* case did not apply to Humphrey because the FTC was "an administrative body created by Congress to carry into effect legislative policies." Therefore, it could not "in any sense be characterized as an arm or an eye of the Executive." Sutherland continued:

> Whether the power of the president to remove an officer shall prevail over the authority of Congress to condition the power by fixing a definite term and precluding the removal except for cause will depend upon the character of the office; the *Myers* decision, affirming the power of the president alone to make the removal, is confined to purely executive officers. [89]

The *Humphrey* decision not only invalidated Roosevelt's removal of Humphrey but also generally limited presidential removal power to officials who could be classified as "purely executive officers." Except for appointees immediately responsible to the president and those exercising nondiscretionary or ministerial functions, such as White House aides, the president's power of removal could be limited by Congress.

The Supreme Court attempted to make a distinction between "executive" and "administrative" functions within the federal bureaucracy. Presidents have complete control over executive functions, or those that deal with the execution of the policy of the administration and are under the direction of the president, such as members of the EOP and cabinet members. The Court ruled that presidents do not, however, have complete control over administrative functions, or those that have quasi-judicial or quasi-legislative roles, such as those of the independent regulatory commissions. Only when Congress chooses specifically to give presidents control over these agencies can they remove officials for merely political reasons.

In 1958 the Supreme Court further clarified the removal power of presidents. In *Wiener v. United States,* the Court held that if officials are engaged in adjudicative functions presidents may not remove them for political reasons. In 1950 President Truman had appointed Wiener to serve on the War Claims Commission. When Eisenhower assumed office, he requested Wiener's resignation. When Wiener refused, Eisenhower removed him from office. Similar to Roosevelt's removal of Humphrey, Eisenhower's removal of Wiener rested on purely political reasons. Congress had created the War Claims Commission to adjudicate damage claims resulting from World War II. It made no provisions for removing commissioners. Wiener sued for his lost salary.

Noting the similarity between the *Wiener* and *Humphrey* cases, the Supreme Court ruled in favor of Wiener. The Court argued that in both cases presidents had removed persons from quasi-judicial agencies for political purposes. Calling the War Claims Commission a clearly adjudicative body, Justice Felix Frankfurter concluded for the Court:

> Judging the matter in all the nakedness in which it is presented, namely, the claim that the President could remove a member of an adjudicative body like the War Claims Commission merely because he wanted his own appointees on such a Commission, we are compelled to conclude that no such power is given to the President directly by the Constitution, and none is impliedly conferred upon him by statute simply because Congress said nothing about it. The philosophy of *Humphrey's Executor,* in its explicit language as well as it implications, precludes such a claim. [90]

These cases have defined more clearly the legal and constitutional authority of presidents over the federal executive branch by addressing their power to remove certain officers. The *Myers* case gave presidents considerable authority to fire executive branch officials appointed by the president and confirmed by the Senate. The *Humphrey* and *Wiener* cases limited presidential removal authority over agencies that exercise quasi-legislative or quasi-judicial functions, such as independent regulatory agencies.

Generally, presidents may remove all heads of cabinet departments and all political executives in the Executive Office of the President. In addition, they may remove at any time the directors of the following agencies: ACTION, the Arms Control and Disarmament Agency, the Commission on Civil Rights, the Environmental Protection Agency, the Federal Mediation and Conciliation Service, the General Services Administration, the National Aeronautics and Space Administration, the Postal Service, and the Small Business Administration.

The Budgeting Power

The power to control the budget process is one of the most important administrative prerogatives of the presidency. The chief executive is an important participant in the budget process, for often it is the president who decides where and how money is spent. As presidential scholar Richard Pious has noted, "To budget is to govern. In a system of separated institutions that share power, the question is which institution, and by what authority, determines spending levels for the departments?" [91] In the last part of the twentieth century, the presidency has assumed an increasingly important role in determining federal spending and thus more responsibility in governing. Although Congress technically controls the purse strings, the president controls the formulation and development of the budget.

The Constitution does not clearly establish a budgetary process or specifically spell out the presidency's role in such a process. Because of this ambiguity, presidents have been able to bring much of the process under their control. Article I of the Constitution gave Congress the powers to tax and spend. Article II, section 3, gave presidents the power to recommend to Congress such measures as they deemed appropriate. ("He shall from time to time give to the Congress Information of the State of the Union, and recommend to their Consideration such Measures as he shall judge necessary and expedient.") Implied in this power is the idea that presidents may present to Congress a financial program.

Historically, presidents have not taken part in budget planning. Even in modern times, presidential involvement in the process has varied from one administration to another. For many presidents, preparing a budget is a job not readily cherished because it has proven to be tedious and time consuming. President Lyndon B. Johnson once wrote, "The federal budget is a dry, unfathomable maze of figures and statistics—thicker than a Sears-Roebuck catalogue and duller than a telephone directory." [92] Some presidents have been able to maintain consistent interest in the budget's complexities throughout their terms in office; others have not. Political scientist Lance T. LeLoup examined the roles that past presidents played in the budget process and found that shortly after the first year in office, Dwight D. Eisenhower and Richard Nixon tired of the tedious budget process. Harry S Truman and Gerald R. Ford, however, were able to maintain their enthusiasm throughout their administrations. [93]

Budgeting gives the presidency a tremendous amount of administrative power, and most presidents have recognized the importance of the budget in controlling their administrations. They usually approach their first budget optimistically, excited about the potential power to eliminate or cut back programs that they may feel have outlived their usefulness. Describing his involvement in his first budget, Lyndon Johnson wrote, "I worked as hard on that budget as I have ever worked on anything.... Day after day I went over that budget with the Cabinet officers, my economic advisers, and the Budget Director. I studied almost every line, nearly every page, until I was dreaming about the budget at night." [94] Yet, LeLoup found that often this enthusiasm wanes after presidents are confronted with the recurring difficulty of the whole process. [95]

Although their enthusiasm may fade, presidents continue to seek to control the budget process. They see their participation in the process as a way of doing things that can benefit the national economy and their own political fortunes. In the words of President Ford, "The budget is the president's blueprint for the operation of government in the year ahead." [96] According to Dennis S. Ippolito in his study of the budget process, presidents become involved in the budget process to achieve a means of administrative management and control: "By affecting the resources available for agencies and programs, the president can seek to promote better planning of what is done, more effective supervision of how it is done, and more systematic evaluation of how well various objectives are accomplished." In addition, Ippolito has pointed out that budget decisions can affect political support. He has written, "By emphasizing particular programs or criticizing others, by challenging Congress' spending preferences, by trumpeting the need for fiscal responsibility, or by reiterating commitments to greater economy and efficiency, a president can attempt to dramatize his leadership role and to generate public support for his economic policies and program preferences." [97]

Attempts to control the budget process often force presidents to play a public relations game. Most presidents want to be considered fiscal conservatives. The overwhelming majority of Americans want a balanced budget and want the president to curtail the growth of federal expenditures. Yet presidents must continue to fund existing programs for various groups and for the American public in general. In addition, presidents are expected to present new initiatives, some of which benefit groups to whom presidents have political obligations. The dilemma is one of holding down public expenditures while trying to solve public problems. It is not an easy task, and it makes presidential participation in the budget process much more demanding and important.

The President's Role in the Budget Process

In the role of chief administrator, presidents had little influence in managing executive branch funds before passage of the Budget and Accounting Act of 1921. Previously, agency budget requests went to the House of Representatives without much interference from the White House. There was very little budget coordination by presidents or their staffs. Congress believed it could handle the budget without much help from the presidency. By the end of World War II, however, both the executive and legislative branches had developed an awareness that the federal government needed better management.

Budget and Accounting Act of 1921

The Budget and Accounting Act of 1921 gave presidents important managerial controls over the budgeting process and made them the dominant force in budgetary politics. Ironically, this act was passed by Congress in an attempt to bring order into its own chaotic budget process. An earlier House committee pointed to the haphazard nature of a budget process that lacked a coherent review of the executive branch's budget request. But in attempting to alleviate the problem, the act placed the presidency squarely in the budgetary process by requiring presidents to submit to Congress annual estimates of how much money it will take to run the federal government during the next fiscal year. (A fiscal year is the twelve-month span in which financial accounting is made. This period for the federal government runs from October 1 to September 30.)

The annual budget messages delivered by the president contain recommendations on how much money should be appropriated by Congress for each department of the federal government. The White House first evaluates all agency budget requests and decides which to accept or reject before submitting the annual budget message. Consequently, presidents become very much involved in the process. They receive more information about the budget than most members of Congress, allowing them to initiate budget discussions on their own terms.

In addition, the Budget and Accounting Act created the Bureau of the Budget (BOB) and placed it under the control of the Treasury Department. Its role was to "assemble, correlate, revise, reduce, or increase the estimates of the several departments or establishments." [98] In 1939, as a result of a growing need for coordination of New Deal programs and recommendations from the Committee on

Administrative Management (the Brownlow Commission), President Roosevelt moved BOB into the Executive Office of the President (EOP).

BOB began instituting a form of "budget clearance" so that the departments could not bypass its budget review process either for authorizations or for appropriations. No longer were the departments on their own in requesting funds from Congress. Bureaus and agencies made requests for funds to their departments, and the departments went through BOB for consideration by the president. From 1939 to 1969, BOB evolved into a highly influential component of the EOP.

Office of Management and Budget

In 1970 President Richard Nixon changed the name and function of BOB. Emphasizing the management functions of the budget agency, Nixon renamed it the Office of Management and Budgeting (OMB). As the word *management* implies, new emphasis was placed on providing departments with advice on ways to improve their efficiency and to reduce the costs of their operations.

Nixon specifically had four major roles for OMB. First, it was to continue many of BOB's functions, especially writing the federal budget. Second, it was to serve as a clearinghouse for programs and new legislation. Third, Nixon wanted some part of the Executive Office of the President to have the capability to track legislation as it moved through Congress. OMB was vested with this capacity. Fourth, OMB was given the specific authority to provide management advice to the various departments and agencies. Since its inception, OMB has served as the centerpiece of presidential budgeting.

Although the president's budget is not submitted to Congress until the January before the first day of the new fiscal year (October 1), the presidential budget process begins at least nineteen months before the submission of the finished budget proposal. *(See Table 2.)* The budget cycle begins in early spring with OMB informing the departments of the fiscal outlook and the spending priorities of the president. During the summer, the OMB director (also called the "budget director") issues specific revenue projections and imposes specific guidelines for departmental spending. On September 1 agencies submit their initial budget requests to OMB. OMB then holds formal hearings on these requests at which departmental officials justify their proposed budgets before OMB examiners.

OMB's director examines the entire budget from November 1 to December 1. Often the director will invite the National Security Council (NSC), the Council of Economic Advisers, and several White House aides to participate in the review. The OMB director makes final decisions subject to the economic forecast and communicates these decisions to the departments. The departments may appeal the decisions directly to the president. Usually, however, each department will revise its formal budget to coincide with the budget director's wishes, for presidents rarely reverse their budget director's decisions.

Congress receives the first official hint of what the president wants in the State of the Union address at the end of January, and specifics are then spelled out in the president's budget message in February. Pending approval by Congress, the budget goes into effect with the new fiscal year, October 1.

Not all agency requests are treated equally. Until the Nixon administration, the Defense Department's budget requests were exempt from control by the president's budgeting organization. During the administrations of John F. Kennedy and Lyndon Johnson, the Pentagon submitted its budget directly to the president without review by the Bureau of the Budget. If BOB believed budget items to be too high, it could appeal to the president. This practice, a reversal of the traditional procedure, placed the burden of proof on the budget office rather than on the department. President Nixon changed the procedure for the Pentagon by leaving final decisions with the NSC and OMB and giving the Defense Department the right of appeal. Subsequent presidents have continued to use OMB as a counterbalance to the Pentagon's budget requests.

Current Services Budget

Under the provisions of the 1974 Congressional Budget and Impoundment Act (PL 93-344), presidents must submit two budget proposals. When they submit their budget for the upcoming fiscal year, they must also submit, through the supervision of OMB, a *current services budget*. The current services budget provides Congress with an indication of the cost of existing budget obligations and a guide for evaluating additional budget proposals. Specifically, the current services budget includes the "proposed budget authority and estimated outlays that would be included in the budget for the ensuing fiscal year ... if all programs were carried on at the same level as the fiscal year in progress ... without policy changes."[99]

Although this procedure was intended to provide Congress with a basis for determining the overall size and direction of existing budget commitments and for assessing and evaluating the president's budget proposals, it has never quite lived up to its potential. Political scientist Howard E. Shuman has noted that the current services budget has little significance or meaning: "Only budget buffs and perennial budget watchers pay much attention to it. It is, however, a useful document in assessing whether any or how much fundamental change has been made in the old budget to produce the new one."[100]

Uncontrollable Spending

In any given year, much of OMB's current service estimates can be classified as *uncontrollable spending*, expenditures mandated by current law or some previous obligation. *(See Table 3.)* To change the spending on these mandated programs would require congressional action. By 1980, 75 percent of the federal budget could be classified as uncontrollable spending. These expenditures can be broken down into three major categories.

The first category, fixed costs, consists of legal commitments made by the federal government in previous years. These require the government to spend whatever is necessary to meet these expenses. The largest and most important component of this category is interest on the national debt. Another fixed-cost expenditure is public housing loans. Fixed costs are virtually "uncontrollable" because they can be eliminated only by such extreme measures as default.

The second category is large-scale government projects that require long-term financing. These multiyear contracts and obligations include the building of dams, weapons systems, aircraft, and the space shuttle. Many of these projects are reviewed annually, and expenditure levels are occasionally modified. Most, however, are not.

Table 2 Budget Timetable in the Executive Branch and Congress

Executive branch	Timing	Congress
Agencies subject to executive branch review submit initial budget request materials.	September 1	
Fiscal year begins.	October 1	Fiscal year begins.
President's initial appropriation order takes effect (amounts are withheld from obligation pending issuance of final order).	October 1	
	October 10	Congressional Budget Office (CBO) issues revised report to Office of Management and Budget (OMB) and Congress.
OMB reports on changes in initial estimates and determinations resulting from legislation enacted and regulations promulgated after its initial report to Congress.	October 15	
President issues final sequester order, which is effective immediately, and transmits message to Congress within 15 days of final order.	October 15	
Agencies not subject to executive branch review submit budget request materials.	October 15	
	November 15	Comptroller general issues compliance report.
Legislative branch and the judiciary submit budget request materials.	November–December	
President transmits the budget to Congress.	1st Monday after January 3	Congress receives the president's budget.
OMB sends allowance letters to agencies.	January–February	
	February 15	CBO reports to the budget committees on the president's budget.
	February 25	Committees submit views and estimates to budget committess.
OMB and the president conduct reviews to establish presidential policy to guide agencies in developing the next budget.	April–June	
	April 1	Senate Budget Committee reports concurrent resolution on the budget.
	April 15	Congress completes action on concurrent resolution.
	May 15	House may consider appropriations bills in the absence of a concurrent resolution on the budget.
	June 10	House Appropriations Committee reports last appropriations bill.
	June 15	Congress completes action on reconciliation legislation.
	June 30	House completes action on annual appropriations bills.
President transmits the mid-session review, updating the budget estimates.	July 15	Congress receives mid-session review of the budget.
OMB provides agencies with policy guidance for the upcoming budget.	July–August	
Date of "snapshot" of projected deficits for the upcoming fiscal year for initial OMB and CBO reports.	August 15	
	August 20	CBO issues its initial report to OMB and Congress.
OMB issues its initial report providing estimates and determinations to the president and Congress.	August 25	
President issues initial sequester order and sends message to Congress within 15 days.	August 25	

Source: Office of Management and Budget, Circular No. A-11 (1988).

The third category of expenditures officially designated as uncontrollable is the largest. These programs, called "entitlements," commit the federal government to pay benefits to all eligible individuals. Any attempt at controlling these expenditures would require changing the laws that set them up. Entitlements include Social Security, Medicare, Medicaid, Supplemental Security Income, food stamps, public assistance, and federal retirement. In some cases the federal government will pay individuals directly; in other cases, the states determine eligibility and administer the programs. Most of these programs have no limit on the amount of spending they may entail. As more people become eligible for benefits, expenditures increase.

From time to time presidents will try to increase or decrease these so-called uncontrollable expenditures. Nixon and Ford, for example, attempted to decrease entitlement expenditures by restricting eligibility and establishing a limit on benefit increases on several programs. In his first full budget year, Reagan proposed an entitlement cut of $11.7 billion. His budget proposal reflected the frustration that many presidents have felt in attempting to deal with uncontrollable expenditures. It said in part, "The explosion of entitlement expenditures has forced a careful reexamination of the entitlement or automatic spending programs.... when one looks behind the good intentions of these programs, one finds tremendous problems of fraud, waste, and mismanagement. Worse than this, the truly needy have not been well served." [101]

Controllable Spending

The president does have some control over several categories of expenditures. Sixty percent of expenditures that can be classified as controllable are used for salaries and fringe benefits for both civilian and military personnel. Although these expenses technically fit the category of controllable expenditures, the practical problems surrounding spending on salaries and fringe benefits make it difficult for a president to control them completely. Seniority and civil service rules protect so many federal employees that it is futile to attempt real cutbacks in expenditures going to salaries.

A second category of controllable federal expenditures is the general operating expenses of the various agencies. Spending for operating expenses constitutes 22 percent of the budget. Although economical measures can be undertaken on such things as heating, cooling, electricity, transportation, and supplies, expenses will always continue if operations continue. And operating expenses usually increase as inflation increases.

The third category of controllable expenditures, research and development of new programs, makes up 18 percent of the controllable portion of the federal budget. Medical research, weapons research, and grants to state and local governments encompass a large proportion of this category. Again, budget cuts can be made in this category, but only within limits. As a result, even the controllable categories of the federal budget give the president little latitude in budget decisions.

Budgeting Theories

One of the most important functions served by the budget is to increase presidential administrative control and management of federal agencies and programs. How-

Table 3 Uncontrollable Spending, 1970-1980 (billions of dollars)

Category	1970	1975	1980
Open-ended programs and fixed costs			
Payments to individuals			
Social Security and railroad retirement	31.3	68.4	120.4
Federal employees' retirement and insurance	5.6	13.3	25.7
Unemployment	3.7	14.0	13.2
Veterans' benefits	6.6	12.4	13.7
Medicare and Medicaid	9.9	21.6	46.2
Housing assistance	.5	2.1	5.1
Public assistance and related programs	4.7	17.1	26.2
Interest	14.4	23.2	46.2
Revenue sharing	—	6.1	6.9
Farm price supports	3.8	.6	2.8
Other	3.8	8.0	9.8
Outlays from prior-year contracts and obligations[a]			
Defense	24.1	22.3	37.1
Civilian	17.4	28.4	50.8
Total	125.8	237.5	404.1

Source: Office of Management and Budget, *The Budget of the United States Government, Fiscal Year 1980* (Washington, D.C.: Government Printing Office, 1980), 560.

a. Excluding prior year contracts and obligations for activities shown as "open-ended programs and fixed costs."

ever, the budget process has always been the subject of criticism aimed at improving the efficiency of government management. Over the years, critics, both within the presidency and outside it, have complained about the lack of coordination and centralization in the executive branch's efforts to control the federal administration. Consequently, since the early 1960s various presidents have introduced reforms aimed at making budgeting more efficient, rational, and comprehensive. Rarely, however, have they been as successful as hoped.

Planning-Programming-Budgeting

In 1961 Secretary of Defense Robert S. McNamara introduced a planning-programming-budgeting (PPB) system into the Pentagon. McNamara brought PPB from the private sector and used it to improve the quality of decision making and budget planning for national security policy. In 1965 President Johnson announced that PPB would be applied to domestic operations as well.

PPB was designed to allow budget decisions to be made by focusing on program goals and on quantitative comparisons of costs and benefits. Once budget officials established priorities among their objectives, they then determined the best expenditure mix in the annual budget to achieve the largest future benefits.

Specifically, PPB had several main characteristics. First, it attempted to improve the planning process before programs were developed and before budget decisions were made. Improving the planning process would allow analysis to be used throughout the budget process and future budget decisions to be based on previously formulated plans.

Second, one of the most important features of PPB was its strong centralization of the budget process. Agencies would base their budget estimates on their objectives and then send the budgets up the hierarchy. This method required strong, centralized control over the composition of executive budget proposals, as well as planning and evaluation of goals.

Third, once each agency identified its goals, it also would have to specify alternative methods for achieving those goals.

Fourth, PPB emphasized cost-benefit analysis. In assessing consequences of policy alternatives, quantitative estimates of costs and benefits were assigned to each alternative. The alternative that produced the greatest benefit at the least cost would be selected. PPB proved to be attractive to budget makers because it appeared logical for the federal government to plan rather than to wander along blindly and wastefully.

By 1971, however, PPB had come into disfavor with executive budget makers. Although many people had looked to PPB to reform budgeting in the executive branch by making it more rational and less "political," PPB failed to gain a permanent place in the budget process for a variety of reasons. It never achieved any great degree of popularity within the departments and agencies in part because it required a very formal structure. One fallacy was the assumption that what worked well in the Defense Department would work well in the entire national government. In reality, comparing alternative defense systems had little resemblance to policy decisions made in, for example, the State Department.

In addition, because the budgeting system largely was forced on BOB from the top down, many BOB staffers lacked commitment to making PPB work. Finally, PPB suffered major resistance from Congress. Advocates of PPB apparently forgot that Congress has an important and jealously guarded role in the budget process. Members of Congress who had spent years building up their contacts and knowledge of agency budgets resented a new budget system that disrupted their channels of influence and information in an effort to make budgeting more rational and less political.

Management by Objective

In the late 1950s, economist Peter Drucker developed a management technique for business called management by objective (MBO). In the early 1970s, OMB adopted the system. Similar to PPB, it was an attempt to make budget decisions more rational. Not quite as ambitious in its comprehensiveness as PPB, MBO simply stated that agencies should specify goals and alternative means of achieving those goals. At each level of the budgeting process objectives would be discussed, agreed upon, and then advanced up the hierarchy. It was a system much less centralized than PPB, with less emphasis on long-range planning, but it still was based on agencies making rational choices about their policy goals.

Despite its simplification, MBO also had a short life in the federal government. By the beginning of Jimmy Carter's administration, it had passed from use.

LeLoup pointed out that many of the problems with PPB remained with MBO. He wrote, "It was difficult to specify and agree on objectives, and to quantify benefits.

MBO was not supported at middle and lower levels of agency management because it was still perceived as a system that increased control at the upper levels." [102]

Zero-Base Budgeting

The most recent attempt at presidential control over the national budgeting process is zero-base budgeting (ZBB). Developed in the private sector (like PPB and MBO) by Peter Pyhrr of Texas Instruments, Inc., ZBB was first applied to state governments.

Under Pyhrr's direction, Jimmy Carter first implemented it in Georgia while he was governor. In 1977, several months after he became president, Carter instructed OMB to implement ZBB. Carter promised that "by working together under a ZBB system, we can reduce costs and make the federal government more efficient and effective." [103] ZBB was primarily designed to avoid "incremental" budgeting where some arbitrary percentage is more or less blindly added to the preceding year's budget. Pyhrr has argued that its main goal is to "force us to identify and analyze what we [are] going to do in total, set goals and objectives, make the necessary operating decision, and evaluate changing responsibilities and work loads . . . as an integral part of the [budget] process." [104]

ZBB entails three basic steps within each administrative entity. First, agencies must identify "decision units," or the lowest-level entities in a bureaucracy for which budgets are prepared. These may be staffs, branches, programs, functions, or even individual appropriations items. Second, budget makers must formulate "decision packages," a listing of objectives and levels of services and resources needed to provide those services. Decision packages usually suggest estimates of how much service would be provided for various amounts of funding (for example, 80, 90, 100, or 110 percent of current amounts). This type of analysis allows budget makers to evaluate how much an agency would lose if its budget were cut and how much it would gain if it were given an increase. Third, at various stages of the budget process, managers must rank decision packages in order of preference. These rankings may then be revised by higher-level agency officials who consider available funding. The higher-priority packages for which there is funding are then included in the agency's budget request, and the others are dropped.

Like PPB and MBO, the appeal of a comprehensive budgeting program such as ZBB is tremendous, but its success has been limited. Budget scholar Allen Schick has concluded that the effect of ZBB on the budgeting activities of the executive branch has been almost negligible. Most budget items have been funded under ZBB at or slightly above past current services levels. [105] In their evaluation of the success of ZBB, Frank Draper and Bernard Pitsvada suggest that the success of ZBB "has been mixed in the sense that while ZBB involved more people in the budget process, it has tended to overextend itself and evolve away from true zero-base reviews. . . . ZBB as a process has not had a major impact on reducing spending, nor did ZBB really change the way agencies budget." [106]

Congressional Response to the President's Budget

Because the presidency traditionally has controlled the compilation and production of the budget, Congress frequently complained that it could get only superficial information from the president on technical budget matters on which it would eventually have to make important decisions. It argued that it did not possess adequate professional staff to evaluate independently the details, proposals, and estimates of the president's budget. Congress had become dependent on OMB and the presidency for all its budgetary information.

Congressional Budget Office

To improve its ability to evaluate the budget, Congress in 1974 created the Congressional Budget Office (CBO) through the Congressional Budget and Impoundment Control Act. CBO was a major innovation for Congress and a major challenge for the presidency. Designed to provide congressional budget committees with a variety of budget and policy information, CBO's professional staff incorporates several functions performed in the executive branch by OMB.

CBO activities fall into five categories. First, CBO prepares an annual report on budget alternatives, including fiscal policy options, levels of tax expenditures, and budget priorities. Second, it issues five-year budget projections for spending and taxation. Third, CBO projects the long-term costs of bills approved by House and Senate committees and sent to the full Congress for consideration. Fourth, CBO performs a "scorekeeping" function by comparing pending and enacted legislation with targets and ceilings specified by Congress. Fifth, CBO provides Congress with special reports on economic and budgetary issues.

CBO's independent data base allows Congress to evaluate presidential budget proposals more effectively. In measuring the success of CBO after its first five years of operation, political scientist Aaron Wildavsky wrote, "The Congressional Budget Office has improved the accuracy of budget numbers by providing a competitive source of expertise, and it has made competent analysis more widely available to those that want it." [107]

This competition in the budget process, however, has irritated more than one president. CBO's economic forecasts usually counter OMB's optimistic and more moderate projections, leading to numerous congressional-presidential confrontations over budget proposals. Shuman notes that in the past, CBO "angered President Carter because it disputed his energy program savings and angered President Reagan by saying that his economic assumptions about inflation, interest rates, and unemployment were unrealistic, overly optimistic, wrong." [108]

Congress and Presidential Lobbying

Since an almost adversarial relationship exists between Congress and the president over development of the budget, presidents must actively lobby Congress for their budget recommendations to become public policy. This difficult task is complicated by the dispersal of congressional budget authority between the House and Senate Appropriations committees and the various standing (ongoing) committees. After the president submits the budget plan, Congress gives different committees jurisdiction over different aspects of it. The House Ways and Means and Senate Finance committees consider revenue proposals. The various standing committees consider proposals for changes in laws that affect the uncontrollable expenses.

The Joint Economic Committee studies the fiscal implications of the president's proposals. The House and Senate Budget committees prepare the budget resolution. The House and Senate Appropriations committees consider expenditure requests. Presidents must exert influence on these different committees if their proposals are to become grants of spending authority for their departments and agencies.

Probably the most important committees with which presidents have to deal are the Appropriations committees. These are also the most difficult for presidents to influence because they are among the most powerful and the most isolated from White House control. Appropriations committees have several independent sources of information from which to work when they consider presidential budget requests. They have the figures prepared by OMB, estimates from the substantive committees of possible expenditures from programs under their jurisdiction, program estimates and options prepared by CBO, and tentative spending guidelines prepared by the various budget committees.

In addition to having sources of information besides that prepared by OMB, the Appropriations committees also are free from the political control of the president. Their members enjoy tremendous electoral freedom, especially those in the House. In 1986 98 percent of House members were reelected. Although the percentages are not as large in the Senate, the number of incumbents reelected has been well above the 60 percent range in recent years. Pious has written, "Each committee member can maintain his position in his district through delivery of goods and services and patronage, from agencies eager to please him. The president cannot oust these members from his party, the committee, or the House by purging them if they cross him." [109]

Still, the initiative remains with the president. A determined president, who exerts the full force of the presidency, can overcome many congressional objections. The president represents one view. Congress often speaks with many confused and chaotic partisan voices. It is therefore difficult for Congress to defeat presidential budget initiatives. Consequently, the momentum in the budget proceedings belongs to the presidency, which usually speaks with unanimity. As Shuman has pointed out, because of this consensus the White House can control the debate: the president's "budget and ... views are the subjects of the lead paragraphs in the early budget stories. Congressional criticism trails as an afterthought at the end of the article." [110] After introducing his first budget in Congress, for example, President Reagan went on the offensive by defending his budget before friendly audiences. Before a joint session of the Iowa legislature, he said, "The budget we have proposed is a line drawn in the dirt. Those who are concerned about the deficits will cross it and work with us on our proposals or their alternatives. Those who are not ... will stay on the other side and simply continue their theatrics." [111]

Presidential Spending

Although Congress has power over the appropriations process, presidents always have a certain amount of *discretionary power* over spending, that is, they may spend certain funds as they please within broad areas of responsibility. Often Congress delegates discretionary power to the president. In a crisis, for example, especially during wartime, Congress has given the president "lump sum," or very broadly defined, appropriations so that the president and executive branch officials who represent presidential wishes may devote funds as they deem appropriate within the congressional limit. For example, Congress set up the Disaster Relief Fund to be administered by the EOP without restrictions. Although the discretionary power does not give presidents unlimited spending authority, it does give them some budget flexibility and some latitude in the actual spending of funds as well as a final opportunity to make policy. As political scientist Louis Fisher has observed, "What is done by legislators at the appropriations stage can be undone by administrators during budget execution."[112]

Sometimes presidents exercise discretionary spending power that Congress has not delegated specifically by interpreting spending authorizations and appropriations as permissive rather than mandatory. In 1959, for example, President Eisenhower simply did not establish a food stamp program that Congress had passed into law. Presidents also can delay setting up appropriated programs in their efforts to frustrate congressional initiatives. In 1975, after Congress had developed a summer employment program, the Ford administration successfully stymied the program by setting it up so slowly that the appropriated funds could not be spent during the fiscal year. Similarly, OMB can delay funding from the Treasury to an agency in an attempt to eliminate the agency or its programs. In 1975 the Ford administration undermined the Community Services Administration by delaying the agency's funds until after the agency's authority expired.[113]

Confidential Funding

Occasionally, Congress grants the president confidential funding for urgent, highly sensitive, or secretive matters. Presidents have complete discretion over such annually funded budget items. For example, during his 1974 visit to Egypt, President Nixon used a presidential contingency fund to give Anwar Sadat a $3 million helicopter as a gift.

Fisher has reported that several confidential accounts are a matter of public record but are not audited by Congress, including four in the White House, six diplomatic agencies, and one each for atomic energy, space, the Federal Bureau of Investigation (FBI), and the Central Intelligence Agency (CIA).[114] One of the most notorious confidential funds was President Nixon's Special Projects Fund that was used to finance a massive spying and sabotage campaign against Nixon's "political enemies."

Secret Funding

In addition to the various confidential funds, presidents may ask Congress for a general appropriation for secret projects. Secret funds do not require either the appropriation (the amount of money granted by Congress) or the expenditure (the amount of money spent by the executive branch) to be a matter of public record.

Secret funding was used for the Manhattan Project during World War II. The development of the atomic bomb required more than $2 billion, which Congress approved with very little scrutiny of the purpose of the appropriation.

Secret funding also is used for intelligence organizations, such as the CIA. The CIA's expenditures are drawn on requests from the agency's director and are not made public or audited by Congress. CIA activities are financed by secret transfers of funds from the appropriations accounts of other agencies, primarily the Defense Department. This process keeps the CIA budget hidden not only from the public, but also from many members of Congress.

In recent years Congress has attempted to restrict the use of confidential and secret funds and bring existing funds under greater congressional scrutiny. In 1974, after revelations of covert operations overseas, Congress prohibited the CIA from funding operations other than activities intended solely for obtaining necessary intelligence.[115] More recently, there has been a move to make the funding of the CIA and other intelligence agencies a matter of public record. Congress has the power either to control or to limit this type of discretionary power, but so far it has chosen to impose only moderate limitations. As Ippolito has pointed out, "[Congress] can insure, as it has done with respect to the CIA, that more of its members participate in the oversight activities. Congress can also provide for review and audit by the Government Accounting Office to insure that confidential or secret funds are expended in accordance with legislative intent."[116]

Transfers

Another method of bypassing the congressional appropriations process is the transfer and reprogramming of funds. In these cases, presidents attempt to use appropriated funds for purposes other than what Congress originally intended. Such transfers occur when Congress permits the executive to shift funds from one appropriation account to another, allowing officials to use appropriated funds for different purposes. As noted earlier, intelligence agencies frequently are funded with transfer funds. The Central Intelligence Agency Act of 1949 allows the CIA to transfer funds to and from other agencies to perform its functions.

In 1970, the Nixon administration used transfer authority to finance the Cambodian intervention with a $108.9 million transfer from military aid accounts for Greece, Turkey, Taiwan, the Philippines, and South Vietnam. In 1972 Congress prohibited transfers of military aid from one nation to another unless the president gave Congress notice. Yet, despite the Nixon administration's agreements to submit transfers to Congress for approval, the war in Cambodia in 1972 and 1973 was financed by more than $750 million in transfer authority already given the president.

Reprogramming

Presidents may also reprogram funds, that is, move funds within an appropriation account from one budget item to another. In some cases, presidents have used reprogramming to frustrate congressional intent by shifting funds for projects that had been approved to projects that had not been approved.

Presidents most frequently reprogram funds within the Defense budget. The Pentagon often reprograms funds in an attempt to develop new weapons systems after the House and Senate Appropriations committees have cut the Defense budget. In the 1960s, for example, as many as one hundred reprogramming actions moved several billion dollars in a single year. Between 1956 and 1972, average annual reprogramming in the Pentagon totaled $2.6 billion.

In the past, congressional committees allowed departments to reprogram first and inform them afterwards. But because some departments maneuvered around the intent of appropriations measures, Congress now requires at least semiannual notification and, in some cases, prior clearance with the committees.

Impoundment Powers

Until 1974, the most powerful presidential tool in overcoming the congressional funding prerogative was the power of impoundment—the president's refusal to spend funds that Congress has appropriated for a particular purpose. Historically, presidents have claimed both constitutional and statutory authority to impound funds either by treating the funding as permissive, that is, optional, rather than mandatory and rescinding spending authority or by deferring spending to future years. The impoundment power is similar to the veto power in that both are attempts to block or thwart congressional actions.

One of the most famous early examples of a president's use of the impoundment power was Thomas Jefferson's refusal in 1803 to spend a $50,000 appropriation for gunboats on the Mississippi River to protect the western frontier. Jefferson carefully informed Congress that the money should be used for the purchase of more advanced boats the following year. Similarly, President Ulysses S. Grant refused to spend funds that Congress had appropriated for public works projects, arguing that they could be completed for less money than had been appropriated. In both cases Congress eventually accepted the president's power to refuse to spend congressionally appropriated money.

Congress eventually gave impoundment authority a statutory basis by passing the Anti-Deficiency Acts of 1905 and 1906. These laws allowed presidents to withhold funds for a period of time to prevent deficiencies or overspending in an agency. In 1921 the Bureau of the Budget established impoundment authority when its director, Charles Dawes, announced that "the president does not assume . . . that the minimum of government expenditures is the amount fixed by Congress in its appropriations." [117]

Under the New Deal, President Roosevelt occasionally used impoundments for budgetary or policy purposes. In some cases, the president acted with at least the implied consent of Congress. During the Great Depression, for example, spending bills were sometimes treated as ceilings, allowing Roosevelt to refuse to spend money that he believed to be unnecessary. During World War II, Roosevelt argued that his war powers gave him the power to cut spending that was not essential to national security. Presidents Truman, Eisenhower, and Kennedy all used impoundments to cut military spending.

President Johnson, however, used impoundments to curtail domestic spending during the Vietnam War. As the war progressed and inflation rose, Johnson impounded funds designated for agriculture, conservation, education, housing, and transportation. These impoundments were usually temporary, and the funds eventually were released. Although Johnson did not use the power of impoundment to cripple congressionally appropriated programs (many of them were his own programs), his actions did set an example of impoundment power being used to combat inflation—a power later adopted and expanded by Nixon.

Both Johnson and Nixon used impoundment to control spending, but Nixon's use was unprecedented in its scope and effects. Whereas Johnson relied on temporary deferrals rather than permanent cuts and worked personally with Congress to soothe tempers, the Nixon administration's impoundments seemed designed to eliminate or to curtail particular programs favored by the Democratic Congress. Between 1969 and 1974 the administration made a determined effort to redistribute the emphasis of governmental services. When Congress overrode Nixon's veto of the Federal Water Pollution Control Act Amendments of 1972, for example, the Nixon administration impounded half of the $18 billion that had been alloted for fiscal years 1973 through 1975, thereby handicapping the program. In addition, the Nixon administration undertook major impoundment reductions in low-rent housing construction, mass transit, food stamps, and medical research programs.

By 1973 Nixon had impounded more than $20 billion, and his budget for fiscal year 1974 contained a list of 109 reductions he wanted to make, 101 of which he said would require no congressional approval. Ippolito concluded, "While administration spokesmen advanced a variety of justifications in support of these impoundments—including precedent, statutory responsibilities, and general executive authority—it was apparent that impoundment was being used to enforce the president's policy preferences and budgetary priorities." [118] More than thirty lower court cases overturned Nixon impoundments. The Supreme Court eventually tackled Nixon's impoundment of funds for water pollution control. In *Train v. City of New York*, the Court ruled that once water pollution control funds had been appropriated by an act of Congress, funds could not be withheld at a later stage by impoundment. [119]

Eventually, public pressure began to build for Congress to do something about Nixon's use of the impoundment power. At first, individual members attempted to intervene personally with the president in an effort to restore funds to certain projects. By 1970 many subcommittees became concerned over the impoundment pattern that was beginning to emerge—a pattern that threatened their control of the policy-making process. In 1973 House and Senate Appropriations committees began holding hearings on the impoundment of funds for low-income housing, and Congress began inserting mandatory language in certain spending bills to eliminate the discretionary authority that had allowed presidential impoundment.

In 1974 Congress adopted the Congressional Budget and Impoundment Control Act. Besides setting up the Congressional Budget Office to improve congressional monitoring and deliberation of the budget, the act also aimed at controlling presidential impoundment. It stipulated two new procedures, *rescissions* and *deferrals,* by which presidents can temporarily override or delay congressional appropriations decisions. If presidents wish to defer (that is, delay) spending, they must tell Congress. If Congress does not agree, it can pass a resolution by a majority vote of both houses requiring immediate spending of the appropriated funds. If presidents wish to rescind (that is, cancel) all or part of the appropriated funds, they also must tell Congress. Unless Congress passes a rescission bill within forty-five days permitting the cancellation of funding, presidents must spend the funds.

Since Nixon resigned in 1974, a few months before the implementation of the impoundment control provisions of the budget act, he never felt the force of the act. The first administration to be confronted with these statutory impoundment limitations was the Ford administration. Of the $9 billion of rescissions requested by President Ford during his term in office, 86 percent of his requests were denied by Congress. Only 24 percent of his deferral requests were rejected, however. This pattern has been followed fairly consistently since the Ford administration. Congress usually grants deferrals; in most years, it allows 90 percent of them. Rescissions are a different matter, however. In recent years, congressional approvals have ranged from 80 percent in 1979 to none in 1980. Usually, Congress approves fewer than half of presidential rescissions.[120]

The President as Chief Law Enforcement Officer

"All is gloom in the eastern states," wrote John Marshall in January of 1787.[121] Farmers, many of them veterans of the American Revolution, sought and were denied legislative or judicial relief from their debt. Under the leadership of Daniel Shays, a former officer of George Washington's army, farmers revolted in Massachusetts. Would, as Marshall plainly worried, the American experiment survive?

It did survive. Shays's Rebellion was suppressed by Massachusetts militia, though not without considerable effort. The national government, such as it existed at the time, was powerless to assist.

Debtors, however, remained resentful, and property owners had become apprehensive. The political leadership of the United States sought a more durable remedy, and a more durable remedy was found.

In February 1787, the thirteen states of the United States were invited by Congress to send delegates to a May convention for the purpose of amending the Articles of Confederation. At the urging of leaders such James Madison and Alexander Hamilton, however, the articles were rejected summarily by the convention as a basis for continued political union among the thirteen states. The convention's new formula for government was proposed by Congress on September 17, 1787, and ratified by the requisite nine states the following year. On June 21, 1788, the U.S. Constitution became the supreme law of the land.

It would be excessive to say that Shays's Rebellion was the singular or even the most significant event leading to the adoption of the Constitution; serious defects in the Articles had been generally known well before the Massachusetts farmers revolted. The contribution of Shays to the Constitution, rather, was to force the political leadership of the various states to do what they already knew had to be done. It aroused "an emotional surge," in favor of a new constitution.[122]

Thus, "We the People of the United States," sought, among other things, to "form a more perfect Union, establish Justice, [and] insure domestic Tranquility."[123] The people would not repeat the mistake of the Confederation; Americans would not render the national government powerless to promote domestic tranquility and justice.

The president, said the Constitution, would "take Care that the Laws be faithfully executed" and would preside as chief executive over what would become a vast law enforcement apparatus. Should such assistance be needed, then the president could invoke the authority of "commander in chief" and deploy the armed forces, including units of state militia, to enforce the law. And, should mercy be a more effective means of promoting domestic tranquility than the sword, then the president would be given extensive clem-

ency authority—the power to grant pardons and reprieves. The president would become chief law enforcement officer of the United States.[124]

Presidential law enforcement power has grown in rough proportion to enlargements in the responsibilities and power of the national government itself. In 1789, the year Washington was inaugurated as the nation's first president, the national government generally restricted itself to activities such as collecting customs taxes, suppressing domestic insurrections, enforcing court orders, and regulating Indian tribes, the mails, and the army and navy. The law enforcement responsibility and power of the national government was potentially great, but actually weak.

This has changed. Congress adds incrementally to the law enforcement responsibility and power of the national government each time it convenes. The process was hastened in the final two decades of the nineteenth century and during the presidential administrations of Theodore Roosevelt, William Howard Taft, and Woodrow Wilson. Increased federal regulatory power was a fundamental element of Franklin D. Roosevelt's New Deal. With the peace following the Second World War came novel and renewed demands for national regulation, demands that have been largely met.

As Congress added to the "police power" of the national government, the power, that is, to regulate the health, safety, morals, and general welfare of the nation, it also increased the enforcement power of the executive branch. It supplemented the authority already vested directly in the president by the Constitution, or prior congressional act, and it gave the president additional resources to exercise these grants more effectively and with more power.

Congress has not relinquished its own considerable power over law enforcement. To the contrary, it has insisted that power in law enforcement be shared between the president and Congress. The role of each actor must be understood, as must be the relationship of each one to the other. So must be the unique contribution of the judicial branch to the power of the president in law enforcement.

Law Enforcement by the U.S. Government

The U.S. Constitution delegates limited power to the government of the United States. This means, essentially, that the U.S. national government possesses only those powers that are specifically granted to it by the Constitution, or those which can be fairly implied from grants that are specifically made and which are not otherwise limited by other constitutional provision. The national government does not possess general law enforcement or police power.

The Constitution itself does not give any branch of the national government explicit authority to regulate the health, safety, morals, or general welfare of the community.[125] Nonetheless, that result has been obtained. Although the Constitution does not make a grant of general police power to the national government, it does grant or enumerate a variety of powers that have been shaped, constitutionally and politically, into what now resembles a general national police power.

Article I, section 8, of the Constitution enumerates a variety of powers that may be exercised by Congress. Congress, to consider only a few such powers, may impose and collect taxes, regulate immigration, print currency and punish counterfeiters, provide postal service, and regulate the armed forces and military bases of the United States. Meriting special mention, Congress also may regulate commerce "among the several States" (the "interstate commerce clause" of the Constitution).

These powers alone may seem neither surprising nor imposing. We would expect Congress to have authority to regulate the collection of taxes, the printing and circulation of a national currency, the operation of a postal service, and trade crossing state lines. These activities, after all, seem national in scope; arguably they are necessary incidents of national power. But alone, these powers do not seem to explain the significant law enforcement power of the national government or, derivatively, of the president.

For an explanation, we must turn to the final clause of Article I, section 8, the "necessary and proper clause" of the Constitution: "The Congress shall have Power ... To make all Laws which shall be necessary and proper for carrying into Execution the foregoing Powers, and all other Powers vested by this Constitution in the Government of the United States, or in any Department or Officer thereof." If the necessary and proper clause of the Constitution is read to enlarge the enumerated powers of Congress, then we have at least a textual basis in the Constitution for Congress exercising expansive police or regulatory powers.

That is precisely how the necessary and proper clause is read by the U.S. Supreme Court. In the 1819 decision of *McCulloch v. Maryland*,[126] the Court was asked to determine whether the Constitution gave Congress authority to charter a national bank when chartering a national bank was (and is) not among those powers specifically granted Congress. If the national government, the state of Maryland argued, was to be a government of limited, enumerated powers, then the Court must find that Congress had exceeded its authority.

Writing on behalf of a unanimous Court, Chief Justice John Marshall agreed completely with Maryland's contention that Congress is granted only limited regulatory power by the Constitution. He also conceded that chartering a national bank is not listed in Article I, section 8. Marshall was too clever a legal logician, however, and too ardent a supporter of national power to allow congressional regulatory authority to be curbed by such a restricted interpretation of the Constitution.

The constitutional authority of Congress, Marshall wrote, consists of those powers that are expressly granted by the Constitution, plus—here is where he ties the necessary and proper clause to the enumerated powers of Congress—those powers that are necessary and proper to the exercise of its expressly granted powers. If the end (for example, collecting taxes or supporting an army) is legitimate (that is, authorized by an enumerated power), then the means chosen by Congress to promote that end (chartering a national bank) will be upheld judicially, as long as those means are not prohibited by some other constitutional provision.

The attention of the Court was then shifted to giving meaning to the enumerated powers. Granted, Congress is authorized to enact any law which helps it, for example, promote the regulation of interstate commerce, but what exactly does "commerce among the several States" mean? Is the Constitution referring to actual transportation of goods between two or more states? Does the commerce clause imply more?

Again, the antecedents of modern constitutional doctrine were established during the tenure of Marshall.[127] But more than a century of judicial review was required before the modern rule became established: Congress has constitutional authority to regulate anything that *affects* interstate commerce, no matter how slight the effect.[128] Little imagination is required to find an affecting relationship between a specified activity and interstate commerce.[129]

The Supreme Court's expansive interpretation of the Constitution did not mandate a particular national role in law enforcement. It did not in any sense require Congress to exercise its police power to the fullest lawful extent. The Court, rather, conferred constitutional legitimacy on an expansive national police power—if and to the extent Congress chose to exercise that power.

Periodically responding to the perceived need and popular demand for national regulation, Congress has added incrementally to the police power of the federal government. The Interstate Commerce Commission (ICC) Act of 1887 provided for federal regulation of the railroads. This was followed by the Sherman Antitrust Act of 1890, Pure Food and Drug Act of 1906, Federal Reserve Act of 1913, and Federal Trade Commission Act of 1914. The notion of an extensive federal police power, and much of the reality, was firmly in place by the time Franklin Roosevelt was inaugurated president in 1933.

The Great Depression was the singular fact faced by Roosevelt and Congress. Congress deferred to the president, and the president responded with the New Deal, a collection of programs adding directly to the regulatory authority of the federal government. The banking industry became more thoroughly regulated with enactment of the Banking Act of 1933. Enactment of the Securities Acts of 1933 and 1934 placed the sale of stocks under direct federal supervision, as did the National Labor Relations Act of 1935 for labor-management relations, and the Civil Aeronautics Act of 1938 for civilian aviation. Wages and hours of employment became the subject of extensive federal regulation with passage of the Fair Labor Standards Act of 1938.

Roosevelt and Congress had inherited the rudiments of a federal police power in 1933. By the time the New Deal had ended, effectively with the 1941 entry of the United States into the Second World War, the regulatory jurisdiction and power of the federal government had been made even more inclusive, intensive, and extensive. Regulating the health, safety, morals, and general welfare of the nation had become a major preoccupation of the federal government.

This role has been expanded in the years following the conclusion of World War II. The Federal Housing Act of 1949, and multiple amendments, made Washington the principal source of money to finance inner-city public housing construction and urban renewal. Money received from the federal government, whether in the form of loans, grants, or payments for goods and services, is accompanied by a plethora of regulations and contractual obligations. Various pieces of legislation—the most important being the employment, housing, and public accommodations provisions of the Civil Rights Act of 1964—banned discrimination based on race, color, religion, sex, and national origin. Examples of other federal measures enacted during this period are the Federal Aviation Act of 1958, Consumer Credit Policy Act of 1968, National Environmental Protection Act of 1969, Occupational Health and Safety Act of 1970, Consumer Product Safety Act of 1972, and Endangered Species Act of 1973.

This summary points out that the police power of the national government has expanded greatly in the past one hundred years. Still, the summary indicates only some of the ways power has grown. It does not mention, for instance, the many and frequent amendments to the Internal Revenue Code (annual amendments that are sometimes mockingly called "Lawyers and Accounts Relief Acts") or to the criminal code. Nor does it touch on more "traditional" exercises of federal police power: immigration, national security, regulation of Indian tribes, imposition of ethical standards on government employees, import restrictions and taxes, and operation of the postal system.

A policy of selective business "deregulation" initiated by President Jimmy Carter, and supported and furthered by his successor, Ronald Reagan, deserves special mention. Supporters of deregulation argued that it would reduce consumer costs by fostering competition and by reducing the costs of regulation (that is, the costs of record keeping, administrative monitoring, and legal advice) previously borne by the regulated businesses and passed on to consumers.

Deregulation efforts to date have been directed at a limited number of industries—primarily transportation, communications, and commercial credit—and at only selected business practices. Deregulation has reduced but not eliminated the national police power over economic activity. American businesses remain thoroughly regulated by the national government.

After enacting laws, members of Congress do not, of course, pin badges on their chests and act as enforcement officers. Rather, Congress makes the laws of the United States and then delegates enforcement jurisdiction and power to agencies and personnel of the executive branch. These agencies are also the creation of Congress.

Development of the federal civilian bureaucracy, and its power, has almost paralleled these diverse bursts of congressional energy. Civilian personnel employed by the federal government in nondefense capacities numbered 4,279 in 1816. Almost 80 percent of these were postal workers. By 1901, the number of such employees had increased to 186,532. Civilian personnel of the national government employed by nondefense agencies in 1986 totaled 1.9 million.[130]

Not all of these increases can be attributed to the growth of the police power of the national government. Space exploration, agricultural advice, and maintenance of national parks, for example, have little to do with law enforcement. When these demands are combined with the demands created by increasing direct regulation, then it can be seen that much, if not all, of the expansion of the federal civilian work force is associated with the increased law enforcement role of the national government.

As chief executive and chief law enforcement officer of the United States, the president has been the most direct and most frequent beneficiary.

Presidential Law Enforcement Authority and Power

John F. Kennedy exercised the legal power of the president when, in September 1962, he deployed U.S. marshals (and an assortment of other federal civilian law enforcement officers), and then regular army troops to Oxford, Mississippi. Kennedy was acting as chief law enforcement officer of the United States; he was, as Article II, section 3, of the U.S. Constitution requires, "tak[ing] Care that the Laws be faithfully executed."

Enforcing the law, in this case, meant backing a federal court order. In 1961, James Meredith applied for admission to the University of Mississippi ("Ole Miss"). Meredith was a Mississippi citizen, a veteran of the Air Force, and he was black. Ole Miss did not admit blacks at the time.

Denied admission by the university, Meredith appealed to the federal courts for assistance. His complaint was initially dismissed by a federal district court, but this decision was reversed by the U.S. Court of Appeals for the Fifth Circuit. A panel of Fifth Circuit judges found that Meredith had been denied admission to the university solely because of his race, and they ordered his enrollment.

Prolonged negotiations between Ross Barnett, the governor of Mississippi, Kennedy, and Kennedy's lieutenants, principally Attorney General Robert F. Kennedy, failed to produce an agreement for the orderly admission of Meredith. Mississippi, it became clear, would not use its own force to protect Meredith and maintain order on the campus. Protection and the maintenance of law and order, if it was to be supplied at all, would have to come from Washington.

Federal protection was provided initially by a contingent of U.S. marshals. A mob formed, however, and the original federal force had to be reinforced. Additional marshals were sent to Oxford, as were almost any federal law enforcement officer who could be spared—game wardens, border patrol, and prison guards. Even this augmented force was threatened by the persistent and violent mob attacks.

On September 30, 1962, President Kennedy ordered the mob to disperse. He backed his order (and the original court order) with the deployment of regular army troops to the Ole Miss campus. Meredith was registered. *(See box, John F. Kennedy, the Law, and the "Ole Miss" Campaign, pp. 36-37.)*[131]

Kennedy enforced the laws of the United States when he ordered U.S. marshals and troops onto the Ole Miss campus. In doing so, however, he—the president of the United States—also was acting according to law. He was, that is, acting according to and within the limitations set by the U.S. Constitution and Congress.

Presidential law enforcement power may be defined by either or both sources. Article II, section 1, of the Constitution vests in the president the "executive Power" of the United States. Section 2 of the second article designates the president commander in chief of the armed forces, including, when ordered into national service, the National Guard of the various states. It also gives the president almost unlimited authority to appoint the principal officers of the executive and judicial branches.

Finally, Article II, section 3, of the Constitution lays responsibility on the president to "take Care that the Laws be faithfully executed."

The second path is less direct; this path goes from the Constitution, to Congress, and from Congress to the president. Article I, section 8, of the Constitution gives Congress authority to make all laws "necessary and proper" to execute its own enumerated authority as well as any other authority conferred by the Constitution in the government or any branch of the United States. According to this authority, Congress has delegated extensive authority to the president and officers of the executive branch who are subordinate to the president.

The Constitution, for example, grants Congress authority "necessary and proper" to "provide for the Punishment of counterfeiting" the currency of the United States. Congress has used this authority by making counterfeiting a crime, by creating the Secret Service of the Treasury Department, and by giving the Secret Service authority to arrest suspected violators.

Although the Constitution and Congress vest considerable law enforcement authority in the president, both also limit that authority. The Constitution provides generally for shared decision making in many aspects of law enforcement. Presidential appointment of officers of the federal government having major law enforcement responsibilities are often subjected to Senate approval. The president must obtain Senate approval for his or her appointment to the office of attorney general, for instance, as well as the deputy and various assistant attorney generals, director of the FBI, and the U.S. attorney for each judicial district.

Presidential power is also limited by direct restrictions placed on the office by the Constitution or Congress. The president is prohibited by the Constitution from spending money for law enforcement unless an appropriation for that expenditure is first made by Congress.[132] Congress has limited the authority of the president to use military force for law enforcement.

A final characteristic of presidential power must be considered. This is the distinction between *discretionary* and *ministerial* authority.

Discretionary authority involves the exercise of judgment and choice. Ministerial authority does not. It involves, rather, the faithful implementation of decisions made by others.

The Constitution, for example, has given the president authority to nominate and, with Senate consent, to appoint justices to fill vacancies on the U.S. Supreme Court. Whom the president appoints, if anyone, is a matter left constitutionally to the discretion of the president; neither Congress nor the courts may compel the president to nominate a particular person.

Paying the salary of the person eventually appointed, however, is a purely ministerial act (with the constitutional proviso that the salary of a sitting federal judge may not be reduced). Congress sets the salary and authorizes payment; the job of the president (actually a subordinate of the president in the Department of Treasury) is to write the check. Writing the check is a ministerial act.

Where discretionary authority is at issue, the president acts as a policy maker, exercising his or her best judgment about law enforcement. Since this authority is bestowed on the president by the Constitution or Congress, a court cannot compel the president to make a particular decision. The issue is considered political, not legal.[133] A court, for instance, cannot compel the president to grant a pardon to a criminal offender; the decision is entrusted to the discretion of the president.

Much of the law enforcement authority of the president is discretionary. Discretion is assigned the president to set law enforcement priorities and to appoint senior law enforcement officials of the executive branch to implement those priorities. These officials, in turn, have been delegated considerable discretion by Congress and the president to set additional law enforcement policies—what types of offenses merit the greatest attention, what resources shall be allocated, and what cases will be prosecuted.

Merely because a power is discretionary does not mean that external political pressure cannot be brought to bear on the president. A sufficiently aroused public can force the president to be more or less aggressive in enforcing a particular law, as can a sufficiently aroused Congress. Congressional and public dissatisfaction with enforcement of the nation's environmental laws in the early years of the Reagan administration, for example, led eventually to the almost wholesale replacement of the top management of the Environmental Protection Agency. The agency became more aggressive in its enforcement efforts as a result. A disappointed public may turn to a candidate from the opposing party. Congress is equipped to retaliate in a variety of ways, escalating from mere public denouncements, to pubic investigation, to removal by impeachment. The uncompleted impeachment proceedings against President Richard Nixon (who resigned "voluntarily") remain a dramatic reminder of the ultimate measure of retaliation.

A reading of the Constitution reveals four general categories of presidential authority in law enforcement. Three of these make intuitive sense without prior understanding of the Constitution or law. These are the executive, military, and clemency powers of the president.

The fourth category of presidential law enforcement authority stems from the "take care clause" of the Constitution. Intuition is not of great use in comprehending at least the dimensions of the resulting presidential power.

Take Care Power of the President

The U.S. Constitution provides in Article I, section 3, that the president "shall take Care that the Laws be faithfully executed." Two principal interpretations of that clause often may be asserted.

One interpretation holds that the take care clause imposes an obligation on the president. The text itself is imperative in mood; it is a command to the president to obey and enforce the law. No separate and independent grant of authority to the president is stated; none can be implied.

Supreme Court Justice Oliver Wendell Holmes, Jr., urged this interpretation in *Myers v. United States:* "The duty of the President to see that the laws be executed is a duty that does not go beyond the law or require him to achieve more than Congress sees fit to leave within his power."[134] Holmes, it should be noted, was writing in dissent.

No one disputes that the president is obliged to obey the law and to enforce the law with the authority that he or she is granted. Such a view is certainly supported by rulings of the U.S. Supreme Court.[135]

The Court, however, has gone further. It has fashioned a power-granting interpretation of the take care clause, one that does not conform to Holmes's more restrictive interpretation.

The primary ruling resulted from an appeal to the Supreme Court in the case of *In re Neagle.*[136] A deputy U.S. marshal was assigned by the attorney general to guard an associate justice of the Supreme Court, Stephen J. Field. The marshal shot and killed an assailant and was prosecuted for murder by the state of California.

The marshal argued that inasmuch as he was performing official law enforcement duties as an officer of the United States at the time the assailant was shot, he was cloaked with immunity from state prosecution.

California did not dispute that U.S. marshals are generally not answerable in state courts for their official actions. It contended, however, that the marshal could not

John F. Kennedy, the Law . . .

U.S. Constitution

The confrontation between President John F. Kennedy and Gov. Ross Barnett is remembered today as an instance in which federal power overwhelmed state resistance to a judicial order. Kennedy faithfully executed the laws of the United States; James Meredith enrolled as a freshman at the University of Mississippi.

But the judicial branch did not just order Meredith's admission to "Ole Miss," and the president did not just enforce that order. The courts and the president acted according to the laws of the United States. Certain of these laws are reproduced here to illustrate how law is connected with the exercise of presidential power.

A number of constitutional provisions were involved in the Ole Miss controversy. These pertained to individual rights, the powers of the president, the powers of Congress, and the power of the national government in general.

Individual Rights. The Fourteenth Amendment, section 1, of the Constitution provides that no state may "deny to any person within its jurisdiction the equal protection of the laws." In 1954 the U.S. Supreme Court interpreted this passage to mean that segregated public educational facilities were constitutionally impermissible.[1] The U.S. Court of Appeals for the Fifth Circuit applied this rule when it ordered the University of Mississippi to admit James Meredith.[2]

Presidential Power. Article II, section 1, of the Constitution vests the "executive Power" of the United States in the president. Section 2 of this article designates the president "Commander in Chief" of the armed forces of the United States and, when called into federal service, of the several state militias. Finally, section 3 of Article II says that the president "shall take Care that the Laws be faithfully executed."

Congressional Power. Congress, under Article I, section 8, of the Constitution, is given power to "make all Laws which shall be necessary and proper for carrying into Execution" its own enumerated constitutional powers "and all other Powers vested by this Constitution in the Government of the United States, or in any Department or Officer thereof." Among the enumerated powers of Congress are the power "To raise and support Armies," "To make Rules for the Government and Regulation of the land and naval Forces," "To provide for calling forth the Militia to execute the Laws of the Union, suppress Insurrection. . . ," and "To provide for organizing,

arming, and disciplining the Militia, and for governing such Part of them as may be employed in the Service of the United States. . . ."

National Power. The "Supremacy Clause" of the Constitution provides that the "Constitution, and the laws of the United States which shall be made in Pursuance thereof; . . . shall be the supreme Law of the Land." State and local officials are bound by interpretations of the Constitution made by federal courts.[3]

Congressionally Enacted Legislation

According to its constitutional authority to make all laws "necessary and proper" to carry out the powers of Congress and of the president that are enumerated above, Congress enacted the following laws.

Section 332. Use of militia and armed forces to enforce Federal authority. "Whenever the President considers that unlawful obstructions, combinations, or assemblages, or rebellion against the authority of the United States, make it impracticable to enforce the laws of the United States in any State or Territory by the ordinary course of judicial procedings, he may call into Federal service such of the militia of any State, and use such of the armed forces, as he considers necessary to enforce those laws or to suppress the rebellion."[4]

Section 333. Interference with State and Federal Law. "The President, by using the militia the armed forces, or both, or by any other means, shall take such measures as he considers necessary to suppress, in a State, any insurrection, domestic violence, unlawful combination, or conspiracy, if it—(1) so hinders the execution of the laws of that State, and of the United States within the State, that any part or class of its people is deprived of a right, privilege, immunity, or protection named in the Constitution and secured by law, and the constituted authorities of that State are unable, fail, or refuse to protect that right, privilege, or immunity or to give that protection; or (2) opposes or obstructs the execution of the laws of the United States or impedes the course of justice under those laws. In any situation covered by clause (1), the State shall be considered to have denied the equal protection of the laws secured by the Constitution."[5]

Section 334. Proclamation to disperse. Whenever the President considers it necessary to use the militia, or the armed forces under this chapter, he shall, by proclamation, immediately order

have been acting officially when he was guarding Field since Congress had not expressly given marshals that authority. Without congressional authorization, the marshal was acting merely in the capacity of a private citizen. He

was, therefore, subject to the jurisdiction of the California courts.

The Court rejected California's argument and rendered an expansive interpretation of the take care clause in

...and the "Ole Miss" Campaign

the insurgents to disperse and retire peaceably to their abodes within a limited time.[6]

Presidential Proclamation and Executive Order

Acting on his constitutional and congressionally delegated authority, President Kennedy ordered federal enforcement of the court desegregation order. First, a force of U.S. marshals and other federal law enforcement personnel were dispatched to the Ole Miss campus. Next, when a mob threatened to overwhelm this force, and when it became apparent that state law enforcement personnel would not assist the beleaguered federal force, the president commanded the secretary of defense to deploy regular army troops to the campus. The following excerpts are from Kennedy's September 30, 1962, proclamation ordering the mob to disperse and from his executive order of the same day, mobilizing the army to enforce the law:

Proclamation 3497
Obstructions of Justice
in the State of Mississippi
By the President of the United States of America
A Proclamation

WHEREAS, the Governor of the State of Mississippi and certain law enforcement officers and other officials of that State, and other persons, individually and in unlawful assemblies, combinations and conspiracies, have been and are willfully opposing and obstructing the enforcement of orders entered by the United States District Court for the Southern District of Mississippi and the United States Court of Appeals for the Fifth Circuit; and

WHEREAS, such unlawful assemblies, combinations and conspiracies oppose and obstruct the execution of the laws of the United States, impede the course of justice under those laws and make it impracticable to enforce those laws in the State of Mississippi by the ordinary course of judicial proceedings; and

WHEREAS, I have expressly called attention of the Governor of Mississippi to the perilous situation that exists and to his duties in the premises, and have requested but have not received from him adequate assurances that the orders of the courts of the United States will be obeyed and that law and order will be maintained:

NOW, THEREFORE, I, JOHN F. KENNEDY, President of the United States, under and by virtue of the authority vested in me by Constitution and laws

of the United States, ... do command all persons engaged in such obstructions of justice to cease and desist therefrom and to disperse and retire peacefully forthwith.[7]

Executive Order 11053
Providing Assistance for the Removal of
Unlawful Obstructions of Justice
in the State of Mississippi

WHEREAS on September 30, 1962, I issued Proclamation No. 3497 reading in part as follows:

[The portions of the proclamation quoted above are reprinted.] and

WHEREAS the commands contained in that proclamation have not been obeyed and obstruction of enforcement of those court orders still exists and threatens to continue:

NOW, THEREFORE, by virtue of the authority vested in me by the Constitution and laws of the United States, ..., it is hereby ordered as follows:

Section 1. The Secretary of Defense is authorized and directed to take all appropriate steps to enforce all orders of the United States District Court for the Southern District of Mississippi and the United States Court of Appeals for the Fifth Circuit and to remove all obstructions of justice in the State of Mississippi.

Section 2. In furtherance of the enforcement of the aforementioned orders of the [specified courts], the Secretary of Defense is authorized to use such of the armed forces of the United States as he may deem necessary.

Section 3. I hereby authorize the Secretary of Defense to call into the active military service of the United States, as he may deem appropriate to carry out the purposes of this order, any or all units of the [national guard] of the State of Mississippi to serve in the active military service of the United States for an indefinite period and until relieved by appropriate orders. In carrying out the provisions of Section 1, the Secretary of Defense is authorized to use the units, and members thereof, ordered into the active military service of the United States pursuant to this section.[8]

1. *Brown v. Board of Education*, 347 U.S. 483 (1954).
2. *Meredith v. Fair*, 306 F2d 374 (5th Cir. 1962)
3. *Cooper v. Aaron*, 358 U.S. 1 (1958).
4. 10 United States Code section 332.
5. 10 United States Code section 333.
6. 10 United States Code section 334.
7. Proclamation 3497, 3 Code of Federal Regulations, 225-226 (1959-1963 compilation).
8. Executive Order 11053, 3 Code of Federal Regulations, pages 645-646 (1959-1963 compilation).

the process. The president's power to enforce the law, wrote Justice Samuel Miller, is not limited to enforcing specific acts of Congress. It also involves enforcing the Constitution and the general peace of the land. California

was ordered to release its prisoner.

Another notable Supreme Court interpretation of presidential enforcement authority arose in response to President Grover Cleveland's suppression of the Pullman

Railroad Strike of 1894. Arguing that the strike was interfering with interstate commerce and delivery of the mails, two activities consigned by the Constitution to the national government, the president sought and obtained a federal court injunction ordering the strikers to desist. Federal troops were dispatched to Chicago to enforce the injunction; those resisting were prosecuted for contempt of court.

Both the injunction and the use of military force to enforce the court order were challenged by the defendants. Congress, they argued, had not given the federal court the authority to issue the injunction, nor had it authorized the use of military force by the president to enforce the injunction. Both challenges were rebuffed by the Court.[137]

Neither Supreme Court decision should be read as giving the president power to override or ignore Congress. The take care clause, rather, was invoked in both instances when Congress had been silent.

Executive Powers of the President

Presidents are elected by the people, presumably to make and supervise the implementation of policy. Presidents are not expected to involve themselves in the details of implementation. With few exceptions, they do not.

The same might be said of the attorney general, secretary of the Treasury, or even the director of the Federal Bureau of Investigation or commissioner of the Internal Revenue Service (IRS). Considerable discretion to act is and must be delegated to the men and women who actually enforce the law: special agents of the FBI who witness a violation of federal law, IRS auditors who discover irregularities in tax filings, assistant U.S. attorneys who uncover evidence of criminal activity in the files of investigative reports.

The law enforcement power of the president, therefore, depends substantially upon the president's ability to affect the behavior of subordinates within the executive branch. And the ability of the president to affect the behavior of these subordinates depends, partially at least, on

the president's legal authority.

The Constitution says little about presidential authority over officers of the executive branch. The first sentence of Article II, section 1, states that the "executive Power shall be vested in a President of the United States of America." This would seem to give the president great power; however, the Constitution does not give a definition of "executive Power." It may be read as merely descriptive; the powers otherwise mentioned in Article II are vested in the president. It may also be read as conferring authority on the office of president that is otherwise not defined in the Constitution. The latter reading of this abuse is applied by the judicial branch.

Appointment and Removal of Law Enforcement Officers. The executive power of the president embraces authority to appoint senior law enforcement officers of the executive branch and judges of the federal judiciary. *(See also "The Appointment Power," p. 16, in this chapter.)* That authority is conferred by the "appointments clause" of Article II, section 2, of the Constitution. *(See text from Article II, section 2, in box, p. 39, and "Instruments of Presidential Control," p. 6, in this chapter.)* Additional provision is made for temporary appointments during Senate recesses.

The appointment power of the president applies generally to the senior officers of the executive branch charged with law enforcement responsibility. All cabinet members serve by virtue of presidential appointment, as do agency heads and members of the so-called subcabinet: policy-making officers immediately subordinate to the cabinet officer and at the level of under secretary, deputy secretary, and assistant secretary. This means that the president appoints not only the attorney general and the principal officers of the Department of Justice, for example, but also the principal political officers of all federal departments and agencies involved in law enforcement.

These appointees generally serve at the pleasure of the president, which means simply that they may be fired by

Drawn by G.W. Peters from sketch by G.A. Coffin; Library of Congress

President Grover Cleveland's suppression of the Pullman Railroad Strike of 1894 is an example of presidential enforcement authority. Left, a meat train leaves the Chicago stockyards under escort of U.S. Cavalry.

the president—for good reason, bad reason, or no reason at all. Such a move may be costly politically, but it does lie within the legal discretion (that is, authority) of the president, and this discretion may not be curbed by Congress.[138]

Less senior but still high-ranking law enforcement officers may also be subject to presidential appointment. The director of the FBI, commissioner of the IRS, and administrator of the Drug Enforcement Administration (DEA) are examples. Other examples include the U.S. attorney for each judicial district of the United States, the chief U.S. marshal, and the commissioner of the U.S. Customs Service.

Presidential authority to fire these officers varies. Since 1973, the director of the FBI has been appointed to a ten-year term and may not be fired without cause. U.S. attorneys, however, may be removed at the will of the president.

Two other classes of presidential appointees deserve special note: board members and other high-ranking officers of independent regulatory boards and commissions, and federal judges.

Independent regulatory boards and commissions are largely the product of the "good government" movement of the later nineteenth and early twentieth centuries. These boards and commissions are the outgrowth of the notion, naively conceived perhaps, that certain aspects of policy implementation could and should be separated from ordinary partisan politics. If the organization implementing policy is legally separated from politics, then the policy makers in that organization will act faithfully to implement policy created by Congress and will not act to promote the partisan advantage of the incumbent president.

The Interstate Commerce Commission (ICC) was established in 1887 to regulate the nation's growing railroad industry and later was assigned jurisdiction over trucking as well. After establishment of the ICC, other independent boards and commissions were created to regulate the following: business trade practices (Federal Trade Commission, or FTC), labor-management relations (National Labor Relations Board, or NLRB), television and radio broadcasting (Federal Communications Commission, or FCC), sale of stocks and bonds (Securities and Exchange Commission, or SEC), banking (Federal Reserve Board, or FRB), and the nuclear power industry (Nuclear Regulatory Commission, or NRC).

The exact authority of these agencies varies. They generally possess power to make law through what is called "rule making" and to adjudicate disputes about the application of the law through quasi-judicial methods. They also have authority to investigate unlawful conduct and, in some cases, actually to prosecute civil violations. (Criminal violations are prosecuted by the Justice Department.) Their authority may extend to rate setting and licensing of businesses and individuals.

Congress has given the president authority to appoint the principal officers of these agencies. Presidential authority to fire them, however, has been limited to reasons specified by law. These limitations have been challenged but upheld by the U.S. Supreme Court.[139] (See "The Removal Power," p. 22, in this chapter.)

Federal judges, including justices of the Supreme Court, are appointed by the president. That ends the president's formal authority over the judicial branch. By explicit constitutional provision, federal judges have life tenure and may not be removed from office except by the impeachment process.[140]

> The President shall be Commander in Chief of the Army and the Navy of the United States, and of the Militia of the several States, when called into the actual Service of the United States. . . .
> —from Article II, section 2

Presidential Authority to Command. So far we have considered two variables, appointment and removal authority, affecting presidential power over the behavior of officers of the national government involved in law enforcement. Some relationship is supposed between presidential power over these officers and presidential authority to appoint and, more important, to remove them. A third variable requires consideration: presidential authority to control their official behavior, that is, to command that they perform (or not perform) specified acts.

This authority over federal judges can be described quickly: there is none. Similarly, presidents lack command authority in most instances over officers of independent regulatory boards and commissions. (See "Regulatory Commissions," p. 4, in this chapter.)

Command authority over officers of the executive branch who do not enjoy independent status is greater, although still not absolute. If the presidential command is lawful, then failure of a subordinate to obey could constitute neglect or insubordination. The president could remove such an officer and justify the decision to do so.

Presidents themselves, however, are obliged to obey the law, and they have no authority to command their subordinates to commit a violation. What happens, for example, if the president orders the attorney general to have a person's home searched illegally and the attorney general refuses. The attorney general could be fired by the president and have no recourse in court—cabinet members serve at the discretion of the president, and may be fired for good reason, bad reason, or no reason at all.

A third situation is presented when a disagreement exists about what the law requires or prohibits. Laws are often stated ambiguously; two or more competing interpretations of a law or of a set of apparently related laws may be held by reasonable people. May the president fire a subordinate for insubordination when such disagreements are reached?

For cabinet members and other appointed officers who may be removed at the will of the president, the answer is clearly yes. In refusing to comply, the FBI director, however, would be taking a chance that his or her interpretation was correct.

The great majority of federal law enforcement personnel are not appointed by the president. They are, rather, career civil servants, who obtain their positions through a competitive and nonpartisan selection process. These law enforcement personnel may be fired only for causes specified by statute or administrative regulation, and only following a neutral and procedurally rigorous judicial-type hearing.

Special agents of the FBI, Secret Service, and Bureau of Alcohol, Tobacco, and Firearms belong to this category. So do deputy U.S. marshals, assistant U.S. attorneys, IRS auditors, and customs inspectors. In fact, just about all investigating and enforcement officers, supporting staff, and many policy-making officers of the executive branch belong to the civil service.

This makes presidential appointment authority especially important to presidential law enforcement power. Civil servants are not obliged to share the same law enforcement goals and priorities as the president. Their goals and priorities, rather, are shaped by their personal values and by their perception of what will promote their own interests. The official behavior of civil servants, therefore, should not be expected to conform in all cases with the goals and priorities of the president.

Civil servants, to be sure, are obliged to obey all lawful commands of the president and of their own bureaucratic superiors. Willful failure to comply will normally constitute legal cause for discipline, including being fired from the job. To be successful, therefore, bureaucratic resistance to the president must be displayed in a less direct, more subtle way. More than a century of accumulated experience has provided civil servants a variety of such methods.

Seasoned bureaucrats know well, for example, the difference between complying with lawful orders and going through the motions of complying. A president might exclaim, "Enough, already!" and direct federal law enforcement agents to be especially aggressive in investigating members of Congress for corruption. Such an order lies within the discretionary power of the president and is entirely lawful.

Most federal agents would comply. That is their job. Other agents, however, may not share the president's enthusiasm for investigating members of Congress. These agents may be concerned that an angry Congress would slice their budgets, or that particularly powerful members of Congress might retaliate in the future by blocking their appointments to high-level agency positions. In such a case, documents will be examined (but not too thoroughly), and leads will be followed (but not too many). All of this will be well documented in reports that pronounce the absence of evidence justifying further investigations. A command was issued, and obeyed.

The chief executive's power over law enforcement, therefore, depends substantially upon the existence of and discretion in exercising three presidential powers: appointment, removal, and command. The appointment power of the president is substantial and even applies to officers of the judicial branch. This is the most comprehensive executive power that can be used by the president to affect law enforcement.

The removal power provides the president a blunt instrument of executive coercion. It is, however, an instrument that can be used unimpeded with only the most senior officers of the executive branch, and then only in certain cases. It does not apply to federal judges at all and can be used against officers of independent regulatory boards and commisioners, certain officers of the executive branch, and civil servants only for reasons specified by Congress.

Command power is tied to removal power. If presidents are to enforce their commands, then they must be capable of removing or otherwise disciplining disobedient or obstructing officials.

The executive power of the president in law enforcement, then, depends substantially on the president's ability to choose trusted appointees who are able to influence the behavior of subordinates. Ideally, subordinates will share the president's values pertaining to law enforcement. Experience shows, however, that at least a degree of bureaucratic resistance may be expected.

Military Power

The significance of the armed forces of the United States to presidential law enforcement power should not be measured by the frequency of their use, which has, especially in this century, been infrequent. The significance, rather, lies in the fact that military coercive power is available to the president to enforce the law when civilian power is unable to do so.

Presidents have used military power to enforce the law in several notable instances. President George Washington used military force to quell the Whiskey Rebellion. His precedent was followed by President Abraham Lincoln, who used a more powerful military force to suppress the southern rebellion. Both presidents were, legally speaking, enforcing the law.

Defiance of court injunctions against labor strikes in the nineteenth century prompted both Rutherford B. Hayes and Grover Cleveland to deploy troops to enforce the law. In the twentieth century, Presidents Dwight D. Eisenhower and John F. Kennedy used force when court desegregation orders were met by local resistance. Lyndon B. Johnson used his military power in 1968 to put down rioting in Detroit.

The military power of the president is derived from the Constitution and Congress.

The U.S. Constitution states in Article II, section 2, that the "President shall be Commander in Chief of the Army and Navy of the United States, and of the Militia of the several States, when called into actual service of the United States." Article IV, section 4, provides that the United States, "on Application of the [state] Legislature, or of the Executive [governor] (when the Legislature cannot be convened)" shall guarantee "against domestic Violence."

The commander-in-chief clause of the Constitution gives the president unquestionable authority to command the men and women of the armed forces. It is authority, however, that is itself shaped by law. The president and Congress share authority over the armed forces of the United States.

Congress, according to its authority to enact laws "necessary and proper" to "make Rules for ... Regulation of the land and naval Forces," and "To provide for calling forth the Militia to execute the Laws of the Union, suppress Insurrections and repel Invasions," has enacted legislation that both authorizes and places limitations on presidential use of the military to enforce the law.[141] (See box, John F. Kennedy, the Law, and the "Ole Miss" Campaign, pp. 36-37, for a reprinting of these laws.)

The Constitution does not seriously impede the ability of the president to use military force to assist civil authorities in enforcing the law. To the contrary, wrote Justice David Brewer: "There is no such impotency in the national government.... If the emergency arises, the army of the nation, and all its militia, are at the service of the nation to compel obedience to the laws."[142]

Nor does Congress impede the president in law enforcement. A careful reading of the relevant legislation reveals that although Congress has specified the conditions in which such force may be deployed, it has worded the statute in a way that leaves to the president considerable discretion in deciding if those conditions have been met.

A different situation arises, however, should the president attempt to declare martial law and supplant civil with military authority within the boundaries of the United

States. The Supreme Court has ruled that for such an action to be maintained constitutionally, the situation must be so desperate that the civil courts are closed.[143] The military might of the United States must support, not supplant, the law.

Clemency Power

[H]e shall have Power to grant Reprieves and Pardons for Offenses against the United States, except in Cases of Impeachment.

—from Article II, section 2

Article II, section 2, of the U.S. Constitution delegates to the president "Power to grant Reprieves and Pardons for Offenses against the United States, except in Cases of Impeachment." It gives to the president an ability to be merciful as well as vengeful.

But mercy for the sake of being merciful was not necessarily what the Framers had in mind when they included clemency in the enumerated powers of the president. Alexander Hamilton explained in *Federalist* No. 74: "But the principal argument for reposing the power of pardoning . . . in the Chief Magistrate [president] is this: in seasons of insurrection or rebellion, there are often critical moments when a well-timed offer of pardon to the insurgents or rebels may restore the tranquility of the commonwealth." [144] Well-timed offers of pardon helped restore domestic tranquillity to Massachusetts after Shays's Rebellion—a fact specially noted by Hamilton.[145] Allow the president, he urged, the same power.

Shortly after the Constitution was ratified, this power was used. In 1792, President George Washington "most earnestly admonish[ed] and exhort[ed]" whiskey manufacturers of western Pennsylvania to cease their disobedience and obstruction of the law. They were, the president's proclamation continued, not only refusing to pay taxes on the whiskey produced, they were also resisting enforcement of the tax law with violence.[146]

Washington tried demands to end the "Whiskey Rebellion," and he tried force. Law and order in the western counties of Pennsylvania, however, was not restored until the president promised and granted the offenders a full and absolute pardon.[147]

A reprieve reduces a sentence already imposed by a judicial-type tribunal. A person sentenced to death by a U.S. district court or military court martial, for example, may have his or her sentence reduced to a long term of imprisonment by presidential reprieve. The guilt is not wiped out, but the severity of the punishment inflicted on the guilty person may be reduced.

Presidential pardons wipe out both guilt and punishment. They restore the person pardoned to his or her full civil rights, as if the offense had never been committed. President Gerald R. Ford, for example, granted a full and unconditional pardon to his predecessor, Richard Nixon, and relieved the former president of the possibility of being prosecuted for any involvement he may have had in the crimes associated with Watergate.

Reprieves and pardons may be granted to individuals or to classes of people in the form of "amnesties." For example, Presidents Abraham Lincoln and Andrew Johnson signed amnesties for Confederate soldiers and political leaders as did Presidents Gerald Ford and Jimmy Carter for draft evaders during the Vietnam War.

The president may attach conditions to either form of clemency. President Nixon, for instance, pardoned labor leader Jimmy Hoffa but with the condition that Hoffa would never again become involved in union activities.

The clemency authority of the president is extensive. It applies to any federal process or offender, except, by express constitutional language, those persons tried (or being tried) and convicted through congressional impeachment. Moreover, it is one of the few constitutional powers of the president that does not require legislative assent. Congress, in fact, may not interfere with presidential clemency authority in any manner, including, the U.S. Supreme Court has held, the imposition of restrictions on those pardoned.[148]

Hamilton's argument in favor of extensive presidential clemency authority received its strongest validation in the events following the Civil War. Harmony among the people of the United States did not occur immediately. In fact, hostility, anger, and resentment on both sides of the conflict made an amicable reunion of the two sides impossible for many decades. Healing took time and the passing of many generations.

The process of healing was nourished, though, by the successful reintegration of Southerners into the American political process. Not only did white Southerners regain the right to vote, they also ascended to high political office. And although no former Confederate soldier or political officer was ever elected president, many later served with distinction in the legislative, executive, and judicial branches of the United States.

Augustus Garland, for example, was appointed attorney general by President Cleveland. President William Howard Taft appointed Edward Douglas White to the position of chief justice of the United States, the titular head of the judicial branch of the nation. Both appointees had previously served the Confederate cause.

The Law Enforcement Bureaucracy

The power of the president in law enforcement has been discussed so far in terms of the legal authority that the U.S. Constitution and Congress give the office. But answering the question, "What does the president command?" is just as important as the question, "By what right?" The president commands a vast law enforcement bureaucracy, comprising scores of departments and agencies.

Perhaps the most familiar element of this bureaucracy is the Federal Bureau of Investigation. Its historical feats (and faults) have been well chronicled. But the FBI is not the national police force of the United States. In fact, the United States has no national police force. Rather, the law enforcement power of the United States is distributed throughout the executive branch.

The FBI is part of the Department of Justice, itself the repository of several other important law enforcement agencies, including the Immigration and Naturalization Service (INS), the U.S. Marshals Service, the Drug Enforcement Administration, and the Criminal Division.

The Justice Department must be considered the lead law enforcement agency at the disposal of the president. The attorney general, statutory head of the department,

Attorneys General of the United States

The attorney general of the United States is the chief legal adviser to the president and is the head of the U.S. Department of Justice. Since virtually every official decision made by the president is governed by law, and since such a large percentage of the work of the federal government is devoted to enforcing the law, the nature of the attorney general's job would almost ensure influence with the president. And indeed it has. The attorney general usually is considered one of the "inside members" of the president's cabinet. It is a position of considerable power.

President George Washington turned to a fellow Virginian, Edmund Jennings Randolph, as his (and the nation's) first attorney general. In Randolph we find two qualities that often have characterized the men (as of January 1989, no woman had been appointed attorney general) who have held that office ever since: talent and controversy.

Before serving with Thomas Jefferson, Alexander Hamilton, and Henry Knox in Washington's first cabinet, Randolph had distinguished himself through his service as military aide to General George Washington, as attorney general and governor of Virginia, as delegate to the Virginia constitutional convention of 1776, as delegate from Virginia to the Continental Congress, and as delegate to the U.S. Constitutional Convention of 1787. Although Randolph refused to sign the product, the U.S. Constitution, because, among other reasons, he opposed vesting the executive power in a single president, he did urge its ratification by Virginia.

When Thomas Jefferson resigned in 1794 as Washington's first secretary of state, Washington picked Randolph to succeed him. Randolph resigned the following year, however, amidst false charges of soliciting bribes and giving secret information to the French government. Although stripped of his public standing by the charges, the capable Randolph led the successful legal defense in the treason trial of Aaron Burr.

Talent and controversy have followed the successors of Randolph. Roger Taney, attorney general to President Andrew Jackson, and Harlan Fiske Stone, attorney general to President Calvin Coolidge, became chief justices of the United States (Stone, after serving sixteen years as associate justice). Other former attorneys general who became Supreme Court justices (and the presidents whom they served) are Nathan Clifford (James K. Polk), Joseph McKenna (William McKinley), James C. McReynolds (Woodrow Wilson), Francis W. Murphy (Franklin D. Roosevelt), Robert H. Jackson (F. D. Roosevelt), and Thomas C. Clark (Harry S Truman).

Harry M. Daugherty was attorney general to President Warren G. Harding and was implicated in the Teapot Dome Scandal. Many people thought that Ramsey Clark, the last attorney general to President Lyndon B. Johnson, should have been indicted for treason, but he was not. Clark remains controversial for visiting Hanoi during the Vietnam War after he left office. Two of President Richard Nixon's attorneys general, John N. Mitchell and Richard G. Kleindienst, went to prison after leaving office and being convicted of crimes.

One attorney general, Charles Joseph Bonaparte, had an unusual family history for an American leader. Bonaparte was the grandson of Jerome Bonaparte, king of Westphalia and marshal of France. Jerome, in turn, was the younger brother of Napoleon I, emperor of France. The American Bonaparte first distinguished himself as a leader of the good-government movement of the late nineteenth and early twentieth centuries, serving consecutively as president of the National Civil Service Reform League in 1904 and as president of the National Municipal League in 1905. This commitment appealed to President Theodore Roosevelt, who rewarded Bonaparte with appointments first as secretary of the navy and then as attorney general.

---

commands a variety of important investigatory and enforcement agencies, the FBI being only one. He or she also commands the principal prosecutorial agencies of the national government, the various U.S. attorneys across the United States, and the centralized prosecutorial divisions in Washington. Finally, the attorney general traditionally serves as the principal legal adviser to the president and supervises for the president the selection of nominees for federal judicial posts and clemency. *(See box, Attorneys General of the United States, this page.)*

Law enforcement responsibility and power is divided and allocated even further. It is allocated in significant respects to the Department of Treasury, which contains the Secret Service, Customs Service, and Internal Revenue Service; to the Department of Labor, which enforces laws regulating labor unions, wages, and occupational health and safety; to the Department of Defense, which contains both civilian and military investigative and enforcement agencies; and to various regulatory agencies.

In one respect, applying the term "chief law enforcement officer of the United States" to the president is misleading. Beginning with the Interstate Commerce Commission in 1887, and continuing with the creation of such agencies as the Federal Trade Commission, National Labor Relations Board, and the Securities and Exchange Commission, Congress periodically has allocated various law enforcement powers to independent boards and commissions within the executive branch but outside the supervisory authority of the president. The power of the president over these agencies generally is limited to appointing board members and other important agency officers. These officials may not be fired by the president except for cause, which is defined by Congress.[149]

Categories of Federal Law Enforcement

Agencies of the executive branch are involved in at least eight categories of law enforcement. These categories overlap in many instances and oversimplify a highly complex regulatory scheme, but they do provide an overview of the law enforcement activities of the executive branch.

Economic. Agencies of the executive branch implement a variety of laws seeking to foster economic growth, stability, and competition. Also included in this category are laws designed to advance fairness in business practices and harmonious labor-management relations. The Antitrust Division of the Justice Department, for example, enforces laws promoting fair trade practices and proscribing monopolies. Financial institutions are subjected to regulation by the comptroller of currency and by the IRS of the Treasury Department. Employment is subject to enforcement actions by the Occupational Safety and Health Administration (OSHA) and by the Employment Standards Administration of the Department of Labor. Despite deregulation, substantial regulation of the transportation industry is still administered by the Federal Aviation Administration of the Department of Transportation. Energy, a relative newcomer to the federal regulatory scheme, is under the jurisdiction of the Departments of Energy and of Interior.

Social. Laws have been enacted that can be said to promote a mélange of social goals: equality, fairness, and material comfort. Antidiscrimination laws, such as the equal employment and fair housing provisions of the Civil Rights Act of 1964, the Age Discrimination in Employment Act, and the Civil Rights Restoration Act of 1988 belong to this category. Their enforcement generally is accomplished by the combined efforts of the Civil Rights Division of the Justice Department, the Equal Employment Opportunity Commission, and the Department of Education. Each agency of the federal government also contains offices charged with enforcing internal compliance with these laws, as well as compliance by firms contracting with them. A multitude of retirement, medical care, and educational assistance acts are administered by the Social Security Administration of the Department of Health and Human Services, the Department of Veterans Affairs, and the Department of Education.

Political. Political decisions are made according to a complex system of procedural laws. The often-stated purpose of these laws is to promote fairness and integrity in government. The Voting Rights Act of 1965, for instance, forbids racial discrimination in voting and is enforced by the FBI and Civil Rights Division of the Department of Justice. Bribery of and extortion by federal government officials of all branches also falls under the jurisdiction of the FBI, and violations are prosecuted by the Criminal Division of the Justice Department.

Judicial. Most judicial orders are complied with voluntarily. Judgment is entered against the defendant, and the defendant complies: that is, the defendant makes payment, stops the unlawful activity, or turns himself or herself over to authorities for completion of a jail sentence. Behind every instance of voluntary compliance, however, is at least the implicit backing of armed force. Armed force may also be necessary on occasion to enforce judicial orders and to protect judges, jurors, witnesses, and other participants in a trial. The U.S. Marshals Service of the Justice Department is the agency that usually enforces the authority of the judicial branch. Their power may, in extreme circumstances, be backed by the armed forces of the United States, principally by the army and by Army National Guard units nationalized by presidential order.

Public Health and Safety. The national government oversees many issues of public health and safety. They include transportation safety, a concern of the Federal Aviation Administration (FAA) of the Department of Transportation; occupational safety and health, consigned by Congress to the aptly named Occupational Safety and Health Administration of the Department of Labor; and food purity, which falls under the jurisdiction of the Food and Drug Administration (FDA) of the Department of Health and Human Services; the Environmental Protection Agency; and the Food Safety and Inspection Service of the Department of Agriculture.

Public health and safety activities of the executive branch also entail enforcement of more commonly known criminal laws, such as those prohibiting interstate kidnapping, prostitution, and transportation of stolen property. Finally, federal laws attempting to stem drug and alcohol abuse in the United States are enforced by the FBI, DEA, FDA, Customs Service, Coast Guard, Border Patrol, and Bureau of Alcohol, Tobacco, and Firearms. Prosecutions are the responsibilty of the Criminal Division of the Justice Department and local U.S. attorneys.

National Security. Treason and espionage are crimes, as are assorted other activities that tend to jeopardize the military and diplomatic interests of the United States. Protection of American security is associated most often with the FBI, but the efforts of the FBI constitute only a part of the whole. A number of agencies of the Department of Defense—such as the Defense Investigative Service, the Naval Investigative Service, the Office of Special Investigations (Air Force), and the Intelligence and Security Command (Army)—have law enforcement duties to protect national security, as do the Coast Guard, Border Patrol, Immigration and Naturalization Service, and Office of Security at the Department of State. The Central Intelligence Agency is *not* given domestic law enforcement authority by Congress, but it may pass to the FBI intelligence it gathers abroad about American national security breaches.

Public Resources. The public resources of the national government consist of money, property, and people. Almost every law enforcement agency of the national government is involved in the protection of one or all of these resources. The better known of these agencies are the FBI and the Secret Service. Others include the Postal Inspection Service, Park Police of the Department of Interior, U.S. Marshals Service, and Federal Protective Service of the General Services Administration. Each department and agency of the executive branch contains an internal capability to investigate theft, fraud, and personal security, usually in the form of an Office of Inspector General.

Public Revenue. As Americans, we should appreciate the law enforcement services provided by the national government, for we pay for them, principally through personal and corporate income taxes, estate taxes, excise taxes, and customs duties. Most of us pay our fair share of taxes, that is, the share we are required to pay by law. But some do not. Enforcing the nation's tax laws falls primarily under the jurisdiction of three agencies of the Department of

Customs agents inspect baggage of all persons entering the United States, searching for illegal possessions such as weapons, drugs, and certain agricultural products.

Treasury: the Bureau of Alcohol, Tobacco, and Firearms (for taxes on alcohol and tobacco products), the Customs Service (for import tariffs and fees), and the Internal Revenue Service (for personal, corporate, and estate taxes). The Tax Division of the Justice Department has been established by Congress to prosecute violations of the various tax laws.

Law Enforcement Functions of the Bureaucracy

The bureaucracy performs four general law enforcement functions: investigation, enforcement, prosecution, and custody.

Investigation. Investigation entails fact finding, that is, a search for facts that may assist an agency in the discharge of its assigned law enforcement responsibilities. The search for facts may be directed toward enactment of new laws or the enforcement of existing laws with more effective strategies, policies, and priorities. Most agencies of the executive branch do this routinely.

For an assortment of reasons—the need for impartiality, prestige, or outside expertise—the president may prefer on occasion that a particular issue in law enforcement be investigated by persons not affiliated with existing agencies. In such instances, the president may appoint a presidential investigatory commission.

The presidential commission normally comprises a bipartisan panel of Americans who may or may not be employed by the federal government but who have distinguished themselves publicly. The commission receives a presidential mandate to answer a question, or a series of questions, and is supported by a professional staff paid for by the president.

The National Advisory Commission on Civil Disorders, better known as the "Kerner Commission" is a good example. In July 1968, Detroit, Michigan, was torn by urban rioting. Unable to control the rioting with state and local forces, including the Michigan National Guard, the governor of Michigan requested the assistance of the president.

The president responded with airborne troops, and order soon was restored. But, as also happened after Shays's Rebellion almost two centuries before, the causes of the rioting presumably remained. And the problem was not confined to Detroit. The president wanted to know the causes, and he wanted to know what could be done to eliminate or control them.

To answer these questions, President Johnson established the Kerner Commission on July 29, 1967.[150] He appointed Otto Kerner, then governor of Illinois, to chair a panel composed of four members of Congress, one mayor, a state official, a local police chief, and a representative each from labor, business, and civil rights.[151] Two advisory panels, a large investigative staff, and outside consultants and witnesses assisted the panel.

The commission's findings followed months of public hearings, statistical analyses, and review of programs, policies, and procedures. Almost all applied and theoretical disciplines of the social sciences influenced the final product: sociology, psychology, political science, economics, criminology, urban planning, and education. Causes were asserted and solutions offered.[152]

Some of the recommendations found their way into national policy; others were talked about but never implemented. The timing of the Detroit riot, and the resulting report, was not good because President Johnson devoted much of his remaining and limited time in the White House to managing the Vietnam War. Richard Nixon, his successor in 1969, was not as receptive to the proposals contained in the report.

The more routine form of law enforcement investigation is directed at enforcing rather than changing policy. This is fact finding aimed at determining whether an unlawful act has been committed, the identity of the perpetrators, and whether evidence can be gathered that is both admissible in court and sufficient to obtain a favorable verdict.

Most enforcement agencies of the executive branch are involved in this phase of law enforcement. The investigation may consist simply of witnessing a crime in progress and interrogating the suspect, in hopes of obtaining a signed confession.

Other investigations take more time, more effort, and considerably more resources. Investigation by the FBI of a national security breach, for example, may require months of investigative work, including surveillance of potential suspects, installation and monitoring of wiretaps, and rigorous background checks.

Certain investigations involve crimes so complex that the resources of multiple agencies from different departments may be mobilized into single task forces. Organized crime falls under this category; agents from the FBI, the IRS, and the DEA often join with their counterparts from state and local police forces and with federal and state prosecutors, to control this persistent problem.

Enforcement. The investigative process is goal directed. In most situations, this goal is the arrest and conviction of a criminal suspect. This is one way in which laws are enforced. Enforcement, however, involves more than arrest and conviction of criminal suspects. It also involves protection of federal resources and execution of judicial orders.

The federal agencies participating in enforcement (most often the same ones that conduct investigations) are too numerous to discuss in this limited space. Nevertheless, a sampling of these agencies are listed and discussed briefly below.

Food Safety and Inspection Service (Agriculture Department). President Theodore Roosevelt is reputed to have been reading Upton Sinclair's *The Jungle* while eating breakfast one morning in the White House. Disturbed by Sinclair's description of the meat-packing industry in Chicago, the president threw his sausage out of the White House window and began working toward enactment of the Pure Food and Drug Act of 1906. Conditions have improved considerably since Roosevelt's day. Meatpacking and other food production and processing industries now are subjected to standards adopted and enforced by the Department of Agriculture. The job of the Food Safety and Inspection Service is to enforce these standards. In fiscal year 1987, this agency employed 8,857 persons and administered a budget of $373 million.[153]

U.S. Department of Defense. By order of the president, units of the armed forces of the United States may be used to suppress domestic violence and to remove obstructions to the enforcement of the law. National Guard units of the states may be "nationalized" for this purpose by presidential order. When they are, they are placed under the operational command of the secretary of defense. The Defense Department, and its component Departments of the Army, Navy, and Air Force, includes a number of internal agencies with law enforcement responsibility and authority. These agencies include both civilian and military personnel and provide protective services to the property and personnel of the department. They also enforce laws pertaining to fraud, corruption, and national security. The Pentagon Procurement Scandal of 1988, for example, was uncovered by investigations conducted by the Naval Investigative Service.

Federal Bureau of Investigation (Justice Department). J. Edgar Hoover, the consummate bureaucratic chief, shaped the FBI into a modern, professional, and semi-autonomous law enforcement agency. Under his almost fifty years of leadership, the bureau gained notoriety in the 1930s by apprehending or killing marauding and overly romanticized criminals, such as John Dillinger. The favorable image Hoover and his agents already enjoyed was only enhanced by the agency's successful apprehension of enemy spies during the Second World War and the ensuing cold war. Always sensitive to public opinion, Hoover insisted that his agents conform to rigid dress and behavioral standards. He also initiated programs cultivating the bureau's reputation for effectiveness—the FBI's "ten most wanted list" is the outstanding example.

The mystique surrounding and protecting the FBI began to decay somewhat in the 1960s. Charges were made that Hoover was insensitive to civil rights issues and refused to commit his resources to the investigation of organized crime. Additional blows to the agency came in the wake of Watergate, when its acting director, L. Patrick Gray, admitted to destroying documents important to the initial investigation and when high bureau officers were convicted of and imprisoned for illegal activities. Under the tutelage of directors Clarence M. Kelley (1973-1978), former police chief of Kansas City, and William H. Webster (1978-1987), former federal appellate judge, the image of the FBI as a professional and competent law enforcement agency has been largely restored. The FBI is the closest thing the United States has to a general police agency in the national government. Its jurisdiciton includes investigation and enforcement of laws pertaining to national security, fraud, corruption, civil rights, elections, kidnapping, and robbery of federally insured banks. In fiscal year 1987, the FBI employed 22,456 persons and had a budget of $1.1 billion.

Peter Main, *Christian Science Monitor*

The U.S. Border Patrol monitors the borders of the United States, detecting and apprehending illegal entrants. Here, U.S. officers pursue illegals into a freight yard in El Paso, Texas.

Gerald R. Ford Library

Secret Service agents surround President Ford and survey the crowd as the president waves from his motorcade. The Secret Service provides security for the president and the first family as well as for past presidents and their families.

Drug Enforcement Administration (Justice Department). Agents of the DEA have perhaps the dirtiest and most dangerous law enforcement job in the federal government: they enforce national drug laws. Most of the work of the DEA is conducted within the boundaries of the United States. Yet, agents may and often do carry their investigations to foreign countries—the drug production, refinement, and transportation centers in Latin America, Europe, Asia, and the Middle East. Here they may advise and exchange intelligence information with their foreign counterparts and, depending on arrangements with their host countries, conduct their own investigations. Although they are subject to reprisals by foreign drug dealers, they are not necessarily authorized to arm themselves. The half-billion dollar budget and 5,680 employees authorized by Congress for the DEA in fiscal year 1987 reflect the agency's importance to federal law enforcement policy.

Border Patrol (Justice Department). The Border Patrol, the uniformed component of the Immigration and Naturalization Service, does just what its name implies: it patrols the borders of the United States. As an agency of the INS, the principal task of the Border Patrol is to detect and apprehend illegal entrants. Performing this task, of course, exposes officers of the Border Patrol to an assortment of other crimes, the most notable of which is drug smuggling across the U.S. border. They have the authority and are expected to make arrests in such circumstances.

U.S. Marshals Service (Justice Department). U.S. marshals have been a law enforcement resource of the president since the administration of President George Washington. In the nineteenth century, marshals acted as the general police force for much of the West; large sections of the American West had not yet achieved statehood and were organized by Congress as territories of the United States. Television has taught us that the U.S. marshal of this period, Wyatt Earp and Matt Dillon being only two, single-handedly stood between the ordinary law-abiding

citizen and a host of predators—gunslingers, horse thieves, and the local cattle baron, all aided, apparently, by corrupt local sheriffs, mayors, and judges.

The job of the marshal in contemporary American society is less romantic but still important. Marshals enforce court orders, serve court papers, maintain security and order in courtrooms, protect witnesses, escort federal prisoners, and suppress domestic disturbances. Marshals possess general law enforcement power and are an all-purpose force at the disposal of the president and attorney general. The 1987 budget for the U.S. Marshals Service was comparatively small—$168 million. The service employed 2,729 persons in fiscal year 1987.

Secret Service (Treasury Department). The men and women wearing business suits, sunglasses, and radio earplugs who surround the president on every occasion are the best-known component of the Secret Service. But guarding the president is just one of the duties of this agency of the Treasury Department. It also provides security for the vice president, former presidents, immediate family members of current and former presidents, the president- and vice president-elect, presidential and vice-presidential candidates, and visiting heads of state. A uniformed branch of the Secret Service guards foreign embassies and missions and assists in guarding the White House. The Secret Service also has primary jurisdiction in enforcing laws pertaining to counterfeiting, credit card fraud, and defrauding of federally insured banks. Congress appropriated $334 million for the Secret Service in fiscal year 1987, a large portion of which was used to pay the salaries of the 4,355 men and women it employs.

Internal Revenue Service (Treasury Department). The IRS has an enviable reputation in Washington for efficiency and impartiality, although many Americans view it apprehensively as the nation's tax collector. Consider its assignment from Congress: The IRS not only collects taxes owed the federal government from individuals and corporations but also processes tax returns from almost every American adult, corporation, partnership, and nonprofit organization. It also calculates and returns any amount previously overpaid by the taxpayer. Usually by computer, certain of these returns are selected for audit, a process designed to detect tax fraud and to deter intentional understatement of future tax liabilities. The IRS includes a criminal investigative division, whose agents are authorized to carry firearms, investigate possible criminal violations of the tax code, make arrests, and serve search warrants. In fiscal year 1987, the IRS employed 29,561 persons and was appropriated a budget of $4.4 billion.

Customs Service (Treasury Department). The men and women of the Customs Service are the ones authorized to inspect the baggage of all persons, citizen or visitor, entering the United States. They are searching chiefly for goods subject to federal tax or prohibited by law from being imported into the United States, such as drugs, weapons, and certain agricultural products. Customs agents board and search incoming ships, airplanes, pleasure boats, trucks, buses, and automobiles, as well as their passengers, baggage, and cargo. Although the Customs Service is principally a tax collection and enforcement agency, it has assumed a lead role in the enforcement of the nation's drug laws by intercepting shipments on the borders of the United States. In fiscal year 1987, the Customs Service had 15,610 employees and a budget of $1.1 billion.

Employment Standards Administration (Labor Department). The Fair Labor Standards Act mandates that employees engaged in interstate commerce not otherwise exempted must be paid a minimum hourly wage—$3.35 per hour as of January 1989. The same act also requires that compensation amounting to the employee's usual hourly wage be paid for any work exceeding forty hours in a given work week. Enforcing these laws is the primary responsibility of the Employment Standards Administration (ESA). In fiscal year 1987, the ESA employed 4,100 persons and had a budget of $191 million.

Occupational Safety and Health Administration (La-

bor Department). Health and safety in the work place are the concerns of OSHA. In accordance with legislation passed by Congress, OSHA has put into effect detailed regulations governing such matters as protective clothing for workers, the handling of hazardous substances, and protective shields on industrial equipment. Inspectors from local OSHA offices inspect work sites and have authority to cite employers who violate or permit violations of the regulations. OSHA employed 2,141 persons in fiscal year 1987 and administered a budget of $226 million.

Federal Aviation Administration (Transportation Department). Americans should appreciate the FAA, for we fly millions of miles each year and are rarely discomforted, much less hurt. Part of the explanation lies in the efforts of the FAA, which administers and enforces laws pertaining to commercial air travel. Its jurisdiction includes pilot licensing, airport safety and security, air traffic control, and airplane safety. It employed 45,266 persons in fiscal year 1987 and administered a budget of $2.3 billion.

Coast Guard (Transportation Department). The Coast Guard traces its origins to the nation's first secretary of the Treasury, Alexander Hamilton, who created a service of revenue cutters (small, armed ships) to help prevent smuggling and the resulting evasion of customs taxes. The Coast Guard still performs this function. It also enforces regulations pertaining to maritime safety, licenses boat captains, patrols waterways for hazards (such as icebergs), and rescues people from sunken or disabled vessels. The Coast Guard has an important role in the current efforts to suppress drug smuggling. During war, operational command of the Coast Guard is transferred to the Navy. In fiscal year 1987, Congress gave the Coast Guard a budget of $1.8 billion, part of which was used to pay its 39,778 uniformed and civilian personnel.

Offices of Inspector General. All federal departments and most federal agencies contain an office of inspector general. The functions vary somewhat by agency but generally include investigations of fraud, abuse, bribery, waste, and personal misconduct within the agency.

U.S. Coast Guard

A Coast Guard crew unloads bails of marijuana seized off the Florida coast.

Prosecution. U.S. attorneys filed 118,237 civil and criminal actions during the 1987 fiscal year. This added to their existing workload of 202,479 docketed cases.[154]

The U.S. attorney is the workhorse of the federal prosecutorial system. Appointed by the president, and located within the Department of Justice, the U.S. attorney assumes the lead responsibility for representing the government in court. One U.S. attorney is appointed for each of the ninety-four judicial districts in the United States and is supported by a professional legal staff.

Although the U.S. attorney represents the government in most cases, there are other prosecutorial resources in the executive branch. The Department of Justice itself comprises different divisions that may, at times, be involved in litigation. Each division is headed by an assistant attorney general. Their jurisdiction is indicated by their division title: Antitrust Division, Civil Division, Civil Rights Division, Criminal Division, Land and Natural Resources Division, and Tax Division.

One other component of the Justice Department is involved in the prosecution phase of law enforcement. This is the Office of Solicitor General. The solicitor general determines which decisions of federal or state appellate courts will be appealed by the United States to the U.S. Supreme Court and represents the government in the appeal. Owing to the considerable influence the Supreme Court has in interpreting the law, including laws allocating power to the president and presidential agencies, this function is particularly critical to the president.

Departments and agencies outside of the Justice Department occasionally are given limited prosecutorial authority and resources by Congress. The solicitor of labor, for instance, has authority to initiate civil actions in federal court to enforce wage-and-hour and occupational health and safety laws.

Custody. Conviction of a crime in federal court may lead to a sentence of imprisonment. When it does, the prisoner is usually remanded to the custody of the Bureau of Prisons for punishment. The Bureau of Prisons is an agency of the Department of Justice and has responsibility for administering the federal prison system. This responsibility includes guarding the inmates (often from one another) as well as supplying them housing, food, recreation, medical care, and rehabilitation services such as education and counseling. The bureau employed 11,257 persons and spent $626 million in fiscal year 1987.

Law Enforcement within the U.S. Political System

Law enforcement responsibility and power are shared in the U.S. political system, first of all by the national government and the fifty states and their units of local government. Responsibility and power for law enforcement are also shared by the three branches of the national government. With the notable exception of the president's constitutional authority to grant reprieves and pardons, all incidents of presidential law enforcement power may be checked by at least one of the two other branches.

Sharing within the Federal System

Federalism refers to a form of political organization whereby at least two levels of government exercise sovereign power over geographically defined and overlapping jurisdictions. The two levels of sovereign government in the United States are the national government and the fifty independent state governments.

Allocation of law enforcement responsibility and power within the U.S. federal system has evolved significantly since George Washington and members of the First Congress took office in 1789. This evolution generally has increased the power and responsibility of the national government at the expense of state power and independence.

National law enforcement responsibility and power were slight in 1789 and remained so until the Civil War. States, however, had significant law enforcement responsibility during this period, and they had power commensurate with that responsibility. Legislating to promote the public's health, safety, morals, and general welfare was the business of the state legislatures, and it was the business of local sheriffs, state militia, and state judges to enforce those laws.

A number of things changed this balance in favor of the national government. First, led by Chief Justice John Marshall, the U.S. Supreme Court handed down rulings in the first decades of the nineteenth century that interpreted expansively the constitutional grants of power to the national government. Congress, the Court ruled, has ample constitutional power to enact any law necessary and proper to carry out its enumerated powers, as long as that law was not proscribed by the Constitution itself.[155] Contrary provisions of state law must yield to laws enacted by Congress in accordance with its constitutional power,[156] and state court interpretations of federal law are susceptible to review and possible reversal by federal courts.[157]

The assumption of significant and broader law enforcement responsibility and power by the national government cannot be attributed to Marshall and his Court; a half-century was to pass before the national government began assuming its modern role and powers. What these early judicial rulings did accomplish, however, was to establish a constitutional doctrine for the assumption when it was to occur.

Marshall and the Supreme Court, then, legitimized an extensive and pervasive national role in law enforcement. Still missing was a workable consensus among the American people and their elected representatives in Congress that such a role ought to be exercised. That consensus was achieved in the latter part of the nineteenth century.

Business in the early decades of the American Republic was largely a local activity and was regulated primarily by state and local governments. By the latter two decades of the nineteenth century, however, it became increasingly apparent that many business activities either could not or would not be regulated effectively by state and local government. The people eventually pressured Washington to assume the burden. Interstate rail transportation came under federal regulatory jurisdiction with enactment of the Interstate Commerce Act of 1887. Today, virtually no business activity is untouched by federal regulation.

The current relationship between the national and the fifty state governments in law enforcement is complex. Some activities are regulated extensively and simultaneously by both levels of government. Retail sales, occupational health and safety, and banking, for example, are subject to a host of national and state laws and regulations.

Other activities tend to be regulated predominantly by either one or the other level of government. The national government exercises a near monopoly in the regulation of interstate and international airline travel, radio and television broadcasting, and nuclear power production. Automobile speed limits, assault and battery, marriage and divorce, and medical licensing are principally matters for state regulation.

The current breakdown of state-national law enforcement responsibility reflects the will of Congress. Congress, without question, is empowered to exert a far wider regulatory reach than it currently exercises. Yet it is content to leave the regulation of most activities to state government. Congress, for example, is quite content to leave the definition and enforcement of many "ordinary" crimes to state governments. Murder, rape, burglary, robbery, and mayhem are offensive to American society. They merit prohibition and punishment throughout the United States. And they are, but not by the federal government (except when a special federal connection exists, such as when the crime is committed by a member of the armed forces and on the premises of a military base). These and other ordinary crimes are generally the object of state, not federal, regulation.

States may already do the job competently, or, in fact, far better than could be expected from the national government. Moreover, Congress understandably wishes to avoid entering additional regulatory fields requiring much additional expense and work—by Congress, as well as the federal executive and judicial branches—and little anticipated benefit.

Consider, for instance, the burden that would be placed on all three branches of the national government should Congress attempt to regulate directly speed limits on federally financed highways. Consider also what, if anything, would be gained.[158]

Congress is susceptible to political pressure as well. When Congress enters a new regulatory field, support for such a move can usually be traced to politically powerful interest groups, or to the American public, or both. Conversely, lack of congressional interest in a regulatory field is understandable when such a move is supported neither by powerful interest groups nor by a significant segment of the American public. This is especially true when a contemplated law is actively opposed.

Little public interest, for example, is aroused by the notion of professional licensing by the national government. But the idea arouses strong opposition from well-organized and assertive interest groups such as national and state bar and medical associations. Attorneys and physicians are licensed by state government.

The relationship between national law enforcement agencies of the executive branch and their counterparts in state and local governments can be characterized most aptly as competitive but cooperative. Federal law enforcement agencies may request, and often receive, investigatory and enforcement assistance from state and local police forces. Such assistance, for instance, may be given to locate and arrest a military deserter, an armed robber of a post office, or a counterfeiter, or it may be given in the form of security for a visiting president or foreign dignitary.

The president and the principal law enforcement officers of the national government will be reluctant to deny a reasonable request from a state governor for law enforcement assistance. The request may be for troops to put down a riot, as occurred when President Lyndon Johnson sent airborne troops to Detroit in the summer of 1967. More commonly, though, it will involve special federal attention to local problems that either are beyond the competence of state and local resources to resolve or can be resolved more effectively and efficiently with federal assistance.

Finally, state and local agencies also receive routine assistance from federal law enforcement agencies. Federal agencies distribute law enforcement assistance grants to state and local governments, offer training in modern law enforcement techniques and technology to state and local enforcement officials, and provide intelligence information about local criminal activity.

Sharing within the National Government

High school civics teaches that laws are made by Congress, enforced by the president, and applied by the courts. It is by this means that tyranny in the United States is averted: political power in the national government is divided and allocated to separate and independent branches. Each branch, therefore, has some check on the goings on (and possible abuses) of the others.

Article I, section 1, of the U.S. Constitution does assign the legislative power to Congress. And Article II vests the executive power of the United States in the president and imposes on the president the obligation to "take Care that the Laws be faithfully executed." Finally, Article III, section 1, delegates the judicial power of the United States to the Supreme Court and to such other courts as Congress chooses to create.

Still, there is more to this arrangement than the division and allocation of power to separate and independent branches. Power is also shared. Congress, the legislative arm of the national government, makes law according to its constitutional grant of power, but is does so subject to presidential approval or veto, and often at the president's urging. Congress also delegates practical law-making power—authority to promulgate binding administrative rules and regulations—to the president and officers of the executive who may or may not report to the president.

The judiciary, if complaints from presidents and members of Congress are any measure, seems to involve itself in functions normally considered legislative or executive. Judges routinely interpret law and by so doing lend their own flavor to its meaning. Occasionally this leads judges to invalidate congressional or executive actions.

Conflicts between the president and Congress or the president and the judiciary attract the attention of the press and, by derivation, of the American public. Intramural conflict is a familiar ingredient of U.S. political life.

Although less attention is drawn to this fact, thus it is less evident to the American people, cooperation also exists among the three branches of American government, more so, perhaps, than conflict. The relationship is not harmonious, nor is it intended to be, but it is generally cooperative.

Congress and Presidential Law Enforcement Power. Article I, section 1, of the Constitution states that "All legislative Powers" of the United States belong to Congress. This power bears directly, extensively, and frequently on the law enforcement obligations and powers of the president. Four categories of power are available to Congress, which, when exercised, may either increase or restrict the law enforcement power of the president. These are law making, investigation, review of presidential appointments, and impeachment.

Congress is, first of all, responsible for defining the laws of the United States. Congress decided that railroads, airlines, and television ought to be regulated by the national government, and Congress determined that national standards ought to apply to production of food and drugs. The expansion of the national police power is the product of congressional action.

The legislative work of Congress does not end with asserting the regulatory power of the national government. A system and a process must be set in place for enforcing the law. Agencies must be created and empowered. They must employ men and women who actually enforce the law, and they must pay them. Finally, law enforcement officers of the executive branch must be granted specific law enforcement authority.

Congress provides the people necessary to staff the president's law enforcement agencies through authorizing legislation, and it provides for payment of their salaries through separate appropriations bills. Through a similar process, it provides enforcement officers the personnel and material support necessary to do a satisfactory job.

Federal law enforcement agencies and personnel receive two principal forms of authority from Congress: jurisdictional and enforcement authority. The former determines the types of laws a given agency is supposed to enforce; the second provides enforcement officers with the specific powers to make their enforcement effective.

Congress, for example, has defined the jurisdiction of the Secret Service to include protection of the current and former presidents and vice presidents of the United States and the members of their immediate families; candidates for the presidency and vice presidency meeting certain conditions; and visiting foreign dignitaries. The Secret Service also has jurisdiction over laws pertaining to currency, enumerated sections of various banking laws, and various forms of electronic and credit card fraud. [159]

Agency jurisdiction occasionally overlaps. The Drug Enforcement Administration has primary jurisdiction over enforcement of the nation's narcotics laws. But that jurisdiction overlaps considerably with the jurisdiction given the FBI, the Customs Service, the Coast Guard, and the Food and Drug Administration. Congress has given all of these agencies, and many more, the authority to enforce various aspects of the nation's drug laws.

Special agents and other FBI personnel have congressional authority to "carry firearms, serve warrants and supoenas issued under the authority of the United States." Congress has also given them authority to "make arrests without warrant for any offense against the United States committed in their presence, or for any felony cognizable under the laws of the United States if they have reasonable grounds to believe that the person to be arrested has committed or is committing such felony." [160]

Congress has made similar grants of authority to U.S. marshals, agents of the Secret Service and Drug Enforcement Administration, and a host of other federal law enforcement personnel. [161]

Congress may limit the authority that it confers on federal law enforcement agencies and personnel. Postal inspectors, for instance, have authority to "make arrests without warrant for offenses against the United States committed in their presence," [162] but only if the offense is related to the property or use of the Postal Service. [163]

The second way Congress may affect the law enforcement power of the president involves the exercise of its inherent authority to investigate. Investigations may be for the purpose of determining whether new laws are needed, or they may be to determine whether existing laws are being enforced in the manner and with the energy that Congress intends.

Congressional investigations frequently are conducted through the device of a committee hearing. Witnesses give their views on the issue before the committee and subject themselves to questions by commttee members and counsel. The testimony may be given voluntarily or under compulsion (subpoena). In most instances a witness will be placed under oath, subjecting him or her to the possibility of prosecution for giving false testimony intentionally.

Impressive resources are available to Congress to assist in these investigations. These may include personal and committee staff, researchers of the Library of Congress, economists of the Congressional Budget Office, auditors of the General Accounting Office, and analysts of the Office of Technology Assessment. The staffs of each of these congressional agencies have established reputations for objective and competent work.

Television has enhanced the significance of congressional investigations. The specter of organized crime in the United States was revealed starkly in the 1950s televised investigations of the Kefauver Committee (Special Committee to Investigate Organized Crime in Interstate Commerce)—the American people heard, for the first time, mention of the "mafia" and "la cosa nostra" from witnesses who testified to the power and pervasiveness of these organizations in American society.

Of more recent vintage, separate Senate and House committees investigated alleged criminal activities committed during the Nixon administration, after burglars traced to the White House were arrested during a break-in of the Democratic National Committee headquarters at the Watergate complex in Washington, D.C. In 1987, a joint committee of Congress investigated the circumstances surrounding the Iran-contra affair.

Most congressional investigations lack such spectacular quality, but they are important nevertheless. A subcommittee of the House Committee on Interior and Insular Affairs, for instance, conducted an investigation into the enforcement of federal law by the Nuclear Regulatory Commission. Its findings were critical, as is indicated by the title of its report: *NRC Coziness with Industry: Nuclear Regulatory Commission Fails to Maintain Arms' Length Relationship with the Nuclear Industry.* [164]

Review of Presidential Appointees. The importance of presidential appointment authority to presidential law enforcement power has already been discussed. Congress exercises an important restraint on presidential law enforcement power by saying (within constitutional limitations) which offices are subject to presidential appointment and what limitations are imposed on the presidential authority to remove commissioned appointees.

Congress also influences presidential appointment authority by specifying the appointments that must receive Senate confirmation before the appointees may take office. The only limitation on this legislative check on presidential law enforcement authority is that nominees to the U.S. Supreme Court must be considered and approved by the Senate—that is not a disabling condition.

Presidential appointees to law enforcement and judicial positions are regularly if not routinely approved by the Senate. Generally, the position of the Senate is that appointment, especially of the president's own subordinates in the executive branch, is the president's prerogative. Refusal to confirm must be based on considerations other than partisan or ideological differences. The reasons heard most often for failure of the Senate to confirm are unfitness for office due to questions of ethical or professional competence for the job.

There are exceptions, however. In 1985, for example, the Senate refused to confirm William Bradford Reynolds as President Reagan's appointee to associate attorney general. An adequate number of senators were not satisfied that Reynolds had performed with sufficient vigor in his previous post, assistant attorney general in charge of the civil rights division.

The effect of Senate approval on presidential appointment power, however, cannot be measured solely by reference to the number of times the Senate refuses to confirm. Knowing that appointees must be examined and confirmed by the Senate may well cause the president to moderate appointments, at least on occasion. Moreover, the knowledge that nominees will be subjected to Senate scrutiny should cause the president to insist that backgrounds of prospective appointees be subjected to searching investigation before names are announced and submitted. It does not always work that way.

Finally, Senate examination of presidential nominees, usually done in public hearings, may result in promises being made by the nominee to Congress. A notable instance was when the Senate Judiciary Committee exacted a promise from Elliot Richardson that if confirmed as attorney general, he would not fire the special prosecutor investigating the Watergate improprieties except for misconduct. Richardson was confirmed and kept his promise. He resigned rather than obey President Nixon's order to fire Archibald Cox, the special prosecutor.

Removal from Office through the Impeachment Process. The ultimate congressional check over executive law enforcement power is removal through impeachment and conviction. Article II, section 4, of the Constitution gives Congress power to remove from office the president, vice president, "and all civil Officers of the United States," upon impeachment for and conviction of "Treason, Bribery, or other high Crimes and Misdemeanors."

The removal process is conducted in two stages: impeachment and trial. The first stage, which is consigned by the Constitution to the House of Representatives, is concerned with whether probable cause exists to believe that misconduct warranting removal has occurred and that the accused is culpable.[165] Acting much like a grand jury in a criminal case, the House considers charges of misconduct, hears evidence concerning the alleged acts of misconduct, makes a preliminary determination of whether the alleged misconduct, if true, warrants removal, and whether the evidence supports the charges. If the House, by a majority vote, considers the allegations of misconduct sufficiently serious to warrant removal, and supported by the evidence, then it reports one or more articles of impeachment to the Senate for trial.

The House functions as a grand jury; the Senate acts much like a trial jury in a criminal case. Its function is to convict or acquit for each article of impeachment, based on evidence heard in a trial conducted in the Senate chambers. Guilt or innocence of the charges contained in the articles of impeachment is determined by a two-thirds vote of the senators present.[166]

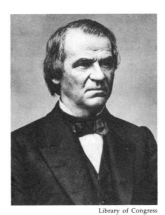

Only one president has been impeached to date — Andrew Johnson in 1868.

"Treason, Bribery, or other high Crimes and Misdemeanors," the constitutionally stated grounds for removal through the impeachment process, do not have a meaning that is agreed upon universally. Alexander Hamilton described the impeachment power as political, for it would be applied to persons committing "injuries done immediately to society itself." [167]

Such injuries, we may safely assume, would include the stated crimes of treason and bribery, as well as such criminal acts as murder, rape, and mayhem. But would they also include, as "high Crimes and Misdemeanors," conduct more in the nature of political misdeeds? Would they include, for example, a violation of the Constitution or a statute not providing criminal penalties? Would they include a *failure* to enforce the law?

Because of a paucity of precedent, no definitive answer can be given. Only one president has been impeached (that is, charged) to date. In 1868, President Andrew Johnson was charged by the House with violating the Tenure of Office Act of 1867.[168] The president was charged with violating his constitutional obligation to take care that the laws are executed faithfully by firing Edwin M. Stanton, his secretary of war, without cause or without prior Senate consent. The Senate, however, failed to muster the two-thirds vote necessary to convict Johnson—by one vote.

The precedent furnished by Johnson's ordeal is primarily negative. A narrow interpretation of the precedent would hold that the Senate merely confirmed that violation of the Tenure of Office Act, a legislative measure of dubious constitutional validity, did not constitute a sufficient basis for removal of the president.[169] A broader reading of the Senate's action would find significant the failure of the Senate to remove a president for what was really political incompatibility.

A more contemporary instance of the impeachment power being used against a president is furnished by the events leading to the resignation of President Nixon in 1974. In 1972, employees of the Committee to Re-elect the President, Nixon's personal campaign organization, were arrested by District of Columbia police during a burglary of the Democratic party headquarters in Washington's Watergate complex.

Investigations by local and federal law enforcement agencies, a federal grand jury, a Senate investigative committee, a special prosecutor, as well as newspaper and broadcast journalists, revealed evidence not only of involvement by high- and mid-level members and former members of the Nixon administration in the burglary but also of various other allegedly unlawful activities. An impeachment bill was introduced on the House floor and referred to the House Committee on the Judiciary.

Following televised hearings, the committee voted to recommend three articles of impeachment to the House. Each one of the three articles charged the president with violating his oath of office and his constitutional obligation to take care that the laws be faithfully executed. The three articles then enumerated specific allegations of misconduct, which, a majority of the committee believed, warranted Nixon's removal: obstruction of justice, abuse of power, abuse of individual rights, misprision (concealment) of felony, and failure to comply with congressional subpoenas.

Nixon was not impeached; that outcome was averted when he resigned from the office on August 9, 1974. Still, the committee action remains a powerful reminder that the removal power of Congress is not entirely dormant. The circumstances warranting its use must be serious, and the charges must be backed by compelling evidence—a "smoking gun" was the phrase often used by some committee members. But the power remains, and it can be used.

The Judiciary and the President. The essential American judicial function is to arbitrate and resolve legal disputes according to the law. In doing this, the judiciary both supports and checks presidential law enforcement authority. It also creates law enforcement opportunities and burdens for the president and makes law through the process of interpreting law.

Presidential law enforcement power is supported by the judiciary when judges lend legitimacy to presidential claims of law enforcement authority by declaring that those claims are in accord with the U.S. Constitution and laws of the United States. Such pronouncements usually settle any immediate disputes between the president and Congress or the states over the existence and extent of specific presidential law enforcement powers, and they offer reassurance to the American people that their president acted within the law.

The judiciary also supports presidential law enforcement power by invalidating efforts by other political actors, usually the Congress and states, to unduly restrict presidential authority.

Americans witnessed the first type of support for presidential power when the U.S. Supreme Court upheld assertions of presidential power to deploy military forces to suppress a domestic insurrection (the Civil War) and to quell strikes inhibiting interstate movement of railroads and delivery of the U.S. mail.[170] Similarly, the Supreme Court upheld presidential discretion to use U.S. marshals to maintain peace in situations neither contemplated nor prohibited by legislation.[171] The Court has protected the president from congressional interference with the power to grant pardons, reprieves, and amnesties.[172]

American judges, however, are an independent lot, constitutionally and in fact. They are not appointed to be mere supporters of the president, and they do not define their own roles in that manner. They have authority to check presidential claims of law enforcement power, and they have the power to make their own authority felt.

Presidential law enforcement authority is checked by the judiciary most often when judges rule against the government in civil or criminal cases. The ruling may be on an important interpretation of law, the admissibility in trial of a critical piece of evidence, or on the facts of the case. An assortment of judicial rulings can lead to the government losing. The result is the same.

When the rulings involve an interpretation of constitutionally or legislatively delegated authority of the president, then the effect may well limit the executive law enforcement capability in future cases as well as in the immediate case. Federal law enforcement agents know well, for example, that a confession obtained through coercion cannot be used as evidence in trial.

Notes

1. Clinton L. Rossiter, *The American Presidency,* 3d ed. (New York: Harcourt Brace Jovanovich, 1963).
2. Woodrow Wilson, *Congressional Government* (1885; reprint, New York: Meridian Books, 1956), 167-168, 170.
3. Peter Woll, *American Bureaucracy,* 2d ed. (New York: W. W. Norton, 1977), 63.
4. Alexander Hamilton, *Federalist* No. 72, in *The Federalist Papers* (New York: Tudor, 1937), 64.
5. Charles T. Goodsell, *The Case for Bureaucracy* (Chatham, N. J.: Chatham House, 1983), 2.
6. H. H. Gerth and C. Wright Mills, *From Max Weber* (New York: Oxford University Press, 1946), 196-199.
7. George J. Gordon, *Public Administration in America,* 2d ed. (New York: St. Martin's Press, 1982), 297.
8. Quoted in Robert Sherrill, *Why They Call It Politics,* 4th ed. (New York: Harcourt Brace Jovanovich, 1984), 260.
9. Michael Nelson, "The Irony of American Bureaucracy," in *Bureaucratic Power, in National Policy Making,* ed. Francis E. Rourke, 4th ed. (Boston: Little, Brown, 1986), 163-187.
10. Ibid., 169.
11. Sherrill, *Why They Call It Politics,* 259.
12. Quoted in ibid.
13. Quoted in Richard Neustadt, *Presidential Power* (New York: Wiley, 1960), 22.
14. Quoted in Mike Causey, "Trying to Activate Bureaucracy," *Washington Post,* May 30, 1972, B-9.
15. Arthur M. Schlesinger, Jr., *The Crisis of Confidence* (Boston: Houghton Mifflin, 1969), 291.
16. Richard M. Pious, *The American Presidency* (New York: Basic Books, 1979), 212.
17. Thomas E. Cronin, *The State of the Presidency,* 2d ed. (Boston: Little, Brown, 1980), 333.
18. Richard Rose, *Managing Presidential Objectives* (New York: Free Press, 1976), 23.
19. Rossiter, *American Presidency,* 129.
20. Stephen Hess, *Organizing the Presidency* (Washington, D.C.: Brookings, 1976), 10.
21. David Truman, *The Governmental Process* (New York: Knopf, 1951); Hess, *Organizing the Presidency;* George Reedy, *The Twilight of the Presidency* (New York: World, 1970).
22. Richard Rose, *Managing Presidential Objectives* (New York: Free Press, 1976), 147.
23. Cronin, *State of the Presidency,* 2d ed., 225.
24. Alexander Hamilton, *Federalist* No. 70, in *The Federalist Papers* (Tudor edition), 49-50.
25. McGeorge Bundy, *The Strength of Government* (Cambridge, Mass.: Harvard University Press, 1968), 37.
26. Woll, *American Bureaucracy,* 2d ed., 241.
27. Ibid., 240.
28. Executive Office of the President, President's Special Review Board 1987, *Report of the President's Special Review Board (Tower Commission Report)* (Washington, D.C.: Government Printing Office, 1987).
29. Anthony Downs, *Inside Bureaucracy* (Boston: Little, Brown, 1967), 116-118.

30. Arthur M. Schlesinger, Jr., *A Thousand Days: John F. Kennedy in the White House* (Boston: Houghton Mifflin, 1965), 683.
31. Cronin, *State of the Presidency*, 226.
32. Louis W. Koenig, *The Chief Executive* (New York: Harcourt Brace and World, 1968), 417.
33. Richard P. Nathan, *The Plot That Failed: Nixon and the Administrative Presidency* (New York: Wiley, 1975), 82.
34. "President Nixon Finds a Real Garbageman to Woo Garbagemen," *Wall Street Journal*, June 21, 1972, 1, 25.
35. Richard P. Nathan, "The Administrative Presidency," in *Bureaucratic Power*, 216. See also Richard P. Nathan, *The Administrative Presidency* (New York: Wiley, 1983.)
36. Dwight D. Eisenhower, *The White House Years: Mandate for Change, 1953-1956* (Garden City, N.Y.: Doubleday, 1963), 114.
37. Hess, *Organizing the Presidency*, 3.
38. Frank Kessler, *The Dilemmas of Presidential Leadership: Of Caretakers and Kings* (Englewood Cliffs, N.J.: Prentice-Hall, 1982), 60.
39. Hess, *Organizing the Presidency*, 3.
40. Quoted in Koenig, *Chief Executive*, 193.
41. Kessler, *Dilemmas of Presidential Leadership*, 72.
42. William Safire, *Before the Fall* (Garden City, N.Y.: Doubleday, 1975); and Henry Kissinger, *The White House Years* (Boston: Little, Brown, 1979).
43. *Congressional Quarterly Weekly Report*, July 21, 1979, 1432.
44. Colin Campbell, *Managing the Presidency: Carter, Reagan, and the Search for Executive Harmony* (Pittsburgh, Pa.: University of Pittsburgh Press, 1986), 61.
45. Kessler, *Dilemma of Presidential Leadership*, 68.
46. Quoted in Campbell, *Managing the Presidency*, 71.
47. Ibid.
48. *Tower Commission Report*, IV-10.
49. Woll, *American Bureaucracy*, 11.
50. Pious, *American Presidency*, 222.
51. Allen Schick, "Politics through Law: Congressional Limitations on Executive Discretion," in *Both Ends of the Avenue: The Presidency, the Executive Branch, and the Congress in the 1980s*, ed. Anthony King (Washington, D.C.: American Enterprise Institute, 1983), 176.
52. Pious, *American Presidency*, 224.
53. Thomas Franck and Edward Weisband, *Foreign Policy by Congress* (New York: Oxford University Press, 1979).
54. Pious, *American Presidency*, 229.
55. *Immigration and Naturalization Service v. Chadha*, 193 S. Ct. 2764 (1983).
56. Executive Office of the President, President's Committee on Administrative Management, *Hoover Commission Report* (Washington, D.C.: Government Printing Office, 1937), 5.
57. Ibid., 6-7.
58. Peri E. Arnold, *Making the Managerial President: Comprehensive Reorganization Planning, 1905-1980* (Princeton, N.J.: Princeton University Press, 1986), 114-115.
59. Commission on the Organization of the Executive Branch of Government, *General Management of the Executive Branch* (Washington, D.C.: Government Printing Office, 1949).
60. Ibid., 34.
61. Arnold, *Making the Managerial Presidency*, 159.
62. Ibid., 177-193.
63. Ibid., 277.
64. Tyrus G. Fain, ed., *Federal Reorganization: The Executive Branch*, Public Document Series (New York: R. R. Bowker, 1977), xxxi.
65. See, for example, Koenig, *Chief Executive*, Chapter 8.
66. James P. Pfiffner, "Strangers in a Strange Land: Orienting New Presidential Appointees," in *The In-and-Outers: Presidential Appointees and Transient Government in Washington*, ed. G. Calvin Mackenzie (Baltimore: Johns Hopkins University Press, 1987), 141. Total number of appointees is based on data from the Center for Excellence in Government, February 1989.
67. Hugh Heclo, *A Government of Strangers: Executive Politics in Washington* (Washington, D.C.: Brookings, 1977), 94.
68. Niccolo Machiavelli, *The Prince* (Harmondsworth, Middle-sex, England: Penguin, 1961), 124.
69. Quoted in Schlesinger, *Thousand Days*, 127.
70. Pfiffner, "Strangers in a Strange Land," 142.
71. Richard F. Fenno, Jr., *The President's Cabinet* (New York: Vintage, 1958), 51.
72. G. Calvin Mackenzie, *The Politics of Presidential Appointments* (New York: Free Press, 1981), 6.
73. Cronin, *State of the Presidency*, 164.
74. U.S. Commission on Executive, Legislative, and Judicial Salaries, *Report of the Commission on Executive, Legislative, and Judicial Salaries* (Washington, D.C.: Government Printing Office, 1980), ix and 1.
75. Quoted in Dick Kirschten, "Why Not the Best?" *National Journal*, June 12, 1982, 1064.
76. Mackenzie, *Politics of Presidential Appointments*, 95.
77. Cronin, *State of the Presidency*, 165.
78. Christopher J. Deering, "Damned If You Do and Damned If You Don't: The Senate's Role in the Appointments Process," in *The In-and-Outers*, 119.
79. Ibid., 117.
80. Dom Bonafede, "The White House Personnel Office from Roosevelt to Reagan," in *Presidential Appointees*, 32.
81. John W. Macy, Bruce Adams, and J. Jackson Walter, *America's Unelected Government: Appointing the President's Team* (Cambridge, Mass.: Ballinger, 1983), 32.
82. Quoted in Edward D. Feigenbaum, "Staffing, Organization, and Decision-Making in the Ford and Carter White Houses," *Presidential Studies Quarterly* (Summer 1980): 371.
83. Bonafede, "White House Personnel."
84. Quoted in Ibid., 48.
85. Macy, Adams, and Walter, *America's Unelected Government*, 39.
86. Bonafede, "White House Personnel," 57.
87. *Meyers v. United States*, 272 U.S. 52 (1926).
88. Quoted in Woll, *American Bureaucracy*, 224.
89. *Humphrey's Executor v. United States*, 295 U.S. 602.
90. *Wiener v. United States*, 357 U.S. 349.
91. Pious, *American Presidency*, 256.
92. Lyndon Baines Johnson, *The Vantage Point* (New York: Holt, Rinehart and Winston, 1971), 34.
93. Lance T. LeLoup, "Fiscal Chief: Presidents and the Budgets," in *The Presidency: Studies in Policy Making*, ed. Stephen A. Shull and Lance T. LeLoup (Brunswick, Ohio: Kings Court, 1979), 211.
94. Johnson, *Vantage Point*, 36.
95. Lance T. LeLoup, *Budgetary Politics*, 2d ed. (Brunswick, Ohio: King's Court, 1980), 148.
96. Gerald Ford, "Budget Message of the President," *The Budget of the United States Government, Fiscal Year 1978* (Washington, D.C.: Government Printing Office, 1977), M-3.
97. Dennis S. Ippolito, *The Budget and National Politics* (San Francisco: Freeman, 1978), 40.
98. 42 Stat. 20, sec. 206.
99. Office of Management and Budget, *Preparation and Submission of 1977 "Current Services" Budget Estimates*, Bulletin No. 76-4 (Washington, D.C.: Government Printing Office, 1975), 1.
100. Howard E. Shuman, *Politics and the Budget: The Struggle Between the President and the Congress* (Englewood Cliffs, N.J.: Prentice-Hall, 1984), 225.
101. *Budget of the United States, Fiscal Year 1983: Major Themes and Additional Budget Details* (Washington, D.C.: Government Printing Office, 1982), 37.
102. LeLoup, *Budgetary Politics*, 271.
103. Quoted in Joel Haveman, "Zero-Base Budgeting," *National Journal*, April 2, 1977, 514.
104. Peter A. Pyhrr, *Zero-Base Budgeting: A Practical Management Tool for Evaluating Expenses* (New York: Wiley, 1973), 10.
105. Allen Schick, "The Road from ZBB," in *Contemporary Approaches to Public Budgeting*, ed. Fred A. Kramer (Cambridge, Mass.: Winthrop, 1979), 216.
106. Frank D. Draper and Bernard T. Pitsvada, "ZBB—Looking

Back After Ten Years," *Public Administration Review* 41 (January/February 1981): 77.

107. Aaron Wildavsky in *The Congressional Budget Process After Five Years,* ed. Rudolph G. Penner (Washington, D.C.: American Enterprise Institute, 1981), 99.

108. Shuman, *Politics and the Budget,* 287.

109. Pious, *American Presidency,* 272.

110. Shuman, *Politics and the Budget,* 60.

111. *New York Times,* February 10, 1982, A1.

112. Louis Fisher, *Presidential Spending Power* (Princeton, N.J.: Princeton University Press, 1975), 7.

113. Pious, *American Presidency,* 278.

114. Fisher, *Presidential Spending Power,* 207.

115. 88 Statute 1804, sec. 32 (1974).

116. Ippolito, *Budget and National Politics,* 135.

117. Quoted in Pious, *American Presidency,* 278.

118. Ippolito, *Budget and National Politics,* 138-139.

119. *Train v. City of New York,* 420 U.S. 35.

120. John Ellwood and James Thurber, "The Congressional Budget Process Re-examined," in *Congress Reconsidered,* 2d ed., ed. Lawrence C. Dodd and Bruce I. Oppenheimer (Washington, D.C.: CQ Press, 1981), 266.

121. Letter of John Marshall to James Wilkinson, January 5, 1787, reprinted in *The Papers of John Marshall, 1775-1788,* vol. 1, ed. Herbert A. Johnson (Chapel Hill: University of North Carolina Press, 1974), 200.

122. Samuel Eliot Morison, Henry Steele Commager, and William E. Leuchtenburg, *The Growth of the American Republic,* vol. 1 (New York: Oxford University Press, 1969), 242. See generally this volume, pp. 227-261, for a description of the events immediately preceding and occurring during the Constitutional Convention.

123. U.S. Constitution, preamble.

124. See generally U.S. Constitution, Article II, for an enumeration of presidential powers.

125. The U.S. Constitution does, in Article I, section 8, give Congress authority to "pay the Debts and provide for ... the general Welfare of the United States." This is interpreted as a grant of authority for Congress to *spend money* to promote the general welfare of the nation. It is *not* interpreted as a grant of authority to enact any regulatory scheme it feels will promote the general welfare.

126. *McCulloch v. Maryland,* 17 U.S. (4 Wheat.) 316 (1819).

127. *Gibbons v. Ogden,* 22 U.S. (9 Wheat.) 1 (1824).

128. *Wickard v. Filburn,* 317 U.S. 111 (1942).

129. What, for example, is the relationship between home-grown food for purely household consumption and interstate commerce? The Supreme Court gave its answer in *Wickard v. Filburn*: If a household grows and harvests food on its own land, and for its own use, then it will be less likely to purchase food products on the commercial market. The effects of this isolated instance of self-sufficiency will be felt eventually across state lines.

130. U.S. Department of Commerce, Bureau of Census, *Historical Statistics of the United States: Colonial Times to 1970,* vol. 2 (Washington, D.C.: Government Printing Office, 1975), table Y 308-317, pp. 1102-1103; and U.S. Department of Commerce, Bureau of Census, *Statistical Abstract of the United States,* 108th ed. (Washington, D.C.: Government Printing Office, 1987), table 494, p. 307.

131. Accounts of the "Ole Miss" incident may be found in Schlesinger, *A Thousand Days,* and Theodore C. Sorensen, *Kennedy* (New York: Harper and Row, 1965).

132. U.S. Constitution, Article I, section 9.

133. The most famous discussion of this distinction is found in Chief Justice John Marshall's opinion for the U.S. Supreme Court in *Marbury v. Madison,* 5 U.S. (1 Cranch) 137 (1803).

134. *Myers v. United States,* 272 U.S. 52, 177 (1926).

135. See, for example, *Kendall v. United States,* 37 U.S. (12 Pet.) 524 (1838); *Youngstown Sheet and Tube Co. v. Sawyer,* 343 U.S. 579 (1952) (also known as the *Steel Seizure Case*); and *United States v. Nixon,* 418 U.S. 683 (1974).

136. *In re Neagle,* 135 U.S. 1 (1890).

137. *In re Debs,* 158 U.S. 564 (1895).

138. *Myers v. United States.*

139. *Wiener v. United States,* 357 U.S. 349 (1958); and *Humphrey's Executor v. United States,* 295 U.S. 602 (1935).

140. U.S. Constitution, Article III, section 1.

141. U.S. Constitution, Article I, section 8.

142. *In re Debs,* 158 U.S. 564, 582 (1895).

143. *Ex parte Milligan,* 71 U.S. (4 Wall.) 2 (1866).

144. Alexander Hamilton, *Federalist* No. 74, in *The Federalist Papers* (New York: Mentor, 1961), 449.

145. Ibid., 448.

146. Proclamation of September 15, 1792, George Washington, *Messages and Papers of the Presidents, 1789-1897,* vol. I, ed. James D. Richardson (Washington, D.C.: Government Printing Office, 1897), 124-125.

147. See Proclamation of July 10, 1795, George Washington, in ibid., 181.

148. *Ex parte Garland,* 71 U.S. (4 Wall.) 333 (1866). See generally *Schick v. Reed,* 419 U.S. 256 (1974).

149. *Wiener v. United States* and *Humphrey's Executor v. United States.*

150. Executive Order 11365, July 29, 1967.

151. Kerner was later rewarded by the president with appointment to the U.S. Court of Appeals for the Seventh Circuit. The judge resigned after being indicted and convicted of a felony.

152. Office of the President, National Advisory Commission on Civil Disorders, *Report of the National Advisory Commission on Civil Disorders* (Washington, D.C.: Government Printing Office, 1968).

153. Employment and budget data in this section are taken from Office of the President, Office of Management and Budget, *Appendix: Budget of the U.S. Government—Fiscal Year 1989* (Washington, D.C.: Government Printing Office, 1988).

154. Office of the President, Office of Management and Budget, *Appendix, Budget of the U.S. Government* (Washington, D.C.: Government Printing Office, 1988), I-06.

155. *McCulloch v. Maryland.*

156. *Gibbons v. Ogden,* 22 U.S. (9 Wheat.) 1 (1824).

157. *Martin v. Hunter's Lessee,* 14 U.S. (1 Wheat.) 304 (1816); *Cohens v. Virginia,* 19 U.S. (6 Wheat.) 264 (1821).

158. Congress has constitutional authority, no doubt, to impose a national speed limit on interstate highways. Despite popular impressions to the contrary, it does not do so. Congress, rather, coerces states that receive federal highway assistance to agree to impose and enforce a sixty-five-mile-per-hour limit. The same thing has occurred with respect to the twenty-one-year-old drinking age: if states want federal highway funds, they must agree to a state drinking age of at least twenty-one.

159. 18 United States Code, section 3056 (a) and (b).

160. 18 United States Code, section 3052.

161. See 18 United States Code, section 3053 (U.S. marshals); 18 United States Code, section 3056 (Secret Service); and 21 United States Code, section 878 (Drug Enforcement Administration).

162. 18 United States Code, section 3061 (a) (2).

163. 18 United States Code, section 3061 (b).

164. U.S. Congress, House, Committee on Interior and Insular Affairs, Subcommittee on General Oversight and Investigations, *NRC Coziness with Industry: Nuclear Regulatory Commission Fails to Maintain Arms' Length Relationship with the Nuclear Industry,* Committee Print No. 5, 100th Cong., 1st sess., 1987.

165. U.S. Constitution, Article I, section 2.

166. U.S. Constitution, Article I, section 3.

167. Hamilton, *Federalist* No. 65, in *The Federalist Papers* (Mentor edition), 396.

168. 14 Stat. 430 (1867)

169. Compare *Myers v. United States.*

170. *The Prize Cases,* 67 U.S. (2 Black) 635 (1863); *In re Debs.*

171. *In re Neagle.*

172. *Ex parte Garland.*

Selected Bibliography

Arnold, Peri E. *Making the Managerial President: Comprehensive Reorganization Planning, 1905-1980.* Princeton: Princeton University Press, 1986.

Bundy, McGeorge. *The Strength of Government.* Cambridge: Harvard University Press, 1968.

Campbell, Colin. *Managing the Presidency: Carter, Reagan, and the Search for Executive Harmony.* Pittsburgh: University of Pittsburgh Press, 1986.

Cronin, Thomas E. *The State of the Presidency.* 2d ed. Boston: Little, Brown, 1980.

Dodd, Lawrence C., and Richard L. Schott. *Congress and the Administrative State.* New York: Wiley, 1979.

Fain, Tyrus G., ed. *Federal Reorganization: The Executive Branch.* Public Document Series. New York: Bowker, 1977.

Fenno, Richard F., Jr. *The President's Cabinet.* New York: Vintage, 1958.

Heclo, Hugh. *A Government of Strangers: Executive Politics in Washington.* Washington, D.C.: Brookings, 1977.

Hess, Stephen. *Organizing the Presidency.* Washington, D.C.: Brookings, 1976.

Ippolito, Dennis S. *The Budget and National Politics.* San Francisco: Freeman, 1978.

Koenig, Louis W. *The Chief Executive.* New York: Harcourt Brace and Jovanovich, 1968.

Kramer, Fred A. *Contemporary Approaches to Public Budgeting.* Cambridge: Winthrop, 1979.

LeLoup, Lance T. *Budgetary Politics.* 2d ed. Brunswick, Ohio: King's Court, 1980.

Mackenzie, G. Calvin, ed. *The In-and-Outers: Presidential Appointees and Transient Government in Washington.* Baltimore: Johns Hopkins University Press, 1987.

_____. *The Politics of Presidential Appointments.* New York: Free Press, 1981.

Macy, John W., Bruce Adams, and J. Jackson Walter. *America's Unelected Government: Appointing the President's Team.* Cambridge: Ballinger, 1983.

Nathan, Richard P. *The Administrative Presidency.* New York: Wiley, 1983.

Rossiter, Clinton L. *The American Presidency.* 3d ed. New York: Harcourt Brace Jovanovich, 1963.

Rourke, Francis E., ed. *Bureaucratic Power in National Policy Making,* 4th ed. Boston: Little, Brown, 1986.

Legislative Leader

The U.S. constitutional system created by the Framers "blends" power among the three branches of government. The Framers made the legislative branch—the U.S. Congress—dominant in formulating law, for they believed that the legislature most accurately reflects mass opinion. By contrast, they limited the president's ability to influence legislation to two "express" powers: the duty to recommend to Congress any measure deemed "necessary and expedient" (Article II, section 3) and, more important, the power to approve or to veto a bill passed by Congress (Article I, section 7). Presidents also gained the power to negotiate treaties, which become law when "two-thirds of the Senators present concur" (Article II, section 2), and to convene "emergency" sessions of Congress (Article II, section 3). But these are extraordinary events.

The Constitution is remarkably reticent about the president's role in legislating, yet the relationship between Congress and the executive is the most important aspect of the U.S. system of governance. Two hundred years of history have seen an immeasurable and fundamental expansion in the array of resources (such as staff and technical expertise) and powers that presidents can use to influence public policy.

Some of these powers were "implied" in the Constitution, awaiting only time and, perhaps, judicial interpretation as new and unforeseen cases arose. Others were delegated by Congress to meet changing economic or social circumstances, emerging government responsibilities, or new public demands. Still more presidential power has arisen from new technologies, like television, or new international responsibilities for the United States, like the defense of Western Europe since the end of World War II. The formal brevity of the executive's role in legislating thus masks the considerable influence that presidents wield over the congressional agenda and the direction of public policy.

Even with the remarkable expansion in the size and power of the executive branch, a modern president's relationship with Congress remains fluid, ambiguous, and frustrating. Much of what presidents want still requires new laws, congressional appropriations, or senatorial approval of appointees or treaties. The president *needs* Congress, but the legislature so often proves stubbornly independent, uncooperative, or even hostile that residents of the White House rarely can take congressional support for granted.

By Christopher J. Bosso

The Veto

Perhaps the chief legal weapon the president possesses is the veto, the ability to block acts passed by Congress that finds its origins in the 1787 debate over the Constitution.

Constitutional Foundations

Those who wrote the Constitution are revered for their efforts at creating a national government that, above all, sought to safeguard the rights and liberties of both the people and the states. We thus recognize today the enduring importance of the web of checks and balances woven into a system of separate institutions—executive, legislative, and judicial—sharing government power, characteristics designed primarily to prevent any single branch (and, by extension, any single individual or group) from wielding potentially tyrannical political power.

Virtually every schoolchild knows well the colonists' complaints against King George III and their subsequent fear of powerful executives. Yet, lost too often in textbook treatments of the Constitution was the Framers' equal dread of unchecked legislative power. After all, Thomas Jefferson's second villain in the Declaration of Independence was the English Parliament, a legislature unobstructed by formal constitutional limits and loathed widely in the colonies for its apparent disregard for due process of law. In addition, the leaders of the new nation met in 1787 expressly because of failures widely seen in the Articles of Confederation (written in 1781), which essentially was a league of friendship among the thirteen states. Because the national government under the articles largely was a creature of the states, and dependent on them for its powers and funds, it proved unable to promote either national unity or effective government.

Another common concern was that the articles provided for no independent national executive, one strong enough to administer the laws and resist legislative tyranny.[1] State legislatures almost without exception dominated governors and were seen by many delegates at the Constitutional Convention as being as dangerous to liberty as unrestrained monarchs. Jefferson, reflecting on his experiences as governor of Virginia, wrote, "All the powers of government . . . result to the legislative body. The con-

He shall, from time to time, give to the Congress information of the state of the union, and recommend to their consideration such measures as he shall judge necessary and expedient....
—from Article II, section 3

centrating of these in the same hands is precisely the definition of despotic government." [2] These experiences were shared by a number of those present at the convention, and it was clear that the new national executive would need some way to check legislative power.

The concept of a *veto* (Latin for "I forbid") was nothing new to the Framers. Indeed, it was as old as ancient Rome, where it was used by the plebeians to protect the common people against the excesses of a senate dominated by aristocrats. It later emerged in medieval Europe as a royal check on newly developing legislatures. In England, for example, the monarch retained the absolute power to deny acts by Parliament, a weapon that Queen Elizabeth I used quite frequently.[3] Finally, and closer to home, a few state constitutions (such as that of Massachusetts) contained some form of executive veto, but the veto was not a widespread practice.

Thus armed with precedence and spurred on by fear of a rapacious legislature, the Framers moved to include some form of executive check on laws passed by Congress in virtually every plan for the new constitution. The Virginia Plan, for example, called for a "council of revision" made up of members of the executive and the judiciary that would prevent the legislature from drawing "all power into its impetuous vortex." [4] George Mason argued that this type of plural veto would be too weak, since disputes within the council would undermine decisive executive action. Furthermore, Mason continued, the veto should be more than a mere defense against legislative intrusion. Instead, it was necessary to discourage demagogy and prevent "unjust and pernicious" laws.[5] Others attending the convention also were uncomfortable with having judges act on bills before they came up as legal cases, so the veto eventually was confined to the president alone.

Some, including Alexander Hamilton, initially supported an absolute veto, giving Congress no opportunity to respond, but such a weapon seemed too powerful to delegates also worried about unresponsive and capricious executives. After much debate, the Framers instituted a "partial negative" whereby the president could reject bills or joint resolutions passed by Congress (excluding constitutional amendments, concurrent resolutions, or resolutions passed by only one chamber),[6] but which legislature could override by extraordinary majorities of two-thirds of the members present in each chamber.

The veto was destined to be the constitutional core of executive independence. As defended during the battle over ratification by Alexander Hamilton in *Federalist* No. 73, "the primary inducement to confering this power in question upon the executive is to enable him to defend himself; the second one is to increase the chances in favor of the community against the passing of bad laws, through haste, inadvertence, or design." [7] The legislature is not infallible, Hamilton argued, and, unless checked, its love of power would ultimately betray both it and the ability of government to function effectively. Additionally, argued

James Madison in *Federalist* No. 48, only by giving each branch some control over the others could power be restrained and rights and liberties protected—a theme he continued in No. 51 with his famous statement, "Ambition must be made to counteract ambition." [8]

Those opposed to the veto included such Anti-Federalists as Thomas Jefferson, who, despite his concerns about potentials for abuse of legislative power, argued ardently that Congress alone represented the people. The veto, Jefferson argued might undermine democratic values by allowing the president to block "good" laws, and opponents viewed the device simply as a means to thwart majority rule. But, Hamilton retorted in *Federalist* No. 73, unrestrained majorities are equally as dangerous as unchecked elites, and "the injury which might possibly be done by defeating a few good laws will be amply compensated by the advantage of preventing a number of bad ones." [9] What is more, allowing the executive to threaten a veto might induce legislative moderation, making actual use of the veto unnecessary.

The Constitution thus gives the president three choices upon being presented with legislation passed by Congress:[10] approve and sign the bill into law; veto the bill by returning it to the chamber where it originated within ten days of passage (Sundays excluded); or, finally, do nothing. If the president does nothing, the bill becomes law after ten days to prevent presidents from killing legislation, and thus thwarting the will of the majority, through simple inaction. The exception to this rule occurs when Congress presents a bill and then adjourns before the required ten days elapse, for any bill not signed by the president when Congress adjourns dies automatically. This procedure is called a *pocket veto*. (See "Pocket Veto," p. 62, in this chapter.)

If the president vetoes a bill, returns it to Congress, and the legislature fails to respond, the bill dies. If two-thirds of the members present *in each house* pass the vetoed bill once again, however, it becomes law despite presidential disapproval.[11] Such overwhelming majorities combine to produce an *override*. Veto overrides are rare (between 1789 and 1988 only 100 of 2,475 presidential vetoes were overridden), because to sustain a veto the president needs to gain only one-third plus one of the votes in either chamber. *(See Table 1.)* Barring an override, Congress either can rewrite the legislation to meet presidential demands (as Hamilton foresaw) or simply can give it up.

Bills vetoed by the president normally are sent back to Congress accompanied by a message stating the reasons for the president's opposition. *(See box, A Veto Message, p. 62.)* Sometimes the reasons given cite constitutional problems, at other times political or issue differences between the branches, but at all times veto messages are aimed at

Every bill which shall have passed the House of Representatives and the Senate, shall, before it become a law, be presented to the president of the United States; if he approve, he shall sign it, but if not, he shall return it, with his objections, to that house in which it shall have originated who shall ... proceed to reconsider it.
—from Article I, section 7

pressing the president's views on the bills in question. Whatever their other purposes, veto messages are political statements and are directed not only toward Congress but to the public at large. In this sense, then, the messages become additional resources in the president's effort to influence public policy.

Historical Development

Early presidents conformed with the prevailing view that Congress best represented the public will and thus confined vetoes to bills deemed unconstitutional. The notion that a president should veto a bill simply because it was "bad" was not yet widely accepted. Indeed, the first six presidents issued few regular vetoes between 1790 and 1830 and in most instances did so on constitutional grounds.

This narrow interpretation of the president's right (and, perhaps, duty) to use the veto underwent significant redefinition during the tenure of Andrew Jackson (1829-1837)—hero of the War of 1812, keen foe of Eastern business and banking interests, and self-styled "Tribune of the People." Jackson was a strong party loyalist who quickly entered into warfare with his congressional foes, and the veto in his hands became an instrument of political as well as constitutional power. In eight years Jackson issued twelve vetoes, more than his predecessors combined, and none of them was overridden. Perhaps most controversial was his 1832 rejection of a bill rechartering the Bank of the United States, which was opposed bitterly by frontier settlers and farmers hurt by its high interest rates. As political scientist Clinton Rossiter suggested, Jackson "revived the veto and purified it of the niceties that had grown up around it" by making it an overtly political instrument.[12]

Whig presidents after Jackson, while professing allegiance to their party's doctrine of congressional supremacy, also proved surprisingly resolute when challenged by the legislature. John Tyler (1841-1845), for example, vetoed two major bank bills supported by his own party, and his 1843 veto of a controversial tariff measure sparked the first formal attempt in Congress to impeach a president. That effort failed, and Tyler's successors showed equally notable bursts of independence. Even so, only fifty-nine bills were vetoed between 1789 and 1865, more than half of them during the terms of Presidents Jackson, Tyler, and Franklin Pierce (1853-1857).

Post-Civil War Era

Presidents and Congress after Abraham Lincoln (1861-1865) clashed increasingly within a national political arena rife with sharp regional and partisan antagonisms, dramatic social and economic changes, and disputes over the proper role of government. This era, although marked generally by congressional dominance, nonetheless saw stark surges in presidential use of the veto as successive executives attempted to grapple with massive numbers of bills spawned by an often antagonistic Congress. The period between the Civil War and the late 1890s saw some of history's keenest partisan battles, which often spilled over into conflict between the branches of government.

Andrew Johnson (1865-1869), for example, wrestled strenuously with Congress immediately after the Civil War and became the first president whose veto of an important bill was overridden. Among all presidents, Johnson in fact had the greatest percentage of regular vetoes overturned by

Table 1 Vetoes and Vetoes Overridden, All Bills, 1789-1988

President	All bills vetoed	Regular vetoes	Pocket vetoes	Vetoes overridden
Washington	2	2	0	0
J. Adams	0	0	0	0
Jefferson	0	0	0	0
Madison	7	5	2	0
Monroe	1	1	0	0
J. Q. Adams	0	0	0	0
Jackson	12	5	7	0
Van Buren	1	0	1	0
W. H. Harrison	0	0	0	0
Tyler	10	6	4	1
Polk	3	2	1	0
Taylor	0	0	0	0
Fillmore	0	0	0	0
Pierce	9	9	0	5
Buchanan	7	4	3	0
Lincoln	7	2	5	0
A. Johnson	29	21	8	15
Grant	93[a]	45	48[a]	4
Hayes	13	12	1	1
Garfield	0	0	0	0
Arthur	12	4	8	1
Cleveland (1st term)	414	304	110	2
B. Harrison	44	19	25	1
Cleveland (2d term)	170	42	128	5
McKinley	42	6	36	0
T. Roosevelt	82	42	40	1
Taft	39	30	9	1
Wilson	44	33	11	6
Harding	6	5	1	0
Coolidge	50	20	30	4
Hoover	37	21	16	3
F. Roosevelt	635	372	263	9
Truman	258	191	67	12
Eisenhower	188	79	109	2
Kennedy	21	12	9	0
L. Johnson	29	18	11	0
Nixon	43	24	19[b]	5
Ford	68	49	19	12
Carter	31	13	18	2
Reagan	68	41	27	8
Total	2,475	1,439	1,036	100

Sources: Guide to Congress, 3d ed. (Washington, D.C.: Congressional Quarterly Inc., 1982), 763; *Congressional Quarterly Weekly Report,* various issues.

a. Veto total listed for Grant does not include a pocket veto of a bill that apparently never was placed before him for his signature.
b. Includes Nixon's pocket veto of a bill during the 1970 congressional Christmas recess later that was ruled invalid by the federal courts.

Congress (fifteen out of twenty-one, or 71 percent). So acrid was the antipathy between the branches that Johnson's refusal to abide by the Tenure of Office Act, a law passed over his veto that forbade presidents from firing political appointees without congressional approval, led directly to his impeachment by the House. Johnson was acquitted in the Senate by only one vote, and the Tenure of Office Act (which many constitutional scholars later viewed as unconstitutional) was repealed in 1887.[13]

Table 2 Private Bills Vetoed, 1789-1988

President	Regular vetoes	Pocket vetoes	Vetoes overridden
Washington	0	0	0
J. Adams	0	0	0
Jefferson	0	0	0
Madison	2	0	0
Monroe	0	0	0
J. Q. Adams	0	0	0
Jackson	0	0	0
Van Buren	0	1	0
W. H. Harrison	0	0	0
Tyler	0	0	0
Polk	0	0	0
Taylor	0	0	0
Fillmore	0	0	0
Pierce	0	0	0
Buchanan	2	0	0
Lincoln	0	1	0
A. Johnson	0	2	0
Grant	29	37	3
Hayes	1	0	0
Garfield	0	0	0
Arthur	1	8	0
Cleveland (1st term)	271	82	1
B. Harrison	5	23	9
Cleveland (2d term)	30	99	2
McKinley	4	32	0
T. Roosevelt	27	31	0
Taft	10	7	0
Wilson	7	2	0
Harding	3	0	0
Coolidge	3	17	0
Hoover	4	6	0
F. Roosevelt	317	180	0
Truman	137	38	1
Eisenhower	43	64	0
Kennedy	8	4	0
L. Johnson	12	4	0
Nixon	0	3	0
Ford	3	2	0
Carter	0	2	0
Reagan	7	5	0
Total	926	650	16

Sources: Guide to Congress, 3d ed. (Washington, D.C.: Congressional Quarterly Inc., 1982), 357; *Congressional Quarterly Weekly Report,* various issues.

Note: The official distinction between public and private bills was rather hazy through the 1930s, although private bills generally were classified as those benefiting a single individual rather than a large segment of society (for example, a private pension bill). Beginning in 1936, however, a Library of Congress publication has listed all private bills.

Johnson's experiences aside, most of the vetoes produced during the rest of the nineteenth century were aimed at "private" bills, actions by Congress that benefited specific individuals, companies, or municipalities. *(See Table 2.)* Most private bills during the late 1800s provided pensions for Civil War veterans, but many were fraudulent or excessive claims that often were passed late in the congressional session. Grover Cleveland (1885-1889, 1893-1897)

vetoed 482 private bills during his eight years in office—43 during one three-day period in 1886 alone.[14] Many were through the use of pocket vetoes, and only three of Cleveland's vetoes of private bills were overridden.

Modern Presidents

Franklin D. Roosevelt (1933-1945) used the veto more vigorously than any other president, was the first to use it against major tax legislation, and crafted the threat of the veto into his legislative strategy. Roosevelt in many ways created the modern presidency, and the veto became yet another instrument of executive influence within an environment of expansive government action and power.

His influence on the presidency endures, particularly because contemporary U.S. government so often is marked by split partisan control over the White House and Congress. Vetoes have been used most frequently when such partisan splits occur. Harry S Truman (1945-1953), for example, in 1947 vetoed the controversial Taft-Hartley Labor Act, a bill the Republican-dominated Congress passed to restrain the power of labor unions. Truman subsequently used congressional overrides of this and other vetoes to great political effect in rallying voters to the Democrats in the 1948 presidential and congressional elections.

Republican president Dwight D. Eisenhower (1953-1961) wrestled with a Congress dominated by Democrats during all but two of his eight years in office. He used the veto often to stop liberal social programs and relied heavily on a "conservative coalition" of congressional Republicans and southern Democrats for support against overrides. One notable case occurred in 1959 when Eisenhower squared off against congressional Democrats intent on pushing a new domestic agenda. Eisenhower's veto warnings went unheeded, but the conservative coalition in Congress held fast throughout the year to sustain successive vetoes against new spending for urban housing, rural electrification, and other domestic programs. Threats of further presidential vetoes persuaded Democrats to cut back drastically on their efforts.[15]

Democrats John F. Kennedy (1961-1963) and Lyndon B. Johnson (1963-1969), blessed with friendly majorities in Congress, seldom used the veto, but Republicans Richard Nixon (1969-1974) and Gerald R. Ford (1974-1977) fared differently. Both Nixon and Ford faced off against Democratic Congresses, so the veto by necessity became central to their legislation strategies. Nixon issued several vetoes on major bills he deemed inflationary and even appeared on national television to veto a massive appropriations bill. As when Eisenhower was in office, the conservative coalition in Congress often proved large enough to derail override attempts.

Because the success of the veto is inextricably tied to a president's overall "strength," Nixon's political troubles eventually weakened his national popularity and influence within Congress. In 1973, for example, a resurgent Congress soundly overrode his veto of the War Powers Resolution, an act aimed at limiting presidential ability to commit U.S. armed forces abroad without congressional approval. Congress also overrode Nixon's veto of the 1974 Budget Impoundment and Control Act, which he opposed because it limited presidential ability *not* to spend funds appropriated by Congress. *(See "Item Veto," p. 64, in this chapter.)*

Ford, who became president after Nixon's resignation

August 9, 1974, used the veto frequently and to great effect. Despite facing a Congress strongly controlled by Democrats, Ford was sustained on all but four of the seventeen vetoes issued in 1975 alone. Ford also used the threat of a veto to derail a consumer protection bill popular in both chambers. His experience showed how the veto can be used to compensate partially for the severe political weakness of being an unelected chief executive succeeding a disgraced president.

Jimmy Carter (1977-1981), like Kennedy and Johnson, relied on the veto less frequently because his fellow Democrats dominated Congress. A notable exception was his rejection of a 1977 energy research bill, a $6 billion authorization measure that Carter successfully opposed because it included funds for a nuclear breeder reactor he thought dangerous and too expensive.[16] Carter was not challenged on that veto, but in 1980 he became the first president since Harry Truman to suffer an override at the hands of his own party.[17] Carter had vetoed a bill to limit the national debt because it contained a provision eliminating import fees on foreign oil. He lost this time, however, because the fees were widely unpopular and, perhaps, because members of Congress were emboldened by the apparent weakening of Carter's public support as the Iran hostage situation dragged on.

The experiences of Ronald Reagan (1981-1989) in many ways mirrored those of Nixon, although Reagan for one term faced a Congress itself split between a Republican Senate and a Democratic House. Like Nixon, Reagan vetoed major spending bills contrary to his program and often warned, "my veto pen is inked up and ready to go," when Congress was on the brink of passing legislation he opposed.[18] Reagan's great popularity with the voters in his first term often was enough to deter congressional action, and his veto of a 1981 continuing appropriations bill proved so potent that Congress reworked the measure to his satisfaction. Reagan found it harder to make veto threats work to his advantage, however, after Democrats regained full control over Congress in the 1986 elections. Indeed, Congress in early 1987 easily overrode his vetoes of major water pollution and highway bills, signaling to many a shift in the president's influence over national policy. (See box, A Veto Message, p. 62.)

An Instrument of Presidential Power

James Bryce, the nineteenth-century English observer of U.S. government, argued that the veto "conveys the impression of firmness." [19] Contemporary scholars of the presidency agree with Bryce only to a point, since most view the veto as both a clumsy instrument of executive power and one whose frequent use displays political weakness, not strength.[20] Thomas Cronin, a political scientist who long has studied the presidency, has argued simply that to see the veto as a tool of "strong presidents" is illusory, since presidents historically have used vetoes predominantly against private bills and seldom have vetoed major tax and appropriations measures.[21] Another scholar of the presidency, George Edwards III, added that the veto is a negative instrument, good for stopping unwanted legislation, but once used, it indicates largely that the president has failed to sway Congress from its course.[22] Having a veto overridden underscores a president's relative political weakness, particularly if Congress is dominated by the president's own party.

In discussions of the veto's strength, Ford's frequent use of the device is often mentioned because scholars of the presidency think he was dealt the weakest political hand of any modern president. After succeeding Nixon, he faced a fiercely independent Congress dominated by liberal Democrats. To defend his prerogatives, he used the veto more frequently than any other twentieth-century president because political circumstances gave him no option. That so many of his vetoes were sustained within a largely hostile Congress suggests the raw power of the veto to stop legislation.

The experiences of other presidents buttress this view. Harry Truman's crafty use of the veto as a political weapon against congressional Republicans did not hide the fact that he often lost important override battles. Ronald Reagan's defeat in successive override episodes during early 1987 emphasized his weakening leverage in light of renewed Democratic dominance in Congress and his own troubles over secret arms sales to Iran. In sum, the veto more often than not is the weapon of last resort, to be used when all other attempts at persuasion fail.

When presidents veto legislation, the move may be viewed as a sign of relative weakness; but when they successfully head off unwanted legislation by *threatening* to use the veto, the tactic is seen as an indicator of presidential strength. Veto threats are useful bargaining tools in the hands of a popular and wily executive. Presidential scholars often point to Franklin Roosevelt, who was known to beg his aides to "find something I can veto" as both a lesson and a reminder to Congress of his potential power.[23] The strength of Ronald Reagan's public popularity during his first term more than once allowed him to challenge Congress with the veto and successfully get legislation reworked to his liking. Even Gerald Ford, despite his problems, effectively used the threat of a veto to deter legislation, although he did so when Congress was about to adjourn.

Congress, however, finds ways to undermine vetoes or threats of vetoes made by even popular presidents. Because the president cannot veto parts of a bill, members of Congress many times will load up major legislation with amendments on a completely different subject (known as "riders") or with pet spending programs that they know the president must accept to ensure passage. To make matters more complicated, Congress in recent years has relied on massive omnibus (or "catch-all") bills to pass the budget, to appropriate funds, and to levy new taxes simultaneously. Ronald Reagan several times had to accept omnibus bills containing programs or provisions he detested simply because he needed other spending contained in the same bill. A prime example was the Boland Amendment, a provision restricting U.S. aid to the rebels opposing the Nicaraguan government, which was tacked onto a 1984 appropriations bill.

Congress also tends to wait until late in each session to pass critical spending bills, which narrows the president's range of possible responses because a veto may not be feasible if Congress has adjourned and the funds needed to run the federal government are contained in the legislation.

Finally, a president cannot totally rely on fellow party members in Congress for support on veto threats, or even during override battles, since most members resist being seen by their constituents as mere rubber stamps for the president's wishes. This is true especially when the bill in question benefits a member's district or state, as when Congress overrode Reagan's vetoes on water treatment and

A Veto Message

A bill passed by Congress is formally vetoed when the president returns it to Capitol Hill unsigned and accompanied by a message stating the reasons for executive opposition. Presidents today rarely write their own veto messages. Instead, the messages typically are composed by professional staff assistants in the Executive Office of the President, often with input from experts in the Office and Management and Budget (OMB) or other executive branch agencies. The president may scan the final draft, and on occasion may pen major parts of controversial veto messages, but the overall process of rebuffing Congress on a piece of legislation largely is a collective one.

Whether the reasons given for a veto are constitutional, fiscal, substantive, or "merely" political—or a combination of reasons—a veto message is designed with more than Congress in mind. In today's media-saturated political atmosphere, any message from the White House to Congress is scrutinized closely for its potential political ramifications. Veto messages thus are crafted carefully, designed above all to sell the president's views on a bill to national opinion makers and to the public, not simply to Congress.

Most veto messages are signed in the relative privacy of the Oval Office and sent by courier to Capitol Hill. They then are delivered to the chamber from whence the bills in question originated, which normally takes the lead in any efforts to override the veto. On vetoes of major bills, however, a president may use the opportunity to convene a public ceremony, complete with supporters and members of the national press, to attack the bill and to generate public sentiment against Congress.

In the following excerpt, President Ronald Reagan explained his objections to amendments to the Clean Water Act passed by Congress in January 1987. Despite Reagan's opposition, however, Congress easily overrode the president's veto by large bipartisan majorities.

TO THE HOUSE OF REPRESENTATIVES:

I am returning herewith without my approval HR 1, the "Water Quality Act of 1987." Because all regulatory, research, enforcement, and permit issuance activities are continued under permanent law and current appropriations—including grants to finance the construction of sewage treatment plants—I emphasize that my veto will have no impact whatsoever on the immediate status of any water quality programs.

The cleanup of our nation's rivers, lakes, and estuaries is, and has been for the past 15 years, a national priority of the highest order. This Administration remains committed to the objectives of the Clean Water Act and to continuing the outstanding progress we have made in reducing water pollution. But the issue facing me today does not concern the ensuring of clean water for future generations. The real issue is the Federal deficit—and the pork barrel and spending boondoggles that increase it.

The Clean Water Act construction grant program, which this legislation funds, is a classic example of how well-intentioned, short-term programs balloon into open-ended, long-term commitments costing billions of dollars more than anticipated or needed. Since 1972, the Federal government has helped fund the construction of local sewage treatment facilities. This is a matter that historically and properly was the responsibility of State and local governments. The Federal government's first spending in this area was intended to be a short-term effort to assist in financing the backlog of facilities needed at the time to meet the original Clean Water Act requirements. When the program started, the cost of that commitment to the Federal taxpayer was estimated at $18 billion. Yet to date, $47 billion has been appropriated. HR 1 proposes to put still another $18 billion of taxpayers' money into this program. Despite all this money, only 67 percent of all municipalities have actually completed the construction needed to comply with the Clean Water Act pollution limits. On the other hand, non-municipal treatment systems, which have received no federal funding, have completed 94 percent of the construction needed for compliance with Federal pollution standards. I want a bill that spends only what we need to spend and no more—not a blank check. For these reasons I must disapprove HR 1, a bill virtually identical to S 1128, which I disapproved last November. . . .

HR 1 gave the Congress the opportunity to demonstrate whether or not it is serious about getting Federal spending under control. The Congress should fulfill its responsibility to the American people and support me on these important fiscal issues. Together we can cut the deficit and reduce spending. But by passing such measures as HR 1, the Congress divides our interests and threatens our future.

Ronald Reagan

The White House,
January 30, 1987

---

highway bills in 1987. So popular were both measures that Republicans abandoned the president in droves, sacrificing his agenda for their constituents' interests.

The veto is a powerful weapon for stopping legislation when all other means have failed. As a tool for crafting policy, however, its utility is limited by a president's popularity, political skills, and timing, not to mention circumstances perhaps beyond the control of the White House.

Pocket Veto

The veto is mentioned specifically in the Constitution, as is the method for congressional override. But, as often is the case with the Founders' handiwork, minor provisions have evolved over time into major constitutional battles between Congress and the presidency. One of the most heated of these battles has been over what has come to be known as the *pocket veto*.

Constitutional Provision

The Constitution gives the president ten days (excluding Sundays) either to sign a bill into law or to return it to Congress with a veto message. A bill not approved by the president becomes law after ten days "unless the Congress by their adjournment prevent its return, in which case it shall not be law" (Article 1, section 7). This provision was intended to ward off last-minute actions by Congress that may prove dangerous or foolhardy. When Congress has left for home after adjournment, the president cannot possibly veto and return bills as prescribed in the Constitution, so the Framers determined that under such circumstances it was better that any bill left unapproved at adjournment simply die.

A *pocket veto* thus results from executive inaction, not anything the president actively does, and the term reflects the notion that the president "pocketed" a bill rather than acted on it.[24] A president technically cannot "issue" a pocket veto; the entire situation occurs simply because Congress has adjourned and the bill cannot be returned with a regular veto message. Even so, not a few presidents have asserted their "right" to use the pocket veto as if it were an active power of the office.

The first president to rely on the pocket veto was James Madison, in 1812, and only twice more did a president use a pocket veto before 1830. The incidence of pocket vetoes increased thereafter, especially against many of the private pension bills passed by Congress in the second half of the nineteenth century. The champion of the pocket veto in absolute numbers is Franklin Roosevelt (263), but Grover Cleveland used the device far more frequently (almost 30 per year in office, compared with Roosevelt's approximately 22 per year) and largely against the many private veterans' pension bills passed in the decades following the Civil War.

Constitutional Issues

The pocket veto is controversial because Congress and the president often disagree over what constitutes congressional adjournment. The Constitution, as so often is the case, is not clear on this point, except for adjournment sine die (Latin for "without a day," meaning "without a day being set for meeting again"). Adjournment sine die marks the end of a two-year Congress. Other circumstances under which a pocket veto is constitutional is a critical question to both branches, since any interpretation narrowing its use to adjournment sine die benefits the legislature. A more expansive definition magnifies executive power over legislation, since presidents might be able to defeat bills through inaction whenever Congress takes a recess, such as between sessions of the same Congress or during holidays occurring within any single session.

This question was not an issue through the nineteenth century, since Congress sat in session, on average, only half a year, and calling members back to Washington could take weeks of travel. But, as Congress began to stay in session almost full time and as new technology made communications to and recall of Congress far easier than the Framers ever envisioned, the issue of when the president legally can use the pocket veto has grown in importance.

The first real shot in this battle came with the 1929 *Pocket Veto Case*, in which the Supreme Court ruled that President Calvin Coolidge could pocket veto an Indian claims bill passed just before a four-month recess.[25] The justices ruled that the term *adjournment* applied to *any* break in the congressional calendar that prevented the return of a bill within the required ten-day period, in this case adjournment between sessions. The ruling, as historian Arthur M. Schlesinger, Jr., noted, "was based in part on the idea that, if Congress was in adjournment, no officer or agent was authorized to receive on behalf of Congress a bill rejected by the President."[26] To close this apparent loophole, particularly as Congress began to convene almost year-round and recess for very short periods, both chambers began to appoint "agents"—usually the clerk of the House and secretary of the Senate—to receive presidential veto messages while members were away, thus theoretically negating a president's rationale for a pocket veto. After all, once Congress returned it could deliberate and perhaps override a presidential veto at any time before adjournment sine die.

Franklin Roosevelt asserted that this strategy was unconstitutional in declaring a pocket veto against a bill passed before Congress went on a three-day recess. In 1938, however, the Supreme Court modified the 1929 ruling and held that pocket vetoes could not occur during brief recesses if agents had been so named.[27] Regular veto procedures, the justices argued, served to give the president time to consider a bill *and* allow Congress the opportunity to respond, so the use of agents to receive presidential veto messages was deemed constitutional. Congress, not surprisingly, made this practice commonplace thereafter.

This issue lay dormant until the early 1970s, when Richard Nixon's application of the pocket veto again sparked controversy about what kind of congressional adjournment "prevents" regular veto procedures. Despite the 1938 ruling, Nixon in 1970 declared that during a six-day congressional holiday recess he would pocket veto the Family Practice of Medicine Act, which provided funds for medical training. Congress had passed the bill unanimously, had appointed agents to receive presidential messages, and arguably would have overridden any regular veto, but Nixon did not give Congress the chance to respond.

Nixon created a furor by asserting that a short holiday was analogous to adjournment sine die. Members of Congress argued that the bill had indeed become law because Nixon could not exercise a pocket veto during a recess, and Sen. Edward M. Kennedy (D-Mass.) subsequently brought suit against the administration.[28] Kennedy's case was upheld by a U.S. court of appeals, which in 1974 ruled that pocket vetoes were disallowed during short recesses so long as Congress established procedures to receive veto messages in its absence.[29]

Kennedy again brought suit after Gerald Ford declared a pocket veto against a bill passed just before the intersession break of the Eighty-eighth Congress. Once again, a federal court of appeals overturned a lower court decision and ruled that pocket vetoes cannot be used except after adjournment sine die so long as both chambers appoint agents.[30] The Ford administration subsequently announced that it would abide by the ruling.[31]

Despite these rulings, Ronald Reagan in 1983 reasserted a more expansive view when he declared a pocket veto against a bill barring aid to El Salvador passed just before the end of the first session of the Ninety-eighth

If any bill shall not be returned by the president within ten days, (Sundays excepted) after it shall have been presented to him, the same shall be a law, in like manner as if he had signed it, unless the Congress by their adjournment prevent its return, in which case it shall not be a law.

—from Article I, section 7

Congress. As with Nixon, Reagan administration officials argued that the pocket veto should apply to any congressional recess longer than three days. And, just as before, many in Congress declared once again that the device applied only to adjournment sine die. Thirty-three House Democrats subsequently sued the administration, and a U.S. court of appeals in 1984 reversed a lower court decision and reaffirmed the standard set in 1976.[32] The administration appealed the decision to the Supreme Court, which in January 1987 declared the particulars of the case moot (since the dispute over aid to El Salvador had long passed) and upheld the decision of the lower court.[33] Members of Congress and administration officials alike voiced disappointment that the high court had not settled the matter once and for all.

What constitutes constitutional application of the pocket veto thus remains a point of contention between members of Congress eager to protect legislative prerogatives and presidents equally keen to expand their weapons against unwanted legislation. The issue of the pocket veto may not be settled until the Supreme Court acts.

Item Veto

The veto is a blunt tool for executive influence precisely because it is an all or nothing matter. For many who support expansive executive power this is a major flaw, since a president cannot separate items deemed wasteful within a major spending bill. Proposals to give the president the ability to pick and choose among specific appropriations, called an *item veto,* have dotted congressional agendas throughout history; but so far the effort has been thwarted by legislators fearful of even greater executive leverage within their domain.

Forty-three states give their governors some form of item veto. Most of these provisions pertain primarily to spending bills, but others expand the governor's power to substantive laws as well. At least ten states allow governors actually to amend spending bills and send them back to the legislature for reconsideration.[34]

The Framers appear to have given no attention to an item veto during the drafting or ratification of the Constitution, which seems surprising until we recall that even the regular veto proved highly contentious. Granting to Congress full power over appropriations and revenues certainly emphasized the Framers' bias, but the option of allowing the president to excise specific parts of spending bills would arise thereafter. The states of the Confederacy included a clause in their constitution allowing the president to "approve any appropriation and disapprove any other appropriation in the same bill" (Article 1, section 7, clause 2), and efforts to pass a constitutional amendment creating similar executive power in the U.S. Constitution have been commonplace since the 1870s.

A number of presidents through the twentieth century have expressed their support for an item veto, most notably Franklin Roosevelt, Dwight Eisenhower, and Ronald Reagan. Roosevelt came closest to realizing his wishes when the House in 1938 voted to give the president that power, but the effort died in the Senate.[35] In 1985, Sen. Mack Mattingly (R-Ga.) and forty-six cosponsors pushed for a two-year trial run, but, despite President Reagan's enthusiastic endorsement in his 1985 State of the Union address, the proposal was rebuffed both then and a year later. Even if the Senate in 1986 had approved the item veto, it was unlikely that the House, which is highly protective of its power of the purse, would have gone along.

"Quasi-Item Vetoes"

Not a few presidents compensated for the lack of formal item veto power through other means. One mechanism was to "impound"—or *not* spend—money appropriated by Congress for fiscal or administrative reasons. The concept of impoundment is not controversial when presidents can show that the expenditure is no longer needed, as when Thomas Jefferson impounded funds earmarked for naval ships because the hostilities prompting the appropriation no longer existed, or when unforeseen circumstances delay spending. But when presidents try to use impoundment for obvious fiscal or policy reasons, sharp conflict with Congress is guaranteed.

Impoundment was used infrequently until the 1970s, largely because presidents sought to avoid major fights with Congress over control of the purse.[36] Richard Nixon, however, relied openly on impoundment to "veto" specific congressional budgetary allocations, even for entire agencies. These efforts proved so controversial that Congress in 1974 passed the Budget and Impoundment Act (over his veto), which forbade impoundments unless approved by both houses of Congress.

Subsequent presidents have continued to "defer" or "rescind" funds under the auspices of the law, although the actions deemed most controversial have had difficulty getting congressional acquiescence. In 1986, for example, President Reagan attempted to defer $5 billion for housing and urban development programs for fiscal reasons because Congress had appropriated more money than he had requested, but a federal appeals court ruled that his actions violated the intent of the 1974 law.[37]

Presidents also on occasion refuse to abide by specific provisions in laws they sign, or they issue their own interpretations when they think Congress has acted unconstitutionally. In 1959 Eisenhower announced that he would disregard a provision for congressional access to secret documents because it would violate the president's need to protect national security. In 1971 Nixon insisted that he was not bound by a provision requiring the president to state a specific time period for withdrawal from Vietnam.[38] Both presidents effectively undermined the provisions in question, but the constitutionality of such actions has not been tested in court.[39]

The Item Veto Debated

Proponents of the item veto argue that such an instrument would help limit federal spending, allow presidents to excise "wasteful" congressional appropriations, and give chief executives greater opportunities to promote their overall budget priorities. Political commentator George Will called it an "effective instrument of allocation" to help presidents carry out their electoral "mandates" and to strengthen presidential responsibility over both the budget and the general direction of the federal government.[40] The proponents' argument, in sum, is that what is good enough for forty-three governors must be good enough for the president of the United States.

Their critics argue that a presidential item veto simply would not affect federal spending profoundly, particularly since it would not apply to the massive "entitlement" programs (like Social Security) that make up so much of the total budget.[41] Presidents also are seen as being just as responsible for budgetary growth as Congress, since they can use the regular veto to force legislative compliance if they wish. Still others point out that any reference to state item veto provisions negates the very real differences that exist between the powers of state legislatures and those possessed by the U.S. Congress.[42]

Practical questions aside, the debate over the item veto is a debate over power, over which branch will be supreme when it comes to federal spending. Those promoting the item veto favor expanded executive power to control both spending and the direction of national policy. Those opposing the item veto fear the effect of such power on congressional control of the purse and argue that the provision would become yet another way for a president to reward friends, hurt enemies, and dominate the legislative process. Whatever the case, the debate over the item veto promises to sizzle as long as the federal budget deficit continues to be a major political issue.

The President's Program

The president's second express duty is to "from time to time give to the Congress information of the state of the Union, and recommend to their consideration such measures he shall judge necessary and expedient" (Article II, section 3). Unlike the veto, which is a limited and somewhat negative instrument for stopping unwanted legislation, the duty to recommend legislation has over time become the primary mechanism by which chief executives influence the nation's political agenda. Given the presidency's relatively weak array of formal mechanisms for mandating government policy, no other facet of the office today is as critical to presidential success or failure when the nation is not in crisis. This is so because the ability to affect the agenda of government—to decide what is or is not a priority—is in essence the power to influence what government will or will not do.

Determining the agenda of government is no paltry matter. As many a high school debate team member discovers, there are rules for debate—the questions to be discussed and the procedure for discussing them—that participants must follow whether they like it or not. Unlike a scholastic debate competition, however, in the political realm the topics to be discussed and the rules for discourse are not set beforehand by a neutral moderator. Rather, deciding the issues to be debated in the first place is a matter of political power, timing, and, perhaps, luck. As political scientist E. E. Schattschneider long ago concluded, "He who determines what politics is all about runs the country, because the definition of the alternatives is the choice of conflicts, and the choice of conflicts allocates power." [43]

At times, unforeseen crises such as natural disasters, war, or sudden shifts in the economy overwhelm the agenda of government. When that happens, the existing agenda is thrown aside and presidential "success" or "strength" is judged by the pace and suitability of executive response. Franklin Roosevelt's answer to the impending collapse of the banking system in March 1933 often is cited as an example of strong presidential leadership, for within a few days Roosevelt moved Congress to reorganize the system and, equally important, persuaded average Americans to return their savings to the banks. In doing so Roosevelt instilled renewed faith in the financial system and began the road to national economic recovery.

Ronald Reagan, however, reaped a great deal of criticism in October 1987 for his allegedly belated and passive response to a sudden plunge in the stock market, which Wall Street analysts blamed largely on the deadlock between the president and Congress over how to resolve the federal budget deficit. Whether the "crisis" over the budget deficit caused the market crash, or whether Reagan responded inadequately, is hard to say, yet common perceptions that the president had not dealt forcefully with the situation eroded confidence in his leadership.

Crises aside, no single institution in the United States so powerfully influences the national agenda of political debate as the presidency. No other institution is so capable of subjecting Congress to so much pressure in so organized a manner, and no other political figure commands so much attention from the public regardless of the issue. The presidency always has been the focal point of U.S. politics because it is the only political office in the United States chosen through a national election, but its importance has burgeoned since the 1930s. The sheer growth in the scope and influence of the federal government, the emergence of the United States as a world economic and military power (which amplified the president's role as commander in chief), and, perhaps most important, the rise of modern telecommunications technology, all have combined to place the presidency squarely in the public psyche both at home and abroad.

The presidency, as political scientist Bruce Miroff has suggested, commands the "public space" in contemporary U.S. politics, largely forcing other participants in the political process to respond to issues as the president defines them.[44] That reality powerfully influences success or failure on policy initiatives, particularly in issue areas where most Americans have no direct experience. Reagan, for example, consistently portrayed the rebels fighting the Nicaraguan government as "freedom fighters," a picture so compelling to so many citizens that those in opposition were forced continually to refute the president's definition even before they could attack his policies. But, each time they came close to defeating further U.S. aid to the rebels, they discovered anew the president's power to reach out to the nation for support. It may be said, in fact, that Reagan alone carried the rebels along through the sheer power of his office to dominate the agenda of discussion.

The president did not define the national agenda throughout most of the nineteenth century. In those days, Congress dominated government, the White House was populated by a succession of largely forgettable figures, and the technologies of mass communication did not yet exist. Presidents were not expected to formulate legislative agendas, prepare and present executive budgets, or do much else except oversee the executive branch, conduct foreign policy (such as it was when the United States was relatively isolated), and oppose Congress whenever necessary and possible. Nor did the dominant view of government hold that presidents should take active roles in initiating or influencing public policy. Not until Franklin Roosevelt did the presidency become a strong *institution,* one that remained potent regardless of the person sitting in the Oval Office.

Congress and the Presidency: Two Cultures

It is impossible to discuss the president's legislative influence without first recognizing the essential differences between the executive and legislative branches. Not only does the Constitution grant to Congress the sole power to make law, generate revenues, and appropriate funds, but it also established in the national government sets of dynamics and roles that fundamentally set Congress far apart from the presidency. Those differences, which have remained remarkably constant throughout history, are important to understanding why presidents succeed or fail in achieving their legislative goals.[45]

First, presidents and members of Congress reach national office through entirely separate paths. The president is the only political figure elected through a nationwide election. That process, combined with the national responsibilities of the office, inevitably gives the president a broad perspective on issues. Members of Congress, by contrast, come to government through local elections, be they district contests for the House of Representatives or statewide races for the Senate. That fact alone ensures, as former speaker of the House Thomas P. (Tip) O'Neill was fond of saying, that for members of Congress "all politics is local." [46] Those in Congress can and do think in national terms on a wide range of policy questions, but their elective roles force them to tend to their home districts first and foremost. More than one House member or senator has paid a political price for not keeping close tabs on local matters.

What is more, presidents and members of Congress serve different terms of office. A president is elected for four years, but members of the House have only two-year terms, which makes them especially sensitive to momentary pressures and local demands.

This also means that, because congressional elections take place in the second year of the president's term, some elections can be construed as public votes of confidence in presidential performance. The president's party almost invariably loses seats in the House of Representatives and the Senate in midterm elections, and members of Congress from the president's party are keenly aware that public disenchantment with their leader may cause them serious electoral problems. The opposition party, for its part, naturally tries to use these contests to its advantage, making gains at the expense of the president's party.

In 1980, for example, the Republicans picked up 34 new House seats in the wake of Ronald Reagan's victory over Jimmy Carter.[47] Although House Democrats still outnumbered Republicans by a 243-192 margin, House Republicans in 1981 were able to build alliances with conservative southern Democrats large enough to give the president a working majority and push through his dramatic budget and tax reduction bills. But an economic recession, and Democrats' effective attacks on administration plans to alter the Social Security program, resulted in the Republicans' losing more than two-thirds of those new seats in the 1982 midterm election. The effect on Reagan's influence was palpable: the Democratic majority in the House was larger and more unified, public approval of the president was weaker, and southern conservative Democrats no longer readily joined Republicans against their own party.

The problem for presidents in the Senate is a bit different. Members of the Senate serve for six years, with only one-third of the body up for reelection every second year. Thus, every other Senate term is not affected directly by a presidential election. This gives senators greater freedom to support or oppose presidential initiatives without as much concern about short-term constituent pressures. Additionally, the Senate retains constitutional leverage over the executive through its power to approve presidential nominees to the federal judiciary and to high-level executive branch positions and through its power to approve or reject treaties with other nations. These roles, and the great independence of senators generally, almost guarantees problems for presidents even of the same party. Jimmy Carter failed to obtain Senate approval for the 1978 Strategic Arms Limitation Treaty despite Democratic dominance in the chamber, and Reagan faced the greatest opposition on the 1987 Intermediate Force Missile Treaty from conservative Republicans.

The two branches also possess widely divergent decision-making cultures and processes, variations that emerge from their fundamentally different governing responsibilities. The president, whose primary responsibilities are implementing the laws and defending the nation, is at the top of an executive hierarchy that speaks with one official voice on policy matters. Decisions frequently are dictated to subordinates from the Oval Office, and policy options often stem from the president's overall ideology and political agenda. Loyalty to the president's program is paramount, and dissenting voices find their influence severely limited, if not completely cut off.

Congress, however, speaks with many voices simultaneously, one for each of the 535 members of the House and Senate. Congress is diverse not principally because of inherent failings in the legislature itself, or because members are by nature disputatious (although many are), but because members of Congress must both represent their constituents and make national policy. These dual roles often conflict, since what may be good for any member's constituents (such as new services or public facilities) may bode ill for the nation (in the form of massive budget deficits, for example). Each member of Congress wields but one vote, regardless of seniority or party position, and no member can be expelled from the legislature simply because of voting behavior or personal opinion. Only constituents have the right to "fire" their representatives.

This inherent equality among members forces the institution itself to operate according to relatively nonhierarchical decision-making processes. To do otherwise would appear antidemocratic. Decisions, in the form of legislation, are achieved by building coalitions of members large enough to win committee and floor votes. Consensus becomes a hallowed norm of behavior. Successful legislating depends on knitting together enough diverse interests and demands to overcome opposition, using whatever tactics seem reasonable or necessary. This is true even in the less hierarchical Senate, where the rules of debate and norms of courtesy, reciprocity (trading favors), and consensus allow a single member to obstruct the majority—and the president—until agreement surfaces.

In 1982, for example, Sen. Jesse Helms, a staunchly conservative Republican from North Carolina, single-handedly held up the Reagan administration's tax bill because he objected to higher levies on tobacco. Throughout the Reagan years Helms stalled appointments to ambassadorial positions because of disagreements with the administration on foreign policy issues. The White House could do little but complain loudly and threaten to withhold favors or federal contracts to firms in his home state, but Helms nonetheless won reelection in 1984.

Presidents usually want to move quickly so they can make the most of their limited opportunities through dramatic and often comprehensive policy initiatives. This is true particularly during the first year, because every president knows that the personal popularity so critical to overcoming the normal inertia of the political system inevitably fades.

But Congress, except in times of crisis or when an issue is especially important, prefers more stately deliberation and a more cautious weighing of the consequences. The needs of each member's constituency must be treated fairly, and coalitions of support must be constructed. These considerations usually are more important to members of the House and Senate than speed or ideological purity. Many a president, resentful of this glacial pace of deliberation, has chastised Congress publicly for its somewhat messy operating style, but the legislature by design marches to its own drummer.

These fundamental differences all too often produce clashes between presidents theoretically acting on behalf of the national interest and members of Congress promoting constituents' needs. Presidents routinely accuse Congress of waste or inertia, but they also find that cumulative local and state interests often overcome any supposed "national" good. Carter, for example, early in his administration attacked spending for public works projects (such as dams and irrigation canals), but he discovered very quickly that these projects are "sacred cows" to legislators eager to serve their constituents.[48] In 1987 Reagan vetoed a popular reauthorization of the Clean Water Act because he felt that its $20 billion appropriation for water and sewage treatment projects was wasteful, but Congress overrode his veto by overwhelming bipartisan margins.

Contrast these conditions with those common in parliamentary systems, where prime ministers typically are selected by the majority party (or party coalition) in the legislature. There is no separation of powers in the American sense, and strong party cohesion is essential to maintaining control over government. Prime Minister Margaret Thatcher, for example, gained her position as a result of Conservative party dominance in Parliament, a solid majority that allows her to push through major legislation far more easily and quickly than any U.S. president could imagine. In the United States, by contrast, members of Congress can and do go against their party and president when constituent interests are on the line. What the Constitution splits apart, party loyalty cannot easily bind together.[49]

In sum, the relationship between the president and Congress is one determined by the Founders through constitutional provisions on terms, powers, and governing responsibilities. Those who wrote the Constitution were far more concerned with checking the potential abuses of power than with speedy or easy legislating. They *wanted* Congress and the president to be at odds, and they endowed Congress with the ability to withstand executive pressure and, indeed, to dictate public policy if it so willed. Even when dominated by a president's party, Congress as an institution insists on playing its constitutional role according to its own needs and internal dynamics. No president seeking to succeed can forget those realities.

Sen. Jesse Helms (R-N.C.) singlehandedly held up the Reagan administration's tax bill. A single member often can obstruct a congressional majority and the president.

Historical Development

"Whether legislator, opinion-maker, commander, or administrator," argued presidential scholar Clinton Rossiter, "the President molds lasting policy in every sector of American life."[50] Indeed, as political scientist Bertram Gross wrote in 1953, "Except in wartime, Presidents are now judged more by the quality of the legislation they propose or succeed in getting enacted than by their records as executive."[51] The presidency today is seen almost as a third house of Congress, with presidents involved deeply in all aspects of the legislative process and judged by how well they can mobilize support for their programs.

Compare these analyses with the experiences of early presidents, and the contrast is staggering. Rather than expecting the president to formulate a legislative program and lobby for its enactment, Congress, through the late 1800s, almost invariably regarded presidential involvement in policy making as nothing less than unwarranted intrusion.[52] Textbook notions that Congress alone makes the law, which the president then simply administers, were taken seriously, and separation of powers meant that presidents left to Congress the responsibility to initiate public policy. Presidents who forgot this constitutional nicety were quickly reminded of it by members of the legislature always on guard against such presumptuousness.

Whether the Founders actually meant the president to play so passive a role is hotly debated. Certainly, they viewed the presidency as a bulwark against congressional mischief or tyranny. Yet, as Alexander Hamilton argued in *Federalist* No. 70, "energy in the executive is a leading character of good government."[53]

The Founders may have rejected decisively the more monarchical schemes for the executive proposed early on by Hamilton and others, but they also emphatically rejected making the president subordinate to or entirely separate from Congress. The legislature was to make national policy, but the president did receive from the Founders a limited number of instruments for influencing legislation. Bringing those resources to bear, however, would be another question.

Early Presidents

George Washington discovered rather quickly the difficulties of influencing legislation. He was the first—and last—president ever to sit in on Congress during actual floor debate. In line with his early view that oral communications were indispensable to fruitful relations between the branches, on August 22, 1789, Washington personally presented to the Senate the particulars of an Indian treaty and requested that body's advice and consent. The president's proposal was read aloud—twice, since some senators could not hear for the noise coming in off the street—but only awkward silence ensued. Sen. William Maclay of Pennsylvania then rose and called for a reading of the treaty itself and its accompanying papers, and afterward supported a move to refer the entire matter to a committee for further study. Maclay, as he later wrote in his journal, "saw no chance of fair investigation of subjects if the President of the United States sat there, with his Secretary of War, to support his opinions and over-awe the timid and neutral part of the Senate." Washington, wrote Maclay, "started up in a violent fret" at the proposal to refer the matter to committee, exclaiming, "This defeats every purpose of my coming here." The president eventually calmed down and agreed to a two-day delay, but on his return he found many senators still uneasy about his presence. After completing the business at hand, Washington vowed that he would not repeat the experience.[54]

Washington thereafter shied away from face-to-face lobbying, but he nonetheless remained active in influencing legislation, particularly treaties, indirectly. Secretary of the Treasury Alexander Hamilton, however, proved unabashedly aggressive in trying to expand executive policy-making resources. Hamilton's belief in an energetic presidency and his tireless use of his department to initiate and lobby for legislation soon sparked a backlash in Congress. Secretary of State Thomas Jefferson, despite his overall support for Washington, objected strenuously in a letter to the president that Hamilton's "system flowed from principles adverse to liberty, and was calculated to undermine and demolish the republic, by creating an influence of his department over the members of the legislature."[55]

Jefferson, whose Democratic-Republican party in principle glorified the concept of congressional supremacy, eschewed personal lobbying when he became president and went so far as to suspend the fledgling tradition of personally delivering an annual State of the Union message. But Jefferson was no passive chief executive. He carefully maintained the forms of separation of powers and congressional supremacy but relied heavily on cabinet members and his strong party caucus organization, which held the majority in Congress, to initiate and dominate legislative activity. Secretary of the Treasury Albert Gallatin acted as his primary liaison to the party caucus, and Jefferson personally picked his own party floor leaders, who then became known as the president's chief congressional spokespersons. The strength of the party caucus, held together in many ways by Jefferson's own political skills (including innumerable and widely acclaimed dinner parties), produced a style of governing that in many ways paralleled parliamentary systems.

After Jefferson, however, "king caucus" gave way to congressional supremacy. Jefferson's model of party government decayed as splits within the Democratic-Republican caucus eroded its usefulness as a mechanism for executive leverage. Power flowed back to Congress as an institution, and strong leaders such as Henry Clay and John C. Calhoun actively set the agenda of government through the 1820s. House Speaker Clay in particular dominated tariff and public works matters and with his allies would force even James Madison against his will to con-

front the British in the War of 1812. Congress also began to develop its own institutional mechanisms for sustained policy-making expertise, particularly in the standing committees, which began to evolve into power centers in their own right as presidents came and went.

Andrew Jackson in the 1830s momentarily reinvigorated the role of the Democratic party and its national convention as a means for setting the national agenda. Even more notable, the breadth and strength of his party organization allowed Jackson to become the first president to appeal directly to the public over the heads of Congress on such issues as the National Bank and the tariff.[56] Overall, however, Jackson's legislative strategy was largely negative, relying primarily on the veto to rebuff congressional actions. The idea that the president should actively propose and shepherd legislation through Congress was still controversial, and the increasing power of the standing committees did not allow Jackson to dominate Congress through the party.[57] Nonetheless, and particularly when compared with the series of Whig presidents to follow him, Jackson temporarily reinvigorated executive leadership in national policy making.

A few relatively active presidents aside, and not including Lincoln's emergency actions during the Civil War, nineteenth-century legislating generally was a congressional affair. The president's constitutional responsibilities over the armed forces and foreign policy mattered little, since the United States during most of this century kept resolutely out of international politics and maintained a minimal defense and foreign policy apparatus. On the domestic side, the federal government concerned itself largely with such parochial matters as post offices and other public works projects. Except in times of crisis, government through the late 1800s did relatively little on a national scale, and the presidency by extension played a secondary role in policy formation. Congress never shied from reminding presidents of their "proper" role, and even Abraham Lincoln toward the end of the Civil War was admonished that the president "must confine himself to executive duties—to obey and execute, not make the laws. . . ."[58]

Shift toward Presidential Leadership

These distinctions began to change in the late 1880s as the American economy and society evolved, and as the United States began to play a greater role in international affairs. The industrial revolution brought with it a transition from a self-sufficient farm economy to an urban manufacturing one, from largely localized business concerns to huge national corporations, and, perhaps as a result, a shift from the view that the federal government should do little to calls for it to do more. The issues of the day—interstate commerce, corporate monopoly, child labor, food and drug purity, monetary policy, agricultural research, and transportation, among others—became more national in scope and often overlapped with international trade and diplomacy questions that were growing in importance as the United States became more active in the world.

These trends also altered the prevailing wisdom about government and, by extension, the role of the presidency. Calls for more active executive leadership on legislation began to be heard as Congress increasingly found itself ill-equipped to handle broad national questions. The legislature by nature is better able to deal with issues that can be broken down by congressional districts or state lines, such as allocation of funds for post offices, than it is with issues having no clear constituency boundaries. Moreover, popular perceptions that Congress was not attentive to emerging national and international problems legitimized the notion of an energetic president. The constitutional forms of the two branches in most respects would stay the same, but their dynamics would change subtly as the nation itself entered a new era.

Theodore Roosevelt, who once said the president "can be as big a man as he can," could be called the first exponent of the "new" presidency.[59] Roosevelt was keenly aware that his was the only purely national voice, and he saw the Oval Office as a "bully pulpit" for stimulating public opinion and pushing legislation through Congress. "In theory the Executive has nothing to do with legislation," Roosevelt later wrote in his *Autobiography*.

> In practice, as things are now, the Executive is or ought to be peculiarly representative as a whole. As often as not the action of the Executive offers the only means by which the people can get the legislation they demand and ought to have. Therefore a good executive under the present conditions of American political life must take a very active interest in getting the right kind of legislation, in addition to performing his executive duties with an eye single to the public welfare. [60]

Roosevelt tried to practice what he preached. Largely on the strength of the president's advocacy and wide newspaper publicity, the Pure Food and Drug Act of 1906, a landmark consumer law that established the Food and Drug Administration, was pushed through a Congress dominated by agriculture and business interests. Roosevelt also established the national park system, attacked monopolies, and negotiated the end to a war between Japan and Russia (for which he won the Nobel Peace Prize).

Even more instructive was Roosevelt's decision to send a U.S. naval squadron on a global tour. Congress refused to appropriate money for the "show the flag" exercise, but Roosevelt scraped together enough funds from other naval accounts to send the fleet halfway around the world. He then publicly challenged Congress to provide enough money to bring the ships home. Public opinion so strongly supported Roosevelt that Congress quickly surrendered.

Although Roosevelt was unique in many ways—boundless in energy, aggressively intellectual, eager for public acclaim—his legacy would not disappear. The nation and Congress had been given a taste of energetic presidential leadership, and succeeding chief executives would find both the public and Congress more receptive to their initiatives.

William Howard Taft, Roosevelt's immediate successor and noted advocate of a far less grandiose view of the office, nonetheless was the first president to present draft legislation formally to Congress.[61] Woodrow Wilson in 1913 became the first president since John Adams to deliver his State of the Union message personally before a joint session of Congress. He thereafter used the address as a statement of his legislative agenda and to put into practice his belief that the president should lead government more actively.[62] Wilson also made bold assertions of his right to guide legislation, arguing in a special address to Congress, "I have come to you as the head of the government and the responsible leader of the party in power to urge action now, while there is time to serve the country deliberately, and as we should, in a clear air of common counsel." [63] The object of his speech, the Federal Reserve Act of 1913, was drafted largely in conferences at the White House, with Wilson personally in charge.

The Roosevelt Model

Despite gradual changes in the presidency during the early 1900s, the office remained a largely negative force in opposition to Congress, not the source of initiative and leadership Americans are used to (and demand) today. Theodore Roosevelt or Woodrow Wilson could take the lead in selected instances, particularly when conditions for presidential initiative were most favorable, but the office itself lacked mechanisms for sustained legislative influence. In the 1930s, however, the office underwent major, permanent changes; in many ways the actions of Franklin Roosevelt prefaced the contemporary presidency.

Franklin Roosevelt came to office in 1933 as the nation faced unprecedented economic and social pressures. The Great Depression devastated the national economy, forcing millions into unemployment and crippling public faith in government. Herbert Hoover (1929-1933) had relied on the market system and its leaders to resolve the crisis, but many voters thought this confidence was misplaced and believed that Hoover was to blame for the country's hardships. As a result, Hoover suffered a humiliating defeat in the 1932 presidential election. The emergency required major action and gave Roosevelt the opportunity to take the lead in ways no peacetime president ever had. Congress, which itself had proved unable to resolve the crisis, awaited strong direction. Conditions for redefining the very essence of the presidency were never so ripe.

Roosevelt's immediate attack on the depression would go down in U.S. history as the most sweeping and sustained rearrangement of national domestic policies ever made. During the famous "first Hundred Days" of Roosevelt's first term, Congress in special session gave the new president a blank check to remold the federal government, to introduce new programs, and to do almost anything to turn the economy around. Roosevelt and his battalions of energetic New Dealers took on the task with an almost joyful gusto, pushing major legislation through a willing Congress with unparalleled speed between March 9 and June 15, 1933. *(See box, The First Hundred Days of Franklin D. Roosevelt, p. 70.)* As presidential scholar Clinton Rossiter said of Roosevelt, "In the first Hundred Days he gave Congress a kind of leadership it had not known before and still does not care to have repeated." [64]

Library of Congress · Library of Congress

President Theodore Roosevelt was an energetic legislative leader, but his cousin Franklin D. Roosevelt went still further. FDR redefined the role of national government through his New Deal legislation and vastly expanded the size of the executive branch.

The First Hundred Days Of Franklin D. Roosevelt

Franklin D. Roosevelt was sworn into office on March 4, 1933, and convened the 73rd Congress into special session on March 9 to consider the Emergency Banking Act, which was passed after eight hours of debate. Roosevelt at first thought about sending Congress back home after passage of the act, but the momentum attained seemed too valuable to waste. As historian Arthur M. Schlesinger, Jr., later wrote, "In the three months after Roosevelt's inauguration, Congress and the country were subjected to a presidential barrage of ideas and programs unlike anything known to American history." [1] The major accomplishments of that first hundred days are:

March 9	Emergency Banking Act: reformed the national banking system
March 20	Economy Act: authorized cuts in federal spending
March 22	Beer and Wine Revenue Act: legalized sale of beer and wine
March 31	Civilian Conservation Corps: created employment for youths in a wide range of conservation efforts
April 19	Abandonment of gold standard: detached value of currency from gold
May 12	Federal Emergency Relief Act: created a national relief system
May 12	Agricultural Adjustment Act: established a national agricultural policy
May 12	Emergency Farm Mortgage Act: refinanced farm mortgages
May 18	Tennessee Valley Authority Act: provided for the unified development of the Tennessee Valley
May 27	Truth in Securities Act: required full disclosure of a firm's financial shape in issuing new securities
June 13	Home Owners' Loan Act: refinanced home mortgages
June 16	National Industrial Recovery Act: created a system of industrial self-regulation under federal supervision and a $3.3 billion public works program
June 16	Glass-Steagall Banking Act: separated commercial and investment banking, guaranteed bank deposits
June 16	Farm Credit Act: reorganized federal farm credit programs
June 16	Emergency Railroad Transportation Act: created greater coordination in national railroad system

1. Arthur M. Schlesinger, Jr., *The Coming of the New Deal* (Boston: Houghton Mifflin, 1959), 20.

Central to Roosevelt's success in 1933 was the link he established between the presidency and the American people, a connection achieved in great part because of his ability to communicate directly over radio. "This great nation will endure as it has endured, will revive and will prosper.... This nation asks for action, and action now," he said in his first inaugural address, which sparked nearly half a million letters of support. "We must act, and act quickly." [65] His speeches, the "fireside chats," and the frequent press conferences, all spoke directly to the American people, and indirectly to Congress, about his dreams and priorities. In the process, Roosevelt focused public attention on the presidency.

The New Deal era and Roosevelt's actions during World War II both redefined the role of national government and thoroughly altered the presidency as an institution. By the time Roosevelt died in 1945, the executive branch had exploded in size and in the scope of its responsibilities, and the presidency itself had gained a wider array of resources for influencing legislation, making budgets, and implementing programs. The presidency no longer was a single person but an institution, one that was growing in size and potency as Congress gave the president more staff and more resources to manage the government, initiate public policy, and lead the nation. Congress delegated these responsibilities both because legislators came to realize that the presidency was better situated to lead and, perhaps more important, because Americans demanded it.

When Harry Truman took up Roosevelt's mantle in 1945, he sat at the center of an office completely transformed during the course of twelve years. Under Roosevelt the presidency had become part national cheerleader, and would become even more so with the advent of television to transmit ideas and symbols. It had become part legislative leader, with the president required both to initiate and to shepherd new policies through a potentially recalcitrant Congress. It had become part chief executive officer of a large and busy government organization, with the need to manage and direct the federal bureaucracy toward the common good. It had become part world ambassador, no longer a safe refuge for those ignorant of or unconcerned about international affairs. And, most important, it had become wholly responsible for the nation's successes or failures, for Roosevelt interjected the presidency forcefully into a role traditionally and constitutionally held by Congress. No longer would the presidency remain a passive office, even if its occupant possessed neither Roosevelt's skills nor his vigor.

The Roosevelt Legacy

Roosevelt's legacy has been problematic for contemporary presidents. The office has grown in power and prestige, but perhaps not proportionately with public and congressional expectations about what presidents can deliver. Those in the Oval Office must present and implement broad national programs, but separation of powers ensures that presidents' futures are not necessarily in their own hands. The emergence of the United States as a world power after World War II demands that presidents exercise their commander-in-chief responsibilities more fully and consistently than when the U.S. played virtually no role in international political and military affairs, but these responsibilities frequently do not coincide well with public demands that domestic matters be given top priority. The coming of television brings the world more intimately into every home, and the pace of events has quickened demonstrably; but coalitions of support also seem more fleeting, and governing appears all the more difficult. The world is smaller, and public expectations about government are greater, creating for the presidency a burden of leadership that may, scholars speculate, prove too great to carry.[66]

This is not to argue that presidents have *no* control over their own destinies, but the extent of their control seems at times to depend less on personal intellect and skill than on the social, political, and economic contexts within which they govern. It also depends on the relative quiescence or independence of other governing institutions, particularly Congress.

Lyndon Johnson, for example, was a master of the legislative process, having had a long career as House member, senator, and, later, Senate majority leader. Nonetheless, in 1965 his ability to promote and attain the most sweeping of social programs since Roosevelt's first Hundred Days depended just as much on the trauma of John Kennedy's assassination, a national mood supporting broad social change, and an especially cooperative congressional majority after his sweeping 1964 election victory as it did on his legislative skills. Johnson's successes in 1965, when Congress approved some 69 percent of his requests, was tempered by knowledge that times would soon change.[67] "I have watched the Congress from either the inside or the outside, man and boy, for more than 40 years," Johnson commented early in 1965, "and I've never seen a Congress that didn't eventually take the measure of the president it was dealing with." [68]

Carter discovered that reality acutely very early in his administration when a Congress strongly dominated by his own party proved skeptical of his comprehensive energy plan. Carter's problems in 1977 and later stemmed not only from his relative lack of experience in and even distaste for Washington politics, but from the very changes to have taken place in Congress, and in American politics generally, during the preceding decade. Congress had become far more open, more fragmented, and more independent in the interim, forcing presidents to adapt to new ways of influencing the legislature. Lyndon Johnson had been able to push through his Great Society programs largely on his ability to rally key committee chairs and other congressional leaders, but Carter found it necessary to lobby virtually every member, a decidedly more difficult and frustrating task. Even Reagan, whose masterful rhetorical skills helped him translate his 1980 election victory into early legislative success, found his later efforts frustrated by his inability to induce Congress to follow his lead. Lyndon Johnson's warning is an apt one.

The question of context thus is essential to analyzing a president's ability to set the agenda of government and to persuade Congress to enact those priorities. According to presidential scholar Louis Koenig, Congress most consistently follows presidential leadership in three situations.[69] The first is during crises, when Congress and the nation almost invariably turn to the president for leadership. Roosevelt and the first Hundred Days is the most-cited example, for it is almost impossible to conceive that the New Deal could have been passed under "normal" political conditions.

Second, matters of national security and foreign affairs, where the Constitution gives the presidency primacy, find Congress generally more amenable to presidential initiatives. This was true particularly between World War II and the end of the Vietnam War, when a general view that party "politics ended at the water's edge" gave postwar presidents an unparalleled range of flexibility. The tendency for Congress to accede to presidential demands in defense and foreign policy issues led more than one president to cloak purely domestic programs in the mantle of national security to obtain easier passage. The interstate highway system, federal education programs, and the space program all were defined as essential to national security or pride—highways for easier movement of defense forces, greater education spending to "catch up" to the Soviets after the launch of Sputnik, and the Mercury, Gemini, and Apollo programs to win the "space race." These programs thus won far greater national support than they might have otherwise.

Third, presidents reap benefits from "abnormal" contexts—the combined effects of skilled political leaders, superior partisan dominance in Congress, changing societal values, and, especially, timing. Virtually every newly elected president enjoys a postelection "honeymoon" with Congress, a period during which the new occupant of the White House can push priorities within an atmosphere of general cooperation. Presidents from Roosevelt to the present usually have had their greatest legislative successes in the first six months following their initial election to office. Their success has varied, depending on the president's own abilities, the dominant national mood, and the strength of congressional majorities.

In sum, the ability of any president to dominate the agenda of government, to plan and propose new initiatives, and to lobby successfully on their behalf depends on more than personal skills or intellect. The character of the U.S. political system, the nature of the times, and the types of issues under debate, all affect the extent to which any president can influence the national agenda and the legislative process.

The State of the Union Address

The annual State of the Union Address has become since the 1930s an essential and powerful instrument by which presidents seek to influence the national agenda. It is today the primary means by which presidents review their past accomplishments and outline their future goals, yet this constitutional requirement that presidents give Congress information on the state of the Union has not always played so central a role in presidential strategies. Both George Washington and John Adams appeared personally before Congress to deliver their annual messages, but Thomas Jefferson in 1801 dropped the practice and instead submitted his reports in writing. Jefferson's action appeared to stem from his dislike of a practice that had its roots in the British Parliament, which opened each session with a speech from the king or queen. By eliminating what he saw as a quasi-monarchical rite, historian Arthur M. Schlesinger, Jr., has noted, Jefferson hoped to instill stronger republican values in the still-new American system of government.[70]

Eighteenth century presidents continued Jefferson's practice, and it was not until 1913 that a president appeared again before Congress and personally delivered an address. Woodrow Wilson, who believed that the role of the presidency included strong personal appeals to the nation and to Congress, revived the ritual begun under Washington. In his first personal appearance before Congress for a special messge on finance, Wilson expressed his general

Presidential Appearances before Congress, 1789-1988

President	Number of Appearances	Occasions
Washington	10	8 annual messages (1789-1796); 2 inaugural addresses (1789, 1793—second inaugural before Senate only)
J. Adams	6	4 annual messages (1797-1800), inaugural address (1797); relations with France (1797)
Wilson	26	6 annual messages (1913-1918); tariff reform, bank reform, relations with Mexico (1913); antitrust laws, Panama Canal tolls, relations with Mexico, new tax revenue (1914); impending rail strike (1916); "Peace without Victory" (Senate only), breaking relations with Germany, arming of merchant ships, request for war declaration against Germany (1917); federal takeover of railroads, "14 points" for peace, peace outlook, need for new revenue, request for ratification of women's suffrage amendment (Senate only), armistice (1918); request for approval of Versailles treaty (Senate only), high cost of living (1919)
Harding	7	2 annual messages (1921-1922); federal problems (1921); 2 on the Merchant Marines (1922); coal and railroads (1922); debt (1923)
Coolidge	2	1 annual message (1923); George Washington's birthday (1927)
Roosevelt	16	10 annual messages (1934-1943); 100th anniversary of Lafayette's death (1934); 150th anniversary of First Congress (1939); Neutrality address (1939); national defense (1940); declaration of war (1941); Yalta conference report (1945)
Truman	17	6 State of the Union messages (1947-1952); prosecution of the war (1945); submission of UN charter (Senate only, 1945); congressional Medal of Honor ceremony (1945); universal military training (1945); railroad strike (1946); Greek-Turkish aid policy (1947); aid to Europe (1947); national security and conditions in Europe (1948); 50th anniversary of the liberation of Cuba (1948); inflation, housing, and civil rights (1948); steel industry dispute (1952)
Eisenhower	7	6 State of the Union messages (1953-1954; 1957-1960); Middle East (1957)
Kennedy	3	3 State of the Union messages (1961-1963)
Johnson	8	6 State of the Union messages (1964-1969); assumption of office (1963); voting rights (1965)
Nixon	7	4 State of the Union messages (1970-1972, 1974); Vietnam policy (1969—separate addresses before House and Senate); economic policy (1971); Soviet Union trip (1972)
Ford[1]	6	3 State of the Union messages (1975-1977); assumption of office (1974); inflation (1974); state of the world (1975)
Carter	6	3 State of the Union messages (1978-1980); energy program (1977); Middle East talks at Camp David (1978); SALT II arms control treaty (1979)
Reagan	11	8 State of the Union messages (1981-1988); budget address (1981); Central America (1983); U.S.-Soviet summit (1985)

Sources: Guide to Congress, 3d ed. (Washington, D.C.: Congressional Quarterly Inc., 1982), 767; *Congressional Quarterly Weekly Report* (various issues).

1. On October 17, 1974, President Gerald R. Ford testified before the Subcommittee on Criminal Justice of the House Judiciary Committee on his pardon of former president Richard Nixon for crimes possibly committed during the Watergate affair.

views about spanning the gulf between the branches:

> I am very glad indeed to have the opportunity to address the two houses directly, and to verify for myself the impression that the president of the United States is a person, not a mere department of the government hailing Congress from some isolated island of jealous power, sending messages, and not speaking naturally and with his own voice, that he is a human being trying to cooperate with other human beings in a common service. After this experience I shall feel quite normal in all our dealings with one another.[71]

The annual messages before Wilson's time usually were laborious recitations of department and agency activities. They seldom contained substantive legislative proposals, in line with the prevailing view that Congress alone made law and that the suggestions made by presidents were to be given no greater weight than those of average citizens. The exception to this informal but ironclad rule in many ways emphasized it. When Grover Cleveland deviated from tradition by devoting his entire 1887 message to ideas about tariff reform, he sparked a tremendous debate in the press, divided his own Democratic party, and, as a result, apparently contributed to his defeat in 1888.[72]

Beginning with Woodrow Wilson, however, the State

of the Union address has become a key vehicle for expounding the president's annual legislative agenda and priorities. This use of the annual message grew even more important with the advent of radio and, later, television. Today the president's annual appearance before a joint session of Congress is a major national event. It is a moment of high ceremony, a pageant attended by the members of Congress, department secretaries, the Joint Chiefs of Staff, justices of the Supreme Court, foreign dignitaries, and other special guests. Television cameras pan the House chamber as the president speaks, recording the reactions of particular members of the audience to various presidential statements or proposals. Media commentators and other political experts routinely judge presidential "performance" almost before the president leaves the House chamber. The issues raised by the president get serious consideration in the press, if not always by Congress, and the opposition party almost always feels compelled to ask for equal time to state its own views. *(See box, Presidential Appearances before Congress, 1789-1988, p. 72.)*

The power of the annual address to shape public opinion and spur on Congress should not be underestimated. Kennedy, for example, used it to push successfully for a national effort to put a person on the moon before the end of the 1960s. Johnson passionately promoted his civil rights and Great Society social programs, and Nixon used the opportunity to propose sweeping reorganization of the federal establishment and to defend U.S. actions in Vietnam. Reagan, a master of television speeches, used the annual address to spark national (and congressional) debate on tax reform, on aid to the rebels in Nicaragua, and on his Strategic Defense Initiative. Whatever presidents discuss, the nation discusses—if only for a while. Often, the president's priorities become those of government.

The State of the Union address thus has become an important part of the "conversation" between presidents and Congress, a constant dialogue that may be as formal as the address or as informal as the daily contact among presidents, presidential aides, members of Congress, and Capitol Hill staff.[73] This dialogue can be examined in part by listing the major themes expressed in State of the Union messages of presidents Johnson through Reagan. *(See Table 3.)* A shift in priorities from foreign to domestic policy during the 1970s stands out, as does a shift back in the 1980s. And, as political scientist Charles O. Jones notes, "Many of the domestic requests by Nixon, Ford, and Carter were reform measures seeking to reshape the structure and substance of programs enacted in the 1960s—a shift from issues requiring expansion of government to those demanding high consolidation or even contraction of government."[74] All of these come out in the State of the Union address.

The address also is a moment for presidents to proclaim successes, express their grand desires for the future, and engage in a little political theater. Reagan, for example, used his time to praise American "heroes," to chastise Congress for the way it prepares budgets *(see box, State of the Union Address as Political Theater, p. 74),* and to recruit potential supporters to the Republican party. Using the address for such purposes had its drawbacks, however, particularly when events outstrip plans. In 1986, for example, the Reagan administration intended to make full use of the launch of the space shuttle *Challenger* to praise "teacher in space" Christa McAuliffe as an example of the bright future for the nation. The *Challenger* was launched on the day the speech was scheduled, but the shuttle acci-

Table 3 Major Themes in Selected State of the Union Addresses

President	Year	Major themes
Kennedy	1961	Economy; social programs
	1962	Getting America moving; economy; military strength
	1963	Cuba; economy; tax reduction
Johnson	1964	JFK legacy; budget
	1965	Great Society domestic programs
	1966	Vietnam, foreign and defense policy
	1967	Maintaining previous momentum
	1968	Vietnam, foreign and defense policy
	1969	Review of achievements
Nixon	1970	Vietnam, foreign and defense policy
	1971	Vietnam; economic and social policy
	1972	Foreign and defense policy; plea for action on previous requests
	1973	Natural resources; economy; social policy
	1974	Energy; economic issues
Ford	1975	Economy; taxes; energy
	1976	Economic and energy issues
	1977	Energy; achievements
Carter	1978	Economic and energy issues
	1979	Inflation; SALT II
	1980	Foreign and defense policy
	1981	Record of progress; budget priorities
Reagan	1982	Economic and budget issues
	1983	Economic and budget issues
	1984	Federal deficit; foreign policy
	1985	Tax reform; government spending
	1986	Foreign policy; welfare reform
	1987	Foreign policy
	1988	Economic and budget issues

Sources: Charles O. Jones, "Presidential Negotiation with Congress," in *Both Ends of the Avenue: The Presidency, the Executive Branch, and Congress in the 1980s,* ed. Anthony King (Washington, D.C.: American Enterprise Institute, 1983), 103; *Congressional Quarterly Weekly Report,* various issues.

dent and the deaths of the eight astronauts forced the postponement of the address. President Reagan instead went on television that night to speak of the tragedy and to express his belief that the nation had to go on.

The State of the Union message is required by the Constitution, but through statute Congress over time has required the president to make other annual reports as well, the volume of which has skyrocketed since the 1920s. The Budget Act of 1921, for example, requires the president to submit an annual budget message, and the Employment Act of 1946 mandates an annual report on the economy. Hundreds of other reports, messages, and legislative proposals are submitted to Congress annually, all bearing the president's imprint and expressing the White House's views on important policy matters. Each one, particularly the budget and economic reports, has potential political influence.

Preparing Legislation

Setting the national agenda of debate is but the initial stage in successful presidential leadership—if *presidential*

The State of the Union Address as Political Theater

Woodrow Wilson in 1913 revived the earlier tradition of presidents personally delivering the State of the Union address to Congress, but it was not until the advent of radio and, later, television that the annual speech took on powerful symbolic meaning. Widespread public access to radio allowed Franklin D. Roosevelt, for example, to speak directly to the American people and rally the nation out of the depression of the 1930s. Television, however, with its particular capacity to present emotional visual images, elevated the State of the Union address to true public theater, complete with an audience (members of Congress assembled) and critics (network commentators). Televised annual addresses have become less a litany of dry statistics than a panorama of past accomplishments, current endeavors, and future dreams. And, increasingly, the State of the Union address has become the primary fixture in setting the nations' annual agenda for action, with presidents judged on how *well* they delivered their messages. The medium and the message indeed have coalesced.

John F. Kennedy arguably inaugurated the use of television to breathe vibrancy into the annual message, but it was Ronald Reagan, the acknowledged master of visual media, who used the address to its greatest effect thus far. Whether to needle Congress, praise heroes, or express his dreams for America, the State of the Union address in Reagan's hands became an eagerly awaited and heavily analyzed event. Reagan may not have written his own words or dreamed up the various symbolic appeals used—such matters were left to professional speech writers—but he was the bringer of the message to the people. What follows, an excerpt from President Reagan's 1988 State of the Union address, shows how one president transformed this once banal annual accounting into the preeminent national political event.

> ... Now, it is also time for some plain talk about the most immediate obstacle to controlling federal deficits. The simple but frustrating problem of making expenses match revenues—something American families do and the federal government can't—has caused crisis after crisis in this city. Mr. Speaker, Mr. President, I will say to you tonight what I have said before—and will continue to say: The budget process has broken down; it needs a drastic overhaul. With each ensuing year, the spectacle before the American people is the same as it was this Christmas—budget deadlines delayed or missed completely, monstrous continuing resolutions that pack hundreds of billions of dollars' worth of spending into one bill—and a federal government on the brink of default.
>
> I know I'm echoing what you here in the Congress have said because you suffered so directly—but let's recall that in seven years, of 91 appropriations bills scheduled to arrive on my desk by a certain date, only 10 made it on time. Last year, of the 13 appropriations bills due by October 1st, none of them made it. Instead, we had four continuing resolutions lasting 41 days, then 36 days, and two days, and three days, respectively. And then, along came these behemoths. This is the conference report—1,053-page report weighing 14 pounds. Then this—a reconciliation bill six months late, that was 1,186 pages long, weighing 15 pounds; and the long-term continuing resolution—this one was two months late and it's 1,057 pages long, weighing 14 pounds. That was a total of 43 pounds of paper and ink. You had three hours—yes, three hours, to consider each, and it took 300 people at my Office of Management just to read the bill so the government wouldn't shut down.
>
> Congress shouldn't send another one of these. No—and if you do, I will not sign it.
>
> Let's change all this; instead of a presidential budget that gets discarded and a congressional budget resolution that is not enforced, why not a simple partnership, a joint agreement that sets out the spending priorities within the available revenues? And let's remember our deadline is October 1st, not Christmas; let's get the people's work done in time to avoid a footrace with Santa Claus. And yes, this year—to coin a phrase—a new beginning. Thirteen individual bills, on time and fully reviewed by Congress....

Source: Congressional Quarterly Weekly Report, January 3, 1988, 221.

leadership is defined simply as getting proposals approved by Congress. A president's priorities generally, though not always, require formal congressional consideration if they are to be realized, and in this process presidents through history have relied on a wide array of personnel and resources.

For the president to take an active part in drafting legislation is a departure from strict interpretations of separation of powers, since only Congress has constitutional power to make law. Nonetheless, presidents since Washington have involved themselves directly in this first stage of the legislative process, although early residents of the office usually tried to avoid any appearance of interposing their views in a realm zealously guarded by Congress. George Washington, for example, quietly discussed ideas for new measures with cabinet officials and members of Congress alike, and he secretly lent a hand in composing the odd bill; but he studiously avoided any open and direct role in forming legislation. Instead, he assigned various cabinet members to consult formally with Congress, an activity seen as more legitimate because department heads appeared regularly before congressional committees on routine business. Congress itself validated this strategy by directing Secretary of the Treasury Alexander Hamilton to draft and submit recommendations for a new national bank, a resolution of state debts, and a promotion of manufacturing—tasks the energetic Hamilton took on with such relish that he eventually sparked severe criticism from members of Congress about his dominance over legislating.[75]

Hamilton's chief critic was Secretary of State Thomas Jefferson, but Jefferson proved no less energetic once he became president in 1801. Despite his party's view that Congress alone made public policy, Jefferson secretly composed bills, which he transmitted through his department secretaries to party loyalists in the legislature. Even more important, Jefferson used his cabinet heavily for maximum influence on legislating. He met with department heads regularly to discuss new proposals and to write bills. Afterwards, cabinet members would meet with the relevant congressional committees. Jefferson's strong party caucus—which enjoyed a solid congressional majority—also enabled him to maintain the fiction of his complete separateness from law making even while wielding a strong hand behind the scenes.

Other nineteenth-century presidents continued the pattern of using cabinet officials to craft and lobby for legislation. They had few alternatives. Presidents during the 1800s had very few personal staff members, since Congress did not appropriate funds for clerical assistance until 1857. Nor did they have extensive networks of personal advisers and assistants.[76] Cabinet officials gave presidents valuable access to congressional committees, acted as the chief executive's political eyes and ears, and, as historian James Young has noted, "allowed Presidents to maintain, for what it was worth, the outward appearance of conformity to community norms which decreed social distance between the President and Congress." [77]

This system had its disadvantages, of course. Chief among them was the political reality that department heads frequently were selected to pay off political favors or to accommodate rival factions within the president's own party. Presidents thus never were entirely sure of their department heads' primary loyalties. They always had to guard against the tendency of strong cabinet officials to cultivate their own power bases in Congress. Lincoln, to cite but one example, was plagued constantly by the need to maneuver around such formidable political figures as Secretary of State William Seward and Secretary of the Treasury Salmon P. Chase, who led their own factions within the Republican party and regularly clashed with Lincoln over Civil War policies.

The Institutional Presidency

The picture of the nineteenth-century presidency generally is one of a lone figure with little reliable assistance. Contemporary presidents, by contrast, reside at the heart of an immense executive institution, aided in their tasks by nearly sixteen hundred special assistants, personal aides, policy experts, and clerical staff distributed among several specialized agencies. *(See Table 4.)*

The Executive Office of the President (EOP) is the chief executive's personal bureaucracy, designed expressly to help the president oversee department and agency activities, formulate budgets and monitor spending, craft legislation, lobby Congress, and, above all, ensure that the president's priorities are promoted.

This support system began to take shape when Congress, in the Budget and Accounting Act of 1921, required the president to coordinate all executive branch spending proposals and present a unified annual budget. These new responsibilities, which grew largely out of the recognition that departments all too often bypassed the chief executive in their pleas for new appropriations, were accompanied by the creation of the Bureau of the Budget (BOB) to assist presidents in their tasks. Thus arose the notion of "central clearance," the use of BOB to monitor all executive branch spending, to judge new funding requests

AP

In his **1988 State of the Union address, President Reagan derided Congress's last-minute passage of 3,296 pages' worth of budget reconciliation and governmentwide appropriations.**

before they went to Capitol Hill, and, especially, to "veto" budget proposals not in line with the president's overall agenda. The president for the first time had a mechanism to coordinate and perhaps even control executive branch activities.[78]

Franklin Roosevelt's New Deal not only spawned a staggering growth in executive branch responsibilities, but also, as a result, strained even the capacity of the presidency to coordinate and control government expenditures and actions. In 1939 the Bureau of the Budget moved to the newly created Executive Office of the President—itself the product of widespread recognition that the president sorely needed sustained personal staff assistance. Roosevelt gradually extended BOB's central clearance functions to include screening bills passed by Congress and recommending to the president whether or not they should be approved.

These central clearance responsibilities were magnified even more during the early 1970s, when Congress transformed BOB into the Office of Management and Budget (OMB) and Richard Nixon made the office into the president's chief instrument of policy advocacy. Subsequent presidents have augmented OMB power and reach even further. Today no legislative proposal generated within the executive branch goes to Congress without OMB approval; no new regulation goes into effect until OMB approves; and no bill passed by Congress hits the president's desk until OMB judges how well it meets the president's policy and budgetary goals and thus should be signed or vetoed. Once a relatively quiet and even neutral accounting department, OMB today is the powerful, parti-

How a Bill . . .

1. Introduction of a Bill. A proposal that will eventually become law must be introduced by a member of Congress. Often when a member introduces a bill he or she will find someone in the other chamber to introduce a "companion bill." Each bill is given a number as it is introduced, and numbering is sequential. House bill numbers start with *HR*, Senate bill numbers start with *S*.

When an executive branch agency or the White House wants Congress to consider a specific proposal they ask a senator or representative to introduce the bill "by request."

2. Referral to Committee. After a bill is introduced it is referred by the parliamentarian to a standing committee. The committee chair then decides which subcommittee will consider the measure.

3. Subcommittee Action. The subcommittee holds hearings on the bill. Testimony may be taken from invited witnesses only, or the committee may issue an open call and hear from anyone who wishes to speak. At this point administration representatives have a chance to urge support for a bill. Subcommittee hearings also provide an opportunity for them to oppose a bill they do not like.

When hearings are completed, the bill is "marked up," that is, rewritten to incorporate the subcommittee's changes. These changes may be designed to, strengthen (or weaken) the provisions, or they may be politically inspired to improve (or reduce) a bill's chance of passage. If the president has objections, it is at this point that friendly committee members and White House lobbyists attempt to amend the bill to meet presidential approval. When the subcommittee has finished its work, the bill is sent to the full committee.

4. Full Committee Action. The full committee may ratify the subcommittee's actions, or it may repeat the subcommittee's steps by holding more hearings and marking up the bill a second time. This second markup gives the administration another chance to alter the bill if its effort to make changes at the subcommittee level failed. Whether or not the subcommittee steps are repeated, only the full committee formally reports the bill back to the chamber for floor action; a subcommittee cannot report a measure directly.

5a. House Rules Committee. After the full committee reports the bill, it is placed on a "calendar" and is ready for floor consideration. In the House, controversial or complicated bills are referred to the Rules Committee, which determines the framework for debate and amendment. A special rule written by the Rules Committee specifies how long debate will last, who will control the time, and how many and what type of amendments may be offered.

After the Rules Committee has recommended a rule, the full House votes on whether to accept it. If the rule does not allow amendments that the president favors, or if the legislation contains provisions the president would like to see deleted, the White House may lobby House members to defeat the rule. The White House is seldom successful in defeating a rule; but when it is, that success is a major victory for the president.

5b. House Floor Consideration. If, as usually happens, the House accepts the rule, the next step is debate on the bill. Normal House rules limit each member to one hour during general debate, but often the rule imposes more rigid time limits. Roll call votes may be requested if a certain number of members agree to the request. Roll call votes are taken electronically in the House and usually last fifteen minutes.

If the bill originated in the House, it is referred to the Senate for action after passage *(see solid line)*. If the House is completing consideration of a measure referred from the Senate and the bill has not been amended, it is cleared for presidential action. If the bill is a referral from the Senate and has been substantially amended, it may be referred to a conference committee *(see No. 6)*.

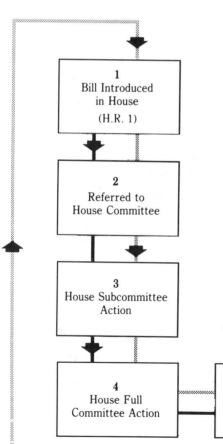

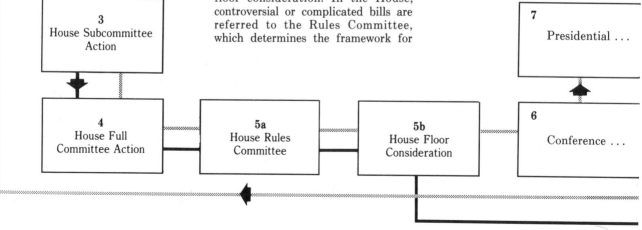

...Becomes a Law

5c. Senate Unanimous Consent.

To expedite floor consideration the Senate has developed a procedure, known as the "unanimous consent agreement," similar to the special rules written by the House Rules Committee. A unanimous consent agreement is worked out informally by the majority and minority leaders and by any senator with an interest in the bill under consideration. The agreement specifies how much time will be allotted for debate, what amendments will be considered, and how the time will be divided. Unlike a House rule, however, which needs a simple majority to pass, a unanimous consent agreement must be accepted by all senators on the floor at the time it is proposed. A single objection defeats the agreement.

5d. Senate Floor Consideration.

Floor consideration under a unanimous consent agreement in the Senate is similar to action under a rule in the House. If a unanimous consent agreement cannot be worked out, however, the Senate operates under its normal rules, which are much less restrictive than House rules. There is no time limit on debate. Members opposed to a bill under consideration sometimes "filibuster"—that is, hold the floor by speaking for an extended period of time—to delay or kill a bill. A filibuster can be ended only if sixty senators agree to a "cloture" petition to limit debate. As a result floor proceedings in the Senate usually take much longer than in the House. Voting in the Senate is not electronic. The roll is called by a clerk who records each senator's vote.

If the bill under consideration originated in the Senate, it is then referred to the House for action after passage *(see broken line)*. If the Senate is completing consideration of a measure referred from the House and the bill has not been amended, it is cleared for presidential action. If the bill is a referral from the House and has been substantially amended, it may be referred to a conference committee *(see No. 6)*.

6. Conference Action.

A bill must be approved by both chambers in identical form before it can be sent to the president. If there are major differences between the versions passed by the House and the Senate, the bill may go to a conference committee, which works out a compromise. The committee usually consists of senior members of the committees that reported the bill. If the president has reservations or objections or prefers the bill passed by one chamber to the version passed by the other, it is in the conference that the White House attempts to influence members to adopt a final version that is acceptable to the administration.

When the conference is completed, the committee files a conference report to which both the House and the Senate must agree. If either rejects the conference agreement, the bill dies. If both agree to the conference report, the measure then goes to the president for final action.

A conference often can be avoided, however. Even if one chamber has amended a bill substantially, it can refer the measure back to the originating chamber, which may accept all the amendments (clearing the bill for the president), accept some and reject others, or even add some amendments of its own (in which case the bill then bounces back to the other chamber for a second time). This back-and-forth can continue until both chambers have agreed to the measure in identical form, thus clearing it for presidential action. In reality, most bills are cleared in this manner, avoiding an official conference.

7. Presidential Action.

The president has several options once a bill is received from Congress. The president may sign the bill, making it law immediately; or the president may veto the bill and return it to Congress. Congress may overturn a presidential veto if both chambers vote by a two-thirds majority (of those present and voting) to "override" the veto. If Congress fails to override the veto, the bill dies. Normally, if the president takes no action the bill becomes law after ten days without a signature. An exception may occur at the end of a session of Congress, when the president may "pocket veto" a bill by not signing it within the ten-day limit.

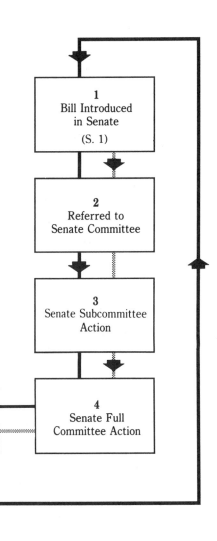

... Action

... Action

5d
Senate
Floor
Consideration

5c
Senate
Unanimous Consent

4
Senate Full
Committee Action

3
Senate Subcommittee
Action

2
Referred to
Senate Committee

1
Bill Introduced
in Senate
(S. 1)

Table 4 Size of Executive Office of the President, Various Offices, 1941-1985

Year	White House Office	Office of Management and Budget	National Security Council [a]
1941	53	305	—
1942	49	459	—
1945	61	565	—
1950	295	520	17
1955	290	444	28
1960	446	434	65
1965	333	524	38
1970	311	633	75
1975	625	673	89
1980	406	616	69
1985	367	566	62

Source: Bureau of the Census, *Statistical Abstract of the United States* (Washington, D.C.: Government Printing Office, various editions).

a. Created in 1947.

san, and often controversial defender of the president's goals and policies.

Other arms within the Executive Office of the President complement OMB's activities, and the EOP as a whole is designed to help occupants of the Oval Office gather information and promote their priorities. The Council of Economic Advisers, normally composed of three noted economists, advises the president on economic matters and how they affect national politics. The National Security Council acts as the president's foreign policy advisory mechanism, designed to transcend the institutional boundaries of the various foreign policy bureaucracies and to give the president a broader view of national security questions.

At the apex of the pyramid sits the White House Office. Home to the president's closest personal aides and special assistants, the White House Office is chiefly responsible for coordinating the executive institution and spearheading the president's agenda.

The contemporary presidency thus is an *institution* with resources and powers that remain potent regardless of the personal traits of individual chief executives. This bureaucracy exists solely because the presidency today is required to design and lobby for legislative proposals, to monitor and coordinate government spending, and to promote an overall national agenda. This is a far cry from the days when presidents crafted legislation in secret or found themselves unable to oversee spending within the various departments.

Ironically, this very institutional capacity to do all these tasks presents presidents with a new dilemma: how to ensure that the Executive Office of the President *itself* can be controlled by the occupant of the Oval Office. Presidents cannot be involved personally with every action that occurs below them and increasingly must rely on subordinates to monitor and guide the behavior of an institution that itself is designed to monitor and guide the behavior of the executive branch as a whole.

If eighteenth-century presidents bemoaned their lack of staff resources, presidents today must wonder how they will be able to make their own vast organization run both well and loyally.

The President's Agenda

Much of the legislation Congress addresses annually originates within the executive branch. No longer do presidents maintain the fiction of separation from the legislative process, and contemporary presidents more often than not are judged by the quality and timing of their annual policy agendas. Congress and the public demand that presidents initiate legislation and criticize severely those who do not. Eisenhower, for example, did not offer a formal legislative agenda during his first year in office, only to receive sharp rebukes from both parties. "Don't expect us to start from scratch on what you people want," said one angry House member to an administration official. "That's not the way we do things here. You draft the bills and we work them over." [79]

A multiplicity of sources provide ideas for the intellectual foundation of the president's program. Before Franklin Roosevelt's administration, presidents could work out their agenda from their personal experiences, since the role of the executive branch was limited and the number of problems requiring presidential attention were relatively few. Theodore Roosevelt's aggressive national park and wildlife conservation policies stemmed at least in part from his background as a western rancher and big-game hunter. Hoover used his experiences as secretary of commerce under Calvin Coolidge (1923-1929) to guide his priorities— until the Great Depression overtook his presidency.

Today, however, as the data compiled by presidential scholar Paul Light suggest, a surprising proportion of a contemporary chief executive's domestic program may come from "outside" sources—Congress, national events, the departments and agencies of the executive branch, and public opinion. *(See Table 5.)* Congress, with its hundreds of members and thousands of staff, is fertile ground for legislative ideas. Many of the formal legislative proposals that come from the White House stem from ideas and proposals that have existed on Capitol Hill for years, waiting to be adopted as the president's own when circumstances permit. [80]

One example of a policy agenda derived from Congress was Kennedy's domestic program, a large portion of which was ideas and options promoted to no avail by liberal congressional Democrats during the Eisenhower years. What Kennedy could not get through Congress, Lyndon Johnson later incorporated into his Great Society program. The same perspective applies to Reagan's vaunted tax reduction bill of 1981, which in many ways was the "offspring" of a Republican tax plan pushed by Rep. Jack Kemp (N.Y.) and Sen. William Roth (Del.) during the late 1970s. Hundreds of policies float about at all times, each awaiting the power of a president to lift it out of the mass of proposals and give it life. [81]

Crises or other events also structure the domestic agenda, probably more than presidents desire or care to admit. This is true particularly as Americans have come to expect government to respond forcefully to new or sudden problems. There is no question, for example, that Hoover's inability to rein in the depression led to his defeat in 1932 and that Franklin Roosevelt attained immortality for his innovative ("try anything") attack on the economic crisis and for his overall leadership during World War II. [82] The 1957 Soviet launch of Sputnik startled Eisenhower into major spending for science education and the space program. The energy crisis of the 1970s, sparked largely by huge hikes in oil prices by producing nations, dominated the fiscal and budgetary agendas of both Ford and Carter.

National concern about the AIDS (Acquired Immune Deficiency Syndrome) epidemic forced the Reagan administration to reverse its policies and to increase research funding to combat that disease. Although presidents enjoy a tremendous institutional capacity to define the agenda of government, many times they are forced to respond to issues or events out of their control.

Executive branch bureaucrats provide another wellspring of policy ideas or options, despite the propensity of presidential candidates to attack the bureaucracy during their election campaigns as bloated and unresponsive. Career civil servants who are deeply dedicated to particular policy realms possess the technical expertise and perspectives that come from long tenure. Their experience can help new presidents initiate new policies or simply avoid repeating the errors of the past.

The degree to which any president adopts ideas generated from within the professional bureaucracy depends in large part on personal ideology and style. The White House staffs of Nixon and Reagan, for example, were highly suspicious of the motives and political leanings of career civil servants and tried whenever possible to draw policy making directly into the White House.[83] Democratic presidents, however, usually seem to share civil servants' fundamental beliefs in the role of government and thus have shown a greater willingness to tap bureaucratic ideas.

Whatever the source of an agenda item, presidents must test its technical, economic, and, particularly, political soundness before sending it off to Congress. Inadequately tested proposals are ripe for disaster. Carter's energy policy, for example, which was hammered out privately by a panel of experts, suffered embarrassing political defeats once it was sent to Congress.

To avoid such problems, presidents ideally seek out a wide range of expertise, but, as they find out, no source is perfect. Professionals within the EOP, for example, are valuable sources of technical expertise or economic analysis, but they may not be attuned to the political climate or understand well the vagaries of Capitol Hill. Personal aides and trusted friends are valued for their political acumen and their ability to say things to the president that others would not dare. Every president has such intimates, be they the Californians making up Reagan's "kitchen cabinet," Carter's "Georgia mafia," or Franklin Roosevelt's "brains trust." But such persons may themselves be new to Washington or blinded to political reality by their loyalty to the president when controversial decisions must be made.

Cabinet secretaries, in contrast to the days when they were the president's primary advisers, today often play a secondary role in judging proposals unless they also enjoy close personal ties to the president or preside over a department particularly important to presidential priorities. Presidents frequently fill the position of attorney general, for example, with a close friend or longtime political ally, who then enjoys ready access to the Oval Office. Kennedy appointed his brother Robert; Nixon looked to friend and former law partner John Mitchell; and Reagan appointed longtime aide Edwin Meese III. Each of these acted as more than a department head; they also were intimates.

By contrast, some cabinet members rarely see the president in private, even when issues central to their departments arise. Department heads often have complained that their phone calls were routed to presidential assistants who they technically outrank. Samuel R. Pierce, Jr., for example, was secretary of the Department of Hous-

Table 5 Sources of Ideas for the President's Agenda

Source	Respondents mentioning source (percent)
External sources	
Congress	52
Events and crises	51
Executive branch	46
Public opinion	27
Party	11
Interest groups	7
Media	4
Internal sources	
Campaign and platform	20
President	17
Staff	16
Task forces	6

Source: Paul C. Light, *The President's Agenda* (Baltimore: Johns Hopkins University Press, 1983), 118.

Note: Number of respondents: 118. Respondents were past and present White House aides who were asked, "Generally speaking, what would you say were the most important sources of ideas for the domestic agenda?"

ing and Urban Development throughout the Reagan presidency, yet he rarely played a central role in policy development because his department was peripheral to the president's agenda. (In fact, as one famous story goes, Reagan even failed to recognize Pierce at a reception for city mayors.) Cabinet members also are regarded with deep suspicion by the president's closest advisers because of their tendency to promote departmental interests over the presidential agenda the longer they stay in office. Cabinet secretaries who "go native" typically find access to the Oval Office cut off and their advice ignored, even when it could prove valuable.

Members of Congress may be keenly sensitive to the political feasibility of new proposals—that is, whether or not they can get through the legislature. But, as elected officials in their own right, even those of the president's party may have their own particular agendas to promote. They also may find, given their distinct electoral and governing roles, that their perspectives differ dramatically from the president's. Carter, for example, deeply distrusted members of Congress, whom he felt were largely parochial in their views. He found, to his dismay, that local interests prevailed within the legislature once his proposals went to Capitol Hill. All presidents find this out sooner or later, and most realize that members of Congress must be heard, if only so that they can warn of the potential obstacles that lie ahead.

Career federal bureaucrats know what is feasible technically and economically, but they may have their own policy and institutional goals to consider beyond the president's own. Besides, career bureaucrats will be in their positions long after a particular president is gone from the White House. They generally can wait out an administration hostile to their views until the political winds change or new leaders come to office.

Outside experts such as academics can offer new ideas and perhaps can lend an aura of expertise and legitimacy to controversial issues, but they may not have enough understanding of what is feasible politically. Moreover, there is no guarantee that any recommendations made by panels of experts ever will be more than reams of paper sitting in a file cabinet.

There are, in sum, many possible sources for ideas and expertise available to any president, but only the individual in the White House can decide which information, and which sources, are to be tapped. Some presidents, such as Franklin Roosevelt and Lyndon Johnson, were voracious consumers of advice from a great number of sources. Roosevelt was known to surround himself with assistants who disagreed violently on major issues so that he could get a broader spectrum of opinion. Johnson was famous for his midnight telephone calls to sleepy senators demanding the latest scoop on a piece of legislation. Both had keen political instincts, and for them information was a resource to be used actively in political battles. This style requires tremendous personal energy and intellect and can be overwhelming if the president does not have some way to reduce the deluge of information hitting the Oval Office daily. Presidents who do not adequately delegate tasks to subordinates risk overload.

Other presidents have preferred to let information and policy options "bubble up" through the ranks of advisers and experts surrounding them, using their closest aides to synthesize advice and present a short list of alternative courses of action. Both Eisenhower and Reagan appear to have operated in this manner. Reagan was particularly content to let his assistants parse out competing choices and to withhold his own views until aides presented him with one or two options. The president's role in this approach is far more passive, but it can work well when those who actually weigh the alternatives keep the president's values and priorities firmly in mind. Problems arise when a president's assistants fail to do so or when they keep the president in the dark about their activities.

Presidents' operating styles hinge most on their personal qualities, overall goals, and perspective on the job itself. Carter saw the president's job as one of problem solving, and he insisted on being informed of or involved in virtually every decision—including, as one story goes, the schedule for the White House tennis courts. His problem, critics charged, was that he was so immersed in the minutiae of policy that he failed to discern or convey to the public the broader goals of public policy or of his office. Reagan, by contrast, apparently viewed the presidency as being like chairman of the board; he was content to dictate broad goals and directions while leaving details to his aides. The tendency to remain aloof from the particulars of policy questions often led him to appear uninformed during press conferences, but even Reagan's critics admitted that the strength and passion of his ideals provided his subordinates with clear guidelines by which to judge and select policies.

Presidential Lobbying

Assuming, perhaps wrongly, that legislation is drafted coherently to begin with, presidents next must convince Congress to go along. Presidential scholar Richard Neustadt has argued that the primary power of the presidency is the power to persuade others, but the Constitution is silent about just *how* presidents are to do so.[84] That silence is convenient: presidents seeking little in the way of change can assert that separation of powers does not allow

them to influence Congress, but aggressive presidents more often than not regard this silence as justification for any means not expressly forbidden by law or accepted practice. In general, then, the way presidents organize their lobbying activities, and the styles they employ to influence Congress, reflects their policy goals, their knowledge about how government works, and their overall personal skills. It also reflects whether—or how much—Congress is willing to be influenced, a state of receptiveness that always is in doubt.

Presidents through the early 1900s were careful to obey the form, if not the substance, of separation of powers. Their instruments for influencing legislation were few and constrained by prevailing beliefs in congressional supremacy. Party loyalty, favorable newspaper coverage, and politically connected cabinet members were a nineteenth-century president's primary resources, and lobbying tended to be loosely organized and discreet.

This picture changed dramatically by the 1940s, as both government and prevailing public attitudes about presidential leadership underwent fundamental changes. But the evolution of presidential lobbying from the indirect and passive styles of earlier presidents to the open and organized practices of today took decades.

Woodrow Wilson was noted for his strongly personal approach, going so far as to sit in on congressional committee deliberations on trade legislation and pulling party strings to ensure Democratic support; nonetheless, he shied away from a direct lobbying strategy. His chief congressional lobbyist was Postmaster General Albert Burleson, a former House Democrat who used postal positions as inducements for loyalty to the president's program. Wilson also craftily used John Nance Garner, another Texas Democrat, as his confidential lobbyist within the House. Garner, who sat on the influential Ways and Means Committee, each week would enter the White House through a side door and consult with Wilson privately on current congressional news and prospects for the president's legislation.

Less than two decades later Franklin Roosevelt abandoned any pretense of regal noninvolvement and employed a far more open and vigorous lobbying strategy. Many consider Roosevelt the father of contemporary lobbying styles, beginning with his own sustained and overt role in policy formation.

Roosevelt personally goaded Congress through radio addresses to the public and careful cultivation of friendly relations with the press. He also directed personal assistants James Rowe, Thomas Corcoran, and Benjamin Cohen openly to write bills and lobby legislators. Like Wilson, Roosevelt relied heavily on patronage to reward loyalty and to punish deserters; Postmaster General James A. Farley, who was also the national Democratic party chairman, acted as his enforcer. Preferential treatment on public works projects and other New Deal spending programs, funds critical to hard-pressed Democrats during election years, and promises for personal campaign appearances by the wildly popular president also served as inducements. Although Roosevelt's overall influence in Congress waxed and waned with changes in political conditions, he constructed for the presidency a new, more vigorous, and central role in the legislative process.

Formalizing the Process

Although Roosevelt inaugurated or perfected many of the lobbying techniques employed by contemporary presidents, he did not make lobbying a formal process. New

Deal legislation instead was presented and fought for piece-meal; Roosevelt would assign a staff person to lobby for a program only if it got into trouble. Legislative liaison—the practice of having assistants constantly cultivate a receptive environment—remained an informal affair, reflecting in many ways Roosevelt's own more personal approach to politics and his dislike of strongly ordered organizational styles. Roosevelt never established a formal liaison office; instead, he used aides to augment his own considerable skills in swaying legislators.[85]

Dwight Eisenhower adopted the antithesis of Roosevelt's highly personal and avowedly disorganized approach. As political scientist Eric Davis has pointed out, Eisenhower was the first president to formalize the executive lobbying process by creating the Office of Congressional Relations (OCR), a specialized structure reflecting his own hierarchical predispositions and general dislike of direct lobbying. Eisenhower, who was uncomfortable in the rambunctious world of politics, also wanted OCR to act as a buffer between himself and members of Congress, even those from his own party.[86] Heading the office was Bryce Harlow, a longtime House committee staff member who had no other responsibilities but to cultivate cordial relations with Congress and, especially, to keep House and Senate Republicans happy. But Harlow's liaison office seldom took an active role in legislative development, largely because Eisenhower spent more time opposing congressional Democrats than in pushing his own agenda.

John Kennedy, by contrast, planned an aggressive agenda and strengthened the liaison office by appointing a longtime political ally, Lawrence F. O'Brien, as chief lobbyist. O'Brien, for his part, thought it critical that liaison staff not only generate support for specific Kennedy programs but also "create a general climate in favor and receptivity toward the president and the administration among members of Congress, and . . . use these positive perceptions as a resource when attempting to obtain support for particular pieces of legislation."[87] O'Brien organized OCR along lines paralleling the structure of Congress by assigning a staff member to interact with virtually every faction and bloc in the legislature. He also constructed cooperative relationships with agency personnel, party leaders, and interest groups—whoever might be useful or necessary to the president's success. Many presidential scholars today consider O'Brien to be the architect of modern legislative liaison practices; the system he established continued through the Carter administration.

Despite O'Brien's efforts, Kennedy generally proved reluctant to push an expansive legislative agenda because conservative Democrats in Congress strongly opposed new social programs and civil rights legislation. Kennedy's narrow victory over Richard Nixon in 1960 did not give him enough leverage in Congress to pressure members for support, even fellow Democrats. Although Kennedy's liaison organization was credited with a handful of notable legislative victories on trade and tax matters, the political climate in Congress was a reality for which no organized lobbying could readily compensate.

Lyndon Johnson, however, fared quite differently. He was successful initially because Kennedy's assassination created in the nation and in Congress a desire to pass some of the slain president's legislation and later because of his own massive 1964 election victory over Barry M. Goldwater. The 1964 election also brought in many new and more liberal House Democrats, thus giving Johnson the necessary political support for his domestic policy agenda.

The Eisenhower administration established the first Office of Congressional Relations. Ike appointed Bryce Harlow, an experienced House committee staff member, but Kennedy was more aggressive in his choice of a longtime political ally, Lawrence F. O'Brien.

Johnson retained the liaison office built up by Kennedy to augment his own considerable personal political skills, and he insisted that O'Brien and his liaison staff be consulted closely before initiatives were taken. Congressional scholar Charles O. Jones has characterized Johnson's style of relations with Congress as akin to a majority leader, which Johnson had been in the Senate during the 1950s.[88] Johnson believed that Congress should be consulted regularly on policy initiatives. He knew how to include its members in decision making and how not to overload the system. And he was sensitive to making loyal supporters look good. Above all, in contrast to later presidents, Johnson sought out compromise behind the scenes, going directly to the people only as a last resort, and his liaison staff worked hard to develop and maintain cooperative relationships all over Capitol Hill.[89]

Richard Nixon cared little for domestic political issues; he preferred instead to focus on foreign policy, which required (in his mind) little congressional involvement. He seldom became personally involved in lobbying and rebelled against the sort of bargaining that Johnson had relished. Where Johnson had integrated the liaison office into his overall congressional strategy, Nixon removed it from the policy-making process and instead relied heavily on his close circle of personal aides for legislative advice and strategy. Where Johnson was accessible to many views and representatives, Nixon shielded himself behind a wall of assistants. And where Johnson relied on compromise, Nixon tended to confront and to stick with his course regardless of political considerations—a style not conducive to lobbying when Congress is in the hands of the other party.

Gerald Ford in many ways operated like Johnson, reflecting their shared congressional experiences. Like Johnson, Ford believed in working with members of Congress, and he deployed his legislative liaison team to cultivate friendly relations with both parties. But Ford was a minority president, since the Democrats controlled both houses of Congress. Unlike Johnson, he had to rely heavily on the veto as a central part of his overall strategy, using his staff to build coalitions in support of his vetoes. In this sense at least, Ford was highly effective; but as an unelected president succeeding a president forced to resign, he did not have the political capital to craft and push through a broad domestic agenda.

Unlike the four previous presidents, Jimmy Carter was an outsider who campaigned and won on that appeal. He had less interest in the process of consensus building than in the substance of policy options, was issue-based rather than party-oriented, and had an overall dim view of traditional Washington politics. "Legislative liaison for Carter," Eric Davis suggested, "simply was a matter of convincing members of Congress of the correctness of his positions on the issues."[90] His liaison team, as a result, was organized initially along issue lines, as opposed to the geographical and voting bloc organizational patterns employed since O'Brien. This meant that no single staff assistant could discuss a wide array of issues—or make deals across issues—with any single member of Congress. Also, unlike the days when O'Brien courted members constantly and doled out favors to loyalists and party leaders, the Carter White House initially turned its back on such traditional ways of cultivating support. Carter aides were either so disdainful or so ignorant of the ways of Washington that even House Speaker Thomas P. O'Neill, who Carter later would need desperately to push through his ambitious energy program, was unable to get good seats for his guests at the inaugural gala—a slight O'Neill never forgot.[91]

Carter usually would present his case directly to the public first, believing that his primary task was to persuade citizens to his side on an issue and thereby create a political climate favorable to congressional action. Congressional leaders often were not consulted in advance, and legislative liaison tended toward the exchange of information rather than the building of coalitions.[92]

In his first year Carter bombarded Congress with dozens of bills all at once, thus overloading the legislative process and spreading lobbying resources thin. After a somewhat disappointing first six months—where what victories Carter did win came because of large Democratic majorities in Congress—the White House reorganized the liaison office in line with the O'Brien model and worked harder thereafter to consult with congressional leaders.

Charles O. Jones characterized Carter as a political layman, a label that was true insofar as traditional styles of negotiation were concerned.[93] But Carter encountered a far more complex and frustrating political climate than had Johnson. Public faith in government and willingness to follow political leaders was at a low point after Watergate and Vietnam, and Congress itself had changed dramatically in the interim. Johnson could rely heavily on congressional leaders to carry his banner, since the congressional hierarchy still was strong enough to keep party members in line. But by the time Carter was elected in 1976, that hierarchy had all but dissolved, and Carter needed to construct temporary coalitions among as many members as possible in order to succeed. Negotiating with Congress thus had become a different ballgame by the time Carter arrived, and, in retrospect, his strategy of going directly to the public on important issues in many ways may have been the best possible approach.

Ronald Reagan in fact used that same strategy to great effect during his first year, although it was augmented by an experienced and well-organized legislative liaison staff. House Speaker O'Neill called Reagan's victory on the 1981 budget package "the greatest selling job I've ever seen." Reagan's success came about through a mixture of dramatic public appeals by the president, the work of administration officials sent to generate support in key Democratic constituencies, and a good deal of old-fashioned bargaining.[94] Jones has likened Reagan's lobbying style to that of Franklin Roosevelt, with emphasis placed on communicating views and ideals to the public and generating pressure on Congress to go along.[95]

Trends in Presidential Lobbying

Although there is no single best way for presidents to lobby Congress, certain devices—such as favors, consultation, and personal phone calls—are always useful. Each president's particular style and the manner in which lobbying is organized reflects personal skills, interests, and views about the relationship between the two branches of government. Presidents who see themselves as partners with Congress, such as Johnson, will operate far differently from those, such as Nixon, who see the presidency as essentially independent of the legislature.[96] Each style has its strengths and weaknesses, but neither guarantees success. After all, pushing a legislative agenda also means having to deal with a Congress that sees itself as the energetic center of U.S. government.

Still, even "failed" presidents enjoyed a modicum of success in Congress, if success is measured by the percentage of bills supported by the president that Congress passes into law. The data show, for example, that Carter, despite his apparent weaknesses, actually enjoyed a great deal of success overall, and that Reagan, for all his popularity and rhetorical skills, on average fared much worse.

The reason for this disparity may be simply that Carter faced large and generally friendly Democratic majorities in Congress and that Reagan constantly encountered at least one house dominated by his political foes. One should point out, however, that Reagan's successes came not on the quantity of bills supported in Congress, but on their scope and importance.

Another trend to emerge is the inevitable decline in congressional support throughout the course of any administration despite the equally inevitable sharpening of an administration's lobbying and organizational skills. This paradox perhaps is less mystifying when one compares presidential success in Congress with the president's own popularity. (See Table 4.) Both scores drop over time, suggesting how presidential popularity affects legislative success. Members of Congress, George Edwards III points out, "respond to the president's current popularity among their supporters" and thus are reluctant to oppose a popular president.[97] They do not, however, hesitate to vote against one whose public support has weakened, particularly if the president is from the opposing party.

Thus, whether a president succeeds or fails may in fact have less to do with personal attributes or styles than with political conditions at the time. Presidents certainly can influence these conditions, but they cannot control them. Successful presidents, therefore, merely may be those whose particular strengths mesh well with the tenor of the times or with prevailing congressional majorities.

Use of Public Appeals

Every president has found it necessary on occasion to go directly to the people to exert pressure on a recalcitrant Congress. Be it through speeches to the nation on television, "leaks" of information to favored newspaper reporters, or orchestrated public demonstrations of support, presidents find some way to recruit public opinion in their fights with Congress when they believe conditions and issues warrant.

Going directly to the people has become far easier and, thus, more desirable as the technology of television has allowed presidents since the 1940s to speak their minds with less worry that their messages will be garbled by intermediaries. The rise of television as the primary means by which most Americans receive their news is a primary factor in the emergence of the contemporary presidency and its power to influence the national agenda. Nonetheless, going directly to the people has its risks, for success hinges largely on the issue in question, a president's own rhetorical skills, and the mood of the public at the moment.

Early Use of Public Appeals

Presidents before the twentieth century neither had the technologies to speak directly to the people nor did they generally conceive of their roles in exactly the same manner as do presidents today. The very earliest presidents were influenced heavily by the Founders' fear of demagogic leaders, which had induced them deliberately to remove presidential election from the popular vote. Congress was meant to represent the people, and Congress generally considered it illegitimate and intrusive for a president to try to pressure members of the legislature on public policy matters.

Even then, however, some presidents did attempt to influence congressional deliberations through indirect, often subtle pressure. Thomas Jefferson, for example, relied heavily on his popular dinner parties to influence key legislators, newspaper reporters, and other important political figures. But it was Andrew Jackson among earlier presidents who began the practice of appealing to the common people for support. Jackson, after all, had come to office as an outsider and a foe of the established ways of doing business, and he used his mass popularity to influence Congress where possible. Jackson in many ways presaged the contemporary presidency by artfully arranging for official documents to be leaked to supportive newspapers, using friendly journalists to convey his views and desires, and relying on his party organization to stir up public support and pressure Congress. "King Andrew," as his enemies came to call him, not surprisingly reaped a great deal of criticism for his unorthodox practices, and most pre-Civil War presidents did not follow his pattern. None had Jackson's popularity with the people, nor his philosophy about the role of the presidency, to continue Jackson's practices.

Abraham Lincoln was almost always on the defensive with Congress over his war policies, but he overcame its opposition by winning public support through the newspapers. Lincoln wrote numerous letters and opinion columns, and friendly publishers, such as Horace Greeley, saw to it they received favorable coverage. Lincoln generated other supportive stories through leaks to reporters. It also was said that Lincoln grew his beard after a supporter remarked that his bare face (and lack of chin) did not look "presidential" enough, and inexpensive lithographs (a new technology) of the newly bearded commander in chief soon graced many a Union household.

Theodore Roosevelt thrived on publicity and made himself easily available to favorite reporters. His love of the press in many ways was reciprocated, for the flamboyant and erudite Roosevelt made for good copy. Roosevelt is credited with creating the official White House press release, which he often issued on Sundays—traditionally the slowest news day—to give newspapers something to print the next day. He also devised off-the-record or "background" press briefings, which he frequently used to float "trial balloons" as one way to assess public and congressional opinion on issues.

Woodrow Wilson, no doubt much to his satisfaction, outdid Roosevelt in going directly to the public by resuming the practice of delivering the State of the Union address personally and by instituting regular and formal press conferences. He was most effective, however, in making direct appeals to people through the newspapers or speeches before Congress. The notable exception was his grueling nationwide tour in 1919 to generate support for the Versailles treaty. The president was followed by a "truth squad" of senators who opposed the treaty, and the journey ruined his health. Wilson's efforts to go to the people went for naught, for the Senate failed to ratify the treaty.

Roosevelt and Radio

Theodore Roosevelt and Woodrow Wilson were, in many ways, masters at generating favorable public opinion through the press, but they lacked the technology to go directly into every citizen's home. Franklin Roosevelt entered the White House as radio entered its heyday, and the ebullient New Yorker made superb use of the new medium.

His public speeches, the twenty-seven "fireside" radio chats, hundreds of formal press conferences, countless informal background sessions with selected reporters, and shrewd use of the newsreels, all constructed a public persona that millions of Americans would recall fondly for decades. So great was the public response to Roosevelt's first inaugural address, in which the president averred that "the only thing we have to fear is fear itself," that humorist Will Rogers wrote, "If he burned down the Capitol, we would cheer and say, 'Well, we at least got a fire started somehow.'"[98]

In his first radio chat to the nation, Roosevelt explained how the banking system worked and why the public should take their money out of their mattresses and put it back into their savings accounts. They did, and Roosevelt was credited with ending the panic. As Arthur M. Schlesinger, Jr., later described the fireside chats, they "conveyed Roosevelt's conception of himself as a man at ease in his own house talking frankly and intimately to neighbors as they sat in their living rooms."[99]

The radio speeches and chats were intended for more than soothing the public: they were meant to move Congress into action on Roosevelt's agenda. According to political scientist Wilfred Binkley, Roosevelt "had only to glance toward a microphone or suggest that he might go on the air again and a whole congressional delegation would surrender. They had no relish for the flood of mail and telegrams they knew would swamp them after another fireside chat to the nation."[100] Roosevelt, particularly after the first year, did not always win when he went to the airwaves, but those in opposition never took his power to move the public for granted.

The Television Presidency

One reason Roosevelt proved so successful with radio was that radio forces listeners to use their imaginations to

Table 6 Television Addresses by Presidents, 1961-1988

President	Year	Topic
Kennedy	1961	Urgent national needs; Berlin Wall
	1962	Racial unrest; quarantine of Cuba
	1963	Civil rights bill; Test ban treaty
Johnson	1963	Kennedy assassination
	1965	Voting rights bill
	1968	Bombing halt/withdrawal from election
Nixon	1969	National unity in Vietnam; Vietnam peace proposals; Vietnam troop reductions
	1970	Vietnam; Cambodia incursion (2); Peace in Indochina
	1971	Withdrawal of troops; economic policy
	1972	Report of trip to the People's Republic of China
	1973	National energy policy
	1974	Resignation
Ford	1974	Post-Nixon resignation speech; inflation
	1975	State of the world
Carter	1977	Energy crisis; energy policy
	1979	Energy crisis; national morale; Soviet troops in Cuba; military spending
	1980	Failure of Iran rescue mission; anti-inflation
	1981	Farewell speech
Reagan	1981	Economic policies and proposals (4)
	1982	Federal budget; Middle East; Lebanon; Arms control
	1983	Strategic Defense Initiative and Central America; Grenada; Lebanon
	1985	Tax reform; U.S.-Soviet summit (Geneva)
	1986	Military spending; aid to contras (2); U.S.-Soviet summit (Iceland); Iran arms sales
	1987	Iran arms sales; economic summit; Iran-contra affair; Bork nomination; U.S.-Soviet summit (Washington)
	1988	Contra aid

Source: Congressional Quarterly Almanac, various issues, and *Congressional Quarterly Weekly Report,* various issues.

Note: Table does not include State of the Union and inaugural addresses, which also are televised; it includes only those addresses that are not part of a ceremonial occasion.

visualize both the speaker and the topic under discussion. He had a powerful voice, creating an image of strength and determination that overcame his own personal disability—stricken with polio at the age of thirty-nine Roosevelt could not walk. Many Americans never knew this because, in a tacit agreement with the press corps, he rarely was photographed below the waist. Those who did know about his disability never seemed to let it detract from the image of strength he projected in his radio addresses. But if Roosevelt had run for the presidency in the age of television—first and foremost a visual medium—he could not have controlled his public image so masterfully. Whether he could have been elected in the first place because of his disability, much less rally a nation through depression and war, is one of the tantalizing "what ifs" of history.

The contemporary presidency in many ways lives—and sometimes dies—by television. Eisenhower was the first president to permit news conferences to be filmed and, later, televised, but he did so only after careful editing by the White House.

John Kennedy, arguably the first president of the television age, was the first to permit live telecasts of his news conferences. For the first time the public saw actual questions and answers as they occurred, with no chance for the president or his aides to edit the president's comments. Kennedy's own ease with television, his intellect, and his humor made television a potent tool for communicating with the American people. His persuasive television appearance was not enough, however, to ensure congressional approval of his programs.

Lyndon Johnson, superb as he was in the art of personal lobbying, proved uneasy with television, although his televised address urging the passage of the 1965 Voting Rights Act did move the nation and Congress. But Johnson discovered how television can be a double-edged sword. Americans absorbed televised images of urban riots and anti-war demonstrations and for the first time could witness the horrors of war by watching the evening news. These televised events frequently appeared to contradict Johnson's own assertions about the pace of social progress at home and the winability of the war in Indochina and therefore shook the nation's confidence in its government. Johnson was particularly wounded by public reaction to a massive North Vietnamese offensive in early 1968, a coordinated assault on south Vietnamese cities that undercut his own statements that the war was winding down, and he decided not to run for reelection. His experience with the powerful impact of television on the American people, one which he could not easily control, was but an early example of how external events can influence a president's own agenda and popularity.

Richard Nixon, who felt that the press had been hostile to his candidacy in 1960 and saw how Johnson had fared with the media, used television extensively to tailor his image and present it directly to the public. His distrust of the Washington press corps, which often proved unwilling to rally around the administration's Vietnam policy, led the president to speak directly to the American people far more often than had his predecessors. In his November 1969 address to the nation on Vietnam, for example, Nixon asserted that a "silent majority" of citizens supported his actions, despite what members of the press wrote.[101] Nixon also held few Washington press conferences, which he felt only offered easy opportunities for his critics to attack him, and instead began to hold press conferences outside the capital, where journalists might be more deferential of his office.

What is more, Nixon used Vice President Spiro Agnew to make vigorous attacks on the news media, a tactic that produced one of the most memorable phrases in American political lore. In a September 1970 speech in San Diego, Agnew railed that the Washington press corps was filled with "nattering nabobs of negativism. They have formed their own 4-H Club—the 'hopeless, hysterical hypochondriacs of history.' "[102] The tactic was clear: discredit the news media and connect the president more directly to the American people.

Nixon also used television successfully to pressure Congress in selected instances, such as his televised veto of a 1970 appropriations bill. The broadcast generated thousands of supportive telegrams to both the White House and

Capitol Hill, and sent the impression of massive popular support for his position. Whether this deluge was spontaneous or orchestrated by Nixon supporters was irrelevant to many members of the House, which upheld the veto.

As with Johnson, however, television played a part in Nixon's downfall. The nation watched in fascination as the daily drama of the 1973 Senate Watergate hearings played out on national television. Nixon's own performances during televised press conferences, and even in speeches to the nation, seemed to many viewers to be the picture of a president trying to deceive the public. Following the emergence of evidence of Nixon's possible complicity in the Watergate coverup, the president resigned in disgrace on August 9, 1974.

His successor, Gerald Ford, worked to reverse the mutual distrust between the White House and the media built up over the previous years. Nixon basked in the trappings of the office, but Ford worked to convey a simpler image; for example, he allowed himself to be photographed while making his own breakfast. Nixon held the rare press conference, but Ford held many—and earned high praise from those in the media for his openness and honesty. Ford did not escape unscathed, however, for his every stumble or slip became grist for the humor mill (an irony, no doubt, for a former football all-American).

Jimmy Carter, given his populist image and belief that Americans had tired of the "imperial presidency," early on cultivated an image as an outsider by holding televised "town meetings" where citizens would call with questions. Carter also tried his own version of Roosevelt's fireside chats, sitting before a fire wearing a cardigan sweater.

But what had worked for Roosevelt in the days of the depression and radio did not work for Carter on television in the post-Watergate era. Too many Americans saw Carter's approach as superficial symbolism, and his efforts to use television to stir the public generally failed. His talk to the nation on the energy crisis, which he called "the moral equivalent of war," evoked no widespread support and even spawned jokes that the acronym for "moral equivalent of war" was MEOW.

Carter's supporters argued that this criticism was unfair, that the president's attempts to rally the American people seemed to come up short less because of Carter's own shortcomings than because the public was far less inclined to follow presidential directions than they may have been before Vietnam and Watergate. Public trust in government had waned measurably in the late 1970s, they noted, making Carter's task all the more difficult. Whatever the cause, Carter's efforts to communicate directly to the public and rally its support frequently fell on deaf ears, and Congress generally went its own way.

Carter's well-known difficulties should not mask his real successes, however. Most notable was the televised signing of the 1979 Camp David Accords, a moment of high drama when Egyptian president Anwar Sadat signed a peace treaty with Israeli prime minister Menachem Begin. Carter, who had been personally instrumental in bringing these longtime adversaries together, used the signing to rally congressional support for significant American aid to both Israel and Egypt.

Generally, however, Carter proved more victim than manipulator of television, particularly after Iranian militants seized and held fifty-three American hostages for over a year. Americans each night witnessed on their television sets the humiliation of the hostage situation and Carter's inability to free the hostages proved instrumental in his loss to Ronald Reagan in 1980.

Reagan, the former movie and television actor, quickly proved a powerful contrast to Carter in his ability to use the media to his political advantage. As radio had been to Franklin Roosevelt, television was to Reagan, and the president relied heavily on his rhetorical talents to whip up massive support for his dramatic budget and tax policy victories in 1981. Of particular potency was Reagan's May 1981 appeal to a joint session of Congress for support on his budget package, his first public appearance since the March 1981 assassination attempt. So powerful was the moment, and so massive was the outpouring of public support for the president, that the Democratic-dominated House passed his package a few days after the speech.

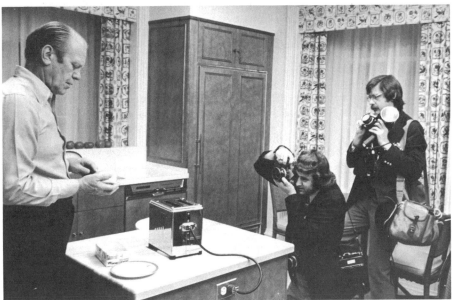

Gerald R. Ford Library

To reverse the mutual distrust between the White House and the media built up during the Nixon administration, Ford worked to convey a simpler image to the press. Here he allows photographers to take pictures as he makes his own breakfast.

No president had used television to establish intimacy with the American people as well as Reagan did. Few could resist the emotional pull of his 1984 speech on the cliffs overlooking Omaha Beach on the fortieth anniversary of the Normandy invasion or of his eulogy for the astronauts who died in the 1986 space shuttle disaster. But even for Reagan the medium had a double-edged effect.

Public responsiveness to televised appeals almost inevitably wanes the more frequently a president relies on them, and Reagan discovered as his time in office went on that the technique has decreasing power. Public confidence in his leadership was eroded by startling revelations about secret arms sales to the Iranian government and their possibly illegal ties to the supply of arms to the contras, or Nicaraguan rebels. Televised congressional hearings on the affair raised broad public concern about Reagan's overall command of his office. By 1988, when the three major networks refused to carry another appeal for aid to the contras because it "was not news," it was apparent that the skills so integral to Reagan's early successes no longer were potent enough to prevail.

The president of the United States has an unparalleled capacity to dominate the national debate because of the office's unique ability to command media attention. Equally important, the president is but one person, whereas Congress is a vast and seemingly disorganized institution. In a battle between the branches, the resident of the White House who possesses good rhetorical skills has a tremendous advantage over the branch of government once given the constitutional mandate to make the law.

Some observers worry that the president's capacity to dominate national debate may drown out many other voices demanding to be heard. Presidents can take credit for ideas that Congress developed, or, conversely, they can blame Congress for their failures. The danger, political scientist Bruce Miroff has concluded, is that presidents could "take over so much of the public space that citizens would perceive the political world chiefly through presidential actions." [103] Should that happen the Framers' fears of a monarchical executive would prove well founded.

Executive Orders

Article II of the Constitution allots to the president the "executive power," one of the least specific but potentially far-reaching phrases in the document. Before 1787, state legislatures generally defined executive power, but the writers of the Constitution (learning from their problems with the Articles of Confederation) shied away from having Congress dictate the boundaries of presidential action. Instead they left the range of such power undefined, open-ended, and ripe for reinterpretation and expansion by later presidents.

Their silence proved critical. When paired with the Article II provision requiring presidents to "take care that the laws be faithfully executed," the executive power clause today provides for a range of "implied" powers whose extent and potency have grown beyond anything the Founders could have foreseen.[104] "Express" powers—those specifically named in the Constitution—like the veto give presidents a limited set of tools for shaping legislation. But powers *implied* in the Constitution, and given substance by years of continuous reinterpretation, are the source of the president's ability to act alone, often without specific con-

> The executive power shall be vested in a president of the United States of America.
> —from Article II, section 1

gressional statute. Much of U.S. history has involved a struggle between presidents claiming the power to act without clear constitutional mandates and their critics arguing to the contrary.

On its face, the take care clause directs the president to administer statutes in ways faithful to legislative language and intent. Like so many constitutional provisions, however, it is a clause vague in meaning and elastic in potential ramifications. In 1890, for example, the Supreme Court ruled that the clause pertained not only to statutes but to any "rights, duties, and obligations growing out of the Constitution itself, our international relations, and all the protection implied by the nature of the government under the Constitution." [105]

The 1890 interpretation of the take care clause provided by that decision alone suggests greater discretionary power inherent in the president's roles as chief executive and commander in chief than the Constitution seems to state specifically. This line of reasoning theoretically means that presidents could undertake any actions deemed necessary to carry out their constitutional duties, to provide for the nation's defense, or to protect the common good. To make matters more complex, the Constitution is mute on exactly what the "common good" entails, another one of those "great silences" that makes the potential of implied powers so controversial.

An offspring of the implied powers doctrine is the *executive order*. This critical instrument of active presidential power is nowhere defined in the Constitution but generally is construed as a presidential directive that becomes law without prior congressional approval. It is based either on existing statutes or on the president's other constitutional responsibilities. Executive orders usually pertain specifically to government agencies and officials, but their effects often reach to the average citizen. For example, Lyndon Johnson in 1965 (Executive Order 11246) required firms that win federal government contracts to create programs for hiring more minorities, thus significantly affecting private sector employment practices. For the most part, orders are issued to establish executive branch agencies, to modify bureaucratic rules or actions, to change decision-making procedures, or to give substance and force to statutes.[106] In Executive Order 12298, for example, President Ronald Reagan moved to implement an interstate cooperative agreement authorized by Congress in 1980 by abolishing one coordinating body to make way for a new one. *(See box, Executive Order 12298, p. 89.)*

There are no specific constitutional procedures for issuing executive orders, and during the first hundred or so years they were issued without any system of publication or

> [The President] shall take care that the laws be faithfully executed....
> —from Article II, section 3

recording. The numbering of executive orders began only in 1907, with numbers assigned retroactively to the time of Abraham Lincoln. Almost thirteen thousand executive orders had been recorded as of 1988, although haphazard reporting and record keeping throughout much of U.S. history prompts scholars to estimate that somewhere between fifteen thousand and fifty thousand directives never were recorded.[107] *(See Table 7.)* To respond to growing concerns that these lax conditions created serious problems for governing and democratic accountability, Congress in the Administrative Procedures Act of 1946 mandated that the number and text of all executive orders must be published in the *Federal Register,* the official U.S. government record, published each weekday; of all executive branch announcements, proposals, and regulations. The exception to this rule applies to "classified" executive orders—those pertaining directly to sensitive national security matters, which are entered into the *Register* by number only.[108]

The Discretionary Presidency

Executive orders are critical to the legislative role of the contemporary presidency precisely because Congress frequently finds itself unable or unwilling to respond to complex national problems with highly detailed laws. Instead, Congress copes by legislating in broad language, setting certain goals and instructing executive branch personnel to hammer out technical matters, regulatory procedures, and rules that both meet those goals and carry the force of law. In 1921, for example, Congress directed the president to coordinate all executive branch budget requests and package them together into a single annual budget document. But Congress never said *how* the president should do so, nor what the limits of that authority should be. As a consequence, the Office of Management and Budget (known until 1970 as the Bureau of the Budget) has grown immeasurably in size and power through presidential initiative. In 1981, in Executive Order 12291, to cite but one case, President Reagan dramatically expanded the OMB's role in substantive policy making by requiring that all executive branch agencies submit new rules and regulations for OMB approval before they can go into effect. Congress nowhere specifically transformed OMB's central role, but one president's use of executive discretion in effect redefined the decision-making process in the federal bureaucracy. The impact was seen immediately in such areas as environmental policy, where Environmental Protection Agency personnel increasingly found their directives overruled by the OMB for budget or policy reasons. The overall effect has been to centralize decision making more in the Executive Office of the President, but Congress at no time passed a law to accomplish this fact.[109]

Even when legislative language is precise, as it usually is in tax legislation, there may emerge policy contradictions, unforeseen circumstances, or technical considerations that require executive branch officials to exercise their judgment in administering the programs legislated by Congress. The Tax Reform Act of 1986, for example, spawned approximately forty-two new Internal Revenue Service regulations, sixty-five announcements, thirty-two rulings, and forty-eight new tax forms within the first thirteen months after passage.[110]

Congress also consciously delegates broad discretionary authority in the name of flexibility, effectiveness, or efficiency.[111] The Smoot-Hawley Tariff Act of 1930, for

Table 7 Executive Orders, by President, 1789-1989

President	Years in office	Number of orders	Average per year
Washington	8.00	8	1.00
J. Adams	4.00	1	.25
Jefferson	8.00	4	.50
Madison	8.00	1	.13
Monroe	8.00	1	.13
J. Q. Adams	4.00	3	.75
Jackson	8.00	12	1.50
Van Buren	4.00	10	2.50
W. H. Harrison	0.08[a]	0	—
Tyler	4.00	17	4.25
Polk	4.00	18	4.50
Taylor	1.25	5	4.00
Fillmore	2.75	12	4.36
Pierce	4.00	35	8.75
Buchanan	4.00	16	4.00
Lincoln	4.00	48	12.00
A. Johnson	4.00	79	19.75
Grant	8.00	217	27.13
Hayes	4.00	92	23.00
Garfield	0.50	6	—[b]
Arthur	3.25	96	29.50
Cleveland (1st term)	4.00	113	28.25
Harrison	4.00	143	35.75
Cleveland (2d term)	4.00	140	35.00
McKinley	4.75	185	38.95
T. Roosevelt	7.25	1081	149.10
Taft	4.00	724	181.00
Wilson	8.00	1803	225.38
Harding	2.60	522	200.77
Coolidge	5.40	1203	222.77
Hoover	4.00	968	242.00
F. Roosevelt	12.33	3522	285.64
Truman	7.67	897	116.96
Eisenhower	8.00	478	59.75
Kennedy	3.00	228	76.00
L. Johnson	5.00	316	63.20
Nixon	5.60	355	63.39
Ford	2.40	152	63.33
Carter	4.00	311	77.75
Reagan	8.00	409	51.13

Sources: Calculated by the author from Gary King and Lyn Ragsdale, *The Elusive Executive: Discovering Statistical Patterns in the Presidency* (Washington, D.C.: CQ Press, 1988), 160-167; *Code of Federal Regulations.*

Note: Includes both numbered and unnumbered executive orders.

a. W. H. Harrison died after only one month in office.

b. Garfield was assassinated after six months in office, during which he issued six executive orders. At that rate his average would have been twelve per year.

example, ran over 170 pages because Congress tried to codify into law virtually every known type of tariff and trade matter. The 1934 Reciprocal Trade Agreements Act, in contrast, ran but 2 pages; this time Congress simply authorized the president to do whatever was necessary to achieve the law's intent.[112] The rigid Smoot-Hawley tariff schedules had been a spectacular nightmare, and Congress thereafter apparently decided that executive branch personnel were better positioned to act flexibly on issues with

Processing Executive Orders

Proposed executive orders can originate from almost anywhere in the executive branch. A few are composed directly in the White House, but most emanate from the various executive departments and agencies. Some orders, such as those imposing trade sanctions on another nation, may be written at the express instruction of the president. Most, however, are composed by career staff personnel in the departments and agencies to implement federal regulations, propose new rules or procedures, or add technical language to congressional statutes. Whatever the case, executive orders have the force of law, so they are crafted largely by professional legal counsel at the instruction of the president's appointees. Rarely does the president take a direct hand in writing an order's language.

Each proposed executive order must be composed and submitted along procedures laid out in the U.S. Code. It must be prepared in a specific format and style (for example, on certain types of paper, in certain language) and must contain language explaining its nature, purpose, background, and effects, along with an assessment of how it relates to existing law. The proposed order is then sent, with seven copies, to the director of the Office of Management and Budget (OMB), where it is examined for adherence to the administration's overall policy and budgetary goals. If approved, the order and its copies are sent next to the attorney general, whose office scrutinizes it for potential legal problems. Since both the attorney general and the director of the OMB typically are among the president's closest personal advisers, clearance by these offices normally can be assumed to signify presidential approval.

Following these steps, the proposed order is transmitted to the director of the Office of the Federal Register, which is part of the National Archives and Records Services of the General Services administration, the federal government's housekeeping arm. The order is reviewed once more for stylistic and typographical errors, after which it and three copies are submitted to the president for final approval. If signed by the president, the order and two copies go back to the director of the Federal Register for publication in the *Federal Register*. It is only upon the moment of publication in the *Register* that the order takes force.

Not all executive orders follow these precise steps. Those relating to some emergency may bypass much of the review process and go directly to the president for final approval. What is more, the text of an order concerning some aspect of national security may be deemed confidential, in which case only the order's number is published in the *Federal Register*. The overwhelming number of executive orders do not fit into these categories, however, so the process for creating and implementing an order typically follows a pattern set by law.

broad domestic and international effects.

Although administrative actions must conform with legislative intent, the line between "making" and "administering" law often becomes blurred.[113] This uncertain distinction occurs most noticeably in international affairs, executive branch operations, and national security, matters where the Constitution gives the president primary authority. Executive branch agencies thus "make" law continuously by interpreting the intent of the law in ways that belie the fiction that presidents only "administer" the will of Congress.

Some scholars argue that for Congress to delegate broad authority to the president is unwise or illegitimate,[114] but executive orders usually are not controversial when based clearly on existing statutory authority. They do, however, spark disputes when based on vaguely defined implied powers. The first such spat with Congress came in 1793 when George Washington unilaterally declared U.S. neutrality in the war between France and England. Washington justified his action with the argument that his constitutional responsibilities in diplomacy included the implied power to keep the United States out of war, but James Madison retorted that the proclamation was invalid because only Congress could decide issues of war and peace.[115] The dispute has simmered ever since, erupting forcefully whenever presidents take actions that Congress deems unconstitutional intrusions into its domains.

Presidents also court controversy when they base executive orders on "implied" legislative consent; that is, when Congress has not legislated *against* some action. Federal courts tend to judge each case individually, but they usually give presidents the benefit of the doubt when Congress has failed to decide an issue over a prolonged period of time. Making matters still more complex, Congress often gives presidents retroactive authority for their unilateral actions, particularly during emergencies. Congress approved Washington's proclamation of neutrality a year later; this pattern has been repeated enough that presidents often proceed on the assumption that Congress will acquiesce.

Finally, presidents maintain that they have the constitutional authority to act unilaterally because they inherit "war" or "emergency" powers during periods of apparent crisis. *(See "Emergency Powers," p. 94, in this chapter.)*

Growth in Executive Discretion

Alexander Hamilton and other Federalists wanted a national government that "left substantial freedom of action to high officials and kept Congress out of most administrative details."[116] As secretary of the treasury under Washington, Hamilton argued strongly that Congress should legislate and appropriate in broad categories, granting to those in the executive branch wide latitude to administer programs. Washington's years in office in fact witnessed a remarkable degree of deference to presidential authority, particularly in the areas of fiscal policy and trade. This did not deter controversies from arising over Hamilton's aggressive claims to executive branch discretion or Washington's proclamation of neutrality, but Congress generally entrusted the president to get the new nation on its feet.

That deference had eroded by 1800, as Jefferson's Democratic-Republicans took control and asserted their view of legislative dominance. Jefferson and his allies, notes historian Leonard White, "emphasized the responsibility of the executive branch and the administrative system to Congress." During the nineteenth century, Congress usually maintained tight reins over executive branch actions through highly detailed statutes, strict budgetary controls, and reviews of even the most mundane administrative matters.[117] Executive orders during these years most often supplemented acts of Congress to carry out rather minor matters like salary increases for individual employees. With the possible exception of Abraham Lincoln's dramatic assumption of power during the Civil War, presidents and legislators alike tended to accept the view that presidents simply administered the law.

The shift toward greater executive discretion began most forcefully with Theodore Roosevelt. His "stewardship" theory of the presidency hinged on "residual" executive powers implied in the Constitution, and it coincided in the late 1800s with growing federal government responsibilities both in the United States and abroad.[118] Residual powers, he concluded, neither were enumerated in the Constitution nor assigned broadly to a specific branch; instead, they resided simply in concepts, like national sovereignty or the public good. Thus, Roosevelt argued, "my view was that every officer, and above all every executive officer in high position, was a steward of the people. . . . My belief was that it was not only his right but his duty to do anything that the needs of the Nation demanded unless such action was forbidden by the Constitution or by the laws."[119] This view contrasted strongly with the more traditional notion that presidents were mere "clerks" who carried out congressional dictates, for it asserted the responsibility of the president to represent the nation as a whole.

The problem with Roosevelt's position was that the Constitution said little about the powers available for presidential stewardship. Clearly, as political scientist Richard Pious suggested, "to use prerogatives effectively the president must first stake out his claims to them. Like Excalibur's sword, he must wrest his powers from the Constitution before he can wield them."[120] Although Abraham Lincoln and Theodore Roosevelt both carved out new areas for unilateral executive initiative, the specter of the truly discretionary presidency did not gain real shape until the administration of Woodrow Wilson. During World War I Wilson issued almost two thousand executive orders and also wielded expansive emergency powers to direct the war and domestic economic production. The powers Wilson asserted in wartime did not dissolve once hostilities ceased. They endured for the benefit of later presidents in a rachet-like expansion in executive power that was to be repeated thereafter.

Rise of the Discretionary Presidency

Franklin Roosevelt gave permanence to the stewardship view of the presidency during the New Deal and World War II. Elected as depression raged and given wide latitude by Congress and the American people, Roosevelt relied heavily on executive initiatives to attack the economic crisis and rally the nation. He issued 654 executive orders in 1933 alone,[121] including his inaugural day proclamation closing all banks for four days to restructure the crumbling financial system and his creation of administrative mechanisms for implementing New Deal programs.

In most cases Roosevelt won quick and retroactive

Executive Order 12298
March 12, 1981
Lake Tahoe Region

By the authority vested in me as President by the Constitution of the United States of America, and in order to eliminate unnecessary and duplicative Federal interference in the responsibilities of the Tahoe Regional Planning Agency (see Public Law 96-351 of December 19, 1980), it is hereby ordered that the Tahoe Federal Coordinating council is terminated and Executive Order No. 12247 of October 15, 1980, is revoked.

Ronald Reagan

The White House,
March 12, 1981.

Source: Office of the Federal Register, *Weekly Compilation of Presidential documents,* March 16, 1981 (Washington, D.C.: Government Printing Office, 1981), 287.

---

congressional approval for his actions. Congress during these years also appropriated massive amounts of money to be used at the president's discretion so that Roosevelt could develop and finance a myriad of special New Deal programs quickly and, perhaps, more effectively than Congress thought possible through traditional procedures.[122] The gravity of the crisis called for decisive action, and Roosevelt stretched the boundaries of his constitutional powers to the limit.

Not only did Roosevelt exercise a highly muscular view of presidential discretion, but the sheer growth in federal government activities during the 1930s brought with it an explosion in executive branch responsibility. Congress found it increasingly difficult to grapple with the size and complexity of new national programs and began the widespread delegation of authority that marks contemporary government. Equally important, scholars and politicians alike began to support the idea that broad executive discretion leads to efficient and effective public administration, arguments that redefined the concept of chief executive away from more traditional views of the president as a mere agent of Congress.[123] Delegating broad authority not only made pragmatic sense but also cohered with views that relatively free executive management and administrative discretion offered unalloyed benefits to a fragmented and decentralized system of government. Traits that the Founders deemed essential for safeguarding citizens' rights and liberties now were seen as impediments to sound government. Strong executive leadership was viewed as the only mechanism able to overcome systemic weaknesses in the federal structure of governance.

The approach of World War II accelerated these trends as Roosevelt gained broad authority to prosecute the war and manage the domestic economy. Roosevelt moved unilaterally in many instances without the benefit of even vague statutory authority, basing his actions instead on powers allegedly inherent in his constitutional duties as commander in chief and chief executive. In 1941, for example, he ordered the seizure of defense plants, shipyards, and thousands of coal mines to prepare the nation for war. Congress more often than not provided the needed statutory authority afterwards and gave Roosevelt tremendous discretionary spending authority because of the national emergency, but even then there were limits to congressional acquiescence. Roosevelt's tendency to use executive orders to create wartime agencies and then to fund them with money appropriated for other purposes eventually stirred a backlash, and Congress in 1944 barred use of any appropriations for an agency created through executive order unless the funds were authorized specifically for that agency.[124]

Perhaps the most controversial of Roosevelt's actions came in 1942, when his Executive Order 9066 authorized the dislocation of Americans of Japanese ancestry from the West Coast and their confinement to camps in the southwestern desert for the duration of the war. This order later came to be viewed as a gross violation of the civil liberties of U.S. citizens, but at the time it was defended as a safeguard against potential sabotage—although the same logic was not applied to citizens of German or Italian heritage. No citizen of Japanese descent ever was convicted of espionage or sabotage, but the Supreme Court in 1944 ruled that Roosevelt had acted legally to protect the nation during wartime.[125]

National security in fact became the primary justification for unilateral executive action in the postwar era. The "cold war" between the United States and the Soviet Union, additional U.S. commitments around the world, and a consensus on the need for assertive executive leadership prompted Congress through the 1960s to accede to presidential dictates across a wide spectrum of domestic and international policy domains. So generous was congressional delegation of foreign policy making power to the presidency during this era, which stood in sharp contrast to the tight reins the legislature had held on executive discretion before World War II, that many scholars regarded this time as one of relative congressional decline. In its reluctance to hobble presidential flexibility in international affairs, Congress appeared to surrender many of its traditional prerogatives. As political scientist Allen Schick noted, "when Congress controls, it legislates the particulars; when Congress withdraws, it legislates in general terms."[126] If one examines a cross-section of postwar statutes, both in domestic and foreign policy realms, it is striking how far less detailed and constraining they were compared to laws passed before the 1930s.

Postwar presidents relied on executive orders less heavily than did presidents before the war. This trend occurred largely because of the accumulation of a body of administrative law that replaced the need for unilateral presidential action in more routine areas, like personnel administration and regulatory procedures. What is more, of almost two thousand executive orders issued between 1945 and 1965, more than 80 percent were based on existing statutory authority, indicating in part the breadth of the statutory web built up since World War II.[127]

Still, the orders issued by postwar presidents were much broader in scope and were used more frequently to bypass a reluctant Congress. Lyndon Johnson, for example, issued an executive order to create minority hiring guidelines for federal contracts after Congress failed to embody affirmative action in the Civil Rights Act of 1964.[128] Rich-

ard Nixon used executive orders to restructure and gain greater control over the executive branch after Congress turned down his reorganization proposals. In 1986 Ronald Reagan preempted possible congressional action in ordering drug testing for federal employees. Thus, while the number of executive orders declined in absolute terms, the tendency of contemporary presidents to use them to bypass Congress made them even more controversial.

Orders as Executive Law Making

Postwar presidents issued executive orders for a wide range of purposes, but three in particular stand out: to combat discrimination, to control executive bureaucracies, and to maintain secrets.

Combating Discrimination

Beginning with Franklin Roosevelt, who directed greater desegregation of defense plants during World War II, presidents have used executive orders to safeguard or promote the civil rights of minorities and women. Many orders were applied to executive branch agencies; others altered federal programs after Congress proved unable or unwilling to act. Harry Truman, for example, in 1948 used Executive Order 9981 to integrate the armed forces, an action that, combined with calls for stronger civil rights protection, split Democrats during the 1948 election. Dwight Eisenhower in 1957 sent federal troops into Little Rock, Arkansas, to enforce Supreme Court decisions forbidding racial segregation in public schools,[129] as did John Kennedy in the early 1960s to protect blacks seeking admission into southern state universities. (See John F. Kennedy, the Law, and the "Ole Miss" Campaign, pp. 36-37, in Chief Executive chapter.) Kennedy also used Executive Order 11063 in 1963 to bar racial discrimination in federally subsidized housing after finding the legislative route blocked by southern conservatives.

Lyndon Johnson's Executive Order 11246 in 1965 directed that firms contracting with the federal government create minority hiring programs after Congress refused to do so in the Civil Rights Act of 1964.[130] Johnson's creation of affirmative action later was redefined somewhat by Nixon's "Philadelphia Plan," a 1969 executive order setting up racial hiring quotas on federal projects. Nixon was challenged on his order's apparent conflict with the 1964 Civil Rights Act (which forbade quotas of any kind), but he was upheld by a federal court of appeals based partly on the implied power of the president to set federal procurement policies.[131]

Controlling Executive Bureaucracies

The Constitution fails to spell out the relationships between presidents and executive branch employees. Presidents thus have made vigorous use of executive orders to mold and control the activities of bureaucrats, efforts that accelerated sharply as the sheer growth in federal responsibilities brought with it an explosion in executive branch size and complexity. In many ways the contemporary presidency's greatest task is to control the federal establishment, and the executive order has become an instrument for government management.[132]

A major problem for presidents and their political appointees is preventing lower-level career bureaucrats from bypassing their superiors and appealing directly to sympathetic congressional committees. William Howard Taft as early as 1909 (Executive Order 1142) prohibited agency officials from applying to Congress for funds without consent of their cabinet secretaries, but it was Franklin Roosevelt who relied most on executive orders to inaugurate the first great effort to centralize control over agencies and their expenditures. Executive Order 6166 in 1933, for example, transferred all executive budget-making authority from department heads to the Bureau of the Budget. Perhaps more important, Roosevelt in 1939 (Executive Order 8248) moved BOB from the Treasury Department to the newly created Executive Office of the President, thus instituting even greater presidential control over bureaucratic actions.

Richard Nixon directed the next powerful effort to impose stricter presidential control. After Congress in 1970 approved the reorganization of the Bureau of the Budget into the Office of Management and Budget, Nixon in Executive Order 11541 directed the new bureau to monitor agency programs and budgets more forcefully. This order effectively began the transformation of OMB from a low-profile budget office into a powerful and controversial policy-making arm of the presidency.

Ronald Reagan went even further in using OMB to monitor and direct agency actions. His Executive Order 12291 in 1981 prohibited federal agencies from proposing or issuing any new rules until OMB ensured that their benefits exceeded their costs. Even more important, Executive Order 12498 in 1985 extended OMB's reach to agency "pre-rulemaking activities," which were defined as almost any activity that could lead to the *consideration* of the need for a regulation. This order also required OMB to approve an annual "regulatory program" submitted by each agency and prohibited actions not in that program unless cleared by OMB observers.

The cumulative effect of these directives has been to endow OMB with expansive powers to supervise the policy development process in all agencies, stop those deemed in conflict with the president's agenda, and insert the president's own priorities more squarely into the routines of agency life. These actions were criticized for accelerating tendencies toward the "overcentralization" of executive branch power, but most complaints seem to come from those opposing the policies of the respective presidents. Future presidents are unlikely to reverse these trends, since the desire to control bureaucratic action is common to Democratic and Republican presidents alike.

Directing policy making is one thing, but there is far less agreement about presidential efforts to control the personal views or behavior of executive branch employees out of a desire for "loyalty" or "proper" lifestyles. These efforts spark heated debates with those who fear the erosion of civil servants' fundamental rights and liberties. Wilson, for example, used an April 1917 executive order to give agency heads the right to fire employees judged "inimical" to the public welfare. The order was seen as a way of dismissing those holding socialist or other "un-American" views as the nation prepared for World War I. Later, as the nation became caught in the grip of the cold war between the United States and the Soviet Union, Truman's Executive Order 9825 in 1947 instituted loyalty oaths for all federal employees to root out possible Communist sympathizers. This order later was codified into law by the Summary Suspension Act of 1950.[133]

In a different vein, Reagan in September 1986 (Executive Order 12564) ordered all executive branch agencies to establish random drug-testing programs for all personnel in "sensitive" positions. The order was controversial because it was not confined to military or intelligence agencies, which already used such tests, but to all agencies. Most government assertions that public employees do not enjoy privacy at work have been contested hotly in the courts.

Maintaining Secrets

Perhaps most controversial has been the use of executive orders to create a system for classifying government documents or other information in the name of national security. Governments always have pursued secrecy in sensitive diplomatic or military matters, but the idea that the United States should maintain a formal classification system did not take hold until the eve of World War II, when Franklin Roosevelt in March 1940 authorized the classification of military intelligence information. The test of what would constitute secrets worth classifying, Roosevelt said, "is what the Commander in Chief of the Army and Navy thinks would be harmful to the defense of this country to give out."[134]

Later executive orders extended classification beyond its original confines as the war progressed, but the practice did not end once hostilities ceased. The onset of the cold war instead led presidents to expand the category of information deemed essential to national security. Truman in two orders extended classification to *any* executive branch agency when secrecy was deemed essential. Whereas Roosevelt based his 1940 executive order on the vague authority provided by a 1938 statute classifying military charts, Truman's expansion of secrecy was based simply on his assertion that inherent executive powers gave him the responsibility to do whatever was "necessary and proper" to protect the general welfare.[135] Constitutional scholars debated Truman's move but worried even more about the effects of greater secrecy on democratic governance. Agencies could classify almost anything, and there were few mechanisms to guard against the overclassification inevitable when agencies consider information a valuable resource or wish to hide mistakes from public view. As presidential scholar Richard Pious noted, "The new system could be used in the conduct of diplomacy to keep Congress uninformed or misinformed."[136]

Eisenhower in 1953 (Executive Order 10501) also based his action on a general claim of presidential authority when he attempted to streamline the classification system and narrow secrecy to information critical to "national defense." As Arthur M. Schlesinger, Jr., argues, however, Eisenhower's order also gave greater power to the secretive Interagency Committee on Internal Security, a panel composed of security officials from various agencies. These officials, who generally supported extensive classification, thereafter would play decisive roles in narrowing public access to government information.

Kennedy, who did not shy away from using secrecy in military and diplomatic ventures when it suited his purposes, nonetheless fought against bureaucratic tendencies toward blanket classification of all information. His Executive Order 10964 in 1962 set up procedures for declassifying or downgrading the classification of information no longer essential to national security, but his efforts were undermined by bureaucrats and congressional conservatives. In fact, notes Schlesinger, the classification system itself eventually because classified.[137]

Secrecy would expand even further under Nixon. Where Eisenhower, for example, sought to confine classification of information to national defense matters, Nixon in 1972 (Executive Order 11652) stretched the boundaries of "national security" to include any information in "the interest of the national defense or foreign relations of the United States," including domestic intelligence activities. Nixon's order was a reaction to the publication of the *Pentagon Papers,* an internal Pentagon study of how the United States became enmeshed in the Vietnam conflict, and critics charged Nixon with both overexpanding secrecy and strangling freedom of the press. That battle has raged to this day.

Potential for Abuse

Executive orders often are controversial because of their great potential for overuse by presidents who are unwilling to work with Congress, frustrated by opposition, or overeager to impose strict secrecy. The discretionary presidency brings with it fears that presidents have become far less accountable to congressional "oversight" (that is, supervision). Another fear is that use of executive orders to tame the bureaucracy may too easily denigrate professional competence and undermine administrative law.

Potential Threats to Civil Liberties

Besides secrecy, another major controversy since the early 1970s has been the use of executive orders to inaugurate domestic surveillance of persons opposed to presidential foreign policy initiatives. Nixon, for example, in 1971 (Executive Order 11605) created sweeping new authority to investigate Americans and determine if they were threats to national security. Most of the domestic surveillance was aimed at groups opposing U.S. action in Vietnam and included secret wiretapping, breaking into offices, and using informers to infiltrate groups. Details of past activities came to light in the mid-1970s, and the ensuing controversies forced Ford and Carter to narrow the range of permissible domestic surveillance actions and to impose stricter control over federal agents.

Reagan, however, in 1981 loosened up considerably on the restrictions through Executive Order 12333, aimed at combating possible domestic terrorism. Civil libertarians were alarmed because the order sanctioned covert surveillance activities based merely on suspicion that there was "probable cause" to believe that some group might be engaged in terrorist actions, as opposed to the more stringent suspicion of actual crimes applied to criminal law. Even more troubling was that the precise guidelines for initiating and conducting investigations themselves were classified.[138]

Revelations in early 1988 that the Federal Bureau of Investigation (FBI) had relied on this sweeping authority to conduct a large-scale covert surveillance program against groups opposed to U.S. policy in Central America sparked outcries. Particularly troubling to many was the breadth of the investigation, which had spread to religious groups and labor unions, and its basis on information allegedly fabricated by an FBI informant. The episode embarrassed the Reagan administration just as it was seeking to generate greater public support for its Latin American policies. Another round of debate ensued about the use of presidential directives for such sweeping purposes.

Secret Orders

Problems also can arise when an executive order is based on information that *itself* is classified for national security purposes. Although federal law mandates the publication of executive orders and proclamations, it also allows for secret orders in the name of the public interest.[139] For example, Truman's 1952 executive order creating the National Security Agency, the largest and most secretive of the nation's intelligence organizations, itself remains classified almost forty years later.

A notable recent example of the problem is Reagan's secret order of September 1986, which retroactively authorized arms shipments to Iran despite an official U.S. embargo against that nation. Reagan failed to notify congressional intelligence committees of the arms sales, asserting later that notification was "deferred" to prevent leaks of information that might harm hostages being held in Lebanon by groups allied with Iran. Trouble for the president came when news of the arms sales came to light in the foreign press, and Americans reacted with shock and anger over the dealings and their links to financial support for rebels fighting the Nicaraguan government (in apparent violation of a congressional ban on such aid). Whatever the merits of the arms sales, or the use of their profits to aid the rebels, the political damage to the administration grew out of the secrecy surrounding the whole affair and the failure to consult with congressional intelligence committees beforehand.

Inertia and Accountability

Heavy reliance on executive orders can take on a life of its own. Presidents may use them instead of seeking congressional action, for example, simply because executive orders have become the normal way of operating. What is more, political scientist Philip Cooper has argued, "as orders move from administration to administration within any given issue area, they tend to spin off more policy elements more widely distributed across the policy space than their predecessors."[140] The accumulation of orders affecting civil rights and government secrecy over time constructed ever more encompassing policy domains that Congress found increasingly difficult to influence. Equally important, federal courts usually grant legitimacy to such policies because they are the products of long and consistent practice. The result is law making by executive decree, a condition antithetical to those who believe that Congress alone has power to make law.

Whether the policies that result from executive orders are good or bad is immaterial. The real question of government by decree is democratic accountability. Executive orders by nature exclude Congress from the process of decision making, often leaving the legislature to catch up after the fact. Few argue that presidents should not enjoy a degree of discretionary authority to administer the laws and carry out functions of the executive branch. The problem with unilateral presidential actions lies with their tremendous influence, lack of consistent congressional input, and prospects for ever greater centralization of policy making in the executive branch.

Reining in the Discretionary Presidency

The period between the New Deal and the Watergate era (roughly 1933, when Roosevelt was inaugurated, to

The Legislative Veto

Beginning in the 1920s, Congress increasingly legislated in broader language and delegated substantial discretionary authority to executive branch departments and agencies. To cope with the potential danger that federal bureaucrats—or the president—might abuse that authority or engage in decisions contrary to the will of Congress, the legislature also began to attach to these bills provisions allowing Congress to pass judgment on new regulations or other bureaucratic actions. These provisions are known as *legislative vetoes.*

Legislative vetoes typically required that no bureaucratic action could go into effect for a prescribed length of time (such as ninety days). During this period, Congress could vote to disallow the regulation or action through a simple resolution of both houses, one house singly, or even one congressional committee, depending on the provision in question.

Congress saw the legislative veto as a way to restrain the executive branch, but presidents of both parties generally opposed the device as an unconstitutional intrusion by Congress into their prerogatives as chief executive. Worse, from a presidential perspective, there was no response to legislative vetoes because simple resolutions do not go to the president for approval. More than one president during the 1970s vetoed a law passed by Congress because it contained one of these provisions.

Despite presidential opposition, use of legislative vetoes mushroomed during the 1970s, particularly after the bruising battles between Congress and Richard Nixon over war powers and impoundment of appropriated funds. By 1983 more than two hundred separate pieces of legislation contained some form of legislative veto.

In June 1983, however, the Supreme Court, in *Immigration and Naturalization Service v. Chadha,* struck down the legislative veto as unconstitutional.[1] The particulars of the case itself are not so important as the Court's ruling that a legislative veto provision attached to an immigration law violated the constitutional doctrine of separation of powers. If Congress wished to prevent the executive branch from undertaking some action, the majority ruled, it must either legislate in greater detail to begin with or pass a regular bill—subject to presidential review—to redress an action it deems unacceptable.

Although the legislative veto itself is dead, the majority decision in *Chadha* left unanswered whether the laws to which the veto provisions were attached also were null and void. As of 1988 the Court seemed reluctant to go that far, and Congress, for its part, appears to be adapting to life after *Chadha* by using more explicit language in bills. It also increasingly is writing provisions into appropriations bills forbidding funding for some specific bureaucratic or presidential actions—language that provides the functional equivalent of a legislative veto if the president accepts the appropriations bill as a whole. Until the Court rules on this strategy, or until the day that the president gains the item veto, use of appropriations bills to restrain executive actions is likely to grow, suggesting how the branches of government adapt to new legal conditions.

1. 462 U.S. 919 (1983).

1974, when Nixon resigned) marked the apogee of the discretionary presidency. By the early 1970s, however, Congress had begun to seek ways to limit what was perceived widely as a gradual but systematic aggregation of expansive executive power and its apparent abuses in both domestic and foreign policy spheres. The war in Vietnam and the incursion into Cambodia, "excessive" use of impoundment (refusal to spend funds appropriated by Congress) domestic surveillance and other abuses of civil liberties, and Watergate suggested to many a presidency out of control.

During the 1970s Congress enacted a wide range of limitations on executive discretion, including: the 1974 Budget and Impoundment Control Act, increased reliance on legislative vetoes *(see box, The Legislative Veto, this page)*, more short-term authorization for federal programs or policies to ensure more frequent reviews of executive agencies as the statutes expire, greater use of provisions in appropriations bills to dictate how funds were to be spent, freedom of information rules, and additional executive branch reporting responsibilities. Congress also dramatically expanded its own institutional capacities for overseeing the executive branch by hiring thousands of additional staff and by creating or expanding congressional support agencies like the General Accounting Office and Congressional Budget Office.

All of these efforts have interposed Congress more forcefully into the routines of federal policy making, but Congress cannot or will not abolish the discretionary presidency. Contemporary government cannot return to congressional government because Congress cannot legislate in the detail necessary to carry out most government functions. There also remains a great reluctance, even by those members of Congress most critical of executive discretion and bureaucratic policy making, to place too many or too strict limitations on the ability of the president to act quickly or flexibly when conditions require.

Tension between Congress and the presidency is nothing new, and it tends to run in cycles. As political scientist Allen Schick has pointed out, "The president and other executive officials try to stretch the authority given them by Congress more broadly than might have been intended. Congress responds by narrowing executive discretion. But the new restrictions hobble executive performance and lead to demands for relaxation." [141]

Neither branch can achieve complete dominance, since the other always retains a range of constitutional and political resources that ensure both independence and a degree of countervailing power.[141] The tension is a dynamic one, and neither presidents nor Congress can dominate for long.

Emergency Powers

In times of crisis presidents often lay claim to extraordinary powers to preserve the nation, to promote the general welfare, or to provide for the common good of the people. Such "emergency" powers neither are granted expressly to the president nor delegated to Congress by the Constitution; instead, they are judged to reside purely in the inherent need for leaders to protect national sovereignty and domestic order. Thus, to many scholars the great silences in the Constitution imply an array of residual powers for each branch to draw on in times of crisis.

The doctrine of emergency powers is a variation of what the Framers knew as the Lockean Prerogative. John Locke, the eighteenth-century English philosopher, believed strongly in a government of laws. But he also argued that, in dire emergencies, "the laws themselves . . . . give way to the executive power, or rather to this fundamental law of nature and government . . . [namely] that, as much as may be, all the members of society are to be preserved." Limited government was the idea; but in emergencies, responsible leaders may have to resort to extraordinary actions because legislatures usually are slow to move, and national self-preservation is superior to legal niceties.

Of equal importance, said Locke, is "the people's permitting their rulers to do several things of their own free choice, where the law is silent, and sometimes, too, against the direct letter of the law, for the public good, and their acquiescing in it when so done." [142] Locke was joined in his views by the French philosopher Jean Jacques Rousseau, who in the 1760s argued simply, "It is advisable not to establish political institutions so strongly as to prevent a possibility of suspending their operation." [143]

The Founders relied on European philosophers such as Locke and Rousseau to supply a great deal of the rationale behind the Constitution, but nowhere in the document did they indicate that government, much less the president, would wield broad emergency powers. The only possible such authority granted to the president in fact was the ability to grant reprieves and pardons (Article II, section 2), which the Founders believed might be useful in resolving domestic insurrections like Shays's Rebellion of 1786-1787 (which had prompted the rewriting of the Articles of Confederation in the first place). The Constitution also provided for suspending writs of *habeas corpus* in cases of rebellion or invasion, which would allow for arrest without due cause, but this provision was enumerated to Congress in Article 1, section 9. [144]

Despite the Constitution's general silence on the subject, the notion of emergency powers arguably remained implicit in the document. Article II mandates, for example, that the president shall "preserve, protect, and defend" the Constitution and uphold its provisions. This duty could require the president to bring to bear the commander-in-chief and chief executive powers from which many implied powers arise. What is more, in *The Federalist Papers* Alexander Hamilton and James Madison both indicated their views that national preservation might be cause for superseding constitutional restrictions. [145] Nonetheless, as Arthur Schlesinger, Jr., argued, they also warned that those claiming emergency powers did so at their own risk and, having acted, must gain support from Congress and the people if constitutional government is to survive. [146]

Philosophic questions aside, the debate over emergency powers also is a highly practical one. The structure of the U.S. system was designed to diffuse political power and safeguard individual rights. As such, it is a system prone to tremendous inertia, even stalemate, since no branch easily or quickly overpowers the others. These conditions might only be maddening to participants in "normal" times, but they could be potentially fatal to the Republic when crisis or war intrudes, particularly in these days of intercontinental ballistic missiles and a highly integrated world economy. That the president alone may be able to act quickly and flexibly when the situation demands speed and dexterity is a reality the Founders recognized when they created the single executive and endowed it with the commander-in-chief and chief executive powers.

The question thus is not who should lead in times of crisis. Rather, the question is how to preserve *both* the nation and the Constitution when crisis threatens the future of the Republic. Abraham Lincoln, in defending his remarkable usurpation of power during the early months of the Civil War, asked simply, "Is there in all republics this inherent and fatal weakness? Must a government of necessity be too *strong* for the liberties of its people, or too *weak* to maintain its own existence?" Or, as Lincoln later asked, "Was it possible to lose the nation and yet preserve the Union?" [147]

Lincoln's experiences during the Civil War were unique, but history is dotted with other moments where this dilemma emerged powerfully. Few doubt the need for presidents to wield extraordinary powers in times of crisis, but debates rage when the "crisis" is not clear to all or when the claims to emergency powers appear overstated. Asserting the powers necessary to defend and preserve the nation under moments of true emergency is one thing, but claiming such powers when the threat is not readily apparent, or when the powers asserted seem disproportionate to the alleged threat, is a far different matter.

That is the dilemma of emergency powers. "Whether intentionally or not," political scientists Erwin Hargrove and Michael Nelson have written, "the Constitution conferred prerogative power in times of emergency on the president. Efforts to define 'emergency' by legislation and thus limit the president in such cases have run up against Locke's warning of the futility of trying to legislate for cases yet unknown." [148]

The history of the nation has been marked by recurrent tensions between presidential claims to extraordinary powers and the right of Congress to impose its will when emergencies occur. It is a struggle yet to be resolved entirely.

Powers in Wartime

The United States has entered into five declared wars, a civil war, and numerous undeclared hostilities in its history. In each instance presidents have relied upon assorted emergency powers to deal with the threat, but as presidential scholar Louis Koenig has argued, they have invoked starkly different justifications of their actions. The "Lincolnian Pattern" asserts an aggressively broad view of the president's inherent war powers, based largely on wedding the presidential oath of office to the commander-in-chief and take care clauses. The "Joint President-Congress Pattern," by contrast, involves broad congressional grants of executive authority to prosecute the war and maintains that presidential powers are statutory as opposed to inherent.[149] Woodrow Wilson and Franklin Roosevelt, during World Wars I and II, respectively, followed this second pattern.

Neither pattern is a pure type, since every president exercises inherent and delegated war powers simultaneously. The difference lies in the fundamental claims presidents make to justify their actions as hostilities loom, distinctions that are increasingly important as the very notion of war itself has changed from the relatively stately styles of the eighteenth century to the short but violent spasms of combat prevalent today.

The Supreme Court through history has upheld presidential claims to *some* extraordinary emergency powers when the nation was involved in hostilities. The earliest important test came during the War of 1812, when several New England governors challenged James Madison's request that their state militias take up specific defense responsibilities. Madison's order was based on authority granted by Congress in the Militia Act of 1795, but the governors' resistance was supported by various state high courts. The Supreme Court, however, in 1827 ruled that Madison could overrule the governors because the president alone could define emergencies when the nation was at war or was faced with imminent hostilities.[150]

The Madison case was the exception to presidential claims of war powers in the years before the Civil War. In most instances, presidents deployed U.S. forces against pirates abroad or Indian uprisings at home to protect American citizens and their property. Their actions usually were based on some specific congressional grant of authority, such as that given to James Monroe to protect merchant ships against pirates. Early presidents, including the headstrong Andrew Jackson, exhibited a great deal of restraint in using their commander-in-chief responsibilities.

Lincoln and Inherent War Powers

Restraint was abandoned during the single greatest threat to national unity yet encountered by the United States. Faced with secession by the Southern states in 1861, Abraham Lincoln claimed numerous emergency war powers to save the Union and in the process became what presidential scholar Clinton Rossiter called a "constitutional dictator."[151] Other scholars saw Rossiter's characterization as unduly harsh, but there is no doubt that Lincoln used remarkable, often unconstitutional, means to quell the rebellion.

Congress was not in session when Fort Sumter fell. With the onset of hostilities, Lincoln unilaterally proclaimed a blockade of Southern ports, mobilized state militias, increased the size of the army and navy, sent weapons to unionists in Virginia (who established the state of West Virginia), authorized construction of ships for the navy, and appropriated funds for purchases of war material.

Lincoln conveniently failed to call Congress back into session for eleven weeks; and when he did, he claimed that his actions were justified by the inherent prerogative powers of the presidency, especially his role as commander in chief. Congress ultimately gave Lincoln retroactive authority for his actions, even though some (such as expanding the army and spending unappropriated funds) clearly were unconstitutional. Legal nuances paled before the emergency at hand, however, and Lincoln continued to assume and exercise independent war powers even with Congress in session.

This same sense of emergency led the courts to sup-

Categories and Examples of Emergency Powers

When emergencies are declared, or during times of crisis, the president has at hand a broad array of potential powers. These emergency powers can be grouped into three categories of actions the president may take:

Powers over Individuals

Confine individuals seen to be threats to national security

Restrict travel of Americans to other nations (such as Cuba) or travel of some foreigners to the United States

Restrict movement of citizens within the United States

Require persons, because of their backgrounds, associations with certain groups, or ownership of particular articles (such as weapons), to register with government officials

Restrict certain persons from working in industries critical to national security

Remove federal employees regarded as threats to national security

Suspend writs of *habeas corpus*

Declare martial law

Assign armed forces to conflicts in foreign nations

Powers over Property

Order stockpiling of strategic materials (such as uranium)

Impose restrictions on exports (such as computer equipment)

Allocate materials in ways necessary to aid national defense

Require industries to give priority to government contracts and seize industries failing to comply with such orders

Fix wages and prices

Powers over Communications

Withhold information from Congress and the public deemed potentially sensitive to national security

Monitor and censor communications between United States and other nations

Require foreign representatives to register with U.S. government

Sources: U.S. Congress, House of Representatives, Subcommittee on Administrative Law and Governmental Relations, Committee on the Judiciary, Hearings on H.R. 3884, *National Emergencies Act,* 94th Cong., 1st sess., March 6-April 9, 1975, 22-23; Robert E. DiClerico, *The American President* (Englewood Cliffs, N.J.: Prentice-Hall, 1979), chap. 8.

port many of Lincoln's claims. In the *Prize Cases* (1863), shipowners whose vessels had been seized trying to run the blockade of Southern ports sued on the grounds that the blockade itself was constitutional because Congress had not declared war.[152] This was true technically, but the Supreme Court ruled that the South nonetheless was enemy territory and Lincoln thus was required to deal with the insurrection. As Arthur Schlesinger, Jr., points out, however, the justices endorsed such executive power only in domestic rebellions or invasions, not, as later presidents asserted, to use against sovereign nations overseas.[153]

The Union also faced tremendous dangers behind its own lines. The problems were keenest around Washington, D.C., with secessionist Virginia on one side and Maryland filled with Southern sympathizers on the other. The mayor of Baltimore was decidedly pro-Confederate; mobs attacked federal troops; bridges were sabotaged; and the state legislature was about to convene with the real possibility of voting to secede. Lincoln responded by declaring martial law and suspending writs of *habeas corpus* behind the Northern lines, thus allowing military authorities to arrest without warrants members of the Maryland legislature and other rebel sympathizers. Lincoln also suppressed opposition newspapers and ordered censorship of postal and telegraph communications.

Some of the president's actions provoked clashes with the judiciary. In *Ex parte Merryman* (1861), the Supreme Court ruled that Lincoln had usurped the sole right of Congress to suspend writs of *habeas corpus* during an emergency.[154] Lincoln flagrantly ignored the ruling, and Congress later affirmed his actions in the Habeas Corpus Act of 1863, but the president's continued reliance on preemptive arrests and use of military courts to try civilians set in motion another confrontation.

In *Ex parte Milligan* (1866), the Supreme Court ruled that Lincoln lacked the constitutional authority to use military courts behind Northern lines so long as the civil judicial system remained intact.[155] A civilian, L. P. Milligan, was arrested in Indiana for treason, but the Court ruled that Indiana was not in the "theater of war" and writs of *habeas corpus* thus could not be suspended. The Constitution worked "equally in war and in peace," said the justices, and national preservation was not cause enough to violate its principles.[156]

By the time the Court ruled, however, Lincoln was dead and the Civil War over, so *Milligan* joined a number of judicial decisions that create doubts whether the courts would challenge a sitting president during national crises. These doubts reemerged during World War II when Franklin Roosevelt ordered some 112,000 Japanese-Americans from their homes on the West Coast to internment camps in the southwestern desert. The forced relocation was challenged in the courts but never to any great effect.[157]

World War and Delegated Powers

Unlike Lincoln, who disregarded the Constitution to preserve the nation, both Woodrow Wilson and Franklin Roosevelt fought foreign wars based largely on powers at least broadly delegated to them by Congress. Both Wilson and Roosevelt faced situations in which the nature of war itself had changed. Twentieth-century war was "total war": the lines between combatants and civilians had become blurred; struggles involved not only armies but the entire social, economic, and industrial capacities of nations; and control over national populations was key to success.

Total war thus required swift, massive, and sustained national organization and mobilization, the capacities for which lay most in the executive branch. Congress for its part prepared for war by delegating broad powers to the presidency to carry out military functions and to regulate the domestic economy. The Lever Food and Fuel Control Act of 1917, for example, empowered Wilson to seize defense-related facilities; to regulate food production, manufacturing, and mining; and to fix prices on commodities. The Selective Service Act of 1917 allowed the president to raise an army. The Espionage Act of 1917 gave him the power to restrict exports. The Trading with the Enemy Act of 1917 allowed for regulation and censorship of all extenal communications.

Wilson also received broad authority to monitor the actions of resident aliens, to regulate or operate transportation and communications facilities, and to reorganize executive branch agencies where necessary. In effect, Wilson was granted almost free rein to conduct the war and to maintain the domestic economy—a pattern that recurred two decades later, although on a greater scale, when Congress delegated broad discretionary powers to Franklin Roosevelt.[158]

Moreover, neither Wilson nor Roosevelt overlooked his constitutional prerogatives as commander in chief. Far from it: both claimed the right to create wartime executive agencies, to enforce "voluntary" press censorship, and to coordinate private industry beyond the scope of congressional authorization. Roosevelt in particular claimed emergency powers to sidestep congressional declarations of neutrality as Europe fell into war. In 1939 he declared a "limited" state of emergency, which allowed him to invoke existing statutes and prepare the nation militarily. In early 1941 he declared an "unlimited" state of emergency under which he reorganized the executive branch and prepared to deal with the domestic economy once the U.S. entered into hostilities. In neither instance did Roosevelt obtain previous authorization, although he usually tried to cloak his actions in existing statutory powers.

Once war was declared, however, Roosevelt dropped even the pretense of delegated powers. His seizure of defense plants immediately after Pearl Harbor, for example, was based on claims of authority given to him by the Constitution and "the laws," although he never made clear *which* laws. Perhaps his most intriguing claim came in 1942, when he asked Congress to repeal legislation dealing with farm prices. If Congress did not do so, Roosevelt warned, he would repeal the provisions himself because, he said, "the president has the powers, under the Constitution and under congressional acts, to take measures necessary to avert a disaster which would interfere with the winning of the war."[159] Whether Roosevelt would have acted on his threat was never tested, for Congress quickly gave in.

Truman and the Limits of Emergency Powers

Neither Wilson nor Roosevelt made sweeping claims to *inherent* emergency powers during either world war. Subsequent presidents operated differently, however, as the United States in the late 1940s began a period of prolonged confrontation with the Soviet Union. The nature of war changed again—from total conventional war to indeterminate potential thermonuclear war at one extreme and localized wars of containment at the other. The postwar world, at least the one inhabited by superpowers jockeying for dominance, would be characterized by permanent military establishments and the "imperial presidency." [160] Boundaries between war and peace no longer were clear, and the sheer scope of the meaning of national security (defense, intelligence, economic health, scientific advances—to name a few) gave presidents greater potential power than ever before in virtually every aspect of national affairs. Presidential influence over both civil liberties and congressional authority never seemed so extensive.

The debate about the use of inherent powers exploded first in 1952. Harry Truman had put the nation on emergency war footing in 1950 with the invasion of South Korea and in late 1951 ordered the seizure of strike-threatened steel mills to avoid potential shortages. Truman based his action not on any statutory authority to resolve labor disputes but "on the authority vested in me by the Constitution and laws of the United States, and as President of the United States and Commander in Chief of the armed forces of the United States." [161] When challenged on this rationale, Truman argued simply, "The President has very great inherent powers to meet national emergencies." [162]

Congress did not respond, despite broad antipathy to Truman's action, but the Supreme Court in *Youngstown Sheet and Tube Co. v. Sawyer* (1952) declared the seizure of the steel mills unconstitutional because in the 1947 Taft-Hartley Labor Act Congress had decided *not* to give presidents the right to take over industrial facilities shut down by strikes.[163] What is more, the majority opinion implied that the president did not possess inherent powers in times of emergency, nor did the commander-in-chief role grant special domestic powers. Four out of the five justices concurring in the majority decision, however, did not reject this notion outright. Their concurring opinions suggested that emergency prerogatives may exist when presidents act in accordance with the express or implied will of Congress or in the absence of congressional action. *(See box, Justice Jackson's Test of Presidential Emergency Powers, p. 99.)* Congressional opposition places the presidency in its weakest constitutional position, and Truman's action could not be supported because it so clearly violated congressional intent.

Truman's greatest problem in the *Steel Seizure Case* probably was that he overstated the gravity of the situation. If both Congress and the people had backed Truman as they had Roosevelt in the internment of Japanese-Americans, it is doubtful the Court would have challenged his claims. But, as Rossiter suggests, "the Court's power of judicial review is least useful when most needed," for it is during emergencies that rash actions are likeliest to occur, actions that may indeed violate constitutional safeguards.[164] Many scholars are concerned that the country's ongoing readiness for war and its worldwide commitments have created conditions for unfettered presidential claims to inherent war powers and have increased the potential for rash executive action even in the absence of clear and broadly perceived emergencies.

Powers in Economic Crises

Outside of wartime, presidents also wield emergency powers when the nation's economic system is seriously unstable. In economic crises it appears that such power emanates exclusively from statutes, although presidents have shown ingenuity in stretching the boundaries of that authority.

Procedures for Emergency Orders

The National Emergencies Act of 1976 (PL 94-412) terminated all states of emergency that were in effect until that time but also set in place procedures for declaring and, more important from the view of many in Congress, terminating future states of emergency. As the brief overview below suggests, the provisions of the National Emergencies Act were intended above all to force Congress and the president, acting singly or together, to take action to ensure that any state of emergency does not outlive the conditions upon which it was based.

The president by law cannot declare a state of national emergency without also specifying the provisions of existing law or constitutional provisions under which the proposed action falls. Furthermore, any proclamation of a national emergency must be transmitted immediately to Congress and published in the *Federal Register*.

During any declared national emergency, the president and all relevant executive branch agencies or departments must maintain files on all rules, regulations, executive orders, or any other activities carried out to address the emergency. All of these must be transmitted promptly to Congress. Matters requiring confidentiality are to be handled in a prescribed manner (for example, delivered only to members of the congressional intelligence committees and those staff members with security clearances). All expenditures made by the executive branch to address the emergency also must be reported to Congress within ninety days after each six-month period following the declaration of the emergency.

The law also specifies how states of emergency are to be terminated, either by the president or congress. No later than six months after an emergency is declared, the two houses of Congress by law must meet to consider a concurrent resolution to determine whether the emergency should be terminated. The resolution must go through the normal congressional procedures, but according to a specific schedule to avoid delays. Should Congress be unable or unwilling to terminate the emergency (perhaps because of some disagreement between the House and the Senate), it must consider another such resolution within the next six-month period.

The president can terminate unilaterally any declared state of emergency when it is deemed that the conditions meriting the emergency have passed. But, to avoid another situation where states of emergency endure legally for decades, the law calls for automatic termination of an emergency upon the anniversary of its declaration, unless the president previously notifies Congress (and publishes in the *Federal Register*) of the need to continue the emergency after the anniversary. One way or another, then, states of emergency are to be terminated.

The Trading with the Enemy Act gave Wilson the authority to impose diverse economic measures in times of war or national emergency. This law, passed on the eve of U.S. entry into World War I, was intended as a wartime measure, but its authority was never revoked after the war ended. Later presidents thus discovered, to their delight, the apparent statutory justification for emergency actions to manage a faltering economy.

The best example is the action of the newly inaugurated Franklin Roosevelt in 1933 when faced with the imminent collapse of the nation's financial system. Roosevelt on March 4 declared a national state of emergency and closed the banks, basing his action on the Trading with the Enemy Act. This interpretation of the wartime statute was dubious, but it nonetheless reflected Roosevelt's desire to cloak his action in legal authority. Congress sanctioned his move when it passed the Emergency Banking Act three days later. In the following months it also granted Roosevelt a wide range of new powers to address the economic emergency. In fact, the single greatest outpouring of major legislation in peacetime U.S. history took place between March 9 and June 16.

In 1933 Roosevelt's actions responded to a starkly imminent crisis, but in August 1971 Richard Nixon's declaration of emergency over a growing imbalance in the U.S. balance of payments struck many observers as overly dramatic. Nixon used the emergency to disconnect the value of the dollar from the gold standard, levy a 10 percent surtax on all imports, and freeze all domestic prices for ninety days. The overall effect was to devalue the dollar, drive down the prices of American goods overseas, and halt inflation temporarily. Nixon based his actions on the 1970 Economic Stabilization Act, which authorized the president to "issue such orders as he may deem appropriate to stabilize prices, rents, wages and salaries," although he had signed the law only because it also had contained provisions affecting national defense.[165]

Powers during Domestic Unrest

Presidential emergency powers also include the authority to call out federal troops or take control over state national guards (descendants of the state militias) to quell domestic unrest or to deter violence. Such authority has been used in the United States to put down illegal labor strikes, to ensure delivery of the mail, to impose order during natural disasters and urban riots, and to prevent other volatile situations from exploding.

Before to the 1940s, and particularly during the late nineteenth century, presidents became involved in domestic disorders most often during labor strikes. Until the passage of the Wagner Act of 1933, which ensured the right of collective bargaining and established procedures for negotiations, strikes usually were considered illegal and often resulted in dramatic outbreaks of violence between strikers and company security forces. This was true especially in the mining, steel, railroad, and, later, automobile industries, where relations between management and labor were sharply adversarial in the best of times. Use of troops to break the 1894 Pullman strike in Chicago is but one of several famous examples of a practice that virtually ended by the 1950s.

During the 1950s and 1960s, presidents relied on federal troops or state national guards to ensure calm in situations involving racial desegregation. The first and per-

haps most notable case came in 1957, when Dwight Eisenhower sent troops into Little Rock, Arkansas, to enforce desegregation of the public shools in the face of resistance from state officials. John Kennedy confronted state officials when he sent in federal troops to ensure peaceful integration at the University of Alabama in 1963, and later took over (or "federalized") the Mississippi National Guard to do the same in that state. Kennedy, and Lyndon Johnson after him, also used troops to protect civil rights marchers on several occasions.

During the later 1960s, troops were used more frequently to quell urban riots and to control demonstrations against U.S. involvement in Vietnam. Most noteworthy was the unrest following the April 1968 assassination of civil rights leader Martin Luther King, Jr., which sparked widespread rioting throughout more than one hundred cities and forced Lyndon Johnson and various governors to call out some 55,000 troops.[166]

Another case entailed the declaration of a state of national emergency. In March 1970 Nixon responded to a postal strike in New York, which threatened to cripple postal service nationally, by declaring a state of emergency and calling out federal troops to take over the New York postal system and keep mail deliveries flowing. Nixon's use of troops to sort and deliver the mail was unusual, but it shows how presidents can react to potential disturbances.

Powers during Natural Disasters

Presidents by statute also have the authority to declare states of emergency in areas of the country hit by hurricanes, floods, earthquakes, or other natural disasters. By declaring a natural disaster area, the president sets in motion the government machinery that can provide immediate aid, such as food, shelter, police protection. Perhaps more critical, however, the president can ensure longer-term assistance like federally guaranteed home and business loans at interest rates significantly lower than most commercial banks might offer at the time. In doing so, the government ensures that the disaster will be softened some for those able to rebuild more quickly and less expensively.

The Permanent Emergency

Most Americans probably never realized that the United States lived under a state of declared national emergency from 1933 to 1975. In 1952 Truman terminated Roosevelt's pre-World War II emergencies (declared in 1939 and 1941) that had granted the president greater discretion to direct defense preparations, organize the executive branch, and mobilize the nation for potential hostilities. But four other states of emergency were still in force as of 1975: Roosevelt's bank emergency (1933), Truman's mobilization following the invasion of South Korea (1950), Nixon's use of troops to maintain mail deliveries (1970), and Nixon's response to international economic conditions (1971).

In none of these six emergencies had a termination date been specified, nor had Congress written into most of the statutes provisions for terminating the president's emergency authority. Emergency declarations usually are drafted in the White House and rushed through Congress. In 1933, legislators approved the law authorizing Roosevelt's emergency powers to alleviate the bank crisis after

Justice Jackson's Test of Presidential Emergency Powers

Justice Robert Jackson's concurring opinion in *Youngstown Sheet and Tube v. Sawyer* (1952) remains a classic analysis of the conditions under which a president may in fact possess extraordinary powers. More important, Jackson's dispassionate examination suggests when those emergency powers may not exist.

Mr. Justice Jackson, concurring:
The actual art of governing under our Constitution does not and cannot conform to judicial definitions of the power of any of its branches based on isolated clauses or even single Articles torn from context. While the Constitution diffuses power the better to secure liberty, it also contemplates that practice will integrate the dispersed powers into a workable government. It enjoins upon its branches separateness but interdependence, autonomy but reciprocity. Presidential powers are not fixed but fluctuate, depending upon their disjunction or conjunction with those of Congress. We may well begin by a somewhat oversimplified grouping of practical situations in which a President may doubt, or others may challenge, his powers, and by distinguishing roughly the legal consequences of this factor of relativity.

1. When the President acts pursuant to an express or implied authorization of Congress, his authority is at its maximum, for it includes all that he possesses in his own right plus all that Congress can delegate. In these circumstances, and in these only, may he be said (for what it may be worth) to personify the federal sovereignty. If his act is held unconstitutional under these circumstances, it usually means that the Federal Government as an undivided whole lacks power. A seizure executed by the President pursuant to an Act of Congress would be supported by the strongest of presumptions and the widest latitude of judicial interpretation, and the burden of persuasion would rest heavily upon any who might attack it.

2. When the President acts in absence of either a congressional grant or denial of authority, he can only rely upon his own independent powers, but there is a zone of twilight in which he and Congress may have concurrent authority, or in which its distribution is uncertain. Therefore, congressional inertia, indifference or quiescence may sometimes, at least as a practical matter, enable, if not invite, measures on independent presidential responsibility. In this area, any actual test of power is likely to depend on the imperatives of events and contemporary imponderables rather than on abstract theories of law.

3. When the President takes measures incompatible with the expressed or implied will of Congress, his power is at its lowest ebb, for then he can rely only upon his own constitutional powers minus any constitutional powers of Congress over the matter. Courts can sustain exclusive presidential control in such a case only by disabling the Congress from acting upon the subject. Presidential claim to a power at once so conclusive and preclusive must be scrutinized with caution, for what is at stake is the equilibrium established by our constitutional system.

Into which of these classifications does this executive seizure of the steel industry fit? It is eliminated from the first by admission, for it is conceded that no congressional authorization exists for this seizure. That takes away also the support of the many precedents and declarations which were made in relation, and must be confined, to this category.

Can it then be defended under flexible tests available to the second category? It seems clearly eliminated from that class because Congress has not left seizure of private property an open field but has covered it by three statutory policies inconsistent with this seizure. In cases where the purpose is to supply needs of the Government itself, two courses are provided: one, seizure of a plant which fails to comply with obligatory orders placed by the Government; another condemnation of facilities, including temporary use under the power of eminent domain. The third is applicable where it is the general economy of the country that is to be protected rather than exclusive governmental interests. None of these were invoked. In choosing a different and inconsistent way of his own, the President cannot claim that it is necessitated or invited by failure of Congress to legislate upon the occasions, grounds, and methods for seizure of industrial properties.

This leaves the current seizure to be justified only by the severe tests under the third grouping, where it can be supported only by any remainder of executive power after subtraction of such powers as Congress may have over the subject. In short, we can sustain the President only by holding that seizure of such strike-bound industries is within his domain and beyond control of Congress. Thus, this court's first review of such seizures occurs under circumstances which leave presidential power most vulnerable to attack and in the least favorable of possible constitutional postures....[1]

1. *Youngstown Sheet and Tube v. Sawyer,* 343 U.S. 579 (1952).

only eight hours of debate.[167] Even more worrisome, these unexpired states of emergency gave the president the technical authority to invoke a wide range of emergency powers, even if no crisis seemed imminent. These powers included the right to seize private property and regulate private enterprise, to organize and control all means of production and transportation, to call up reservists and assign military forces overseas, to institute martial law, and to restrict travel.[168]

The potential gravity of the situation hit home for many in 1972 as a result of friction between Congress and the Nixon administration following the 1970 U.S. incursion into Cambodia. Members of the Senate Foreign Relations Committee asked Secretary of Defense Melvin R. Laird what would happen if Congress cut off funds for continued

U.S. involvement. They were surprised when Laird stated that the president could bypass Congress entirely and spend unappropriated funds through emergency authority granted under a 1799 statute. The law was still on the books, and, at least theoretically, so too was the president's emergency power.[169]

Disturbed greatly by this assertion and concerned that other such laws might still apply years after their passage, the Senate created the Special Committee on National Emergencies and Delegated Powers to investigate the possible extent of presidential emergency powers. This committee, through hearings and investigations, discovered approximately 470 statutes dealing with emergency situations still on the books. It also learned that four states of emergency technically remained in effect.[170]

As a result of these findings, and during a period when efforts were made to rein in the "imperial presidency," Congress in 1976 passed the National Emergencies Act terminating, as of 1978, the states of emergency in effect since 1933. The law also terminated the presidential emergency powers stemming from those declarations, established the president's authority to declare future states of national emergency in ways that clearly defined presidential powers during the emergency, provided for congressional review, and mandated that states of emergency will lapse after six months unless renewed.[171] The act does not require the president to consult with Congress before declaring a state of emergency, which everyone realized might be impossible, but it does force the president to specify clearly the nature of the emergency and the statutory powers to be invoked. Congress did not try to legislate for all emergencies; it sought principally to ensure presidential accountability.[172]

In 1977 Congress curbed executive authority to impose economic controls during presidentially declared states of emergency by amending the 1917 Trading with the Enemy Act and by confining the act's broader authority to wartime. The 1977 law also defined economic controls that presidents could employ without calling a state of national emergency, including the ability to regulate foreign currency transactions, to institute embargoes against other nations, and to freeze foreign assets. These powers would be more restricted, however, than might be the case during wartime. This condition was implied in the 1917 law, but presidents beginning with Franklin Roosevelt interpreted it far differently.

Conclusion

There is an understandable tendency to examine the presidency in a context of crisis. Crises, after all, force presidents to act forcefully, and some have done so in ways that expanded presidential power thereafter. Lincoln, for example, claimed for the office a range of inherent war powers that endure today. Roosevelt established the president's capacity to address economic problems, to aid allies in times of trouble, and to prepare the nation for war.

If we study the presidency exclusively through the lens of crisis response, however, we introduce systematic inaccuracies into our understanding of how the institution works and how it relates to the other components of the national government. After all, episodes like the 1962 Cuban missile crisis, the subject of innumerable studies on presidential leadership, remain the exception to the rule. Emergencies are extraordinary times, and to focus on them as the epitome of presidential leadership fosters the impression of greater presidential power than may in reality exist in a system where political authority is shared among separate branches. It also may foster in the White House a view of leadership that may exist only during crises: the need to respond quickly to problems with little or no consultation with Congress, to resort to extraconstitutional or even unconstitutional means to achieve ends, and to function as if the presidency is above the law. Such attitudes—which some observers saw in Nixon's 1970 decision to invade Cambodia and Reagan's efforts to support rebels in Nicaragua—may do the presidency more harm than good since they invite congressional and public backlash. The ultimate lesson of emergency powers is to know when they are appropriate, not merely expedient.

Notes

1. Louis Fisher, *The President and Congress* (New York: Free Press, 1972), 18-21.
2. Thomas Jefferson, "Notes on Virginia," in *The Life and Selected Writings of Thomas Jefferson,* ed. Adrienne Koch and William Peden (New York: Random House, Modern Library, 1944), 237.
3. *Guide to Congress,* 3d ed. (Washington, D.C.: Congressional Quarterly Inc., 1982), 770. The power theoretically exists to this day, although no English sovereign has used the veto since 1707.
4. James Sundquist, *Constitutional Reform and Effective Government* (Washington, D.C.: Brookings, 1986), 30.
5. Ibid., 30-31.
6. The exemption of constitutional amendments from the presidential veto was established by the Supreme Court in *Hollingsworth v. Virginia,* 3 Dall. 378 (1798).
7. Alexander Hamilton, James Madison, and John Jay, *The Federalist Papers,* ed. Clinton Rossiter (New York: New American Library, 1961), 443.
8. Ibid., 322.
9. Ibid., 444.
10. The Constitution gives presidents the authority to approve or veto legislation within ten days after a bill is *presented* to the White House, as opposed to after it is *passed* by Congress. Bills passed by Congress cannot be presented to the president until they have been signed by the Speaker of the House and the president of the Senate (that is, the vice president, although this function is performed normally by the president pro tempore). Therefore, an indefinite gap can occur between passage and presentation. There have been times, in fact, when Congress has delayed presentation of bills because the president has been out of the country. There also have been times when presidents have maneuvered to delay presentation to create opportunities for pocket vetoes. In 1970, for example, Richard Nixon had Vice President Spiro Agnew exercise his authority to sign legislation, which Agnew then delayed in carrying out so that several bills would not be presented to Nixon until just a few days before adjournment. For a discussion of this sort of maneuver, see Eric Redman, *The Dance of Legislation* (New York: Simon and Schuster, Touchstone Books, 1973).
11. As upheld by the Supreme Court in *Missouri Pacific Railway Co. v. United States,* 248 U.S. 277 (1919).
12. Clinton Rossiter, *The American Presidency* (New York: Harcourt Brace and World, 1960), 91.
13. See James Bryce, *The American Commonwealth,* 2d ed., vol. 1 (New York: Macmillan, 1911), 64. The Supreme Court in 1926 ruled that the power to remove political appointees resided with the president alone. See *Myers v. United States,* 272 U.S. 52 (1926).
14. Louis Fisher, *Presidential Spending Power* (Princeton, N.J.: Princeton University Press, 1975), 25.
15. See, for example, Neil MacNeil, *Forge of Democracy: The House of Representatives* (New York: David McKay, 1963), 244-245.
16. Jimmy Carter, *Keeping Faith: The Memoirs of a President* (New York: Bantam Books, 1982), 101.
17. *Guide to Congress,* 771.
18. Robert Pear, "Court Is Asked to Define Power of the Pocket Veto," *New York Times,* November 9, 1986, sec. 4.
19. Bryce, *American Commonwealth,* 59.
20. See Richard E. Neustadt, *Presidential Power: The Politics of Leadership from FDR to Carter* (New York: Wiley, 1980).
21. Thomas Cronin, *The State of the Presidency,* 2d ed. (Boston: Little, Brown, 1980), 81.
22. George C. Edwards III, *Presidential Influence in Congress* (San Francisco: Freeman, 1980), 24.
23. Neustadt, *Presidential Power,* 63.
24. See, for example, Redman, *Dance of Legislation,* 243.
25. *Pocket Veto Case,* 279 U.S. 644 (1929).
26. Arthur M. Schlesinger, Jr., *The Imperial Presidency* (New

York: Popular Library, 1974), 237.

27. *Wright v. United States,* 302 U.S. 583 (1938).

28. See Redman, *Dance of Legislation,* 275-277.

29. *Kennedy v. Sampson,* 511 F.2ds 430 (D.C. Cir. 1974).

30. *Kennedy v. Jones,* Civil Action no. 74-194 (D.D.C.).

31. Pear, "Power of the Pocket Veto," 4.

32. *Barnes v Carmen,* 582 F. Supp. 163 (D.D.C. 1984); *Barnes v. Kline,* 759 F.2d 21 (D.C. Cir. 1985). The lone dissenter was Judge Robert Bork, who argued that members of Congress had no right to sue the president in the first place and the court had no jurisdiction over such issues. Lawyers for Congress argued that the courts have every right to adjudicate disputes between Congress and the executive.

33. *Barnes v. Burke,* 479 U.S., 93 L.Ed. 2d 732, 107 S.Ct. (1987).

34. See Louis Fisher, *The Politics of Shared Power,* 2d ed. (Washington, D.C.: CQ Press, 1987), 210.

35. Ibid., 209.

36. Edwards, *Presidential Influence in Congress,* 20.

37. Stuart Taylor, Jr., "Court Rebuffs Reagan on Deferral of Spending Ordered by Congress," *New York Times,* January 21, 1987, sec. A.

38. Edwards, *Presidential Influence in Congress,* 21.

39. Fisher, *Politics of Shared Power,* 20.

40. George Will, "Power to the President," *Newsweek,* October 12, 1981, 120.

41. Sundquist, *Constitutional Reform,* 209-215.

42. See Fisher, *Politics of Shared Power,* 210-213.

43. E. E.Schattschneider, *The Semi-Sovereign People: A Realist's View of Democracy in America* (Hinsdale, Ill.: Dryden Press, 1975), 66.

44. Bruce Miroff, "Monopolizing the Public Space: The President as a Problem for Democratic Space," in *Rethinking the Presidency,* ed. Thomas E. Cronin (Boston: Little, Brown, 1982), 218-252.

45. For a cogent discussion of the constants of American governance and the effects that they have on presidential leadership, see Bert A. Rockman, *The Leadership Question: The Presidency and the American System* (New York: Praeger, 1984), chap. 3.

46. For an honest defense of this perspective, see Thomas P. O'Neill, Jr., with William Novak, *Man of the House: The Life and Political Memoirs of Speaker Tip O'Neill* (New York: Random House, 1987).

47. Norman J. Ornstein, Thomas E. Mann, and Michael J. Malbin, *Vital Statistics on Congress, 1987-1988* (Washington, D.C.: Congressional Quarterly Inc., 1987), 51.

48. For a president's perspective on this phenomenon, see Carter, *Memoirs of a President,* 83-84.

49. Neustadt, *Presidential Power,* 33.

50. Rossiter, *American Presidency,* 140.

51. Bertram Gross, *The Legislative Struggle: A Study of Social Combat* (New York: McGraw-Hill, 1953), 101.

52. See, for example, James Sundquist, *The Decline and Resurgence of Congress* (Washington, D.C.: Brookings, 1981).

53. Hamilton, Madison, and Jay, *Federalist Papers,* 423.

54. For discussion of Washington's experience, see George M. Haynes, *The Senate of the United States: Its History and Practice,* vol. 1 (Boston: Houghton Mifflin, 1938), 62-63.

55. George B. Galloway, *History of the House of Representatives* (New York: Thomas Crowell, 1969), 12.

56. Edward S. Corwin, *The President: Office and Powers, 1789-1957,* 4th ed. (New York: New York University Press, 1957), 21.

57. Ibid., 23.

58. Galloway, *History of the House,* 245-246.

59. Corwin, *President: Office and Powers,* 28.

60. *Theodore Roosevelt: An Autobiography* (New York: Macmillan, 1913), 282.

61. Sundquist, *Decline and Resurgence of Congress,* 130.

62. Corwin, *President: Office and Powers,* 269.

63. Special address to a joint session of Congress, June 23, 1913. As cited in Corwin, *President: Office and Powers,* 269.

64. Rossiter, *American Presidency,* 140.

65. Arthur M. Schlesinger, Jr., *The Age of Roosevelt: The Coming of the New Deal* (Boston: Houghton Mifflin, 1959), 1.

66. See, for example, Rockman, *Leadership Question.*

67. *Guide to Congress,* 762.

68. Roland Evans and Robert Novak, *Lyndon B. Johnson: The Exercise of Power* (New York: New American Library, 1966), 490.

69. Louis Koenig, *The Chief Executive,* 5th ed. (New York: Harcourt Brace Jovanovich, 1986), 145-146.

70. "Annual Messages of the Presidents: Major Themes of American History," in *The State of the Union Messages of the Presidents, 1790-1966,* ed. Fred L. Israel (New York: Chelsea House, 1966), xiv.

71. *Public Papers of Woodrow Wilson,* vol. 1, 32; as cited in Corwin, *President: Office and Powers,* 269.

72. Fisher, *Shared Power,* 26; see also H. Wayne Morgan, *From Hayes to McKinley* (Syracuse, N.Y.: Syracuse University Press, 1969), 274-319.

73. Charles O. Jones, "Presidential Negotiation with Congress," in *Both Ends of the Avenue: The Presidency, the Executive Branch, and Congress in the 1980s,* ed. Anthony King (Washington, D.C.: American Enterprise Institute, 1983), 99.

74. Ibid., 102.

75. Fisher, *President and Congress,* 52-53.

76. Cronin, *State of the Presidency,* 118.

77. James S. Young, *The Washington Community* (New York: Columbia University Press, 1966), 167.

78. For a superb discussion of the evolution of "central clearance," see Fisher, *Presidential Spending Power.*

79. Richard E. Neustadt, "The Presidency and Legislation: Planning the President's Program," *American Political Science Review* 49 (December 1955): 1015; see also Stephen J. Wayne, *The Legislative Presidency* (New York: Harper and Row, 1979), 19.

80. Paul Light, "Presidents as Domestic Policymakers," in *Rethinking the Presidency,* ed. Thomas E. Cronin (Boston: Little, Brown, 1982), 360.

81. See, for example, John W. Kingdon, *Agendas, Alternatives, and Public Policy* (Boston: Little, Brown, 1984).

82. See William Manchester, *The Glory and the Dream: A Narrative History of America, 1932-1972* (Boston: Little, Brown, 1974), 95.

83. See Joel D. Aberbach and Bert A. Rockman, "Clashing Beliefs within the Executive Branch: The Nixon Administration Bureaucracy," *American Political Science Review* 70 (June 1975): 456-468.

84. Neustadt, *Presidential Power.*

85. Eric L. Davis, "Congressional Liaison: The People and the Institutions," in *Both Ends of the Avenue,* 60.

86. Ibid., 61.

87. Ibid., 62.

88. Jones, "Presidential Negotiation with Congress," 106.

89. See Davis, "Congressional Liaison," 78-79.

90. Ibid., 65.

91. O'Neill, *Man of the House,* 310-311.

92. Davis, "Congressional Liaison," 65.

93. Jones, "Presidential Negotiation," 118.

94. Roger H. Davidson and Walter J. Oleszek, *Congress and Its Members* (Washington, D.C.: CQ Press, 1981), 299. For an insider's view of the 1981 tax and budget battles, see David Stockman, *The Triumph of Politics: The Inside Story of the Reagan Revolution* (New York: Harper and Row, 1986).

95. Jones, "Presidential Negotiation," 126.

96. Ibid., 123-125.

97. Edwards, *Presidential Influence,* 110.

98. As quoted in Manchester, *The Glory and the Dream,* 91.

99. Schlesinger, *New Deal,* 559.

100. Wilfred E. Binkley, *President and Congress* (New York: Vintage Books, 1962), 305.

101. As cited in William Safire, *Safire's Political Dictionary* (New York: Ballantine Books, 1978), 649.

102. Ibid., 444. The phrase "nattering nabobs. . ." was penned by William Safire, who later became a popular newspaper col-

umnist and expert on the English language. The term *nabob* is Hindi in origin and has come to mean in English a self-important person.

103. Miroff, "Monopolizing the Public Space," 230.
104. Corwin, *President: Office and Powers*, 7; Richard Pious, *The American Presidency* (New York: Basic Books, 1979), 38.
105. *In re Neagle*, 135 U.S. 1(1890). By contrast, see the Court's opinion in *Myers v. United States*, 272 U.S. 52 (1926), where Justice Oliver Wendell Holmes argued, "The duty of the President to see that the laws be executed is a duty that does not go beyond the laws or require him to achieve more than the Congress sees fit to leave within his power." This view of executive discretion is generally superseded by the view propounded in *Neagle*. See Corwin, *President: Office and Powers*, 169, for discussion.
106. *Proclamations*, in contrast to executive orders, are directed specifically at private individuals. Proclamations generally encompass such hortatory matters as Thanksgiving Day or National Black History Month, although some involve substantive issues that carry the force of law. The Supreme Court in *Wolsey v. Chapman*, 101 U.S. 755 (1879), ruled that there is no material difference between proclamations and executive orders, so this section will not make any distinctions between the two. This discussion focuses primarily on executive orders.
107. Phillip J. Cooper, "By Order of the President: Administration by Executive Order and Proclamation," *Administration and Society*, 18 (August 1986): 239.
108. Ibid., 239.
109. See Christopher J. Bosso, *Pesticides and Politics: The Life Cycle of a Public Issue* (Pittsburgh: University of Pittsburgh Press, 1987).
110. *Newsweek*, February 29, 1988, 40.
111. For Supreme Court decisions supporting congressional delegation of authority to the executive branch, see *Field v. Clark*, 143 U.S. 649 (1891); *Butterfield v. Stranahan*, 192 U.S. 471 (1904); *United States v. Grimaud*, 220 U.S. 506 (1911); *Clark Distilling Co. v. West Maryland Railway Co.*, 242 U.S. 311 (1917).
112. Allen Schick, "Politics Through Law: Congressional Limitations on Executive Discretion," in *Both Ends of the Avenue*, 162.
113. See Corwin, *President: Office and Powers*, 126. In the *United States v. Grimaud*, the court made the distinction between "legislative" and "administrative" powers but noted that it was impractical for Congress to provide for every detail or possible occurrence.
114. See, for example, Theodore Lowi's indictment of the practice in *The End of Liberalism*, 2d ed. (New York: W. W. Norton, 1989).
115. Corwin, *President: Office and Powers*, 178-179.
116. Leonard White, *The Federalists* (New York: Macmillan, 1948), 512.
117. Leonard White, *The Jeffersonians* (New York: Macmillan, 1951), 552.
118. Corwin, *President: Office and Powers*, 152.
119. Theodore Roosevelt, *An Autobiography* (New York: Scribners's, 1931), 388.
120. Pious, *American Presidency*, 49.
121. *Executive Orders and Proclamations*, Committee on Government Operations, House of Representatives, 85th Cong., 1st sess., December 1957, 36.
122. See Fisher, *Presidential Spending Power*, 61-64.
123. Schick, "Politics Through Law," 160.
124. Fisher, *Shared Power*, 36.
125. *Korematsu v. United States*, 323 U.S. 214 (1944).
126. Schick, "Politics Through Law," 161.
127. See Ruth Morgan, *The President and Civil Rights* (New York: St. Martin's Press, 1970), 5.
128. Cooper, "By Order of the President," 238.
129. *Brown v. Board of Education of Topeka*, 349 U.S. 483 (1954) and *Brown v. Board of Education of Topeka*, 349 U.S. 294 (1955).

130. Cooper, "By Order of the President," 238.
131. Fisher, *President and Congress*, 51.
132. For a good discussion of these efforts, see Fisher, *Presidential Spending Power*.
133. Corwin, *President: Office and Powers*, 100.
134. Schlesinger, *Imperial Presidency*, 324.
135. Ibid., 325.
136. Pious, *American Presidency*, 348.
137. Schlesinger, *The Imperial Presidency*, 325.
138. *New York Times*, February 13, 1988, 33.
139. See Pious, *American Presidency*, 347.
140. Cooper, "By Order of the President," 254.
141. Schick, "Politics Through Law," 157, 181.
142. John Locke, *The Second Treatise on Government* (Indianapolis: Bobbs-Merrill, 1952), 91-96. See also discussion in Corwin, *President: Office and Powers*, chap. 1; Pious, *American Presidency*, chap. 2; Robert E. DiClerico, *The American President* (Englewood Cliffs, N.J.: Prentice-Hall, 1979), chap. 8; Schlesinger, *Imperial Presidency*, chap. 2.
143. Jean Jacques Rousseau, *The Social Contract* (New York: Hafner Press, 1947), 110.
144. A writ of *habeas corpus* (Latin for "present a body") is a court order requiring that authorities must present a prisoner in court and show cause for that person's detention. The Constitution otherwise generally forbids detention of prisoners without due cause.
145. See *Federalist* No. 28 and No. 41 in *Federalist Papers*.
146. Schlesinger, *Imperial Presidency*.
147. Ibid., 69; Clinton Rossiter, *Constitutional Dictatorship* (Princeton, N.J.: Princeton University Press, 1948), 19.
148. Erwin C. Hargrove and Michael Nelson, *Presidents, Politics, and Policy* (Baltimore: Johns Hopkins University Press, 1984), 26.
149. Koenig, *Chief Executive*, 235-237.
150. *Martin v. Mott*, 12 Wheat. 19, 23-33 (1827).
151. See Rossiter, *Constitutional Dictatorship*.
152. *Prize Cases*, 2 Black 635, 17 L.Ed. 459 (1863)
153. Schlesinger, *Imperial Presidency*, 75.
154. *Ex parte Merryman*.
155. *Ex parte Milligan*, 71 U.S. (4 Wall.) 2, 18 L.Ed. 281 (1866).
156. Schlesinger, *Imperial Presidency*, 78-79.
157. See *Hirabayashi v. United States*, 320 U.S. 81 (1943); *Korematsu v. United States*, 323 U.S. 214 (1944); *Ex parte Endo*, 323 U.S. 284 (1944). In *Hirabayashi*, the Court narrowed, but did not overturn, the ability of military officials to impose special curfews on Japanese-Americans. In both *Korematu* and *Endo* the Court reluctantly upheld the internment itself.
158. Corwin, *President: Office and Powers*, 235-236.
159. See John Roche, "Executive Power and the Domestic Presidency: The Quest for Prerogative," *Western Political Quarterly* 5 (December 1952): 607.
160. See Schlesinger, *The Imperial Presidency*.
161. J. Malcolm Smith and Cornelius Cotter, *Powers of the President During Crises* (Washington, D.C.: Public Affairs Press, 1960), 134.
162. DiClerico, *American President*, 322.
163. *Youngstown Sheet and Tube Co. v. Sawyer*, 343 U.S. 579 (1952).
164. Rossiter, *American Presidency*, 53.
165. William Manchester, *The Glory and the Dream: A Narrative History of America, 1932-1972*, vol. 2 (Boston: Little, Brown, 1974), 1535-1536.
166. Ibid, 1382.
167. See Frank Church, "Ending Emergency Government," *American Bar Association Journal* 63 (February 1977): 198.
168. *Congress and the Nation*, vol. 4 (Washington, D.C.: Congressional Quarterly Inc., 1977), 802.
169. See Fisher, 240, *Presidential Spending Power*, 240.
170. *Congress and the Nation*, vol. 4, 801.
171. P.L. 94-412; see, House Subcommittee on Administrative Law and Governmental Relations, Committee on the Judiciary, Hearings on H.R. 3884, *National Emergency Act*, 94th

Cong., 1st sess., March 6-April 9, 1975.
172. See DiClerico, *American President*, 327-329.

Selected Bibliography

Binkley, Wilfred E. *President and Congress.* New York: Vintage, 1962.

Bryce, James. *The American Commonwealth.* Vol. 1, 2d ed. New York: Macmillan, 1911.

Corwin, Edward S. *The President: Office and Powers.* 4th ed. New York: New York University Press, 1957.

_____ . *Presidential Power and the Constitution: Essays.* Ed. Richard Loss. Ithaca, N.Y.: Cornell University Press, 1976.

Cronin, Thomas E., *The State of the Presidency.* Boston: Little, Brown, 1980.

Cronin, Thomas E., ed. *Rethinking the Presidency.* Boston: Little, Brown, 1982.

Dodd, Lawrence C., and Bruce I. Oppenheimer, eds. *Congress Reconsidered.* 3d ed. Washington, D.C.: CQ Press, 1985.

Edwards, George C., III. *Presidential Influence in Congress.* San Francisco: Freeman, 1980.

Fenno, Richard F. *The President's Cabinet.* New York: Vintage Books, 1959.

Fisher, Louis. *President and Congress: Power and Policy.* New York: Free Press, 1972.

_____ . *Presidential Spending Power.* Princeton, N.J.: Princeton University Press, 1975.

_____ . *The Politics of Shared Power: Congress and the Executive.* 2d ed. Washington, D.C. CQ Press, 1987.

Hamilton, Alexander, James Madison, and John Jay. *The Federalist Papers.* Ed. Clinton Rossiter. New York: New American Library, 1960.

Hargrove, Erwin C. *The Power of the Modern Presidency.* New York: Knopf, 1974.

Hargrove, Erwin C., and Michael Nelson. *Presidents, Politics, and Policy.* Baltimore: Johns Hopkins University Press, 1984.

Heclo, Hugh. *A Government of Strangers: Executive Politics in Washington.* Washington, D.C.: Brookings, 1977.

Hess, Stephen, ed. *Both Ends of the Avenue: The Presidency, the Executive Branch, and Congress in the 1980s.* Washington, D.C.: American Enterprise Institute, 1983.

Koenig, Louis. *The Chief Executive.* 5th ed. New York: Harcourt Brace Jovanovich, 1986.

Mansfield, Harvey C., Sr., ed. *Congress against the President.* New York: Academy of Political Science, 1975.

Nelson, Michael, ed. *The Presidency and the Political System.* 2d ed. Washington, D.C.: CQ Press, 1988.

Neustadt, Richard. *Presidential Power: The Politics of Leadership from FDR to Carter.* New York: Wiley, 1980.

Pious, Richard. *The American Presidency.* New York: Basic Books, 1979.

Polsby, Nelson W. *Congress and the Presidency.* New York: World, 1970.

Polsby, Nelson W., ed. *The Modern Presidency.* Washington, D.C.: University Press of America, 1973.

Rockman, Bert A. *The Leadership Question: The Presidency and the American System.* New York: Praeger, 1984.

Rossiter, Clinton. *Constitutional Dictatorship.* Princeton, N.J.: Princeton University Press, 1948.

_____ . *The American Presidency.* 2d ed. New York: New American Library, 1960.

Schlesinger, Arthur M., Jr., and Alfred DeGrazia. *Congress and the Presidency: Their Role in Modern Times.* Washington, D.C.: American Enterprise Institute, 1967.

Smith, J. Malcolm, and Cornelius Cotter. *Powers of the President during Crises.* Washington, D.C.: Public Affairs Press, 1960.

Sundquist, James. *Politics and Policy.* Washington, D.C.: Brookings, 1968.

_____ . *The Decline and Resurgence of Congress.* Washington, D.C.: Brookings, 1986.

Wayne, Stephen J. *The Legislative Presidency.* New York: Harper and Row, 1978.

Young, James S. *The Washington Community.* New York: Columbia University Press, 1966.

Chief Diplomat

John F. Kennedy expressed the importance of foreign affairs to the presidency when he observed, "The big difference [between domestic and foreign policy] is that between a bill being defeated and the country [being] wiped out." [1] Most contemporary presidents would have agreed with Kennedy's appraisal of the importance of foreign affairs. In the nineteenth century when U.S. foreign interests were limited primarily to trade and to disputes about western expansion, presidents often could concentrate on domestic policy. Today the dangers of the international environment and the wide array of U.S. economic, political, and military commitments virtually ensure that presidents will spend at least half of their time on foreign affairs.

Even during periods of relative international calm, foreign policy has remained an area of unique importance to the presidency. Foreign affairs issues usually have offered presidents the greatest freedom to exercise their power and the best opportunity to affect policy personally. Important foreign affairs decisions often have been made by the president alone or during intimate consultations with a few trusted advisers. In contrast, it is more common for domestic policy decisions to originate in the bureaucracy, involve many officials, require less secrecy, be affected by interest group politics, and be subject to strict congressional constraints. In addition, whereas presidents always have expected their domestic policies to be criticized by political opponents and a significant portion of the general public, the desire of political friends and foes alike to project a united front frequently has produced initial support for many foreign policies. Consequently, presidents may choose to retreat to the refuge of foreign affairs where they can exercise their powers most freely and feel like the leader of the nation.

Presidents who are concerned with establishing an enduring place in history often are drawn to foreign affairs. Steadfast wartime leadership, the prevention or resolution of dangerous crises, bold diplomatic initiatives, and historic summit meetings with important foreign leaders can create presidential legends. The most memorable acts of many of the most famous U.S. presidents have involved foreign affairs. George Washington and John Adams kept the United States out of the war between Britain and France; Thomas Jefferson bought Louisiana from France; James Monroe announced the Monroe Doctrine declaring the in-

tention of the United States to resist European intervention in the affairs of independent nations in the Western Hemisphere; Theodore Roosevelt maneuvered to build the Panama Canal; Woodrow Wilson negotiated and unsuccessfully campaigned for the Treaty of Versailles; Franklin D. Roosevelt led the nation through World War II; Harry S Truman ordered the use of the atomic bomb and oversaw the creation of the North Atlantic Treaty Organization (NATO), the United Nations (UN), and the postwar bipolar balance of power; and Kennedy made the Soviets withdraw missiles from Cuba.

The experiences of three recent presidents who upon entering office possessed greater expertise and interest in domestic policy than in foreign policy demonstrated the centrality of foreign affairs to the modern presidency. Lyndon B. Johnson, Jimmy Carter, and Ronald Reagan each found his administration overwhelmed by foreign affairs issues. Johnson's plans for a "Great Society" were undercut by the resource demands of the Vietnam War and the divisions the war created in the American public. Carter, a former governor with little foreign policy experience, became personally absorbed with foreign policy issues such as recognition of the People's Republic of China, arms control, and the Camp David peace process between Egypt and Israel. At the end of his term the Iran hostage crisis dominated his presidency almost as much as the Vietnam War had dominated Johnson's. Reagan, another former governor, did not display Carter's enthusiasm for learning the details of U.S. foreign policy, preferring instead to outline broad policies and to delegate the authority to implement them. Despite Reagan's relative detachment from foreign affairs, his administration probably will be best remembered for its arms control treaty with the Soviet Union, its bouts with terrorism, and the scandal surrounding the sale of arms to Iran and the diversion of funds to the Nicaraguan resistance.

Distribution of Foreign Policy Power

The Constitution specifically grants remarkably few foreign affairs powers to the president. It states: "He shall have Power, by and with the Advice and Consent of the Senate, to make Treaties, provided two-thirds of the Sena-

By Daniel C. Diller

> He shall have Power, by and with the Advice and Consent of the Senate, to make Treaties, provided two-thirds of the Senators present concur; and he shall nominate and, by and with the Advice and Consent of the Senate, shall appoint Ambassadors, other public Ministers and Consuls.... He shall receive Ambassadors and other public Ministers.
> —from Article II, sections 2, 3

tors present concur; and he shall nominate and, by and with the Advice and Consent of the Senate, shall appoint Ambassadors, other public Ministers and Consuls.... He shall receive Ambassadors and other public Ministers." The Constitution also bestows upon the president the responsibility to be the commander in chief of the army and navy and to execute the laws of the United States.

The Constitution assigned to Congress the powers "to ... provide for the common Defence and general Welfare of the United States; ... to regulate Commerce and foreign Nations; ... to define and punish Piracies and Felonies committed on the high Seas and Offences against the Law of Nations; to declare War ... and make Rules concerning Captures on Land and Water; to raise and support Armies; ... to provide and maintain a Navy; ... to make all Laws which shall be necessary and proper for carrying into Execution the foregoing Powers...."

At a glance the congressional powers in foreign affairs appear at least as broad as those granted to the president. The president commands the armed forces, but Congress declares war; the president makes treaties, but not without the advice and consent of the Senate; the president appoints ambassadors, but they must be confirmed by the Senate. Only the power to receive ambassadors, a seemingly ceremonial function, was left unchecked by a corresponding congressional power. In contrast, Congress has several specific foreign affairs powers, including the important responsibility of regulating foreign commerce, that are unchallenged by a specific presidential power. More important, the legislative branch's general power to make laws, control appropriations, and "provide for the common defense and general welfare of the United States" gave it broad authority to become involved in any foreign policy decision or action not specifically reserved for the president by the Constitution.[2]

Yet beyond the enumerated foreign affairs powers, the president has other constitutional resources that may be used to shape foreign policy. Since it is impossible clearly to define where policy making stops and policy implementation begins, the executive power gives the president an inherent influence on foreign policy decisions and actions. The veto power supplies the president with another check over Congress's ability to dictate foreign policy. In addition, several presidential foreign affairs powers are implied in the Constitution. As chief of state, negotiator of treaties, and manager of the diplomatic corps, the president is recognized as the official spokesperson of the nation. As commander in chief of the armed forces, presidents can make foreign policy by taking or threatening to take military actions short of declared wars. Finally, the power to send and receive ambassadors is interpreted as implying the president's authority to recognize the legitimacy of other governments.

Still, the affirmative grants of power in the Constitu-

tion do not begin to answer all the questions about how foreign policy decisions shall be made and implemented. For example, the Constitution does not say how the president is to receive Senate advice on treaties, whether the president can make international agreements without using the treaty process, who can declare neutrality, whether the president needs congressional approval to sustain military action that might commit the United States to war, or what foreign policy actions the president can take under the general executive authority of the office. The authors of the Constitution formulated a very ambiguous distribution of shared foreign policy powers between the president and Congress, which could be unraveled only by events. In the famous words of presidential scholar Edward S. Corwin, the Constitution is "an invitation to struggle for the privilege of directing American foreign policy." [3]

Presidential Dominance of Foreign Policy

In 1948, addressing members of the Jewish War Veterans, President Truman stated, "I make foreign policy." [4] Most historians and political scientists would agree that although Truman's assessment of presidential power was an exaggeration, it reflects modern presidents' relative autonomy over foreign policy compared with their more limited authority in domestic affairs. Since the beginning of the Republic and especially since World War II presidents have won most of the interbranch struggles for primacy in foreign relations. Although Congress has retained an important role in foreign affairs, its actions almost always have been responses to presidential policies. On many occasions Congress has been able to frustrate, delay, modify, or negate presidential foreign policy when a majority of members has been willing to oppose the chief executive. The president, however, has dominated the formulation and initiation of foreign policy, and the American public and foreign governments expect the president to make decisions and to implement them. Presidents perceived as indecisive or weak in foreign relations quickly lose popularity. It is even common for members of Congress from both parties to criticize a president for failing to provide foreign policy leadership.

Since the constitutional division of foreign affairs powers between the executive and legislative branches is relatively ambiguous, one cannot attribute the establishment of presidential control over foreign relations to the affirmative grants of power in the Constitution. The ambiguity of the document ensured that customs and precedents would be developed that would fill in the gaps left by its brief treatment of the foreign affairs powers. In this vague constitutional environment, the branch most capable of asserting its own interests and demonstrating its ability to make effective foreign policy would likely emerge as the more powerful. This branch proved to be the executive.

Presidential Advantages

Since its creation, the presidency has possessed inherent practical advantages that make it better suited than Congress to the conduct of foreign relations. First, as head of the foreign policy bureaucracy, the diplomatic corps, the intelligence agencies, and the military, the president controls information that is crucial to effective foreign policy decision making. Second, because only 1 person occupies the office of the president, whereas 525 make up the Congress, the president is able to work with speed and secrecy—two capabilities that are indispensable in many diplomatic situations, especially crises that threaten the security of the nation. Third, since it is a responsibility of the presidency to communicate with foreign governments through treaty negotiations and diplomatic channels, the president can most easily formulate policy that is consistent with negotiating positions and official statements. Fourth, as the executor of foreign policy, commander in chief of the armed forces, and appointer of diplomatic personnel, the president and presidential advisers should be in the best position to judge the capacity of the U.S. government to carry out a given foreign policy initiative. Fifth, because presidents are elected every four years, they can provide more continuity to foreign policy than Congress, which must sustain an election every two years. Sixth, because presidents, unlike members of Congress, are elected by a national constituency, they are usually more inclined than Congress to focus on international problems that affect the entire nation. Finally, the president is the most identifiable leader and visible symbol of the nation and is, therefore, the most capable of rallying national support in a crisis.

At various times throughout U.S. history, each of the three branches of government has recognized these inherent practical advantages of the president. The resulting episodes of legislative acquiescence, judicial interpretation in favor of the president, and executive assertiveness have contributed to the president's primacy in foreign affairs.

Precedents Set under Washington

George Washington exercised his foreign affairs power with great restraint by today's standards. He conducted international business through the treaty process rather than through executive agreements between himself and foreign leaders; he consulted with the Senate more closely on treaty matters than subsequent presidents have; he proposed legislation, but thereafter did not attempt to influence congressional debate; and he considered his veto over legislation as a tool to be used only if a resolution were unconstitutional.

Yet Washington and his closest adviser, Secretary of the Treasury Alexander Hamilton, believed the president had the constitutional authority and the practical duty to take the initiative in foreign policy. As a result Washington set several precedents that enlarged the foreign affairs powers of the young presidency beyond a literal reading of the enumerated powers in the Constitution. He established the president's authority to recognize foreign governments, to demand that foreign ambassadors be recalled, to negotiate treaties without congressional involvement, and to withhold from Congress documents pertinent to treaty negotiations. Most important, Washington demonstrated that in foreign affairs the president could use the office's inherent executive power to take actions that were authorized neither by Congress nor by a specific presidential foreign policy power in the Constitution.

Neutrality Proclamation of 1793

Washington set the precedent for unilateral presidential action by keeping the United States neutral in the war that broke out between France and Great Britain in 1793. Although the treaty of alliance with France signed in 1778 was still in effect, and most Americans favored the French, Washington was anxious to avoid involving the United States in the conflict, fearing that it would disrupt the strengthening of the American economy and political institutions.

On April 22, 1793, he issued a proclamation which declared that the United States would be "friendly and impartial" toward the belligerents. The proclamation carefully avoided using the word "neutrality" in deference to Secretary of State Thomas Jefferson, who had opposed the proclamation. Among other objections, Jefferson was not convinced that the president's action was constitutional. Jefferson reasoned that since only the Congress could declare war, the president did not have the power to decide unilaterally that the nation would not fight a war.[5] Although the proclamation was unpopular with many Americans, Congress followed Washington's lead by passing the Neutrality Act of 1794, which endorsed the policy of neutrality already in effect. Washington had shown that the president's executive power could be used to make foreign policy rather than just execute congressional directives.

Hamilton-Madison Debate

Washington's action set off a famous debate between Alexander Hamilton and James Madison—then a member of the House of Representatives from Virginia—on the subject of presidential power. In a series of articles printed in the *Gazette of the United States,* a Federalist newspaper published in Philadelphia, Hamilton defended Washington's authority to issue the proclamation. Writing under the pseudonym "Pacificus," Hamilton argued that the "executive power" granted to the president by the Constitution empowers the president to conduct all facets of foreign policy that do not usurp the powers specifically granted to the Congress. Hamilton reasoned that the president's enumerated powers "ought therefore to be considered, as intended merely to specify the principal articles implied in the definition of executive power; leaving the rest to flow from the general grant of that power, interpreted in conformity with the other parts of the Constitution, and with the principles of free government." [6]

This expansive interpretation of presidential power alarmed the pro-French Democratic-Republicans led by Secretary of State Jefferson. Jefferson had reluctantly agreed to Washington's proclamation, but he wanted to prevent it from establishing a precedent that would greatly enlarge presidential power. Since Jefferson was a member of Washington's cabinet, he felt it would be improper for him publicly to refute Hamilton's article. He therefore urged Madison to respond to Hamilton. Jefferson wrote to Madison, "Nobody answers him and his doctrines are taken for confessed. For God's sake, my dear Sir, take up your pen, select the most striking heresies and cut him to pieces in face of the public." [7]

Writing as "Helvidius," Madison stated that Congress's authority to declare war and its role in the treaty-making process made it the branch of government properly entrusted to formulate foreign policy, including declarations of neutrality. He rejected Hamilton's broad interpretation of the president's executive powers by claiming that "the natural province of the executive magistrate is to execute laws, as that of the legislature is to make laws. All his acts, therefore, properly executive, must presuppose the existence of the laws to be executed." [8] Thus, according to

Supreme Court Cases Related to the President's Foreign Policy Powers

Ware v. Hylton, 3 Dall. 199 (1796). The Court ruled 4-0 that treaties made by the United States overrode any conflicting state laws. The 1783 Treaty of Paris with Britain, which ended the American Revolution, provided that neither Britain nor the United States would block the efforts of the other nation's citizens to secure repayment of debts in the other country. This provision rendered invalid a Virginia law allowing debts owed by Virginians to British creditors to be "paid off" through payments to the state.

Foster v. Neilson, 2 Pet. 253 (1829). By a 5-0 vote, the Court refused to rule on a boundary dispute involving territory east of the Mississippi River claimed by both the United States and Spain. Chief Justice John Marshall described the matter as a "political question," which it was not the business of the judiciary to resolve.

Holmes v. Jennison, 14 Pet. 540 (1840). A fugitive from Canada, detained in Vermont, sought release through a petition for a writ of *habeas corpus*. After the state supreme court denied his petition, he asked the Supreme Court to review that action. The Court dismissed the case for lack of jurisdiction, but Chief Justice Roger B. Taney declared in his own opinion that states were forbidden by the Constitution to take any independent role in foreign affairs, and thus state governors could not surrender a fugitive within their jurisdiction to a foreign country who sought the fugitive's return.

The Prize Cases, 2 Black 635 (1863). These cases involved the capture of four ships seized while trying to run the Union blockade of Confederate ports, which Lincoln instituted in April 1861 and Congress sanctioned in July. By a 5-4 vote, the Court sustained the president's power to proclaim the blockade without a congressional declaration of war. A state of war already existed, the majority said, and the president was obligated "to meet it in the shape it presented itself, without waiting for Congress to baptize it with a name. . . ."

Geofroy v. Riggs, 133 U.S. 258 (1890). The Court ruled 9-0 that it is within the scope of the treaty power of the United States to regulate the inheritance by aliens of land and other property in the United States. The Court declared that the treaty power was unlimited except by the Constitution.

Missouri v. Holland, 252 U.S. 416 (1920). After lower courts ruled an act of Congress protecting migratory birds an unconstitutional invasion of powers reserved to the states, the U.S. government negotiated a treaty with Canada for the protection of the birds. After the Senate approved it, Congress again enacted protective legislation to fulfill the terms of the treaty. The Court sustained this second act by a 7-2 vote. It ruled that in order to implement a treaty, Congress may enact legislation that without a treaty might be an unconstitutional invasion of state sovereignty.

United States v. Curtiss-Wright Export Corp., 299 U.S. 304 (1936). By a 7-1 vote the Court upheld an act of Congress authorizing presidents, at their discretion, to embargo arms shipments to foreign belligerents in a South American war. Justice George Sutherland described the power of the president in foreign affairs as "plenary and exclusive" and called the president "the sole organ of the federal government in . . . international relations."

United States v. Belmont, 310 U.S. 324 (1936). In the executive agreements that established diplomatic relations between the Soviet Union and the United States in 1933, the two nations had agreed that Soviet assets in the United States would be used to pay the claims of U.S. citizens for property seized in the Soviet Union at the time of the Russian revolution. When U.S. government officials tried to recover funds from the accounts of Russian nationals in New York banks, the state maintained that its laws prohibited the action. The Supreme Court, however, ruled that the executive agreements upon which the action was based constituted an international compact that, like a treaty, superseded conflicting state laws.

Goldwater v. Carter, 444 U.S. 996 (1980). In December 1978, President Jimmy Carter announced that the United States would terminate the 1945 Mutual Defense Treaty with the Republic of China (Taiwan) as part of the process of establishing diplomatic relations with communist China. Sen. Barry Goldwater (R-Ariz.) brought a suit to stop the action, maintaining that treaty termination, like treaty ratification, required the prior approval of the Senate. The Court tacitly sided with the president by dismissing the case as a political question outside the realm of judicial review.

Madison, the president's role in foreign affairs was restricted to executing the laws, treaties, and declarations of war made by Congress and performing those duties specifically enumerated in the Constitution.

Over time Hamilton's conception of presidential power has triumphed. Presidents have almost always prevailed when the Constitution is silent on foreign affairs. Indeed,

many presidents have behaved as if they had a general, comprehensive power to conduct foreign affairs, while Congress could only participate if it found an opportunity to use one of its specific powers. Congress has enjoyed short periods of ascendancy, but even during these periods, it has usually exercised its influence by reacting to presidential initiatives.

Judicial Endorsement of Presidential Power

Although the Supreme Court has preferred not to rule on disputes between the executive and legislative branches that involve international affairs, when the Court has acted, it has tended to support the president's claims to power. The most important and often cited Supreme Court decision dealing with the president's foreign affairs powers is *United States v. Curtiss-Wright Export Corporation,* delivered in 1936.

In 1934 Congress passed a joint resolution empowering the president to embargo shipments of arms to warring nations. When President Franklin D. Roosevelt imposed an embargo on Bolivia under the resolution, the Curtiss-Wright Export Corporation was prohibited from shipping aircraft armaments to that country. The corporation conspired to send Bolivia arms in spite of the embargo, but its activities were discovered. In court Curtiss-Wright's lawyers argued that Congress's delegation of power to the president was unconstitutional.

With only one dissenting vote, the Supreme Court held that while Congress could not delegate its law-making authority over internal affairs, it could do so with respect to foreign affairs. Justice George Sutherland, delivering the opinion of the Court, explained:

> We are here dealing not alone with an authority vested in the President by an exertion of legislative power, but with such an authority plus the very delicate, plenary, and exclusive power of the president as the sole organ of the federal government in the field of international relations—a power which does not require as a basis for its exercise an act of Congress.... It is quite apparent that if, in the maintenance of our international relations, embarrassment—perhaps serious embarrassment—is to be avoided and success for our aims achieved, congressional legislation which is to be made effective through negotiation and inquiry in the international field must often accord to the President a degree of discretion and freedom from statutory restriction which would not be admissible were domestic affairs alone involved.[9]

U.S. v. Curtiss-Wright was a landmark decision because, as historian Arthur M. Schlesinger, Jr., observed, "the Court thus did in foreign policy what it had been reluctant to do in domestic policy: it affirmed the existence of an inherent, independent and superior presidential power, not derived from the Constitution and not requiring legislation as the basis for its exercise." [10] Sutherland's statements supporting vast presidential foreign affairs powers were contained in the decision's dicta (legal observations not essential to the main issues of the case). Nevertheless, they continue to exercise great influence over conceptions of presidential power in foreign relations.

Congressional Cooperation and Conflict

In spite of the president's advantages in the conduct of foreign policy, the political customs and precedents that favored presidential leadership in foreign affairs, and judicial interpretations that supported the president's claims to authority, presidents have not always controlled U.S. foreign policy. At times Congress has refused to follow the president's leadership and has attempted to legislate its own policy course. Even when presidents have dominated foreign policy, Congress has demonstrated that no chief executive can sustain a foreign policy program for long without its support. Cooperation between the two branches, therefore, has been crucial to establishing effective foreign policies.

Early Cooperation

Congressional majorities often were willing to cooperate with early presidents on foreign affairs matters. Congress passed the Neutrality Act of 1794 a year after President Washington had declared American neutrality in the war between Britain and France, even though many members of Congress had opposed the original proclamation. In 1803, the Senate followed Jefferson's lead by ratifying the treaty with France that transferred the Louisiana Territory into U.S. control.

In 1816 a report by the Senate Foreign Relations Committee demonstrated Congress's recognition of the advantages of presidential leadership in foreign affairs:

> The President is the Constitutional representative of the United States with regard to foreign nations. He manages our concern with foreign nations and must necessarily be most competent to determine when, how, and upon what subject negotiations may be urged with the greatest prospect of success. For his conduct he is responsible to the Constitution. The committee considers this responsibility the surest pledge for the faithful discharge of his duties. They think the interference of the Senate in the direction of foreign negotiations [is] calculated to diminish that responsibility and thereby to impair the best security for the national safety. The nature of transactions with foreign nations, moreover, requires caution and unity of design, and their success frequently depends on secrecy and dispatch.[11]

Nineteenth Century

Presidents during much of the last two-thirds of the nineteenth century exerted less foreign policy leadership than had earlier presidents. The resolution of the slavery question, the development of the American West, and the Reconstruction of the South following the Civil War were the most important political issues of the period. Consequently, presidents spent most of their time on domestic policy. In addition, foreign trade and the acquisition of territory from foreign governments, two matters in which Congress has a large role, were often the primary foreign relations issues. Also, presidents were rarely able to carry out major foreign policy initiatives during this time because they were seldom in office long enough to establish their own foreign policy strategy. From the end of Andrew Jackson's administration in 1837 to the turn of the century, only Ulysses S. Grant served two consecutive four-year terms, and seven presidents served less than one four-year term. Four of these seven died in office, and three of the succeeding vice presidents were not reelected as president.

Congressional power was at its peak during Reconstruction. The executive branch suffered a number of serious setbacks, including the impeachment and near removal of President Andrew Johnson from office and the passage of the Tenure of Office Act in 1867, which gave the

Senate the power to veto a president's decision to remove an appointee from office.[12] The Spanish-American War in 1898 marked a major turn in foreign policy, which Congress strongly supported. Under President William McKinley, the country dropped its traditional policy of nonintervention, went to war to rid Cuba of Spanish rule, and emerged from the conflict with overseas outposts as far distant as the Philippines in the western Pacific.

Theodore Roosevelt's Administration

Following the Spanish-American War presidents expanded their control over foreign affairs. In 1901 McKinley was assassinated, and his vice president, Theodore Roosevelt, succeeded him as president. For the next seven and a half years, Roosevelt frequently ignored or circumvented Congress while using his executive prerogatives aggressively to pursue his perception of U.S. interests abroad. In 1903 he used U.S. naval power to back a small Panamanian revolt against Colombian rule; recognized the state of Panama, which emerged from the revolution; and quickly negotiated a treaty with the new Panamanian government giving the United States the right to dig the Panama Canal. In 1905, Roosevelt implemented an executive agreement with Santo Domingo (now the Dominican Republic) that gave the United States control of that nation's customs in order to guarantee its European debts, even though Congress would not approve the pact. The same year, Roosevelt personally directed mediation efforts between Russia and

Japan without consulting Congress. His efforts led to the Portsmouth Conference in New Hampshire, which ended the Russo-Japanese War and won him the Nobel Peace Prize. In 1907 Roosevelt decided to send the U.S. fleet on a world cruise, primarily to impress the Japanese with U.S. naval strength. Congress threatened to deny funding for the mission but relented when Roosevelt declared he had sufficient funds to send the navy to the Pacific—and Congress would be responsible for funding its return.[13]

Roosevelt freely admitted that he had avoided involving Congress in major foreign policy actions. In 1909, while still in office, he wrote: "The biggest matters, such as the Portsmouth peace, the acquisition of Panama, and sending the fleet around the world, I managed without consultation with anyone; for when a matter is of capital importance, it is well to have it handled by one man only." [14]

Versailles to World War II

Presidential disregard for Congress's role in foreign policy reached its height in 1919. Woodrow Wilson traveled to Versailles, France, to participate personally in the negotiation of a peace treaty to end World War I. Under strong pressure from Wilson, the conference agreed to include provisions in the treaty establishing a League of Nations. The president brought the treaty back to the United States and began a vigorous national campaign for Senate approval.

During the war, Congress had cooperated with Wilson by granting him unprecedented war powers. Once the

Theodore Roosevelt, middle, won the Nobel Peace Prize for his effort in ending the war between Russia and Japan. In 1905, he met with delegates from both sides in Portsmouth, New Hampshire.

threat had passed, however, the Senate was ready to reassert legislative influence over foreign policy. Many senators resented Wilson's refusal to involve them in the Versailles negotiations or even to inform them of U.S. negotiating positions. In 1919 and 1920, the Senate refused to approve the treaty, thus keeping the country out of the League of Nations.

The demise of the Versailles treaty signaled a new period of congressional activism in foreign policy. During the next two decades Congress limited U.S. involvement overseas, with little resistance from the executive branch. When war threatened in Asia and Europe in the second half of the 1930s, Congress, reflecting the isolationism of the public, tried to legislate neutrality.[15] But when war finally began, Franklin Roosevelt, like presidents before him in times of crisis, acquired enormous powers through his own assertiveness and Congress's grants of authority, which were motivated by the need for national unity.

Postwar Presidential Power

After World War II ended, however, presidential authority in foreign affairs continued to grow. The period brought many new responsibilities and dangers that seemed to require a chief executive capable of quick, decisive action. The United States had emerged from the war as the most powerful nation on earth and the leader of the non-Communist world. The fear of Communist expansion brought the whole globe into the sphere of U.S. interest. The United States had swung from isolationism in the late 1930s to unprecedented international involvement in the late 1940s, aligning itself with virtually any willing country and sending billions of dollars in economic and military aid overseas.

Dangers to the security of the United States grew along with its commitments. The advancement of missile technology and Soviet development of the atomic bomb in 1949 and the hydrogen bomb in 1953 made a devastating attack on the American homeland a possibility. The fall of China to Communist forces in 1949 reinforced the belief of many Americans that the United States had to be ready to use troops if necessary to stop Communist expansion.

This complex and hostile international environment contributed to a consensus for strong presidential leadership in foreign policy. Congress recognized that only the executive branch had the means to collect and analyze the huge amount of information on foreign policy issues and to act with the speed that seemed necessary to manage U.S. global commitments. In addition, the presidential role of keeper of the nuclear switch magnified the commander in chief's stature as guardian of the free world, thereby enhancing presidential authority in other areas of defense and foreign policy.

Congress repeatedly passed resolutions supporting presidential policy and authorizing the president to use force if necessary to deal with particular international problems. In 1955, Congress authorized the president to use force to defend Formosa (Nationalist China) and the Pescadores Islands if they were attacked by Communist China. An even broader resolution was passed in 1957 that supported the "Eisenhower Doctrine," which announced the intention of the United States to defend Middle Eastern countries "against aggression from any country controlled by international communism." The House and Senate passed resolutions in 1962 declaring their support for any presidential action, including the use of force, that was necessary to defend the rights of the United States in Berlin. The same year Congress adopted similar resolutions pertaining to the Cuban missile crisis.

In August 1964 Congress passed the sweeping Tonkin Gulf resolution with only 2 senators out of 535 members of Congress in opposition. The resolution had been proposed by the Johnson administration in response to cloudy evidence of North Vietnamese torpedo boat attacks on U.S. vessels off the coast of Vietnam.[16] It authorized the president to take "all necessary measures to repel any armed attacks against the forces of the United States and to prevent further aggression." At least two months before the incident, Johnson's National Security Council staff had prepared a draft of a similar resolution supporting presidential freedom to act in Vietnam.[17] Since Johnson never asked Congress for a declaration of war, he used the Tonkin Gulf resolution in subsequent years as evidence of congressional support for his expansion of U.S. involvement in the conflict in Vietnam.

Congressional Rebellion

By the late 1960s, however, Congress began to rebel against what many members considered the aggrandizement of presidential foreign policy power. They objected to the growing tendency of presidents to avoid including Congress in foreign and defense policy issues. Following the Tonkin Gulf resolution, for example, President Johnson never sought congressional approval for any policy or strategy decision about the Vietnam War, except the appropriations bills necessary to continue U.S. military involvement in Southeast Asia. Members of Congress were also unhappy with the increasing use of executive agreements—pacts concluded between the president and other governments that had the force of law but were not subject to congressional approval—to make international commitments.

The Congress was partly responsible for the expansion of executive power between 1945 and 1969. In the interests of national unity and anti-Communism, the legislature had consented to and even encouraged presidential initiative in foreign affairs. Congress became accustomed to following whatever policy direction the president chose and failed to recognize that by granting the president discretion to handle specific foreign affairs problems it enlarged presidential interpretations of executive power.[18] In June 1969, by an overwhelming 70-16 vote, the Senate adopted a "national commitments" resolution, which declared the sense of the Senate that a national commitment by the United States results "only from affirmative action taken by the executive and legislative branches of the United States government by means of a treaty, statute, or concurrent resolution of both houses of Congress specifically providing for such a commitment." In 1969 and 1970, Congress repeatedly attempted to terminate funds for U.S. military activities in Indochina. During that period, Congress also used its investigative powers to probe the extent of U.S. commitments abroad.

In the early 1970s, the revelations of a secret Defense Department study of the decision-making process surrounding the Vietnam War, known as the *Pentagon Papers*, the unwillingness of presidents Johnson and Nixon to include Congress in foreign policy decisions, and the Watergate scandal spurred movements in Congress to recapture foreign affairs power lost to the executive branch. In

1972, Congress passed the Case Act, which established more rigorous requirements for the reporting of international agreements to Congress by the executive branch. The following year Congress passed the War Powers Act over President Nixon's veto. The measure set a sixty-day limit on any presidential commitment of U.S. troops to hostilities abroad, or to situations where hostilities might be imminent, without specific congressional authorization.

In 1974, Congress passed a major trade reform bill only after approving the Jackson-Vanik amendment, which linked trade concessions for Communist countries to their emigration policies. The same year Congress imposed a ban on military aid and arms shipments to Turkey. In 1978, the Senate conducted a long and contentious debate on the Panama Canal treaties and approved them only after adding numerous amendments. During this period Congress also conducted investigations of the intelligence community and began to take a more active interest in the specifics of the Defense Department's budget.

Congressional activism in foreign affairs has continued into the 1980s and appears to have become a permanent feature of U.S. foreign policy. Although Congress often supported President Reagan's actions, many of his foreign policies, such as military assistance to the Nicaraguan resistance and arms sales to moderate Arab nations, were accompanied by tough and sometimes unsuccessful battles for congressional approval. Congress also has routinely submitted alternative plans for weapons acquisition, arms control, and policies on regional problems. In addition, it has passed nonbinding resolutions stating its concerns on a variety of foreign policy issues.

Still, Congress has not superseded the contemporary president's role as formulator, initiator, and negotiator of U.S. foreign policy. Foreign policy remains an area of presidential dominance. Because of Congress's increased willingness and ability to assert itself in foreign affairs, however, congressional support has become more important to the success of a president's foreign policies.

Power of Communication

The Constitution's separation of powers between independent branches created a question that was unique to the United States: Who had the power to receive communications from foreign countries and to speak for the nation? Under the Articles of Confederation, these responsibilities belonged to Congress. The presidency created by the Constitution, however, had strong claims to the communication power. Negotiating treaties and sending and receiving ambassadors, two communicative powers, were specifically assigned to the president. Perhaps more important, communications was a function more suited to an office occupied by a single person with executive power than a large deliberative body composed of many individuals.

Washington was anxious to establish the presidency as the only organ of government empowered to communicate officially with foreign governments. He recognized that if both the president and Congress presumed to speak for the nation, diplomacy would be impossible, and foreign governments might try to exploit the confusion. During the first year of his administration, Washington received a letter from King Louis XVI of France notifying "the President and Members of the General Congress of the United States" that Louis's son had died. Washington told Con-

gress that he had received the letter and that he would send a reply to France. The president informed the king that "by the change which has taken place in the national government of the United States, the honor of receiving and answering your Majesty's letter of the 7th of June to 'the President and Members of Congress' has devolved upon me." [19]

In 1793 Washington's secretary of state, Thomas Jefferson, echoed this assertion when he explained to the French ambassador, Edmond Genêt, that the president is "the only channel of communication between this country and foreign nations, it is from him alone that foreign nations or their agents are to learn what is or has been the will of the nation; and whatever he communicates as such, they have the right, and are bound to consider, as the expression of the nation." [20]

Washington's conception of the president's role as national communicator was accepted without serious challenge. In 1799 John Marshall reaffirmed the president's position as the instrument of communication with foreign governments when as a member of the House of Representatives he declared, "The President is the sole organ of the nation in its external relations, and its sole representative with foreign nations." [21] The same year Congress passed the Logan Act, which prohibited any person other than presidents or their agents from communicating with another country with the intention of affecting its policy toward an issue of contention with the United States. [22] The act has never been enforced against a member of Congress, although it remains in the United States Code. Informal discussions with foreign leaders by members of Congress have become accepted practices, but presumably the Logan Act could be invoked if a senator or representative attempted to usurp the president's power to communicate officially with foreign nations. [23]

Foreign Policy Declarations

The president's authority to communicate with other nations is not merely a ceremonial power. From George Washington to the present, presidents have found they can make foreign policy simply by making a statement. Presidents have used their communications power to make commitments, formalize decisions, or institutionalize broad policy goals.

The president's ability to make foreign policy through declarations derives from the president's position as "the sole representative with foreign nations." Only the president can speak for the United States. Consequently, Congress often is forced to choose between supporting a presidential commitment or decision it had no part in making or undermining that commitment or decision, which the world has accepted as U.S. policy. How a president expresses U.S. interests and intentions, therefore, can shape U.S. foreign policy. Kennedy's famous speech at the Berlin Wall in 1963, for example, encouraged the people of Berlin to expect U.S. protection, thereby committing the United States to its defense. Theodore Roosevelt explained the connection between communication and policy:

> The president carries on the correspondence through the State Department with all foreign countries. He is bound in such correspondence to discuss the proper construction of treaties. He must formulate the foreign policies of our government. He must state our attitude upon questions constantly arising. While strictly he may not bind our

government as a treaty would bind it, to a definition of its rights, still in future discussions foreign secretaries of other countries are wont to look for support of their contentions to the declarations and admissions of our secretaries of state in other controversies as in a sense binding upon us. There is thus much practical framing of our foreign policies in the executive conduct of our foreign relations.[24]

Presidential Doctrines

Presidents have not only made specific commitments through statements and declarations, they have also outlined broad foreign policy themes and strategies that they intended to pursue. The most famous and durable policy statement by a president has been the Monroe Doctrine. In 1823 President Monroe announced during his annual message to Congress that the United States would resist any attempt by a European power to interfere in the affairs of a Western Hemisphere country that was not already a European colony. Monroe did not consult Congress before his announcement, and some of its members believed the president had overstepped his authority. Henry Clay proposed a joint resolution supporting the president's policy, but it never was acted upon. Not until 1899 did the Monroe Doctrine receive a congressional endorsement.[25]

Theodore Roosevelt built upon the Monroe Doctrine in 1904 when he announced what came to be known as the Roosevelt Corollary in his annual message to Congress. Roosevelt claimed for the United States the right to act as the Western Hemisphere's policeman if "chronic wrongdoing or impotence" in a country required U.S. intervention.

Statements of broad foreign policy strategy, or "doctrines," are associated with the administrations of many contemporary presidents. The Truman Doctrine stated that "it must be the policy of the United States to support free peoples who are resisting attempted subjugation by armed minorities or outside pressures."[26] The Eisenhower Doctrine, which was supported by a joint resolution, claimed for the United States the right to intervene militarily in the Middle East to protect legitimate governments from attacks by Communist forces. The Nixon Doctrine (also known as the Guam Doctrine) proposed to continue giving allies military and economic aid while encouraging them to reduce their reliance on U.S. troops. The Carter Doctrine declared the Persian Gulf area to be a vital U.S. interest and warned that the United States would use force to prevent any attempt by an outside power to gain control of it. The Reagan Doctrine declared the Reagan administration's intention to support anti-Communist insurgencies around the world. These broad foreign policy declarations are not always accepted by Congress and do not always last beyond the administration that announces them. Yet, only the president's policy declarations have a chance to become accepted as national policy.

The Treaty Power

The authors of the Constitution used only one clause to explain how treaties were to be made. Article II, section 2, clause 2, declares that the president "shall have the Power, by and with the Advice and Consent of the Senate, to make Treaties, provided two-thirds of the Senators present con-

John F. Kennedy Library

A large crowd gathers as John F. Kennedy delivers his famous "Ich bin ein Berliner" speech at the Berlin Wall in 1963.

cur. . . ." This concise statement sets up a classic division of power between the legislative and executive branches. The primary responsibility for conducting treaty negotiations is a presidential duty but the president cannot conclude a treaty without first obtaining the consent of the Senate and probably will be deterred from negotiating a treaty that the Senate is unlikely to approve. The Constitution, therefore, ensures that no formal treaty can be concluded without a strong interbranch consensus.

Nevertheless, the executive branch has established itself as the dominant branch in treaty making. As the sole organ of communication with foreign countries, commander in chief, and head of the foreign policy bureaucracy, presidents have been equipped with the means necessary to control most phases of the treaty-making process. The president decides what treaties to negotiate, chooses the negotiators, develops the negotiating strategy, and submits completed draft treaties to the Senate for approval. The president, not the Senate as commonly believed, even has the final power of ratification. Once the Senate has approved a treaty, it does not become law until the president ratifies it. If the president decides to ratify a treaty the Senate has approved, an exchange of ratifications occurs between the signatories. Then the treaty is promulgated—that is, officially proclaimed to be law—by the president. At any time the president may stop the treaty-making process, and after a treaty is ratified, the president has the authority to terminate it without Senate consent. Thus, the president has the power of initiative over a treaty from its conception to its ratification and beyond.[27]

Creation of the Treaty Power

In the eighteenth century, treaties were considered to be the primary tool of foreign policy, and the authors of the

Constitution deliberated extensively on how treaties should be made. Under the Articles of Confederation, the treaty power was completely entrusted to Congress. It selected negotiators, wrote and revised their orders, and made the final decision whether a treaty would be accepted or rejected. At the Constitutional Convention, delegates initially assumed that this congressional power would be given to the legislative body created by the new Constitution. After much debate and committee work, however, the convention adopted a proposal on September 8, 1787, to divide the treaty-making power between the executive and legislative branches.

By giving the president the power to make treaties "by and with the advice and consent of the Senate," the authors of the Constitution bolstered the prestige of the office of president, making it possible for future chief executives and their representatives to have the same authority as other world leaders in negotiating treaties. The convention also recognized that the president could conduct treaty negotiations with more speed and secrecy than Congress. John Jay emphasized this consideration in *The Federalist Papers:*

> It seldom happens in the negotiation of treaties, of whatever nature, but that perfect secrecy and immediate dispatch are sometimes requisite. There may be cases where the most useful intelligence may be obtained, if the persons possessing it can be relieved from apprehensions of discovery. Those apprehensions will operate on those persons whether they are actuated by mercenary or friendly motives; and there doubtless are many of both descriptions who would rely on the secrecy of the president, but who would not confide in that of the Senate, and still less in that of a large popular assembly.[28]

The delegates were not willing, however, to place too much treaty-making authority in the hands of the executive. Consequently, they required that two-thirds of the senators voting on a treaty be in favor of it before it could be ratified. The Founders did not unanimously support the two-thirds percentage, but this number, as well as the exclusion of the House of Representatives from the formal treaty approval process, survived several late attempts to change it.

Alexander Hamilton and John Jay defended the exclusion of the House from the treaty-making process in *The Federalist Papers.* Using similar arguments, they contended that the legislative role in treaty making should be limited to the Senate because decisions on treaties would thus be placed in the hands of persons chosen by the "select assemblies" of the states instead of by the rank and file, because the longer and overlapping Senate terms would provide relatively greater continuity, because the smaller size of the Senate would aid "secrecy and dispatch," and because agreement among the president, the Senate, and the House would be more difficult to obtain.[29]

One weakness of the Articles of Confederation that the Constitutional Convention was determined to correct was its dependence on the states to implement treaties. Congress had the power to make treaties with other countries, but it could not force the states to recognize treaty provisions as law. As a result, several states had violated certain articles of the Peace Treaty of 1783 with Great Britain. The convention's answer to this problem was Article VI, clause 2, of the Constitution, which states that

> all Treaties made, or which shall be made, under the Authority of the United States, shall be the supreme Law of the Land; and the Judges in every State shall be bound thereby, any Thing in the Constitution or Laws of any State to the Contrary notwithstanding.

Chief Justice John Marshall interpreted this clause in his opinion on *Foster v. Neilson* in 1829. He confirmed that any treaty or portion of a treaty that did not require legislation to fulfill its provisions was binding on the states and had equal force to federal law. Therefore, although Congress may have to enact legislation to carry out acts stipulated by a treaty, any self-executing treaty or part of a treaty automatically attains the status of a law, enforceable by the courts. Provisions of various treaties periodically have been the target of legal challenges, but the Supreme Court has never declared a treaty or provision of a treaty made by the United States to be unconstitutional.[30]

Presidential Primacy in Treaty Negotiations

The ambiguity of the language in the Constitution that describes the treaty-making power created inevitable questions about how treaties would be made. That both the president and the Senate had a role in treaty making was clear, but the form of the Senate's advice on treaty matters and its influence over negotiations had to be worked out.

President Washington's initial interpretation of the treaty-making clause was that "advice" meant he was to seek Senate opinions in person before his representatives began negotiations. On August 21, 1789, Washington and his secretary of war, Henry Knox, questioned the Senate in its chambers about a treaty to be negotiated with the Creek Indians. After some debate, the Senate decided to postpone its response to Washington's questions until the following week so it could discuss the negotiations further. Washington, who had expected an immediate reply, returned on Monday, August 24, and received answers to his questions, but he was apparently angered by the Senate's indecisiveness and pessimistic that he could rely on that body for timely consultations on treaty matters. He never again attempted to use it as an executive council before treaty negotiations.[31]

It is interesting to speculate whether the history of U.S. foreign policy making would have been different had the Senate given Washington satisfactory answers when he came to consult on the treaty with the Creek Indians. The Senate's role in treaty negotiations would likely have been enhanced had Washington established a presidential precedent of consulting with that body in person. Subsequent presidents, however, agreed with Washington that the advice and consent of the Senate was best obtained from a distance. Several twentieth-century presidents, including Wilson and Truman, went to the Senate to propose or lobby for a treaty, but no president has ever returned to the Senate chamber to seek direct advice on treaty matters.

Washington's handling of the important Jay Treaty of 1794, which avoided war with Great Britain, demonstrated that he had abandoned his initial interpretation of the Constitution's treaty-making clause. During the early years of his presidency, Washington had conscientiously written to the Senate for advice on treaty matters before and during negotiations. He also had routinely submitted the negotiator's instructions to the Senate and kept that body informed of the progress of talks. In preparation for the Jay Treaty negotiations, however, Washington only submitted the appointment of his negotiator, Chief Justice John Jay, to the Senate for approval. He withheld from the Senate Jay's instructions about the sensitive negotiations, and the negotiations were held in London without Senate involvement.

Rather than challenging the president's power to make a treaty independently of the Senate, that body responded by amending the completed Jay Treaty in a manner similar to the method by which it amended legislation. Washington accepted the Senate's authority to do this, and after initial protests, the British ratified the amended treaty. The Jay Treaty established a process of treaty making that subsequent administrations and Senates would emulate. As Corwin observed, "The Senate's function as an executive council was from the very beginning put, and largely by its own election, on the way to absorption into its more usual function as a legislative chamber, and subsequent developments soon placed its decision in this respect beyond all possibility of recall." [32]

Washington's actions established the power of the executive branch to make treaties on its own before submitting them for Senate approval. Today, the right of either house of Congress to offer advice is not questioned, but the advice of the legislative branch is merely persuasive, not compelling. In its landmark decision in the 1936 *Curtiss-Wright* case, the Supreme Court ruled: "The president . . . alone negotiates. Into the field of negotiation the Senate cannot intrude, and Congress itself is powerless to invade it." [33]

The degree of congressional participation in negotiations has become entirely a matter of presidential preference. When presidents have cooperated closely with the Senate in the negotiation of a treaty, they usually have been motivated by their recognition that Senate involvement would increase the chances for approval. Thus, the sporadic influence the Senate has retained in treaty negotiations is largely derived from its legislative veto over treaties, rather than from the constitutional provision that the president should consider the Senate's advice when making treaties.

The Treaty-making Process

The first step in making a treaty is negotiating with a foreign power. This stage is controlled by the president and presidential advisers and representatives. During or before this phase Congress may offer advice to the president or express its views on the negotiations individually or collectively. One or both houses of Congress may choose to pass a resolution containing advice on treaty matters. If Congress strongly opposes a treaty under negotiation, a resolution communicating its disapproval may cause the president to change negotiating strategies or abandon a treaty altogether. A supportive resolution, however, may contribute to the executive branch's enthusiasm for a particular treaty. In 1948, for example, the Senate's Vandenberg Resolution, which preceded the development of NATO and other alliance systems, advised the president to negotiate regional security agreements. [34] Regardless of congressional protests or encouragement, the president and representatives of the president cannot be constrained from initiating and conducting treaty negotiations with another country.

Although the executive branch has the power to negotiate a treaty without Congress, many presidents have found that involving individual senators in the negotiating process can be a useful political tool. Such involvement can take several forms. During most treaty negotiations influential senators are at least asked for their opinions on the proceedings, but a president may also ask senators to help select the negotiating team, observe the negotiations, follow the progress of the talks through briefings, or even be negotiators. [35] Up to the end of Madison's administration in 1817, the names of treaty negotiators were referred to the Senate for confirmation. The Senate repeatedly protested subsequent presidents' neglect of that practice, but the Senate never was able to establish firmly its right to confirm negotiators. Presidents seem to have abandoned the practice because of the need for secrecy in employing special agents, whose appointments were recognized as the right of the executive.

On various occasions since Madison's administration, however, presidents have sought Senate confirmation of treaty negotiators. James K. Polk submitted the names of his appointees to negotiate a treaty with Mexico. Grant sought Senate confirmation for the commissioners who negotiated the Treaty of Washington, which settled American claims against Great Britain, which had occasionally violated its neutrality during the Civil War by aiding the Confederacy. Warren G. Harding submitted the names of his appointees to the World War Foreign Debt Commission in 1922, but this submission was required by a provision of the act that created the commission. [36]

The practice of sending the instructions of treaty negotiators to the Senate for review, which Washington had done early in his presidency, proved to be even more temporary than the custom of senatorial confirmation of the negotiators. After Washington's administration, no president asked the Senate to consider the terms of a treaty not yet agreed upon, until Polk submitted the skeleton of a treaty ending the war with Mexico in 1846. Preliminary drafts of treaties were sent to the Senate in a few instances by four other presidents—James Buchanan, Lincoln, Johnson, and Grant. In 1919, the Senate requested a copy of the proposed Treaty of Versailles as presented to the representatives of Germany. The secretary of state replied: "The president feels it would not be in the public interest to communicate to the Senate a text that is provisional and not definite, and finds no precedent for such a procedure." [37]

Wilson's refusal to inform the Senate about the Versailles treaty negotiations contributed to that body's rejection of the treaty. Several of Wilson's successors learned from his mistake and sought to include the Senate at an early stage in controversial treaty negotiations. While World War II was still being fought, Franklin Roosevelt established the Joint Advisory Committee on Postwar Foreign Policy to provide a forum where members of Congress and the executive branch could discuss the composition of an international peace organization. This committee, along with the administration's private consultations with Senate leaders, helped create bipartisan support for the United Nations. [38] When the negotiations on the United Nations Treaty began in 1945, Truman included senators from both parties in the U.S. delegation. The Carter administration also tried to limit Senate objections to the SALT II (Strategic Arms Limitation Talks) treaty it hoped to negotiate with the Soviet Union by encouraging senatorial participation in the treaty-making process. Selected senators were allowed to observe the negotiations, and the administration consulted closely with Senate leaders while the negotiations were in progress. During these consultations senators voiced suggestions and concerns that prompted Carter to instruct his negotiators to modify their position on several issues.[39]

Once U.S. negotiators have agreed upon the terms of a treaty with a foreign government, the president must decide whether to submit the draft to the Senate for consideration. If it appears that Senate opposition to a treaty will make approval unlikely, the president may decide to withdraw the treaty to avoid a political defeat. Also, international events may change the president's mind about the desirability of ratifying a treaty. President Carter came to this conclusion after the Soviet Union invaded Afghanistan in December 1979. He withdrew the SALT II treaty from Senate consideration to protest the Soviet presence in Afghanistan, even though before the invasion he had pressed the Senate to approve the treaty.

If the president does decide to submit a treaty to the Senate for consideration, the Constitution requires that a two-thirds majority of senators voting be in favor of the treaty for it to be approved.

The Senate is not compelled by the Constitution either to approve or to reject a treaty as it has been negotiated by the executive branch. It may attach amendments to a treaty that require the president to renegotiate its terms with the other signatories before the Senate grants its approval. In 1978 Congress added a number of conditions and reservations to the treaty that provided for the transfer of the Panama Canal to Panamanian control after the year 2000. The most notable of these amendments was

Library of Congress

During the eighteenth and nineteenth centuries, a precedent developed of presidents not traveling outside the United States while in office. Teddy Roosevelt became the first president to break this precedent when he visited Panama in 1906 to inspect the canal under construction.

written by Sen. Dennis DeConcini (D-Ariz.). It claimed for the United States the right to take whatever steps were necessary, including military force, to open the canal if its operations ceased.[40] The Panamanian government agreed to accept the Senate amendments without renegotiation. Such amendments, however, often make agreement between the United States and its negotiating partner impossible.

U.S. presidents have accepted without serious challenge the Senate's power to force renegotiation of parts of a treaty. In effect, when the Senate gives its consent on condition that its amendments are accepted by the negotiating partner of the United States, it is rejecting the treaty while outlining a revision of the treaty to which it grants its consent in advance.[41] Presidents in turn may decide not to renegotiate if they believe the senatorial amendments make the treaty undesirable.

The Senate also has the power to add nonbinding written reservations to a treaty before approving it. This option can be used when the Senate agrees to the basic terms of a treaty but believes it must state its interpretation of the document to dispel ambiguity and to influence the treaty's implementation. Nonbinding resolutions, however, can have a profound effect on the conclusion of a treaty if the foreign government involved disagrees with the resolutions or finds them insulting. Ratification of the 1976 Treaty of Friendship and Cooperation with Spain was delayed several months by Spanish objections to nonbinding Senate resolutions attached to the treaty. The issue was resolved by an agreement between Congress, the Ford administration, and the Spanish government to attach the resolutions to the U.S. instrument of ratification, the document outlining the U.S. understanding of the treaty, but to exclude them from the Spanish instrument of ratification and the treaty ratification document exchanged by the two countries.[42]

After the Senate approves a treaty and the president ratifies it, it may require legislation to fulfill its intent. Such treaties are referred to as "non-self-executing." For example, the Migratory Bird Treaty of 1916 between the United States and Canada pledged the two nations to make and implement laws to protect migratory birds. Therefore, complying with the terms of the treaty required subsequent legislative action by the Congress and the president.[43] Treaties that require the appropriation of funds or the enactment of criminal laws for their implementation would also be non-self-executing, since these tasks can only be accomplished through laws made by the Congress.[44] Consequently, non-self-executing treaties give Congress another chance to pass judgment upon them after ratification. Although Congress rarely has chosen to undermine a treaty by refusing to appropriate funds or enact implementing legislation, its right to do so is well established.[45]

Treaty Approval

Even though the executive branch often has ignored or minimized the Senate's advisory function, the Senate has approved without changes about 70 percent of the treaties submitted to it.

This apparent Senate acquiescence to the executive branch's will on treaty matters is not as striking as it seems. To avoid a political defeat, presidents often have withdrawn treaties from consideration that were in jeopardy of Senate rejection. Other treaties were neither approved nor

On September 7, 1977, President Jimmy Carter and Panamanian leader Brig. Gen. Omar Torrijos Herrera signed the treaty that transferred control of the Panama Canal to Panama after the year 2000. The Senate ratified the treaty the following spring.

rejected by the Senate, but instead left without action in political limbo. For example, the Genocide Treaty, which instructed signers to prevent and punish the crime of genocide, was approved by the Senate in 1986, almost thirty-seven years after Truman submitted it to that body. Many more pacts that could have taken the form of treaties were concluded as less formal executive agreements between the president and a foreign government to avoid the possibility of Senate rejection.

Nevertheless, the Senate seldom has been willing to disapprove of a completed draft treaty without serious cause. The high percentage of Senate approval can be attributed to several political factors. First, because presidents and executive branch officials are mindful that they will eventually need the Senate's approval, they usually take the Senate's concerns into account even when they do not closely consult with that body.

Second, senators, as well as their counterparts in the House, historically have been inclined to follow the president's lead in foreign affairs in the interest of projecting a united front abroad, unless they have serious objections to the administration's course of action. Members of Congress do not wish to be seen as saboteurs of presidential policy, especially when U.S. troops are engaged in hostilities overseas. Since the Vietnam War, however, the Congress has been more willing to challenge the president's leadership in foreign affairs.

Third, when a president concludes a draft treaty with another nation, in the eyes of the international community the United States has made a commitment. Even though the Senate is exercising a constitutionally granted power when it votes to reject a treaty, rejection usually causes both the United States and the president to lose some credibility with other nations. The Senate, therefore, must balance its reservations about a particular treaty against the damage rejection would inflict on international confidence in U.S. ability to make commitments.[46] Finally, the executive-legislative relationship is not purely adversarial. All presidents have their share of allies in the Senate who will work for approval of virtually any treaty the president

submits. Furthermore, senators of the president's party often will side with the president on a particular treaty for the sake of the party's welfare and unity even if they have reservations about the agreement. If the president's party happens to be in control of the Senate, obtaining approval for a treaty may require the support of fewer than half of the senators from the opposition party.

Although the Senate's approval record has been overwhelmingly favorable, there have been significant exceptions. The most famous rejection of a draft treaty by the Senate was its refusal in 1919 to approve the Treaty of Versailles, which ended World War I and established the League of Nations. Wilson campaigned vigorously for approval of the treaty after it had been negotiated, but his failure to include the Senate in the treaty-making process contributed to its defeat.

Proposed Changes in Approval Process

The method by which Congress approves treaties has been the target of much criticism. John Hay, secretary of state under McKinley and Roosevelt who fought several losing battles with the Senate over treaty approval, called the power of the Senate to veto treaties the "original mistake of the Constitution." [47] In particular, the constitutional requirement that two-thirds of the senators present must consent to a treaty before it can be ratified has been the subject of proposed changes. After the Senate refused to approve the Versailles treaty, proposals surfaced in both the executive and legislative branches to reduce the fraction of Senate members needed to approve a treaty. Most proposals advocated a simple majority; others suggested lowering the requirement from two-thirds to three-fifths of the senators voting.

None of the proposals has come close to being implemented, but if the requirement for a two-thirds majority were lowered, the effect would be significant. The president probably would be less inclined to substitute executive agreements for treaties on matters that should receive congressional review. Yet, the two-thirds vote requirement has ensured that important treaties requiring a sustained U.S. commitment—such as the treaty that established NATO—have been concluded with strong bipartisan support.[48]

Another periodic reform proposal has been the inclusion of the House of Representatives in the treaty-making process by requiring a majority vote of both houses of Congress before ratification. Madison and James Wilson argued unsuccessfully for this method of treaty approval at the Constitutional Convention in 1787. Several resolutions to make the House a partner in treaty making were introduced in Congress during the 1920s and 1940s, but they met with no more success than the proposals of Madison and Wilson.

A third reform that has been suggested in the twentieth century is to change the Senate's rules of procedure to prevent approval of a treaty from being blocked by inaction or a filibuster. The Senate could eliminate the possibility of a small minority of its members effectively defeating a treaty if it prohibited filibusters in treaty debates and required votes on draft treaties set before it by the president. This proposal would require only the Senate itself to adopt such rules.[49]

Termination of Treaties

Although Article VI, clause 2, of the Constitution declares that treaties are the "supreme Law of the Land," the federal government is not legally constrained from terminating a treaty through agreement with the other party, in response to the other party's violations of the treaty, or for any other reason. It is unclear, however, which branch has the authority to terminate a treaty. The Constitution provides no guidelines as to who determines that a treaty should be revoked and what sort of approval is needed from another branch. Consequently, both the president and Congress at various times have claimed the power to terminate treaties.[50]

In 1979 this issue was brought before the Supreme Court when the Carter administration sought to terminate the 1954 Mutual Defense Treaty with the Republic of China (Taiwan) as part of the process of establishing formal relations with the People's Republic of China (PRC). The treaty had a clause permitting withdrawal, but President Carter took the action without consulting the Senate in advance. Since the president cannot ratify a treaty without Senate consent, his authority to revoke an existing treaty unilaterally was uncertain.

Sen. Barry Goldwater and twenty-three other members of Congress objected to Carter's termination of the treaty and brought suit against the president to prevent it. U.S. District Court Judge Oliver Gasch ruled in October 1979 that treaty termination is a shared power, one that requires the consent of two-thirds of the Senate or a majority of both houses of Congress. He concluded that President Carter's action therefore was unconstitutional on the grounds that it violated the principle of separation of powers.

After a U.S. court of appeals overturned Gasch's decision by a 6-1 vote, Goldwater appealed to the Supreme Court. The Court ruled 7-2 in favor of the president's authority to terminate the treaty on his own. Four justices said that the termination of the treaty was a political issue that the executive and legislative branches would have to resolve themselves.[51]

Executive Agreements

An executive agreement is a pact other than a treaty made by the president or representatives of the president with a foreign leader or government. Presidents have asserted that their power to execute the laws, command the armed forces, and function as the sole organ of foreign policy gives them the legal authority to make these pacts without obtaining the specific approval of the Senate. The executive agreement is a particularly powerful foreign policy tool. The president can make agreements with foreign governments without congressional consent, and these agreements have the force of law. Unlike treaties, they do not supersede U.S. laws with which they conflict, but in every other respect they are binding.

The vast majority of executive agreements are either routine extensions of existing treaties or are based upon broad legislative directives.[52] Agreements made by the president to carry out legislation or treaty obligations are often called "congressional-executive international agreements." Presidents have maintained that their responsibility to execute the laws of the United States gives them the right to make these routine pacts. Other executive agreements have been supported by joint resolutions. Presidents occasionally have chosen to seek the approval of a majority of both houses of Congress for executive agreements when they did not have the support of two-thirds of the Senate but did want some type of specific congressional consent. Although presidents have used joint resolutions to circumvent the formal treaty process, this practice has not elicited strong objections, since it does involve Congress in foreign policy.

The small percentage of agreements that do not fall under these categories are the "pure" executive agreements, which are not accompanied by any congressional approval. These are usually the most important and controversial pacts made under the president's authority.

The use of executive agreements has grown dramatically in the twentieth century. During the eighteenth and nineteenth centuries presidents concluded on average only one executive agreement per year.[53] By the 1930s executive agreements had become more common than treaties.[54] Between 1946 and 1973 a mere 6 percent of all international agreements were treaties.[55] Executive agreements not only have grown in number, they also have been used to conduct business once reserved for treaties. Contemporary presidents can accomplish virtually anything through an executive agreement that can be accomplished through a treaty. Trade agreements, the annexation of territory, military commitments, and arms control pacts have all been concluded through executive agreements.

Constitutional Dilemma

The power of the president to make agreements without congressional approval has created much concern and occasionally resentment on Capitol Hill. Although the Constitution does not prohibit executive agreements, the Founders' careful division of the treaty power in the Constitution must be interpreted as an attempt to ensure that Congress has a direct voice in making international commitments. The growing use of executive agreements by presidents and their representatives to avoid the advice and consent of the Senate has been widely regarded by constitutional scholars and members of Congress as a serious deterioration of constitutional checks and balances in the area of foreign policy.

The development of the United States into a world power with security commitments and economic interests in every corner of the world has made some degree of executive flexibility in making executive agreements desirable. Like Jefferson, who was confronted with the irresistible opportunity to buy the Louisiana Territory, contemporary presidents are sometimes faced with an international situation that calls for making commitments with speed and secrecy. Also, executive agreements often provide a simpler method of transacting less important international business that would overload the already tight legislative schedule if treaties were used. Therefore, there are compelling arguments against legislation or constitutional amendments that would seriously limit the president's ability to make executive agreements.

The crux of the problem is that there are important international agreements that should receive Senate approval in accordance with the Constitution, but there are no concrete guidelines to indicate which agreements need Senate consent and which could be handled simply by executive agreement. Presidents may, therefore, use their discretion in deciding how to make a particular agreement. Numerous presidents, faced with the prospect of fighting for two-thirds approval in the Senate, have used executive agreements to skirt the treaty requirements imposed by the Constitution rather than abandon a diplomatic initiative they believed to be good for the nation or important for their own political future. Treaties, therefore, have become an exception to the rule of presidential policy making.

Despite the use of executive agreements to avoid the treaty ratification process, the Supreme Court has repeatedly upheld the president's power to make international agreements without the consent of the Senate. The Court's ruling on *U.S. v. Belmont* in 1936 was particularly significant. At issue was the president's authority to conclude unilaterally several agreements connected with the 1933 recognition of the Soviet Union. In delivering the Court's opinion, Justice George Sutherland wrote:

> The recognition, establishment of diplomatic relations, the assignment, and agreement with respect thereto, were all parts of one transaction, resulting in an international compact between the two governments. That the negotiations, acceptance of the assignment and agreements and understandings in respect thereof were within the competence of the president may not be doubted. Governmental power over internal affairs is distributed between the national government and the several states. Governmental power over external affairs is not distributed, but is vested exclusively in the national government. And in respect of what was done here, the Executive had the authority to speak as the sole organ of that government.[56]

Justice Sutherland could have based his opinion that the president had the authority to make these agreements on the president's indisputable power to recognize foreign governments. Although he did mention the relevance of this presidential power, he seemed to find authority for the agreements in the president's broader power as the sole organ of foreign policy.[57]

Landmark Executive Agreements

Ironically, Thomas Jefferson, the leader of the Democratic-Republican party, which officially opposed the enhancement of the federal government's power, was the first president to conclude a major international agreement without obtaining the required constitutional approval from the Senate.[58] He agreed to purchase Louisiana from France and delivered the payment before he sent the deal to the Senate for confirmation.

Jefferson acted without the advice and consent of the Senate and against his own political beliefs because he feared that the inevitable delay of a Senate debate would ruin the sale. Napoleon was anxious to sell the territory, and Jefferson did not want to risk the possibilities that Britain might take control of the area or that Napoleon might even sell the land to the British while the Senate debated the purchase. Many future presidents would use executive agreements to avoid lengthy Senate consideration of urgent diplomacy. Since Jefferson eventually did obtain Senate approval, historians generally do not consider the Louisiana Purchase to have been an executive agreement, but it clearly presaged the use of executive agreements by future administrations.[59]

The first major executive agreement concluded between a president and a foreign power was the Rush-Bagot agreement with Great Britain.[60] The pact, which imposed limitations on naval forces on the Great Lakes, was concluded under the supervision of President Monroe in 1817. A year after the agreement was put into operation Monroe decided that he wanted congressional acquiescence to his act of diplomacy. He sent the agreement to the House and Senate and asked if they thought it required the consent of the Senate. The Senate endorsed the "arrangement" with a two-thirds vote but did not consider its action to be an approval of a treaty, and instruments of ratification were never exchanged between the United States and Great Britain.[61]

Although Monroe's executive agreement was significant in establishing a precedent, President John Tyler's annexation of Texas by executive agreement in 1845 was even more important, because it was the first time a president had used an executive agreement to accomplish what could not have been done through the treaty process.[62]

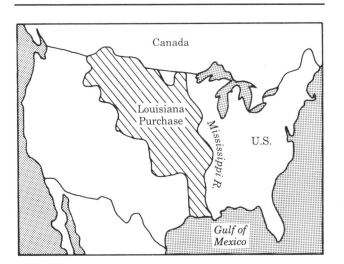

In 1803 President Thomas Jefferson bought the Louisiana territory from France for $15 million, or about four cents an acre, nearly doubling the size of the United States. Jefferson was the first president to conclude a major international agreement without Senate approval.

Tyler wished to bring Texas into the Union to keep it out of foreign hands and to strengthen the slave states, but he was not close to having the necessary two-thirds support in the Senate for conclusion of a treaty of annexation. Late in his term, however, public support in favor of annexation was reflected in Congress, and he called for a joint resolution to bring Texas into the nation. The House easily passed the resolution 120-98, but the Senate gave its approval by only two votes, 27-25, a margin far short of the two-thirds majority that would have been required for Senate approval of a treaty. Armed with this resolution, Tyler invited Texas to become a state. In 1898 McKinley annexed Hawaii as a territory by the same method.[63]

Theodore Roosevelt frequently used his commander-in-chief and executive powers to avoid congressional checks on his authority. Predictably, he was not timid about using executive agreements to accomplish foreign policy objectives that would have been delayed or undermined by the treaty process. One of Roosevelt's most famous executive agreements involved the Caribbean nation of Santo Domingo (now the Dominican Republic). The president wished to block European influence anywhere in the Western Hemisphere. When Santo Domingo fell into heavy debt to European creditors in 1905, Roosevelt oversaw negotiations of an agreement that extended U.S. protection to Santo Domingo and put the United States in control of collecting the country's customs. The United States would turn over a percentage of the revenue to the Dominican government and pay the country's creditors gradually with the rest. Roosevelt hoped that the Senate would consent to the draft treaty, but he immediately implemented it as an executive agreement. When the Senate refused to approve the treaty, Roosevelt continued the arrangement under the executive agreement.[64]

Franklin Roosevelt also used an executive agreement to avoid the treaty process when he provided destroyers to the British in 1940. The United States was still officially neutral at that time, and the persistent isolationist mentality in Congress precluded any possibility that a treaty could be approved to provide Britain with badly needed fighting ships to defend against German submarine attacks. Roosevelt therefore used an executive agreement to trade old U.S. destroyers for the right to lease several British naval bases in the Western Hemisphere. Since the deal was in violation of two statutes and threatened the neutral status of the United States, it was clearly an agreement that should have been accompanied by some sort of congressional approval.[65]

The development of NATO illustrates another use of executive agreements. NATO was established by a short treaty containing only fourteen articles that pledged the signatories to maintain and improve their collective defense capabilities. Upon this foundation, the contracting parties constructed an organization with an integrated command structure, detailed battle plans, extensive transportation and communications facilities, and routinely scheduled multinational maneuvers.

Executive agreements were used to expand the NATO treaty, which had received much bipartisan support. Although the senators who voted for ratification could not have foreseen the enormous development of NATO that would take place through executive agreements, the original treaty did provide the Senate with an opportunity to approve the concept of an alliance with Western European nations.[66]

A dramatic contemporary example of damage that can be caused by a secret informal executive agreement was President Nixon's written assurance to President Nugyen Van Thieu of South Vietnam in 1973 that the United States would "respond with full force," if North Vietnam violated the Paris Peace Agreement, which ended the U.S. military presence in Vietnam. Thieu had consented to the Paris Agreement based on Nixon's personal promise, which was not kept when the North Vietnamese invaded South Vietnam in 1975. Thieu regarded Nixon's pledge as a national commitment, and the United States lost credibility when the promise was not kept.[67]

Nixon's promise, however, was not supported by a corresponding congressional resolution and did not reflect the mood either of Congress or of the American people at the end of the Vietnam War. It is virtually inconceivable that Congress would have consented to a major reescalation of the war by appropriating large sums to fight the North Vietnamese assault that conquered South Vietnam in 1975. Therefore, Nixon's promise, which helped persuade Thieu to accept the Paris agreement, was little more than the optimistic personal promise of a president who almost certainly would not have had the means to keep it, even if he had remained in office.

Attempts to Limit Executive Agreements

Since the end of World War II, Congress has made two major attempts to limit the president's power to make international agreements and commitments without the advice and consent of the Senate. The first was a movement in the 1950s led by Sen. John W. Bricker (R-Ohio), who had proposed a constitutional amendment that would have placed restraints on the president's power to make executive agreements and decreased the effect of the agreements on domestic law. The second occurred in the early 1970s and culminated in the Case Act of 1972, which was intended to compel the executive branch to report all executive agreements to Congress or to selected congressional committees. Except for a clarification of the Case Act passed in 1977, subsequent efforts by Congress to make the executive branch more accountable for its agreements with other nations have been unsuccessful.

Bricker Amendment

Senator Bricker, a conservative Republican, chaired the Foreign and Interstate Commerce Committee. He and his followers were concerned about the implications of Article VI, clause 2, of the Constitution in the postwar environment where the United States was expanding its defense commitments and its participation in international organizations.

The clause provides that treaties made by the United States are the supreme law of the land and binding on the states. The 1936 Supreme Court ruling written by Justice Sutherland in U.S. v. Belmont had extended the force of law to "all international compacts and agreements from the very fact that complete power over international affairs is in the national government and is not and cannot be subject to any curtailment or interference on the part of the several states."

The Brickerites believed that the president's broad power to make international agreements that have the force of law over the states threatened the constitutionally guaranteed rights of the American people.[68] In particular, many senators were alarmed by the growing tendency to use executive agreements to implement military alliance pacts and UN programs. In January 1953 Bricker and sixty-three cosponsors introduced an amendment aimed at establishing congressional review of executive agreements and making treaties unenforceable as domestic law without accompanying legislation. The amendment stated:

> 1. A provision of a treaty which denies or abridges any right enumerated in this Constitution shall not be of any force or effect.
> 2. No treaty shall authorize or permit any foreign power or any international organization to supervise, control, or adjudicate rights of citizens of the United States within the United States enumerated in this Constitution or any other matter essentially within the domestic jurisdiction of the United States.
> 3. A treaty shall become effective as internal law in the United States only through the enactment of appropriate legislation by the Congress.
> 4. All executive or other agreements between the President and any international organization, foreign power, or official thereof shall be made only in the manner and to the extent to be precribed by law. Such agreements shall be subject to the limitations imposed on treaties or the making of treaties in this article.
> 5. The Congress shall have power to enforce this article by appropriate legislation.

The third and fourth provisions would have radically altered the way the United States enters into agreements with foreign governments. Every treaty and executive agreement would have required implementing legislation to make them enforceable as domestic laws, and any executive agreement made by a president would be subject to regulation by Congress. As a result, the ability of presidents to make foreign policy through executive agreements and to negotiate treaties without involving Congress would have been severely curtailed. The amendment did not, however, come to a vote by the time Congress adjourned in August. In 1954 a milder version of the Bricker amendment came within one vote of passing the Senate with a two-thirds majority. Thereafter, support for the amendment ebbed, in part because President Dwight D. Eisenhower strongly opposed it.

The Case Act

In the early 1970s a more modest movement surfaced in Congress to restrain the indiscriminate use of executive agreements. The impetus for this effort was a Senate subcommittee's discovery in 1969-1970 that the executive branch had made secret commitments and terms of agreements during the 1960s. The Security Agreements and Commitments Abroad Subcommittee of the Senate Foreign Relations Committee, chaired by Sen. Stuart Symington (D-Mo.), uncovered secret agreements with Ethiopia, Laos, Thailand, South Korea, Spain, the Philippines, and other countries.

The Nixon administration deepened congressional resentment by concluding important executive agreements with Portugal and Bahrain about military bases. The Senate passed a resolution asserting that the agreements should have been made in the form of treaties, which would have required Senate consent.

Congress responded by passing the Case Act in 1972. The act obligates the executive branch to inform Congress of all executive agreements within sixty days after they have been concluded. It also requires the executive branch to inform Congress of all executive agreements in existence at the time the law was signed. Finally, it provides that the House Foreign Affairs Committee and the Senate Foreign Relations Committee be informed of any executive agreements that the president determines need to be kept secret to ensure national security. The Senate passed the bill by a unanimous 81-0 vote and the House by voice vote.[69] Several bills were proposed in the years following passage of the Case Act that were intended to establish a congressional procedure for disapproving executive agreements. In 1974, such a bill introduced by Sen. Sam J. Ervin, Jr. (D-N.C.), passed in the Senate, but the House did not act upon it. Hearings on two similar bills were held in 1975 by the Senate Judiciary Subcommittee on the Separation of Powers, but they did not lead to legislation.

After several years, Congress found that many executive agreements were not being reported under the provisions of the Case Act because executive branch officials did not define them as executive agreements. Congress reacted by passing legislation in 1977 that required Congress to be informed of any verbal or informal understanding made by any representative of the U.S. government that might constitute a commitment.

Although the Case Act and the legislation that followed it do not limit the president's power to make executive agreements, legislators are more likely to be able to check this executive branch power if they know what sort of agreements the president is making. Given that Congress can conduct investigations, issue resolutions, pass legislation, and control appropriations, it does have tools with which it can challenge executive agreements it believes are unwise or improper. This is especially true since many executive agreements depend on supporting legislation.[70]

The Recognition Power

Although the Constitution does not explicitly grant presidents the power to recognize foreign governments, it is generally accepted that they have this power as a consequence of the authority to send and receive ambassadors. Article II, section 2, of the Constitution says the president "shall appoint Ambassadors," and section 3 of the same article grants the president the power to "receive Ambassadors and other public Ministers" of foreign nations. Since the acts of sending an ambassador to a country and receiving its ambassador imply recognition of the legitimacy of the foreign government involved in the exchange, presidents have successfully claimed exclusive authority to decide which foreign governments will be recognized by the United States. Also, given that presidents decide which nations will be recognized, it follows that they have the power to terminate relations with another nation.

This extension of presidential power was not taken for granted at the beginning of the Republic. Madison, writing as Helvidius, argued that the duty to receive ambassadors did not give the president the power to rule on the legitimacy of foreign governments.[71] In *The Federalist Papers,* Hamilton did not appear even to notice the potential connection between the ceremonial power to receive ambassadors and the recognition of nations. Despite his inclination to see many implied executive powers in the Constitution, Madison wrote that the president's power to receive ambassadors "is more a matter of dignity than of authority. It is a circumstance which will be without consequence in the administration of the government; and it was far more convenient that it should be arranged in this manner than that there should be a necessity of convening the legislature, or one of its branches, upon every arrival of a foreign minister." [72]

The first use of the president's power of recognition occurred in 1793 when Washington agreed to receive Edmond Genêt, the ambassador of the new French Republic. Since most of the members of Congress who were inclined to resist the growth of executive power into areas not specifically granted in the Constitution were also supporters of the new republican regime in France, this expansion of the president's power to receive ambassadors was not questioned.[73] All subsequent presidents have assumed the right to make recognition decisions.

Congress has no role in the recognition process other than to approve the president's nominees for ambassadorships. As with treaties, however, Congress can offer its nonbinding advice to the president on matters of recognition. After France was conquered by the Nazis in World War II, for example, the House and Senate passed resolutions supporting the Roosevelt administration's agreement with other nations in the Western Hemisphere not to allow the transfer of the sovereignty of any European colony in the Americas to another European power.[74]

Genêt Affair

Washington's decision to accept Genêt's credentials soon began to cause the president problems. Genêt attempted to exploit the American people's sympathy for revolutionary France by privately enlisting their support against his country's enemies, Great Britain and Spain. He encouraged settlers in Kentucky and other territories in the West to take up arms against the Spanish in Louisiana, and he took steps to outfit French pirates willing to attack British and Spanish shipping from U.S. ports. These activities undercut Washington's Proclamation of Neutrality and threatened to draw the United States into the European hostilities. Washington, therefore, demanded that the French government recall Genêt. The French ordered their ambassador to return home, but retaliated by demanding that Washington recall the U.S. minister to France, Gouverneur Morris, on the grounds that he had supported plots to restore the French monarchy.[75] Washington thus established a second implied presidential power related to sending and receiving ambassadors. He demonstrated that the president could expel a foreign representative whose conduct was judged unacceptable.

Principles of Recognition

Many countries determine whether they will recognize a particular foreign government according to that government's ability to maintain its authority over its people and to meet its international obligations. The ideological system and the moral character of the regime in question are irrelevant under this conception of recognition. In 1913 President Wilson set a precedent by refusing to recognize the Mexican regime of Victoriano Huerta on the grounds that it was immoral and did not represent the will of its people.[76] Since Wilson, the ideology and morality of a foreign regime have become accepted factors in determining whether a government should be recognized. As a result, successive presidents refused to recognize the revolutionary Communist regimes in Russia from 1917 to 1933, and China from 1949 to 1979, even though these regimes were in firm control of their countries long before the United States established diplomatic relations. In the late 1980s, several Communist countries, including Cuba and Vietnam, did not have diplomatic relations with the United States.

A president also can recognize the rights or interests of national or political groups that do not hold political power. In 1978 Jimmy Carter announced a qualified recognition of the interests of the Palestinians living in Israeli occupied territories by saying that any Middle East peace settlement must recognize "the legitimate rights of the Palestinian people" and "enable the Palestinians to participate in the determination of their own future." [77] A president may also deny recognition of a government's legal authority over a part or all of the territory claimed by that government. For example, the United States has continued to refuse to recognize the legitimacy of the Soviet Union's annexation of Latvia, Lithuania, and Estonia, which occurred in 1940.

Recognition as a Policy Statement

A decision to recognize or not to recognize a nation can be a major policy statement that expresses the attitudes and intentions of the United States toward the nation in question, and sometimes toward an entire region. Such policy statements can have profound consequences, including war. In 1836 Andrew Jackson realized that the act of recognizing the Republic of Texas could have the effect of a declaration of war against Mexico, which regarded Texas as a Mexican territory. Although Jackson did not repudiate his authority to recognize Texas or any other nation, he announced his willingness to allow Congress to decide if Texas should be recognized: "It will always be considered consistent with the spirit of the Constitution, and most safe, that it [the recognition power] should be exercised when probably leading to war, with a previous understanding with that body by whom war can alone be declared, and by whom all the provisions for sustaining its perils must be furnished." [78]

Theodore Roosevelt's recognition of Panama in 1903 following its U.S.-backed revolt from Colombia paved the way to a treaty that gave the United States the right to dig the Panama Canal. It also led to a treaty in 1921 between Colombia and the United States that provided for the United States to pay Colombia $25 million in reparations for the loss of its Panamanian territory.

Truman's recognition of Israel on May 15, 1948, was also controversial. A few minutes after Jews in Palestine had proclaimed the state of Israel, Truman rejected the advice of his State Department and made the United States the first nation to recognize the new country. The recognition indicated U.S. support for Israel and effectively blocked a United Nations plan to keep Palestine under a temporary trusteeship.[79]

The president's power to sever diplomatic relations has been used as an ultimate sanction to protest another country's behavior. Severance of relations is usually reserved for situations when the differences between the two nations are so great that there is no hope they may be

U.S. Legal Relationship with Taiwan

The repercussions for U.S. relations with Taiwan from President Carter's recognition of the People's Republic of China (PRC) illustrated the effect a recognition decision can have on U.S. laws and relations with other nations. Successive presidents had refused to recognize the PRC since it was established in 1949. Instead, the United States recognized the Republic of China, the nationalist Chinese government which had fled to Taiwan after its defeat by the Communist Chinese armies. Growing cooperation and friendship between the United States and the PRC in the 1970s, however, made the establishment of diplomatic relations with Beijing a matter of practical importance. In December 1978, the Carter administration announced that it intended to recognize the PRC as the "sole legal government of China" on January 1, 1979.

This recognition could be accomplished only by withdrawing U.S. recognition of the Republic of China as China's legal government. Since many laws and agreements involving commercial, cultural, and security relations with other countries depend on a nation's diplomatic status, the legal framework of the U.S. relationship with Taiwan had to be rebuilt. Without new legislation establishing a special relationship with the Republic of China, the United States could not deal with Taiwan as another nation.

Consequently, Congress passed the Taiwan Relations Act in March 1979. The act was intended to ensure that normal relations would continue between Taiwan and the United States, even though the United States no longer recognized the Republic of China regime that governed the island. The legislation established the American Institute in Taiwan through which the United States would conduct relations with Taiwan. The institute was created as a private, nonprofit corporation that was authorized to enter into, execute, and enforce agreements and other transactions with Taiwan and perform consular functions for U.S. citizens. The act also authorized U.S. government employees, especially Foreign Service officers, to take temporary leaves of absence from their posts in order to work for the institute. While in Taiwan, they would not be considered U.S. government employees, but they would retain their seniority, pensions, and other benefits when they returned to work for the government. Thus, the Taiwan Relations Act created a nonprofit corporation that could do virtually anything done by an embassy.

In addition to creating the American Institute in Taiwan, the act recognized the validity of Taiwan domestic law, contracts entered into under Taiwan law, and all U.S. agreements and treaties with Taiwan except the 1954 mutual defense treaty, which was terminated at the end of 1979. It also authorized the president to grant Taiwan's unofficial representatives in the United States diplomatic privileges and treat Taiwan as a nation with its own immigration quota equal to that of the PRC. These and dozens of other provisions of the Taiwan Relations Act addressed the legal difficulties created by the withdrawal of U.S. recognition of the Republic of China.

---

resolved through normal diplomatic procedures. It is customary to break diplomatic ties with a country before declaring war against it, but many events short of war have prompted presidents to terminate relations. In 1979, President Carter ended diplomatic relations with Iran in response to the hostage crisis.

Even when relations have been broken with a particular country, communication usually continues. "Interests sections" may be established in each country's capital in the embassies of a third country. For example, U.S. interests in Cuba and Iran are represented by the Swiss embassies in those countries. Foreign nations without diplomatic relations with the United States also have used their representatives to the United Nations to communicate with U.S. officials. Nevertheless, such measures do not accommodate international business between the two countries with the same efficiency as normal diplomatic exchanges. A less drastic method employed by presidents to communicate their displeasure with another nation is the temporary recalling of the U.S. ambassador in that country for "consultations." President Carter used this tactic after the Soviet invasion of Afghanistan, when he recalled Thomas J. Watson, the U.S. ambassador in Moscow, to Washington.

Power to Appoint Diplomatic Personnel

Article II, section 2, of the Constitution states that the president shall, "nominate, and by and with the Advice and Consent of the Senate, shall appoint Ambassadors, other public Ministers and Consuls." Since the president was to be the sole organ of foreign communications, the power to appoint those individuals who would be communicating directly with foreign leaders was properly a presidential duty. The success of a president's foreign policy program depends greatly on the personalities and abilities of the people who fill important diplomatic and advisory posts.

The difficulty of selecting ambassadors and high-level foreign policy officials has increased dramatically for presidents since the early years of the Republic. George Washington and his immediate successors had only a few posts to fill and were able to appoint men whom they knew personally. As the U.S. government grew and expanded its involvement in world affairs, presidents were increasingly forced to delegate responsibility to their advisers for selecting candidates for less important posts.

Although the president appoints officials, the Congress has the constitutional power to create offices. Nevertheless, presidents have used executive orders to create government bodies that required them to make appointments. Kennedy established the Peace Corps in this manner, and Gerald Ford unilaterally created the Committee on Foreign Intelligence and the Intelligence Oversight Board.[80]

Senate confirmation of presidential nominees for diplomatic posts often has been routine, but there have been exceptions. For example, Eisenhower's appointment of Charles E. Bohlen as ambassador to the Soviet Union barely survived the confirmation vote, even though Eisenhower's own party controlled the Senate.[81]

Political Appointees versus the Foreign Service

A question that complicates the diplomatic appointments of contemporary presidents is how to divide ambassadorships and important State Department posts between political appointees and the State Department's own career foreign service officers. Senior foreign service officers can offer a president valuable diplomatic experience that can prevent foreign policy mistakes. Also, since they serve successive presidents, they can provide continuity in foreign policy between administrations.[82] Yet, presidents often have been reluctant to entrust important ambassadorships and assistant secretary posts to foreign service officers, who are less likely than political appointees to be responsive to the president's directives. Because their careers are not dependent on the president but on a self-run promotion system, and because many regard foreign policy as an endeavor that should not be subject to partisan politics, foreign service officers have a greater reputation for resisting presidential policies than do political appointees.

Political appointees can more easily be found who share the president's philosophy, are politically minded, and appreciate how their job fits into the president's comprehensive domestic and foreign policy goals. If an administration favors political appointees, however, the president may gain a measure of diplomatic control at the expense of greater diplomatic expertise at U.S. embassies, the goodwill of the State Department, and the morale of the Foreign Service. An option open to the president is to balance appointments by reserving many ambassadorships for foreign service officers while nominating political appointees to posts crucial to the execution of the president's particular foreign policy goals.[83]

Symbolism and Politics of Appointments

Presidents must take into account more than a candidate's abilities and qualifications when making an appointment. They must consider how the appointment will be perceived. The symbolism of presidential appointments can profoundly affect foreign policy, especially at the beginning of the president's term. Appointments provide the president with an opportunity to indicate to Congress, the American public, and foreign governments the foreign policy goals the new administration intends to pursue. Reagan's appointment of conservative Jeane Kirkpatrick as

ambassador to the United Nations reaffirmed his intention to make anti-Communism a foreign policy theme of his administration, just as Carter had underscored his commitment to human rights and third world issues with his appointment of Andrew Young to the same post.

Diplomatic appointments also give presidents certain political opportunities. They may choose to broaden their base of support within their party by appointing people to ambassadorships who originally opposed their nomination. Presidents also can try to build up trust and cohesion within their new administration by giving department and agency heads broad discretion in selecting subordinates.

Presidents sometimes have used appointments to create an atmosphere of bipartisanship. Kennedy believed that by appointing Republicans to senior foreign policy posts in his administration he could disarm potential congressional resistance to his policies. Treasury Secretary Douglas Dillon, Defense Secretary Robert McNamara, national security adviser McGeorge Bundy, director of the Central Intelligence Agency (CIA) Allen Dulles, and disarmament chief John J. McCloy were all Republicans, as were John A. McCone and William C. Poster who eventually replaced Dulles and McCloy, respectively. Other presidents have made appointments with bipartisanship in mind, though no modern president has appointed as many members of the opposing party to such important foreign policy jobs as Kennedy did.[84]

Presidential Envoys

Many presidents have used personal emissaries not subject to Senate confirmation to conduct foreign policy. Often such presidential representatives have been employed to carry out specific diplomatic missions. The use of personal envoys allows presidents to inject their own ideas and proposals directly into negotiations without having to go through the State Department or other official channels through which information may be leaked, misinterpreted, or opposed. The presence of a personal envoy sent by the president sometimes can stimulate stalemated negotiations by lending greater prestige to the talks and demonstrating the president's interest in them. Presidential represen-

Bill Auth

Reagan's appointment of conservative Jeane Kirkpatrick, left, as ambassador to the United Nations reaffirmed his intention to make anti-Communism a foreign policy theme, just as Carter had underscored his commitment to human rights with his appointment of Andrew Young, right, to the same post.

tatives also can provide the president with an additional source of information that is relatively free of institutional biases.

The use of presidential envoys is not specifically allowed or disallowed in the Constitution. The practice contradicts the apparent intention of the Constitution, however, since the president is supposed to appoint ambassadors "with the advice and consent of the Senate." The employment of personal envoys, therefore, is a means by which presidents have circumvented the Senate's check on their diplomatic appointment power.

Washington did not believe that the Constitution prohibited him from using private representatives to conduct diplomacy. In 1791, Gouverneur Morris, who held no public office at the time, carried out important negotiations with the British at Washington's direction. By using a personal representative Washington could explore the possibilities for a treaty without having to involve Congress or deal with the formalities of official treaty negotiations.

The first major controversy over the appointment of diplomats not confirmed by the Senate occurred during Madison's presidency. In 1813, Madison sent a delegation to the negotiations in Europe that produced the Treaty of Ghent, which ended the War of 1812 with Great Britain. The president had dispatched the negotiators without submitting their names for confirmation by the Senate, which was on recess. Madison's critics argued that he could not appoint ministers to offices that had not been authorized by Congress and that the appointments were illegal since the Senate did not have the chance to approve them. The president responded by claiming that it was unnecessary for Congress to create a diplomatic post if the president determined that a need had arisen for one, and the president was free to fill any vacancy that happened to occur during a congressional recess.[85] Since Madison's time, however, Congress has enacted legislation that gives it control over the creation of new ambassadorships.

Many subsequent presidents have found this practice to be useful at some time during their administration. In 1831 Jackson sent unconfirmed representatives to Turkey to conclude a trade and navigation treaty, and in 1893 Cleveland gave his own emissary, J. H. Blount, "paramount authority" over the Senate-approved resident minister in Honolulu at talks on the annexation of Hawaii.[86] Two twentieth-century presidents established the use of personal representatives as a common diplomatic device of the president. Wilson made extensive use of his close friend Col. Edward House to perform diplomatic missions in Europe before and during World War I. Wilson also named House to the U.S. delegation to the peace talks in Paris at the end of the war and sent former secretary of state Elihu Root to Russia in 1917 during World War I to urge the Russian government not to make a separate peace with Germany. Franklin Roosevelt employed Harry Hopkins, a personal aide, as a negotiator in Great Britain and the Soviet Union during World War II. Among other accomplishments, Hopkins helped negotiate and direct the lend-lease agreements under which the United States supplied war materiel to Great Britain and other countries at war with Germany.

Presidents have not felt compelled to submit their appointments of private representatives to the Senate for approval. In addition to the precedent set by Washington, there are strong justifications for this position. Personal envoys of presidents function outside of permanent government positions, do not have their duties enumerated in the Constitution, serve only as long as the president asks them, and often receive no compensation.[87]

Summit Meetings

Presidents are responsible for the conduct of diplomacy. They appoint diplomats, formulate diplomatic policy, and send and receive ambassadors and treaty negotiators. The State Department, the National Security Council (NSC), and other executive branch agencies involved in diplomacy are servants of the president. Yet, despite presidential control over diplomatic activities, presidents themselves rarely met with foreign leaders until World War II. The difficulties of travel, the isolated location of the United States, and the traditional belief that presidents should stay close to their administrative and legislative responsibilities in the capital prevented presidents from acting as their own negotiators.

Today the American public takes for granted meetings between their president and other world leaders. They regard these meetings, which have become known as "summit meetings," as an established and useful tool of presidential foreign policy making. Indeed, if a modern president were to avoid meetings with leaders of foreign governments, the press and public alike would invariably criticize the chief of state as being uninterested in international affairs, or even isolationist. Presidents have found that a highly publicized summit tends to raise their public approval rate. *(See "Presidential Popularity," p. 194, in Chief of State chapter.)*

Winston Churchill is credited with coining the term *summit*. In 1953 he used the word when he called for a conference between the leaders of the Soviet Union and the Western powers. The media picked up the term and used it to describe the Geneva conference between Soviet and Western leaders in 1955. After Geneva, meetings between national leaders increasingly were referred to as *summits*.[88] The term is used to distinguish between meetings that are actually attended by the recognized leaders of states and meetings between foreign ministers or lower-level officials.

Presidential Diplomacy

Although presidential travel to foreign nations was impractical before the twentieth century, presidents throughout U.S. history have conducted personal diplomacy with foreign leaders through direct exchanges of letters. Personal letters between leaders could accomplish some of the goals of the modern summit meeting. They gave a president the chance to send and receive information, ideas, and proposals without using intermediaries and to establish a personal rapport with a foreign leader. Presidential letters were especially important to early presidents who did not have the benefit of an extensive diplomatic network with representatives in many foreign capitals. President Jefferson, whose years as secretary of state under Washington had provided him with extensive diplomatic experience, had an ongoing correspondence with Czar Alexander I of Russia during the Napoleonic wars.[89]

Early presidents also met with foreign leaders who traveled to the United States. The first high-ranking official of a foreign government to visit the United States was a personal emissary of the ruler of Tunis who came to Amer-

National Archives

FDR made a series of trips overseas to confer with Allied leaders about military strategy and the composition of the postwar world. Left, in February 1945, Roosevelt confers with Winston Churchill and Joseph Stalin at Yalta in the Crimea.

ica in 1805 to discuss the passage of U.S. commercial ships in the Mediterranean. The marquis de Lafayette, who had led colonial troops against the British in the American Revolution, was the first official guest to be invited to the United States by the U.S. government. President Monroe received him in 1824 after he arrived on an American ship that Congress had dispatched to France.[90] During the rest of the nineteenth century visits to the United States by foreign dignitaries were common. Visits by the heads of state of other nations, however, remained rare. Up to the end of World War I, presidents received only about thirty heads of state.[91]

Presidential Travel

During the eighteenth and nineteenth centuries a precedent developed against presidents traveling outside the country during their term. Theodore Roosevelt became the first president to break this precedent when he visited Panama in 1906 to inspect the canal under construction. Presidential travel abroad remained uncommon until World War II when Franklin Roosevelt made a series of trips to Canada and overseas to confer with allied leaders about military strategy and the composition of the postwar world. Truman followed Roosevelt's example by attending the Potsdam Conference in 1945 with Joseph Stalin and Churchill (and, later, Clement R. Attlee).

President Eisenhower, however, institutionalized the role of the president as international diplomat with his foreign trips, including his 22,000-mile "Quest for Peace" tour of eleven nations in 1959. He believed that establishing good will toward the United States in foreign nations was an important presidential function. Accordingly, many of his stops in foreign countries were devoted to ceremony and speech making. After Eisenhower, presidential visits abroad were an accepted part of the president's job and

were highly coveted by the leaders of foreign nations.

Eisenhower's successors continued his practice of frequent overseas visits. President Kennedy met with Premier Nikita Khrushchev in Vienna in 1961 and toured Europe in 1963, at which time he delivered his famous *Ich bin ein Berliner* speech in Berlin. President Johnson initially declined taking trips abroad because he had no vice president, but after the election in 1964 he made several overseas trips, including visits to Australia, the Philippines, Vietnam, and Latin America. Nixon embarked on a major European tour in 1969 only a month after he became president. In 1972 he signed the SALT I treaty in Moscow and became the first U.S. president to visit the People's Republic of China. President Ford also went to the Soviet Union, meeting Leonid Brezhnev in Vladivostok in 1974. Carter and Reagan both traveled to numerous foreign countries and met with Soviet leaders overseas.

Constitutional Questions

The Constitution does not specifically sanction the president's authority to meet with other world leaders, but the power to appoint, send, and receive ambassadors and to negotiate treaties clearly establishes the president's right to conduct diplomatic negotiations personally. A more controversial constitutional question about summit meetings was whether a president could properly fulfill the obligations of office while out of the country. The Constitution states that if the president is unable "to discharge the powers and duties of the said office, the same shall devolve on the vice president." The authors of the Constitution did not specify if being absent from the country could render a president incapable of fulfilling the constitutional responsibilities of the office.

No one questioned the constitutionality of Theodore Roosevelt's short trip to Panama in 1906 or Taft's meeting with the Mexican president just across the border in 1909. When President Wilson announced in late 1918 that he planned to go to Europe to attend the peace conference in Versailles, however, numerous critics objected that Wilson's safety could not be ensured and that he would lose touch with the everyday business of running the country during the lengthy Atlantic crossing.[92]

Many of the protests were politically motivated, but some critics sincerely questioned the constitutionality of Wilson's proposed venture. Resolutions were introduced in both houses of Congress that would have declared the presidency vacant and required the vice president to assume the president's powers if Wilson left the country. Former president Taft defended Wilson's plans, however. He argued in an article in the *Washington Post* on December 5, 1918, that the president could properly fulfill the duties of his office while overseas. He wrote: "There is no constitutional inhibition, express or implied, to prevent the president's going abroad to discharge a function clearly given him by the Constitution. That instrument says that he shall make treaties.... It is a curious error to assume that the president himself may not attend a conference to which he can send a delegate." [93] The congressional resolutions against Wilson's trip never got out of committee. Wilson's critics continued to attack the wisdom of his policy, but he went to Europe without a major confrontation over the constitutionality of his trip.[94]

The jet airplane and modern means of communication eliminated any lingering concern that presidential travel could make a chief executive incapable of performing the tasks of office. Modern presidents travel with large staffs and stay in constant touch with administration and con-

gressional officials in Washington, D.C. Although presidents taking a lengthy foreign trip will spend less time on domestic affairs while out of the country, they have the means to carry out virtually any presidential function from any place in the world.

Superpower Summitry

The most famous summit meetings have been those between the U.S. president and the leader of the Soviet Union. U.S. and Soviet leaders have met sporadically since 1943, when Franklin Roosevelt traveled to Tehran for a wartime conference with Stalin and Churchill. Since Roosevelt, every president has met with a Soviet leader at least once. These meetings recently have been associated with arms control negotiations. In some cases, like the summits in Moscow in 1972, Vienna in 1979, and Washington in 1987, the meeting is a culmination of the arms control process where an agreement is signed. In other cases, like the 1985 Geneva Summit and the 1986 Reykjavik Summit, the leaders hoped to stimulate arms control negotiations. The media and public attention that accompanies these meetings between the leaders of the superpowers is inspired by hopes that they can produce an agreement or understanding that will reduce the chances of war and lead to a more cooperative coexistence.

The continuing threat of nuclear war gives the leaders of the superpowers reason to pursue summit meetings despite the mistrust between the two nations. The U.S. president and the leader of the Soviet Union each controls huge arsenals of nuclear weapons targeted on the other super-

White House

In 1972, Richard Nixon became the first U.S. president to visit the People's Republic of China. Here he is greeted by Chinese Communist party chairman Mao Tse-tung.

U.S.-Soviet Summit ...

Date	Place	Leaders	Topic
July-August 1945	Potsdam	President Harry S Truman, Soviet leader Joseph Stalin, British prime ministers Winston Churchill and Clement R. Attlee	Partition and control of Germany
July 1955	Geneva	President Dwight D. Eisenhower, Soviet leader Nikolai A. Bulganin, British prime minister Anthony Eden, French premier Edgar Fauré	Reunification of Germany, disarmament, European security
September 1959	Camp David, Md.	President Eisenhower, Soviet leader Nikita S. Khrushchev	Berlin problem
May 1960	Paris	President Eisenhower, Soviet leader Khrushchev, French president Charles de Gaulle, British prime minister Harold Macmillan	U-2 incident
June 1961	Vienna	President John F. Kennedy, Soviet leader Khrushchev	Berlin problem
June 1967	Glassboro, N.J.	President Lyndon B. Johnson, Soviet leader Aleksei N. Kosygin	Middle East

power and its allies. Prevention of nuclear war depends in part upon the calculations of these leaders about the behavior of their counterpart. A summit provides the leaders of the two countries with a chance to assess each other and clarify their goals and intentions so the chances of miscalculation are reduced.

Former president Nixon has argued that developing mutual understandings between the superpowers of their respective interests and patterns of behavior should be the primary purpose of a superpower summit. These understandings, which he calls "rules of engagement," do not resolve differences between the two countries or end their adversarial relationship; rather, they reduce the possibility that a crisis will lead to war. He rejects the popular notion that summit meetings are valuable because they create a "spirit" of friendship.[95] Indeed, the superpower summits declared to have created a new spirit of cooperation have been among the least successful at producing substantive progress on major issues: Geneva in 1955, Camp David in 1959, Vienna in 1961, Glassboro in 1967, and Geneva in 1985. Unfounded optimism following a summit can contribute to international disillusionment and hostility if public expectations are inflated beyond what is warranted by progress on tangible diplomatic issues.

Careful preparation is especially important in super-

power summits, since the president is dealing with an adversary who is seeking not only an agreement, but also an advantage. The Soviets come to summits with propaganda goals in addition to their bargaining goals. At the Paris summit in 1960, for example, Khrushchev abandoned the opportunity for negotiation in favor of milking the U-2 incident for its propaganda value. The propaganda opportunities of a summit meeting can undermine negotiations if the agenda is not set and if the Soviets have not agreed to measures to ensure serious private negotiations.

The Soviets possess several bargaining advantages that dispose them to be patient negotiators. Unlike the United States, the Soviet Union is under less domestic pressure to conclude an agreement since the government controls the news media. Soviet leaders also do not have to worry about negotiating an agreement that will be acceptable to a legislative body. In addition, if the Soviets are displeased with the negotiating positions of a particular U.S. president, they have the option of waiting until a new one is elected before pursuing an agreement. Summits are most likely to succeed when they are held after the negotiations of lower-level officials who have made substantial progress toward resolving the issues to be discussed at the summit.

Without careful preparation, international pressure and the personal desire to make a diplomatic breakthrough

... Meetings, 1945-1988

Date	Place	Leaders	Topic
May 1972	Moscow	President Richard Nixon, Soviet leader Leonid I. Brezhnev	SALT I, anti-ballistic missile limitations
June 1973	Washington, D.C.	President Nixon, Soviet leader Brezhnev	Détente
June-July 1974	Moscow and Yalta	President Nixon, Soviet leader Brezhnev	Arms control
November 1974	Vladivostok	President Gerald R. Ford, Soviet leader Brezhnev	Arms control
June 1979	Vienna	President Jimmy Carter, Soviet leader Brezhnev	SALT II
November 1985	Geneva	President Ronald Reagan, Soviet leader Mikhail S. Gorbachev	Arms control, U.S.-Soviet relations
October 1986	Reykjavik	President Reagan, Soviet leader Gorbachev	Arms control
December 1987	Washington, D.C.	President Reagan, Soviet leader Gorbachev	INF Treaty, Afghanistan
May-June 1988	Moscow	President Reagan, Soviet leader Gorbachev	Arms control, human rights
December 1988	New York City	President Reagan, Soviet leader Gorbachev	U.S.-Soviet relations

may cause presidents to agree to a proposal they would reject if they were considering it within the framework of the normal diplomatic process. The 1986 "mini-summit" in Reykjavik between Reagan and Mikhail Gorbachev, which was intended as a preparatory meeting to a full summit later in the year, turned into a bargaining session on an extensive arms control agreement. Reagan hastily accepted in principle Soviet proposals to eliminate all ballistic missiles within a decade—a notion from which the administration later distanced itself.

Many U.S. policy makers and foreign policy experts have advocated concluding an agreement with the Soviet Union to hold annual summit meetings. Nixon pointed out three advantages to holding regular summit meetings, in addition to whatever business could be concluded at such meetings. First, regular summits could reduce the risk that a war could be started through a miscalculation, since leaders of both countries would better understand the limits beyond which the other could not be pushed. Second, before regularly scheduled summits, both sides would be inhibited from taking actions that could be perceived as contrary to the interests of the other. Third, regular summits would stimulate movement in the bureaucracies of the Soviet Union and the United States that might lead to further agreement.[96]

Evaluating Summit Diplomacy

Despite its popular appeal, summit diplomacy can be ineffective and even counterproductive. Diplomatic historian Elmer Plischke has pointed out numerous disadvantages and risks of summit meetings compared with conventional diplomacy.

The extensive media attention given summits may distort their substance or lead to popular disillusionment by raising public expectations of improved relations with another country beyond what is warranted. The spontaneity possible at summits may yield agreements that have not received proper scrutiny or that personally commit the president to a policy without allowing for the option to modify it after further review. Summits may also distract presidents from their other responsibilities, place presidents in a location where it is difficult to ensure their safety, and cause physical strain that could threaten the president's health. Because the success of a summit depends on the performance of the president, relations with other countries can be harmed if the president is inexperienced or inadequately prepared. Moreover, if diplomacy with another country is grounded on the personal relationship between a president and that country's leader, relations may suffer when one of them leaves office. Frequent summits may even harm the morale of professional diplomats if they perceive that their talents are being ignored in favor of direct presidential negotiations.[97]

Despite these dangers, a summit meeting has the potential to be a valuable diplomatic tool, if the president and the president's advisers understand the risks and pursue prudent, realizable goals.

Plischke also cites ten advantages of summit meetings that can make them valuable additions to conventional diplomacy. First, by becoming personally acquainted, a president and a foreign leader may reduce tensions, clarify national interests, and establish mutual respect. Second, personal friendship between a president and a foreign statesman may lead to improved relations between the two countries. Third, summits allow presidents to focus national attention on specific issues and to improve public understanding of them. Fourth, presidents engaging in personal diplomacy are more capable than professional diplomats of understanding the domestic policy consequences of a given diplomatic action. Fifth, foreign leaders can be sure that they are dealing with the source of foreign policy power when they negotiate with the president at a summit. Sixth, summit negotiations can yield quick results if desired, since discussions are between leaders with the power of decision rather than between representatives who must receive instructions, make reports, and relay new proposals. Seventh, summit meetings may produce broad agreements that can resolve differences or lead to specific agreements worked out in lower-level forums. Eighth, diplomatic impasses may be overcome at summits by shifts in policy that only the top leaders are empowered to make. Ninth, if presidents desire an international forum for their diplomatic policies, a summit meeting can provide one. Tenth, successful summits can enhance the image of the president and the United States.[98]

As these lists indicate, summit meetings are neither inherently good nor inherently bad. Their advantages and disadvantages are products of the same diplomatic conditions. For example, the potential for a summit to produce a quick breakthrough in stalemated negotiations and the risk that a summit can lead to a hasty, poorly conceived agreement both arise from the president's authority to modify bargaining positions and conclude an agreement on the spot. A summit, therefore, is a special diplomatic environment that offers opportunities but also conceals traps. This environment can be used profitably by skilled, prepared presidents with a firm conception of what they are trying to accomplish and what they are willing to risk; or it can produce a diplomatic disaster if inexperienced or unprepared presidents are influenced by domestic political pressure, media attention, or the desire to make history.

AP/Wide World

President Reagan and Soviet leader Gorbachev discuss arms control and other superpower concerns. The Soviet leader came to Washington, D.C., for three days of summit negotiations in December 1987.

Manager of the Foreign Policy Bureaucracy

The president's management of the foreign policy bureaucracy is less visible than the president's performance as a diplomat, but it is as important to the success of U.S. foreign policy. The "foreign policy bureaucracy" loosely refers to all executive branch personnel whose primary duties pertain to foreign affairs. Almost every department and agency has employees engaged in activities that affect foreign relations, but the State Department, the Defense

Department, the intelligence agencies, and the National Security Council staff dominate the foreign policy-making process. Other agencies, such as the Arms Control and Disarmament Agency, the U.S. Information Agency, and the Agency for International Development, deal with specific aspects of foreign policy.

Although the president is responsible for the conduct of foreign affairs, modern foreign policy can not be made by one person. Policy results from a process of consultation and compromise among the president and the president's top foreign affairs advisers. Moreover, the lower levels of the bureaucracy perform functions that are essential to the success of foreign policy. Presidents Kennedy and Nixon preferred to base their decisions on the advice of a small, close-knit group of advisers, but even presidents such as these need a bureaucracy to collect information and intelligence, research policy problems, plan for long-range contingencies, represent the United States abroad, implement presidential directives, and oversee the daily functions of U.S. foreign policy.

Expansion of the Foreign Policy Bureaucracy

During George Washington's administration, the foreign policy bureaucracy consisted of the secretary of state, a small group of clerks, and a few carefully chosen ambassadors to key European states. Although U.S. contacts with other nations expanded during the next hundred years, the foreign policy apparatus of the executive branch remained small. In addition, the low salaries of diplomats and the practice of appointing wealthy campaign contributors and party functionaries to diplomatic posts hindered the development of a professional diplomatic corps.[99] At the end of the nineteenth century the United States began to upgrade the quality and status of its diplomats to correspond with the nation's growing involvement in international trade and politics. Presidents increasingly relied upon the State Department for information, analysis, and staff support.

With the coming of World War II and the emergence of the United States as the most powerful nation on earth, presidents needed greater bureaucratic resources to support their foreign policy decision making. The United States saw itself as an international leader and the protector of the non-Communist world. In the postwar years, it entered into numerous alliances and mutual defense agreements, distributed massive amounts of military and economic aid, hosted the United Nations, and actively participated in most international organizations. This new U.S. involvement in world affairs multiplied the president's foreign policy responsibilities. An expanded bureaucracy was required to administer the growing number of U.S. programs and activities overseas and to provide the president with the information and analysis necessary for constructing effective foreign policies.

As a result, not only did the State Department increase in size, but other departments and agencies were created or expanded to provide military, economic, scientific, and intelligence-gathering expertise that the State Department was not equipped to provide. The State Department thus lost its preeminent role in foreign policy making. It became one player among many in the field of foreign policy. Nevertheless, it has remained the president's primary instrument of negotiation with foreign countries and an important source of information, analysis, and advice on foreign relations.

In 1949, Congress created the Defense Department by unifying the individual armed services. Although the United States rapidly demobilized after World War II, the North Korean invasion of South Korea in 1950 and the growing Soviet threat convinced U.S. leaders that, for the first time in American history, the country needed a large standing military.[100] The size of the unified military budget and the number of people in the armed services ensured that the civilian and military leaders of the new Defense Department would have considerable bureaucratic clout. Moreover, most foreign policy issues had become indistinguishable from national security issues. Containing Soviet expansionism, forming and maintaining an anti-Communist alliance network, and remaining ahead in the nuclear arms race were among the most important international goals for the United States. Defense officials consequently became important players in foreign policy decision making. *(See "Department of Defense," p. 165, in Commander in Chief chapter.)*

The Central Intelligence Agency (CIA) was created by the National Security Act of 1947 to gather and analyze information from every corner of the globe and to provide the president with a covert operations capability. The CIA along with other intelligence-gathering agencies constitute the intelligence community. The community's members include the Defense Intelligence Agency, the intelligence offices of the individual armed services, the State Department's Bureau of Intelligence and Research, the Federal Bureau of Investigation, and the massive National Security Agency, which intercepts and analyzes communication signals. The director of the CIA was given preeminent status

Oversight of Intelligence Activities

Because of the requirements of secrecy, the National Security Act of 1947 gave the president nearly exclusive responsibility for oversight of covert intelligence activities. Before the mid-1970s, Congress rarely showed an interest in covert operations, and the president and the intelligence agencies did not willingly offer information about them. Congress routinely approved billions of dollars in funds for the intelligence community with only a few members of its appropriations committees knowing how the money was being spent.

In the mid-1970s, however, numerous revelations of unethical, unauthorized, and illegal activities by the CIA and other intelligence units were uncovered by congressional investigations. Among other abuses, the CIA had helped overthrow the democratically elected government of Socialist president Salvador Allende in Chile. In addition, the FBI and other intelligence agencies were found to have conducted illegal surveillance operations and engaged in other activities that violated the civil liberties of individual Americans.

In response, Congress passed a series of laws that created House and Senate intelligence committees and strengthened congressional oversight of intelligence activities. The Hughes-Ryan Amendment to the 1974 foreign aid bill and the 1980 Intelligence Oversight Act required that the president report all U.S. covert intelligence operations to designated congressional committees in a timely fashion. To complement Congress's actions, Gerald Ford established the Intelligence Oversight Board, a White House three-member panel to oversee intelligence activities and report any questions of illegality to the president through the attorney general.

in the intelligence community with primary responsibility for coordinating intelligence activities and advising the president on intelligence matters.

The CIA inherited many of the functions and personnel of the Office of Strategic Services, which had carried out covert operations during World War II. The Japanese sneak attack on Pearl Harbor had impressed the U.S. leadership with the need to have sources of information beyond those provided by U.S. embassies. In addition, Moscow's aggressive use of its intelligence apparatus and the difficulty of extracting information from the closed Soviet society by conventional means seemed to demand a similar intelligence effort by the United States.

National Security Council

In addition to creating the CIA, the 1947 National Security Act established the National Security Council

(NSC). The NSC is a presidential advisory body consisting of the president, vice president, and secretaries of Defense and State. In addition to these statutory members, the director of the Central Intelligence Agency and the chairman of the Joint Chiefs of Staff are designated as statutory advisers to the NSC. Presidents were to convene the NSC as often or as seldom as they liked and invite whomever they wanted to attend in addition to its statutory participants.

Although presidents could call cabinet meetings to consider national security matters, the cabinet was a large and unwieldy body that included heads of departments unrelated to national security policy. The NSC gave presidents a forum that was smaller and more focused than the cabinet but would allow them to draw together their top defense, diplomatic, economic, and intelligence advisers to consider broad issues of national security.

The National Security Act stated that the NSC's responsibility was "to advise the President with respect to the integration of domestic, foreign, and military policies relating to the national security so as to enable the military services and other departments and agencies of the government to cooperate more effectively in matters involving the national security." In addition to integrating the efforts of agencies and officials concerned with national security policy, the NSC has performed several other functions. Some presidents have used the NSC as a forum for generating and discussing policy options, while others have made decisions outside the NSC and then asked the council to approve them. The NSC occasionally has been used as a decision-making forum during crises, including the North Korean invasion of South Korea in 1950, the Soviet invasion of Czechoslovakia in 1968, and the *Mayaguez* incident in 1975. At various times the NSC also has been used for less dramatic functions such as policy planning and budget review.[101]

In addition to creating the National Security Council, the National Security Act established an NSC staff, which would be independent of other departments and agencies. This staff, created to serve the president and the members of the National Security Council, has become a major player in foreign policy making. At times it has rivaled or eclipsed the State Department in influence.

The NSC staff is headed by the assistant to the president for national security affairs, a post established by Dwight Eisenhower. Since the Nixon administration, it has commonly been referred to as the "national security adviser." Originally, the national security adviser was supposed to facilitate foreign policy making by coordinating NSC meetings and overseeing the staff that served the NSC, but under Eisenhower's successors the national security adviser often had power equal to cabinet members. As a presidential aide, the national security adviser is not confirmed by the Senate and does not possess the vast legal authority of a cabinet member. Rather, the power of the national security adviser within the administration depends entirely upon the president. The NSC staff has a unique position within the foreign policy bureaucracy. Since the national security adviser and most NSC staffers owe their position and status to the president, they have few competing loyalties. Some NSC staffers who are drawn from other departments and agencies may retain institutional loyalty to their parent organization, but during their tenure on the NSC staff they are responsible only to the president. In addition, the NSC staff is virtually beyond the reach of the legislative branch since it has no statutory responsibility to report to Congress. Presidents therefore can use the NSC staff to fulfill any function they choose. National security advisers such as Henry Kissinger and Zbigniew Brzezinski have served as negotiators, policy advisers, and national security analysts in addition to their duties as manager of the NSC staff. The Iran-contra investigations in 1986 and 1987 revealed that the NSC staff also could be used (in this case unwisely) to implement covert operations.

Foreign Policy-making Process

Although the National Security Council and the executive departments and agencies that deal with foreign affairs are established by law, it is up to the president to create and maintain a responsive and effective foreign policy-making process. Because numerous executive branch units are working on foreign policy, their work must be coordinated to minimize the duplication of their efforts, to avoid institutional conflict, and to ensure that each unit has access to the president. Therefore, as managers of the foreign policy bureaucracy, presidents must establish procedures through executive orders and their personal management style that determine how policy options and information should be presented to them, who should have access to intelligence, how the efforts of various departments and agencies should be coordinated, how the agendas of foreign policy meetings should be set, who should regularly attend these meetings, who should chair these meetings, and who should be responsible for overseeing policy implementation.

Managing the Foreign Policy-making Process

Since World War II, the central question about the process of producing foreign policy has been who should manage that process. The president must ultimately be the referee of the inevitable bureaucratic struggle within the administration for influence, resources, and prestige, but the responsibility of determining the substance of policy leaves the president little time for matters of management. Therefore, some executive branch unit must serve as the facilitator of the foreign policy-making system. The main rivals for this responsibility have been the State Department under the secretary of state and the National Security Council staff under the national security adviser. Since the Kennedy administration, presidents have tended to look to their national security advisers to manage their foreign policy-making system. Critics of this trend have maintained that the oversight, coordination, and leadership of the foreign policy-making system properly belong to the State Department.[102] They argue that the State Department was intended to be preeminent in foreign affairs, and its foreign policy expertise, accountability to Congress, and network of embassies in foreign capitals make it the best choice to run the president's foreign policy-making system.

The State Department, however, has institutional interests like any department that inhibit its ability to be an arbiter between competing departments and agencies. Just as the military mission of the Defense Department or the intelligence mission of the CIA disposes those units to approach foreign affairs from a unique perspective, State's diplomatic mission disposes it to prefer its own foreign policy strategies. Even if State Department officials were able to mediate disputes impartially between other bureaucratic units, those units would never regard State as a neutral department.

Although a foreign policy-making system coordinated by the NSC staff denies the State Department its traditional role as the manager of foreign policy, the NSC has a better chance of succeeding as a referee between competing departments and agencies and ensuring that the president remains in control of foreign policy. This is because the NSC is answerable to the president and has no institutional mission beyond serving the president.

The question of who should lead the foreign policy-making system pertains not only to the NSC staff and the State Department, but to their leaders as well. Some secretaries of state, including John Foster Dulles of the Eisenhower administration and George Marshall and Dean Acheson of the Truman administration, were their presidents' foremost foreign policy advisers. The influence of other secretaries, however, most notably William P. Rogers who served in the Nixon administration, was eclipsed by other officials. Kissinger, Nixon's assistant for national security during his first term, served as the administration's principal foreign policy spokesperson and negotiator. Rogers's activities were confined primarily to ceremonial tasks and administering the State Department. In 1973 Kissinger became secretary of state, thereby occupying the office that traditionally went with the power he already possessed.

Foreign Policy Decision-making Systems

The National Security Act of 1947 established a forum presidents could use as the focus of their foreign policy decision-making system. Presidents were not obliged, however, to convene meetings of the NSC or to regard the meetings that were held as decision-making forums. Congress had mandated the existence of a National Security Council and a staff to support it, but it was up to the president to decide how to use them, if at all. Many presidents have chosen to deemphasize NSC meetings, preferring to rely on ad hoc meetings with small groups of trusted advisers. Others have used the NSC as the formal centerpiece of an extensive web of committees and interagency groups considering foreign policy. Every post–World War II president, however, has brought a unique leadership style to the management of foreign policy decision making.

Harry Truman's suspicion that Congress had created the NSC to check his authority and Truman's strained relationships with his first two secretaries of defense, James Forrestal and Louis Johnson, initially led him to ignore the NSC. He attended only twelve of the first fifty-seven NSC meetings.[103] During the Korean War the NSC developed a more important policy-making role. Truman attended most meetings and the group was used to forge presidential foreign policies. Nevertheless, Truman still emphasized its advisory nature and frequently consulted its individual members or ad hoc groups rather than relying on the entire NSC for policy advice.

Dwight Eisenhower's foreign policy decision-making system reflected his military background. He presided over highly structured weekly meetings of the NSC and created NSC subcommittees to consider specific policy issues. He also established the "Planning Board," a staff body charged with foreign policy planning, and the "Operations Coordinating Board," an interagency committee charged

Henry Kissinger served as Nixon's principal foreign policy spokesperson and negotiator. In 1973 he became secretary of state.

The White House

with overseeing implementation of executive decisions.[104] Although Eisenhower's system had the advantages of ensuring that all parties would participate in decision making and the president would not become bogged down in details better left to subordinates, it often has been criticized as being too rigid and formalistic. Meetings were sometimes held because they were routinely scheduled rather than because they were necessary. Eisenhower also insisted that his top advisers reach a consensus on issues. His demand for unanimity led to policy papers that were too general and vague to provide direction to lower-level personnel charged with implementing policy.

John Kennedy replaced Eisenhower's formal committees with a less structured collegial decision-making system. Kennedy's reliance on the advice of departmental experts who had advocated the disastrous U.S.-supported Bay of Pigs invasion of Cuba by Cuban nationals in April 1961 had convinced him that he needed independent sources of national security advice in the White House. As a result, the NSC staff under the direction of the national security adviser, McGeorge Bundy, not only facilitated the decision-making process, it generated and evaluated policy options for the president. Formal NSC meetings also were deemphasized. During the Cuban missile crisis Kennedy relied on an assembly of his closest advisers known as the "Executive Committee." Unlike the NSC, membership in this ad hoc group depended not on statutory requirements, but on the trust and confidence of the president.[105]

Lyndon Johnson made few changes in either Kennedy's national security decision-making system or the personnel who ran it. The number of advisers involved in ad hoc policy-making sessions declined, however, especially when the Vietnam War was the topic. Johnson developed the practice of discussing the war at Tuesday lunch meetings attended by five or six close advisers. NSC meetings were used primarily to announce and discuss decisions that had already been made. In 1966, Johnson created formal interdepartmental groups to develop and coordinate policy proposals that would flow up to the NSC, but the work of these groups was largely confined to peripheral issues unrelated to the war. [106]

Richard Nixon tried to create a foreign policy-making system that incorporated the best aspects of the Eisenhower and Kennedy-Johnson systems. He created a formal interagency committee structure like Eisenhower's to ensure that all departments and agencies would be heard. Unlike Eisenhower's committee system, however, Nixon's was intended to produce several policy options for the president's consideration rather than an interdepartmental consensus. The committees also were designed to make less important decisions, thereby allowing the president and his top advisers to concentrate on the most important issues. Nixon established a strong NSC staff that enabled the president and his national security adviser, Henry Kissinger, to monitor the activities of the committees.

Although most scholars consider Nixon's NSC system to be a well-conceived blueprint for national security decision making, that blueprint was not always followed. His strong interest in national security affairs and the delicate nature of the negotiations to end the Vietnam War and improve relations with the Soviet Union and Communist China led to a centralization of decision making in the hands of Nixon, Kissinger, and the NSC staff that excluded other top advisers and departments. Late in Nixon's presidency, the Watergate scandal dominated the president's time, causing the president to rely even more on Henry Kissinger and a small circle of trusted advisers. [107]

Nixon's successor, Gerald Ford, was able to restore balance to the foreign policy decision-making system. Ford used the NSC staff and national security adviser Brent Scowcroft primarily as coordinators of national security decision making rather than as policy advisers. The president still relied heavily on Kissinger who had become secretary of state in 1973, but the views of other departments and agencies were integrated more often into national security decisions than they had been during the latter years of Nixon's presidency.

Like Richard Nixon, Jimmy Carter leaned heavily on the NSC staff and his national security adviser, Zbigniew Brzezinski. Nevertheless, Carter also tried to encourage a decentralized advisory system that would filter proposals up to his office from the bureaucracy. To ensure that he would not be insulated from a diversity of opinion, he had department and agency leaders report directly to him rather than through a chief of staff or the national security adviser. Carter's system, however, suffered from the frequent disagreements of Brzezinski and Secretary of State Cyrus Vance, who resigned his post in May 1980 after U.S. forces failed to rescue American hostages in Iran.

Ronald Reagan initially announced his intention to give his secretaries of defense and state dominant roles in national security policy making. Nevertheless, Reagan rejected a plan submitted by Secretary of State Alexander Haig to designate the State Department as the manager of foreign policy. The president took a whole year before setting up a formal foreign policy-making system that stressed cabinet predominance.[108] From the beginning of the administration, however, the NSC staff was given a smaller role than it had had under Presidents Nixon, Ford, and Carter. Reagan's first national security adviser, Richard Allen, did not even have direct access to the president. Although subsequent national security advisers William Clark, Robert McFarlane, John Poindexter, Frank Carlucci, and Colin Powell did have daily access to the president, none dominated the policy-making process as Henry Kissinger and Zbigniew Brzezinski had under Nixon and Carter.

The most distinguishing feature of the Reagan foreign policy-making system was the president's hands-off leadership. Ronald Reagan allowed his cabinet secretaries and other subordinates vast discretion in responding to the day-to-day issues affecting their area of foreign policy. He limited his own participation primarily to the articulation of broad themes and the performance of ceremonial duties.

Reagan's style of leadership was praised by some observers during his presidency as an example of how presidents should delegate responsibilities to save their energies for the most important decisions and avoid being overwhelmed by the details of foreign policy. The Iran-contra scandal, which was uncovered in 1986, however, demonstrated the dangers of Reagan's detached leadership of the foreign policy-making system. NSC staff member Lt. Col. Oliver North along with national security adviser Vice Adm. John Poindexter and other administration officials attempted to use funds acquired from secret arms sales to Iran to aid the Nicaraguan "contra" rebels, even though Congress had prohibited U.S. government military aid to the contras. The Tower Commission, appointed by the president to review his NSC system in the wake of the affair, commented on Reagan's management style in its 1987 report:

> The President's management style is to put the principal responsibility for policy review and implementation on the shoulders of his advisors. Nevertheless, with such a complex, high-risk operation and so much at stake, the President should have ensured that the NSC system did not fail him. He did not force his policy to undergo the most critical review of which the NSC participants and the process were capable. At no time did he insist upon accountability and performance review. Had the President chosen to drive the NSC system, the outcome could well have been different.

The scandal forced the resignation of several White House officials and led the president to project a more visible role in foreign policy making.

The Bureaucracy as a Source of Presidential Power

The foreign policy bureaucracy can be a great asset to presidents in their struggle with Congress for control of foreign policy and their efforts to provide effective foreign policy leadership. The bureaucracy's most obvious benefit is that it enables presidents and their closest advisers to concentrate on the decisions and initiatives they deem most important while the bureaucracy deals with the many small foreign policy matters the executive branch must handle daily. President Nixon and his national security adviser, Kissinger, spent the vast majority of their foreign policy time during Nixon's first term on three problems: ending the Vietnam War, opening up China, and improving relations with the Soviet Union. Most other foreign policy matters were left to the bureaucracy. Although Nixon and Kissinger certainly neglected other important matters as a result, the extraordinary attention they were able to give these principal issues made progress possible.

The bureaucracy's capacity to supply the president with information and advice is another asset. No institution, including Congress, has information sources in foreign affairs that can compare with the array of channels supplying the president with current intelligence and professional opinions. Most modern presidents have been briefed daily on foreign policy issues by their secretary of state, national security adviser, or other top aides. These officials in turn receive information and proposals that have been distilled and funneled up to them from their respective departments. Presidents also frequently order studies of particular topics. This information and advice make it possible for a president to address foreign policy issues intelligently without being an expert.

In addition to the information available from normal advisory and diplomatic resources, the nation's vast intelligence-gathering capabilities are at the president's service. The director of the CIA coordinates intelligence activities and relays important intelligence directly to the president. Many foreign policy decisions, particularly those that involve the use of force, cannot be made without access to intelligence information. For example, President Kennedy decided to blockade Cuba during the Cuban missile crisis after he and his advisers had carefully analyzed all intelligence information.[109] The president's access to intelligence has provided a rationale for presidential autonomy over foreign policy. Congress's recognition of this presidential advantage contributed to its frequent willingness to accept presidential leadership in foreign affairs following World War II. Since the Vietnam War, however, Congress has more actively sought access to intelligence and has been more reluctant to accept presidential evaluations of international issues.

The professional foreign policy bureaucracy also provides continuity between the policies of successive administrations. When a new president takes office the general policy directives that provide guidance to the bureaucracy change and the political appointees who head the various departments and agencies are new, but the bureaucrats continue to collect intelligence, write reports, and make recommendations. Useful initiatives begun by the previous president have a chance to find a place in the new administration, and foreign governments that are frustrated by the frequent changes in presidential leadership can take comfort in the continuing presence of career officials with whom they have dealt in the past.

The Bureaucracy as an Impediment to Presidential Power

Although presidents have authority over the foreign policy bureaucracy, it does not always serve their purposes. Indeed, since the end of World War II, executive branch departments and agencies often have been a greater obstacle to presidential will in foreign affairs than has Congress. This has occurred because the goals and interests of the bureaucracy often have conflicted with those of the president. Political scientist Richard Neustadt has explained why presidents have found it difficult to control the bureaucracy:

> Everything somehow involves the President. But operating agencies owe their existence least of all to one another—and only in some part to him. Each has a separate statutory base; each has its statutes to administer; each deals with a different set of subcommittees at the Capitol. Each has its own peculiar set of clients, friends, and enemies outside the formal government. Each has a different set of specialized careerists inside its own bailiwick. Our Constitution gives the President the 'take-care' clause and the appointive power. Our statutes give him central budgeting and a degree of personnel control. All agency administrators are responsible to him. But they also are responsible to Congress, to their clients, to their staffs, and to themselves. In short, they have five masters.[110]

The president must, therefore, do more than order bureaucrats to perform a given function. As Neustadt said, the president must "convince such men that what the White House wants of them is what they ought to do for their sake and on their authority."[111]

Such persuasion is not always easy for presidents and their staff. Foreign service officers, military personnel, members of the intelligence community, and other career executive branch employees involved in foreign affairs are neither dependent on the president for their jobs nor necessarily in agreement with presidential goals and policies. Career bureaucrats naturally are concerned with the welfare of their particular department or agency. They usually will fight against policies that could diminish their responsibilities or resources, and they often will resent decisions that show an obvious disregard for their institutional point of view. In addition, foreign policy bureaucrats may regard presidents and their political appointees as temporary invaders of the foreign policy realm whose political goals threaten the permanent interests of the United States.

Members of the foreign policy bureaucracy have several means by which they can resist presidential will in foreign affairs. They can delay or undermine the execution of presidential directives, provide the president only with information and options that do not conflict with their own interpretation of an issue, leak details of a controversial or covert policy to Congress or the media, publicly oppose a policy, or resign in protest. The president may have the constitutional power to order an agency to carry out a particular task, but if that agency drags its feet or otherwise undermines implementation of the order, the president's power can be neutralized.

The most important means available to presidents of controlling the bureaucracy and communicating to it their foreign policy vision is the power to appoint the officials who will head the departments and agencies. These officials serve as department managers as well as members of the inner circle of presidential advisers. In choosing these appointees the president must reconcile, on the one hand, the need to find a qualified person with administrative talent who will be respected by the department he or she heads, with, on the other hand, the president's desire to maintain control over the bureaucracy. Even the most loyal presidential appointee, however, usually will develop a competing loyalty to the department or agency, which may at times conflict with the goals of the president.[112]

Notes

1. Theodore C. Sorensen, *Kennedy* (New York: Bantam, 1966), 573.
2. Louis Henkin, *Foreign Affairs and the Constitution* (New York: Norton, 1972), 76-77.
3. Edward S. Corwin, *The President: Office and Powers 1787-1984*, 5th rev. ed. (New York: New York University Press, 1984), 201.
4. Quoted in Clinton Rossiter, *The American Presidency*, 2d ed. (New York: Time, 1960), 15.
5. Robert F. Jones, "George Washington and the Establishment of Tradition," in *Power and the Presidency*, ed. Philip C. Dolce and George H. Skau (New York: Scribner's, 1976), 19.
6. Alexander Hamilton, *The Gazette of the United States*, June 29, 1793, quoted in Robert S. Hirschenfield, ed., *The Power of the Presidency* (New York: Atherton, 1968), 51.
7. Quoted in Corwin, *The President*, 210.
8. James Madison, *The Gazette of the United States*, August 24, 1793, quoted in Hirschenfield, 57-58.
9. Quoted in Howard Ball, *Constitutional Powers: Cases on the Separation of Powers and Federalism* (St. Paul, Minn.: West, 1980), 176.

10. Arthur M. Schlesinger, Jr., *The Imperial Presidency* (Boston: Houghton Mifflin, 1973), 102-103.
11. Quoted in Arthur Bernon Tourtellot, *The Presidents on the Presidency* (Garden City, N.Y.: Doubleday, 1964), 272.
12. James MacGregor Burns, *Presidential Government: The Crucible of Leadership* (Boston: Houghton Mifflin, 1965), 46-48.
13. Richard Harmond, "Theodore Roosevelt and the Making of the Modern Presidency," in *Power and the Presidency,* ed. Dolce and Skau (New York: Scribner's, 1976), 72-73.
14. Theodore Roosevelt to H. C. Lodge, January 28, 1909, quoted in Schlesinger, *The Imperial Presidency,* 89.
15. Richard M. Pious, *The American Presidency* (New York: Basic Books, 1979), 53.
16. For a discussion of the Tonkin Gulf incident, see Leslie H. Gelb and Richard K. Betts, *The Irony of Vietnam: The System Worked* (Washington, D.C.: Brookings, 1979), 100-104; Eugene Windchy, *Tonkin Gulf* (New York: Doubleday, 1971).
17. Gelb, *The Irony of Vietnam,* 103-104.
18. Robert E. DiClerico, *The American President,* 2d ed. (Englewood Cliffs, N.J.: Prentice-Hall, 1983), 59.
19. Tourtellot, *The Presidents on the Presidency,* 274.
20. Quoted in Pious, *The American Presidency,* 334.
21. Quoted in Corwin, *The President,* 207-208.
22. Henkin, *Foreign Affairs and the Constitution,* 301.
23. Arthur Miller, *Presidential Power in a Nutshell* (St. Paul, Minn.: West, 1977), 134.
24. Quoted in Tourtellot, *The Presidents on the Presidency,* 298.
25. Schlesinger, *The Imperial Presidency,* 27.
26. Ibid., 128.
27. Cecil V. Crabb, Jr., and Pat M. Holt, *Invitation to Struggle: Congress, the President and Foreign Policy* (Washington, D.C.: CQ Press, 1984), 14-15.
28. John Jay, "No. 64," in *The Federalist Papers,* Alexander Hamilton, James Madison, and John Jay (New York: New American Library, 1961), 392-393.
29. George H. Haynes, *The Senate of the United States* (Boston: Houghton Mifflin, 1938), 575.
30. Buel W. Patch, "Treaties and Domestic Law," *Editorial Research Reports,* March 28, 1952, 241.
31. Abraham D. Sofaer, *War, Foreign Affairs and Constitutional Power: The Origins* (Cambridge, Mass.: Ballinger, 1976), 95-96.
32. Corwin, *The President,* 240.
33. Quoted in Ball, *Constitutional Powers,* 175.
34. Joseph E. Kallenbach, *The American Chief Executive: The Presidency and the Governorship* (New York: Harper and Row, 1966), 505.
35. Pious, *The American Presidency,* 336.
36. F. M. Brewer, "Advice and Consent of the Senate," *Editorial Research Reports,* June 1, 1943, 350.
37. Ibid., 352.
38. Louis W. Koenig, *The Chief Executive* (New York: Harcourt Brace and World, 1968), 211-212.
39. DiClerico, *The American President,* 48.
40. Theodor Meron, "The Treaty Power: The International Legal Effect of Changes in Obligations Initiated by the Congress," in *The Tethered Presidency: Congressional Restraints on Executive Power,* ed. Thomas M. Franck (New York: New York University Press, 1981), 116-117.
41. Henkin, *Foreign Affairs and the Constitution,* 134.
42. Meron, in *The Tethered Presidency,* 105-108.
43. Kallenbach, *The American Chief Executive,* 507.
44. Henkin, *Foreign Affairs and the Constitution,* 159.
45. Corwin, *The President,* 205-206.
46. Dorothy Buckton James, *The Contemporary Presidency,* 2d ed. (Indianapolis: Bobbs-Merrill, 1974), 238.
47. Quoted in Henkin, *Foreign Affairs and the Constitution,* 377.
48. Francis O. Wilcox, *Congress, the Executive, and Foreign Policy* (New York: Harper and Row, 1971), 161.
49. Kallenbach, *The American Chief Executive,* 508.
50. Henkin, *Foreign Affairs and the Constitution,* 168-170.
51. Crabb, *Invitation to Struggle,* 15.

52. Loch K. Johnson, *The Making of International Agreements: Congress Confronts the Executive* (New York: New York University Press, 1984), 12. Johnson estimates from his analysis of international agreements made between January 1, 1946, and December 31, 1972, that 87 percent have been made in accordance with treaties or legislation.
53. Lawrence Margolis, *Executive Agreements and Presidential Power in Foreign Policy* (New York: Praeger, 1986), 95.
54. Edward M. Borchard, "Treaties and Executive Agreements," *American Political Science Review* 40 (August 1946): 735.
55. Johnson, *The Making of International Agreements,* 12.
56. Henkin, *Foreign Affairs and the Constitution,* 177-178.
57. Ibid., 178-179.
58. Margolis, *Executive Agreements,* 6-7.
59. Ibid., 6-7.
60. Schlesinger, *The Imperial Presidency,* 86.
61. Ibid., 86-87.
62. Margolis, *Executive Agreements,* 7-9.
63. Ibid., 9.
64. Tourtellot, *The Presidents on the Presidency,* 277.
65. DiClerico, *The American President,* 49.
66. Wilcox, *Congress, the Executive, and Foreign Policy,* 160-161.
67. DiClerico, *The American President,* 51.
68. Johnson, *The Making of International Agreements,* 86-87.
69. *Congressional Quarterly Almanac, 1972* (Washington, D.C.: Congressional Quarterly Inc., 1972), 619.
70. Koenig, *The Chief Executive,* 212.
71. Corwin, *The President,* 212.
72. Alexander Hamilton, "No. 69," in *The Federalist Papers,* 420.
73. Schlesinger, *The Imperial Presidency,* 14.
74. Koenig, *The Chief Executive,* 213.
75. Kallenbach, *The American Chief Executive,* 493.
76. Crabb, *Invitation to Struggle,* 18-19.
77. Seth P. Tillman, *The United States in the Middle East* (Bloomington: Indiana University Press, 1982), 221.
78. Quoted in Tourtellot, *The Presidents on the Presidency,* 291.
79. Pious, *The American Presidency,* 335.
80. Miller, *Presidential Power in a Nutshell,* 37.
81. Koenig, *The Chief Executive,* 213.
82. Robert E. Hunter, *Presidential Control of Foreign Policy: Management or Mishap* (New York: Praeger, 1982), 79-80.
83. Ibid., 84.
84. Koenig, *The Chief Executive,* 217.
85. Corwin, *The President,* 235.
86. Ibid., 236.
87. Henkin, *Foreign Affairs and the Constitution,* 46.
88. Elmer Plischke, *Diplomat in Chief: The President at the Summit* (New York: Praeger, 1986), 13.
89. Kallenbach, *The American Chief Executive,* 498-499.
90. Plischke, *Diplomat in Chief,* 121.
91. Kallenbach, *The American Chief Executive,* 499.
92. James, *The Contemporary Presidency,* 127-128.
93. Quoted in Plischke, *Diplomat in Chief,* 202.
94. Ibid., 200-202.
95. Richard Nixon, "Superpower Summitry," *Foreign Affairs* 64, no. 1 (Fall 1985): 1.
96. Ibid., 9-10.
97. Plischke, *Diplomat in Chief,* 460-473.
98. Ibid., 456-460.
99. Marcus Cunliffe, *American Presidents and the Presidency* (New York: American Heritage, 1972), 286.
100. Amos A. Jordan and William J. Taylor, *American National Security: Policy and Process* (Baltimore: Johns Hopkins University Press, 1984), 64.
101. John E. Endicott, "The National Security Council," in *American Defense Policy,* 5th ed., ed. John F. Reichart and Steven R. Sturm (Baltimore: Johns Hopkins University Press, 1982), 521-522.
102. For an outline of a state-centered foreign policy-making system see I. M. Destler, *Presidents, Bureaucrats, and Foreign Policy* (Princeton, N.J.: Princeton University Press, 1974), 254-294.

103. Endicott, "The National Security Council," 522.
104. Zbigniew Brzezinski, "The NSC's Midlife Crisis," *Foreign Policy* 69 (Winter, 1987-1988): 84-85.
105. Jordan, *American National Security*, 91.
106. Ibid., 91-92.
107. Charles W. Kegley, Jr., and Eugene R. Wittkopf, *American Foreign Policy: Pattern and Process* (New York: St. Martin's Press, 1979), 258-259.
108. Brzezinski, "The NSC's Midlife Crisis," 90.
109. Graham T. Allison, *Essence of Decision* (Boston: Little, Brown, 1971), 46-62.
110. Richard E. Neustadt, *Presidential Power: The Politics of Leadership from FDR to Carter,* 2d ed. (New York: Wiley, 1980), 30-31.
111. Ibid., 26.
112. Hunter, *Presidential Control of Foreign Policy*, 18.

Selected Bibliography

Corwin, Edward S. *The President: Office and Powers 1787-1984.* 5th ed. New York: New York University Press, 1984.

Crabb, Cecil V., and Pat M. Holt. *Invitation to Struggle: Congress, the President and Foreign Policy.* 2d ed. Washington, D.C.: CQ Press, 1984.

Destler, I.M. *Presidents, Bureaucrats, and Foreign Policy.* Princeton, N.J.: Princeton University Press, 1974.

Henkin, Louis. *Foreign Affairs and the Constitution.* New York: Norton, 1975.

Hunter, Robert E. *Presidential Control of Foreign Policy: Management or Mishap.* New York: Praeger, 1982.

Johnson, Loch. *The Making of International Agreements: Congress Confronts the Executive.* New York: New York University Press, 1984.

Kallenbach, Joseph E. *The American Chief Executive: The Presidency and the Governorship.* New York: Harper and Row, 1966.

Margolis, Lawrence. *Executive Agreements and Presidential Power in Foreign Policy.* New York: Praeger, 1986.

Neustadt, Richard E. *Presidential Power.* 2d. ed. New York: Wiley, 1980.

Pious, Richard M. *The American Presidency: The Politics of Power from FDR to Carter,* New York: Basic Books, 1979.

Plischke, Elmer. *Diplomat in Chief: The President at the Summit.* New York: Praeger, 1986.

Schlesinger, Arthur M. *The Imperial Presidency.* Boston: Houghton Mifflin, 1973.

Wilcox, Francis O. *Congress, the Executive, and Foreign Policy.* New York: Harper and Row, 1971.

Commander in Chief

The Framers of the Constitution distrusted both executive and military power and believed the potential for tyranny was great when the two were combined. Among the colonial grievances cited in the Declaration of Independence were the charges that the British monarch had "kept among us, in times of peace, Standing Armies without the Consent of our legislature" and "affected to render the Military independent of and superior to the Civil Power." The document also denounced the quartering of troops in American homes, the impressment of American sailors for British warships, and the unjust war being waged against the colonies. The delegates to the Constitutional Convention were determined to restrain military power to prevent the new government from committing the type of offenses that they believed the British had perpetrated on the colonies. Their main instrument of accomplishing this constitutional goal was the separation of powers. They therefore rejected a proposal to grant the president the authority to declare war and divided the war-making power between the executive and Congress.

Nevertheless, the Founders of the United States were practical people who recognized that they must not cripple their young nation's ability to defend itself, especially against sudden attack, through their efforts to prevent the misuse of military power. While many war powers, including the decision to go to war, could be given to Congress, command of U.S. forces during a conflict necessitated the unified and flexible leadership that only a single person could provide. As Alexander Hamilton noted: "Of all the cares or concerns of government, the direction of war most peculiarly demands those qualities which distinguish the exercise of power by a single hand." [1] The Framers therefore assigned the commander-in-chief power to the presidency and took comfort in the certainty that George Washington would be the first person to hold that office.

Few presidents, however, have been as well suited for the role of commander in chief as George Washington. Many have mismanaged military affairs, and a few have abused their military power. In addition, the dramatic expansion of presidential authority over national security affairs in the decades following World War II led to a confrontation between the executive and legislative branches over the war power that has not been entirely resolved. Yet it is difficult to imagine that the historical record of the United States could have been improved had

By Daniel C. Diller

the Framers separated the role of commander in chief from the presidency. The Civil War, World War I, and World War II demonstrated that a strong president willing to interpret the commander-in-chief power broadly is in the best position to lead the military, unite the American people, and focus the efforts of the nation on victory when war threatens its security. As political scientist Clinton Rossiter wrote: "We have placed a shocking amount of military power in the President's keeping, but where else, we may ask, could it possibly have been placed?" [2]

Constitutional Distribution of War-making Power

There was general agreement at the Constitutional Convention that the person who occupied the highest civilian office should also be the commander in chief of the nation's military forces. Article II, section 2, of the Constitution states: "The President shall be Commander in Chief of the Army and Navy of the United States, and of the Militia of the several States, when called into the actual Service of the United States." This statement is all the Constitution says about the president's war-making power. Unlike all other constitutional grants of power to the presidency, the commander-in-chief clause confers an office rather than a function on the president. [3] Since the precise authority of this office was left undefined, presidents have been able to argue that they possess any power or duty traditionally associated with the office of supreme military commander, rather than just the single function of commanding the armed forces. Consequently, virtually any action that improves the nation's defenses in peacetime or helps it prevail over an enemy in wartime without usurping the power of the other branches or violating the law can be justified under a broad interpretation of the commander-in-chief clause.

In addition, foreign policy and chief executive powers give presidents responsibilities in the area of national security that are not specifically enumerated in the commander-in-chief clause. Through their power to negotiate treaties and executive agreements, presidents may establish an alliance or conclude an armistice. As chief executive, commander in chief, and the occupant of the only elected national office that never is out of session, the president is

> The President shall be Commander in Chief of the Army and Navy of the United States, and of the Militia of the several States, when called into the actual Service of the United States.
> —from Article II, section 2

also recognized as being responsible for the defense of the nation if it is attacked. This role is reinforced by the presidential oath of office in the Constitution, which pledges the president to "preserve, protect, and defend the Constitution of the United States."

The constitutional authors did not, however, regard war making as a function to be dominated by the executive branch. By giving Congress significant war powers, the Framers hoped to prevent the president from making war alone. In contrast to the single phrase designating the president as commander in chief, the clause outlining Congress's war powers is detailed and specific. Article I, section 8, of the Constitution grants Congress the authority:

> To declare War, grant Letters of Marque and Reprisal, and make Rules concerning Captures on Land and Water; To raise and support Armies...; To provide and maintain a Navy; To make Rules for the Government and Regulation of the land and naval forces; To provide for calling forth the Militia to execute the Laws of the Union, suppress Insurrections and repel Invasions; To provide for organizing, arming and disciplining the Militia, and for governing such Part of them as may be employed in the Service of the United States, reserving to the States respectively, the Appointment of the Officers, and the Authority of training the Militia according to the discipline prescribed by Congress.

As Congress's enumerated war powers indicate, the Framers intended Congress to have authority over the raising, equipping, and organizing of the armed forces, while the president would direct the military in times of war. The two branches would share power over the military, an instrument of government often abused if controlled by a single master. A president seeking to become a military dictator would be hindered by Congress's exclusive authority to raise, equip, and organize an army and navy. Presidents might wish to fight a war, but without Congress's support they would lack the necessary tools to do so. Conversely, Congress's ability to legislate a war would be restricted by the president's command of the military during hostilities and authority to negotiate treaties.

Power to Declare War

Although Congress's power to raise armies and fund wars and the president's command of the military in times of war are unquestioned, the authority over the decision when and where to employ military force has been the subject of conflict between the executive and legislative branches. The Framers' suspicions of executive power ruled out granting the president the exclusive authority to declare war. Yet their decision to give Congress alone the power to declare war is significant, since they could have divided this power between the legislative and executive branches. For example, they could have given the president the power to declare war with the "advice and consent of the Senate" as they had with the treaty power. Instead, the authors of the Constitution deliberately delegated to Congress the entire decision to declare war. Moreover, it is clear from the writings of the Framers that they regarded the act of declaring war as more than a formality. By giving Congress the power to declare war they sought to ensure that the decision to risk American lives in the defense of the United States or in pursuit of its perceived interests would be made by the democratically elected representatives closest to the people who would be called upon to fight and die. James Madison wrote:

> Those who are to conduct a war cannot in the nature of things be proper or safe judges whether a war ought to be commenced, continued, or concluded. They are barred from the latter functions by a great principle in free government, analogous to that which separates the sword from the purse, or the power of executing from the power of enacting laws.[4]

The delegates to the Constitutional Convention, however, did not expect Congress to authorize every use of military force. In an early draft of the Constitution, Congress was given the power to "make war," but Madison and Elbridge Gerry convinced their colleagues to change the phrase to "declare war" so as to give the president the prerogative to repel sudden attacks.[5] The Framers recognized that the speed and secrecy only a single decision maker could provide was essential to the safety of the nation if it came under attack.

Despite this concession to executive power the Framers believed they had sufficiently checked the president's war-making authority. In the The Federalist Papers, Hamilton, one of the foremost advocates of a strong chief executive at the Constitutional Convention, narrowly interpreted the commander-in-chief power:

> The president is to be commander-in-chief of the army and navy of the United States. In this respect his authority would be nominally the same with that of the King of Great Britain, but in substance much inferior to it. It would amount to nothing more than the supreme command and direction of the military and naval forces, as first general and admiral of the Confederacy; while that of the British king extends to the *declaring* of war and to the *raising* and *regulating* of fleets and armies—all of which, by the Constitution under consideration, would appertain to the legislature.[6]

The constitutional distribution of authority over the decision to go to war seems clear. Congress decides when to go to war unless the United States is attacked, in which case the president defends the nation. Yet this simple formula is full of ambiguities. How is war to be defined? Are there military missions short of war that the president can order without congressional authorization? Can the president order an attack to preempt an assault from a potential enemy? Can the president order U.S. forces to invade the territory of a neutral nation in pursuit of enemy forces? Can the president incite an attack through actions that are clearly provocative to a potential enemy? The legislative and executive branches were left to battle over these and other war power ambiguities. That Congress has declared war only five times—the War of 1812, the Mexican War, the Spanish-American War, World War I, and World War II—despite U.S. involvement in over one hundred violent military conflicts and incidents illustrates that the Framers' original division of the war power did not address all the situations in which hostilities might be initiated. Because presidents have direct command of military forces and they are charged with defending the nation, they have been in a better position to exploit this ambiguity than Congress. Consequently, when presidents have believed that a war or military action was necessary, they usually have found ways to maneuver the nation into a conflict.

Power to End War or Declare Neutrality

As commander in chief, presidents have the power to order the military to stop fighting or to withdraw from an area of conflict. In addition, their sole authority to negotiate treaties gives them the power to conclude an armistice with an enemy. If Congress has declared war, however, the president cannot unilaterally end the legal state of war that exists. Congress must take some action that supersedes its declaration of war. Usually this action is accomplished through Senate ratification of a treaty negotiated by the president ending the war and establishing peaceful relations with the enemy nation. The Mexican War, the Spanish-American War, and hostilities in the Pacific theater of World War II were officially terminated in this manner. Congress also may formally end a state of war by repealing its declaration of war. This method was used in 1921 after Congress had refused to ratify the Versailles treaty at the end of World War I and in 1951 formally to end war with Nazi Germany.[7]

A more troublesome question is who has the power to declare neutrality. Since only Congress has the authority to declare war, some students of the Constitution have reasoned that only Congress has the power to declare that the nation will not become involved in a war. Secretary of State Thomas Jefferson made this argument in 1793 when President Washington proclaimed that the United States would remain "friendly and impartial" toward the warring British and French.[8] Many Americans wanted to honor the treaty of alliance with France that had been signed during the American Revolution, but Washington believed U.S. involvement in the conflict would disrupt the nation's development. Jefferson supported Washington's proclamation despite his reservations about the constitutionality of the president's declaring neutrality. As a concession to Jefferson, Washington left the word "neutrality" out of his proclamation.

Washington's declaration of neutrality set off a famous debate in the *Gazette of the United States* between Hamilton, who supported Washington's action, and Madison, who opposed this expansion of executive power. Hamilton conceded that the legislature had the exclusive right to declare war but asserted that until war is declared, the executive has the responsibility to maintain peace. Madison saw the declaration of neutrality as a usurpation of Congress's power to declare war. Hamilton and Madison were less concerned with neutrality than with the larger issue of whether a president could declare unilaterally what U.S. foreign policy would be. Over time, Hamilton's view that the president can make U.S. foreign policy has prevailed over Madison's strict interpretation of presidential power. *(See "Hamilton-Madison Debate," p. 107, in Chief Diplomat chapter.)*

Washington's decision to ask Congress to pass judgment on the proclamation created the precedent that declarations of neutrality were subject to congressional approval. Congress eventually did ratify the president's action by passing the Neutrality Act of 1794.

Subsequently, the custom also developed that Congress would not declare war without a presidential request. Yet on two occasions Congress demonstrated that it could move a president to accept a war even if the president had reservations about the wisdom of doing so. In 1812 a majority of members of Congress convinced President James Madison that war against the British was necessary. In 1898, with public opinion on its side, Congress pressured a reluctant William McKinley to ask for a declaration of war against Spain.

Development of Presidential War Powers

The Constitution's assignment of the office of commander in chief to the president created the basis for presidential war powers, but a more precise outline of these powers had to evolve through events. Most early presidents held a narrow view of their commander-in-chief role that was similar to Hamilton's description of the president as the nation's "first general or admiral." Gradually, however, the commander-in-chief power grew. The Civil War and the two world wars provided the most dramatic boosts to presidential authority.

Presidential war powers expanded during these national security emergencies because the flexibility, secrecy, speed, and unity of command associated with the president were seen as crucial to the preservation and defense of the United States. According to political scientist Edward S. Corwin, "The principal canons of constitutional interpretation are in wartime set aside so far as concerns both the scope of national power and the capacity of the President to gather unto himself all constitutionally available powers in order the more effectively to focus them upon the task of the hour."[9] Presidential actions that would have raised a storm of protest in peacetime were accepted in the name of necessity when the security of the nation was at stake.

This is not to say that when wartime emergencies were over presidents continued to wield exceptional power as if an emergency still existed, but every extension of presidential power set a precedent to which a future president could refer when an emergency of similar gravity appeared. Woodrow Wilson's expansion of presidential war power paved the way for Franklin D. Roosevelt's extraordinary wartime authority, just as Wilson had referred to Lincoln's exercise of power when justifying his own.

Following World War II, the cold war between the United States and the Soviet Union, the development of nuclear weapons, and the U.S. participation in two lengthy undeclared wars in Asia led to a series of national security emergencies. Under these conditions presidential commander-in-chief authority continued to expand until the late 1960s and early 1970s when Congress reacted to executive branch abuses of power by attempting to reassert its role in national security affairs. Although the executive branch still dominates national security policy, Congress has scrutinized national security affairs more closely and has been able to restrict presidential policies on a variety of issues including funding for selected weapons systems and military aid to allied nations and guerrilla organizations.

Ironically, until the latter stages of the Vietnam War the expansion of the president's war powers usually had been accomplished with Congress's approval and often with its active support. Congress validated many of Lincoln's actions, passed legislation delegating sweeping wartime powers to both Woodrow Wilson and Franklin Roosevelt, and acquiesced to the accumulation of power by presidents after World War II.

Although the Supreme Court has occasionally ruled against exercises of presidential war power, it seldom has done so when a war was in progress. Often the Court has in effect approved presidential actions by declining to make a ruling on the grounds that such actions are political matters that should be resolved between the executive and legislative branches. Moreover, as the Court's approval of the internment of Americans of Japanese descent during World War II demonstrates, the high court has recognized the authority of the president acting in concert with Congress to take virtually any action in response to a grave national emergency.[10]

Early Presidents

Early presidents generally adhered to the principle that Congress was responsible for committing the United States to war. John Adams consulted with Congress in 1798 before allowing U.S. naval forces to attack French vessels that were preying on U.S. commercial shipping. Congress refrained from declaring war but passed legislation that authorized the president to order U.S. military forces to battle the French.[11] Similarly, Jefferson and Madison believed presidents should carefully respect Congress's warmaking powers. Yet the events of their administrations demonstrated the desirability of a strong commander in chief when war did come.

Jefferson and the Barbary Pirates

Like Adams, Jefferson faced the problem of a limited naval war. In 1801, American ships in the Mediterranean were being attacked by pirates from Tripoli and the other Barbary Coast states of Algeria, Morocco, and Tunisia. Jefferson wanted to take quick action to resolve the problem, but he also wished to uphold Congress's power to order U.S. troops into hostilities. He therefore dispatched a squadron of ships to the Mediterranean with instructions to offer the rulers of the Barbary Coast states payments to leave U.S. shipping alone. Jefferson anticipated trouble, however, and provided the following instructions to the commodore of the squadron:

> But if you find on your arrival in Gibralter that all the Barbary Powers have declared war against the United States, you will then distribute your forces in such a manner, as your judgment shall direct, so as best to protect our commerce and chastise their insolence—by sinking, burning, or destroying their ships and vessels wherever you shall find them.[12]

Jefferson did not disclose these orders to Congress when he went before that body December 8, 1801, to request approval to take the offensive in the naval war that was already being fought. Rather, he emphasized the constitutional restraints under which the squadron operated:

> I sent a small squadron of frigates into the Mediterranean, with assurance to that power [Tripoli] of our desire to remain in peace, but with orders to protect our commerce against the threatened attack.... One of the Tri-

politan cruisers ... was captured, after a heavy slaughter of her men, without the loss of a single one on our part.... Unauthorized by the Constitution, without the sanction of Congress, to go beyond the line of defense, the vessel, being disabled from committing further hostilities, was liberated with its crew.[13]

Congress passed legislation early in 1802 authorizing the naval war that eventually led to a treaty with the Barbary powers. Jefferson had used deception and a *fait accompli* to secure the Mediterranean for U.S. commercial shipping while publicly asserting Congress's right to determine when military force would be used.[14]

Hamilton, however, found Jefferson's consultations with Congress ridiculous. He asserted that the president did not need to ask Congress's permission to turn loose the navy because: "When a foreign nation declares or openly and avowedly makes war upon the United States, they are then by the very fact already at war and any declaration on the part of Congress is nugatory; it is at least unnecessary." [15]

Despite Jefferson's occasional willingness to violate his own principles in pursuit of objectives he considered important, he genuinely believed that the president should not order military operations without congressional approval except in defense of the nation. In 1805 when Spanish subjects in Florida made incursions into the newly acquired Louisiana Territory, Jefferson told Congress: "Considering that Congress alone is constitutionally invested with the power of changing our condition from peace to war, I have thought it my duty to await their authority for using force.... The course to be pursued will require the command of means which it belongs to Congress exclusively to yield or to deny." When Congress chose not to grant Jefferson the authority to attack the Spanish in Florida, he accepted its decision.[16]

The War of 1812

The War of 1812 was the first declared war in U.S. history. Sentiment for the war had been aroused by British captures of American commercial ships and their crews, allegations that the British were supplying hostile Indians on the frontier with arms, and a desire to acquire foreign territory in Canada and Florida. The initial advocates of the war were not President Madison and his close advisers, but members of Congress from the South and the West. These "War Hawks" represented areas that were troubled by Indian attacks and falling agricultural prices. In contrast, the Federalist merchants of the Northeast, who were making large profits on export shipments that avoided capture, were against the war. They feared that war would interfere with their commerce much more than sporadic British seizures of their ships.

Although Madison had tried sincerely to resolve disputes with the British through diplomacy, he was eventually persuaded that the nation must go to war to protect its rights. On June 1, 1812, the president asked Congress for a declaration of war. Madison, like Jefferson, believed strongly that Congress should determine whether the nation should initiate hostilities. In his address to lawmakers asking for a declaration of war Madison called war making a "solemn question which the Constitution wisely confides to the legislative department of the Government." [17] The declaration was passed 79-49 by the House and 19-13 by the Senate. Members of Congress from the South and the West prevailed over their colleagues from the Northeast.

Not only was the nation divided over the war, it was unprepared to fight. The small American navy was hopelessly outmatched, and despite the war's popularity in the South and West the army had difficulty recruiting volunteers. In the Northeast there was talk of secession, and the governors of Massachusetts, Rhode Island, and Connecticut refused to authorize the use of their troops. U.S. forces suffered a string of humiliating defeats including the capture and burning of Washington, D.C., by the British in August 1814.

After the British forces withdrew from the capital, Congress assembled to consider the war effort. Yet, with the army still at only about half its paper strength and enlistments falling off, Congress failed to agree on a conscription bill proposed by James Monroe, Madison's secretary of war and state. Fortunately, the Treaty of Ghent ending the war was signed on Decemeber 24, 1814. Before the news of the treaty reached New Orleans, however, Gen. Andrew Jackson's militia inflicted a stunning defeat on British regulars attacking the city on January 8, 1815. This victory restored some of the nation's pride, but the war had proven that a president's ability to wage a successful war depended not just on the encouragement of Congress but also on public consensus supporting the war.

The Annexation of Texas and the Mexican War

Texas declared its independence from Mexico in 1836 and indicated that it was interested in becoming part of the United States. Although most Americans supported the principle of expansion, the slavery issue made annexation of a new state a tricky political problem for any president. Presidents Andrew Jackson and Martin Van Buren avoided actions on the Texas issue that would anger voters in the North who were opposed to an extension of slavery. John Tyler, who succeeded to the presidency following the death of William Henry Harrison in 1841, however, was a proslavery Virginian who wished to strengthen the slave states and limit English influence over Texas.[18] He began secret negotiations on annexation with Texas and initiated a pro-annexation campaign. The Texans, however, were concerned that if they agreed to annexation they would be invaded by Mexico. They informed Tyler that they would be reluctant to agree to annexation without guarantees that he would protect them with U.S. forces. This created a dilemma for Tyler, whose narrow interpretation of the Constitution had led him to reject presidential authority to use military force without congressional approval except in defense of the nation. In early 1844 Tyler showed that he valued the acquisition of Texas more than his own strict constructionist principles when he ordered the deployment of U.S. forces in Texas and the Gulf of Mexico while the secret negotiations proceeded. When the needed two-thirds of the Senate refused to approve the annexation treaty produced by the negotiations, Tyler sidestepped the Constitution by asking Congress to validate the agreement with a majority vote of both Houses. The joint resolution was passed, thereby establishing a new type of congressionally approved executive agreement.[19]

In the spring of 1846 President Polk ordered Gen. Zachary Taylor to deploy his army in a strip of disputed territory near the Rio Grande that was claimed by Texas but occupied exclusively by Mexicans. Polk had decided to ask Congress for a declaration of war even before Mexican forces attacked Taylor's army, killing a number of American soldiers. The clash ensured the passage of a declaration of war since Polk could claim that Mexico was the aggressor. He told Congress: "Now, after reiterated menaces Mexico has invaded our territory and shed American blood on American soil."[20] On May 13, 1846, Congress recognized "a state of war as existing by act of the Republic of Mexico." Polk's successful maneuvering to place the country in a "defensive" war demonstrated the power of presidents to initiate hostilities through their responsibility to defend the nation.

Library of Congress

U.S. and Mexican forces clash at the Battle of Buena Vista in 1847. In hopes of securing territory occupied by Mexico but claimed by Texas, President Polk maneuvered the country into a "defensive" war after U.S. soldiers were attacked by Mexican forces.

Lincoln and the Civil War

President Lincoln's extraordinary exercise of power during the Civil War demonstrated how far the authority of the presidency could be expanded in wartime. Lincoln believed he faced a choice between preserving the Union and adhering to a strict interpretation of the Constitution. He feared that if he carefully observed the law he would sacrifice the flexibility necessary to prevent the destruction of the nation. In April 1864 he explained his reasoning in a letter to Albert Hodges:

> I did understand, however, that my oath to preserve the Constitution to the best of my ability impressed upon me the duty of preserving by every indispensable means, that government—that nation, of which that Constitution was the organic law. Was it possible to lose the nation and yet preserve the Constitution? By general law, life and limb must be protected, yet often a limb must be amputated to save a life; but a life is never wisely given to save a limb. I felt that measures otherwise unconstitutional might become lawful by becoming indispensable to the preservation of the nation. Right or wrong, I assumed this ground and now avow it.[21]

Lincoln did not come to this conclusion lightly. As a member of the House of Representatives, he had questioned the legality and propriety of President Polk's actions that led to the Mexican War. *(See box, Lincoln's Attack on Presidential War Powers, p. 145.)* Lincoln's expansion of his own

Mathew Brady, 1862; Library of Congress

In conducting the Civil War, Lincoln believed he faced a choice between preserving the Union and adhering to the Constitution. "Was it possible to lose the nation and yet preserve the Constitution?" he wrote. "By general law, life and limb must be protected, yet often a limb must be amputated to save a life."

war-making powers as president, therefore, did not result from a cavalier attitude toward the Constitution but from his recognition of an unprecedented emergency.

Lincoln's Expanded Powers

On April 12, 1861, the Civil War began when Confederate forces attacked Fort Sumter. Recognizing that strict constructionists in Congress might object to emergency measures he thought necessary to deal with the crisis, Lincoln delayed the convocation of Congress until July 4. He used this three-month period to order a series of executive actions to meet the military emergency.[22]

On May 3, 1861, he called for the mobilization of seventy-five thousand state militia subject to his orders under a 1795 act that authorized the president to issue such a call. Although this action was considered within the powers of the president, most of Lincoln's actions during the early months of the war had no constitutional or congressional sanction. In the same proclamation used to mobilize the militia Lincoln unilaterally increased the size of the regular army by twenty-three thousand troops and the navy by eighteen thousand. In addition he ordered nineteen vessels added to the navy and directed the secretary of the Treasury to advance $2 million to authorized persons to pay for military requisitions. Lincoln also ordered a blockade of Southern ports, suspended the writ of *habeas corpus* (the constitutional guarantee against illegal detention and imprisonment) in the vicinity of routes used by Union forces between Washington, D.C., and Philadelphia, ordered foreign visitors to observe new passport regulations, restricted "treasonable correspondence" from being carried by the Post Office, and directed the military to arrest and detain persons "who were represented to him" as contemplating or participating in "treasonable practices."[23]

When Congress finally convened on July 4, Lincoln asked the members to ratify the actions he had taken in their absence. He maintained that some of his emergency measures "whether strictly legal or not, were ventured upon under what appeared to be a popular demand and a public necessity, trusting then, as now, Congress would readily ratify them." In justifying his suspension of *habeas corpus* Lincoln made the constitutional argument that in spite of the placement of the provision on *habeas corpus* suspension in Article I, the Framers must have intended the president to share with Congress the authority to suspend *habeas corpus* since emergencies requiring such action would not always occur when Congress was in session. Yet Lincoln defended his action on practical grounds as well, asking Congress, "Are all the laws but one to go unexecuted, and the Government itself go to pieces lest that one be violated?" In asking this question Lincoln implied that a national emergency threatening the existence of the nation may empower the president to ignore parts of the Constitution to defend the whole.[24]

During the summer, Congress debated a joint resolution that sanctioned Lincoln's acts. Nagging doubts about the legality of his suspension of *habeas corpus* and blockade of Southern ports prevented a vote on the resolution. Near the end of the session, however, a rider attached to a pay bill for army privates that approved Lincoln's actions was rushed through Congress. On August 6, 1861, Congress passed the bill and its rider, which declared the president's acts pertaining to the militia, the army, the navy, and the volunteers "in all respects legalized and made valid, to the same intent and with the same effect as if they had been issued and done under the previous express authority and direction of Congress." [25]

Throughout the war, Lincoln continued to extend his commander-in-chief power beyond its constitutional limits. In 1862, when voluntary recruitments were not adequately supplying the army's need for additional troops, Lincoln ordered a militia draft. The same year he extended his suspension of the writ of *habeas corpus* to persons throughout the entire nation who were "guilty of any disloyal practice." He also declared that these persons could be tried by military courts. On January 1, 1983, Lincoln issued the Emancipation Proclamation freeing "all persons held as slaves within any State or designated part of a State, the people whereof shall then be in rebellion against the United States." Lincoln maintained that his commander-in-chief power gave him the authority to issue the proclamation, since the liberation of slaves reduced the labor force of the South, thus hindering its ability to carry on the war.[26]

Prize Cases

Although the Supreme Court eventually objected to Lincoln's order that civilians could be tried in military courts, it did sanction his prosecution of a total war against the South. When hostilities began, the president had ordered a blockade of Confederate ports to prevent the South from selling cotton to England and importing supplies. The owners of four vessels seized by the blockade sued for redress on the grounds that the seizures were illegal since Congress had not declared war against the South. They argued that Lincoln's duty to suppress the insurrection was not equivalent to the power to wage war. Therefore, an act of war such as a blockade could not legally be ordered by the president in the absence of a declaration of war.

In 1863 the Supreme Court rejected these arguments in its 5-4 decision on the *Prize Cases*. Writing for the majority Justice Robert C. Grier explained:

It is not necessary to constitute war, that both parties should be acknowledged as independent nations or sovereign states. A war may exist where one of the belligerents claims sovereign rights as against the other. . . . A civil war is never solemnly declared; it becomes such by its accidents—the number, power, and organization of the persons who originate and carry it on. When the party in rebellion occupy and hold in a hostile manner a certain portion of territory; have declared their independence; have cast off their allegiance; have organized armies; have commenced hostilities against their former sovereign, the world acknowledges them as belligerents, and the contest a *war*.[27]

The decision supported Lincoln's interpretation that the insurrectionist South was without sovereign rights, while the North possessed all rights of a belligerent in wartime. Moreover, the decision gave Lincoln confidence that the Court would not restrict his expansive interpretation of his commander-in-chief powers in the future. Although this case dealt specifically with the president's power to respond to a general insurrection, advocates of a strong presidency have often cited it when arguing in favor of a broad interpretation of presidential war power.[28]

Spanish-American War

The 1895 Cuban rebellion against Spanish rule occurred when the United States was ready to seek a wider

Lincoln's Attack on Presidential War Powers

As president, Abraham Lincoln stretched presidential power until it approached dictatorship. He justified his extraordinary emergency powers under the commander-in-chief clause and his duty "to take Care that the Laws be faithfully executed." Ironically, as a young member of the House of Representatives, Lincoln had argued for a limited interpretation of the president's war-making authority. In a letter to William H. Herndon, his law partner in Illinois, Lincoln asserted his strict view of presidential power:

Washington, Feb. 15, 1848

Dear William:

. . . Let me first state what I understand to be your position. It is, that if it shall become *necessary, to repel invasion,* the President may, without violation of the Constitution, cross the line, and *invade* the territory of another country; and that whether such *necessity* exists in any given case, the President is to be the *sole* judge.

. . . Allow the President to invade a neighboring nation, whenever *he* shall deem it necessary to repel an invasion, and you allow him to do so, *whenever he may choose to say* he deems it necessary for such purpose—and you allow him to make war at pleasure. Study to see if you can fix *any limit* to his power in this respect, after you have given him so much as you propose. If, to-day, he should choose to say he thinks it necessary to invade Canada, to prevent the British from invading us, how could you stop him? You may say to him, "I see no probability of the British invading us" but he will say to you "be silent; I see it, if you dont."

The provision of the Constitution giving the war-making power to Congress, was dictated, as I understand it, by the following reasons. Kings had always been involving and impoverishing their people in wars, pretending generally, if not always, that the good of the people was the object. This, our Convention understood to be the most oppressive of all Kingly oppressions; and they resolved to so frame the Constitution that *no one man* should hold the power of bringing this oppression upon us. But your view destroys the whole matter, and places our President where kings have always stood. Write soon again.

Yours truly,
A. Lincoln[1]

1. *The Collected Works of Abraham Lincoln,* ed. Roy P. Basler (New Brunswick, N.J.: Rutgers University Press, 1953), 451-452.

role in global affairs. For some Americans the Cuban crisis offered an opportunity to flex American muscle against a European power and extend U.S. influence. Others, aroused by slanted reports in the press of Spanish atrocities in Cuba, wished to rescue the island's inhabitants from Spanish tyranny. This combination of forces resulted in a popular crusade in the United States to aid Cuban independence.

President Grover Cleveland resisted the temptation to satisfy the nation's appetite for war with Spain during the last two years of his term. William McKinley entered office in 1897 similarly determined to avoid war. After the mysterious sinking of the U.S. battleship *Maine* in Havana harbor in February 1898, however, he could no longer stand up to congressional belligerence and public opinion. He asked Congress on April 11, 1898, to approve American armed intervention in Cuba. Spain already had conceded to most American demands for a settlement of the Cuban crisis, but on April 25, Congress passed a declaration of war authorizing the president to use military force to expel Spain from the island. It was adopted by the Senate 42-35 and by the House 310-6.

Although American forces were poorly equipped, trained, and commanded, superior American naval power enabled the United States to oust the Spanish from Cuba, Puerto Rico, and the Philippines. The brevity of the war, the ease with which victory was won, and the popularity of the conflict made McKinley's job as commander in chief an easy one. The issue of what to do with the Philippines, however, was more controversial. McKinley decided to take possession of the islands and, as he later told a group of clergymen, "educate the Philipinos, and uplift and civilize and Christianize them." [29]

On December 10, 1898, Spain signed a treaty relinquishing its control over Cuba and ceding the Philippines along with Puerto Rico and Guam to the United States. Yet many senators had reservations about McKinley's idealistic plans for the Philippines, and the treaty was not assured of ratification. In spite of news that Philippine insurgents had taken up arms against U.S. forces, the Senate approved the treaty after a month of debate by a vote of 57-27, only one vote more than the necessary two-thirds majority. For the first time a president and Congress had acquired territory for the United States outside the North American continent through war.

The World Wars

The first involvement of the United States in an overseas war of massive scale provided the occasion for the most dramatic expansion of presidential powers since the Civil War. The basis for Woodrow Wilson's power differed from Lincoln's, however, in that Lincoln had taken emergency actions independently of Congress, while Wilson was handed most of his expanded war-making authority by statute.[30] Congress gave Wilson not only expanded control of the military and discretion to fight subversion and espionage but also unprecedented control over industries and the allocation of scarce resources. For example, the Lever Food and Fuel Act gave the president "full authority to undertake any steps necessary" for the conservation of food resources. In addition, the Overman Act gave the president complete authority to reorganize the executive branch. Congress was willing to make these broad delegations of power to Wilson because most members believed that the scope and urgency of the war required unified control and direction of all operations and resources related to the the war effort.

Many delegations of authority to the president simply stated their objectives and left Wilson to decide how to achieve them. He commandeered plants and mines, requisitioned supplies, fixed prices, seized and operated the nation's transportation and communications networks, and managed the production and distribution of foodstuffs. The Council of National Defense, an umbrella agency created by Wilson, administered the economy during the war. Wilson created the War Industries Board using his authority as commander in chief. Wall Street broker Bernard Baruch, who had been appointed by Wilson to head the board, became a virtual dictator over American industry. The president also established by executive order the Committee of Public Information, under whose direction a system of voluntary news censorship was instituted and various government publicity services were organized. On April 28, 1917, Wilson imposed strict cable censorship, which later was extended to other forms of communication with foreign countries under authority of the Trading with the Enemy Act of October 6, 1917.

In essence, Congress did not just give Wilson broad discretion in implementing its statutes, it abdicated legislative power to him for the duration of the war. Wilson's confidence in his presidential prerogatives fostered by his wartime authority backfired on him, however, when Congress refused to ratify the Treaty of Versailles after Wilson had ignored lawmakers during its negotiation.[31]

Presidential war power reached its apex during World War II. Constitutional scholar Edward S. Corwin wrote, "The relation ... of the First World War to the Second as regards constitutional interpretation is that of prologue and rehearsal." [32] Like Wilson during World War I, Franklin Roosevelt was delegated wide powers by Congress to manage the economy and direct the war effort, but Roosevelt went beyond Wilson in asserting his prerogative to take any action he deemed necessary to the war effort.

Overcoming Neutrality

Ironically, Franklin Roosevelt's war powers were tightly restrained during the 1930s by the prevailing mood of isolationism in Congress and among the American people. Congress had enacted a series of laws designed to keep the United States out of the conflicts brewing in Europe and Asia. These laws included the Neutrality Acts of 1935 and 1937, which prohibited shipments of arms, ammunition, or implements of war to any belligerent nation, including those that had been the victims of aggression. Isolationist sentiment was so strong that Roosevelt did not denounce these acts until after Hitler's invasion of Poland in September 1939, which brought Great Britain and France into the war against Nazi Germany.[33] Even after the Nazis' aggressive intentions had become obvious, Roosevelt had to maneuver the country toward active support of Britain and the other allies, whose survival he believed was crucial to U.S. security.

On September 3, 1940, Roosevelt announced that he had concluded an agreement with Great Britain under which that country would receive fifty "overage" destroyers in return for the right to lease certain British territory in the western Atlantic for U.S. naval and air bases. Roosevelt's destroyer deal was accomplished through an executive agreement—a legally binding pact between the president and the British government—rather than a Senate ratified treaty. The trade violated at least two congressional statutes, but Roosevelt's attorney general, Robert Jackson, asserted that the president acted legally under his commander-in-chief authority to "dispose" of the armed forces.

On March 11, 1941, Congress passed the Lend-Lease Act, described by Corwin as the most "sweeping delegation of legislative power" ever given to a president.[34] It authorized the president to manufacture any defense article and to "sell, transfer title to, exchange, lease, lend or otherwise dispose of" the defense articles to the "government of any country whose defense the President deems vital to the defense of the United States." The act gave the president the power to aid the Allied cause as he saw fit by virtually any means short of using the armed forces.

Yet Roosevelt did use the armed forces to aid the Allied cause despite the absence of any congressional sanction for acts of war. After Germany occupied Denmark in April 1941, Roosevelt ordered U.S. troops to be stationed in Greenland. Three months later, American forces occupied Iceland. Both moves were made without consulting Congress, which had forbidden the deployment of U.S. reserves and draftees outside the Western Hemisphere in the Reserves Act of 1940 and the Selective Service Act of 1941.[35] Moreover, by the summer of 1941, U.S. naval vessels under presidential orders were escorting allied convoys across the Atlantic. After the *U.S.S. Greer* exchanged shots with a German submarine on September 4, the president declared that henceforth U.S. warships providing protection to supply convoys bound for Britain would be under orders to attack Axis vessels on sight. Three months before Congress declared war, therefore, Roosevelt had maneuvered the nation into an undeclared naval war in the Atlantic.[36]

Roosevelt's "Dictatorship"

The U.S. entry into World War II was accompanied by the concentration of virtually all war powers in the president's hands. Congress delegated vast authority to the president to prosecute the war as it had during World War I, but it also acquiesced to Roosevelt's many unsanctioned appropriations of power and his broad interpretations of congressional statutes. Although Roosevelt saw the wisdom of obtaining Congress's approval for controversial actions, he was far more assertive than Wilson in using his commander-in-chief power to establish complete control over the war effort. Roosevelt created dozens of executive regulatory agencies that were not based on a specific statute, such as the Office of Emergency Management, Board of Economic Warfare, National War Labor Board, Office of Defense Transportation, and War Production Board. Anything remotely connected to the nation's war effort, including its resources and economic activity, was regulated by these war management agencies, which were responsible to the president rather than to existing departments or independent regulatory agencies. Roosevelt justified their creation by citing general delegations of power from Congress, the powers available to him under his emergency proclamations of 1939 and 1941, and his own prerogatives as commander in chief.[37]

On September 7, 1942, the president demonstrated how far he believed his war powers extended. In a speech to Congress, Roosevelt issued an ultimatum to lawmakers to repeal certain provisions contained in the Emergency Price Control Act of 1942:

> I ask the Congress to take this action by the first of October. Inaction on your part by that date will leave me with an inescapable responsibility to the people of this country to see to it that the war effort is no longer imperiled by threat of economic chaos.
>
> In the event that the Congress should fail to act, and

act adequately, I shall accept the responsibility and I will act.

> At the same time farm prices are stabilized, wages can and will be stabilized also. This I will do.
>
> The President has the power, under the Constitution and under Congressional acts, to take measures necessary to avert a disaster which would interfere with the winning of the war....
>
> I have given the most thoughtful consideration to meeting this issue without further reference to the Congress. I have determined, however, on this vital matter to consult with Congress....
>
> The American people can be sure that I will use my powers with a full sense of my responsibility to the Constitution and to the country. The American people can also be sure that I shall not hesitate to use every power vested in me to accomplish the defeat of our enemies in any part of the world where our own safety demands such defeat.
>
> When the war is won, the powers under which I act automatically revert to the people—to whom they belong.[38]

With this declaration, Roosevelt claimed, according to Corwin, "the right and power to disregard a statutory provision which he does not deny, and indeed could not possibly deny, that Congress had full constitutional authority to enact, and which, therefore, he was under obligation by the Constitution to 'take care' should be 'faithfully executed.' "[39] Roosevelt was threatening to suspend the Constitution in the interest of national security if Congress did not act. Not even Abraham Lincoln during the Civil War had claimed the power to repeal a specific congressional statute. Many members of Congress were shaken by Roosevelt's ultimatum, and a few denounced it. Republican senator Robert A. Taft of Ohio called the speech "revolutionary and dangerous to the American form of government . . . an assertion that the laws of this country can be made by executive order."[40] The American public, however, supported Roosevelt's position; and with the war raging, there was little desire in Congress to engage the president in a constitutional showdown. Congress therefore amended the law to meet Roosevelt's objections.

Postwar Congressional Acquiescence

After World War II differences between the United States and the Soviet Union brought on the cold war, a state of continuous international tension that contributed to increased presidential control over national security policy. The specter of an aggressive Soviet Union pushing out wherever the West failed to resist made Congress reluctant to impose restrictions on executive action. A consensus developed that since presidents possessed both the capacity to act immediately and access to the most detailed and reliable information, they alone were suited to direct foreign and military policy. Their status as leaders of the free world and caretakers of the U.S. nuclear arsenal, the most devastating military force ever created, contributed to their unchallenged authority.

Korean War

When the North Korean army swept into South Korea on June 24, 1950, Harry S Truman believed he had to act to save South Korea and discourage further Communist aggression. The next day the United States called an emergency session of the United Nations (UN) Security

Council, which passed a resolution condemning the invasion and asking UN members to "render every assistance" to South Korea. By coincidence the Soviets were boycotting the Security Council to protest the exclusion of the new Communist government of China from the UN. Consequently, their representative was not present to veto the resolution. That evening Truman made up his mind to use air and naval forces to defend South Korea. He authorized Gen. Douglas MacArthur to evacuate Americans from South Korea, transport supplies to the South Koreans, and bomb military targets below the thirty-eighth parallel.

On June 27, Truman met with congressional leaders for the first time since the attack. Members of Congress overwhelmingly supported Truman's decision to commit U.S. forces. A few Republicans, however, protested Truman's failure to involve Congress in the decision. Influential Senate Republican Robert Taft announced on June 28 that while he agreed that U.S. forces should be used in Korea, the president had "no legal authority" to send them without the approval of Congress. Truman had indeed asked Secretary of State Dean Acheson and chairman of the Senate Foreign Relations Committee Tom Connally (D-Texas) if his armed reponse to the invasion required a declaration of war or other congressional action. Both men advised Truman that his commander-in-chief power and the UN Security Council resolution gave him ample authority to use the armed forces.

After Truman announced his intention to defend South Korea, the UN Security Council provided an additional justification for armed intervention by passing a second resolution explicitly calling on members to give military assistance to South Korea. By June 30 Truman had authorized MacArthur to use U.S. ground forces and to bomb targets in North Korea, thereby completing the U.S. commitment to defend South Korea.[41]

Truman could easily have secured a congressional resolution approving his use of military forces in Korea, but the president wished to avoid an appearance of dependence on Congress. According to Secreatary of State Acheson, Truman considered the presidency "a sacred and temporary trust, which he was determined to pass on unimpaired by the slightest loss of power or prestige."[42] Throughout American history, presidents had ordered U.S. forces to rescue Americans overseas, intervene in a foreign country, or undertake some other type of limited military mission. The Truman administration cited these precedents in justifying its unilateral actions in Korea.[43] Initially, there was reason to hope that U.S. military involvement in Korea would be short and limited, but soon the United States found itself in an undeclared war without precedent in American history. Although the president's power to use the armed forces for limited missions was unquestioned, presidential authority to commit the nation to a bloody war of undiscernible length involving hundreds of thousands of military personnel was not. By every definition the United States was waging war in Korea, regardless of the Truman administration's restrictions against the use of military force against Chinese territory and its assertions throughout the war that U.S. involvement amounted to participation in a UN "police action."[44]

Congress, however, was not quick to challenge presidential authority. During the fall of 1950, the war remained popular as UN forces were successful in driving the North Koreans up the peninsula. In November General MacArthur's forces had occupied most of North Korea and appeared close to reunifying North and South.[45] In November and December, however, Communist Chinese forces entered the war and drove UN forces back across the thirty-eighth parallel into South Korea.

With Congress already alarmed by the reversal of the war in Korea, Truman announced on December 19 that he planned to send four more divisions to Europe to bolster Allied defenses. Truman's intention to send so many troops abroad without congressional approval triggered a congressional reevaluation of U.S. defense and foreign policy that was known as the "great debate." The debate, which lasted from January to April of 1951, was principally concerned with Truman's deployment of troops to Europe, but it also addressed the issue of the president's authority to involve the United States in the Korean War. In the end the Senate passed two resolutions approving the dispatch of four divisions to Europe. One of the resolutions declared that it was the sense of the Senate that Congress should approve any future deployment of U.S. ground troops to Europe.

Truman hailed the resolutions as an endorsement of his policies. Indeed, the great debate had confirmed Congress's unwillingness to challenge the president's power to deploy U.S. forces around the world or send them into battle without congressional approval.

Truman's actions set the stage for a period of unquestioned presidential primacy in foreign and national security policy. Truman did suffer a setback in 1952 when the Supreme Court ruled in *Youngstown Sheet and Tube Co. v. Sawyer* that he did not have the authority to take over steel mills to prevent a strike that would damage the Korean War effort. Nonetheless, as historian Arthur M. Schlesinger, Jr., has written: "By bringing the nation into war without congressional authorization and by then successfully defending his exercise of independent presidential initiative, Truman enormously expanded assumptions of presidential prerogative."[46]

Joint Resolutions

The period following the Korean War was characterized by the passage of congressional resolutions granting presidents the authority to use such force as they deemed necessary to repel armed attacks or threats against designated nations or regions. Between 1955 and 1962 four joint resolutions of this type were passed. The Formosa Resolution, signed into law January 29, 1955, authorized presidents to use U.S. forces to protect Formosa and the Pescadores Islands against attack from Communist China. The Middle East Resolution, signed into law March 9, 1957, proclaimed U.S. intentions to defend Middle East countries "against any country controlled by international communism." The Cuban Resolution, signed into law October 3, 1962, authorized presidents to take whatever steps they believed necessary to defend Latin America against Cuban aggression or subversion and to oppose the deployment of Soviet weapons in Cuba capable of threatening U.S. security. The Berlin Resolution did not have the force of law but expressed the sense of Congress that the United States was determined to defend West Berlin and the access rights of the Western powers to that city.

These resolutions received wide support in Congress, although they did have critics who charged that the resolutions gave too much discretionary power to the president and absolved Congress from any responsibility for national security. Schlesinger described the extent of congressional abdication during this period:

In the decade after Korea Congress receded not alone from the effort to control the war-making power but almost from the effort to participate in it, except on occasions when national-security zealots on the Hill condemned the executive branch for inadequate bellicosity. Mesmerized by the supposed need for instant response to constant crisis, overawed by what the Senate Foreign Relations Committee later called "the cult of executive expertise," confused in its own mind as to what wise policy should be, delighted to relinquish responsibility, Congress readily capitulated to what Corwin at the start of the fifties had called "high-flying" theses of presidential prerogative.[47]

Vietnam War

No single president was entirely responsible for U.S. participation in the war in Vietnam. A succession of presidents gradually increased U.S. military involvement in Southeast Asia. In 1954 Vietnamese revolutionary forces defeated the French, who had controlled the region as a colonial power. President Dwight D. Eisenhower had continued the Truman administration's policy of sending aid to the French, but Eisenhower refused to intervene militarily to prevent a French defeat. After the French departed, Vietnam was temporarily partitioned with the Communist government of Ho Chi Minh ruling the North and anti-Communists in Saigon controlling the South. Eisenhower undercut reunification efforts, which he feared would result in Communist control over the entire country, by ignoring the scheduled reunification elections in 1956 and supporting the non-Communist regime in the South. The North Vietnamese and their supporters in the South launched a guerrilla war in an effort to achieve reunification through force. Although Eisenhower stepped up economic and military aid to the Saigon government, which included a small number of advisers, he avoided U.S. military involvement.

President John F. Kennedy, however, fearing the collapse of the Saigon government, responded to South Vietnamese requests for greater assistance by sending additional military advisers and counterinsurgency units to South Vietnam. Before he was assassinated, Kennedy had deployed 16,500 U.S. military personnel in Vietnam.

President Lyndon B. Johnson continued the gradual escalation of U.S. involvement in the widening war. The Gulf of Tonkin incident in August 1964 resulted in a resolution granting the president broad authority to combat North Vietnamese aggression. *(See box, Tonkin Gulf Resolution, p. 150.)* Armed with this congressional sanction and fearing an imminent Communist takeover, Johnson ordered the first regular combat troops to Vietnam in 1965. Their mission was to defend the U.S. airbase at Danang, but soon they were conducting patrols and actively engaging the enemy in combat.

Although Johnson believed his commander-in-chief powers and the Tonkin Gulf resolution gave him the authority to send the troops to Vietnam, he nevertheless wanted Congress on record as approving the move. He therefore requested a specific appropriation of $700 million for U.S. military operations in Vietnam. Within two days, both houses had passed the bill with little dissent.[48] By 1968, Johnson had increased U.S. troop strength in Vietnam to 500,000. The Communists' Tet offensive early that year, although militarily unsuccessful, caused Americans including Johnson to begin to lose confidence that the war could be won.

President Richard Nixon began slowly withdrawing U.S. forces from Vietnam in 1969. Nixon's goal was to extricate the United States from the Vietnam quagmire

Library of Congress

American citizens protesting the Vietnam War contend that President Johnson, who ordered the first regular combat troops to Vietnam in 1965, is a "War Criminal."

while achieving "peace with honor." In January 1973, the United States and North Vietnam signed a peace accord. The North Vietnamese returned U.S. prisoners of war and allowed the regime of South Vietnamese president Thieu to remain in power. In return the United States withdrew its forces from Vietnam and allowed North Vietnamese army units already in South Vietnam to remain there. Without U.S. support, however, South Vietnam was unable to defend itself against a 1975 North Vietnamese offensive that resulted in the fall of Saigon. Although President Nixon had promised Thieu that the United States would intervene if Communist forces threatened to conquer the South, Nixon had resigned the presidency in 1974, and Congress and the American public were firmly against further involvement in Southeast Asia.

The Vietnam War, like the Korean War, was a presidential war. Decision making about goals and strategy in Vietnam was dominated by the executive branch with little input from Congress. Neither Johnson nor Nixon sought congressional approval for their prosecution of the war after 1965. Nevertheless, the picture of these presidents carrying on military activities in Indochina without congressional consent often was overdrawn by critics of the war. Congress continually voted in favor of military appropriations and the draft, without which Johnson and Nixon could not have carried on the war for long. Once troops and materiel had been committed to battle, most members of Congress believed denying U.S. forces the money and reinforcements they needed to wage the war would be perceived as unpatriotic.

Congressional Resurgence

Not until 1969, when Congress recognized that the growing number of U.S. casualties in Vietnam, the fading

Tonkin Gulf Resolution

Each of the joint resolutions sanctioning presidential use of force passed by Congress between 1955 and 1962 represented a declaration of national policy upon which there was broad agreement. The supporters of these resolutions considered them to be effective tools by which Congress could create a united front behind presidential action. This was the intention of members of Congress when they voted almost unanimously in favor of the Tonkin Gulf resolution in 1964. Unlike the other resolutions, however, the Tonkin Gulf resolution revealed the dangers of congressional willingness to hand the president broad discretion in determining national security policy.

On August 2, 1964, the U.S. destroyer *Maddox*, which the navy contended was on a routine mission in the Tonkin Gulf off the coast of North Vietnam, was attacked by North Vietnamese patrol boats. Two nights later the *Maddox*, which had been joined by another destroyer, the *C. Turner Joy*, reported a second patrol boat attack. Neither ship was damaged. President Lyndon B. Johnson responded to the incidents by ordering U.S. warplanes to bomb North Vietnamese torpedo boat bases.

Johnson informed Congress that U.S. ships had been attacked and asked both houses to pass a resolution empowering him to respond to further North Vietnamese aggression. The administration depicted the incidents as unprovoked acts of belligerence. On August 7, Congress passed the Gulf of Tonkin Resolution by votes of 88-2 in the Senate and 416-0 in the House. The resolution stated that "Congress approves and supports the determination of the President, as Commander-in-Chief, to take all necessary measures to repel any armed attack against the forces of the United States and to prevent further aggression." It also declared that the United States was "prepared, as the President determines, to take all necessary steps, including the use of armed force, to assist any member or protocol state of the Southeast Asia Collective Defense Treaty requesting assistance in defense of its freedom." [1]

Members of Congress understood that the resolution would give the president great authority to prosecute the war. In the debate on the resolution, Sen. John Sherman Cooper (R-Ky.) questioned chairman of the Foreign Relations Committee J. William Fulbright (D-Ark.) on its implications:

> Cooper: In other words, we are now giving the President advance authority to take whatever action he may deem necessary? . . .
> Fulbright: I think that is correct.
> Cooper: Then, looking ahead, if the President decided that it was necessary to use such force as could lead into war, we will give that authority by this resolution?
> Fulbright: That is the way I would interpret it. [2]

By overwhelmingly passing the resolution, Congress was following the practice set during the previous decade of deferring to the president's judgment in national security matters in the name of expediency and unity.

This resolution has often been described as a "blank check" for presidential war making in Southeast Asia. Members of the Johnson administration and the president himself frequently cited the resolution as evidence of congressional authorization of their policies in Vietnam. Although the resolution in combination with U.S. membership in the Southeast Asia Treaty Organization may not have been the "functional equivalent" of a declaration of war, as Under Secretary of State Nicholas Katzenbach had claimed in 1967 during testimony before the Senate Foreign Relations Committee, it did provide a justification for almost any presidential military decision in Vietnam.

Investigations by the Senate Foreign Relations Committee in 1968 revealed that the *Maddox* was actually gathering sensitive intelligence within the territorial waters claimed by the North Vietnamese and that a South Vietnamese naval attack against North Vietnam was taking place near the time and place of the *Maddox* patrol. Furthermore, the investigations showed that the administration anticipated the North Vietnamese attacks. U.S. intelligence had warned that the North Vietnamese navy was under orders to respond to U.S. vessels in the vicinity of the South Vietnamese operation as if they were part of that operation, and U.S. ships had been moved to reinforce the *Maddox* before it was attacked. [3]

The Johnson administration had deceived Congress. Not only had the president permitted the ships to be sent into a situation where they were likely to be attacked, when the attack did occur, he maintained that it was a completely unprovoked act against an American ship on a routine mission in international waters. In addition, although the crews of the *Maddox* and *Turner Joy* did fire at what they believed were enemy vessels, evidence suggested that the second attack may have been the product of nervousness and poor visibility. In 1965, Johnson remarked on the second attack, "For all I know, our Navy was shooting at whales out there." [4] Nevertheless, the second attack was presented to Congress as completely factual.

The 1968 revelations about the Tonkin Gulf incidents and growing congressional discontent with the war led to the repeal of the Tonkin Gulf resolution on December 31, 1970. The repeal provision was added to a foreign military sales bill, which was signed by President Richard Nixon on January 12, 1971. The measure was largely symbolic and had no effect on the continuing prosecution of the war by the Nixon administration, which claimed that the president's commander-in-chief power gave him the authority to carry on the war.

1. Cecil V. Crabb, Jr., and Pat M. Holt, *Invitation to Struggle: Congress, the President and Foreign Policy,* 2d ed. (Washington. D.C.: CQ Press, 1984), 141.
2. Leslie H. Gelb with Richard K. Betts, *The Irony of Vietnam: The System Worked* (Washington, D.C.: Brookings, 1979), 103.
3. Richard M. Pious, *The American Presidency* (New York: Basic Books, 1979), 387.
4. Gelb, *The Irony of Vietnam*, 104.

prospects that the war could be won, and doubts about the morality of U.S. involvement had begun to turn the American public against the war did Congress begin to assert its war powers. In that year the Senate passed the National Commitments Resolution, which stated that a national commitment "results only from affirmative action taken by the legislative and executive branches ... by means of a treaty, statute, or concurrent resolution of both houses of Congress specifically providing for such commitment." Although the resolution only expressed the sense of the Senate and had no force of law, it represented Congress's growing dissatisfaction with its exclusion from national security and foreign policy decisions. Later in the year Congress adopted an amendment supported by President Nixon prohibiting the use of U.S. ground forces in Laos and Thailand. For the first time in three decades, Congress had exercised its authority to limit military activities overseas.[49]

In 1970, even as U.S. forces were being withdrawn from Southeast Asia, President Nixon secretly ordered U.S. forces into Cambodia to attack Communist sanctuaries. When Nixon announced the operation on April 30, 1970, college campuses around the United States erupted in protest against the expansion of the war. Four student demonstrators were killed by National Guard troops at Kent State University in Ohio, and 60,000 to 100,000 protestors marched on Washington. After months of debate, a lame-duck Congress passed an amendment in December 1970 barring the use of U.S. ground forces in Cambodia. This amendment did not lead to a confrontation with the Nixon administration since lawmakers had backed away from prohibiting the use of aircraft over Cambodia and Nixon had withdrawn U.S. ground troops from Cambodia months before the amendment passed. Nevertheless, Congress would not have passed such an amendment several years earlier. Later in December, Congress also repealed the Tonkin Gulf Resolution.

During the early 1970s momentum for legislation that would restore Congress's role in the foreign policy process continued to build in Congress. President Nixon undertook a series of controversial military actions without consulting Congress that underscored the legislative branch's inability to affect policy. He provided air support for South Vietnam's 1971 invasion of Laos, ordered North Vietnam's Haiphong harbor mined in May 1972, and launched massive bombing raids against North Vietnam in December 1972. Furthermore, Nixon's "secret" war in Cambodia in 1970, the publication of the Pentagon Papers in 1971 (which disclosed the deception of the executive branch during the 1960s), and the revelations about secret national security commitments uncovered by a Senate Foreign Relations subcommittee chaired by Stuart Symington (D-Miss.) contributed to the growing perception of lawmakers that executive branch secrecy was out of control. After three years of work and debate, Congress's attempts to construct a bill that would reestablish its foreign policy and national security powers culminated in the passage of the War Powers Act in 1973.

War Powers Act

Implicit in the passage of the War Powers Act (HJ Res. 542, PL 93-148) in November 1973 over President Nixon's veto was an admission by Congress that it had contributed to the debacle in Vietnam by abdicating its war-making responsibilities to the executive branch. The passage of the Tonkin Gulf resolution with only two senators dissenting and Congress's acquiescence to presidential budget and troop requests allowed the Kennedy, Johnson, and Nixon administrations to pursue a costly war that in retrospect had limited strategic significance and questionable chances for success. The results of the Vietnam War had belied the assumption that the executive branch with its superior intelligence resources, its unity of command, and its ability to act quickly should be responsible for determining when and how the nation should go to war. With the passage of the War Powers Act Congress attempted to ensure that it would have a decision-making role on matters of war and peace. The bill's preamble stated that its purpose was:

> To fulfill the intent of the framers of the Constitution of the United States and ensure that the collective judgement of both the Congress and the President will apply to the introduction of U.S. armed forces into hostilities, wherein situations where imminent involvement in hostilities is clearly indicated by the circumstances, and the continued use of such forces in hostilities or in such situations.

The most important and controversial provisions of the legislation outlined the situations under which presidents could commit troops, permitted Congress at any time by concurrent resolution to order the president to disengage troops involved in an undeclared war, and required presidents to withdraw armed forces from a conflict within sixty days—ninety if the president certified that further military action was necessary to disengage U.S. military personnel from a conflict safely—unless Congress specifically authorized its continuation. *(See box, War Powers Provisions, p. 152.)* Other provisions included in the act obligated presidents to report to Congress within forty-eight hours on large troop movements abroad and urged them to consult with Congress "in every possible instance" before ordering U.S. forces into hostilities or a situation where hostilities might be imminent.

Passage of the bill was heralded by its supporters as a major step in reasserting Congress's war-making powers. Republican senator Jacob K. Javits of New York, a chief architect of the Senate version of the legislation declared:

> With the war powers resolution's passage, after 200 years, at least something will have been done about codifying the implementation of the most awesome power in the possession of any sovereignty and giving the broad representation of the people in Congress a voice in it. This is critically important, for we have just learned the hard lesson that wars cannot be successfully fought except with the consent of the people and with their support.[50]

In President Nixon's October 24, 1973, veto message of the war powers bill, he stated that the resolution would impose restrictions on the authority of the president that would be "both unconstitutional and dangerous to the best interests of the nation."[51] Nixon's attempted veto of the legislation was supported by some conservatives in both houses and a small group of liberals who agreed that the measure was unconstitutional, but for different reasons.

The leading liberal opponent of the resolution's final form, Democratic senator Thomas F. Eagleton of Missouri, called the the act "the most dangerous piece of legislation" he had seen in his five years in the Senate.[52] Eagleton and other liberal critics of the War Powers Act charged that while it may force the president to deal with Congress within ninety days after troops are committed, it sanctions

War Powers Provisions

The 1973 War Powers Resolution:

~ stated that the president could commit U.S. armed forces to hostilities or situations where hostilities might be imminent only pursuant to a declaration of war, specific statutory authorization or a national emergency created by an attack upon the United States, its territories or possessions, or its armed forces

~ urged the president "in every possible instance" to consult with Congress before committing U.S. forces to hostilities or to situations where hostilities might be imminent, and to consult Congress regularly after such a commitment

~ required the president to report in writing within forty-eight hours to the Speaker of the House and president pro tempore of the Senate on any commitment or substantial enlargement of U.S. combat forces abroad, except for deployments related solely to supply, replacement, repair or training; required supplementary reports at least every six months while such forces were being engaged

~ authorized the Speaker of the House and the president pro tempore of the Senate to reconvene Congress if it were not in session to consider the president's report

~ required the termination of a troop commitment within sixty days after the president's initial report was submitted, unless Congress declared war, specifically authorized continuation of the commitment, or was physically unable to convene as a result of an armed attack upon the United States; allowed the sixty-day period to be extended for up to thirty days if the president determined and certified to Congress that unavoidable military necessity respecting the safety of U.S. forces required their continued use in bringing about a prompt disengagement

~ allowed Congress at any time U.S. forces were engaged in hostilities without a declaration of war or specific congressional authorization by concurrent resolution to direct the president to disengage such troops

~ set up congressional procedures for consideration of any resolution or bill introduced pursuant to the provisions of the resolution

~ provided that if any provision of the resolution was declared invalid, the remainder of the resolution would not be affected

virtually any use of the military by the president during those ninety days. Eagleton believed that an act that recognized unlimited presidential authority to commit forces to a conflict would enhance rather than restrict presidential war-making power. He warned: "By failing to define the president's powers in legally binding language, the bill provided a legal basis for the president's broad claims of inherent power to initiate a war. Under the formula, Congress would not participate in the warmaking decision until *after* forces had been committed to battle." [53] Although the resolution gave Congress the power to withdraw troops from a conflict, Eagleton believed Congress would rarely have the political will to do so, since such action would be seen by many constituents as unpatriotic or lacking in resolve.

On November 7, the House overrode the president's veto with a vote of 284-135—only four votes over the required two-thirds majority. Later in the day the Senate followed with a 75-18 override vote. The congressional override was made possible, in part, by the Watergate scandal, which had weakened Nixon's support among legislators of his own party.

Presidential Compliance

Since the passage of the War Powers Act, presidents have used military force on a number of occasions. Several of these actions, such as President Gerald R. Ford's evacuation of Saigon, Danang, and Phnom Penh in 1975, were uncontroversial and received the general approval of Congress. In most of the military operations undertaken since 1973, however, presidents have violated the letter or at least the spirit of the law. Presidents Gerald Ford, Jimmy Carter, and Ronald Reagan seldom consulted Congress before using the military, and efforts by Congress to force these presidents to start the sixty-day war powers clock were usually ignored. These operations have underscored the act's inability to control presidential war making in the absence of Congress's determination to assert its authority. They also have demonstrated the president's unrestrained prerogative to use military force during the initial sixty-day period allowed by the act.

Mayaguez Incident

The first major test of the War Powers Act occurred on May 12, 1975, when Cambodian Communist gunboats seized the U.S. merchant ship *Mayaguez* and its crew of thirty-nine off the disputed island of Poulo Wai in the Gulf of Siam. President Ford unilaterally ordered U.S. forces to free the sailors and their ship and to bomb Cambodian targets in retaliation. The rescue attempt succeeded in freeing the *Mayaguez* and its crew but resulted in the deaths of forty-one marines.

In this case, there was general agreement that the president had the authority to commit U.S. troops without receiving congressional authorization. Although Ford complied with the war powers provision that required him to report to Congress within forty-eight hours, some legislators complained that his consultations with selected members of Congress after the order to attack had been issued were inadequate and did not provide an opportunity for meaningful congressional involvement.

Ford, however, defended his decision not to consult with Congress before the operation in his report to that body. He argued: "When a crisis breaks out, it is impossible to draw the Congress in with the decision-making process in an effective way." Ford went on to criticize the resolution itself as "a very serious intrusion on the responsibilities of the President as Commander-in-Chief and the person who formulates and ought to execute foreign policy." [54]

Iran Hostage Rescue Attempt

In April 1980, President Carter sent U.S. forces into Iran in an attempt to rescue forty-nine American embassy personnel held hostage in Tehran. The president ordered the action without any prior consultations with members of Congress except a guarded reference made to Senate Majority Leader Robert Byrd (D-W.Va.) about the rescue attempt the day before it occurred. Equipment failure forced the mission to be aborted after eight commandoes died in a helicopter crash.

Carter justified his decision not to consult with Congress by citing the mission's dependence on secrecy. Many members of Congress agreed with Carter's assertion of the need for absolute secrecy. Sen. John Glenn (D-Ohio) remarked, "If I were on that raid, I wouldn't want it all over Capitol Hill."[55] Carter also maintained that the mission was a "humanitarian" rescue attempt rather than a military action against an enemy nation and therefore fell outside the scope of the act.[56]

Lebanon

In 1982 President Reagan sent U.S. troops to Lebanon as part of a multinational peace-keeping force. Marines initially were introduced into that country on August 24, 1982, with the specific mission of observing the evacuation of Palestine Liberation Organization (PLO) forces from Beirut under an agreement mediated by the United States. The marines left Beirut on September 10, after the PLO withdrawal had been completed. Before this operation, the president held constructive consultations with the foreign relations committees of both houses.[57] Reagan had reported to Congress on the deployment of marines the day before it took place. He nevertheless would not concede the validity of the War Powers Act and stated only that he was reporting to Congress "consistent" with the resolution rather than "under" it.[58]

After the assassination of President Bashir Gemayel of Lebanon on September 14, 1982, and the massacre of Palestinians at the Sabra and Shatila refugee camps by Lebanese Christian militia on September 16, President Reagan ordered twelve hundred U.S. Marines to return to Lebanon. The mission of the peace-keeping force, which arrived on September 29, was to join with Italian, French, and British forces in providing a buffer between warring factions, thereby improving stability in Lebanon and the Middle East in general.

Congress debated whether the marines were in a situation where hostilities were "imminent," but it did not demand that the War Powers clock be started. By the end of the summer of 1983, the marines had become targets of terrorist groups and other combatants in the region. On August 29, 1983, U.S. forces sustained their first casualties. President Reagan authorized the marines to fight back from their positions to defend themselves. On September 8, the president increased U.S. involvement in the conflict by ordering warships in the Mediterranean to shell positions in the hills outside of Beirut from which the marines had been receiving hostile fire.

The obvious escalation of U.S. involvement in Lebanon forced the president to negotiate with Congress on terms for keeping the marines there. On October 12, President Reagan signed a joint resolution empowering him to keep the marines in Lebanon for eighteen months. The compromise resolution stated that the marines had been in a situation of imminent hostilities, since August 29, 1983, and that this legislation was "the necessary specific statutory authorization under the War Powers Resolution for continued participation by United States Armed Forces in

the Multinational Force in Lebanon." President Reagan had conceded that the War Powers Act was applicable and agreed to a time limitation that had little possibility of forcing a withdrawal. In return Congress sanctioned his policies in Lebanon. Despite this congressional involvement, the compromise favored the president and demonstrated Congress's reluctance to use the War Powers Act to restrict presidential use of the military.[59]

On October 23, 1983, the suicide terrorist bombing of the marine headquarters in Lebanon killed 241 Americans and weakened public support for the deployment of U.S. troops there. During the winter the chaotic situation in Lebanon failed to stabilize, and the president ordered the marines to withdraw on February 7, 1984.

Grenada

On October 25, 1983, nineteen hundred U.S. troops under President Reagan's orders invaded the small Caribbean island of Grenada. The action, which Reagan referred to as a "rescue mission" was undertaken to overthrow Grenada's pro-Cuban, Marxist government, to restore order to the island, and to ensure the safety of approximately one thousand American citizens living there, most of whom were medical students. U.S. forces were joined by troops from six Caribbean nations belonging to the Organization of East Caribbean States, which had officially asked the United States to intervene.

Both houses of Congress overwhelmingly voted that the sixty-day clock of the War Powers Resolution had begun when U.S. troops invaded Grenada. The United States declared an end to the fighting on November 2, after U.S. troops had evacuated the medical students, overcome light resistance, and secured the island.[60]

Because U.S. troops had quickly achieved their objectives while sustaining few casualties, and the invasion was very popular among the U.S. public, Congress generally supported the Grenada action. The president, however, was sharply criticized by many members of Congress for failing to consult with them meaningfully before the invasion. Reagan had briefed selected congressional leaders about the mission on the evening of October 24, but this briefing was called merely to inform them that troops had already begun their voyage to Grenada. Sen. Charles McC. Mathias (D-Md.) observed after the invasion that the British prime minister was informed of the invasion before top congressional leaders.[61]

Libyan Bombing Raids

On April 14, 1986, President Reagan ordered U.S. warplanes to bomb targets in the Libyan cities of Tripoli and Benghazi. The surprise coordinated air strike resulted in the deaths of two U.S. fliers and, according to the Libyan government, dozens of Libyan military personnel and civilians. The attack was in response to the alleged involvement of Libyan leader Col. Muammar Qaddafi in recent terrorist acts. The operation received broad support from members of Congress of both parties.

Many prominent lawmakers, however, again criticized President Reagan's method of consulting with Congress. Reagan informed twelve congressional leaders of the attack on April 14 when the planes were halfway to their targets. Senate Minority Leader Robert Byrd complained that the meeting amounted to "notification" rather than consultation. Senate Foreign Relations Committee chairman Richard G. Lugar (R-Ind.) disputed Byrd's interpretation, saying the president indicated he would call off the mission if it met with strong congressional objections.[62]

The Libyan bombing highlighted the issue of presidential compliance with the consulting provision of the War Powers Act in cases where the president orders a military strike against terrorists or a nation known to support them. Two approaches to this issue surfaced in Congress in 1986. One advocated early presidential consultation with a designated body of lawmakers before the president ordered a military strike against terrorists. The other sought to exempt counterterrorist military operations from the usual consultation procedures required by the War Powers Act. Neither approach has yet been enacted into law.

Persian Gulf Naval Escorts

Since the war between Iran and Iraq began in 1980, the United States had avoided becoming involved in the conflict. By 1987, however, Iranian attacks on neutral ships threatened to slow the flow of Arab oil through the Persian Gulf. Because Kuwait, a small Persian Gulf state with large oil reserves, supported Iraq in the gulf war, its ships had become a favorite target of Iranian gunboats. In response to Kuwaiti pleas for assistance, President Reagan offered on March 10, 1987, to place tankers owned by Kuwait under the U.S. flag so they could be escorted through the gulf by U.S. warships. The administration's offer to escort the Kuwaiti tankers was intended to ensure the flow of oil through the gulf and to prevent the Soviet Union, which Kuwait also had asked for help, from increasing its influence among moderate Arab nations and its naval presence in the gulf.[63]

On May 17, before the escort operation had begun, the U.S.S. *Stark* was mistakenly attacked by an Iraqi warplane. The ship was struck by a missile that killed thirty-seven crew members. The attack prompted Congress to ask the Reagan administration for a report detailing the risks and objectives of its Persian Gulf policy. Many members of Congress pressed the administration to delay the reflagging operation, but no binding legislation was passed.

On July 24, two days after the escort missions began, a reflagged Kuwaiti tanker was damaged by an Iranian mine. Critics of the administration's Persian Gulf strategy pointed to the incident as evidence that the naval escorts could involve the United States in the gulf war, and many lawmakers called on the president to invoke the War Powers Act. The Reagan administration refused, however, to acknowledge that the escort missions placed U.S. forces into hostilities or an area of imminent hostilities. Several Democratic members of Congress responded by filing suit to force the president to invoke the War Powers Act. In December 1987, a U.S. district court judge dismissed the suit as a political issue that should be settled by the executive and legislative branches.[64]

Legal Questions

The failure of the War Powers Act substantially to change presidential war-making prerogatives is partly due to its questionable constitutionality. Many of its critics and even a few of its supporters have expressed doubts that all of its provisions would stand up to judicial review. President Nixon denounced the war powers bill as unconstitutional when he vetoed it in 1973. The major provisions of

the bill, he contended, would "purport to take away, by a mere legislative act, authorities which the president has properly exercised under the Constitution for almost 200 years." They were unconstitutional, he asserted, because "the only way in which the constitutional powers of a branch of the government can be altered is by amending the Constitution—and any attempt to make such alterations by legislation alone is clearly without force."[65]

President Reagan also stated his reservations about the constitutionality of the War Powers Act in 1983 when he signed the resolution that contained the compromise on U.S. military action in Lebanon. He wrote:

> I do not and cannot cede any of the authority vested in me under the Constitution as President and as Commander-in-Chief of the United States Armed Forces. Nor should my signing be viewed as any acknowledgement that the President's constitutional authority can be impermissibly infringed by statute, that congressional authorization would be required if and when the period specified in ... the War Powers Resolution might be deemed to have been triggered and the period had expired, or that [the 18-month authorization] may be interpreted to revise the President's constitutional authority to deploy United States Armed Forces.[66]

Neither the executive branch nor a majority of members of Congress has appeared anxious to let the Supreme Court decide if the War Powers Act is an unconstitutional legislative intrusion into the commander-in-chief powers of the president. Both branches undoubtedly have preferred to avoid a constitutional clash that could divide the government. It is also likely, however, that both branches have believed they have more to lose than win from such a confrontation. On the one hand, since presidents have been able to ignore the most potent provisions of the War Powers Act, they have had little incentive to seek a decision on the issue in court that might force them to comply more strictly with its provisions. On the other hand, although a Supreme Court ruling that supported the constitutionality of the act would be a major victory for Congress, a decision striking it down would further strengthen the president's authority to use the armed forces. Such a decision would deprive lawmakers of any leverage provided by their threats to invoke the act and would symbolically weaken Congress's claim to a place in the national security decision-making process. In addition, Congress may have been dissuaded from mounting a legal challenge to presidential war making by the Supreme Court's historic tendency to favor the presidency on matters of foreign policy and national security.

Orlando v. Laird and Berk v. Laird

Two 1970 cases tried before district court judges, *Orlando v. Laird* and *Berk v. Laird*, addressed the question of whether the Vietnam War was illegal because Congress had not issued a declaration of war. In independent verdicts two judges ruled that congressional actions short of a formal declaration of war sanctioned U.S. participation in the conflict. The judges cited Congress's continued passage of military appropriations bills to fund the war and its renewal of the Selective Service Act as evidence of congressional support for the war.[67] Indeed, at any time Congress could have withdrawn its support by stopping the draft and refusing to appropriate funds for the war, thereby forcing the executive branch to pull troops out of Vietnam. The rulings did not deny any power to the legislative branch or justify the war on the grounds that presidents possessed inherent authority to use military force whenever they believed it to be in the best interest of the United States. Yet the rulings did indicate that if Congress collaborated with the executive branch in the pursuit of a war through appropriations or other measures, it must be considered to have sanctioned U.S. participation, with or without a declaration of war.

In response to these rulings and the Johnson administration's use of the Tonkin Gulf resolution to justify its expansion of the Vietnam War, Congress included a provision in the War Powers Act denying that a president could infer a congressional sanction for the introduction of troops into hostilities or potentially hostile situations "from any provision of law ... including any provision contained in any appropriation Act, unless such provision specifically authorizes the introduction of United States Armed Forces into hostilities or into such situations and states that it is intended to constitute specific statutory authorization within the meaning of this resolution." The provision went on to deny the president the authority to infer congressional sanction for presidential war making from a ratified treaty. Thus Congress attempted to restrict to declarations of war and other explicit sanctions of military actions the means through which Congress could be said to have approved presidential war making. Regardless of this provision, however, it is unclear whether the courts would declare a president's use of force illegal on the grounds that Congress had not approved the conflict, if lawmakers had passed specific appropriations bills to pay for military operations as it did during the Vietnam War.

The Chadha Decision

In 1983 the Supreme Court's decision on a case unrelated to the War Powers Act struck down at least one provision of the legislation. The Court ruled 7-2 in *Immigration and Naturalization Service v. Chadha* that legislative vetoes over presidential policy are unconstitutional because they circumvent the president's constitutionally granted executive and veto powers. Legislative vetoes are provisions of laws that give Congress the power to review and rescind executive actions. They had been used by Congress for over fifty years primarily to maintain some control over executive implementation of congressional regulations. Writing for the majority, Chief Justice Warren Burger emphasized, "The hydraulic pressure inherent within each of the separate branches to exceed the outer limits of its power, even to accomplish desirable objectives, must be resisted." [68]

The ruling affected the War Powers Act because that legislation empowered Congress to compel the president to withdraw U.S. forces engaged in hostilities by passing a concurrent resolution. Such a concurrent resolution constitutes a legislative veto over executive action.[69] In addition, the *Chadha* decision casts doubt on the legality of the War Powers provision that requires automatic termination of a military action after sixty or ninety days in the absence of congressional approval. If Congress cannot stop U.S. military involvement in hostilities by a concurrent resolution, it is questionable whether those hostilities could be stopped automatically without any specific congressional action.

The *Chadha* ruling did not affect the reporting and consultation provisions of the War Powers Act or the provision delineating the types of situations under which the president could use the armed forces. Presidents have not, however, considered themselves bound by the latter provision. Independent of *Chadha* they have questioned its constitutionality on the grounds that it places unreasonable restrictions on the president's freedom to defend the nation.[70]

Effect of the War Powers Act

During hearings on the war powers legislation on April 23, 1971, Sen. Barry Goldwater (R-Ariz.) warned a House Foreign Affairs subcommittee:

> The war powers bill is not the correct way to tackle this issue. To my mind, the bill is improper, unwise, and perhaps illegal. It would leave the United States helpless to prevent the annihilation of Israel. It would emasculate NATO. It would unwittingly allow a militant Congress to initiate a nuclear holocaust. And it may incite one of the gravest constitutional crises in American history.[71]

The passage of the war powers bill has not resulted in the dire consequences that Senator Goldwater feared. Although different interpretations of how and when the act should be implemented have at times divided the executive and legislative branches, the act has not proven to be an unreasonable hindrance on the president's ability to protect the United States and its allies.

Since the passage of the War Powers Act in 1973, neither congressional action nor the automatic sixty- to ninety-day time limit has forced a president to disengage U.S. troops from a conflict. Moreover, presidents have appeared undaunted by the act's potential to limit their use of American armed forces. Only once—during President Reagan's deployment of Marines in Lebanon in 1982 and 1983—did the prospect of the invocation of the War Powers Act result in a formal compromise between the legislative and executive branches on the limits of a military operation. Even in this case, the compromise favored the president, and it had little effect on his eventual decision to withdraw the troops. The War Powers Act has remained a potentially powerful congressional tool that for better or worse lawmakers have been unwilling or unable to use.

Nevertheless, world events have never provided a major test for the War Powers Act. It was a product of the Vietnam War, and legislators hoped above all that it would help them prevent a future president from waging another protracted conventional war without congressional approval. The painful experience of Vietnam, however, has created a lingering national aversion to military actions that have the potential to develop into long-term conflicts and to cost the lives of thousands of U.S. military personnel. Presidents have been able to initiate small-scale military operations, usually of short duration, without being seriously challenged by Congress or the public, but every post-Vietnam president has carefully avoided any appearance that the United States might be slipping into a war reminiscent of Vietnam. Even conservative public officials and members of Congress who have argued for a more activist policy against "international Communism" have rarely advocated the use of U.S. forces except for limited missions and the defense of vital, widely agreed upon U.S. interests. Thus, the War Powers Act has never been called into service against the type of presidential war that lead to its passage. Still, one cannot infer from its history that it will never be used by Congress to restrict the deployment of military forces by a future president.

The years since the passage of the War Powers Act have shown that it cannot be a substitute for congressional resolve. Presidents have demonstrated that they will not be automatically restrained by the act if they believe the use of American forces is in the best interest of the United States. Thus, the War Powers Act alone has not and will not reestablish Congress as the branch that decides when to go to war. Like the legislature's power to cut off funding for a particular military action, the effectiveness of the act depends upon the collective will of Congress to challenge presidential leadership. If this collective will exists, Congress has ample means to check the president's war-making power and to expand its role in deciding when and how military force should be used.

President as Military Commander

The commander-in-chief clause gives presidents clear authority to command the military as the nation's first general and admiral. They possess all decision-making powers accorded any supreme military commander under international law. Presidents not only order troops into battle, they are expected to approve major strategic decisions and keep a watchful eye on the progress of any military campaign. Most presidents since World War II have even regarded specific tactical decisions related to certain military operations to be among their commander-in-chief responsibilities.

In making the president the commander in chief the Framers attempted to ensure that civilian authority would always direct the armed forces. Military leaders who might use their authority over the army and navy to accumulate political power or enhance their personal reputation would be subordinate to the president who was elected by the entire country and was responsible for the welfare and security of all the people. Designating the president as commander in chief also aided effective military leadership by establishing a single leader at the top of the military hierarchy who was recognized by all as being the legitimate and indisputable supreme military commander.

Military experience has been common among presidents. Although some presidents who have led the nation during wartime, such as James Madison and Woodrow Wilson, had no military experience, twenty-six of forty chief executives served in the military. A remarkably high number of these were high-ranking officers. Twelve served as generals, and six of these twelve—George Washington, Andrew Jackson, William Harrison, Zachary Taylor, Ulysses S. Grant, and Dwight Eisenhower—attained at least the rank of major general.[72] Three presidents—Grant, Eisenhower, and Carter—graduated from a military academy. Franklin Roosevelt, another wartime president who never entered the military, gained defense-related experience as assistant secretary of the navy. Although few presidents could be classified as military experts, as a group they possessed more knowledge of military affairs than they did of many other policy areas.

Presidential Direction of Military Operations

The degree to which presidents have become involved in the direction of military operations has varied according

Dwight D. Eisenhower Library

Eisenhower was one of twelve generals who served as president. On D-Day—June 6, 1944—he personally encouraged American paratroopers of the 101st Airborne Division before their drop into France as the vanguard of the invasion.

During the early stages of the Civil War, Abraham Lincoln became deeply involved in battlefield strategy. He occasionally issued direct orders to his generals regarding their troop movements and frequently conferred with them at the front.

to their own military expertise and the circumstances of the military situation. Once troops have been committed to battle, presidents have usually delegated authority for battlefield stategy to their generals and admirals. The Constitution, however, does not prohibit a president from taking direct command of troops in the field. Several delegates to the Constitutional Convention suggested that the president should be prohibited from taking personal command of troops, but the Convention rejected these proposals.[73]

George Washington was regarded as his nation's greatest general, and neither Congress nor the American public would have thought it wrong for him to have led U.S. troops into battle while he was president. In 1794 Washington came close to doing just that when he personally supervised the organization of the militia charged with putting down the Whiskey Rebellion.[74] In 1799 when an undeclared naval war with France threatened to spread to the North American continent, John Adams delegated his authority as commander in chief to George Washington. Adams, who recognized his own lack of military experience and the advantages of enabling the country to rally around a national legend if war came, asked Washington to accept the post of "Lieutenant General and Commander-in-Chief of all the armies raised or to be raised in the United States." Washington agreed on the condition that he would not have to take command of the army unless "it became indispensable by the urgency of circumstances." War with France remained confined to the high seas, and Washington never had to leave his retirement at Mount Vernon to assume active command of U.S. forces.[75]

The poor performance of Union generals during the early stages of the Civil War and the proximity of the fighting to Washington, D.C., caused Abraham Lincoln to become deeply involved in battlefield strategy. He occasionally issued direct orders to his generals regarding their troop movements and frequently conferred with them at the front. Although Lincoln's interference in purely military matters has been criticized by some historians and applauded by others, he did allow his generals broad dis-

cretion in their implementation of his orders. After Lincoln had given command of the army to General Grant, in whom he had confidence, the president ceased to involve himself in tactical decisions.[76]

President Wilson, like John Adams, recognized his own lack of military experience and delegated responsibility for strategy and tactics to military leaders. Moreover, the distance between the president and the fighting made personal leadership impractical. He confined his commander-in-chief role during World War I to the domestic war effort and broad military decisions, such as his rejection of a French and British proposal in 1918 to have the U.S. open a major front in Russia to prevent the Germans from transferring troops to the West after the Russians had negotiated a separate peace with Germany.[77]

World War II created conditions that necessitated involvement of the president in strategic decisions. Because the war effort against Germany and Japan depended on the concerted action of the United States, Great Britain, the Soviet Union, and other nations, Allied strategy had to be determined through negotiations between the top leaders of each country. As a result, decisions such as when to launch the invasion of Europe and where to concentrate U.S. forces were decisions that presidents Roosevelt and Truman had to make not just because they were the commander in chief, but also because they were the nation's chief diplomat.

The tendency of presidents to become involved in planning the details of military actions increased with the advent of the nuclear age. Nuclear weapons created an environment of constant danger where any use of U.S. armed forces could escalate into a global nuclear confrontation. Consequently, modern presidents have seldom been willing to order a military operation without personally overseeing its execution. Perhaps the most extreme example of presidential involvement in planning military operations in the nuclear era was Lyndon Johnson's participation in the selection of specific bombing targets in North Vietnam.[78]

Governing Conquered Territory

On many occasions U.S. military forces have occupied enemy territory during hostilities. Presidential authority to administer a recently occupied territory through the armed forces is nearly absolute. Neither the Constitution of the United States nor the former laws of a conquered nation constrain the president. Several hundred Supreme Court cases have upheld the president's authority to function as a dictator over occupied territory subject only to the "laws of war."[1] Presidents and their appointed military representatives may set up new government institutions, make laws by decree, establish a court system, collect taxes, or do anything else they believe necessary to administer the conquered area.

Presidential rule over occupied territory lasts until it is annexed to the United States or a treaty is concluded that transfers power back to a local government. The president may not, however, unilaterally annex acquired territory. Article IV of the Constitution grants Congress the power to "dispose of and make all needful Rules and Regulations respecting the Territory or other Property belonging to the United States." Therefore, Congress must approve a treaty of cession or pass legislation annexing the territory before it can become part of the United States.[2]

1. Clinton Rossiter, *The Supreme Court and the Commander in Chief* (Ithaca, N.Y.: Cornell University Press, 1976), 122-123.
2. Joseph E. Kallenbach, *The American Chief Executive: The Presidency and the Governorship* (New York: Harper and Row, 1966), 541.

Sophisticated communication technologies also have contributed to presidential involvement in military operations by making contact between the president and local military commanders possible. For example, in April 1988, the pilot of a navy aircraft patrolling the Persian Gulf observed Iranian gunboats attacking a set of oil rigs. Because U.S. forces in the Persian Gulf were authorized to respond to attacks only on American aircraft, ships, and facilities, the pilot radioed his aircraft carrier for permission to attack the Iranian vessels. The pilot's request was transmitted up the chain of command from the aircraft carrier commander to the admiral in charge of the naval task force. Then the request was relayed via satellite through the chief of the U.S. Central Command in Florida to the chairman of the Joint Chiefs of Staff and the secretary of defense at the Pentagon who called President Reagan. The president authorized U.S. planes to bomb the Iranian gunboats, and the order was relayed back through the chain of command to navy pilots who moved to attack only three minutes after permission had been requested.[79]

Command of Nuclear Weapons

Despite the absurdity of a modern president ever leading U.S. troops into battle, the realities of nuclear warfare have made the president the nation's "first soldier." The decision to use nuclear weapons or to delegate the authority to use them to local military commanders is entirely the president's. Presidential authority over the nation's nuclear arsenal is derived from the commander-in-chief power and the necessity of making the decision to use nuclear weapons with speed and secrecy. If the Soviet Union were to launch an attack on the United States from their nuclear missile submarines, the president would have no more than ten to twelve minutes to receive positive verification of the attack, decide how to respond, and transmit orders to the military commanders in charge of U.S. nuclear forces. Even if the attack were launched from missile silos in the Soviet Union, the president would have little more than twenty to thirty minutes between the launch of the missiles and their impact.[80] A decision that has to be made this quickly must be assigned to a single individual with indisputable authority. The nature of nuclear weapons, therefore, necessitates presidential control over them.

Theoretically, a first-strike nuclear attack by the United States against another nation would be illegal without a congressional declaration of war, since such an attack would be an initiation of hostilities on an unprecedented scale. Few observers, however, believe there is a significant chance that a U.S. president would purposely order a nuclear strike unless the United States, U.S. forces, or close U.S. allies were under a nuclear or massive conventional attack. Consequently, most scenarios for the use of nuclear weapons by the president without congressional approval can be justified on the grounds that the president is responsible for repelling attacks and defending the United States. Even a presidential order to launch nuclear weapons to preempt a nuclear attack perceived as imminent could probably be justified under the president's power to defend the country, although the ensuing nuclear war would likely diminish the significance of any legal debate.

Regardless of the nuclear decision-making role to which Congress might be entitled under a strict interpretation of the Constitution, the demands of secrecy and speed that accompany crisis decision making in the nuclear age disqualify Congress from taking part in decisions to use nuclear weapons, except through their consultations in advance of potential crises. No president could tentatively make the decision to launch nuclear weapons, then present the plan to Congress for approval. Command over nuclear weapons, therefore, literally gives the president the power to destroy the world. Yet, if a president ordered a surprise nuclear attack during peacetime when no crisis existed, it is likely those orders would be questioned and resisted by civilian and military advisers.

Logistical Limits to Presidential Control

Although presidents alone have the authority to order the use of nuclear weapons, they do not possess perfect central control over them. The U.S. nuclear arsenal consists of thousands of nuclear warheads based throughout the world, delivery vehicles for all types of nuclear missions, and a vast network of personnel, computers, communications equipment, and information and intelligence gathering and processing systems necessary to manage the

Presidential Nuclear Command Procedures

An important component of deterrence is maintaining reliable command procedures for the launch of nuclear weapons. The goal of these procedures is to identify positively that a nuclear attack has been launched against the United States, to characterize the attack for the president and other national leaders, to receive orders from the president based on this characterization, and to transmit these orders to the officers in charge of nuclear weapons.

Because the decision to retaliate with nuclear weapons must be made under conditions of extreme stress, nuclear planners provide the president with the Single Integrated Operational Plan (SIOP). This highly classified document contains the possible U.S. nuclear responses to a variety of attacks. Its purpose is to familiarize the president and other top defense officials with nuclear attack options from which they can quickly choose in a crisis.

If the North American Aerospace Defense Command (NORAD)—the underground post in Colorado charged with processing early warning information—detects evidence of a possible nuclear attack against the United States, NORAD, the Strategic Air Command (SAC), the Pentagon's National Military Command Center, and the Alternate National Military Command Center at Fort Ritchie, Maryland, begin procedural steps to verify the authenticity of the attack. If after a series of conferences, NORAD and the other units determine that the attack is real, the president is informed of the attack and its characteristics. The president then consults with defense leaders and considers SIOP options.[1]

Because the Soviets would almost certainly use submarine-launched nuclear missiles, which would reach their targets in ten to twelve minutes or less, the president would probably have no more than three or four minutes to decide on a response. If a nuclear attack option is chosen, the president transmits the launch codes that unlock the nuclear weapons and assure the officers in charge of the weapons that the launch order is authentic. The launch codes are carried in an ordinary black bag known as the "football" by a military officer who is always near the president. The exact procedures for ordering nuclear forces to launch their weapons are highly classified and probably change depending on the global situation and the incumbent president's preferences.[2]

Before or after a president decides how to respond to a nuclear attack, the president and other top leaders may choose to evacuate Washington, D.C. Underground command posts within range of helicopters were built in the 1950s in Virginia and Pennsylvania from which the president could direct a nuclear war. Since advances in Soviet military technology have made these underground posts vulnerable to nuclear attack, the president may choose instead to rush by helicopter to Andrews Air Force Base ten miles from the White House and take off in one of the National Emergency Airborne Command Posts (NEACP). These aircraft remain on constant alert for the president's use and contain communications equipment that would enable the president to transmit orders to U.S. nuclear forces.[3]

If the president is killed by a nuclear attack or is unable to communicate with nuclear forces, nuclear command devolves upon the president's successors as specified in the Twenty-fifth Amendment and the Presidential Successsion Act of 1947.

Presidents, however, may give authority to launch nuclear weapons to specified military leaders rather than depending on the survival of statutory presidential successors. For example, the president may authorize the officers in charge of the Strategic Air Command's airborne command posts, one of which has been aloft every moment since February 3, 1961, to order a nuclear launch if a Soviet strike kills the president and destroys the Washington, D.C., area, where many of the president's successors reside. Such a plan would have the advantage of ensuring that the decision to use nuclear weapons did not fall to a cabinet official completely unfamiliar with nuclear strategy and procedures. It would also decrease the chances that a Soviet nuclear strike would disable U.S. nuclear forces by killing U.S. leaders or interrupting their communications. Yet, bypassing the chain of presidential succession would have the disadvantages of removing nuclear decision making from civilian control and of creating doubts about who was leading the country.[4]

1. Miroslav Nincic, *United States Foreign Policy, Choices and Tradeoffs* (Washington, D.C.: CQ Press, 1988), 265.
2. Walter Slocombe, "Preplanned Operations," in *Managing Nuclear Operations*, ed. Ashton B. Carter, John D. Steinbruner, and Charles A. Zraket (Washington, D.C.: Brookings, 1987), 132.
3. William Sweet, "Civil Defense: Nuclear Debate's New Element," *Editorial Research Reports*, June 4, 1982, 419.
4. Slocombe, "Preplanned Operations," 133.

weapons.[81] Because of the size and complexity of the U.S. nuclear weapons arsenal and the requirements of deterrence, presidents cannot depend on controlling every weapon by simply pushing a button or making a phone call. Their control could be undermined by the failure or destruction of U.S. early warning and communications systems, of personnel who manage the nuclear weapons, or of the weapons themselves.

Presidential control of nuclear weapons has been aided by permissive action links (PALs), or electronic locks that prevent nuclear weapons from being fired without prior presidential authorization. Intercontinental ballistic missiles (ICBMs) based in missile silos and nuclear warheads carried by U.S. strategic bombers are equipped with PALs.[82] The military commanders of certain other types of nuclear weapons, however, have the physical capability,

Table 1 Major Arms Control Agreements

President	Year signed	Agreement	Senate action	Provisions	Parties
Eisenhower	1959	Antarctic Treaty	Ratified	Prohibits all military activity, including deployment of nuclear weapons in Antarctica	Multilateral
Kennedy	1963	Partial Nuclear Test Ban Treaty	Ratified	Prohibits nuclear tests under water, in the atmosphere, and in outer space	Multilateral
Johnson	1967	Outer Space Treaty	Ratified	Prohibits all military activity, including deployment of nuclear weapons in outer space	Multilateral
Johnson	1968	Nuclear Nonproliferation Treaty	Ratified	Prohibits acquisition of nuclear weapons by nations not already possessing them and establishes international safeguards to prevent the spread of nuclear weapons capability	Multilateral
Nixon	1971	Sea Bed Treaty	Ratified	Prohibits deployment of nuclear weapons on the ocean floor	Multilateral
Nixon	1972	SALT I ABM Treaty	Ratified	Limits size and number (two) of antiballistic missile systems in U.S. and Soviet Union. A 1974 executive agreement reduced number of sites permitted to one.	U.S.-Soviet Union
Nixon	1972	SALT I Interim Offensive Arms Agreement	Executive agreement No action	Established a five-year freeze on number of intercontinental ballistic missiles and submarine-launched ballistic missiles deployed by U.S. and Soviet Union	U.S.-Soviet Union
Nixon	1974	Threshold Nuclear Test Ban Treaty	Unratified	Prohibits underground nuclear test explosions greater than 150 kilotons	U.S.-Soviet Union
Ford	1976	Peaceful Nuclear Explosions Treaty	Unratified	Prohibits nuclear explosions greater than 150 kilotons for excavation and other peaceful purposes	U.S.-Soviet Union
Carter	1979	SALT II Offensive Arms Treaty	Unratified	Limits numbers and types of strategic nuclear weapons	U.S.-Soviet Union
Reagan	1987	Intermediate Nuclear Forces Treaty	Ratified	Mandates the removal and destruction of all land-based nuclear missiles with ranges between 300 and 3,400 miles	U.S.-Soviet Union

although not the authority, to launch them without receiving a presidential order. Nuclear missiles deployed in submarines, for example, are not equipped with PALs and therefore could be fired by the officers of a submarine who mistakenly believed that the president had issued a launch order. Since each Trident, the fleet's most modern missile launching submarine, carries twenty-four missiles equipped with eight warheads each, such a mistake would be catastrophic. The navy seeks to minimize the danger of an unauthorized nuclear launch through elaborate launch procedures that require the action of several officers and intensive psychological screening of submarine personnel.

Because of the possibility that the president might be killed or the president's means of communicating with nuclear forces might be destroyed by an enemy nuclear attack, crisis contingency plans exist through which the president could delegate authority to use nuclear weapons to the military commanders in charge of the weapons. Implementation of such a plan during a crisis would require the president's approval, but since "decapitation"—the destruction of the enemy's leadership and communications capabilities—is a central tenet of the nuclear contingency plans of both superpowers, the president may be forced to delegate away the decision to use at least a portion of U.S. nuclear forces.[83] The president could make such a delegation of authority during a crisis as a precaution against a surprise attack, or the president could wait to delegate authority until an enemy launches missiles that threaten the president, secretary of defense, and other leaders in Washington.

When the threat from a potential attack is perceived to be greater than the danger of an accidental or premature launching of nuclear weapons, the president also has the option to put the nuclear missile submarine fleet on a "fail deadly" launch status. Under this arrangement, the submarines receive orders at regular intervals not to launch their missiles, rather than a positive order to launch. If the crews fail to receive an order not to launch, they assume that the president and other top officials have been killed in a nuclear attack, and they fire their missiles. Such a plan is meant to deter an attack by convincing leaders of an enemy nation that their country cannot emerge unscathed from a nuclear war by decapitating the U.S. command and control system.[84]

Nuclear Arms Control

Since the development of atomic weapons, presidents have tried to enhance U.S. security by controlling the nuclear arms race. Arms control agreements have become one of the most important measurements of a president's diplomatic success, and every president since Dwight Eisenhower has concluded some agreement with the Soviet Union or the international community that contributed to the reduction or prevention of the spread of nuclear weapons. *(See Table 1.)*

Arms control has numerous implications beyond its effect on the balance of nuclear forces. It affects U.S. relations with its allies; it can benefit the U.S. economy by reducing the financial burden of defense; it can be the catalyst for the improvement of diplomatic relations with adversaries; and it has become an emotional and moral issue for many groups and individuals. Consequently, arms control is not exclusively a military matter. The president, the official elected by the whole country to oversee the nation's defenses, foreign relations, and economic prosperity, is in the best position to mold a coherent arms control strategy that considers military and diplomatic realities, the nation's economic condition, and the dangers of an unchecked arms race.

As commander in chief and the possessor of the treaty negotiation power, presidents have dominated arms control policy. Although the Senate can exercise negative control over arms control agreements by blocking ratification of a treaty, the president has complete control over the initiation and execution of arms control negotiations. Because arms control agreements are perceived to be among the most important agreements made by the president, they generally have been concluded as treaties. The Senate usually has chosen to approve arms control treaties, but ratification has not been automatic. Three nuclear arms control treaties have remained unratified: the 1974 Threshold Nuclear Test Ban Treaty, the 1976 Peaceful Nuclear Explosions Treaty, and the 1979 Strategic Arms Limitation Treaty (SALT II).

Presidents may choose to avoid the Senate treaty ratification process, however, by concluding arms control accords in the form of executive agreements. In 1972 President Nixon signed the SALT I Interim Offensive Arms Agreement which imposed limitations on the strategic nuclear arsenals of both superpowers, but he did not submit the agreement to the Senate as a treaty. Presidents may also choose to abide by an arms control treaty that the Senate has refused to ratify. President Carter announced in 1980 that the United States would not violate the provisions of the unratified SALT II treaty if the Soviet Union also did not violate it. President Reagan continued Carter's policy of observing SALT II until late 1986 when the ad-

U.S. Navy

A submarine-launched cruise missile is test fired in the Pacific. During the 1980s, the United States deployed hundreds of nuclear-tipped cruise missiles aboard bombers, surface ships, and submarines.

ministration announced that because of Soviet violations the United States would no longer consider itself bound by the treaty. Even the Senate's treaty ratification power, therefore, may not constrain a president who believes a particular arms control measure is in the interests of national security.

Evolution of Presidential Nuclear Decision Making

Since Franklin Roosevelt directed U.S. scientists to build the atomic bomb, presidents have dominated nuclear weapons policy and the formulation of nuclear strategy. Nuclear age presidents have counted nuclear decision making as among their most important and burdensome responsibilities. Dwight Eisenhower once remarked in a speech:

> When the push of a button may mean obliteration of countless humans, the President of the United States must be forever on guard against any inclination on his part to impetuosity; to arrogance; to headlong action; to expedience; to facile maneuvers; even to the popularity of an action as opposed to the righteousness of an action. . . . He must worry only about the good—the long-term, abiding, permanent good—of all Americans.[85]

U.S. Nuclear Monopoly

Harry Truman asserted that the welfare of Americans had motivated him to use the atomic bomb against Japan. In the summer of 1945, after the war against Nazi Germany had been won, President Truman decided to drop newly manufactured atomic bombs on the Japanese cities of Hiroshima and Nagasaki to bring an end to World War II. Truman officially maintained that using the atomic bombs was the only way to end the war without an invasion of Japan. In a radio address to the American public on August 9, 1945, after both atomic bombs had been dropped, Truman explained that he had ordered the attacks "to shorten the agony of war, in order to save the lives of thousands and thousands of young Americans." [86]

Historical evidence suggests, however, that the decision was not a simple choice between forcing the Japanese to surrender by dropping the bomb and sacrificing tens of thousands of U.S. soldiers in an island assault. Throughout the summer the Japanese had made peace overtures that were not fully explored by the Truman administration. Although Truman may genuinely have been convinced that Japan was unwilling to surrender on acceptable terms without witnessing the power of the atomic bomb, it is also possible he had additional motives for dropping it. Truman wanted to end the war abruptly to prevent the Soviet Union, which was about to enter the war against the Japanese, from having a role in the occupation of Japan. He also may have regarded the bomb as an impressive demonstration of American power that would cause the Soviets to be more conciliatory toward the West.[87]

From the bombing of Hiroshima to the early 1950s, the United States enjoyed a nuclear monopoly. The Soviet Union tested its first atomic bomb in 1949, but it did not have an operational capability for several more years. The U.S. ability to destroy Soviet population centers with atomic weapons served as an effective deterrent against the threat to Western Europe from superior numbers of Soviet conventional forces.[88] Although the U.S. nuclear advantage prevented war with the Soviet Union through the 1940s and 1950s, the Korean War demonstrated the difficulty of using nuclear weapons in limited wars. Truman rejected their use in Korea because allied opinion was squarely against the move, and he believed the limited U.S. nuclear arsenal needed to be conserved to defend against a Soviet attack on Western Europe. A moral prohibition against the use of nuclear weapons also had developed, especially against the citizens of an underdeveloped nation like North Korea who were victims of communist expansion.

U.S. Nuclear Superiority

The small Soviet nuclear arsenal developed in the 1950s was much inferior in number and quality to the U.S. nuclear force. President Eisenhower attempted to use U.S. nuclear superiority to deter Soviet aggression. He believed that maintaining a conventional military force capable of countering the Soviets and their clients anywhere in the world would be disastrous for the federal budget and would not be supported by the American public. In addition, a threat to use nuclear weapons against China had helped end the Korean War. The administration therefore declared in 1954 that the United States would respond to Communist aggression by using nuclear weapons against appropriate targets. These targets were not necessarily to be limited to the region where the Communist aggression was occurring. Thus, the United States threatened to attack the Soviet Union (or China) with nuclear weapons not only in response to a Soviet attack on Western Europe, but also in response to unspecified lesser provocations.[89]

The problem with this strategy, which was known as "massive retaliation," was that it lacked credibility. A U.S.

nuclear strike was an inappropriate response to limited acts of Communist aggression such as Soviet-supported guerrilla movements or political subversion. Furthermore, as the Soviet nuclear capability grew during the 1950s, the possibility that the United States could launch a nuclear attack against the Soviet Union without itself and its allies receiving a nuclear counterblow became remote. The successful Soviet launch of the Sputnik satellite in 1957 even engendered false speculation that the gap in military technology that Americans assumed to be in their favor actually favored the Soviets.

John Kennedy sought to bring declared nuclear policy in line with global realities. Upon taking office, he announced a new strategy of "flexible response." Kennedy and his advisers saw that improvements in the Soviet nuclear arsenal had diminished the capacity of U.S. nuclear forces to deter anything but a Soviet nuclear attack or massive invasion of Western Europe. Kennedy also recognized that the United States was faced with many forms of Communist aggression that called for limited responses. Kennedy, therefore, ordered wide-ranging improvements in U.S. military capabilities. Nuclear deterrence remained the centerpiece of U.S. defense, but conventional and counterinsurgency forces also were built up to deal with limited wars.

Soviet placement of medium-range nuclear missiles in Cuba in 1962 precipitated a crisis that pushed the United States to the brink of nuclear war with the Soviet Union. Kennedy refused to accept this alteration of the balance of forces. He ordered a blockade of Cuba to prevent further construction of the Soviet missile sites and demanded that the Soviets withdraw the missiles. After two tense weeks, during which Kennedy estimated the chances of nuclear war at "between one out of three and even," the Soviets agreed to remove their missiles.[90] The Cuban missile crisis highlighted the threat to U.S. security from the growing Soviet nuclear arsenal and stimulated a further modernization of nuclear weaponry.

Like the Korean War, the Vietnam War demonstrated the doubtful utility of nuclear weapons in limited conflicts. Although the Johnson administration found itself committed to a bloody war upon which it had staked its own reputation and the honor of the country, it refused to use nuclear weapons against North Vietnam. The closest the administration came to considering their use was one hypothetical study commissioned in 1967 by Gen. William Westmoreland, the commander of U.S. forces in Vietnam.[91] Johnson refused to employ nuclear weapons because he did not want to risk a wider war with the Soviet Union or China, and he recognized the moral prohibition against their use.

Nuclear Decision Making in the Era of Parity

Presidents Nixon and Ford ascribed to the basic nuclear strategy established by Kennedy and Johnson. The concept of strategic defense—building defensive weapons systems capable of destroying attacking enemy missiles and bombers—had been widely debated during Johnson's presidency. President Nixon, however, concluded a treaty in 1972 with the Soviet Union that placed strict limitations on anti-ballistic missile systems. This formalized the doctrine of "mutual assured destruction" (MAD) that had characterized the nuclear relationship between the superpowers since the Soviets achieved strategic nuclear parity

Presidential Civil Defense Policy

An all-out nuclear war would be a national disaster unrivaled in U.S. history. Tens of millions of civilians would likely be killed, and U.S. governmental structures might cease to exist in many areas of the country. Even a limited nuclear war in which several nuclear weapons exploded on the territory of the United States would create unprecedented medical, communications, transportation, and environmental problems. Because a nuclear war would blur the distinctions between soldiers and civilians and create a civil emergency of enormous magnitude, the commander-in-chief power contributes to the president's authority over civil defense preparations. These preparations are intended to maximize the number of citizens who would survive a nuclear war and provide for the reconstitution of the nation's government and economy.

Rise and Fall of Civil Defense.   Civil defense has never been a high priority in the United States. In the first two decades after the Soviet acquisition of the atomic bomb in 1949, the United States pursued a modest civil defense program. Presidential budget requests for civil defense always exceeded the funds appropriated by Congress for that purpose. Because the deliverable Soviet nuclear arsenal was inferior in number and quality to the U.S. arsenal, there was some justification that civil defense preparations could save the lives of many Americans and enable U.S. society to recover more quickly from a nuclear war.

President Kennedy was the strongest advocate of civil defense among presidents of this era. In a televised address delivered on July 25, 1961, he called for an extensive civil defense program that would include marking fallout shelters, stocking them with food, water, and medical supplies, and creating an elaborate nuclear warning system. Congress initially gave Kennedy the money for his civil defense project but within two years, it had cut back civil defense funding.[1]

By the late 1960s, the increase in the numbers and sophistication of Soviet nuclear weapons to a level of rough parity with the U.S. nuclear arsenal convinced most U.S. citizens that regardless of civil defense measures they would be killed in a nuclear war. Given that U.S. strategic doctrine was based on deterring war by maintaining the mutual vulnerability of the populations of the Soviet Union and the United States, the costs of building shelters and developing procedures to warn and relocate citizens in times of crisis seemed unjustified. Moreover, most Americans had a negative attitude toward civil defense planning because these preparations reminded them of nuclear war and seemed to imply that the government accepted its possibility. Civil defense, therefore, remained a low priority during the late 1960s and most of the 1970s.

Civil Defense Revival.   In the late 1970s, however, the number of civil defense advocates began to grow. Central Intelligence Agency reports of a $2 billion a year Soviet civil defense program prompted some officials to call for a similar program in the United States. These civil defense advocates feared that the Soviet program, which stressed evacuation of cities, would convince Kremlin leaders that they could protect their population in a nuclear war while the U.S. urban population remained vulnerable. President Carter consolidated civil defense efforts in the new Federal Emergency Management Agency created in 1978 but did not substantially increase civil defense funding, which averaged only about $100 million a year during his term.

With the election of Ronald Reagan, civil defense was thrust into the public spotlight. On March 30, 1982, President Reagan proposed a seven-year, $4.2 billion civil defense program. The plan called for evacuating tens of millions of urban residents to rural areas in the event of a nuclear crisis. Government officials had estimated that a timely evacuation could enable as much as 80 percent of the U.S. population to survive a Soviet nuclear attack. Reagan argued that such a program was needed to counter the extensive Soviet civil defense preparations and to strengthen deterrence by ensuring that a larger portion of American society would survive a nuclear war.[2]

Reagan's civil defense plan was criticized by peace activists who contended that it would make a nuclear war more likely by creating the illusion that death and destruction could be minimized. Several ill-chosen statements by top civil defense officials in the Pentagon brought accusations that the administration believed casualties of a nuclear war could be limited to acceptable numbers. The most notorious statement was made in the fall of 1981 by T. K. Jones, a deputy undersecretary of defense, who stated in an interview that personal fallout shelters constructed by digging a hole in the ground and covering it with a door and three feet of dirt could dramatically reduce deaths caused by a nuclear war. "If there are enough shovels to go around," asserted Jones, "everybody's going to make it."[3]

Congress reacted to the debate by increasing funds for civil defense, but appropriations fell far short of Reagan administration requests. Congress authorized only $152 million out of a requested $252 million for fiscal year 1983, the first year of Reagan's civil defense program.[4] Congress continued to trim the administration's civil defense budget proposals in subsequent years. Although Reagan had succeeded in modestly increasing funding for emergency planning, neither the public nor Congress showed much enthusiasm for significantly expanding the role of civil defense in national security strategy.

1. William Sweet, "Civil Defense: Nuclear Debate's New Element," *Editorial Research Reports*, June 4, 1982, 415-416.
2. Ibid., 411-413.
3. Robert Scheer, *With Enough Shovels: Reagan, Bush and Nuclear War* (New York: Vintage Books, 1983), 18.
4. Pat Towell, "Strategic Arms Top List of Defense Cuts," *Congressional Quarterly Weekly Report*, August 21, 1982, 2059.

in the late 1960s. The MAD doctrine asserted that neither superpower could attack the other with nuclear weapons without its rival launching a devastating counterstrike. Both nations, therefore, would achieve security by holding the populations of the other hostage. It is unclear whether the Soviets accepted the desirability of MAD, but the doctrine did reflect strategic realities.

During the Carter administration, U.S. nuclear war strategy was reevaluated. The result was Presidential Directive 59 (PD-59), which was signed by the president in July 1980. PD-59 stressed that the United States had to be prepared to fight a protracted nuclear war lasting up to sixty days. The directive ordered nuclear planners to develop a wider range of limited nuclear war options and assigned a higher priority to destroying the Soviet's leadership, military capabilities, and economic base if nuclear war occurred. It also called for an improvement of U.S. command, control, and communications to ensure that the president and other top leaders could direct a protracted nuclear war effectively.[92] Critics of PD-59 charged that U.S. officials had made nuclear war more likely by promoting the perceptions that a nuclear war could be fought like any other war and that nuclear destruction could be limited to an acceptable degree. Nevertheless, PD-59 did not represent a movement toward an acceptance of nuclear war by President Carter and the defense establishment. Rather, it was an assertion that preparing to fight a nuclear war was the the best way to deter one.

Ronald Reagan took over the presidency in 1981 vowing to rebuild U.S. defenses, including its nuclear forces. He contended that during the 1970s while the United States observed the letter and spirit of nuclear arms control agreements, the Soviets had continued to build nuclear weapons that would give them an advantage in a nuclear war. Reagan asserted that these developments had created a "window of vulnerability" in the U.S. deterrent that could only be closed by building new U.S. weapons. Most experts discounted Reagan's claims that the U.S. nuclear deterrent was threatened since a large number of nuclear warheads—over 5,000—were deployed at sea aboard nuclear submarines that were invulnerable to Soviet attack. Nevertheless, a consensus had begun to develop during the late stages of the Carter administration that a defense buildup was needed, and much of Reagan's nuclear modernization program was approved.

On March 23, 1983, a proposal by Reagan sparked the most significant change in U.S. nuclear strategy since flexible response. In a nationally televised address he urged the scientific community to develop the technology for a space-based antiballistic missile defense that would someday make nuclear weapons "impotent and obsolete." [93] Implicit in the plan was a rejection of the status quo doctrine of mutual assured destruction. Reagan proposed to achieve security in the future not solely by deterring a Soviet nuclear attack, but also by being able to destroy most incoming Soviet missiles.

Although Reagan's optimistic vision led to an extensive research and development program, many scientists admitted that even if insulating the United States from a Soviet missile attack were possible, it would take decades of research and hundreds of billions of dollars to accomplish. By 1987, budget constraints and growing scientific skepticism that Reagan's "Peace Shield" could be built led to a reorientation of the plan. An authoritative classified document prepared by the Joint Chiefs of Staff called for the development of limited antiballistic missile defenses designed to stop about 30 percent of incoming Soviet warheads.[94] The Reagan administration had abandoned the goal of basing U.S. security on strategic defense and settled for the more attainable goal of using defensive weapons to enhance deterrence.

President as Defense Manager

Before World War II the United States maintained a small peacetime defense establishment. The isolation and size of the nation rendered it nearly immune to serious invasions by the armies of Europe. This geographic advantage and the antimilitaristic tradition of the United States worked against the maintenance of large standing armies. When the United States found itself in a war, it mobilized troops and resources until the war was won, after which the armed forces demobilized and the country returned to a state of peace and nonalignment.

After World War II a national consensus developed that the United States should adopt an internationalist defense policy designed to contain the expansion of Communism and limit the coercive potential of Soviet military strength. In pursuit of these regional objectives presidents signed a number of regional alliance treaties that pledged the United States to defend allied nations that came under attack. The most important of these regional alliances was the North Atlantic Treaty Organization (NATO), which committed the United States to the defense of Western Europe. The expanded defense commitments of the United States and its adversarial relationship with the Soviet Union caused the United States to maintain for the first time in its history a huge peacetime military establishment.

Although the Constitution gives Congress the complete authority to raise and equip an army and navy, much of the task of administering the defense bureaucracy and maintaining the nation's defenses in the post-World War II era has been delegated to or assumed by the president and the executive branch. The growth in the size and activities of the military and the perception that nuclear weapons and the Cold War had created a condition of constant emergency combined to legitimize the president's role as defense manager. Presidents functioned not just as the commander in chief in wartime but also as the manager of the routine operations and preparations of the military in peacetime.

Robert S. McNamara, defense secretary from 1961 to 1968, greatly expanded the role of the Office of the Secretary of Defense.

Library of Congress

Presidents and the Defense Establishment

As commander in chief, the president is positioned at the top of a large and complex defense establishment. The Defense Department is made up of three military services and numerous agencies, offices, and unified multiservice commands all under the leadership of the secretary of defense. During the 1980s the number of active duty military personnel has remained over two million, and in 1987 the Defense Department employed over one million civilians. In addition to the Defense Department, other executive departments and agencies have national security roles. The Central Intelligence Agency (CIA) and State Department provide intelligence about foreign governments and groups; the Federal Bureau of Investigation is responsible for combating espionage; the Energy Department develops, tests, and produces nuclear warheads; the Federal Emergency Management Agency oversees civil defense programs; and the Selective Service System conducts draft registration. The Defense Department, however, is the president's principal means of executing national security policy.

Department of Defense

Before 1947 the War and Navy Departments functioned independently of each other. Both had their own cabinet-level secretary, military command structure, and procurement operations. The National Security Act of 1947 created the post of secretary of defense, but its occupant was not given a staff or significant power over the individual services. The defense secretary functioned as the coordinator between the loose confederation of the Departments of the Army (the old War Department) and Navy, and the new Department of the Air Force. A 1949 amendment to the National Security Act created the Defense Department and recognized the primacy of the defense secretary, but in practice the individual services retained authority over their budgets and were administered autonomously by the service secretaries. The three services were not unified into one military organization because reformers believed such an organization could more easily threaten civilian primacy over the military.

The Department of Defense Reorganization Act of 1958 placed the secretary of defense at the top of the military command structure, second only to the president. The act gave the secretary the means to centralize authority over defense operations and planning within the Office of the Secretary of Defense (OSD). In 1961 Robert S. McNamara became defense secretary with a mandate from President Kennedy to take control of the Defense Department. McNamara greatly expanded the role of OSD and demanded unequivocal support from the military for the administration's programs.[95] McNamara ramained defense secretary until 1968. He established four major roles of the modern defense secretary: principal adviser to the president on defense issues, deputy commander in chief behind the president, director of the Defense Department and its huge military budget, and representative of the Defense Department before Congress and within the executive branch. This enlargement of the role of the secretary of defense gave presidents greater control over the defense establishment and assisted in the integration of defense and foreign policy.

Joint Chiefs of Staff

The Joint Chiefs of Staff (JCS) is the body of military officers responsible for formulating unified military strategy and providing the president with advice on military matters. The JCS consists of a chairman appointed from any of the services, the chiefs of staff of the Army and the air force, the chief of naval operations, and the commandant of the Marine Corps.

All five of the chiefs are appointed by the president with the advice and consent of the Senate. Since 1967, the chairman has been appointed for a two-year term, which can be renewed once by the president. The four service chiefs serve one, nonrenewable, four-year term.

A president can appoint several types of officers to the Joint Chiefs of Staff depending on the president's conception of its advisory role. Most chiefs have been officers nominated by their services and accepted by presidents with little consideration of their political compatibility with the administration. The president may receive the good will of the services for endorsing their choices, but the president will have little political control over these nominees. Presidents also have looked beyond the service's candidates and chosen officers whose professional reputation has come to their attention. These appointments may displease the services, but they allow a president to choose an officer with experience and temperament compatible with the administration. Finally, a few presidents have appointed close associates to the JCS. For example, John Kennedy appointed Gen. Maxwell Taylor chairman of the JCS in 1962. Taylor had earlier been offered the post of director of the CIA in 1961 but had chosen instead to become a special military representative to the White House. When the general was appointed chairman of the JCS he quickly became a member of Kennedy's inner circle of advisers. The military usually dislikes such nominees because their first priority is promoting the policies of the president rather than protecting their service's interests.[96]

Since 1947 when the JCS was created it has been criticized by many observers including influential service chiefs and blue ribbon panels commissioned to study its organization. These critics identified several problems with the JCS. First, the joint chiefs were given the conflicting tasks of being service chiefs responsible for the welfare of their services and members of the JCS responsible for developing unbiased policy plans and proposals for the president. The chiefs have seldom been able to do both and have usually put service interests first. Second, because the entire JCS was considered to be the president's military adviser, the chiefs have been compelled to develop consensus positions. As a result, their advice has consisted of uncontroversial compromise recommendations of little value to the president. Third, although the JCS was supposed to develop military plans, it was outside the military's chain of command. Consequently, JCS budgetary, procurement, and strategy proposals often have been unrelated to the needs of the commanders in chief (CINCs) of the multiservice operational commands in specified geographic areas.[97]

In 1986 President Reagan signed a bill reorganizing the JCS. The intent of the legislation was to improve interservice coordination and to create an organizational framework that would streamline the chain of command and minimize the influence of service parochialism on the military advice given to the president by the JCS.

The reorganization bill sought to accomplish these

Truman and General MacArthur

The most famous clash between a president and a member of the armed forces was Harry Truman's dispute with Gen. Douglas MacArthur during the Korean War. The conflict led to Truman's dramatic firing of MacArthur and tested the principle of presidential control of the military.

Few military leaders in the history of the United States were as respected and revered by the American public as General MacArthur was in the early stages of the Korean War. He had been a decorated hero of World War I, the triumphant commander of U.S. forces in the Pacific in World War II, and the successful military governor of Japan, overseeing that nation's transformation into a modern democratic state. When the Korean War broke out he was made supreme commander of the UN forces in Korea. His landing at Inchon behind North Korean lines in September 1950 reversed the tide of the war and reinforced his reputation as a tactical genius. Many Americans and members of Congress saw MacArthur as indispensable to the success of the Korean War effort. Republican leaders regarded the well-known, eloquent, and handsome general as a potential candidate in a future presidential election.

The conflict between Truman and MacArthur arose over their differing opinions of the goals to be pursued in the Korean War. The United States had sent forces to Korea under the authority of the United Nations in June 1950 after the North Koreans had invaded South Korea. Truman's original intention had been to drive the North Korean forces out of South Korea and reestablish a secure border at the thirty-eighth parallel. By October 1950, U.S. troops had accomplished this goal, but the successful military campaign led Truman and his advisers to order MacArthur to cross into North Korea and attempt to unify the nation.[1] Nevertheless, Truman was concerned about provoking Communist China and prohibited MacArthur from attacking North Korean bases in China.

MacArthur, however, envisioned an Asian strategy in which the United States would seek to overthrow the Communist Chinese by encouraging guerrilla war inside China, bombing Chinese targets, and supporting an invasion of China by hundreds of thousands of Nationalist Chinese troops from Formosa. At the least, MacArthur wanted the latitude to bomb North Korean sanctuaries and supply lines inside China. During the fall of 1950 he openly criticized Truman's policies and encouraged his supporters in Congress to press the administration to give him discretion to widen the war.

In November 1950, with U.S. forces close to crushing the North Korean Army, Communist China entered the war and pushed U.S. forces back across the thirty-eighth parallel. MacArthur blamed his retreat on Truman's constraints. Truman responded with a presidential directive on December 5 that instructed overseas military commanders and diplomats to clear all public statements with Washington, but MacArthur continued to make inflammatory comments. In a March 7 press statement the general characterized Truman's Korean strategy as "Die for [a] Tie."[2]

On March 24, MacArthur interfered with ongoing diplomacy. He undercut Truman's efforts to arrange cease-fire negotiations with the Chinese by issuing a statement that the United Nations might "depart from its tolerant efforts to contain the war to the area of Korea...."[3] MacArthur failed to explain or apologize for the communiqué. On April 5, House Minority Leader Joseph Martin (R-Mass.), a MacArthur ally, read a letter from the general on the floor of the House. It described Korea as the arena where "the communist conspirators have elected to make their play for global conquest," and concluded, "... we must win. There is no substitute for victory." Truman could no longer tolerate MacArthur's insubordination. After a week of meetings with his top advisers, the president announced in a 1:00 a.m. news conference on April 11 that he was relieving MacArthur of command.

Truman's public approval ratings, as measured by the Gallup organization, slipped from 28 percent in late March to just 24 percent after he fired MacArthur. Sixty-one percent of Americans disapproved of the way he was doing his job. Impeachment became a common topic of discussion as members of Congress accused the president and his top advisers of appeasing Communism or even being under the influence of Communist agents.[4] MacArthur's welcome home as a war hero intensified the pressure on the Truman administration. The general delivered an emotional farewell address before Congress on April 19 and received a New York City parade attended by an estimated seven million people.

The Truman administration, however, was able to focus attention away from MacArthur's patriotic appeals and denunciations of Truman's policies to the general's insubordination and the constitutional principle of civilian control of the armed forces. At the joint Senate Foreign Relations and Armed Services Committee hearings on MacArthur's firing and Korean War strategy, administration officials united behind the president in denouncing MacArthur's actions and endorsing military restraint in Korea. Most important, Truman received the support of the military. Chairman of the Joint Chiefs of Staff Gen. Omar Bradley told the committees that MacArthur's Korean strategy "would involve us in the wrong war, at the wrong place, at the wrong time, and with the wrong enemy."[5] Talk of impeachment subsided, and Congress took no action against the president. Truman had successfully defended his commander-in-chief authority and reaffirmed the principle of civilian control over the military.

1. John Spanier, *American Foreign Policy Since World War II*, 11th ed. (Washington, D.C.: CQ Press, 1988), 76.
2. James A. Nathan and James K. Oliver, *United States Foreign Policy and World Order*, 2d ed. (Boston: Little, Brown, 1981), 147.
3. R. Gordon Hoxie, *Command Decision and the Presidency* (New York: Reader's Digest Press, 1977), 180.
4. Nathan and Oliver, *United States Foreign Policy*, 149.
5. Hoxie, *Command Decision and the Presidency*, 181.

goals by increasing the authority of the chairman of the JCS. By making the chairman of the JCS the president's supreme military adviser, the bill's advocates theorized that the chairman would be free to develop advice and options independent of service interests. The bill created the post of vice chairman and placed the JCS staff under the direct control of the chairman to bolster the chairman's bureaucratic resources. To ensure that the service chiefs would continue to have an advisory role, the chairman is required to forward their dissenting views to the president and secretary of defense upon the chiefs' request. The bill also enhanced the authority of the CINCs, giving them greater control over the training, supply, organization, and operations of their command.[98]

Presidential Control of the Military

Despite the enhanced authority of the civilian leadership of the Defense Department since 1947, presidents have not dominated the military. Like any government organization, the military has its own organizational objectives and is capable of resisting policies it believes are against its interests. Military leaders have been particularly successful in cultivating friends in Congress who pressure the administration to accept the military's perspective on given issues.

In addition to the military's political clout, presidential control over the armed forces is limited by the president's dependence on the military for evaluations of the nation's military capabilities. Civilian advisers can offer opinions on many military problems, but their assessments must depend on the factual information supplied by the military. Moreover, estimates about the force requirements and prospects for success of a given combat operation can only be supplied by the military.[99] The president may be confident that a particular military operation is justified on moral and political grounds, but the president rarely will order the operation if the military is pessimistic about its chances for success. Presidents also depend on the military to implement their military orders. Whereas presidential initiatives in other areas such as diplomacy can be accomplished through several channels, only the military can carry out a combat operation.

The political leverage of the armed services and their monopoly on military information and resources, therefore, has forced the White House to bargain with the services for cooperation in implementing its programs. Presidents, however, are not always willing and able to compromise with the military. Presidents seeking to reduce their dependence on military sources of defense information and overcome military opposition to their orders and plans can take several steps. They can support defense reorganizations, bring a military officer into the White House as an adviser, rely on the secretary of defense and other civilian advisers for military advice, give the Office of Management and Budget (OMB) greater authority over defense spending, and appoint presidential commissions to study defense problems.[100]

Presidents also can exercise control over the military through their appointments of military officers. Congress establishes the ranks to which officers can be promoted, and the Senate confirms presidential appointees, but the power to assign military officers to posts including the Joint Chiefs of Staff gives presidents the opportunity to shape the leadership of the military. Moreover, one of the most important instruments of presidential control over

Library of Congress

President Truman pins a medal on Gen. Douglas MacArthur at their October 15, 1950, meeting on Wake Island. Truman called the meeting to discuss MacArthur's strategy in Korea. Six months later, Truman would fire MacArthur for insubordination.

the military is the commander in chief's prerogative to dismiss military subordinates in wartime who are incompetent or insubordinate.

Defense Budget

The most frustrating and complicated aspect of presidential defense management is the defense budget. Every year the executive branch must submit a defense budget to Congress, which proposes both defense spending levels and the specific military programs on which funds will be spent. The first question is a highly visible political issue on which most Americans have an opinion and presidential candidates must announce their intentions. The second, however, must be determined through a complex process of conflict and compromise between the president, the Congress, the defense department's civilian leadership, and the individual armed services all under the lobbying pressure of defense contractors and public interest groups.

The amount of money devoted to the defense budget and the manner in which it is spent affect the defense capabilities of the United States by determining what defense programs will be funded. In addition, the defense budget profoundly affects diplomacy. The size and composition of the defense budget create a backdrop for U.S. international relations. Adversaries and allies alike scrutinize it for clues about U.S. global intentions. For example, increases in defense spending, particularly for items such as naval vessels and aircraft, may signal to foreign governments an administration's intention to pursue a more activist foreign policy. Cuts in defense spending may indicate an effort to scale back U.S. defense commitments.

The defense budget also has enormous consequences for the U.S. economy. Even in 1980 before the Reagan administration's military buildup, defense spending accounted for 22.5 percent of all federal expenditures and was equal to 5 percent of the gross national product. By 1986 these figures had climbed to 26.8 and 6.3 percent, respectively.[101]

Defense makes up the largest part of the discretionary budget—the part of the budget that can be cut or shifted from year to year. *(See "The Uncontrollable Budget," p. 262, in Chief Economist chapter.)* The amount of funds spent on defense, therefore, is a major determinant of the size of the budget deficit or surplus. The sharp increases in the budget deficits that occurred during the 1980s were partially attributable to President Reagan's insistence on dramatically raising defense spending without increasing taxes. Defense spending affects the economy in other ways as well. Although most economists believe that tax cuts have a greater stimulative effect on the economy than increased military expenditures, boosting defense spending can create greater demand for goods and services that can reduce unemployment and lift the country out of a depression or recession. Increases in defense expenditures, however, also may increase inflation by creating excessive competition for the goods and services produced by the economy. Vietnam War expenditures sparked an inflationary spiral that plagued the U.S. economy during much of the late 1960s and 1970s.

Defense Budget Process

The defense budget is a large and complex document that is prepared with the participation of numerous bureaucratic entities including the National Security Council, Office of Management and Budget, and many Defense Department agencies. About a year and a half before a fiscal year begins, the defense secretary issues the Defense Guidance. This document assesses military threats and defines departmental goals and spending priorities. Using this outline the military services develop budget requests. These requests are reviewed and amended by the defense secretary and OMB who reevaluate them in the context of defense and nondefense spending priorities. The resulting comprehensive defense budget is then submitted to Congress.[102]

Presidential participation in the defense budget process is limited by the size and complexity of the budget. Although many presidents have served in the military, few have had executive branch experience with the defense budget. They therefore must rely heavily on career military officers and defense department bureaucrats familiar with the process. Even if a president were a defense expert, the many demands of the presidency would not allow its occupant to become immersed in defense budget details.

Nevertheless, presidents affect the defense budget more than any other individual or group because their assessments of U.S. military capabilities and the threats to U.S. national security create the atmosphere under which the defense budget is formulated. No president can be expected to review every item in the defense budget, but they do determine the approximate level of defense spend-ing, and their defense philosophy affects which types of programs will be emphasized. For example, a president rarely will participate in discussions of budgetary details such as how much to pay privates, but a presidential decision that the military needs to improve the quality of recruits will pervade those discussions.

Besides establishing a national security philosophy, presidents function as the final arbiter of disputes between executive departments and agencies over specific defense budget decisions. OMB and the Defense Department in particular are likely to oppose each other on budget issues since OMB's mission of overseeing spending often clashes with Defense's mission of ensuring national security. Early in his term, Reagan had to choose between the conflicting defense budget recommendations of Defense Secretary Caspar Weinberger, who had been charged with building up the nation's defenses, and OMB Director David Stockman, who had been given the task of reducing the federal deficit despite tax cuts. Reagan sided with Weinberger, thus subordinating budget reduction to the defense buildup.[103]

Since World War II, Congress usually has given presidents most of the funds they requested for defense. Few legislators have wanted to be tagged as "soft on defense," and most of them have defense industries or bases in their states and districts, which their constituents expect them to protect from budget cuts. Nevertheless, Congress has scrutinized the defense budget more carefully since the Vietnam War. The executive branch has retained the initiative over the defense budget, but Congress has challenged the president on funding for individual weapons systems and defense programs such as the MX missile. In addition, the creation of the Congressional Budget Office in 1974 and the expansion of congressional committee staffs that deal with the defense budget have enhanced Congress's ability to detect waste and fraud in the spending programs that are approved.[104]

Weapons Development and Procurement

Presidents and their scientific and military advisers must choose which weapons systems to develop and build from a wide variety of options. Numerous agencies and offices within the Pentagon engage in weapons research, development, and acquisition including the Defense Advanced Research Projects Agency, Defense Logistics Agency, and the offices of Research and Advanced Technology, Research and Engineering, Operational Test and Evaluation, and Spares Program Management. In 1986 Congress enacted laws creating the office of under secretary of defense for acquisition and designating the under secretary as the Pentagon's third-ranking official in an attempt to centralize oversight and direction of the huge procurement bureaucracy.

Weapons procurement decisions seldom are based solely on rational calculations of how a particular weapons system may contribute to national security. The individual services press presidents and top defense officials to adopt various procurement strategies. The development of the U.S. nuclear triad—the policy of deploying some nuclear weapons on land-based missiles, others on bombers, and the rest on submarines and surface ships—resulted in part because the individual services each wanted a nuclear mission. Even groups within the services will maneuver to protect their share of their service's procurement funds.

Technological advances also drive weapons procure-

Presidential Promotion of Weapons Systems

The progress of a weapons system from conception to deployment may depend on the president's ability to create a favorable impression of the program among the American public, Congress, and U.S. allies. The fate of two weapons systems illustrates how major decisions dealing with the development and procurement of weaponry have become public issues that hinge as much on an administration's salesmanship as on the weapon's potential contribution to national security.

Jimmy Carter's plan to produce the neutron bomb, a small nuclear warhead intended for deployment in Europe, was hindered by the negative image of the weapon. The Carter administration argued that the bomb's reduced blast, heat, and fallout would reduce civilian casualties if a tactical nuclear war broke out in Europe, while the bomb's emission of an enhanced wave of neutron radiation would be a more effective weapon against Warsaw Pact tanks built to resist the blast and heat of "regular" nuclear weapons.

These arguments disturbed antinuclear activists in Europe and the United States who mounted a public relations campaign against the weapon. They saw the neutron bomb not as strengthening deterrence, but rather as increasing the chances of nuclear war by making nuclear weapons more usable. The bomb also was criticized as the ultimate capitalistic weapon because it killed people with its enhanced radiation, but its diminished blast left buildings standing. The controversy over the neutron bomb in Europe and the United States and the failure of allies in the North Atlantic Treaty Organization (NATO) to commit themselves firmly to its deployment persuaded Carter in 1978 to abandon his plans to produce the weapon.

In contrast, Ronald Reagan succeeded in harnessing popular opinion for the Strategic Defense Initiative (SDI), a controversial weapons program proposed by Reagan in a dramatic televised speech on March 23, 1983. SDI, which came to be known as "Star Wars," was a research and development project intended to produce a space-based defense against a nuclear ballistic missile attack. That Reagan's vision of a space-based missile defense was possible and desirable was unclear. The scientific community did not reach a consensus on the feasibility of such a defense, and even the most ardent supporters of SDI admitted that a workable system capable of defending the entire United States depended on scientific breakthroughs that were more than a decade away. Moreover, the plan was projected to cost hundreds of billions of dollars, would not solve the problem of defending against Soviet bombers and cruise missiles, and would have unpredictable effects on arms control and the strategic nuclear balance.

Nevertheless, to build public support for the expensive development program the Reagan administration promoted it as a project designed to produce a "Peace Shield" that would free the United States and eventually the world from the threat of nuclear destruction. A majority of Americans agreed with the president that SDI was a worthy goal. Members of Congress responded to their constituents' support of SDI by approving dramatic increases in funding for the project. As with the neutron bomb, popular perceptions of SDI were as important to the decision-making process as the weapons system's strategic value and technical feasibility.

---

ment. Since the end of World War II the defense establishment has operated under the consensus that the quality of weapons is more important than their quantity. Defense planners have relied on U.S. technological superiority to compensate for the Eastern bloc's advantage in numbers of troops and tanks. This strategy has led defense planners to accept almost any technological improvement in a weapon regardless of its cost.[105] Presidents must serve as a mediator between competing factions in the procurement process and attempt to develop a mix of weapons that best meets the needs of national security at an affordable cost.

Presidents seldom become personally involved in minor procurement matters, but major decisions about purchases of highly visible and expensive items such as ships, missiles, and large numbers of aircraft must ultimately be approved by presidents and often result from their appraisal of the balance of forces. For example, in the early 1980s, Ronald Reagan's determination that U.S. strategic nuclear forces were threatened by a window of vulnerability led to the deployment of the MX missile and a revival of the B-1 bomber project that had been scrapped under Jimmy Carter.

Yet the changes any one president can make on the U.S. arsenal are limited by the length of time required to

develop a weapon. Weapons systems often take more than a decade to move from conception to deployment and may be conceived under one president, tested under another, and mass produced under a third. Weapons systems in their early stages of development may not survive once the president who presided over their conception leaves office. At the other end of the process presidents have been reluctant to cancel weapons systems that have reached the production stage because of the time and money that have already been spent on their development. In addition, the longer a weapons program has been in existence, the more likely it will have developed constituencies in the defense bureaucracy and Congress who will resist its cancellation. President Carter's decision not to build the B-1 bomber in 1977 was a rare example of a president cancelling a major weapon after it was completely developed and ready for production.[106]

Ultimately, presidents must secure congressional approval for appropriations to pay for the projects they favor. Not only must presidents contend with members of Congress who do not share their views of procurement priorities, presidents must deal with lawmakers who defend weapons because they happen to be built in their home states and districts.

McNamara Reforms

Robert McNamara became secretary of Defense in 1961 with a mandate from President Kennedy to restructure the budget and procurement process within the Defense Department. McNamara viewed the defense planning and budgeting system that existed during the 1950s as arbitrary and wasteful. Funds were divided among the services, which spent the money according to their parochial conceptions of the nation's defense needs. McNamara sought to centralize budgetary authority within the Office of the Secretary of Defense. By centralizing authority away from the services, he believed he and his staff would be able to make unbiased, cost-effective decisions on budgeting, weapons procurement, and other important resource allocation issues that previously had been decided by the services through a process of conflict and compromise. Although McNamara'a reforms did not eliminate inefficiency and duplication of effort, they did create lasting improvements in the defense budgeting process.

The device McNamara used to centralize power in the OSD was systems analysis. Systems analysis used computer-aided statistical techniques to evaluate the relative costs and effectiveness of alternative defense programs.[107] He instituted a new philosophy of defense management that considered defense programs according to their mission rather than which service would receive funds. His planning, programming, and budgeting system (PPBS) was intended to link budget decisions to overall military strategy and existing force levels. For example, under PPBS the OSD would consider the number and types of forces needed to accomplish the goal of strategic nuclear deterrence given existing U.S. forces, Soviet forces, and budgetary constaints. Then it would determine the most cost-effective method of achieving this goal before allocating funds. Under the old budgeting system an individual service did not consider what weapons the other services possessed or were planning to build before submitting its budget and procurement proposals. Thus, the navy determined how many missile launching submarines it needed without considering how many bombers and missiles the air force had or planned to procure.

The services protested the centralization of authority within the OSD and the domination of defense planning and budgeting by civilian systems analysts. They saw their traditional decision-making role eroding and complained that they were not adequately consulted by OSD. Military leaders also criticized the new system for placing too much emphasis on quantifiable aspects of weapons and programs while devaluing military intuition.[108] McNamara's reforms were implemented, however, with the support of presidents Kennedy and Johnson. McNamara left the Defense Department in 1968, and Johnson left office in 1969, but McNamara's PPBS system, his emphasis on systems analysis, and his conception of a strong defense secretary have survived.

Defense Budget Inefficiency

Despite the introduction of systems analysis in the 1960s, defense department funds continue to be wasted through mismanagement and fraud. Perceptions that the defense budget was out of control were heightened during the Reagan administration. Numerous anecdotes of the defense department buying inexpensive items at ludicrous prices demonstrated the problems with defense procurement and budgeting. For example, the air force purchased a twelve-cent allen wrench for $9,606 and toilet seats for military transport planes for $640. In addition, several major defense contractors were found guilty of price gouging, bribery, and tax fraud. In June 1988 the Justice Department disclosed evidence of a major procurement scandal involving dozens of defense contracts costing tens of billions of dollars that threatened to dwarf all defense budget scandals that had come before it.

Although waste occurs in every government department and agency, several characteristics of the Defense Department have made its problem particularly acute.

First, the enormous size of the defense budget not only creates more opportunities for waste, it makes central control of its details nearly impossible.[109] Neither the president, the secretary of defense, OMB, nor Congress can judge the worthiness of every one of the thousands of line items that make up the defense budget.

Second, the Pentagon's unique buyer-customer relationship with the contractors that supply it with weapons and equipment has led to corruption and waste. The Defense Department has applied the same standards to defense contractors that an average consumer would apply to a manufacturer of consumer goods. The Pentagon often has paid contractors for unexpected expenses incurred in the production of a weapons system rather than letting the company assume the risk of cost overruns. Arms manufacturers also have been given primary responsibility for testing their own products and have not been required to provide warranties for the equipment they sell to the Pentagon.

Third, interservice rivalries still adversely affect the coherence of defense budget planning. Each service and defense agency initially develops its own budget requests. Each service tends to promote its own interests at the expense of the others. Moreover, the services often have failed to consult with one another when developing budget and procurement proposals. They have sought weapons and funding that will enable them independently to perform missions they perceive as traditional and glamorous regardless of the needs of the other services.

It is beyond the capacity of the president to ensure that all defense dollars will be spent efficiently. Yet because the defense budget makes up such a large share of the federal budget and the potential for waste is so great, presidents, as manager of the nation's defenses and economy, must make an effort to promote honest and efficient defense spending practices. This must be done primarily by appointing and supporting the efforts of defense officials who have defense budget experience and are committed to vigorous oversight of defense spending.

Military Personnel Policy

Although the Constitution charges Congress with the responsibility to "make rules for the government and regulation" of the army and navy, the executive branch has substantial authority in military personnel policy. Much of this authority has been delegated to the executive branch by Congress, but authority also has been claimed by presidents under the commander-in-chief power to make regulations that do not conflict with congressional statutes. As a result, the laws passed by Congress governing the armed forces have been supplemented by a body of executive rules and regulations.[110]

Presidents have usually taken the initiative in proposing changes in the size of the armed forces, the methods by which the ranks are filled, and where U.S. forces will be stationed. Ultimate authority for raising an army resides in Congress, but legislators often have accepted presidential actions and recommendations on these issues.

Recruitment and the Draft

Conscription was not used in the United States until the Civil War. The 1863 Enrollment Act set up a draft system run by the War Department and administered by military officers. During World War I Congress again authorized conscription to fulfill troop goals. The 1917 Selective Service Act was challenged in the courts, but the Supreme Court upheld Congress's authority to draft Americans in a series of cases known as the *Selective Draft Law Cases.* Moreover, the Court held that military service was one of a citizen's duties in a "just government."

Not until 1940, however, did Congress pass a draft bill while the nation was at peace. Although the United States had not yet become involved in World War II, President Franklin Roosevelt urged Congress to adopt the measure. In the summer of 1941, with the threat of war looming larger, Roosevelt had a difficult fight before winning enactment of amendments that widened the draft. The measure was passed in the House by just one vote. Whereas earlier drafts had been administered by the War Department, the Selective Training and Service Act of 1940 established an independent Selective Service System, headed by a presidential appointee, to oversee the draft.

In 1947, Congress followed President Truman's recommendation to allow the 1940 draft act to expire. A year later when enlistments failed to meet troop needs, Truman proposed a renewal of the draft and universal military training. Truman's plan would have required all physically and mentally able men to receive one year of military training and serve six months in the reserves. Congress rejected universal military training but passed the Selective Service Act of 1948, which renewed the peacetime draft.

Congress extended the draft several times during the next two and a half decades with the support of a series of presidents. In January 1973 the Paris peace accords were signed ending U.S. involvement in the Vietnam War. Congress followed the recommendation of President Nixon and allowed the draft to expire on July 1 of that year. On April 1, 1975, President Ford announced that eighteen-year-old males no longer had to register for the draft.

The draft's expiration was the first step in establishing an all-volunteer armed forces, which had been under study since 1969. Military pay was raised dramatically to attract volunteers. Since 1973 the armed services have succeeded in meeting their personnel requirements. Although some observers' warnings that the volunteer armed forces would lead to a reduction in the quality of military personnel seemed prophetic in the early years of the volunteer army, during most of the 1980s more than 90 percent of recruits have been high school graduates.

In his State of the Union address on January 23, 1980, Jimmy Carter asked Congress to reinstitute draft registration. Carter was motivated to make the proposal by the international tension created in late 1979 by the takeover of the U.S. embassy in Tehran and the invasion of Afghanistan by the Soviet Union. Draft registration was intended to reduce the time required to bring draftees into the armed services after a mobilization. Congress approved

the plan, although it rejected Carter's request to register women. The measure provided only for registration and did not empower the president to draft young men without a further authorization from Congress.[111] Although Reagan opposed draft registration during the 1980 presidential campaign, he ordered its continuation in January 1982.

Peacetime Military Deployments

When U.S. forces become involved in hostilities, presidents have the indisputable authority as commander in chief to determine where those forces will be deployed. In peacetime, however, Congress has occasionally made rules governing the deployment of military personnel. These rules have been justified under Congress's powers to make laws and raise and support the armed forces. Although the commander-in-chief power provides presidents with a justification to determine unilaterally where troops should be deployed even in peacetime, they have generally respected laws limiting their freedom to deploy troops.[112] In 1940 Congress attached a proviso to the Selective Training and Service Act that prohibited troops drafted under the act from being used outside the Western Hemisphere. Franklin Roosevelt accepted this limitation, although he maintained that Iceland was part of the Western Hemisphere and sent troops there in 1941.

A more recent example of a congressional limit on troop deployments occurred in 1982. In that year, Congress attached to a defense appropriations bill an amendment limiting the number of active-duty U.S. military personnel stationed in Europe to 315,000. The Reagan administration argued against the limit, saying that increases in U.S. troop strength in Europe might be required by changes in the military balance between NATO and the Soviet Union and its allies. Despite the administration's objections, Defense Secretary Caspar Weinberger assured Congress that the troop ceiling would be observed. The amendment included a provision that allowed the president to waive the troop limit if the president certified that "overriding national security requirements" made such action necessary. This provision was a recognition by Congress that the purpose of peacetime military deployments is to deter war and that the president as commander in chief should have wide authority to redeploy troops for that purpose.

If a president did refuse to observe limitations Congress placed on peacetime troop deployments, Congress still would have the option of cutting off funds for the base where the troops are stationed or for the supplies needed to sustain the troops. Such action would require a united Congress since presumedly it would have to override a presidential veto of any bill that stopped funds for a troop deployment favored by the president.

Presidential Wartime Emergency Powers

After Thomas Jefferson had left the presidency, in 1810 he wrote:

A strict observation of the written laws is doubtless one of the higher duties of a good officer, but it is not the highest. The law of necessity, of self-preservation, of saving our country when in danger, are of higher obligation. To lose our country by a scrupulous adherence to written law would be to lose the law itself, with life, liberty, property . . . thus sacrificing the end to the means.[113]

This argument, that presidents have the authority to violate the Constitution to ensure the security of the nation, has been used by wartime presidents to justify extraordinary exercises of power.

When it is evident that conditions of national peril exist, Congress and the American public have turned to the president for leadership. Under such conditions Lincoln and Franklin Roosevelt stretched, reinterpreted, and in some cases brazenly violated the Constitution in the name of national security. Their claim to an inherent executive power to safeguard the nation was accepted because the American people generally agreed with their assessment of the gravity of the emergency at hand.[114] Presidential claims of an inherent executive power during a doubtful national emergency, however, will likely fail the test of public and judicial scrutiny. President Nixon was not able to convince the American people or the courts that his administration's use of wiretaps and break-ins was in the interest of national security.

Nowhere does the Constitution mention presidential emergency powers, but the courts often have been sympathetic to exercises of emergency power by presidents in wartime, especially when action is taken with the cooperation of Congress. Yet this approval has not been automatic, especially when the rights and property of U.S. citizens is involved. Total war in any age requires sacrifices from civilians and security measures at home, but a wartime emergency does not give the president unrestrained freedom to violate the rights of Americans.

Martial Law and Civil Rights

The most extreme wartime emergency measure a president may take is the declaration of martial law. Under such a declaration, civilian government is temporarily replaced by military rule. Substitution of military for civilian authority may be absolute, or it may involve only the appropriation of a specific civil function by the military. Even cases of limited martial law, however, invariably result in the curbing of individual rights.

The Constitution does not provide for a power to declare martial law, although it does mention the suspension of *habeas corpus* under Article I, which outlines Congress's powers. The declaration of martial law, however, is usually presumed to be a presidential function flowing from the president's powers to command the armed forces and execute the laws. Because there is no specific constitutional basis for martial law, presidents must justify their decision to proclaim it on the grounds that the welfare and security of the nation requires them to govern through military force rather than established laws.

No president has ever declared a condition of absolute martial law that applied to the entire country. Moreover, not since President Lincoln placed several areas of the nation under martial law during the Civil War has any president directly proclaimed martial law on behalf of the national government. Martial law has been declared, however, by presidential agents or military officers often with the explicit or implied approval of the president. For example, Gen. Andrew Jackson declared martial law in New Orleans before his battle with the British there in 1814; the commander of federal troops sent to Idaho in 1899 to quell labor unrest declared martial law with President McKin-

ley's approval; and after the Japanese attack on Pearl Harbor on December 7, 1941, the territorial governor of Hawaii declared martial law on the islands with the support of Franklin Roosevelt.[115]

Although the courts may reject the president's assessment of the necessity of martial law, historically they have done so only after the emergency has passed. In 1866 the Supreme Court ruled in *Ex parte Milligan* that Lincoln's suspension of the the civil court system in Indiana during the civil war was illegal.[116] Similarly, in 1946 the court declared in *Duncan v. Kahanamoku* that the establishment of martial law during World War II in Hawaii by the governor with President Roosevelt's approval had been unlawful.[117] Yet neither decision had any effect on either president's ability to abrogate civil liberties during the wars.

Suspension of Habeas Corpus

The only emergency power mentioned in the Constitution is the suspension of the writ of *habeas corpus*—the right of prisoners to have the legality of their detention reviewed by the courts and to be released upon the court's orders. The Constitution states: "The Privilege of the Writ of Habeas Corpus shall not be suspended, unless when in Cases of Rebellion or Invasion the public Safety may require it." The Framers did not, however, specify who had this power, although their placement of it in Article I has led many legal scholars, judges, and legislators to argue that it was intended as a congressional power.

The issue of presidential suspension of *habeas corpus* arose most dramatically during the Civil War. In response to sabotage by Confederate sympathizers, President Lincoln ordered in the spring of 1861 that *habeas corpus* be suspended along the route between Washington and Philadelphia. Lincoln believed this and other emergency measures were essential to the survival of the Union. On May 25, John Merryman, a prominent Maryland citizen who had been involved in secessionist activities in that state, was arrested by military authorities. Merryman immediately appealed to Chief Justice Roger Taney for a writ of *habeas corpus*. Taney reviewed the case and ordered the army to release Merryman, but Lincoln defiantly refused to permit his release. Taney denounced Lincoln's action and wrote an opinion asserting that the Constitution had conferred authority to suspend the writ on Congress, not the president. Lincoln maintained that since the suspension of *habeas corpus* was an emergency measure and emergencies could occur when Congress was out of session—as it had been in this case—presidents must have authority to suspend the writ unilaterally.

The conflict between the president and the chief justice showed that a president willing to defy legal procedures during a genuine crisis that was widely recognized as such could suspend *habeas corpus* regardless of the president's legal authority to do so. Presidential scholar Clinton Rossiter remarked,

> The one great precedent is what Lincoln did, not what Taney said. Future Presidents will know where to look for historical support. So long as public opinion sustains the President, as a sufficient amount of it sustained Lincoln in his shadowy tilt with Taney and throughout the rest of the war, he has nothing to fear from the displeasure of the courts. . . . The law of the Constitution, as it actually exists, must be considered to read that in a condition of martial necessity the President has the power to suspend the privilege of the writ of habeas corpus.[118]

Trial of Civilians by Military Courts

In addition to suspending *habeas corpus*, President Lincoln also declared that for some crimes civilians could be tried by military courts. On September 24, 1862, he announced that as long as the Civil War continued

> all rebels and insurgents, their aiders and abettors, within the United States, and all persons discouraging volunteer enlistments, resisting militia drafts, or guilty of any disloyal practice affording aid and comfort to rebels against the authority of the United States, shall be subject to martial law and liable to trial and punishment of courts-martial or military commissions.

Lincoln went on to suspend *habeas corpus* for such persons and declared that they could be imprisoned in military facilities. Although Congress had passed legislation approving many of Lincoln's emergency measures, it never approved his subjection of civilians to military courts.[119]

Lambdin P. Milligan, a citizen of Indiana, was arrested in 1864 by military authorities who charged him with aiding a Confederate raid into Indiana from across the Ohio River. On May 9, 1865, he was found guilty and sentenced to death. Milligan's case eventually came before the Supreme Court.

The Court held 9-0 in *Ex parte Milligan* that the president did not have the authority to subject civilians to military tribunals in an area where civilian courts were functioning.[120] The Court also ruled 5-4 that even the president and Congress together lacked power to authorize trials of civilians by military courts outside of a war zone. The majority opinion, written by Justice David Davis admitted:

> If, in foreign invasion or civil war, the courts are actually closed, and it is impossible to administer criminal justice according to law, then, in the theatre of active military operations, where war really prevails, there is a necessity to furnish a substitute for the civilian authority, thus overthrown, to preserve the safety of the army and society; and as no power is left but the military, it is allowed to govern by martial rule until the laws can have their free course.

The Supreme Court rejected the idea, however, that such conditions existed in Indiana—hundreds of miles from the front—where civilian courts were functioning normally.

Beyond their verdict, the justices used *Ex parte Milligan* to defend the inviolability of the Constitution. Justice Davis wrote:

> The Constitution of the United States is a law for rulers and people, equally in war and in peace, and covers with the shield of its protection all classes of men, at all times, and under all circumstances. No doctrine involving more pernicious consequences was ever invented by the wit of man than that any of its provisions can be suspended during any of the great exigencies of government.

Milligan is regarded as significant by legal scholars for demonstrating that even during the most dire military emergency there are constitutional limits to presidential power.

Korematsu v. United States

When the Supreme Court ruled on *Milligan* in 1866, the war was over and Lincoln was dead. Consequently, the Court was able to strike down a presidential emergency action without confronting an incumbent president during a wartime crisis. Three-quarters of a century later, however, a case involving the violation of individual rights by an exercise of wartime emergency power came before the Court while the emergency still existed.

Following the Japanese attack on Pearl Harbor on December 7, 1941, President Roosevelt ordered several controversial measures to enhance security on the West Coast. These included the imposition of a curfew on persons of Japanese descent and the relocation of 120,000 Japanese Americans to internment camps in the U.S. interior. Both the curfew and the relocation applied to persons of Japanese ancestry regardless of their citizenship or loyalty. Congress subsequently passed legislation validating the president's directives.

This wholesale suspension of the rights of American citizens led to several Supreme Court cases. The Court ruled unanimously in *Hirabayashi v. United States* that together the president and Congress had the power to impose the curfew and that the extreme emergency created by Japan's threat to the Pacific Coast made the curfew justifiable.[121]

The Court did not reach a consensus, however, on the more severe violation of rights involved in the relocation of Japanese-Americans. In *Korematsu v. United States* it ruled 6-3 that the threat to national security justified the joint action of Congress and the president.[122] Writing for the majority, Justice Hugo Black explained, "Compulsory exclusion of large groups of citizens from their homes, except under circumstances of direct emergency and peril, is inconsistent with our basic governmental institutions. But when under conditions of modern warfare our shores are threatened by hostile forces, the power to protect must be commensurable with the threatened danger." In a bitter dissenting opinion, Justice Francis Murphy rejected the premise of the Court's decision that the emergency on the West Coast warranted the exclusion from the West Coast of all persons of Japanese ancestry. "Such exclusion," he wrote, "goes over 'the very brink of Constitutional power' and falls into the abyss of racism."

Although *Korematsu* is now generally regarded as an embarrassing moment in Supreme Court history, it reinforced the prerogative of the president and Congress jointly to take almost any emergency action in time of war, even if that action violates the most basic rights of U.S. citizens.[123]

Seizure of Property

During wartime it sometimes is necessary for a government to seize property of its citizens that is vital to the war effort. Congress has traditionally passed legislation governing the seizure of property belonging to U.S. citizens. Before and during World War I, Congress empowered the president to seize transportation and communications systems if such actions became necessary. President Wilson used these statutes to take over railroad, telephone, and telegraph operations, which were returned to civilian control after the war. Similarly, Franklin Roosevelt was authorized by the War Labor Disputes Act of 1943 to seize industries important to the war effort that were in danger of being shut down by labor disputes.[124]

Presidents have not always waited, however, for Congress to grant them the authority to seize property before they took action. Lincoln personally authorized military units to take possession of telegraph lines during the Civil

War, and Wilson ordered the seizure of a wireless station in 1914 that refused to comply with naval censorship rules. Franklin Roosevelt took control of several strike-threatened industries before Congress authorized such action with the War Labor Disputes Act. Yet unilateral seizures of property by presidents have been exceptions to accepted practice, and the courts generally have rejected the proposition that presidents possess inherent emergency powers that authorize them to seize private property.

The most famous court case dealing with the president's power to seize private property in wartime was *Youngstown Sheet and Tube Co. v. Sawyer,* also known as the *Steel Seizure Case.* In it the Supreme Court ruled that President Truman did not have the authority to seize steel mills about to be closed by strikes despite the ongoing Korean War emergency. United Steel workers threatened to strike on April 9, 1952. Truman believed that the strike would damage the Korean War effort by causing steel shortages. On April 8, he directed Secretary of Commerce Charles Sawyer to seize and operate the steel mills. He justified his seizure of the mills solely on his power as commander in chief and his responsibility to execute the laws. Truman conceded in his report to Congress that it had the authority to countermand his directive, but Congress failed to approve or reject the president's action.

The steel companies brought suit against the government seeking an injunction to stop the president's action. The case quickly reached the Supreme Court, where, by a vote of 6-3, Truman's action was held unconstitutional. The Court claimed that the president had usurped Congress's law-making power. It cited several acts in which Congress had provided procedures for responding to strikes that Truman had ignored. In the debate on one of these laws, the Taft-Hartley Act of 1947, Congress had considered empowering the government to seize an industry to prevent strikes but had refused to include such a provision in the law. Truman, therefore, had not just taken action without congressional authorization, he had taken an action that Congress had rejected.[125]

Although it is unclear whether the Court would have ruled differently had the emergency been more grave or had Congress not rejected the inclusion of property seizure provisions in the Taft-Hartley Act, the decision was a blow to the president's commander-in-chief authority. In a concurring opinion Justice William O. Douglas explained:

> There can be no doubt that the emergency which caused the president to seize these steel plants was one that bore heavily on the country. But the emergency did not create power; it merely marked an occasion when power should be exercised. And the fact that it was necessary that measures be taken to keep steel in production does not mean that the President, rather than the Congress, had the constitutional authority to act.[126]

In an era of rapidly expanding presidential power, the *Steel Seizure Case,* as Clinton Rossiter observed, "revived, for the moment, the notion that Presidents were subject to congressional limitations in foreign affairs."[127]

Armed Forces as a Tool of Presidential Foreign Policy

The armed forces of the United States have assisted presidents in achieving foreign policy goals. A president con-

fronted with an international problem often has the option to use the military to solve that problem. Military strength has enabled presidents to intimidate potential aggressors, impress trading partners, reassure allies, and mediate international disputes. Presidents have been reluctant to deploy armed forces in a crisis, but nearly every twentieth-century president has done so, sometimes with negative results. Beyond the military's potential to use or threaten force in a specific international hotspot, the strength of U.S. armed forces since World War II has allowed presidents to improve relations with other countries by offering them security guarantees and memberships in multinational alliances.

Peacetime Military Missions

From the time the Constitution was ratified until the present, presidents have used the military to accomplish limited missions in peacetime. Presidents have ordered the armed forces to protect settlers from Indians, repel bands of foreign outlaws, punish nations and groups for belligerent or criminal behavior, rescue U.S. citizens abroad, support friendly governments and train their armies, fight pirates and terrorists, warn potential enemies from taking aggressive action, and secure disputed lands. As chief executive, presidents also have used troops to put down domestic insurrections and enforce federal law. The Constitution does not specifically sanction these peacetime military operations, but presidents have justified them under their power to command the military, defend the United States and its citizens, enforce the laws, and conduct foreign policy.

Police Actions and Rescue Missions

Of all peacetime military operations, the most consequential have been police actions and rescue missions ordered by presidents to protect U.S. citizens and interests abroad. The vast majority of these operations have been minor incidents that did not require Congress to declare war. Indeed, many of them were so brief that Congress would not have had time to deliberate on a declaration of war even if the president had asked for one. Presidents have argued that these limited missions require no congressional sanction since they have limited goals and often depend on speed and secrecy. As long as military operations did not threaten to involve the United States in a wider war and casualties remained low, presidential popularity usually has been bolstered by limited uses of force.

Congress and the courts generally have refrained from challenging the president's authority to protect U.S. citizens and property overseas even when military actions taken under presidential orders have been unjust. For example, in 1854 a naval commander acting on the vague but belligerent orders of President Franklin Pierce completely destroyed the Nicaraguan city of Greytown when it refused to pay inflated damage claims filed by a U.S. company. Congress investigated the incident but failed to condemn the Greytown bombardment or make Pierce account for his actions. A U.S. district court dismissed a suit filed by a Greytown property owner against the naval commander on the grounds that the bombardment was a political matter.[128]

Not all presidents have believed the commander-in-chief clause gave them the power to order limited military

Military Responses to Terrorism

Throughout U.S. history, presidents have called on the military to battle not just other nations but also extra-governmental groups that have threatened Americans and their interests. For example, the navy often fought pirates in the eighteenth and nineteenth centuries, and in 1916 President Woodrow Wilson sent Gen. John J. (Blackjack) Pershing and six thousand troops into Mexico in pursuit of the Mexican bandit Pancho Villa after he had raided Columbus, New Mexico.

During the 1970s and 1980s international terrorist groups have threatened the safety of U.S. citizens much as international pirates and bandits did in earlier centuries. Terrorist groups have used violence to gain media attention and strike back at powerful nations they perceive as contributing to their particular plight. Often these terrorist acts have involved attacks on or captures of innocent civilians. Since the mid-1970s the U.S. military has placed greater emphasis on antiterrorist preparations. Intelligence agencies have expanded their efforts to identify terrorists, and elite counterterrorist units have been formed to provide presidents with a more credible military option should they decide to use force against terrorists.

While terrorist groups cannot match the military power of the United States or other industrialized nations, military operations against them have seldom been a practical option. Terrorists have been difficult to identify, and they often have blended into the populace of foreign nations or surrounded themselves with hostages. Presidents who use force indiscriminately risk harming innocent civilians, endangering the lives of hos-

tages, lending credibility to terrorist claims of U.S. injustice, and creating a cavalier image of the United States within the international community. Presidents therefore generally have refrained from using military force against terrorists except when those responsible for a terrorist act could be positively identified and attacked with precision.

Two developments during the Reagan administration increased the likelihood that presidents will use military force against terrorists in the future. First, the administration's popular military operations against terrorists and their sponsors showed that military force could be used to strike back at the roots of terrorism. In October 1985, the president ordered navy fighters to intercept an Egyptian airliner carrying terrorists who had seized a passenger ship and killed a U.S. citizen in the Mediterranean. On April 14, 1986, Reagan directed U.S. warplanes to bomb targets in Libya after U.S. intelligence obtained evidence that Libyan leader Col. Muammar Qaddafi sponsored a terrorist bombing of a Berlin nightclub. The attack set a precedent for U.S. military retaliation against any state proven to sponsor terrorist attacks against U.S. citizens. Regardless of the effectiveness of these operations in deterring terrorism, both satisfied a public impulse to strike back at terrorism and improved President Reagan's standing in public opinion polls. Second, the administration's embarrassing attempt to free U.S. hostages in Lebanon by selling arms to Iran created the perception in government and among the public that negotiating with terrorists will usually be counterproductive.

missions in the absence of congressional approval. For example, Pierce's successor, James Buchanan, claimed that without the consent of Congress he could not "fire a hostile gun in any case except to repel the attacks of an enemy." [129] Most twentieth-century presidents, however, have interpreted the commander-in-chief power broadly to fit the needs and goals of the moment.

No president did more to expand presidential authority to order limited military missions than Theodore Roosevelt. In 1904 he asserted the president's right to exercise an "international police power" in Latin America. In what became known as the Roosevelt Corollary to the Monroe Doctrine he declared that the United States had the right to intervene in Latin America to protect its interests and ensure peace. He justified this position by asserting that those governments in Latin America that were unable to rule justly, maintain order, or meet their international obligations were jeopardizing the security of the hemisphere and violating the rights of the United States. Roosevelt already had acted in the spirit of this proclamation in 1903 when he used military force to protect an American-backed revolt in Panama against Colombian rule. The revolution enabled Roosevelt to conclude a treaty with the new Panamanian government allowing the United States to construct the Panama Canal on favorable terms. In 1905 Roosevelt put his corollary to use when he ordered U.S.

forces to seize and operate the custom offices of Santo Domingo, which was failing to pay its foreign debts.

After Roosevelt presidents exercised the "police power" in the Western Hemisphere with little hesitation or consultation with Congress. William Taft, Woodrow Wilson, Calvin Coolidge, John Kennedy, Lyndon Johnson, and Ronald Reagan all used U.S. forces—or foreign troops trained and supplied by the United States—to intervene in the affairs of Latin American nations.[130]

Even if the president's power to order limited military missions is conceded, there is still the problem of defining which missions fall under the president's police and rescue powers and which should be authorized by a congressional sanction if not a declaration of war. Like the prerogative to repel invasions, the police and rescue powers can be manipulated by presidents to justify military actions that Congress might not sanction.

President Johnson sent twelve hundred troops to the Dominican Republic in 1965 in response to a plea by the U.S. ambassador there to protect Americans from the chaos brought by a coup attempt. The goals and size of the intervention soon changed, however, as the president became concerned that the Dominican faction reputed to be controlled by Communists might seize power. Johnson expanded the U.S. military force on the island to twenty thousand troops and ordered its commanders to help establish a provisional government. The troops remained until the following year when elections were held and the candidate favored by the Johnson administration was elected.

Similarly, President Reagan ordered six thousand troops to the tiny Caribbean island of Grenada in 1983 on what he called a "rescue mission." The administration maintained that a pro-Cuban military coup had placed U.S. citizens on the island in danger and threatened to turn Grenada into a Cuban-supported Communist military base. U.S. troops evacuated about one thousand Americans from the island and proceeded to depose Grenada's new leadership.[131]

In both interventions presidents used armed force to accomplish geopolitical goals without the consent of Congress. U.S. actions in the Dominican Republic and Grenada clearly were more than rescue missions or police actions. Nevertheless, the historical precedent supporting the authority of presidents to order military missions and the perceived urgency of the situation at hand have predictably influenced presidents and the U.S. public more often than strict interpretations of the Constitution and of international law.

Military Exercises and Shows of Force

Throughout U.S. history presidents have ordered conspicuous deployments of U.S. military power to dissuade potential aggressors, support allies, and reinforce U.S. diplomatic bargaining positions. Shows of force were initially limited by the weakness of the U.S. military. The demonstrations of force that presidents did order before World War II almost always involved the navy.

Millard Fillmore sent a squadron of ships under Commodore Matthew Perry to Japan in 1853. The Japanese had kept their ports closed to westerners and had abused U.S. seamen shipwrecked off their shores. Perry was instructed to show the Japanese U.S. naval power, demand that U.S. sailors be treated with respect, and propose a commercial relationship between the two countries. Perry's expedition resulted in the Treaty of Kanagawa, which declared friendship between the United States and Japan, opened several Japanese ports to U.S. commercial vessels, and established provisions for the treatment of U.S. citizens shipwrecked off Japan.

Perhaps the most famous show of force by a president was Theodore Roosevelt's dispatch of the U.S. fleet in 1907 on a cruise around the world. The cruise was primarily intended to impress Japan with U.S. naval power. Roosevelt was concerned by indications of Tokyo's belligerence and wished to demonstrate his own resolve to oppose any act of aggression by the Japanese. He believed the "Great White Fleet's" cruise also would be a valuable exercise and would promote respect and good will for the United States throughout the world. The trip went smoothly with the navy observing protocol at each port of call. Roosevelt later asserted, "The most important service that I rendered to peace was the voyage of the battle fleet around the world."[132]

Shows of force may be used to reassure a friendly government as well as warn a belligerent one. On March 17, 1988, President Reagan sent 3,150 additional U.S. troops to Honduras in response to the incursion of Nicaraguan government troops into Honduras. The Nicaraguan forces reportedly crossed the Honduras border to destroy a supply depot of the antigovernment Nicaraguan contra rebels supported by the Reagan administration. Secretary of State George Shultz said of the troops: "They're not near where the fighting is taking place, but they're designed to say to the Government of Honduras that, 'we are your friend and we stand with you, and if you are invaded you can count on the United States.'"[133] The contingent of troops conducted maneuvers in Honduras and withdrew from the country after ten days without engaging in combat.

Training and Advising Foreign Troops

Military advisers have become an established part of the superpowers' struggle for influence. Both the United States and the Communist bloc have sent military personnel into third world countries to instruct the local armed forces in organization, tactics, and the use of weapons. Often these military advisers are sent specifically to teach local troops how to use military equipment that has been given or sold to that nation.

Since U.S. military advisers usually are instructed not to participate in combat, their deployment traditionally has not required congressional approval. Sending military advisers to a foreign country, however, can be controversial. Many Americans see the introduction of U.S. military advisers into a foreign country as a first step toward greater involvement in that country's problems. This perception was created by the gradual escalation of U.S. involvement in the Vietnam War, which began with the deployment of military advisers in that country. Dwight Eisenhower first sent small numbers of advisers to Vietnam. By the end of 1960, 835 U.S. military personnel were training the South Vietnamese Army. Since South Vietnam was fighting a guerrilla war against Communist Vietcong forces in the South, U.S. advisers could not avoid combat entirely. John Kennedy and Lyndon Johnson dramatically increased the number of advisers in Vietnam to meet the growing military threat to the Saigon government. By the end of 1963 over 16,000 advisers were in Vietnam. A year later this number had swelled to 23,210.[134] Beginning with the Kennedy administration, although U.S. forces were still called "advisers," they had active combat roles.

When President Reagan introduced military advisers into El Salvador in 1981, critics of Reagan's policy charged that the U.S. military involvement in Central America could escalate as it had in Vietnam. Reagan promised to limit U.S. military advisers in El Salvador to fifty-five, but the House Foreign Affairs Committee was concerned enough to outline in a report what it considered to be unacceptable activities for U.S. military advisers in all countries. These included accompanying local units into combat, arming or fueling combat aircraft, and delivering weapons and supplies to local troops in combat areas. Although these guidelines did not have the force of law, they did set a standard for the conduct of U.S. military advisers.[135]

United Nations Peace Keeping

Presidents often have promoted UN peace-keeping missions and, when appropriate, have offered the services of the U.S. military to those missions. The advantages that UN peace-keeping missions have over unilateral U.S. action in many regions are that UN peace-keepers are less threatening to local nations, the economic costs to the United States are minimized, and a UN peace-keeping force can promote a spirit of international accountability and cooperation in solving a particular regional problem.

The primary responsibility for the peace and security function of the United Nations resides with the Security Council. The council assesses threats to peace and attempts to use peaceful measures to prevent aggression. If nonmilitary actions fail or are inappropriate, the Security Council may vote to use military force.[136]

A Security Council decision to use military force or to create a detachment of military observers cannot be adopted without the unanimous approval of its members. Since the United States and the Soviet Union are permanent members of the Security Council along with Great Britain, France, and the People's Republic of China, the relevance of the peace-keeping role of the United Nations to conflicts between allies of the superpowers has been limited. UN peace-keeping forces have been used to separate combatants, monitor cease-fire agreements, and protect civilians in places such as the Congo, Cyprus, Indonesia, West New Guinea, and the border between India and Pakistan. The last three included U.S. personnel.

Neither superpower has been willing to allow UN peace-keeping forces to be used against the perceived interests of its clients. Nevertheless, the Security Council has sanctioned limited peace-keeping missions when the interests of the United States and the Soviet Union have converged. During the late 1980s the status of UN-sponsored peace-keeping forces grew as UN peace-keepers were awarded the 1988 Nobel Peace Prize and the Soviet Union and United States both advocated the use of UN peace-keeping troops to monitor negotiated settlements of several regional conflicts. The United Nations created new peace-keeping forces to oversee peace accords in Afghanistan and Angola and between Iran and Iraq.

The most contentious issue in the Senate debate on U.S. membership in the UN was who had the power to commit U.S. forces to Security Council peace-keeping operations. The Senate did not want to hand the executive exclusive authority to provide the United Nations with troops. Such a power would have allowed the president to commit the United States to UN military operations without the congressional consent required by a declaration of war.[137]

The United Nations Participation Act of 1945 outlined the rules under which U.S. forces could be placed at the disposal of the United Nations:

> The President is authorized to negotiate a special agreement or agreements with the Security Council which shall be subject to the approval of the Congress by appropriate Act or joint resolution, providing for the numbers and types of armed forces, their degree of readiness and general location, and the nature of facilities and assistance, including rights of passage, to be made available to the Security Council on its call for the purpose of maintaining international peace and security....

Thus presidents are expressly prohibited by the Participation Act from unilaterally concluding an agreement with the Security Council under their powers to negotiate treaties, execute the laws, or defend the United States. The president cannot legally aid or commit U.S. forces to UN peace-keeping missions without an approving congressional resolution.[138]

The most dramatic use of the UN security function was the Security Council's response to the North Korean invasion of South Korea in 1950. Because the Soviets were boycotting the Security Council to protest the exclusion of Communist China from the council, they were not present to exercise their veto when the council voted to ask UN member nations to aid South Korea.

Section 6 of the United Nations Participation Act required President Truman to secure congressional approval of the agreement between the U.S. and the Security Council that provided for the use of American forces. No such agreement was ever negotiated. Truman based the U.S. intervention in Korea on the Security Council's call to UN member nations to render assistance to South Korea. Truman's consultations with congressional leaders amounted to an information session shortly before he announced to the press that he had ordered U.S. troops into combat.[139]

Not all U.S. peace-keeping missions have been undertaken under UN auspices. For example, as part of the 1979 Camp David Peace accords the United States promised Egypt and Israel that it would organize a peace-keeping force to monitor the withdrawal of Israel from the Sinai Peninsula if the United Nations did not provide such a force. Since the Soviet Union threatened to exercise its Security Council veto to block the creation of any UN peace-keeping force for the Sinai, the United States created a multinational force that included U.S. troops. The United States also sent military forces to Lebanon in 1982 as part of a multinational peace-keeping force. The U.S. contingent of Marines reached 2,000 in 1983 but was withdrawn in February 1984 by President Reagan four months after the terrorist bombing of the Marine barracks in Beirut killed 241 Marines.

Alliances and Mutual Security Agreements

The armed forces have served as a tool of presidential foreign policy not just when presidents have used or threatened force. U.S. military strength since World War II has enabled presidents to offer security commitments and alliance partnerships to countries concerned with their ability to defend themselves. In doing so presidents have improved relations with many other countries, extended U.S. global influence, and strengthened U.S. defenses.

Before World War II, the United States had shunned alliances. Its size and isolated location on the North American continent made it an unattractive target of military adventures. In addition, during most of the nineteenth and early twentieth centuries the military establishments of the great powers of Europe were primarily concerned with defending against threats from their neighbors. Since the security of the United States did not depend on having allies, the American people generally had preferred to remain isolationist. They considered the possibility of becoming imbroiled in a foreign war while honoring an alliance commitment a greater danger than being forced to defend the United States without allies. With the exception of the Franco-American Alliance of 1778, which was effectively voided by George Washington's 1793 neutrality proclamation toward Britain and France, the United States had never participated in a formal peacetime alliance until after World War II.[140] Even when the United States entered World War I against Germany in 1917, U.S. leaders demonstrated the national aversion to alliances by claiming to be only an "associated power" of Britain and France.

World War II shattered the isolationist policies of the United States. The nation emerged from the war not just as a member of the international community, but as a world leader. The growth of Soviet military power and the establishment of Soviet control over Eastern Europe after World War II led many nations to seek the security of an alliance or friendly relationship with the United States. Under Truman and Eisenhower the United States enthusiastically erected a global network of multilateral and bilateral alliances intended to contain Soviet expansionism. The Rio Pact, signed in 1947, reaffirmed the longstanding U.S. commitment to defend the Western Hemisphere. The 1949 North Atlantic Treaty created the North Atlantic Treaty Organization (NATO), an alliance between the United States, Canada, and most Western European democracies that developed into the cornerstone of U.S. containment strategy. The ANZUS alliance was formed between Australia, New Zealand, and the United States in 1951. The United States also joined the Southeast Asia Treaty Organization (SEATO) in 1954 and established ties with, although not membership in, a Middle Eastern alliance known as the Central Treaty Organization (CENTO) in 1956. These multilateral alliances were complemented by bilateral alliances with Japan and the Philippines in 1951, Korea in 1953, Taiwan in 1954, and Iran, Pakistan, and Turkey in 1959.[141]

Although many of these alliances, including SEATO and CENTO, no longer function, maintaining a web of U.S. security relationships has remained a goal of U.S. foriegn policy. In addition to formal alliances, the United States increased its international defense capabilities through agreements on base rights, intelligence sharing, and informal defense cooperation with other countries.

Power to Form Military Alliances

Alliances often can be a contentious political issue because commitments to fight beside alliance partners under attack can draw a nation into a war. Theoretically, participation in an alliance should involve Congress since the Constitution gives it the power to declare war. Although most major alliances have been based on treaties ratified by the Senate, presidents have claimed the authority to make alliances unilaterally by virtue of their commander-in-chief, negotiation, and recognition powers.

Since World War II presidents often have exercised their alliance-making power without formal action by Congress. On August 14, 1941, for example, President Roosevelt signed the Atlantic Charter, which laid the groundwork for an Anglo-American alliance once the United States had entered World War II. Roosevelt then signed the Declaration of United Nations on January 1, 1942, which pledged the United States and, by the end of the war, forty-five other nations to support the Allied war effort and not make a separate peace with the enemy nations.[142] After the war, Presidents Truman and Eisenhower used executive agreements to expand NATO into a unified defense organization with a standing military structure. Although no formal alliance treaty exists between the United States and Israel, presidents since Truman have maintained the extensive U.S. commitment to Israeli security. Even Carter's 1979 declaration that the Persian Gulf was vital to U.S. national security created the potential for de facto alliances with gulf states if their security were threatened.

Presidential Alliance Responsibilities

U.S. membership in an alliance creates additional presidential responsibilities. The most important of these is the president's obligation, as commander in chief and the person who executes the laws, to fulfill the terms of a treaty by coming to the defense of an allied nation that is attacked. This obligation depends on the terms of the alliance agreement and the declared policy of the United States. The NATO treaty states that "an attack on one or more [of the parties] shall be considered as an attack against all of the parties." Advocates of presidential power could argue that by ratifying a treaty with such language Congress has given presidents the same authority to repel an invasion of a NATO country as they have to repel an attack on the United States. An alliance, therefore, can expand the number of situations under which presidents can order troops into battle without a declaration of war by extending their prerogative to repel attacks to alliance partners.[143]

The declared policy of the United States, however, may be even more relevant to the president's authority to defend an alliance partner than the language of a treaty. With over 300,000 troops and many nuclear weapons committed to the defense of Western Europe, no matter how one interprets the language of the NATO treaty and its effect on presidential authority, the president is expected to direct U.S. troops to repel any Soviet attack on NATO. Similarly, presidents have complete authority to respond to attacks on South Korea and Japan, not only because of treaties with those nations, but because many U.S. troops are based there and numerous acts of Congress have recognized and supported U.S. defense commitments in East Asia.

Presidential authority to come to the aid of many other nations with which the United States has less formal mutual security agreements is ambiguous. It is not certain that the president has the legal authority to commit U.S. forces to the defense of Israel, for example, where the United States has no troops and defense cooperation is based on executive agreements rather than a Senate-ratified treaty. Nevertheless, such executive agreements do provide presidents who are determined to defend an ally with a justification for using troops in its defense.

A second presidential alliance responsibility is maintaining alliance cohesion. An alliance that is not unified will likely be ineffective and will contribute little to U.S. security. Therefore, the president is compelled to consider the effect of U.S. foreign and military policy on the cohesion of its alliances and public opinion within the allied countries. For example, since the citizens of the West European allies of United States fear both the arms race and Soviet military strength, modern presidents can neither ignore arms control that would affect Europe nor conclude an agreement that significantly reduces NATO's military capabilities unless such an agreement is supported by allied governments. Even when a foreign policy action does not directly involve an alliance, a president must weigh its effect on alliance countries. The concerns of Presidents Johnson and Nixon that other U.S. allies would see abandonment of South Vietnam as evidence of U.S. inability to fulfill its commitments contributed to their refusal to withdraw American troops from Vietnam without attempting to ensure South Vietnamese security. Membership in an alliance, therefore, can be a powerful restraint on presidential freedom of action.

In addition to being a caretaker of alliance unity, the president is expected to take the lead in developing new alliance policies. In every alliance in which the United States has participated since World War II, it has been the dominant military power. This status gives the president a considerable bargaining advantage over alliance partners but does not enable presidents to dictate alliance policy. Presidents must lobby allied leaders to support their initiatives just as they must lobby members of Congress to support their legislative proposals. To the extent that a president can persuade allies to support U.S. foreign policies, alliances enhance the president's domestic power. When U.S. presidents are able to take strong action with allied support, they increase their prestige and authority over foreign policy at home. Congress is less likely to challenge the foreign policy of a president who is perceived as an effective international leader than one who has not been able to deliver allied support for U.S. programs and actions.

Notes

1. Alexander Hamilton, *Federalist No. 74*, in *The Federalist Papers* (New York: New American Library, 1961), 447.
2. Clinton Rossiter, *The American Presidency*, 2d ed. (New York: Time, 1960), 13.
3. Samuel P. Huntington, *The Soldier and the State* (New York: Vintage, 1964), 178.
4. James Madison, *The Gazette of the United States*, August 24, 1793, quoted in *The Power of the Presidency*, ed. Robert S. Hirschenfield (New York: Atherton, 1968), 59.
5. Arthur M. Schlesinger, Jr., *The Imperial Presidency* (Boston: Houghton Mifflin, 1973), 4.
6. Hamilton, *Federalist No. 69*, 417-418.
7. Joseph E. Kallenbach, *The American Chief Executive: The Presidency and the Governorship* (New York: Harper and Row, 1966), 535-536.
8. Michael P. Riccards, *A Republic, If You Can Keep It: The Foundation of the American Presidency, 1700-1800* (New York: Greenwood Press, 1987), 152-153.
9. Edward S. Corwin, *The President: Office and Powers, 1787-1984*, 5th rev. ed. (New York: New York University Press, 1984), 297.
10. Clinton Rossiter, *The Supreme Court and the Commander in Chief* (Ithaca, N.Y.: Cornell University Press, 1976), 48-52.
11. Robert E. DiClerico, *The American President*, 2d ed. (Englewood Cliffs, N.J.: Prentice-Hall, 1983), 37.
12. Richard M. Pious, *The American Presidency* (New York: Basic Books, 1979), 392.
13. James D. Richardson, *A Compilation of the Messages and Papers of the Presidents, 1789-1910*, (New York: Bureau of National Literature, 1917), 1:314-315.
14. Pious, *The American Presidency*, 392.
15. Quoted in Corwin, *The President*, 229.
16. Schlesinger, *The Imperial Presidency*, 23.
17. Thomas Eagleton, *War and Presidential Power* (New York: Liveright, 1974), 23.
18. Lawrence Margolis, *Executive Agreements and Presidential Power in Foreign Policy* (New York: Praeger, 1986), 9.
19. Schlesinger, *The Imperial Presidency*, 39-41.
20. Wilfred E. Binkley, *The Man in the White House* (Baltimore: Johns Hopkins University Press, 1964), 192.
21. John Nicolay and John Hay, eds., *The Complete Works of Abraham Lincoln* (New York: Francis Tandy, 1891), 10:66.
22. Schlesinger, *The Imperial Presidency*, 58.
23. Corwin, *The President*, 264.
24. Ibid., 265.
25. Carl B. Swisher, *American Constitutional Development*, 2d ed. (Boston: Houghton Mifflin, 1954), 29.
26. Binkley, *The Man in the White House*, 194.
27. *Prize Cases*, 67 U.S. (2 Black), 635, 1863.
28. Rossiter, *Supreme Court*, 71-75.
29. Eagleton, *War and Presidential Power*, 45.
30. Corwin, *The President*, 271-272.
31. Jacob K. Javits, *Who Makes War* (New York: Morrow, 1973), 207-209.
32. Corwin, *The President*, 272.
33. R. Gordon Hoxie, *Command Decision and the Presidency* (New York: Reader's Digest Press, 1977), 11.
34. Corwin, *The President*, 272.
35. Eagleton, *War and Presidential Power*, 64.
36. Javits, *Who Makes War*, 225-226.
37. Schlesinger, *The Imperial Presidency*, 115.
38. Quoted in Corwin, *The President*, 285-286.
39. Edward S. Corwin, *Presidential Power and the Constitution* (Ithaca: Cornell University Press, 1976), 114.
40. Javits, *Who Makes War*, 230.
41. Cecil V. Crabb, Jr., and Pat M. Holt, *Invitation to Struggle: Congress, the President and Foreign Policy*, 2d ed. (Washington, D.C.: CQ Press, 1984), 130-131.
42. Dean Acheson, *Present at the Creation: My Years in the State Department* (New York: Norton, 1969), 415.
43. Schlesinger, *The Imperial Presidency*, 133.
44. James L. Sundquist, *Decline and Resurgence of Congress* (Washington, D.C.: Brookings, 1981), 109.
45. Hoxie, *Command Decision and the Presidency*, 178.
46. Schlesinger, *The Imperial Presidency*, 141.
47. Ibid., 169.
48. Sundquist, *Decline and Resurgence of Congress*, 124-125.
49. Ibid., 249.
50. Quoted in *Congressional Quarterly Almanac 1973* (Washington, D.C.: Congressional Quarterly Inc., 1974), 906.
51. Ibid., 907.
52. Ibid., 906-907.
53. Eagleton, *War and Presidential Power*, 203.
54. Larry Berman, *The New American Presidency* (Boston: Little, Brown, 1987), 75.
55. Ibid., 76.
56. DiClerico, *The American President*, 45.
57. Jacob Javits, "War Powers Reconsidered," *Foreign Affairs* (Fall 1985): 135.
58. Crabb and Holt, *Invitation to Struggle*, 146.
59. Javits, "War Powers Reconsidered," 136.
60. Crabb and Holt, *Invitation to Struggle*, 149-150.
61. Javits, "War Powers Reconsidered," 137.
62. Pat Towell, "After Raid on Libya, New Questions on Hill," *Congressional Quarterly Weekly Report*, April 19, 1986, 839.
63. Mary H. Cooper, "Persian Gulf Oil," *Editorial Research Reports*, October 30, 1987, 567.
64. Pat Towell, "New Gulf Incident Rekindles an Old Debate," *Congressional Quarterly Weekly Report*, April 23, 1988, 1051-1058.
65. Quoted in *Congressional Quarterly Almanac 1973*, 907.
66. Quoted in Crabb and Holt, *Invitation to Struggle*, 147.
67. Schlesinger, *The Imperial Presidency*, 290.
68. *Immigration and Naturalization Service v. Chadha*, 103 U.S. 2764 (1983).
69. *Congressional Quarterly Almanac 1983* (Washington, D.C.: Congressional Quarterly Inc., 1984), 568-569.
70. Pious, *The American Presidency*, 404-405.
71. U.S. Congress, Senate, *Congressional Record*, daily ed., 92d Cong., 1st sess., April 26, 1971, 11914.
72. Kallenbach, *The American Chief Executive*, 531.
73. Charles A. Beard, *The Republic* (New York: Viking Press, 1944), 101.
74. Riccards, *A Republic, If You Can Keep It*, 164-166.
75. Jacob E. Cook, "George Washington," in *The Presidents: A Reference History*, ed. Henry F. Graff (New York: Scribner's, 1984), 24.
76. Corwin, *The President*, 294.
77. Kallenbach, *The American Chief Executive*, 530.
78. Amos A. Jordan and William J. Taylor, Jr., *American National Security: Policy and Process* (Baltimore: Johns Hopkins University Press, 1984), 85.
79. Molly Moore, "Stricken Frigate's Crew Stitched Ship Together," *Washington Post*, April 22, 1988, A1.

80. Jordan and Taylor, *American National Security*, 231.
81. For a detailed description of the U.S. nuclear infrastructure, see William Arkin and Richard W. Fieldhouse, *Nuclear Battlefields* (Cambridge: Ballinger, 1984).
82. For a discussion of permissive action links, see Donald R. Cotter, "Peacetime Operations, Safety and Security," in *Managing Nuclear Operations*, ed. Ashton B. Carter, John D. Steinbruner, and Charles A. Zraket (Washington, D.C.: Brookings, 1987), 46-51.
83. Paul Bracken, *The Command and Control of Nuclear Forces* (New Haven: Yale University Press, 1983), 232-237.
84. Ibid., 229.
85. *Public Papers of the Presidents of the United States, Dwight D. Eisenhower, 1960-1961* (Washington, D.C.: Government Printing Office, 1963), 851.
86. *Public Papers of the Presidents of the United States, Harry S Truman, 1945* (Washington, D.C.: Government Printing Office, 1961), 212.
87. James A. Nathan and James K. Oliver, *United States Foreign Policy and World Order*, 2d ed. (Boston: Little, Brown, 1981), 41-42.
88. Hoxie, *Command Decision and the Presidency*, 13-14.
89. Miroslav Nincic, *United States Foreign Policy: Choices and Tradeoffs* (Washington, D.C.: CQ Press, 1988), 292.
90. Theodore Sorensen, *Kennedy* (New York: Harper and Row, 1965), 705.
91. Leslie H. Gelb with Richard K. Betts, *The Irony of Vietnam: The System Worked* (Washington, D.C.: Brookings, 1979), 264-265.
92. Arkin and Fieldhouse, *Nuclear Battlefields*, 87.
93. For text of speech and further commentary, see *Historic Documents 1983* (Washington, D.C.: Congressional Quarterly Inc., 1984), 305-316.
94. R. Jeffrey Smith, "Pentagon Scales Back SDI Goals," *Washington Post*, March 27, 1988, A1.
95. Lawrence J. Korb, "The Evolving Relationship between the White House and the Department of Defense in the Post-Imperial Presidency," in *The Post-Imperial Presidency*, ed. Vincent Davis (New Brunswick, N.J.: Transaction, 1980), 103.
96. Richard K. Betts, *Soldiers, Statesmen, and Cold War Crises* (Cambridge: Harvard University Press, 1977), 52-68.
97. For discussions of the problems that led to the reform of the JCS, see James Buck, "The Establishment: An Overview," in *Presidential Leadership and National Security: Style, Institutions, and Politics*, ed. Sam C. Sarkesian (Boulder, Colo.: Westview Press, 1984), 59-64, and John G. Kestor, "The Role of the Joint Chiefs of Staff," in *American Defense Policy*, ed. John F. Reichart and Steven R. Sturm (Baltimore: Johns Hopkins University Press, 1982), 527-545.
98. Pat Towell, "Major Pentagon Reorganization Bill Is Cleared," *Congressional Quarterly Weekly Report*, September 20, 1986, 2207-2208.
99. Morton Halperin, "The President and the Military," in *The Presidency in Contemporary Context*, ed. Norman C. Thomas (New York: Dodd, Mead, 1975), 277.
100. Ibid., 280-284.
101. Mary H. Cooper, "The Military Build-Down in the 1990s," *Editorial Research Reports*, April 22, 1988, 211.
102. Alice Maroni, "The Defense Budget," in *Presidential Leadership and National Security*, 194-196.
103. Ibid., 196.
104. Richard Haass, "The Role of the Congress in American Security Policy," in *American Defense Policy*, 558-560.
105. For a discussion of the quality-versus-quantity defense procurement debate, see James Fallows, *National Defense* (New York: Random House, 1981).
106. Jordan and Taylor, *American National Security*, 106.
107. Ibid., 187.
108. Ibid., 192.
109. George F. Brown, Jr., and Lawrence Korb, "The Economic and Political Restraints on Force Planning," in *American Defense Policy*, 583.
110. Kallenbach, *The American Chief Executive*, 543.

111. Marc Leepson, "Draft Registration," *Editorial Research Reports*, June 13, 1980, 427-430.
112. Kallenbach, *The American Chief Executive*, 537.
113. Quoted in Berman, *The New American Presidency*, 57.
114. Robert S. Hirschfield, "The Scope and Limits of Presidential Power," in *Power and the Presidency*, ed. Philip C. Dolce and George H. Skau (New York: Scribner's, 1976), 301-302.
115. Kallenbach, *The American Chief Executive*, 553-554.
116. *Ex parte Milligan*, 4 Wallace 2 (1866).
117. *Duncan v. Kahanamoku*, 327 U.S. 304 (1946).
118. Rossiter, *Supreme Court*, 25.
119. Ibid., 27.
120. *Ex parte Milligan*, 4 Wallace 2 (1866).
121. *Hirabayashi v. United States*, 320 U.S. 81 (1943).
122. *Korematsu v. United States*, 323 U.S. 214 (1944).
123. Rossiter, *Supreme Court*, 54.
124. Kallenbach, *The American Chief Executive*, 557.
125. Corwin, *Presidential Power and the Constitution*, 124-125.
126. *Youngstown Sheet and Tube Co. v. Sawyer*, 343 U.S. 579 (1952).
127. Rossiter, *Supreme Court*, xxi.
128. Javits, *Who Makes War*, 104-115.
129. Quoted in Arthur Bernon Tourtellot, *The Presidents on the Presidency* (Garden City, N.Y.: Doubleday, 1964), 326.
130. Donald L. Robinson, *"To the Best of My Ability"* (New York: Norton, 1987) 224.
131. Nincic, *United States Foreign Policy*, 231-233.
132. Henry R. Pringle, *Theodore Roosevelt* (New York: Harcourt Brace, 1931), 409.
133. Steven V. Roberts, "3,000 G.I.'s and Questions," *New York Times*, March 18, 1988, A1.
134. Timothy J. Lomperis, *The War Everyone Lost and Won* (Washington, D.C.: CQ Press, 1984), 60.
135. Crabb and Holt, *Invitation to Struggle*, 150-151.
136. Corwin, *The President*, 249.
137. Sundquist, *Decline and Resurgence of Congress*, 105-106.
138. Corwin, *The President*, 251.
139. Sundquist, *Decline and Resurgence of Congress*, 108.
140. Hoxie, *Command Decision and the Presidency*, 130.
141. Jordan and Taylor, *American National Security*, 473.
142. Hoxie, *Command Decision and the Presidency*, 40.
143. Pious, *The American Presidency*, 395-396.

Selected Bibliography

Corwin, Edward S. *The President: Office and Powers, 1787-1984.* 5th rev. ed. New York: New York University Press, 1984.

Crabb, Cecil V., Jr., and Pat M. Holt. *Invitation to Struggle: Congress, the President and Foreign Policy.* 2d ed. Washington, D.C.: CQ Press, 1984.

Eagleton, Thomas. *War and Presidential Power.* New York: Liveright, 1974.

Hoxie, R. Gordon. *Command Decision and the Presidency.* New York: Reader's Digest Press, 1977.

Nincic, Miroslav. *United States Foreign Policy: Choices and Tradeoffs.* Washington, D.C.: CQ Press, 1988.

Javits, Jacob K. *Who Makes War.* New York: Morrow, 1973.

Jordon, Amos A., and William J. Taylor, Jr. *American National Security, Policy and Process.* Baltimore: Johns Hopkins University Press, 1984.

Kallenbach, Joseph E. *The American Chief Executive: The Presidency and the Governorship.* New York: Harper and Row, 1966.

Pious, Richard M. *The American Presidency.* New York: Basic Books, 1979.

Rossiter, Clinton. *The Supreme Court and the Commander in Chief.* Ithaca, N.Y.: Cornell University Press, 1976.

Sarkesian, Sam C., ed. *Presidential Leadership and National Security: Style, Institutions, and Politics.* Boulder, Colo.: Westview Press, 1984.

Schlesinger, Arthur M., Jr. *The Imperial Presidency.* Boston: Houghton Mifflin, 1973.

Chief of State

Every government must have a chief of state who presides over ceremonial functions. In many countries this responsibility is fulfilled by a monarch with little governmental authority or an official whose post was created to shelter the chief executive from ceremonial drudgery. In the United States, however, this task has fallen to the chief executive. The ceremonial activities for which presidents are responsible are as diverse as those that monarchs must perform, but presidents also must perform their duties as chief executive, commander in chief, chief diplomat, chief legislator, and head of their party. Presidents, therefore, can devote only a fraction of their time to ceremonial activities.

The chief of state role, however, involves more than presiding over ceremonial functions for which the president must put on a smile and put the business of the nation on hold. Like monarchs, U.S. presidents are, in some ways, the living embodiment of the American people. They symbolize the country's history, liberty, and strength. Presidents can delegate ceremonial functions to their representatives, but while they are in office they cannot escape their chief of state role. At every moment they represent the United States to the international community and to the American people.

Ceremonial Duties and Functions

As chief of state, presidents preside over an endless series of ceremonies that range in tone from the solemnity of the inauguration to the informality of a White House barbecue. They greet foreign ambassadors, dedicate monuments, pin medals on war heroes, buy Easter seals and Girl Scout cookies, visit schools, throw out the first ball on opening day of the baseball season, and hold state dinners for foreign chiefs of state. National ceremonies have much the same purpose for the country as religious rituals have for a church. Ceremonies create shared symbols and emotional sentiments that comfort, motivate, and unify the American congregation.

Although presidents may occasionally find ceremonial

By Daniel C. Diller

events tiresome, they provide presidents with opportunities to dramatize and personalize their presidency. At ceremonial occasions presidents campaign for their reelection, make policy proposals, espouse their political philosophies, underscore the need for unity, create an atmosphere of confidence, and promote patriotism and national pride. Presidents who neglect ceremonial duties may find they have more time to develop policy and run the government, but they are sacrificing a tool of leadership that can be used not only to inspire the nation to greater accomplishments, but also to improve their own popularity.

Constitutional Ceremonial Duties

The Constitution designated several ceremonial duties that presidents are obliged to perform. They are required to take an oath of office, periodically inform Congress of the state of the union, and receive "Ambassadors and other public Ministers." These constitutional ceremonial duties supported the assumption of the chief of state power by George Washington and his successors because they made the president appear as the leader of the whole nation. Both the oath of office ceremony and State of the Union address physically place the president out in front of other government officials and focus the nation's attention on the president's opinions and recommendations. In addition, the president's duty to receive ambassadors implies that foreign governments are to regard the president as the official representative of the United States. Given that the international community sees the president as chief of state, domestic chief of state responsibilities could not be assumed gracefully by anyone but the president.

Oath of Office and Inauguration

Article II, section 1, clause 8, of the Constitution requires the president-elect to recite the following oath before assuming the presidency: "I do solemnly swear (or affirm) that I will faithfully execute the Office of President of the United States, and will to the best of my Ability preserve, protect, and defend the Constitution of the United States." The occasion for this oath taking was not described in the Constitution, but the inaugural ceremony where it is administered has become one of the U.S. government's most important traditions and the president's first chief of state function.

Constitutional Basis of Presidential Chief of State Role

The Framers of the Constitution did not specifically designate the president as the nation's chief of state, but they created no other office that reasonably could claim the chief of state power. Presidents are the logical possessors of the title of chief of state under the Constitution because they are chosen by a national electorate, are never out of session, and are recognized as the voice of U.S. foreign policy. Consequently, the president can be said to represent the entire nation, is always available to provide ceremonial leadership, and is positioned to perform both international and domestic ceremonial functions.

The Framers never considered establishing a chief of state office separate from the presidency. The creation of a single office that would be filled by one person serving as both the ceremonial and executive leader of the nation, however, was not their only option. The continuing transfer of executive power from the monarch to the prime minister in Great Britain provided the Framers with a model of a political system where the ceremonial and executive functions were separated.[1] Given the objections of many members of the convention to any pretense of royalty in the presidency and the unanimous concern that no president would have the means to become a despot, it is somewhat surprising the Framers accepted the fusion of the two roles without debate.

One can imagine the convention designating a member of Congress such as the Speaker of the House or president pro tempore of the Senate as chief of state, especially since most of the delegates considered the legislature to be the most important branch of government. Such an arrangement would have augmented Congress's power by making it the ceremonial focus of the government, while diminishing the symbolic resources available to any president who sought dictatorial power.

The Framers also could have created an executive council composed of several persons instead of a unitary presidency. The Framers seriously considered this option, but the focus of their debate was on the safety of lodging enormous executive powers in the hands of one person, not on dividing presidential functions between executive officials. The original proposal for a single executive, made by James Wilson of Virginia, was strongly opposed by Benjamin Franklin, Edmund Randolph, George Mason, Roger Sherman, and other prominent members of the convention who feared that having a single executive would lead to despotism or the subordination of the country's interests to the interests of the executive's home region. After several days of debate, however, the Framers decided to reject proposals for a plural executive or an executive advisory committee attached to the presidency in favor of a single executive.[2] Presumably, had the convention opted for an executive committee instead of a single president, the chief of state power would have resided in the entire committee, rather than with one specified member.

According to political scientist Rexford G. Tugwell, an executive committee would not have captured the imagination of the American people the way individual presidents have:

> Since he [the president] would not have been alone in the White House in semi-royal state, with relatives and associates of consuming interest to all his fellow citizens, it would not have been a matter of such consequence whether or not he had an invalid wife and irresponsible children, . . . or whether he possessed social graces as well as wisdom and political talent. He would not, in other words, have been the focus of interest and the symbol of Union for the whole American people, watched with avid curiosity and criticized inevitably by those with standards of conduct differing from his own.[3]

By creating a single executive, the Framers guaranteed that public attention and therefore symbolic power would flow to the president.

1. Erwin C. Hargrove and Michael Nelson, *Presidents, Politics, and Policy* (Baltimore: Johns Hopkins University Press, 1984), 20.
2. Donald L. Robinson, *"To the Best of My Ability"* (New York: Norton, 1987), 69-76.
3. Rexford G. Tugwell, *The Enlargement of the Presidency* (Garden City, N.Y.: Doubleday, 1960), 481.

Like a coronation the inaugural ceremony symbolically invests presidents with the power of their office. At the inauguration the president appears before the people not as the manager of one of the three coequal branches of the federal government but as the paternal leader of the nation who swears to "preserve, protect, and defend" the Constitution.

Benjamin Harrison commented on the significance of the oath of office in his 1888 inaugural address:

> . . . from the beginning of the government the people, to whose service the official oath consecrates the officer, have been called to witness the solemn ceremony. The oath taken in the presence of the people becomes a mutual covenant. The officer covenants to serve the whole body of the people by a faithful execution of the laws, so that they may be the unfailing defense and security of those who observe them.

The oath of office also conjures up heroic images of the nation's heritage. The new president's recitation of the same oath that George Washington, Thomas Jefferson, Abraham Lincoln, Woodrow Wilson, Franklin Roosevelt, and every other president has repeated conveys a sense of historic continuity and links the incumbent to the glories of past presidencies.

George Washington established the tradition that presidents should deliver an inaugural address after taking the oath of office. Most presidents have used this speech not to outline specific policy proposals but to restate their political philosophies, establish a mood of optimism, challenge the nation to pursue ambitious goals, and appeal for unity.

Unity is an important and common theme of inaugural addresses because presidential elections tend to divide the nation along party lines.[1] After the bitterly divisive election of 1800, which led outgoing president John Adams to snub Thomas Jefferson's inauguration, Jefferson declared, "We have called by different names brethren of the same principles. We are all Republicans. We are all Federalists." John F. Kennedy called for unity in 1961 after his close election victory over Richard Nixon: "We observe today not a victory of party, but a celebration of freedom." Jimmy Carter opened his inaugural address by praising his 1976 election opponent, Gerald Ford: "For myself and for our nation, I want to thank my predecessor for all he has done to heal our land."

The inauguration and the parades and parties that have usually followed it also provide the first glimpse of the new chief of state's ceremonial style. After the stiff formality and royal pomp observed during the Washington and Adams administrations, Jefferson wanted his inaugural to symbolize the democratic spirit he intended to bring to the presidency. He therefore eschewed a carriage in favor of walking unceremoniously from his boardinghouse to the Capitol to take the oath of office.

Andrew Jackson's election was regarded as a triumph for common people. To symbolize his link with the average person he opened the doors of the White House to anyone who wished to attend his post-inaugural party. Thousands of enthusiastic supporters descended on the White House, thereby destroying furniture, china, glassware, and other household items.

Kennedy's inaugural was a formal affair that reflected the intellectual and cultural sophistication he would bring to his presidency. Kennedy sent 155 special inaugural invitations to noted writers, artists, and scholars, had Robert Frost read a poem at the inaugural ceremony, and decreed that male participants in the ceremony should wear top hats.

Jimmy Carter, like Thomas Jefferson, used his inaugural to project a simpler presidential image. He wore a business suit instead of formal dress and chose to walk in his inaugural parade rather than ride in a limousine.

Pomp came back into style with the election of Ronald Reagan. His 1981 inaugural festivities—the most expensive in history up to that time—included a parade with eight thousand marchers, eight $100-a-ticket balls, and a nationally televised inaugural "gala" that featured many Hollywood celebrities.

State of the Union Address

The Constitution also states that the president "shall from time to time give to the Congress information of the State of the Union, and recommend to their Consideration such Measures as he shall judge necessary and expedient." From this clause developed the ritual of the president's annual message, or "State of the Union address" as it has been known since 1945.

George Washington delivered the first annual message on January 8, 1790. John Adams, who enjoyed royal for-

malities, followed Washington's precedent, but Thomas Jefferson objected to having presidents deliver their annual messages in person. Like many of his Democratic-Republican colleagues, he thought the custom, which had derived from the British monarch's speech from the throne at the opening of Parliament, had royal pretensions. As part of his effort to "put the ship of state back on its republican tack" he submitted his report to Congress in writing.[2]

Subsequent presidents followed Jefferson's example until 1913 when Woodrow Wilson took the suggestion of journalist Oliver Newman and went before Congress to read his annual message. Wilson saw the change as a way to make the address more personal and dramatic. He explained in the address that he wanted to verify "that the President of the United States is a person, not a mere department of the Government hailing Congress from some isolated island of jealous power, sending messages, not speaking naturally and with his own voice—that he is a human being trying to cooperate with other human beings in a common service." Some members of Congress echoed Jefferson's objections to the practice, but the response to Wilson's speech was generally favorable. Delivering the annual message in person was once again acceptable for presidents. Since Franklin Roosevelt, every president has chosen to deliver the annual message in person.[3]

Like the inauguration, the symbolism of the contemporary State of the Union address reinforces the image of the president as the preeminent leader of the nation, rather than the leader of one of its coequal branches. The Congress, cabinet, and Supreme Court assemble in the House chamber and wait for the president to arrive, like courtiers awaiting a king. After being announced, the president is greeted by a bipartisan standing ovation. Moreover, the event itself implies presidential preeminence, since the president's opinion of the state of the union is the reason for the assemblage. Neither Congress nor the judiciary has a similar opportunity to address the top representatives of the entire government in a formal, ritualistic setting.

The invention of radio and television changed the primary audience of the address from Congress to the American people. Presidents still address Congress, but their remarks are intended primarily for public consumption. Presidents have used this opportunity to put pressure on Congress to vote for their legislative agenda by appealing to the American public for support.

Reception of Ambassadors

The Constitution gives the president the responsibility to "receive Ambassadors and other public Ministers." The authors of the Constitution regarded the reception of foreign visitors as a purely ceremonial responsibility. It was to be given to the president, according to Alexander Hamilton, because Congress could not conveniently perform this function. He wrote in the *Federalist* No. 69 that presidential reception of ambassadors "is more a matter of dignity than of authority. It is a circumstance which will be without consequence in the administration of the government; and it was far more convenient that it should be arranged in this manner than that there should be a necessity of convening the legislature, or one of its branches, upon every arrival of a foreign minister."[4] Subsequently, however, the presidential responsibility to receive ambassadors was used by presidents as a constitutional justification of their authority to recognize or deny recognition to foreign governments. *(See "Recognition Power," p. 121, in Chief*

Robert Frost's Inaugural Poem

Presidents have sometimes attempted to use the celebrity and visibility of their office to promote changes in the lifestyle of the nation. John Kennedy intended to use his position to encourage interest in the fine arts and U.S. culture. He and his wife, Jacqueline, set an example for the nation by frequently patronizing the work of artists, musicians, and writers.

Kennedy began his patronage of the fine arts the day he became president. He asked the famous poet Robert Frost to recite a poem at his inauguration ceremony on January 20, 1961. The eighty-six-year-old Frost planned to read a short introductory verse he had composed for the occasion followed by his poem "The Gift Outright." After Boston's Cardinal Cushing delivered a long invocation, the chairman of the Inaugural Committee, Sen. John Sparkman, introduced Frost. The poet began reading his introductory verse, but the bright sunlight magnified by the glare from the snow that had fallen the day before blinded him. Frost read only three lines before stopping:

> Summoning artists to participate
> In the august occasions of the state
> Seems something artists ought to celebrate.

He said, "I'm not having a good light here at all. I can't see in this light." He tried to continue with the help of Vice President-elect Lyndon B. Johnson, who shaded the poet's manuscript with a top hat, but Frost still could not see. He gave up on the introductory verse, saying, "This was to have been a preface to a poem which I do not have to read." He then recited "The Gift Outright" from memory in a clear voice, changing the last phrase at Kennedy's request from "such as she *would* become" to "such as she *will* become."

The Gift Outright

The land was ours before we were the land's.
She was our land more than a hundred years
Before we were her people. She was ours
In Massachusetts, in Virginia,
But we were England's, still colonials,
Possessing what we still were unpossessed by,
Possessed by what we now no more possessed.
Something we were withholding made us weak
Until we found out that it was ourselves
We were withholding from our land of living,
And forthwith found salvation in surrender.
Such as we were we gave ourselves outright
(The deed of gift was many deeds of war)
To the land vaguely realizing westward,
But still unstoried, artless, unenhanced,
Such as she was, such as she would become.

Diplomat chapter.)

In the spirit of this constitutional provision, presidents have customarily received the official ambassador of every recognized foreign government. Unfortunately, the growth of the Washington diplomatic corps during the twentieth century and the overcrowded presidential schedule have forced presidents to receive most ambassadors, especially those from smaller countries, in groups at the White House to save time.

Customary Ceremonial Functions

Presidents and their representatives perform numerous chief of state functions that do not have their origins in the Constitution and are not based on a specific legal sanction. Some of these activities have been established as annual events by a succession of presidents. Others are seized upon by individual presidents for their public relations value. Presidents can choose to deemphasize their chief of state role by delegating ceremonial functions to the vice president and others, but they cannot escape many events and practices that the American people have come to regard as part of the president's job. A president who claimed to be too busy to light the national Christmas tree or congratulate the World Series baseball champions would waste valuable opportunities to score political points and would risk being perceived as cold or indifferent to American culture. Like the three ceremonial functions based on the Constitution, these informal chief of state activities emphasize the president's role as the leader of the nation, but in addition, many of them serve to humanize the president and symbolically bridge the gap between the president and the people.

National Voice

The president serves as a ceremonial spokesperson for the nation. A presidential proclamation or dedication is a national stamp of approval for cultural events, national monuments, public works projects, charity drives, and special weeks and days. Such proclamations promote national concern and awareness of worthy organizations and causes by indicating that the president thought the object of the proclamation was important enough to recognize. Often presidents highlight their recognition of a charity, organization, or movement by inviting its leaders to the White House. Such an invitation is a further measure of the group's importance since the president's schedule must be interrupted to accommodate the visit.

Presidential recognition gives an event, cause, group, or monument a place in the national consciousness. It also emphasizes the unity of the United States and can inspire patriotic sentiments. A new hydroelectric dam is said to be not just a source of power for a particular region, but an engineering feat and a symbol of American industrial might and technological ingenuity. The work of a charitable organization such as the American Red Cross is praised as an example of the nation's caring spirit.

Presidential endorsements are constantly in demand by organizations and charities, and the president's staff must choose which will receive presidential time. Many of the causes presidents endorse from year to year are determined by precedent. The United Way, Easter Seals, American Cancer Society, and many others receive annual presidential endorsements. Yet the number and type of causes

John F. Kennedy's inaugural was a formal affair that reflected the intellectual and cultural sophistication he would bring to his presidency. Robert Frost reads a poem while vice president Lyndon Johnson uses his top hat to block out the sun.

that receive presidential recognition may also reflect the incumbent's political interests or philosophies. For example, Ronald Reagan's frequent endorsement of charities was consistent with his goal of promoting an increase in the nation's charitable giving as a partial alternative to increased government spending on social services.

Conveyor of Awards and Congratulations

In accordance with their role as national spokesperson, presidents are expected to be the conveyors of national awards and congratulations. Presidents routinely invite citizens to the White House, where they congratulate them on their accomplishments and present them with an award or memento of their visit. Presidents also bestow a variety of official awards, the most prominent of which is the Presidential Medal of Freedom.

Congratulating worthy Americans has been used by presidents as a tool of moral and patriotic leadership. When presidents congratulate popular American heroes they make a moral statement by holding up those individuals to the nation as examples to emulate. Presidential congratulations encourage citizens to be as dedicated as a spelling bee champion, as brave as a war hero, as creative as a great artist, or as resilient as a person celebrating a hundredth birthday.

Such congratulations can improve the morale and sense of well-being of the nation. Amidst news reports of war, recession, crime, natural disasters, and other sobering problems, the congratulations of a hero by an appreciative president speaking for the nation can be a reassuring and uplifting event. President Reagan developed presidential

congratulations into a political art when he made a practice of weaving the introduction of carefully selected heroic Americans into his upbeat State of the Union addresses. His heroes have included an infantry medic who rescued wounded soldiers in Grenada, a twelve-year-old prodigy of gospel music, a woman about to graduate from West Point despite having escaped to the United States from Vietnam only ten years before with no possessions or knowledge of English, and a seventy-nine-year-old Harlem woman who cared for infants born of mothers addicted to heroin.

Congratulating a famous hero brings obvious political benefits to presidents. For example, members of championship sports teams are now routinely invited to the White House where they will joke with the president and present the chief executive with a jersey, game ball, or other memento of their victory. The president can become identified with their sport, demonstrate good humor, and be photographed with America's current sports idols as they are reduced to wide-eyed excitement by their White House reception. Presidents gain similar public relations benefits from congratulating artists, scientists, heroic members of the armed forces, and others who have performed feats of skill, intelligence, or courage.

First Average American

Alexis de Tocqueville, a French aristocrat and author who traveled widely in the United States during the first half of the nineteenth century, observed that "public officers themselves are well aware that the superiority over their fellow citizens which they derive from their authority they enjoy only on condition of putting themselves on a

Presidential Proclamations

The following list of days, weeks, and months recognized by the Reagan White House during October 1987 demonstrates the variety of causes, charities, groups, and holidays that are promoted during a typical month through presidential proclamations.

National Poison Prevention Week
National Medical Research Day
General Casimir Pulaski Memorial Day
Columbus Day
German-American Day
Polish American Heritage Month
Benign Essential Blepharospasm Awareness Week
Leif Erickson Day
Minority Enterprise Development Week
National Farm-City Week
National Down's Syndrome Month
National School Lunch Week
National Job Skills Week
World Food Day
National Safety Belt Use Day
White Cane Safety Day
National Forest Products Week
National Immigrants Day
National Adult Immunization Week
National Hospice Month

level with the whole community by their manners." [5] Most presidents have understood that although Americans want their president to be an exceptional person who is intelligent, decisive, and inspiring, they also want a leader with common tastes and experiences. Americans want to believe that their president, like the log cabin presidents of the nineteenth century, rose to the top through hard work, moral integrity, and a little ambition. The public values common sense as much as an Ivy League education. The ability to understand the needs and desires of the average American is as important as understanding the most complicated foreign policy or economic problems. In short, they want their president to be an exceptional example of an average American.

Presidents have realized that while the regal trappings of the presidency fortify their power and prestige, they must also project a populist image to satisfy the democratic ideals of the American people. Presidents who appear too urbane or who flaunt the privileges of their office risk alienating many citizens who are attracted to politicians with folksy images. Presidents John Quincy Adams and Martin Van Buren lost their reelection bids to Andrew Jackson and William Henry Harrison, respectively. The challengers in these two elections successfully contrasted their self-made, populist personas with the stiff and educated styles of the incumbents. Similarly, in the 1952 and 1956 presidential elections Adlai Stevenson's sophisticated image was not much of an asset against Dwight D. Eisen-

hower, an unpretentious war hero with an engaging smile.

Presidents therefore seek out opportunities to display their common touch. Often this is done simply by publicizing a president's hobbies, habits, and family life. The American public was told that Ronald Reagan chopped his own firewood and snacked on jellybeans, Jimmy Carter played softball and liked Willie Nelson's music, Gerald Ford took a daily swim and cooked his own breakfast. The day after Lyndon B. Johnson's reelection in 1964 he was photographed roping steers on his Texas ranch like any hard-working cowboy. Jimmy Carter made a media event out of his construction of a tree house on the White House grounds for his daughter, Amy.[6]

Presidential appearances at cultural events can reinforce the image of a president as an average person. Presidents attend historical and artistic exhibits, ethnic festivals, and other events where they can display their interest in American life. Presidents have been especially fond of attending sporting contests. Since William Howard Taft threw out the first baseball of the 1910 major league season in Washington, most presidents have observed the tradition. Kennedy wanted to make such a good appearance at the yearly event that he secretly practiced his throwing on the White House grounds.[7] Since the Washington Senators baseball franchise moved to Texas in 1971, presidents who have wished to throw out the first ball have had to travel to other cities. Several presidents, including Kennedy and Nixon, were avid football fans. In December 1969 Nixon attended a highly publicized college football game in Fayetteville, Arkansas, between the Universities of Texas and Arkansas. The president not only was interviewed at halftime in front of a national television audience, he also was filmed visiting both locker rooms after the game.

Observer of Holidays

National holidays reduce societal divisions by emphasizing universal patriotic themes and common traditions. Hundreds of millions of Americans of all races, religions, and regions share the common experience of watching fireworks on the Fourth of July or preparing a banquet on Thanksgiving. On Veterans Day virtually every American citizen will recall someone who served in the military, and on Memorial Day most will remember someone who died in a war. Holidays, therefore, draw a nation together and enhance a citizen's sense of belonging to a single national culture.

As chief of state, presidents usually lead the nation's observation of a holiday. They light the national Christmas tree, deliver a patriotic address on the Fourth of July, and lay a wreath at the Tomb of the Unknown Soldier on Memorial Day. Details of the traditional holiday activities observed by the first family, such as what they ate on Thanksgiving and what gifts they exchanged at Christmas usually are reported to the nation.

Presidents traditionally have issued statements celebrating official holidays such as Memorial Day and Thanksgiving and unofficial holidays like St. Patrick's Day. Presidents, however, cannot proclaim an official federal holiday without an act of Congress. George Washington was the first president to proclaim a national holiday. In response to a congressional recommendation, he declared that a national day of thanksgiving should be observed on Thursday, November 26, 1789.[8] This proclamation contributed to the development of the Thanksgiving holiday now observed in the United States. The most recent holiday

Library of Congress

For years after President William Howard Taft threw out the first baseball of the 1910 major league season in Washington, most presidents observed the tradition.

established by the government was Martin Luther King Day. After initial opposition, Ronald Reagan signed legislation November 2, 1983, declaring the third Monday in January beginning in 1986 to be a legal federal holiday honoring the civil rights leader.

Mourner and Eulogizer

When a prominent American dies the president is expected to lead the nation in mourning. The president routinely issues statements eulogizing Americans who have died. During the first five months of 1983, for example, President Reagan signed statements mourning the deaths of such diverse Americans as Alabama University football coach Paul (Bear) Bryant, entertainer Arthur Godfrey, presidential aide Joseph R. Holmes, three Secret Service agents who were killed in an auto accident, and sixteen Americans who died when the U.S. embassy in Beirut, Lebanon, was bombed by terrorists. Presidential attendance at funerals, however, generally is reserved for former presidents, high government officials, or people who had a close personal or political relationship with the president. When presidents do attend funerals in the United States in their role as chief of state, they usually address the mourners. President Nixon delivered the eulogy at Eisenhower's state funeral at the U.S. Capitol on March 30, 1969.

Presidents also must respond to the deaths of Americans who died while serving their country. Perhaps the most famous of all presidential speeches, Lincoln's Gettysburg Address was delivered during Lincoln's visit to the site of the great battle where thousands of Union and Confederate troops lost their lives. During a war when many soldiers are dying, presidents rarely have time to memorialize individual members of the armed services. In peacetime, however, presidents usually honor any American hero whose death captures the attention of the nation. For example, President Reagan met with the family of Robert Stethem, a Navy diver killed by terrorists who

hijacked TWA Flight 847 in 1985. Reagan also addressed the nation on January 31, 1986, at the memorial service for the seven astronauts killed in the *Challenger* space shuttle disaster.

As head of state, presidents receive invitations to the funerals of foreign leaders. Johnson attended Konrad Adenauer's funeral in Cologne in April 1967, and Nixon traveled to Paris to attend Charles de Gaulle's funeral in November 1970. Presidents rarely go to funerals overseas because of the difficulty of postponing other business and arranging security measures on short notice.

If the president does not go to the funeral, a representative is sent in the president's place. The decision of who to send to a foreign funeral depends on the importance of the country to the United States, the current state of diplomatic relations between the two nations, and the deceased leader's political relationship with the United States. The vice president or secretary of state usually represents the president and the nation at the funerals of prominent world leaders. Former presidents who worked closely with a fallen leader also sometimes attend. President Reagan and Vice President Bush did not attend Anwar Sadat's funeral in October 1981 for security reasons, but Reagan asked former presidents Nixon, Ford, and Carter to represent the United States. At the funerals of leaders of countries that had a strained or minimal relationship with the United States, the U.S. ambassador to that country often will represent the president.

American Tourist

George Washington firmly established the precedent that presidents should travel out among the American people. He made two regional tours as president: New England in 1789 and the South in 1791. Washington thought the purpose of these tours of the states was "to become better acquainted with their principle Characters and internal Circumstances, as well as to be more accessible to numbers

George Washington as. . .

When George Washington became president it was inevitable that the chief of state role would become a prominent aspect of the presidency. His status as a military hero and the leader most identified with the Revolution both in the United States and abroad made him a national symbol even before he became president. Because he had embodied the higher purposes of the Revolution, his acceptance of the presidency brought legitimacy to the Constitution. Presidents since Washington have derived respect and authority from their presidential office and powers. With Washington, however, the flow of benefits was reversed. It was he who brought legitimacy and prominence to an office that had no tradition or established operating procedures and would have been distrusted by the people had he not held it.[1]

Washington believed his primary task as president was to unify the country and establish strong political institutions. In no other presidency were ceremony and symbolism more important to the fulfillment of the president's goals. John Adams saw George Washington as a master of dramatic, symbolic leadership. Many years after Washington's death he commented, "We may say of him, if he was not the greatest President he was the best Actor of the Presidency we have ever had. His address to The States when he left the Army: His solemn Leave taken of Congress when he resigned his Commission: his Farewell Address to the People when he resigned his Presidency. These were all in a strain of Shakespearean and Garrickal excellence in Dramatic Exhibitions."[2]

Washington understood that everything he did as president would set a precedent for future presidents and that even small matters of ceremony could affect the reputation and success of the new government and his office. He wrote: "Many things which appear of little importance in themselves and at the beginning, may have great and durable consequences from their having been established at the commencement of a new and general government. It will be much easier to commence the administration, upon a well adjusted system, built on tenable grounds, than to correct errors or alter inconveniences after they shall have been confirmed by habit."[3]

Washington, therefore, carefully performed ceremonial functions so as to strike a balance between the dignity and accessibility of the presidency. He traveled to his New York inauguration in a carriage, acknowledging the cheers of crowds, but gave a highly formal speech at his inauguration and did not participate in the public revelry surrounding the occasion. Early in his presidency he established a system of formal receptions known as "levees," which allowed him to frequently receive members of government and the public but also to maintain a solemnity that preserved his aura of authority. He also accepted the formal title of "President of the United States" granted by Congress but did not endorse or participate in Vice President John Adams's campaign to have Congress establish the ostentatious presidential title: "His Highness the President of the United States and Protector of the Rights of the Same."[4]

Washington's attention to the details of his chief of state role had significance beyond establishing the proprieties of his office. Washington was also determined to strengthen the common identity of Americans and the primacy of the federal government over the states. The weakness of the federal government and its dependence

---

of well-informed persons."[9] Since then, presidents have been expected to leave the capital to occasionally reacquaint themselves with the nation's problems and listen to the public's needs and complaints. Franklin Roosevelt explained his own need for such travels: "I have always thought it was part of the duty of the Presidency to keep in touch, personal touch, with the Nation . . . now I am going to the Coast . . . to have a 'look-see,' to try to tie together in my own mind the problems of the Nation, in order that I may, at first hand, know as much about the questions that affect all the forty-eight states as possible."[10]

Citizens may become apathetic toward politics and government if they perceive that it is a game played in the capital by leaders who do not care what happens in the rest of the country. By traveling out to the people in the "provinces" presidents can show their interest in the culture of particular regions. They can reawaken public interest in their administration's programs and in government in general.

The concerns of citizens that presidents remain in touch with the needs of the whole country were demonstrated by the successful presidential campaigns of Jimmy Carter in 1976 and Ronald Reagan in 1980. As former governors, both men campaigned against the "Washington establishment," which they said had lost touch with the desires of the people. To emphasize his accessibility and interest in local problems, President Carter journeyed to several small towns during his presidency where he answered the questions of citizens at town meetings and stayed overnight with local families.

Chief of State Role and Presidential Power

The chief of state role has received less scholarly attention than other presidential roles. The ceremonial and symbolic aspects of the presidency appear less important than the responsibilities that come with the president's other powers. When presidents veto bills, sign treaties, nominate Supreme Court justices, issue pardons, or order military actions it is obvious that they have exercised presidential power. As chief of state, however, the president acts neither as a commander nor as an administrator. The effects of ceremonial leadership are less observable and impossible to quantify. Consequently, the chief of state duties are seldom described as a "power" and are sometimes denounced as a waste of the president's time.

... the First Chief of State

on the states under the Articles of Confederation had greatly disturbed Washington and had been the motivation behind the establishment of the new government.

Convincing the nation of the primacy of the federal government and inspiring in the American people a sense of common identity was a difficult task. The Constitution clearly gave the federal government legal preeminence over the states. Nevertheless, most Americans felt a greater allegience to their state than to the Union, and state officials naturally tended to resist federal authority as an intrusion into their jurisdictions. The fledgling government lacked tools to implement government policy. In particular, the federal government had no army or navy and only a few federal marshals who could gather information and enforce federal laws. Consequently, Washington had to rely on state governors to provide militia and law enforcement officers to deal with violations of federal statutes.

Washington used his chief of state role to counter impressions that the federal government lacked authority and did not deserve the primary loyalties of the people. Washington traveled to every state to underscore national unity during trips to the northern states in 1789 and the southern states in 1791. He also insisted that foreign governments deal with him, the representative of all the people, rather than with Congress, which was chosen by local constituencies. When Congress voted for a day of thanksgiving in November 1789, Washington issued the proclamation rather than having Congress ask the states to issue it as had been done with similar declarations under the Articles of Confederation.[5]

Even when seemingly trivial matters of protocol were concerned, Washington was careful to assert the primacy of the presidency and the federal government. During his tour of New England in 1789 he asked to dine with John Hancock, the governor of Massachusetts, but indicated that Hancock should call on him first. When Hancock claimed to be too ill to visit the president, Washington canceled dinner and wrote a stiff note to the governor: "The president of the United States presents his best respects to the Governor, and has the honor to inform him that he shall be at home 'till 2 o'clock. The President of the United States need not express the pleasure it will give him to see the Governor; but at the same time, he most earnestly begs that the Governor will not hazard his health on the occasion."[6] Washington scored an important symbolic victory for the presidency and the Constitution when Hancock relented after a two-day standoff. The governor, who continued to profess an illness, was carried to the president's lodgings by several servants.[7]

1. Glenn Phelps, "George Washington and the Founding of the Presidency," *Presidential Studies Quarterly* 17 (Spring 1987): 352.
2. Clinton Rossiter, *The American Presidency*, 2d ed. (New York: Harcourt Brace and World, 1960), 92.
3. James Hart, *The American Presidency in Action 1789* (New York: Macmillan, 1948), 12.
4. Joseph E. Kallenbach, *The American Chief Executive* (New York: Harper and Row, 1966), 274.
5. Phelps, "George Washington and the Founding of the Presidency," 351.
6. Ibid., 351-352.
7. Hart, *The American Presidency in Action 1789*, 20.

Although the president's right to dedicate a monument or congratulate an astronaut may mean little, the symbolism of the chief of state role constitutes a real power because it enhances presidential authority and legitimizes and magnifies other presidential powers. As political scientist Clinton Rossiter explained, "No President can fail to realize that all his powers are invigorated, indeed are given a new dimension of authority, because he is the symbol of our sovereignty, continuity, and grandeur."[11]

The presidency, therefore, is elevated above other offices and institutions not just by its legal authority, but by its symbolic mystique. This mystique has been built up by two centuries of veneration for an office that has been occupied by many of our greatest national heroes. Rossiter wrote:

> Lincoln is the supreme myth, the richest symbol in the American experience. He is, as someone has remarked neither irreverently nor sacrilegiously, the martyred Christ of democracy's passion play. And who, then, can measure the strength that is given to the President because he holds Lincoln's office, lives in Lincoln's house, and walks in Lincoln's way? The final greatness of the Presidency lies in the truth that it is not just an office of incredible power but a breeding ground of indestructible myth.[12]

Symbolic Leadership

Effective government requires more than rational deliberations and actions. Hearts are stirred and ranks are closed more easily by symbols than by reasoned arguments. Consequently, every government that hopes to provide effective leadership must provide symbols that unify, inspire, and reassure the people. The most powerful symbols are human symbols. Journalist Michael Novak, who worked for the Muskie and McGovern campaigns in 1972, wrote of the necessity of human symbols: "Causes, institutions, and administrative processes must be personified before humans can passionately engage them. Humans are flesh and blood, and they understand best what is flesh and blood. . . . Thus the general law of politics: political movements depend for their general acceptance on the greatness of their leaders."[13] In the United States, the president, as chief of state, is the dominant political symbol for most Americans.

This symbolic stature enables presidents to exercise inspirational leadership from the stage of the White House. Americans want more from a leader than efficiency and honesty. They want a dramatic leader who can articulate their goals, motivate them, and even amuse them. Skillful presidents can use their symbolic assets to build the nation's morale and confidence and call on patriotic sentiments in a crisis. Political scientist Harold J. Laski explained the importance of a symbolic and inspiring leader to the people:

> They must see someone who can say in the grand way what they half-articulately feel. They must have the sense that they are a part of significant events. Dull government can only endure when government is unimportant; a long period of extraordinary prosperity will, as in the Coolidge regime, persuade men that dullness is the same as soundness. But where any significant part of the population is hard pressed, it looks to the president for relief; and it is then urgent that he give the appearance of active intervention on their behalf. A dull president will not last long in a period of crisis. His temptation, just because he is dull, is to throw the burden of responsibility upon the leaders in Congress. He thus ceases to be the symbol of action, and the nation feels deprived of that leadership to which it feels itself entitled.[14]

The chief of state role equips presidents with several symbolic assets through which they can reinforce their executive leadership. Presidents are seen as the symbol of national unity, the symbol of national continuity, and the symbol of the federal government. Although presidents may have varying success at using these assets to further their policies, all presidents possess them. Merely by holding office and exercising presidential powers presidents will represent the nation's unity, continuity, and government to many Americans.

Symbol of National Unity

The Constitution provided for three independent branches of government, but the president, rather than Congress or the courts, has become the symbol of national unity. The presidency's emergence as a unifying symbol was predictable. George Washington, who was a national symbol even before he became president, saw his presiden-

White House

Rutherford B. Hayes was the first president to use an eagle as the official presidential seal. In 1903 Theodore Roosevelt added a circular seal around it, bearing the words, and in 1945 Truman changed the eagle's head from one side to the other. He also added two new stars for the two new states.

tial role primarily as a national unifier who would draw together the citizens of the thirteen states and followers of various political philosophies into one nation. Although no president has been able to remain as nonpartisan as Washington, few presidents have been slaves to their parties and most have worked in some way to reduce national divisions. In addition, presidents are the most identifiable national leaders and the only elected officials (with the exception of vice presidents) who have a national constituency. As such they are seen as the guardian of the interests of the whole nation against the narrow demands of partisan and sectional groups.

The president's status as a symbol of national unity is an especially valuable political asset because much of what the president does as chief executive and party leader divides the nation. Political scientist Thomas E. Cronin has observed that presidents

> necessarily divide when they act as the leaders of their political parties, when they set priorities that advantage certain goals and groups at the expense of others, when they forge and lead political coalitions, when they move out ahead of public opinion and assume the role of national educators, and when they choose one set of advisers over another. A President, as a creative executive leader, cannot help but offend certain interests.[15]

Being a symbol of national unity allows presidents to heal some of the wounds they open while acting in their other roles and to maintain the public's confidence in them as leader of the entire nation. Eisenhower was particularly adept at projecting an image of an amiable unifier while hiding his political side, thereby maximizing the unifying potential of his chief of state role.[16]

The power of the presidency as a unifying symbol is demonstrated by the public's reaction to international crisis. Even when Americans disagree with the president's policies, they have tended to rally around their president when the nation's interests are threatened by a foreign power.

Public opinion polls have shown that presidential approval ratings usually improve when the nation becomes involved in a war or other international crisis. For example, President Kennedy's public approval rating jumped 13 percent in 1962 after the Cuban missile crisis. In 1975 Ford's public approval rating shot up eleven points after he ordered marines to rescue the crew of the merchant ship *Mayaguez*, which had been seized by Cambodian forces.

Although presidential approval ratings will improve the most when the public perceives that the president has acted skillfully or boldly to meet an international crisis, even clear foreign policy failures can add to a president's popularity. In May 1960, the Soviets shot down an American U-2 spy plane over Soviet territory. Eisenhower denied that the United States was conducting intelligence overflights of the Soviet Union, but when Moscow produced the captured pilot, the president took responsiblity for the missions. Eisenhower's approval rating jumped 6 percent following the incident, despite heightened East-West tensions and the collapse of a summit meeting in Paris later in the month. Similarly, after the U.S.-sponsored Bay of Pigs invasion of Cuba by exiled Cuban nationals in 1961, Kennedy's approval rating improved eleven points to 83 percent, even though the invasion was universally considered a disaster.[17] The public rallied around Eisenhower and Kennedy in these situations not because they achieved anything, but because they were the symbols of the United States during a time of international confrontation.

Symbol of Continuity

Presidents also benefit from occupying an office that is identified with the continuity of the United States and the stability of its political institutions. Before taking office presidents pledge in their oath of office to "preserve, protect, and defend the Constitution of the United States." Lincoln, perhaps the most celebrated U.S. president, is remembered primarily for preserving the Union. The American people see the president as not only the current national leader but also the latest president in a long line of presidents who have guarded the freedom and laws of the United States. Consequently, when political rivals challenge the president they are in the uncomfortable position of confronting the defender of the Constitution and the heir of Washington, Jefferson, Lincoln, and the Roosevelts.

The history of the presidency itself demonstrates the stability of the nation's political institutions. Power has always been transferred peacefully from one president to the next. The unbroken chain of presidents has survived assassinations, civil war, impeachment proceedings, election fraud, and a presidential resignation. Even before the presidency faced any of these trials its continuity impressed Martin Van Buren who wrote, "The President under our system, like the king in a monarchy, never dies." [18]

When presidents leave office they continue to symbolize the United States of a past era and the continuity of the nation's democratic institutions. Although there have been exceptions, retiring presidents customarily attend the inaugural ceremonies of their successors, thereby symbolically demonstrating the strength of the Constitution, which provides for the peaceful and orderly transfer of presidential power.[19] Former presidents also can contribute to an image of stability during crises. At John Kennedy's funeral, Herbert Hoover, Harry Truman, and Dwight Eisenhower sat with Lyndon Johnson in a show of nonpartisan support. Together they constituted a powerful symbol of continuity that reassured a nation not yet recovered from the shock of Kennedy's assassination.[20]

Symbol of Government

As chief of state the president symbolizes not only the nation but also its government. Because the presidency is occupied by a single familiar individual who has broad executive powers including the prerogative to initiate policy, it is the most dynamic and understandable element of the federal government. For many Americans what the president is doing becomes synonymous with what the government is doing. For example, a president unveiling a tax reform proposal to a national television audience is more easily understood than the bargaining and consultations within the executive branch that produced the proposal or the complex political and procedural battles that will be fought over the tax reform issue in Congress. The proposal is not seen as emanating from the Treasury Department or the executive branch, but rather from the president. Policy programs, military conflicts, and economic conditions all become identified with the president who was serving at the time they occurred, even if that president was not primarily responsible for them. The presidency, therefore, is used by many Americans as a "cognitive handle," which personalizes and simplifies the detailed processes of governing the nation.[21]

Being the most visible symbol of government can work against presidents as well as for them. Public expectations of the president tend to be very high and often unreasonable. Since it is easier to blame an individual for society's problems than understand all the complicated factors contributing to them, presidents receive much unjust criticism. Public dissatisfaction with federal government policies or local conditions over which the president has little control may be translated into disapproval of the president.

Yet being a symbol of the entire government upon which the media and public focus attention gives presidents the power to dominate issues. When any significant event occurs, Americans look to the president for an assessment and a response. Michael Novak wrote of the power presidents have because they command the attention of the nation:

> If on television the president says our ships were attacked in the Gulf of Tonkin, then that attack (even if it did not occur) occupies our attention and demands that we refute it or accept it or dismiss it. Whatever we do, there stands the president's assertion, solid until painstakingly disproved. This power over our attention, over our power to structure issues, is so enormous that it dwarfs all others.[22]

Tool of Foreign Policy

As chief of state, the president is the ceremonial representative of the United States before the international community. Presidents make ceremonial visits to foreign countries and greet foreign dignitaries who visit the United States. Whether presidents are receiving visitors in the White House or touring the world, they are expected to fulfill both their diplomatic and ceremonial responsibilities. When U.S. presidents visit Great Britain, for example, they usually have a ceremonial meeting with the reigning monarch and a policy meeting with the prime minister.

The international chief of state role, however, cannot be neatly separated from the president's activities as the architect of U.S. foreign relations. State visits and other international ceremonies and spectacles that the president undertakes as chief of state are tools of foreign policy. They are a means of communicating the intentions and attitudes of the administration and improving the relationships of the United States with foreign governments.

Presidents and their representatives also use international ceremonial appearances and events to lobby for the support of foreign peoples and leaders. The foreign public observes U.S. presidents most often in their chief of state role. When presidents admire landmarks, make speeches, and attend state dinners on their foreign trips, they are trying to increase their popularity overseas and establish a reservoir of good will to benefit U.S. interests. International respect for a president will enhance the image of the United States, the confidence of the U.S. public, and the president's ability to exert leadership in the international arena. President Eisenhower, who made the image of the United States a high priority, wrote near the end of his presidency that he had tried to maintain "a respectable image of American life before the world. Among the qualities American government must exhibit is dignity. In turn the principal governmental spokesman must strive to display it."[23]

The president's international chief of state role also creates unscheduled diplomatic opportunities. Between November 1982 and February 1985, three Soviet general secretaries died—Leonid Brezhnev, Yuri Andropov, and

In May 1860, President James Buchanan greets Japan's first envoys to the United States.

Konstantin Chernenko. As chief of state of an important nation, President Reagan received invitations to their funerals in accordance with international protocol. These occasions provided Reagan with opportunities to meet face to face with Soviet leaders during a period when poor U.S.-Soviet relations would have made a scheduled meeting difficult, if not impossible to arrange. President Reagan's decisions to send Vice President Bush as the U.S. representative to each funeral rather than attend himself underscored the hard line he was taking toward the Soviet Union at the time. Nevertheless, the funerals allowed the vice president to meet the succeeding Soviet general secretaries and speak to them about U.S. interests.

Greeting Foreign Leaders

Presidents must entertain many visiting chiefs of state, prime ministers, and other foreign dignitaries every year. These visits often include a photo session and a state dinner attended by selected members of Congress, administration officials, and national celebrities.

The manner in which presidents receive a foreign chief of state sends a signal to that leader and other nations about U.S. policy. President Carter's friendly greeting of Chinese Vice Premier Deng Xiaoping in January 1979 was a ceremonial act with profound diplomatic implications. Before, during, and after Deng's visit to the United States, the vice premier had pointedly attacked the leaders of the Soviet Union for pursuing an aggressive foreign policy. The Carter administration's warm reception of Deng and its refusal to condemn his belligerent rhetoric signaled tolerance for the vice premier's views and a clear tilt toward the Chinese in the trilateral relationship.

Presidents also can make a statement about their foreign policy priorities through their invitations to visit the United States. In 1977, for example, Carter wished to emphasize the importance of U.S. relations with its North American neighbors. Consequently, the first two foreign leaders he invited to the White House were President José López Portillo of Mexico and Prime Minister Pierre Trudeau of Canada.

Making International Tours

International tours of presidents and their delegated representatives often consist of more ceremonial activities than policy discussions with foreign leaders. Because U.S. presidents have limited time and ensuring their security is such a difficult and expensive task, a ceremonial visit to a foreign country is a sign of the value the United States attaches to its relations with that country. To be worthwhile, presidential visits do not have to produce a diplomatic breakthrough or even progress in ongoing negotiations. A president may visit a foreign nation solely to reaffirm U.S. interest in that nation or to focus global attention on a particular region or problem.

Before the 1950s, presidential travel to foreign countries was uncommon. When presidents did go abroad they almost always did so to hold negotiations with foreign leaders. Woodrow Wilson went to Europe in 1918 to negotiate the Treaty of Versailles, which ended World War I. Franklin Roosevelt and Harry Truman traveled abroad to confer with Winston Churchill, Joseph Stalin, and other allied leaders during World War II.

Dwight Eisenhower's "Quest for Peace" tour of eleven Asian, European, and Middle Eastern nations in 1959 established the precedent that presidents could go abroad on good-will missions designed primarily to increase foreign support of U.S. policies. Eisenhower traveled twenty-two thousand miles in nineteen days and was met in many cities by enthusiastic crowds numbering in the hundreds of thousands. His trip was almost entirely devoted to ceremonial activities. On December 3, in a televised speech to the nation before his departure, Eisenhower declared he was about to "set forth as your agent to extend once again to millions of people across the seas assurances of America's sincere friendship." [24] Eisenhower conceived of his trip as so purely symbolic that he declined Pakistani president Ayub Khan's request to discuss the contentious issue of the Pakistani-Indian border with Indian prime minister Jawaharlal Nehru unless the prime minister raised the issue first.

Host nations expect a president who is visiting their country to sample their culture and make a pilgrimage to their most cherished landmarks. In 1972, when Nixon made the first trip to the People's Republic of China by a U.S. president, he traveled to the Great Wall and toured the Forbidden City, the ancient home of Chinese emperors. This sightseeing expressed U.S. respect for Chinese culture and symbolized the desire of the administration to widen contacts between the people of the two nations. Given the vast cultural differences and recent animosity between the United States and the People's Republic of China, this symbolism was an important element in establishing a lasting rapprochement. Similarly, President Nixon attended the Bolshoi Ballet and several state dinners during his historic visit to Moscow the same year.

Kennedy's trip to West Berlin in June 1963 demonstrated how the chief of state role could be used to add force to a foreign policy commitment. For several years the Soviet Union had made veiled threats against the city, which existed as a democratic enclave deep within Communist East Germany. In 1961 the Soviet and East German Communist leaders ordered a wall to be built to prevent East Germans from emigrating to West Berlin. The U.S. commitment to defend West Berlin was not new, but the vulnerability of the city to Soviet attack and the great consequences of nuclear war inevitably caused Berliners, as well as other Western Europeans, to question the U.S. commitment to the city. No matter how adamantly U.S. officials insisted that the United States would defend Berlin, establishing the credibility of the commitment was difficult.

While traveling in Europe in 1963 Kennedy delivered a speech at the Berlin Wall in which he declared "Ich bin ein Berliner" (I am a Berliner). The spectacle of the U.S. chief of state standing before the symbol of Communist oppression and declaring to 400,000 Berliners in their own language that he was one of them added a new force to the U.S. commitment. As the commander in chief and manager of U.S. foreign policy, Kennedy had made the decision to reaffirm the standing U.S. policy to defend West Berlin. It was Kennedy's role as chief of state, however, that gave him the opportunity to infuse the U.S. commitment with a dramatic promise that linked the prestige of the United States and his own presidency to the defense of Berlin and Europe.

In 1985 President Reagan planned to make another dramatic presidential trip to West Germany to commemorate the fortieth anniversary of the end of World War II in Europe. To symbolize U.S.-West German reconciliation and friendship that had been accomplished since the war, the president agreed to visit the German military cemetery at Bitburg and lay a wreath at a tomb for German casualties of the war. After the president had made a commitment to visit the cemetery, however, reports revealed that among its dead were members of the infamous Nazi SS, the group that oversaw the execution of millions of Jews in concentration camps before and during the war. Jewish and veterans groups immediately protested Reagan's itinerary. In an attempt to placate the president's domestic critics, the White House added a stop at the site of the Bergen-Belsen concentration camp to his trip. Nevertheless, the protests continued, and Reagan was confronted with the choice of offending significant numbers of American voters or his West German hosts. Reagan chose to absorb the domestic criticism of the cemetery visit to avoid embarrassing West German chancellor Helmut Kohl and undercutting his symbolic message of reconciliation to the German people.

Partisan Politics

When a political system separates the chief of state role from that of the chief executive, the chief of state can

---

Foreign Chiefs of State

The United States is one of the few developed nations that combine the chief of state and chief executive roles in a single office. The division of these roles between two or more individuals in most Western governments and several Communist nations demonstrates that a nation's top leader does not also need to be its figurehead. In many nations, including Great Britain, Belgium, The Netherlands, Sweden, Denmark, and Norway, a king or queen serves as chief of state even though the monarchy has lost any meaningful executive powers. In these countries the monarchs have become integrative figures who embody the history and ideals of their nations.

In other countries, such as France, Israel, Italy, and West Germany, the chief of state role is assigned to an elected official who serves alongside the head of the government.[1] In many Communist nations there is a triumvirate of leaders: the president, the premier, and the general secretary of the Communist party. The president is the official chief of state, while the premier is formally in charge of the Soviet government. It is the general secretaryship, however, that often is the most powerful post.

Significantly, even when a nation has a full-time chief of state, the official who wields executive power will often perform many chief of state functions. No chief executive can be entirely insulated from ceremonial duties. Even when a chief of state's office is a cherished part of the national culture grounded in centuries of tradition, like the British monarchy, or has retained influence in the government, like the Spanish monarchy,[2] the person who actually wields power will be expected to preside at some ceremonial functions. In particular, chief executives must greet important foreign visitors who want to meet with the most powerful person in the country, not just the reigning figurehead.

1. Merlin Gustafson, "Our Part-Time Chief of State," *Presidential Studies Quarterly* 9 (Spring 1979): 164.
2. William V. Thomas, "World Royalty: Pomp and Circumspection," *Editorial Research Reports*, May 8, 1981, 332-333.

---

transcend partisanship. The British monarch takes no official position in the political struggles between British political parties. Such nonpartisanship is impossible for the U.S. president who must function as the leader of a political party as well as chief of state.

Although the president may genuinely promote a nonpartisan atmosphere on some occasions, presidents frequently exploit their standing as chief of state for partisan purposes. Virtually everything the president does in public as chief of state has political significance. The dignity and status conferred on presidents as the nation's ceremonial and symbolic leader increase their popularity with the American public and their bargaining advantages over other government officials.

The chief of state role also provides presidents with a

Jimmy Carter's Attempt to Depomp the Presidency

During Jimmy Carter's presidential campaign leading up to his 1976 election he perceived correctly that the American people were still disturbed by the Watergate scandal and wanted the next president to reaffirm their trust in government. Carter's emphasis on establishing an honest and unpretentious administration helped propel him to the White House past several better known Democratic candidates and the Republican incumbent Gerald Ford. As president, Carter was determined to eliminate barriers between the presidency and the people.

Carter began his campaign to depomp the presidency on his first day as president. Following Carter's inauguration ceremony he and his family left their limousine and walked up Pennsylvania Avenue to the White House. This gesture symbolized his intention to cut back on the pretentions and privileges surrounding his office as part of his efforts to run a just and open presidency. After Carter's term was over he wrote about his decision to walk back to the White House:

> I began to realize that the symbolism of our leaving the armoured car would be much more far-reaching than simply to promote exercise. I remembered the angry demonstrators who had habitually confronted recent Presidents and Vice Presidents, furious over the Vietnam war and later the revelations of Watergate. I wanted to provide a vivid demonstration of my confidence in the people as far as security was concerned, and I felt a simple walk would be a tangible indication of some reduction in the imperial status of the President and his family.[1]

Thereafter Carter continued his efforts to simplify the imperial presidency. He sold the presidential yacht, carried his own garment bag, donated blood, and ordered the White House thermostat to be set at sixty-five degrees in the winter.[2] In addition, he stopped the practice of having "Hail to the Chief" played when he entered the scene of an official event, delivered an FDR-style fireside chat, and was often photographed in informal clothing.

Carter also attempted to destroy the imperial atmosphere surrounding the presidency by emphasizing his accessibilty. During the first several months of his presidency he held frequent press conferences and question-and-answer sessions with federal employees. He also attended town meetings in rural communities, conducted a phone-in talk show in which members of the public could ask him direct questions, and, when traveling within the country, lodged in the homes of American families.[3] Carter even invited John B. Shanklin, a Wash-

ington, D.C., hotel worker, to the White House as he had promised during a 1974 encounter with Mr. Shanklin at the outset of Carter's campaign for the Democratic nomination.

During his first months in office, Carter's openness appealed to the American people, and he enjoyed high public approval ratings. As time passed, however, Carter and his aides suspected that they had gone too far in eliminating pomp from the presidency. As the president's popularity dropped throughout most of his first year and a half in office, it appeared that Carter's accessibility and populist style had made him seem less presidential than past chief executives and had muted the patriotic message contained in presidential symbols. For some people, Carter's actions also seemed to be weakening the office of the president.[4] Carter recalled: "I overreacted at first. We began to receive many complaints that I had gone too far in cutting back the pomp and ceremony, so after a few months I authorized the band to play 'Hail to the Chief' on special occasions. I found it to be impressive and enjoyed it."[5] As his term progressed Carter tried to establish a balance between the regal symbols that contributed to an image of himself as a powerful, decisive president and the populist symbols that had helped him get elected.

Carter had initially misinterpreted what the public wanted following the Watergate scandal. Undoubtedly, they longed for honesty and openness in the White House, but not at the expense of the symbolic trappings that contributed to the presidency's historic and paternal image. Indeed, the "imperial" presidency of Richard Nixon did not end in disgrace because he enjoyed the glamour and ceremonial display of his office, but rather because he had broken the law, cut himself off from everyone but a handful of advisers, and cynically betrayed the trust of the American people. Carter learned that the symbols and privileges of the presidency contribute to presidential power, and no president can reject them without risking an erosion of popular support.

1. Jimmy Carter, *Keeping Faith* (New York: Bantam Books, 1982), 17-18.
2. Larry Berman, *The New American Presidency* (Boston: Little, Brown, 1987), 314.
3. Harold Barger, *The Impossible Presidency* (Scott, Foresman, 1984), 378.
4. Thomas E. Cronin, *The State of the Presidency,* 2d ed. (Boston: Little, Brown, 1980), 159.
5. Jimmy Carter, *Keeping Faith,* 27.

justification to preside over events with obvious public relations appeal. Chief of state activities can be staged to make presidents look patriotic, amiable, concerned, skilled, and noble. Because chief of state activities are built into the president's job description, the role allows presidents to campaign subtly throughout their term without having to appear overly political or self-serving.

Presidential Popularity

One of the most important factors affecting presidents' domestic political power is the public support they receive. When a solid majority of Americans backs the president on a particular issue, other political institutions, including Congress, rarely will challenge the president. The chief of state role is a political asset primarily because it fortifies the president's popularity.

Many Americans will support the office of the presidency because it symbolizes the nation and the government even when they disagree with the incumbent's policies. The popularity of the presidency is demonstrated by the high public approval ratings enjoyed by new presidents. Political scientists Erwin C. Hargrove and Michael Nelson have written that the "honeymoon" period between the American people and new presidents

> is, in a sense, an affirmation of faith in the office.... New presidents invariably receive the initial approval of millions of citizens who voted against them; vice presidents who succeed to the office, for whom no one voted, actually fare better. Even after experiencing two highly unpopular presidencies in a row, the second culminating in the near-impeachment and resignation of President Nixon, citizens rallied to the support of President Ford by a margin of 71 percent to 3 percent.[25]

Even the outcome of the Watergate scandal can be viewed as evidence of the presidency's popularity and strength rather than its fragility, since Nixon was not forced to resign until long after the depth of the scandal became known.[26]

Given that the presidency is more consistently popular than any incumbent can hope to be, presidents benefit from chief of state activities because they make them appear "presidential." Formal ceremonies such as the State of the Union address and a state dinner for a foreign head of state appeal to public patriotism and allow the president to look like the nation's leader and guardian. They also underscore the president's links with history and cause people to associate the incumbent with the past glories of the office. Nixon attempted to exploit the history of the presidency by placing a bust of Lincoln on his desk and wearing an American flag pin when he appeared on television during the Watergate scandal to assure the American public that he was innocent of any wrongdoing.[27]

The chief of state role also contributes to presidential popularity by personalizing the president. Less formal ceremonies such as a trip to a sporting event or a White House reception for a civic group make the president appear as an average friendly person who shares the everyday interests and concerns of Americans. Ceremonial activities, therefore, can be used to build the fondness, as well as the respect, the public has for a president.

Finally, many Americans will support an incumbent's foreign policies because the president is seen as the representative and symbol of the United States before the world. Few events make a president look more like a statesman than a summit meeting with a prominent head of state or a reception in a foreign country by hundreds of thousands of cheering foreign citizens hoping to catch a glimpse of the U.S. chief of state. Presidents attempt to maximize the public relations benefits of their chief of state role by dramatizing their foreign tours and staging them for television. President Nixon timed his historic arrival in Beijing in 1972 to coincide with Sunday night prime-time television viewing hours. The president's return to Washington was also timed to coincide with prime time even though this required a nine-hour "refueling stop" in Alaska.[28]

Intragovernmental Relations

Although the public often thinks of presidents as leaders who "run the country," they are far from omnipotent.

Congress can block most presidential initiatives, and the courts can declare a presidential action unconstitutional. Even cabinet officers and other members of the executive branch can check presidential power by withholding information, slowing down implementation of presidential directives, leaking details of controversial policies to the media, publicly announcing their opposition to a policy, or resigning to protest a presidential decision. Consequently, presidential power depends not only on the authority of presidents to issue orders and make proposals, but also on their ability to persuade others that those orders and proposals are correct.

The president's status as chief of state strengthens the president's ability to influence other members of the government. Political scientist Richard Neustadt observed:

> Presidential "powers" may be inconclusive when a President commands, but always remain relevant as he persuades. The status and authority inherent in his office reinforce his logic and his charm.... few men—and exceedingly few Cabinet officers—are immune to the impulse to say "yes" to the President of the United States. It grows harder to say "no" when they are seated in his oval office at the White House, or in his office on the second floor, where almost tangibly he partakes of the aura of his physical surroundings.[29]

Such presidential lobbying is hard to resist, especially for members of the president's own party who risk political isolation if they do not have a good record of supporting the president. Presidents, therefore, can exploit the symbolic power of their office to pressure an official or member of Congress for support.

Presidents can also use the glamour and social prestige of the White House to influence members of Congress and other public leaders by granting or denying them access to White House meetings and social functions. Officials want to be close to the president not just because they have use for the chief executive's authority, but because they wish to bask in the glow of presidential celebrity. An invitation to a White House dinner or reception can be one of the most sought after "tickets" in Washington. It allows an individual to rub elbows with the most powerful and famous people in the country, and it is a confirmation of the recipient's importance to the nation and the president. Although presidents and their staffs will invite members of the other party to White House events in the name of bipartisanship, political allies of the president obviously will receive more invitations than political enemies. Politicians who engage the president in a particularly bitter political battle or become enmeshed in a scandal may be cut off from the president's presence entirely.[30]

Furthermore when presidents are faced with a stubborn Congress, their status as chief of state contributes to their ability to appeal to the people over the head of the legislative branch. Presidents have done this by presenting their case to the people on an issue and hoping that favorable popular opinion and active public pressure on individual legislators will force Congress to back presidential policy. Franklin Roosevelt had great success with this tactic. His popularity with the American people weakened resistance in Congress to his New Deal programs. Reagan also used this strategy successfully. During his first year in office, he asked the public to pressure Congress to support his efforts to change dramatically the federal government's taxing and spending policies. Despite a solid Democratic majority in the House of Representatives, he was able to pass a large tax cut and sweeping spending reductions totaling over $35 billion.

Other presidents have been less successful at using public opinion. In September 1919 Woodrow Wilson undertook a cross-country crusade to promote U.S. entry into the League of Nations. After making dozens of speeches in twenty-nine cities across the Midwest and West, he became ill and returned to Washington, D.C., where he suffered a stroke on October 2. Despite Wilson's efforts, the public remained skeptical of an activist foreign policy, and the Republican-controlled Senate refused to ratify the Treaty of Versailles, which established the League.

Jimmy Carter saw himself as a Washington outsider who enjoyed a direct relationship to the people that would help him to deal with Congress on contentious issues. Carter discovered, however, that his election victory and initial personal popularity—which exceeded 70 percent during his first months in office—did not translate into public enthusiasm for his programs. His expectations of being able to confront Congress with strong public backing led him to neglect executive-legislative relations and made passage of his programs more difficult.[31]

Extragovernmental Power

The president is indisputably the nation's first celebrity. One 1969-1970 survey found that 98 percent of adult Americans knew who was president, a much higher percentage of recognition than for any other public figure except the vice president, who was known by 87 percent. In contrast, only 57 percent knew the name of one senator from their state, and only 39 percent could identify their representative in the House of Representatives.[32]

Presidents, first ladies, and former occupants of the White House frequently head the list in "most admired person" polls. Most national radio and television news broadcasts will discuss the president's major activity of the day, and few adult Americans would not be able to recite some basic details about the president's personal and political background. Each year almost two million people, many of whom stand in line for more than an hour, visit the White House. Over nine million people tried to call the White House during President Carter's call-in radio press conference in 1977. This constant attention not only contributes to the president's political power it also gives presidents and their families great influence over national culture and attitudes.

Spiritual Leadership

Although one of the most cherished and accepted principles embodied in the U.S. Constitution is the separation between church and state, many Americans look upon presidents as moral and spiritual leaders. Presidents attend church services and national prayer breakfasts, address religious groups, discuss issues with religious leaders, and frequently invoke God in their speeches. Religious influence flows to presidents because they are the nation's foremost celebrities and the symbols of traditional American values. The moral and religious example they set affects the religious climate of the nation during their term.

The president's role as an unofficial spiritual leader was first exercised by George Washington, who said in his first inaugural address that

> it would be improper to omit in this first official act, my fervent supplications to that Almighty Being who rules

over the Universe.... No people can be bound to acknowledge and adore the invisible hand, which conducts the Affairs of men, more than the People of the United States. Every step, by which they have advanced to the character of an independent nation, seems to have been distinguished by some token of providential agency.

Since then all presidents have mentioned God in their inaugural addresses.[33] Washington also added the words "so help me God" after the oath of office. Every president has followed Washington's example, thereby making an acknowledgement of God part of the president's first official act.

No self-proclaimed atheist has ever been elected president. Thomas Jefferson, who was accused of being one during the 1800 presidential campaign, asserted his faith in God in his inaugural address. He referred to "that Infinite power which rules the destinies of the universe" and "an overruling Providence."

Although Americans expect their president to profess a belief in God and occasionally participate in religious ceremonies and rituals, they are ambivalent about the president's religious role. The majority of Americans want their president to be a religious person, affirm religious values, and set a moral example, but they do not want the president to govern the country according to a private conception of God's will or to use the presidency to promote a specific religious faith. Carter, who considered himself a "born again" Christian, understood this ambivalence. He openly professed a deep faith in God but denied that he considered himself to be a religious leader.[34]

Above all, presidents are expected to take an ecumenical approach to religion that does not offend any faith with significant numbers of adherents. Eisenhower often professed his faith in God and spoke of the importance of religion in American society, but he was careful not to define God narrowly. In a 1959 speech to the National Council of Churches he stated that the spiritual unity of the West included not only Judeo-Christian traditions but also "the Mohammedans, the Buddhists and the rest; because they too, strongly believe that they achieve a right to human dignity because of their relationship to the Supreme Being."[35] Rather than promoting a particular faith, presidents have generally promoted the concept of religion and the basic values common to most religions.

Style

People want to know the details of the life of presidents and their families. Just as the British scan their newspapers and magazines for information about the royal family, the American public avidly follows the private lives of the first family, the closest American equivalent to royalty.

The national spotlight gives presidents and their families influence to affect the lifestyles and habits of Americans. Presidents will often spark new trends in clothing, foods, hobbies, or athletics even if they do not try to do so. Franklin Roosevelt increased the popularity of cigarette holders and scotty dogs. John Kennedy's preference for rocking chairs, which he favored because of his chronic back ailment, led many Americans to get one for their own home. Lyndon Johnson's taste for Mexican food convinced many Americans to try Mexican cuisine for the first time and stimulated the growth of fast food chains selling Mexican dishes. The company that manufactured Ronald Reagan's favorite kind of jelly bean reported that its sales

Public Reaction to the Death of a President

The reaction of Americans to the death of a president provides dramatic evidence of the American public's emotional attachment to the presidency. The deaths of presidents have produced periods of simultaneous public grief more intense than those caused by any other type of national event. Americans regard the death of an incumbent president not just as the death of their elected leader, but as the death of the symbol of the government, the guarantor of the nation's security and stability, and a person almost as familiar as a family member.

Although no systematic studies were done of public reactions to the deaths of incumbent presidents before John F. Kennedy, anecdotal evidence suggests that Americans have often experienced a traumatizing grief when an incumbent president has died. Hundreds of thousands of people lined the railways to view the train carrying Abraham Lincoln's body from Washington, D.C., to Albany, New York, and west to its grave site in Springfield, Illinois. The massive outpouring of grief for Franklin Roosevelt, who had led the nation through the Great Depression and World War II, demonstrated that not only an assassination but also an imcumbent's death by natural causes could produce a national spasm of emotion.

Nor was it necessary for the president to have been perceived as a great historical figure. After the shooting of James Garfield in 1881, large crowds took to the streets of major cities seeking news of the president's condition. The attack was the main topic of church sermons the following Sunday, and Garfield, who had entered office only four months before as a dark-horse candidate from Ohio, was lionized in the press as a great statesman.[1] Similarly, William McKinley and Warren Harding were mourned deeply by the public despite their unexceptional leadership and relative lack of historical prominence.

Following the assassination of President Kennedy on November 22, 1963, social scientists at the National Opinion Research Center at the University of Chicago hastily constructed a survey designed to probe the American people's feelings in the aftermath of the tragedy. The interviewers asked 1,384 persons a series of questions about their reactions to the assassination. The responses indicated that the president's death had a much stronger effect on people than news of other kinds of disasters such as earthquakes or airline crashes.[2]

Only 19 percent of the respondents said they were able to continue their day "pretty much as usual" after hearing of the assassination. Sixty-eight percent of the respondents reported that at some time during the four-day period between the assassination and the president's funeral they "felt very nervous and tense." Fifty-seven percent said they "felt sort of dazed and numb." Fifty-three percent said they had cried.

The survey showed that the death of President Kennedy produced feelings in the American people usually associated with the death of a relative or close friend. Seventy-nine percent said when they first heard about the assassination, they "felt deeply the loss of someone very close and dear." Seventy-three percent felt anger, and 92 percent felt sorry for Kennedy's wife and children.

Paul B. Sheatsley and Jacob J. Feldman of the National Opinion Research Center observed:

> The presidential assassination seems clearly to have engaged the "gut feelings" of virtually every American. Events of this order are extremely rare. Survey after survey has consistently shown that most people are normally preoccupied with their own health, their own families, their own problems, and those of their friends and neighbors.... The election of an Eisenhower, the defeat of a Stevenson, a revolution in Cuba, the death of a Stalin—the surprise drop of an atomic bomb or the launching of a sputnik—such infrequent events, in contrast to the ordinary run-of-the-mill news, arouse the interest of almost everyone, but even they do not produce the cessation of ordinary activities, the almost complete preoccupation with the event, and the actual physical symptoms we have here described.[3]

1. Charles E. Rosenberg, *The Trial of the Assassin Guiteau* (Chicago: University of Chicago Press, 1968), 7.
2. Paul B. Sheatsley and Jacob J. Feldman, "The Assassination of President Kennedy: A Preliminary Report on Public Reactions and Behavior," *Public Opinion Quarterly* (Summer 1964): 189-215.
3. Ibid., 206.

tripled, and new orders were backlogged for more than a year after the media reported Reagan's fondness for their product in 1981.

First Ladies can have an equally dramatic effect on national trends. Uncounted women, fascinated by the glamorous Jacqueline Kennedy, adopted her hairstyle and clothing tastes. Many Americans disapproved of Nancy Reagan's consultations with an astrologer, but popular interest in astrology increased after knowledge of her hobby was made public.

Some presidents have deliberately tried to influence the lifestyle of the nation. Theodore Roosevelt not only urged Americans to live an active life full of outdoor pur-

suits, he also set an example for his fellow citizens to emulate. He climbed trees on the White House grounds, swam in the Potomac, played marathon tennis matches, and went for "obstacle walks" in which he would go over or through any obstacle that stood in his way. Roosevelt also promoted vigorous activity by inviting athletes, explorers, cowboys, and other citizens who led a strenuous life to the White House. In addition, Roosevelt waged a campaign to make simplified phonetic spelling acceptable but found that such a controversial cultural reform was beyond even his powers.[36]

John and Jacqueline Kennedy promoted artistic and intellectual pursuits during their years at the White House.

Their patronage of cultural events and recognition of the achievements of writers, artists, and performers awakened American interest in the fine arts. The Kennedys invited famous entertainers and musicians to the White House for "command performances." The president and first lady also promoted interest in science and history. At one famous dinner in 1962 honoring American Nobel Prize winners, the president declared: "This is the most extraordinary collection of talent . . . that has ever been gathered together at the White House—with the possible exception of when Thomas Jefferson dined alone." [37] Mrs. Kennedy, dismayed by the meager White House library, stocked it with 1,780 great works of literature selected by James T. Babb, Yale University's librarian. She also recovered many historical pieces from museums, private collections, and White House storage areas and had the executive mansion redecorated in authentic early nineteenth-century decor.

Chief of State Burdens

One of the justifications of the British monarchy offered by its contemporary proponents is that it shelters the prime minister from many ceremonial duties. Prime ministers can devote their time and energies to formulating policy and dealing with Parliament and foreign governments while the royal family presides at ceremonial functions and absorbs media and public attention. Presidents have no shield against ceremonial activities equivalent to the British monarchy. Although family members, vice presidents, cabinet secretaries, and other presidential associates can lighten the president's ceremonial burden, the president is responsible for innumerable ceremonial functions and never ceases to be chief of state. Between lobbying a member of Congress to support a bill and meeting with the National Security Council to discuss an international hot spot, the president may have to greet Olympic athletes, officials of the United Way, or Miss America. The president's chief of state duties, therefore, may interrupt or even interfere with the president's duties as chief executive.

Calvin Coolidge, who as president refused to overcrowd his schedule, warned:

> The duties of the Presidency are exceedingly heavy. The responsibilities are overwhelming. But it is my opinion that a man of ordinary strength can carry them if he will confine himself very strictly to a performance of the duties that are imposed upon him by the Constitution and the law. If he permits himself to be engaged in all kinds of outside enterprises, in furnishing entertainment and amusement to great numbers of public gatherings, undertaking to be the source of inspiration for every worthy public movement, for all of which he will be earnestly besought with the inference that unless he responds civilization will break down and the sole responsibility will be on him, he will last in office about 90 days. [38]

Few presidents, however, have been able or have wanted to limit their activities the way Coolidge did, and several have driven themselves to exhaustion. Because the chief of state duties increase the presidential workload, one can argue that they are an onerous burden. In addition to the drain on a president's time and energy, the chief of state role can make the president more vulnerable to assassination attempts, reinforce unreasonable public expectations of the president, and contribute to an atmosphere of deference that may warp the president's judgment. In response to these problems some observers of the presidency have suggested that the office be reformed so that the president, like the British prime minister, is free of ceremonial responsibilities.

Demands on Time

Presidential time is a scarce resource. Presidents are ultimately responsible for everything that the executive branch does. They must have time to preside over policy meetings, review the work of their staff and cabinet, establish working relationships with members of Congress, read intelligence reports, study new policy proposals, hold press conferences, make decisions, and perform numerous other functions necessary to the operation of the government and their administration. In addition, they must find time for political campaigning, personal relaxation, and ceremonial functions.

No chief executive can begin to satisfy all the requests for presidential attention. Woodrow Wilson and Franklin Roosevelt, two presidents with a hands-on managerial style, complained of the burdens of their office. Wilson called the presidential workload "preposterous," and Roosevelt claimed to work fifteen-hour days. [39] Lyndon Johnson related in his memoirs: "Of all the 1,886 nights I was President, there were not many when I got to sleep before 1 or 2 a.m., and there were few mornings when I didn't wake up by 6 or 6:30." [40] Even presidents like Eisenhower and Reagan, who were noted for their willingness to delegate responsibility and authority to their subordinates, faced daily decisions about which activities would have to be sacrificed to the pressures of time.

Although presidential responsibilities have expanded greatly in the twentieth century, eighteenth- and nineteenth-century presidents also had more work than time in which to do it. George Washington found himself overwhelmed by the number of visitors he had to receive and civic functions he had to attend. He complained: "From the time I had done breakfast and thence till dinner and afterwards till bedtime I could not get relieved from ceremony of one visit before I had to attend to another." [41] Washington approached the problem in his typical manner—by asking the advice of colleagues he trusted. He solicited the opinions of Alexander Hamilton, John Jay, James Madison, and John Adams. After hearing their recommendations, Washington decided to limit his public entertaining to a dinner every Thursday at four o'clock for government officials and their families, a public levee on Tuesday afternoons for men, and a public tea party on Friday evenings for men and women. [42]

The enormity of presidential responsibilities received a judicial validation in 1807. Chief Justice John Marshall subpoenaed President Thomas Jefferson to appear before the grand jury in Richmond considering former vice president Aaron Burr's indictment for treason. Jefferson refused to appear. He justified his decision in part by explaining that a president's duties as chief executive should not be set aside for an appearance at a trial: "The Constitution enjoins his constant agency in the concerns of six millions of people. Is the law paramount to this, which calls on him on behalf of a single one?" [43] The court accepted Jefferson's refusal to appear and withdrew its request for his testimony. The president cooperated fully with the investigation and offered to give a deposition, but the court never asked him for one.

George Tames, *New York Times*

This candid photo of JFK in the Oval Office has come to signify the heavy burden of the presidency.

Numerous other nineteenth-century presidents commented on the burdens of their office. James Monroe wrote to Congress just before his second term expired that the higher duties of the presidency, consisting primarily of legislative and administrative tasks, were "sufficient to employ the whole mind, and unceasing labors of any individual." [44] James Polk, who died less than four months after he left office, complained in his diary that his presidential duties left him "almost prostrated by fatigue." [45]

Of all presidential activities, ceremonial functions are usually regarded as the most expendable and are frequently delegated to other individuals. Each year the White House turns down hundreds of requests for the president's time from groups and organizations seeking to publicize their cause through an appointment with the president. When a crisis erupts, ceremonial functions that have been scheduled are sometimes cut to accommodate time constraints. Despite the White House's ability to trim the president's ceremonial schedule, chief of state functions still occupy blocks of the president's time. Many ceremonies over which presidents preside are trivial when compared with the weighty affairs of state. For example, in spite of tradition, appearing at the annual White House Easter egg outing is a questionable use of the president's time considering the unending procession of problems that require the president's attention.

There is evidence, however, that although international ceremonial functions occupy much presidential time, the demands of the domestic chief of state role are less than one might expect. A study of the years 1952 and 1960 from the presidencies of Harry Truman and Dwight Eisenhower revealed that they spent only about one hundred hours per year, or about two hours per week, on domestic ceremonial functions. Sample surveys of the appointment calendars of Herbert Hoover, Franklin Roosevelt, Lyndon Johnson, Gerald Ford, and Jimmy Carter indicated that these presidents spent about the same amount of time as Truman and Eisenhower in their domestic chief of state role. [46]

International chief of state duties, however, took up a much greater percentage of presidential time. For example, Eisenhower spent 376 hours in 1960—the equivalent of 47 eight-hour days—on foreign trips or in meetings in Washington with other heads of state. [47] Taken together, therefore, the international and domestic chief of state responsibilities constitute a significant drain on the president's time and may cause unwanted interruptions in the president's workday.

Risks to the President's Health

Scholars and presidents generally have agreed that the presidency is a tremendous physical burden. [48] The pressures of the presidency can weaken the health of even the strongest person. Presidents usually work long hours, must occasionally take extended trips that require physical and mental stamina, and must endure enormous emotional stress rising out of the responsibilities of their job. Presidents seldom look as vigorous when they leave office as when they entered it.

One study of presidential longevity has shown that most presidents have failed to reach the age to which they were expected to live at the time of their election. Excluding the four presidents who were assassinated, twenty-two of the thirty-two presidents who have died of natural causes failed to reach their life expectancy. As the nation and presidential responsibilities have expanded, so has the tendency of presidents to die prematurely. Only four deceased presidents who were elected after 1836 reached their life expectancy. [49]

Illnesses can and have inhibited the execution of presidential duties. Four presidents—William Henry Harrison, Zachary Taylor, Warren Harding, and Franklin Roosevelt—died of natural causes before their terms expired. Several other presidents, including Wilson and Eisenhower, were incapacitated by illness during their incumbency.[50]

Given the consequences of presidents becoming ill, reducing their workload without diminishing their effectiveness is a worthwhile goal of reform. Since common practice has demonstrated that many of the president's ceremonial duties can be delegated, these duties seem to be the logical starting place of efforts to trim the president's schedule.

George Reedy, who served as press secretary under Lyndon Johnson, has argued that even if ceremonial functions do take up valuable presidential time, the primary source of strain on presidents is not long workdays but the knowledge of the consequences of their actions.[51] From war to welfare reform, presidential policies can have life and death consequences. For presidents who have served during the atomic age, the knowledge of their responsibility as the person who must decide to use nuclear weapons can be particularly stressful. Lyndon Johnson wrote that he felt relief after hearing Richard Nixon complete the oath of office in part because "I would not have to face the decision any more of taking any step, in the Middle East or elsewhere, that might lead to world conflagration—the nightmare of my having to be the man who pressed the button to start World War III was passing."[52]

Reedy maintains, as others have, that chief of state duties can provide a psychological release to presidents from the overwhelming responsibilities of their office.[53] These ceremonial events allow presidents to get away from the strains of decision making, and since ceremonies are an accepted presidential responsibility, presidents are unlikely to feel as if they are neglecting their duties.

The effect of the chief of state role on a president's mental and physical health may depend on that individual's personality. For those presidents who revel in the spotlight of national attention, or are stimulated by an affirmation of public affection, like Theodore Roosevelt, Franklin Roosevelt, or Ronald Reagan, chief of state duties can be the most enjoyable and rejuvenating aspect of the presidency. Those presidents, however, who are uncomfortable with the public attention showered upon them, like William Howard Taft and Herbert Hoover, or who feel like they are wasting time when they avert their attention from policy matters, like James Polk, will likely regard chief of state duties as a burden rather than a release.

Risks to the President's Safety

The assassination of a president is an even greater national disaster than the death of a president by natural causes. There may be time to prepare for the transfer of power to the vice president when a president dies from an illness, but an assassination usually does not allow for a period of administrative or emotional preparation. An assassination not only can cause governmental confusion, it can send the country into shock because people perceive an attack upon the president, the symbol of the United States, as an attack upon the nation itself.

Assassination attempts against presidents have not been uncommon. Lincoln, Garfield, McKinley, and Kennedy were killed by their assailants. Jackson, Truman,

Ford, and Reagan, who was wounded, each survived attempts on their lives. In addition, president-elect Franklin Roosevelt was attacked three weeks before his first inauguration; and three presidential candidates, Theodore Roosevelt, Robert F. Kennedy, and George Wallace, all were shot—with Kennedy being killed. In all, presidents, presidents-elect, and presidential candidates have been attacked thirteen times. All but three of these attacks have occurred in the twentieth century. Moreover, threats against the president's life and attempts by individuals to enter the White House grounds illegally have become increasingly frequent.[54]

The most dangerous presidential activities are those that require the president to appear before a large crowd outside the White House grounds.[55] Since the chief of state role often involves such appearances, it contributes to the danger of assassination. The symbolic goal of many chief of state events is to bridge the gap between the government and the people. This goal is difficult to accomplish from inside a bullet-proof limousine or behind a wall of Secret Service agents. Consequently, presidents, especially those running for reelection, still occasionally seek personal contact with unscreened gatherings of voters while nervous Secret Service agents scan the crowd for possible danger. Yet the benefits of a ceremonial event or symbolic gesture in a location where the president's safety cannot be absolutely guaranteed must always be weighed against the risk of an assassination attempt.

The threat of assassination and the cumbersome security measures necessary to ensure the president's safety have forced changes in the way presidents perform their chief of state role. The days when presidents were expected to wade unprotected into a crowd of citizens to shake hands are gone. Just before leaving office Ronald Reagan commented that he would have liked to have gone to see a college football game between Army and Navy as many other presidents had done, but he did not because "nobody wants to run 75,000 people through a magnetometer." Reagan even justified his lack of church attendance, a traditional ceremonial activity of the president, on the grounds that security measures necessary to ensure his safety would disrupt the congregation. Orchestrated events in front of carefully screened groups and televised speeches and press conferences have become the usual methods by which presidents communicate with the American people. This development has contributed to the isolation of presidents. Now, when they spontaneously place themselves before a crowd, as Carter did when he left his limousine and walked up Pennsylvania Avenue after his inauguration in 1977, it is considered a brave and confident gesture.

Excessive Public Expectations

For better or worse, the presidency is an idealized and romanticized office of which the American people have high expectations. With each election the public hopes for a president who will combine the best qualities of past presidents. They want a president with the confidence of Franklin Roosevelt, the international popularity of Dwight Eisenhower, the charisma of John Kennedy, and the legislative skill of Lyndon Johnson. Few individuals can ever live up to such expectations

Moreover, the American people do not want just a president who will combine the skills and insight of past presidents; they want a leader who will satisfy requirements that are often contradictory. Political scientist Thomas Cronin has identified several paradoxes of the presidency that make the president's job nearly impossible. For example, the president must be gentle and decent but also forceful and decisive; a crusader with an agenda and a pragmatic compromiser; a leader able to inspire the nation but one who does not make unrealistic promises; and a common person who understands the American people but a leader of exceptional intellect and sophistication.[56]

Political scientist Godfrey Hodgson has agreed that the expectations of the American people are not easily reconciled:

> The things "the people" want are mutually inconsistent. They want lower taxes *and* higher benefits. They want to be sure of the supply of gasoline, *and* they do not want to pay higher prices for it. They want national security *and* disarmament. They do not want American boys to be sent abroad to be killed, *and* they want the United States to be respected and feared in Vietnam and Ethiopia and Iran.[57]

The public disillusionment created when presidents fail to meet the public's contradictory demands can lead to declining public approval over the course of a president's term. Public opinion polls have shown that presidential popularity usually peaks shortly after the president takes office. It then tends to fall steadily before reaching its nadir late in the second half of the four-year term. After hitting bottom the president's popularity may rise somewhat, but it never reaches the levels enjoyed during the president's first months in office. Although the exact causes of this pattern are uncertain, the public's unrealistic expectations work against presidential popularity.[58]

The chief of state role contributes to high public expectations of the presidency by causing the public to believe presidents have more power than they actually do. As chief of state and the official who represents the entire country, the president is the personification of the nation and the closest American equivalent to royalty. The president's familiarity and symbolic status cause the media and the public to focus their hopes and expectations upon the president. Political scientist Merlin Gustafson wrote, "When one person exercises both symbolic and political authority his public image tends to become distorted. A substantial portion of the public may be led to identify the presidential person with the governmental process, and assume that he alone determines national policy or 'runs the country.'"[59]

The public tends to blame and praise presidents for virtually everything that occurs during their terms regardless of their actual responsibility for conditions. For example, the public holds presidents responsible for economic prosperity even though the natural swings of the business cycle, foreign economic conditions, and economic shocks such as droughts and oil embargoes guarantee that even the best presidential economic policies will not yield economic growth all the time.

When judging presidents, the public often ignores that the Constitution was designed to prevent any one person from completely dominating the government. Presidents must work with a Congress that may be controlled by the opposing party and is always composed of members primarily concerned with serving their home states and districts. Presidents also must avoid unconstitutional actions and motivate their executive branch subordinates who are capable of undermining presidential policies and initiatives. Presidents who cannot get their bills passed or pro-

grams implemented often are accused of being weak leaders or poor compromisers. In short, even though presidents are constrained by the Constitution, they are expected to be as effective as if they were absolute monarchs.

The danger of high public expectations and their negative effect on presidential approval ratings is that presidents may become obsessed with maintaining their popularity. This can cause presidents to take actions that are popular but that are not in the public's interest. In the worst case, presidents may be tempted to skirt legal constraints in pursuit of effective leadership. Cronin has commented: "Our expectations of, and demands on, the office are frequently so paradoxical as to invite two-faced behavior by our presidents. We seem to want so much so fast that a President, whose powers are often simply not as great as many of us believe, gets condemned as ineffectual. Or a president often will overreach or resort to unfair play while trying to live up to our demands."[60] Even if a president is willing to sacrifice public approval to do what is right, the decline in popularity will make the president's task of leading the nation more difficult.

Dangers of Deference

Because presidents are partisan political leaders they are routinely attacked by their political opponents and scrutinized by a combative press. Yet because they are the chief of state, the symbol of the unity and majesty of the United States, they are also treated with deference.

Presidents are provided with a mansion, guards, aircraft, and custom-made automobiles and are waited upon by a host of servants. They are addressed as "Mr. President" even by close friends they have known for many years. The strains of "Hail to the Chief" greet them when they enter the scene of an important occasion. An omnipresent contingent of reporters seeks their thoughts on any subject, no matter how mundane or irrelevant to national policy. Despite the democratic origins of the presidency, the president enjoys the luxury and veneration usually reserved for monarchs.

The intoxicating effects of the deference given to presidents is reinforced by the historic significance of the presidency and the White House. Newly elected presidents become members of an elite and celebrated club. No matter how ordinary their political career might have been before their succession or election, as soon as they take the oath of office they become a major historical figure. They know historians will be rate them on lists with Lincoln, Washington, and other immortal presidents. Election to the presidency ensures that many books will be written about their lives. When they have left office politicians and journalists will continue to seek their opinions as elder statesmen. A presidential library will be constructed to hold their official papers, and when they die their graves will become national landmarks.

Presidents are daily reminded of their place in history as they live in a house that is one of the nation's most cherished monuments and was occupied by every president except George Washington. In the White House they are surrounded by the artifacts of past administrations. They can view the portrait of George Washington that was rescued by first lady Dolley Madison in 1814 when the British burned the capital, or they can write at the desk given to President Rutherford B. Hayes by Queen Victoria in 1880 and used by many presidents since.

Outside the White House presidents can take a walk through the gardens past the magnolia tree planted by Andrew Jackson in memory of his wife, Rachel, or the Rose Garden originally planted by Ellen Wilson and redesigned under John Kennedy. George Reedy, who served as Lyndon Johnson's press secretary has observed:

> The atmosphere of the White House is calculated to instill in any man a sense of destiny. He literally walks in the footsteps of hallowed figures—of Jefferson, of Jackson, of Lincoln. The almost sanctified relics of a distant, semimythical past surround him as ordinary household objects to be used by his family. From the moment he enters the halls he is made aware that he has become enshrined in a pantheon of semidivine mortals who have shaken the world, and that he has taken from their hands the heritage of American dreams and aspirations.[61]

The deference shown presidents because they are chief of state and the mythic atmosphere created by presidential privileges and the regal White House environment may enoble some presidents by giving them a sense of destiny or historic duty, but the royal trappings of the office also can have damaging effects. During the Nixon administration, the well-being of the president and the presidency became more important than the law. The respect given to Nixon as chief of state and the privileges of the presidency, which he relished, undoubtedly enabled Nixon and his staff to justify more easily to themselves violations of the law and unethical political tactics.

In addition, if the deference shown presidents causes them to believe they are always right and above criticism, meaningful debate on presidential policies may be squelched. Presidents who become overconfident of their own judgment may feel resentment toward staff members who disagree with their opinions. Such an attitude will likely cause subordinates to avoid expressing negative opinions to preserve their own influence with the president. Political scientist Robert DiClerico has written:

> Presidents have a tendency to become intoxicated by the deference and veneration shown to the Office they hold. They begin to see themselves as deserving of praise and come to view challenge and disagreement as an affront.... The isolation of presidents from the disquieting advice of staff members was especially pronounced in the Johnson and Nixon administrations. Both men were lacking in a sense of security, and consequently they were especially susceptible to the arrogance generated by the intoxicating atmosphere of the Presidency.[62]

Presidents accustomed to being treated like monarchs inside the White House grounds may also develop a deep resentment of criticism coming from outside the White House. This may cause a president to rely exclusively on a small group of loyal advisers. Even if the president permits disagreement and frank discussion within this group, an isolated decision-making process will deprive the president of valuable sources of insight and information.

Proposals for Change

Given the problems inherent in having a president who is both the nation's chief executive and chief of state, observers of the presidency have occasionally put forward proposals to reform the chief of state role. Change could be accomplished in two ways: through executive orders or practices that formalize the delegation of most chief of state duties away from the president or through a constitutional amendment that assigns ceremonial duties to some other official or creates a new office of chief of state separate from the presidency. More sweeping reforms of the presidency, such as the creation of a plural executive or the incorporation of parliamentary elements into the American political system, also would affect the chief of state role.

Altering the president's chief of state role has not been a major concern of presidents and their advisers. The most prominent executive branch study of the issue was done by Eisenhower's Advisory Committee on Government Organization, also known as the Rockefeller Committee. The committee, which functioned throughout Eisenhower's tenure in office and studied the organization of the entire executive branch, recommended merely that the vice president perform many ceremonial duties to lighten the president's chief of state burden.[63] Presidents have commonly delegated ceremonial duties to the vice president and other individuals, but no president has set up formal rules concerning which officials would preside at which events. Even if such rules were implemented, the succeeding president might overturn whatever precedent had been set.

Most proposals for changing the president's chief of state power by amending the Constitution have come from scholars and public officials who have speculated on ways to make the presidency more efficient while acknowledging the difficulty of convincing the American people that such reforms are desirable.

One such proposal was a constitutional amendment introduced by Rep. Henry S. Reuss (D-Wis.) in 1975. It would have created an office of "Chief of State of the United States" separate from the presidency. The office as conceived by Reuss would be a purely ceremonial position. The president would nominate a candidate for chief of state who would be confirmed by a majority vote of both houses of Congress. To promote the office's nonpartisanship, the chief of state's four-year term would begin two years into the president's term and last two years into the next administration. There would be no limit on the number of terms a chief of state could serve. The amendment designated the chief of state as "the ceremonial head of the United States" and "the sole officer of the United States to receive ambassadors and other public ministers." In addition the chief of state would carry out ceremonial duties "as recommended by the president." The chief of state was to be paid a salary identical to the president and be subject to the same impeachment provisions.

When introducing the amendment, Reuss acknowledged that tinkering with the Constitution was controversial. He maintained, however, that the demands of the chief of state role on the president's time and the dangers of the "symbolic deification of the president" warranted amending the Constitution.[64]

Neither Congress nor the American people showed much interest in Reuss's amendment. Most Americans are not eager to alter an institution to which they are accustomed and with which they associate many of the nation's foremost heroes. Since Abraham Lincoln, Franklin Roosevelt, and other great presidents were able to use the power of the presidency to meet the nation's great crises, they reason, the solution to the nation's problems will not be found by changing the presidency but by electing leaders who can make it work.

Delegation of Chief of State Functions

Since George Washington, presidents have sought ways to control the number of ceremonial events over which they must preside. There are always more worthy causes to recognize and important events that deserve presidential attention than the president can attend. Presidents have managed to bridge part of this gap by delegating ceremonial tasks to family members, the vice president, cabinet officers, close associates, and staff members. Like representatives sent to negotiate with foreign governments, these substitute chiefs of state have authority because they either occupy an important office within the administration or have a personal relationship with the president. Because they do not possess the power of the presidency, their presence does not have the symbolic force of a presidential appearance, but they are substitutes that most groups readily accept.

First Lady and Family

Presidents have often delegated ceremonial functions to their spouses. First ladies are fitting presidential representatives because they are nearly as well-known as the president and are themselves recognized symbols of American history and culture. When a first lady addresses an organization or presides over a ceremonial event, the audience understands that the president is being represented by an intimate confidant and adviser.

Eleanor Roosevelt's ceremonial activism set the standard for modern first ladies. Franklin Roosevelt, who was crippled by polio, frequently sent his wife to the scene of strikes, disasters, and centers of poverty as his personal representative. She also traveled to England, South America, and the South Pacific during World War II to encourage U.S. troops and allies.

Most succeeding first ladies also performed chief of state duties. Pat Nixon traveled widely with her husband and on her own. In 1972 she toured West Africa after representing the United States at the inauguration of the president of Liberia. Rosalynn Carter made an ambitious good-will tour of Latin America in 1977 in which she carried out diplomatic as well as ceremonial missions. Nancy Reagan visited several foreign countries as her husband's representative, including Great Britain in 1981 for the wedding of Prince Charles and Lady Diana, Monaco in 1982 for the funeral of Princess Grace, and Mexico in 1985 to express concern for the victims of an earthquake.

First ladies not only have served as substitute chiefs of state for their husbands, they also have performed their own traditional ceremonial roles. First ladies are expected to serve as hostesses at state dinners and other White House social functions. In addition, during international trips, while presidents have met with foreign leaders, their wives have often taken part in ceremonies or visited local sights where the international press can photograph them admiring an example of the host country's culture. For example, First Lady Pat Nixon visited the Moscow circus and the GUM department store while her husband met with Soviet leaders in 1972. First ladies have also enter-

tained the wives of foreign leaders who have visited the United States.

Other first family members also have been used as ceremonial representatives by presidents. Julie Nixon Eisenhower and Maureen Reagan both occasionally represented their fathers before civic groups. Jimmy Carter's son Chip was employed by the president as his personal roving emissary. The president explained Chip's role in response to a question asked on his famous nationally broadcast radio talk show in 1977: "When we have a special problem anywhere in the nation, and I want the people there to know how deeply concerned I am about it, I would like to have the opportunity to use members of my family to go and represent me personally, along with professionals who serve in the government." [65] Chip's travels included trips to Buffalo to express concern over a severe winter storm, to China as the president's representative in a congressional delegation, to Great Britain to participate in a ceremonial event with the royal family, and to the Middle East as part of a delegation seeking Arab approval for the Camp David peace accords. President Carter's mother, Lillian Gordy Carter, also represented him at ceremonial occasions, including the funeral of Fakhruddin Ali Ahmed, the president of India, in February 1977.

Vice President

During John Adams's tenure as the first U.S. vice president he remarked, "My country has in its wisdom contrived for me the most insignificant office that ever the invention of man contrived or his imagination conceived." Many of the vice presidents who followed Adams agreed with his appraisal of the office. The Constitution had given the vice president no formal policy-making or administrative powers other than to preside over the Senate and break tie votes in that body. Vice-presidential involvement in governing the country depended on the president's inclination to include the vice president in the policy-making process. Few vice presidents of the nineteenth and early twentieth centuries had a significant role within their administrations. Although vice presidents who have served since World War II have become more involved in policy making, the office has remained one that takes on many ceremonial functions.

Vice presidents are well-positioned to act as substitute chiefs of state not only because they have the time to do it, but also because their office is associated with the presidency. Vice presidents run on the same ticket as their presidential running mates and are the only officials besides presidents who are elected by the entire nation. In addition, although their office may at times seem trivial, vice presidents are first in line for the presidency. Fourteen vice presidents have become president, including eight who succeeded to the presidency when the incumbent died in office and one when the incumbent resigned. The political and historic link between the two offices makes the vice president an appropriate stand-in for the president at ceremonial functions.

Since the advent of the jet airplane, presidents have frequently sent their vice presidents on ceremonial missions overseas. Occasionally these missions have included serious negotiations with leaders of important nations, but often their purpose was more symbolic than substantive. Hubert Humphrey explained the vice president's diplo-

Nixon Project, National Archives

Henry Kissinger became the most recognized symbol of President Richard Nixon's foreign policy. Originally national security adviser, he became secretary of state in 1973.

matic role: "He can perform assignments that the President feels would be unwise for him to take on himself, but for which an official lower than Vice President would be unsuitable." [66]

These assignments have included representing the United States and the president at inaugurations, coronations, and funerals of foreign leaders and major world figures. George Bush, who traveled more than one million miles and visited more than seventy countries as vice president, frequently took President Reagan's place at ceremonial functions overseas. Bush's attendance at the funerals of foreign dignitaries became so common he joked that his motto should be: "I'm George Bush. You die, I fly." [67] Vice presidents generally welcome any overseas trip regardless of its importance because foreign travel makes them appear busy and brings them more press attention than their usually undramatic domestic policy role.[68]

Presidents can enhance the symbolic effect of a vice-presidential trip by demonstrating their interest in it and designating the vice president as their personal envoy. John Kennedy would usually hold a publicized meeting with Lyndon Johnson before the vice president left on a foreign mission. Immediately after entering office, Jimmy Carter sent Walter Mondale on a tour of Europe and Japan to demonstrate the importance of close allied cooperation to the Carter administration. In a South Lawn ceremony President Carter bolstered his vice president's status by declaring: "Vice President Mondale has my complete confidence. He is a personal representative of mine, and I'm sure that his consultation with the leaders of these nations

will make it much easier for our country to deal directly with them on substantive matters in the future." [69]

Sending vice presidents on foreign tours not only relieves presidents of their international ceremonial burdens, it gives the president's "understudy" foreign policy experience. Vice presidents whose previous work in Congress or as governor of a state may not have given them extensive foreign policy experience can become better acquainted with world leaders and the process of international diplomacy in case they should have to assume the presidency. Most foreign leaders welcome a vice-presidential visit and recognize that the vice president one day could become president.

Cabinet Members and Personal Advisers

Cabinet members often operate as assistant chiefs of state within the area of their department's concern. For example, the education secretary makes ceremonial visits to public schools; the housing and urban development secretary tours inner-city housing projects; the commerce secretary speaks to business groups; the interior secretary addresses environmentalist groups; and the defense secretary inspects military installations and presides at ceremonies honoring war heroes and veterans. These events symbolize the administration's concern with a particular issue or group. In addition, cabinet members often use ceremonial occasions or symbolic settings to make speeches that unveil a new program or announce a policy decision affecting their department.

The secretary of state has a special ceremonial role. After the president and vice president, the secretary of state is the nation's highest diplomatic and ceremonial representative. The secretary receives foreign ministers who visit the United States and often heads U.S. delegations at funerals, inaugurations, and other special ceremonies overseas that are not attended by the president or vice president. In matters of protocol the secretary of state also is considered to be the highest ranking cabinet officer. This unofficial rank is reinforced by the Succession Act of 1947, which designates the secretary of state as the first cabinet officer in line for the presidency and the fourth government official after the vice president, Speaker of the House, and president pro tempore of the Senate.

Presidents occasionally have used close friends and White House advisers to perform chief of state duties. Unlike cabinet members these chief of state stand-ins derive their legitimacy not from an office, but from their close political or personal relationship with the president. Woodrow Wilson sent his friend and confidant Col. Edward House, who held no government office, on five diplomatic missions to Europe. Franklin Roosevelt used Harry Hopkins, who carried the title "special assistant to the president," as his personal emissary to allied leaders during World War II. Although both of these men functioned primarily as diplomatic operatives rather than as presidential representatives at ceremonial functions, they became so closely identified with Wilson and Roosevelt that they not only spoke for their presidents when they met foreign leaders, they symbolized the presidency.

During the Nixon administration, National Security Adviser Henry Kissinger transformed his post from a behind-the-scenes presidential aide into a rival of the secretary of state for the diplomatic spotlight. The force of

Kissinger's personality, his close relationship to President Nixon, and his celebrated diplomatic missions to the People's Republic of China and the Soviet Union made him the most recognized symbol of Nixon's foreign policy. During Kissinger's second trip to the People's Republic in October 1971, he performed ceremonial activities including visits to the Great Wall of China and other Chinese landmarks. Kissinger also was constantly at the president's side during the historic 1972 summit meetings in Beijing and Moscow. Kissinger's activities resembled those of the secretary of state so much that he was criticized by some defenders of the State Department for having usurped the role of the secretary. After Secretary of State William Rodgers resigned, Kissinger assumed the post in September 1973.

Notes

1. Karlyn Kohrs Campbell and Kathleen Hall Jamieson, "Inaugurating the President," *Presidential Studies Quarterly* 15 (Spring 1985): 396-397.
2. Arthur M. Schlesinger, Jr., "Annual Messages of the Presidents: Major Themes of American History," in *The State of the Union Messages of the Presidents 1790-1966,* vol. 1 (New York: Chelsea House, 1966), xiv.
3. Ibid., xvi.
4. Alexander Hamilton, *Federalist No. 69,* in *The Federalist Papers,* Alexander Hamilton, James Madison, and John Jay (New York: New American Library, 1961), 420.
5. Cited in Richard Pious, *The American Presidency* (New York: Basic Books, 1979), 5.
6. Harold M. Barger, *The Impossible Presidency* (Glenview, Ill.: Scott, Foresman, 1984), 382.
7. Theodore C. Sorensen, *Kennedy* (New York: Harper and Row, 1965), 368.
8. James Hart, *The American Presidency in Action 1789* (New York: Macmillan, 1948), 24-25.
9. Ibid., 17.
10. *Public Papers of the Presidents of the United States, Franklin Roosevelt, Containing the Public Messages, Speeches, and Statements of the President, 1937* (Washington, D.C.: Government Printing Office, 1938), 379.
11. Clinton Rossiter, *The American Presidency,* 2d ed. (New York: Harcourt Brace and World, 1960), 18.
12. Ibid., 102-103.
13. Michael Novak, *Choosing Our King* (New York: Macmillan, 1974), 8.
14. Harold J. Laski, *The American Presidency, An Interpretation* (New York: Harper and Brothers, 1940), 38.
15. Thomas E. Cronin, "The Presidency and Its Paradoxes," in *The Presidency Reappraised,* 2d ed., ed. Thomas E. Cronin and Rexford G. Tugwell (New York: Praeger, 1977), 79.
16. Fred I. Greenstein, *The Hidden-Hand Presidency: Eisenhower as Leader* (New York: Basic Books, 1982), 5.
17. Erwin C. Hargrove and Michael Nelson, *Presidents, Politics, and Policy* (Baltimore: Johns Hopkins University Press, 1984), 23.
18. Quoted in Arthur Bernon Tourtellot, *The Presidents on the Presidency* (Garden City, N.Y.: Doubleday, 1964), 36.
19. Four presidents who finished their terms chose not to attend the inaugural ceremonies of their successor: John Adams, John Quincy Adams, Martin Van Buren, and Andrew Johnson.
20. Pious, *The American Presidency,* 7.
21. Dale Vinyard, *The Presidency* (New York: Scribner's, 1971), 5.
22. Novak, *Choosing Our King,* 5.
23. Cited in Greenstein, *The Hidden-Hand Presidency,* 240.
24. *Public Papers of the Presidents of the United States, Dwight Eisenhower, Containing the Public Messages, Speeches and Statements of the President, 1959* (Washington, D.C.: Government Printing Office, 1960), 799.
25. Hargrove and Nelson, *Presidents, Politics, and Policy,* 21.
26. Pious, *The American Presidency,* 8-9.
27. Barger, *The Impossible Presidency,* 377.
28. Robert E. DiClerico, *The American President* (Englewood Cliffs, N.J.: Prentice-Hall, 1979), 171.
29. Richard E. Neustadt, *Presidential Power: The Politics of Leadership From FDR to Carter,* 2d ed. (New York: Wiley, 1980), 27.
30. Herman Finer, *The Presidency: Crisis and Regeneration, an Essay in Possibilities* (Chicago: University of Chicago Press, 1960), 103.
31. Larry Berman, *The New American Presidency* (Boston: Little, Brown, 1987), 314-317.
32. Fred Greenstein, "What the President Means to Americans," in *Choosing the President,* ed. James David Barber (Englewood Cliffs, N.J.: Prentice-Hall, 1974), 125.
33. James David Fairbanks, "The Priestly Functions of the Presidency: A Discussion of the Literature on Civil Religion and Its Implications for the Study of Presidential Leadership," *Presidential Studies Quarterly* 11 (Spring 1981): 225.
34. Arthur J. Hughes, " 'Amazin' Jimmy and 'A Mighty Fortress Was Our Teddy': Theodore Roosevelt and Jimmy Carter, the Religious Link," *Presidential Studies Quarterly* 9 (Winter 1979): 80-81.
35. Quoted in James David Fairbanks, "Religious Dimensions of Presidential Leadership: The Case of Dwight Eisenhower," *Presidential Studies Quarterly* 12 (Spring 1982): 264.
36. Joseph E. Kallenbach, *The American Chief Executive* (New York: Harper and Row, 1966), 280.
37. Sorensen, *Kennedy,* 384.
38. Quoted in Tourtellot, *The Presidents on the Presidency,* 366.
39. Ibid., 365 and 369.
40. Lyndon Johnson, *The Vantage Point* (New York: Holt, Rinehart and Winston, 1971), 425.
41. Michael P. Riccards, *A Republic, If You Can Keep It: The Foundation of the American Presidency* (New York, Greenwood Press, 1987), 87.
42. Ibid., 88.
43. Hart, *The American Presidency in Action 1789,* 46.
44. U.S. Congress, House, *Congressional Record,* daily ed., 94th Cong., 1st sess., July 21, 1975, 23717.
45. Emmet John Hughes, *The Living Presidency* (Baltimore: Penguin Books, 1972), 86.
46. Merlin Gustafson, "Our Part-time Chief of State," *Presidential Studies Quarterly* 9 (Spring 1979): 166-167.
47. Ibid., 167.
48. Robert E. Gilbert, "Personality, Stress and Achievement: Keys to Presidential Longevity," *Presidential Studies Quarterly* 15 (Winter 1985): 33.
49. Ibid., 35.
50. Louis W. Koenig, *The Chief Executive,* 4th ed. (New York: Harcourt Brace Jovanovich, 1981), 81-84.
51. George E. Reedy, *The Twilight of the Presidency* (New York: New American Library, 1970), 24.
52. Johnson, *The Vantage Point,* 566.
53. Reedy, *The Twilight of the Presidency,* 24-25. See also Gustafson, "Our Part-Time Chief of State," 167; and Thomas E. Cronin, *The State of the Presidency,* 2d ed. (Boston: Little, Brown, 1980), 158.
54. Frederick M. Kaiser, "Presidential Assassinations and Assaults: Characteristics and Impact on Protective Procedures," *Presidential Studies Quarterly* 11 (Fall 1981): 545-548.
55. In seven of the nine attacks on incumbent presidents, the assailants assaulted the president with a handgun while the president was near a crowd. The exceptions were the attack in 1950 by two men with automatic weapons on Blair House in Washington, D.C., where Harry Truman was staying while the White House was being renovated, and the fatal shooting of John F. Kennedy by Lee Harvey Oswald, who used a high-powered rifle to kill the president as Kennedy traveled through Dallas in a motorcade in 1963.
56. Cronin, "The Presidency and Its Paradoxes."
57. Godfrey Hodgson, *All Things to All Men, The False Promise*

of the Modern American Presidency (New York: Simon and Schuster, 1980), 241.

58. Cronin, "The Presidency and Its Paradoxes," 81.
59. Gustafson, "Our Part-Time Chief of State," 169.
60. Cronin, "The Presidency and Its Paradoxes," 69.
61. Reedy, *The Twilight of the Presidency,* 15.
62. DiClerico, *The American President,* 221.
63. Gustafson, "Our Part-Time Chief of State," 164.
64. *Congressional Record,* July 21, 1975, 23716-23719.
65. *Public Papers of the Presidents of the United States, Jimmy Carter, Containing the Public Messages, Speeches, and Statements of the President, 1977,* Book 1 (Washington, D.C.: Government Printing Office, 1977), 295.
66. Cited in Joel K. Goldstein, *The Modern American Vice Presidency* (Princeton, N.J.: Princeton University Press, 1982), 160.
67. David S. Cloud, "Loyal Lieutenant Bush Seeks Job at the Top," *Congressional Quarterly Weekly Report,* August 6, 1988, 2176.
68. Goldstein, *The Modern American Vice Presidency,* 160.
69. *Public Papers of the Presidents of the United States, Jimmy Carter 1977,* Book 1, 11.

Selected Bibliography

Barger, Harold M. *The Impossible Presidency.* Glenview, Ill.: Scott, Foresman, 1984.

Campbell, Karlyn Kohrs, and Kathleen Hall Jamieson. "Inaugurating the President." *Presidential Studies Quarterly* 15 (Spring 1985): 395-411.

Cronin, Thomas E., and Rexford G. Tugwell, eds. *The Presidency Reappraised.* 2d ed. New York: Praeger, 1977.

Greenstein, Fred I. *The Hidden-Hand Presidency: Eisenhower as Leader.* New York: Basic Books, 1982.

Gustafson, Merlin. "Our Part-time Chief of State." *Presidential Studies Quarterly* 9 (Spring 1979): 163-171.

Hargrove, Erwin C., and Michael Nelson. *Presidents, Politics, and Policy.* Baltimore: Johns Hopkins University Press, 1984.

Hart, James. *The American Presidency in Action 1789.* New York: Macmillan, 1948.

Kallenbach, Joseph E. *The American Chief Executive.* New York: Harper and Row, 1966.

Novak, Michael. *Choosing Our King.* New York: Macmillan, 1974.

Phelps, Glenn. "George Washington and the Founding of the Presidency." *Presidential Studies Quarterly* 17 (Spring 1987): 345-363.

Pious, Richard. *The American Presidency.* New York: Basic Books, 1979.

Reedy, George E. *The Twilight of the Presidency.* New York: New American Library, 1970.

Riccards, Michael P. *A Republic, If You Can Keep It: The Foundation of the American Presidency.* New York: Greenwood Press, 1987.

Rossiter, Clinton. *The American Presidency.* 2d ed. New York: Harcourt Brace and World, 1960.

Chief of Party

Presidential leadership involves role playing. In Harry S Truman's apt analogy, the president wears many hats: chief executive, chief of state, commander in chief, chief diplomat, chief economic manager, legislative leader, and chief of party. Presidential role playing, or hat wearing, is simultaneous, however, rather than sequential. A president does not doff one hat and replace it with another but wears several at a time.

This recognition is especially meaningful in considering the presidential role of party chief. Rarely will a president act solely as party leader. It is equally rare that other roles will be performed without regard for party leadership.

Paradox pervades the presidential role of party leader. Party chieftainship both stands apart from and connects diverse presidential roles. It is simultaneously on the periphery yet at the center of presidential leadership. It clearly divides, and yet more subtly and significantly, it complements and integrates. It is not so much a power as an opportunity; yet under certain conditions, it becomes an obstacle.

The Constitution does not authorize party leadership. It developed outside the framework formed by the constitutionally enumerated presidential powers. Moreover, the assignment of presidential leadership responsibilities over a specific part of the public conflicts with the general expectation that as head of state the president presides over the entire nation.

Yet, because political parties play significant linkage roles in politics, party leadership also is situated at the hub of the varied array of presidential responsibilities. Through the party, the president establishes and maintains connections with other elements in the political order, both inside and outside the government. These connections produce cohesion rather than division.

The exercise of presidential party leadership is often shrouded because of perceived presidential role conflicts and public antagonism toward the concept of partisanship. Given the structure and character of the United States political order, however, turn-of-the-century political scientist Woodrow Wilson's observation remains pertinent: the president's responsibility as chief of party is virtually inescapable.[1]

Party chieftainship calls for particular leadership skills. Political scientist James MacGregor Burns has conducted a general study of leadership in which he identifies two basic types: transactional and transforming. Transactional leadership operates within the framework of exchange: It features bargaining and negotiation. The more complex and potent transforming leadership has an elevating, even moralistic quality. Burns places party leadership in the transactional category.[2] And yet, certain exercises of party leadership are surely transformational.

The generally accepted concept of party in the United States embraces three analytically separate structural elements of party membership: the party in the electorate, the party organization, and the party in office (sometimes referred to as "the party in the government"). The party in the electorate is those voters who with varying degrees of intensity support the party's candidates and causes. The party organization consists of the variably linked network of activists who hold membership and leadership positions in party headquarters throughout the country. The party in office comprises the public officials who hold their positions under the banner of the party along with those who aspire to do so. This group includes both elected officials and those appointed under partisan auspices. According to political scientist Frank Sorauf, the president is chief among the officeholders who have "captured the symbols of the party and speak for it in public authority."[3]

Origins of Presidential Party Leadership

The presidential role of party leader emerged outside the constitutional framework of expectations and powers established in 1787. The reason is simple. In 1787, political parties were not a part of the existing political order. Moreover, to the extent that the Founders' generation contemplated the prospect of political parties, it was generally antagonistic toward them. It is significant that George Washington, the first president, stood second to no one in upholding this position.

Looking from a distance at the Whig and Tory parliamentary factions in Great Britain, the Framers perceived them as divisive and detrimental to national unity. In contrast, the appropriate model of executive leadership appeared in the concept of a patriot king provided a half-century earlier by the British author and statesman Lord

By Harold F. Bass, Jr.

Bolingbroke. Such an ideal figure would stand above party and faction and would rule benevolently in the public interest.

Nevertheless, almost immediately following the onset of the new government, political parties appeared on the scene. At least in part, their origins can be found in an increasingly acute division within the newly-formed cabinet of President Washington. This division pitted the secretary of the Treasury, Alexander Hamilton, against the secretary of state, Thomas Jefferson.

Their conflict had roots in ambition, interest, and ideology. Each saw himself as heir to President Washington. Moreover, each realized that the new constitutional order provided a skeletal framework for development that would inevitably need to be fleshed out; and their respective visions of what the new nation should become were in conflict.

Hamilton glorified the urban areas and their resident merchants and financiers; Jefferson idealized the rural setting and saw the real America embodied in the hard-working farmer. Hamilton perceived the need for strong, dynamic national government; Jefferson professed not to be the friend of energetic central government. During the early years of the Washington administration, conflict between these two principals rocked the cabinet. Among the issues of controversy were those of assumption of the state debts, establishment of a bank of the United States, and the protective tariff. Subsequently, foreign policy differences arose that intensified the cleavage.

In the federal framework created by the Constitution, with its decentralized separation of powers, these disputes could not be contained within the national executive branch. Inevitably, they extended beyond its bounds into the Congress and the states.

Consequently, organization of the respective Hamiltonian and Jeffersonian interests took place. The Hamiltonians took the name "Federalists"; Jefferson's followers were variously titled "Republicans" or "Democratic-Republicans." In contrast to Hamilton, Jefferson himself was not especially visible in the early stages of this process. Rather, his longstanding ally James Madison, a member of the House of Representatives, propelled their common cause and opposed Hamilton's measures in Congress.

George Washington

President Washington viewed these developments with alarm and despair, in keeping with his virulent antipathy toward party. He implored Hamilton and Jefferson to mute their differences, and he steadfastly insisted on holding himself above the emerging partisan battles dividing the government and indeed the entire political community. The president could not remain oblivious, however, to the disputes over policy that were occurring. Indeed, his office forced him to take a stand. Regularly, he opted for the Hamiltonian alternative, even as he denied the legitimacy of partisan conflict. Washington's legacy to presidential party leadership thus emphatically rejects its propriety while very tentatively embracing its inevitability.

John Adams

Washington's successor as president, John Adams, found himself in an exceedingly awkward position in the ongoing party conflict, which was not of his making. In contrast to Washington, Adams viewed parties as natural and inevitable in a free society. However, his theory of government was built on a similar foundation of disinterested executive leadership. He viewed the executive as the balance wheel in a political order featuring a bicameral legislature that represented distinct class interests.

During the Washington administration, Adams generally had supported Hamilton's public policies while maintaining his distance from Hamilton's organizational maneuvering. Personally, he was far closer to Jefferson than to Hamilton. Adams's occupancy of the vice-presidential office made him the logical successor when Washington chose to retire; and the Federalists readily embraced his candidacy in 1796, claiming him as their own. Nevertheless, he had not played any significant organizational role within the party—this was indisputably Hamilton's domain. Meanwhile, Jefferson was thrust forward as a candidate by Madison and other Democratic-Republican partisans. Adams won a narrow electoral vote victory in the first presidential election conducted along partisan lines.

In the presidency, Adams's claims to party leadership foundered on his own theoretical objections to the president's assumption of the role and on Hamilton's ongoing claims. The tension between Adams and his supporters on the one hand and Hamilton and his followers on the other grew until by the end of Adams's term, the Federalist party clearly had split into two wings. Thus, President Adams can be said to have been the leader of, at most, a party faction.

Thomas Jefferson

The third president, Thomas Jefferson, is truly the father of presidential party leadership.[4] By the time Jefferson ascended to the presidency, partisan institutions had begun to take shape. Within the executive, appointments to federal positions were being made with partisan affiliation in mind. Inside the legislature, assemblies or caucuses of like-minded partisans were meeting, not only to plot legislative strategy but also to nominate party candidates for president. Finally, at the state and local level, electoral organizations had formed to secure the selection of partisan candidates to public offices.

The Democratic-Republican partisans looked unequivocally to Jefferson for leadership. While sharing many of his predecessors' prejudices against presidential party leadership, he nevertheless exercised it in a pioneering and exemplary fashion that established high expectations of his successors.

Early on in Washington's presidency, Jefferson acknowledged partisan division as natural but nevertheless deplored its presence. In the ensuing years, he came to defend and justify party activity on grounds of expediency and even honor. Confronted with the realities of Hamilton's initiatives, and disagreeing profoundly with so many of them, he increasingly saw party organization as an exigent and appropriate response. He did not retreat from his antiparty position so much as he superimposed on it a temporary acceptance of party.

For Jefferson, republicanism, or representative government, was the preferable alternative to monarchism, which he associated with arbitrary, hereditary government.

Republicanism derived governmental authority from popular sovereignty and held public officials accountable to popular control. As such, the republican form of government had distinctly democratic implications, although Jefferson was not an advocate of direct democracy. Thus, the Jeffersonian party promoting this cause was labeled "Republican" or "Democratic-Republican."

It is important to note that Jefferson did not clearly endorse the notion of institutionalized party competition. He was never really willing to accord legitimacy to those who opposed him and the republican cause he associated with his party. Furthermore, he demonstrated no abiding commitment to the concept of the Democratic-Republican party. Instead, he viewed the party as dispensable once it had accomplished the restorative tasks for which it had been formed.

Executive-Legislative Relations

Jefferson's party leadership had its chief influence on executive-legislative relations. For Jefferson, presidential party leadership enabled him to overcome an ideological restraint well-established in republican thought: an antipathy toward executive power and a corresponding preference for legislative autonomy. While it is accurate to say that Jefferson never embraced this position with the enthusiasm and extremism of some of his fellow partisans, still he honored it.

For him, the problem was how to exercise positive presidential leadership in the face of republican ideological objections. Here, the presence of party provided a convenient façade facilitating leadership on his part without compromising a fundamental position of his republican followers. He could justify actions taken under the protection of party that, according to republican ideology, might be considered inappropriate under purely executive auspices. In this sense, from his followers' perspectives, Jefferson the party leader had more legitimacy than Jefferson the chief executive. Thus, in adding party leadership to the president's powers, he substantially increased the president's strength in the political arena.

The tactics and techniques Jefferson developed in using party leadership in legislative relations remain the standard in this area. He participated in recruiting candidates. He enlisted members of the legislature as his agents and worked through them in pursuit of his objectives. He deployed the executive department secretaries who constituted his cabinet as emissaries on Capitol Hill.

Not content to rely exclusively on surrogates, Jefferson sought to establish personal relations with rank-and-file legislators. He corresponded extensively with members of Congress. He also regularly scheduled dinner parties in which the guest lists were limited to small groups of legislators who shared his partisan affiliation.

Further, the president sought to generate cooperation and good will with Democratic-Republican legislators through patronage. Although departmental secretaries and state and local officials also were involved in this process, he consistently solicited recommendations and evaluations from individual legislators for prospective appointees.

Jefferson did not choose to continue the practice inaugurated by his predecessors of personally delivering an annual message to Congress. Instead, he tended to work informally, behind the scenes, and through his agents. From this vantage point, however, he was quite willing to make suggestions about details of proposed legislation. Indeed, he often provided trusted legislators with drafts of actual bills for them to introduce according to prescribed procedures, accompanying these communications with admonitions of secrecy and disavowals of meddling.

During his presidency, the opposition Federalist press alleged that Jefferson met with and oversaw the deliberations of the Democratic-Republican party caucus. *Caucus* was the term used to refer to the meetings of the partisan legislators. One well-documented practice was the quadrennial meeting to nominate party candidates for the presidential ticket. In addition, numerous reports make reference to informal assemblies of sizable numbers of legislators to plot legislative strategy and tactics. Unfortunately, the historical record cannot clearly establish the nature and extent of the president's relationship with this early partisan institution.

In exercising party leadership through these various processes, President Jefferson based his partisan appeals for support on four main foundations. The first was principle. His correspondence is replete with references to the promotion of common republican principles. The mirror image of this appeal was one that invoked the specter of the Federalist opposition. Often nothing produces unity as well as a common adversary, and Jefferson frequently sought to keep his followers together by denouncing the other party. Third, Jefferson traded on the immense personal regard in which he was held by his fellow Democratic-Republicans. Finally, as president, he tried to make legislators see that his preferences were in their own self-interests.

Effect of Parties on the Presidency

By the end of Jefferson's presidency, some twenty years into the constitutional era, the unforeseen emergence of political parties had transformed the character of the presidency and indeed the U.S. political system in several respects. Their assertion and assumption of nominating responsibilities for the presidential ticket necessitated a formal change in the balloting arrangements of the electoral college. Originally, the Constitution required presidential electors to cast a single ballot with the names of two presidential candidates listed on it. After the counting of the assembled ballots, the candidate with the most votes, provided that number was a majority, was elected president. The candidate with the next largest number of votes became vice president.

Under this procedure, the election of 1800 produced a tie. The Democratic-Republican party objective before the election was to secure the selection of presidential electors committed to the slate of Jefferson for president and Aaron Burr for vice president. It did so to ensure that as president, Jefferson might not be bedeviled by the presence of a Federalist adversary in the secondary slot, as he himself had acted in quiet opposition to President Adams.

The party effort was too successful. Every elector who voted for Jefferson also voted for Burr, and vice versa; and more electors voted for Jefferson and Burr than for any other contenders. The electoral college tie sent the presidential election to the House of Representatives, where the lame-duck Federalist majority eventually consented to the choice of Jefferson.

Before the next presidential election in 1804, Congress

proposed and the state legislatures ratified the Twelfth Amendment. The change separated the ballots for president and vice president, thus allowing presidential electors effectively to vote for party tickets. This amendment fundamentally altered the status of the electors. They quickly lost the independent agent status envisioned by the Framers. Instead, they became instruments of party will.

Moreover, the parties' monopoly over presidential selection had the result of adding a new, extraconstitutional presidential eligibility requirement above and beyond those enumerated in the Constitution: a party nomination. The expectations and requirements for presidential candidates, heretofore considerable public service and esteem, came to include not only party affiliation but also party nomination.

In turn, the presence of a party's candidate for president at the head of the party ticket for elective public offices conferred on that individual the status of party leader. Once elected, that figure could presume to be something more than the head of the executive branch. Indeed, there was now a basis for claiming government chieftainship, with the idea and organization of party unifying separated national institutions under the leadership of the president.[5]

Evolving President-Party Relationship

Although aspects of presidential party leadership as developed by Thomas Jefferson endure to this day, the president-party relationship has not been static since the first decade of the nineteenth century. Rather, the relationship has gone through a number of changes. Few of these changes have been sudden and dramatic. Instead, they have been mostly gradual and evolutionary, occurring over several presidencies with their essences emerging in clear form only in retrospect.

After Jefferson's retirement in 1809, the congressional party caucus that had responded in a generally positive fashion to his leadership proved to be less accommodating to his immediate successors. Indeed, the caucus came to perceive its role in nominating and, in effect, electing presidents as subordinating the president to congressional authority.

By 1828, however, the caucus was in disarray; and the new president, Andrew Jackson, presided over important transformations in the president-party relationship. Two developments in particular were taking form at this time: the growth of national party organization and the emergence of a mass party—ordinary citizens who identified with a political party and provided electoral support for a party's candidates.

These developments significantly enhanced the president's party leadership role. The presidency became linked with a national party organization that in turn connected state and local party organizations throughout the country. This came about with the advent of the national party convention as the nominator of the president. Further, the presidency became directly tied to the citizenry of the Republic. With Jackson, a general and a popular hero, paving the way, the presidency became the focus of popular attention and representation. Meanwhile, under the astute direction of Jackson's vice president and successor in the

White House, Martin Van Buren, presidential patronage assisted the creation and strengthening of the party organizational machinery.

The next important shift in the character of president-party relations occurred in the immediate aftermath of the Civil War. The congressional Republicans reacted against President Lincoln's assertive wartime leadership by restraining his successors. Also, party leaders at the state and local levels—fortified by patronage resources and strong party identifications and loyalties in the electorate—increased in stature and significance in national politics in the latter part of the nineteenth century. They came to dominate the presidential nomination process, and the presidential nominee was usually beholden to the party organization sponsors.

After the turn of the twentieth century, the balance of power began to shift in favor of the president. Strong, assertive occupants of the White House such as Theodore Roosevelt and Woodrow Wilson invigorated the office of the presidency by dint of personality. An increasing world role for the United States enhanced the visibility and power of the presidential offices. Further, advancing communications technology focused more popular attention on the president. In keeping with these developments, the president's party leadership position gradually became more commanding.

Franklin Roosevelt ushered in the modern era in president-party relations with his long presidential tenure, 1933-1945. In responding to the Great Depression and World War II, Roosevelt effected a dramatic increase in the size and scope of the federal executive. This had important implications for party relations, because Roosevelt came to rely on executive branch personnel to perform many of the political and social service roles that had traditionally been the province of the political party.

Since then, further advancements in communications technology, especially television, served to connect the president even more directly with the public. This weakened the party's traditional position as intermediary between the two. In addition, and indeed in response, party identification in the electorate began to decline. Party reforms reduced the power of the party organization in the nomination of the president.

Thus, the president-party relationship has gone through a number of twists and turns over the years. Jefferson's legacy persists, but it has been augmented by numerous additional trends. The present status of the relationship has been shaped by and remains rooted in these various and conflicting patterns. Further changes, no doubt, will be forthcoming.

The President and the National Party Organization

Within a quarter-century of Jefferson's retirement from the presidency in 1809, a new arena of presidential party leadership opened up with the establishment of national party organizations.[6] This institution arose after the collapse of the congressional party caucus as a nominating device. Beginning in the 1790s, congressional party caucuses had assumed responsibility for nominating the parties' presidential tickets. The gradual demise of the Federalist party following Jefferson and the Democratic-Republicans' electoral success in 1800 left the Democratic-

Republican caucus in effect as the designator of the president, with the electoral college eventually ratifying its choice.

The caucus effected reasonably smooth party leadership transitions from Jefferson to James Madison in 1808-1809, and from Madison to James Monroe in 1816-1817. The culmination of the Virginia dynasty following Monroe's retirement from the White House in 1824 left the party caucus without an obvious consensus choice. Internal division ensued. The decline of interparty competition had served eventually to heighten intraparty competition for the presidential nomination that was tantamount to election.

Further, the very concept of the caucus came under attack from various outside sources. States and congressional districts not in the hands of the dominant Democratic-Republican party had no voice in the caucus proceedings. These areas found themselves excluded from meaningful participation in presidential selection.

In 1824, the supporters of Andrew Jackson's presidential candidacy assaulted the caucus procedure as too elitist. Embracing values of popular participation and reflecting the interests of outsiders in the political order, Jackson's cause did not draw much support from the members of the Washington-based caucus.

Alternatively, others perceived the caucus to be a de facto denial of the constitutional principle of separation of powers, since it allowed a congressional majority to choose the president. Under the weight of these onslaughts, the caucus as a nominating device virtually disintegrated in the mid-1820s, although for a brief time state legislative party caucuses engaged in nominating activities.

The controversy over the caucus was part of a larger issue, the growing division within the dominant Democratic-Republican party. Jackson's 1824 candidacy, followed by his successful run for the presidency in 1828, clearly split the party into two irreconcilable wings. Before the 1832 presidential election, with the caucus discredited and inoperative, a new format for presidential nominations came into being.

The Jackson faction, now styling itself the Democrats, along with the anti-Jackson elements, calling themselves National Republicans, and a third group, the Anti-Masons, separately convened to name their presidential tickets. These conventions, the first in U.S. history, brought together delegations from state parties, thus opening up participation in the nomination process to representatives of the rank-and-file party members. The concept took hold, and since then the quadrennial conventions have been the standard feature of the presidential nominating process.

In 1848, the Democratic national convention inaugurated the practice whereby that body authorized and established a national party committee consisting of leaders of state parties to conduct presidential campaigns and to guide the national party's fortunes between elections. Traditionally, the national committees comprise representatives designated by the state party organizations and ratified by the national conventions. These committees chose individuals to head them, thus creating the office of national party chair.

During the 1920s, national party chairs began staffing national party headquarters on a permanent basis. These national organizations formed the apex of a hierarchical party organization pyramid, atop the similarly constituted state and local party organizations. These, then, are the elements of the national party organization: the convention, the committee, the chair, and the headquarters staff.

Changing Patterns of Interaction

The traditional patterns of interaction between president and national party organization emerged out of mutual needs. A presidential aspirant needed the party nomination to legitimize the candidacy. Further, a nominee needed the resources of the party organization to conduct the general election campaign. Following a successful effort to elect its nominee, the party organization could then justifiably claim the fruits of federal patronage distributed through the executive to its loyal laborers.

Over the past half-century, three important developments have altered the traditional nature of the relationship between the president and the national party organization: changes in the structure of the presidential campaign organization, the emergence of the civil service, and the establishment and expansion of the White House Office.

The critical question in the structure of the presidential campaign organization is the status of the national party organization. A century ago, the contemporary expectation was that it would be peripheral.

Vast patronage resources once awaited the victorious party assuming control of the executive branch, but the expansive coverage of civil service has reduced drastically the quantity of political appointments. The remaining appointments are at such high and specialized levels that the party organization is less often able to provide qualified candidates.

Finally, the establishment and expansion of the White House Office has provided the president with an in-house assemblage of loyalists willing and able to do the sorts of political chores previously delegated to the national party organization. Their presence, and the president's reliance on them, render the party organization less meaningful in presidential politics.

Forms of Interaction

The president and the national party organization interact in selecting and deploying the party chair, managing party headquarters, establishing financial and organizational plans, arranging and running the convention, and managing the nomination and election campaigns.

Selection of the Party Chair

The party chair sits at the hub of the relationship between the president and the national party organization. The national party committee formally names its chair.

The national party committee traditionally represents the state parties. The Republican National Committee is organized according to the principle of state equality, with each state party designating a national committeeman, national committeewoman, and state chair. In addition to the states, the District of Columbia and the territories of Guam, Puerto Rico, and the Virgin Islands receive similar representation.

The Democratic National Committee is over twice as large as its Republican counterpart, and its representational basis is much more complicated. In addition to state and territory party representatives and officers, proportionally represented, ex officio membership is granted to representatives of the party's governors, mayors, county officials, members of Congress, and headquarters officials. Provision is also made for at-large members.

The committee organizes and conducts the national convention, and it asserts responsibility for the conduct of national election campaigns. Normally, its most significant collective action is to elect its chair.

More than a century of custom and practice provide, however, that immediately following the nominating convention, the presidential nominee recommends a candidate for the party chair. The national committee then ratifies that choice. This procedure developed to unify the presidential campaign with the party effort. It carries over to the victor's incumbency, making the national party chair of the president's party in effect a presidential appointee.

The average tenure for post-World War II national chairs of the party controlling the White House is approximately two and one-half years. Thus, virtually all presidents have the opportunity to interact with the national party in selection of the national chair. Among modern presidents, only Lyndon Johnson never exercised the opportunity to choose a party chair. *(See "Lyndon B. Johnson," p. 239, in this chapter.)*

Customarily, when a vacancy exists, perhaps at the instigation of the president, the national committee sends a delegation of its members to call on the president at the White House to be informed of the president's choice. The national committee then convenes to elect that person. Having done so, the national committee's subsequent interaction with the president typically is limited to occasional presidential addresses and receptions scheduled in conjunction with regular meetings of the committee.

Traditionally, the eligibility requirements for the position of national party chair have been very loose, affording the president discretion. As often as not, the chair has not been a member of the committee at the time of selection. Under rules established in the 1970s, both major parties now require that the chair's position be full-time. In 1982, however, the requirement was relaxed when President Ronald Reagan wanted to designate Sen. Paul Laxalt of Nevada to succeed Richard Richards as party chair. The Republican National Committee obliged the president by creating a new unsalaried position of general chair of the Republican party especially for Laxalt. In that role, Laxalt became nominally responsible for coordinating Republican party political operations on Capitol Hill, at party headquarters, at the White House, and in the forthcoming presidential campaign. In addition, to conform with party rules, the national committee elected Frank Fahrenkopf, a Laxalt associate and former Nevada state GOP chair, as its titular salaried chair with responsibility for party headquarters management.

Most observers of this development assumed that Laxalt would be the dominant partner in a tandem arrangement. Over the years, however, it became increasingly clear that Laxalt's title was honorary, and Fahrenkopf emerged as a relatively strong party chair. After Laxalt declined to run for reelection to the Senate in 1986, he quietly abandoned his title as general chair, and the position was not filled. Meanwhile, Fahrenkopf remained as party chair through the end of the Reagan administration.

As the top leadership position in the party organization hierarchy, the position of party chair unquestionably has high symbolic value, especially to the activists who make up the party organization at all levels. Its high visibility makes it something of a plum for persons and factions within the party. Its substantive significance varies considerably according to the expectations of the nominee or president and the orientations of the designated chair.

Looking at decisions made by nonincumbent presidential nominees, some generalizations can be made about patterns of recruitment for the party chair. In recognition of services on the nominee's behalf, the position is often awarded to a personal loyalist from the preconvention campaign organization or to a state organizational leader who has delivered crucial delegate support. *(See Table 1.)*

Examples of personal loyalists serving nominees include Democrat James A. Farley (chosen by Franklin D. Roosevelt in 1932), Republican Herbert Brownell (by Thomas E. Dewey in 1944), Democrat Stephen A. Mitchell (by Adlai E. Stevenson in 1952), Republican Dean Burch (by Barry Goldwater in 1964), and Democrat Lawrence F. O'Brien (by Hubert H. Humphrey in 1968). All were recruited from the preconvention personal organization of the nominee. Loyalty and personal sponsorship brought them to their position. With the exception of O'Brien, each had come from the same state as the nominee and had worked in previous campaigns on the nominee's behalf. In selecting a personal loyalist as party chair, the nominee rewards a trusted associate, takes steps to ensure the responsiveness of the party machinery, and stamps a personal imprint on it.

In past instances of closely contested nominations, the position of party chair became a bargaining gambit for delegate support. Traditionally, the key units of bargaining have been state delegations under the control of powerful state party chieftains. In 1948, Dewey was obligated to the Pennsylvania delegation for its vital support. He reciprocated by naming as party chair a then obscure member of that delegation, Rep. Hugh D. Scott, Jr. In 1952, the national chair was Michigan party leader Arthur Summerfield's prize for declaring for Dwight D. Eisenhower at a crucial moment.

The nominee may use the prerogative of naming the party chair to cultivate or mollify important party and electoral constituencies. Symbolic demographic variables such as region, religion, and sex have come into play here. For example, nominees have used the position of party chair to reinforce the geographical distribution of party power (as they do by balancing the ticket with the vice-presidential nomination) or to recognize a regional center of party power. Summerfield's selection gave representation to the traditional heartland of the Republican party. In 1960, Sen. Henry Jackson, hailing from Washington in the Pacific Northwest, complemented a balanced Democratic ticket composed of a northeasterner, John F. Kennedy, for president and a southwesterner, Lyndon B. Johnson, for vice president.

For more than three decades, from 1928 to 1960, every national chair of the Democratic party was an Irish Catholic. This tradition recognized the influence of that powerful constituency within the party organization. It also compensated for the absence, except for the ill-fated Al Smith, of a Roman Catholic among the party's presidential nominees. Since the 1960 nomination of John Kennedy, the relevance of this consideration has receded.

Democratic nominee George S. McGovern's 1972 selection of Jean Westwood, the first woman to chair a national party committee, reflected two important new developments in nominating politics. The first was the growing clout of women in party affairs. The second was the emergence of new bargaining units at the convention transcending the state party delegations, caucuses that represented pressure groups in the larger political order.

Similar symbolic considerations have turned the party

Table 1 Campaign Party Chairs Chosen by Nonincumbent Presidential Nominees, 1948-1989

Name, Party, Years of Service	Chosen by	State	Age	Religion	Political background
Hugh D. Scott, Jr. (R, 1948-1952)	Dewey	Pennsylvania	47	Episcopalian	U.S. representative
Arthur Summerfield (R, 1952-1953)	Eisenhower	Michigan	53	—	State organization leader
Stephen Mitchell (D, 1952-1955)	Stevenson	Illinois a	49	Catholic	Personal associate of nominee
Paul Butler (D, 1955-1960)	Stevenson b	Indiana	50	Catholic	State organization leader
Thruston B. Morton (R, 1959-1961)	Nixon b	Kentucky	52	Episcopalian	U.S. senator
Henry M. Jackson (D, 1960-1961)	Kennedy	Washington	48	Presbyterian	U.S. senator
Dean Burch (D, 1964-1965)	Goldwater	Arizona a	37	—	Personal associate of nominee
Ray Bliss (D, 1966-1969)	Nixon b	Ohio	58	Episcopalian	State organization leader
Lawrence F. O'Brien (D, 1968-1969)	Humphrey	Massachusetts	51	Catholic	Federal executive
Jean Westwood (D, 1972)	McGovern	Utah	49	Mormon	State organization leader
Robert Strauss (D, 1972-1977)	Carter b	Texas	55	Jewish	State organization leader
William E. Brock III (R, 1977-1981)	Reagan b	Tennessee	46	Presbyterian	Former U.S. senator
Charles Manatt (D, 1981-1985)	Mondale b	California	48	Methodist	State organization leader
Paul Kirk (D, 1985-1989)	Dukakis b	Massachusetts	50	Catholic	National party official
Frank Fahrenkopf (R, 1983-1989)	Bush b	Nevada	48	Catholic	State organization leader

Source: From Harold F. Bass, Jr., "The President and the National Party Organization," in *Presidents and Their Parties: Leadership or Neglect?* ed. Robert Harmel (New York: Praeger, 1983), 63.
Note: Dash (—) means no religious affiliation.
a. Nominees chose party chair from home state.
b. Nominees chose to retain the incumbent party chair.

chair into a potential consolation prize to an unsuccessful aspirant for a spot on the presidential ticket. At the 1960 Democratic convention, nominee John Kennedy offered the vice-presidential nomination to his defeated rival, Lyndon Johnson. After opposition to Johnson's proposed nomination quickly developed among certain elements within the liberal wing of the party, Robert F. Kennedy, his brother's campaign manager, informed Johnson that should he wish to withdraw, he could be named party chair instead. Johnson declined and accepted the initial offer. The position of party chair then went to Henry Jackson, who had been a leading contender for the vice-presidential nomination.

On numerous occasions, presidential nominees have elected to forgo their prerogatives of designating the party chair in favor of retaining the incumbent. In performing their responsibilities, party chairs can develop strong and vocal personal followings, which provide pressures and incentives for their retention, in recognition of jobs well done and in the interests of party unity. Between 1948 and 1988, eight party chairs were retained by nonincumbent presidential nominees: Democrat Paul Butler was kept on by Stevenson in 1956; Republican Thruston Morton by Nixon in 1960; Republican Ray Bliss by Nixon in 1968; Democrat Robert Strauss by Carter in 1976; Republican William Brock by Reagan in 1980; Democrat Charles Manatt by Mondale in 1984; Democrat Paul Kirk by Dukakis in 1988; and Republican Frank Fahrenkopf by Bush, also in 1988.

A final consideration taken into account by the nominee about the selection of the party chair is the primary role the chair is expected to play in the upcoming general election campaign. Traditionally, that role was one of management, concentrating energies and talents on problems of campaign organization and strategy. A recently emerging role is that of spokesperson and campaigner, highly visible but largely separated from the centers of campaign decision making.

Presidents-elect and incumbent presidents exercise selection prerogatives when vacancies exist in the position of

party chair. From an examination of such selections in the years since World War II, certain patterns emerge. *(See Table 2.)*

Chairs have been recruited from diverse political backgrounds, with state organization leaders and legislators predominating. All have been identified with the political causes and campaigns of their presidents, but relatively few can be considered close associates. Geographically, most of these chairs have come from the East and Midwest. Two came from the same state as their presidential sponsors, six from the same region, and nine from different regions. Most of the Democratic chairs have been Catholics, while Methodists and Episcopalians have predominated among Republicans. Their average age at election has approached fifty. Gerald Ford chose the only woman, Mary Louise Smith (1974).

Vacancies between the quadrennial nominating conventions come about for a variety of reasons. On several occasions, presidential promotions of chairs to high-level government positions have created openings. Truman made Sen. Howard McGrath attorney general; Richard Nixon chose Rep. Rogers C. B. Morton to head the Interior Department; and Ford sent George Bush to the People's Republic of China to head the United States Liaison Office.

Several chairs have left for personal reasons or to pursue their own political interests. Although presidential dissatisfaction has not loomed particularly large in the departures of party chairs, press speculation has addressed this possibility; and scandal tainted the resignations of both Democrat William Boyle (1951) and Republican Wesley Roberts (1953).

A brief review of presidential decisions about party chairs since World War II illustrates some of the dynamics of the selection process. When Harry Truman became president on the death of Franklin Roosevelt in 1945, the Democratic party chair was Robert Hannegan, an old Missouri friend and ally of the new president. When Hannegan resigned in poor health in 1947, President Truman named Senator McGrath to succeed him.

Table 2 National Chairs, President's Party, 1944-1989

Name, Party, Years of Service	Chosen by	State	Age	Religion	Political background
Robert Hannegan (D, 1944-1947)	Roosevelt	Missouri	41	Catholic	State organization leader, federal executive
J. Howard McGrath (D, 1947-1949)	Truman	Rhode Island	44	Catholic	U.S. senator
William Boyle (D, 1949-1951)	Truman	Missouri	47	Catholic	Presidential associate, national party official
Frank McKinney (D, 1951-1952)	Truman	Indiana	47	Catholic	State organization leader
C. Wesley Roberts (R, 1953)	Eisenhower	Kansas	49	Methodist	State organization leader
Leonard W. Hall (R, 1953-1957)	Eisenhower	New York	53	Episcopalian	Former U.S. representative
H. Meade Alcorn (R, 1957-1959)	Eisenhower	Connecticut	50	Congregationalist	State organization leader
Thruston B. Morton (R, 1959-1961)	Eisenhower	Kentucky	51	Episcopalian	U.S. senator
John Bailey (D, 1961-1968)	Kennedy	Connecticut	57	Catholic	State organization leader
Rogers C. B. Morton (R, 1969-1971)	Nixon	Maryland	55	Episcopalian	U.S. representative
Robert J. Dole (R, 1971-1973)	Nixon	Kansas	48	Methodist	U.S. senator
George Bush (R, 1973-1974)	Nixon	Texas	49	Episcopalian	Former U.S. representative, federal executive
Mary Louise Smith (R, 1974-1976)	Ford	Iowa	59	Protestant	State organization leader, national party official
Kenneth M. Curtis (D, 1977-1978)	Carter	Maine	45	Protestant	Former governor
John White (D, 1978-1981)	Carter	Texas	54	Baptist	Federal executive
Richard Richards (R, 1981-1983)	Reagan	Utah	49	Presbyterian	State organization leader
Paul D. Laxalt (R, 1983-1986) [a]	Reagan	Nevada	60	Catholic	U.S. senator
Frank Fahrenkopf (R, 1983-1989)	Reagan	Nevada	43	Catholic	State organization leader
Lee Atwater (R, 1989-)	Bush	South Carolina	37	Methodist	Political consultant

Source: From Harold F. Bass, Jr., "The President and the National Party Organization," in *Presidents and Their Parties: Leadership or Neglect?,* ed. Robert Harmel (New York: Praeger, 1983), 74.

a. General chair

Ten months after the 1948 election, Truman moved Senator McGrath into the executive branch as attorney general and elevated William Boyle, the executive vice chair of the Democratic National Committee, to the position of chair. Boyle was an old family friend of the Trumans and a longstanding political ally who had been very active in the 1948 presidential campaign. Boyle's tenure concluded in 1951, ostensibly because of his health. Allegations of his involvement in an influence-peddling scandal, however, were circulating at the time of his resignation.

Truman's choice as his successor was Frank McKinney, a state party leader in Indiana. McKinney served through the 1952 national convention, after which he stepped aside in favor of Stephen Mitchell, the choice of presidential nominee Adlai Stevenson.

After winning the 1952 presidential election, Dwight Eisenhower brought his choice as campaign party chair, Arthur Summerfield, into his cabinet as postmaster general. To fill the vacancy in the party chair, the president chose a longtime party organization leader from his home state of Kansas, Wesley Roberts. Roberts had worked at the national party headquarters during the presidential campaign as organization director, where he coordinated the party's role in the presidential campaign with that of the Citizens for Eisenhower. He had served only two months as chair when he resigned amid charges of influence peddling back in Kansas.

Eisenhower's choice to fill the position was representative Leonard W. Hall of New York. Hall had previously chaired the Republican congressional campaign committee and had traveled with the Eisenhower campaign, providing liaison with the Republican National Committee. Hall served for the remainder of Eisenhower's first term. After directing the successful reelection campaign, he resigned to pursue his own political objectives in New York.

Hall's successor was H. Meade Alcorn of Connecticut. Long active in state and local party politics, Alcorn had supported Eisenhower's candidacy in 1952 and had been a member of the national committee since 1953. He stepped down as chair in 1959, after the party's poor showing in the midterm congressional elections.

Eisenhower chose Sen. Thruston Morton of Kentucky to replace Alcorn. A member of a prominent Kentucky family, Morton was a former member of Congress who also had served in the Eisenhower administration as the State Department's legislative liaison before his election to the Senate. Morton remained party chair through the 1960 nomination and general election campaigns. He resigned midway through 1961, in preparation for his successful senatorial reelection campaign in 1962.

After receiving the 1960 Democratic nomination, John Kennedy designated Sen. Henry M. Jackson of Washington as a party chair for the duration of the campaign. Jackson, passed over for the vice presidential nomination in favor of Lyndon Johnson, received public visibility and performed a valuable service as a campaign spokesman throughout the fall contest. After the election, Jackson resigned to devote full attention to his senatorial responsibilities. Jackson's departure freed Kennedy to install Connecticut party leader John Bailey, a long-time supporter, as national party chair.

When Lyndon Johnson became president after Kennedy's assassination, he kept Bailey on as party chair, although he inserted his own loyalists at the party headquarters. Bailey stayed on as party chair through the 1968 national convention. Afterward, deferring to the wish of nominee Hubert H. Humphrey, he gave up the position to Lawrence F. O'Brien, manager of Hubert H. Humphrey's successful nomination campaign. Serving for seven and one-half years, Bailey has the longest tenure among the post-World War II national party chairs.

After winning the Republican nomination in 1968, Nixon responded to strong party organization support for the retention of incumbent party chair Ray Bliss by keeping Bliss in that position until after the victory in the November election.

At that time, Bliss resigned with Nixon's blessing, enabling the president to install someone of his own choosing. The new president indicated his preference for Rep. Rogers Morton of Maryland (brother of Thruston Morton) to take the reins of the party organization. Morton served for two years. Shortly after the 1970 congressional elections, Nixon appointed him secretary of interior, and he resigned as party chair.

Nixon chose Sen. Robert Dole of Kansas to succeed Morton. Dole served through the 1972 reelection campaign and dutifully resigned, in response to the president's expectation, to be replaced by George Bush, a Texas political figure fresh from a tour of duty as ambassador to the United Nations. Bush stayed in office for the rest of Nixon's tenure. After Nixon resigned in 1974, the new president, Gerald Ford, named Bush to head the U.S. Liaison Office in the People's Republic of China. Ford then elevated the vice chair Mary Louise Smith of Iowa to the position, where she remained through the conclusion of Ford's term.

When Jimmy Carter won the Democratic presidential nomination in 1976, he chose to keep on incumbent party chair Robert Strauss through the election campaign. After the election, Carter appointed Strauss and named former Maine governor Kenneth Curtis to be party chair. Within a year, Curtis resigned amid reports of persistent squabbling between the White House and the party headquarters. Carter then named Texas politico John White as his choice for the party chair. White continued in office until after the

party's defeat in the 1980 presidential election.

In 1980 Ronald Reagan's nomination as the Republican candidate resulted in the temporary retention of William Brock as party chair. After the election victory, Brock moved into the same administration position that Strauss had occupied. On Reagan's recommendation, the party chair went to Utah party leader Richard Richards. Richards resigned following the 1982 midterm congressional elections because of longstanding rumors of White House dissatisfaction with his performance.

Existing party rules required that the position of party chair be full time, which seemed to preclude the choice of an incumbent legislator. President Reagan arranged, however, for Sen. Paul Laxalt of Nevada to assume the specially created position of general chair of the Republican party. This position was superimposed on the traditional national committee chair, which went to Frank Fahrenkopf, one of Laxalt's associates in the Nevada Republican party.

When Laxalt retired from the Senate after the 1986 elections, he also took leave of his position as general chair and was not replaced. Fahrenkopf remained as chair to the end of the Reagan presidency. His replacement, the choice of president-elect George Bush, was campaign manager Lee Atwater.

In sum, the selection of the national party chair is a presidential prerogative, although it is usually exercised in a fashion mindful of pressures within the party and the larger body politic. Presidents and presidential nominees can reward trusted loyalists, repay political debts incurred, or reach out to new party constituencies.

Deployment of the Party Chair

Installed in office by the president, and serving at the president's pleasure, national chairs encounter their party leaders in circumstances that vary considerably in both frequency and substantive significance. The tendency is toward infrequent meetings in rather formal, ceremonial

Lyndon B. Johnson Library

President Lyndon Johnson talks with Democratic party chair John Bailey in the Oval Office in 1968. Serving for seven and one-half years, Bailey has the longest tenure among the post-World War II national party chairs.

settings. To be sure, President Truman had a standing appointment every Wednesday afternoon with the Democratic national chair to discuss party politics. Somewhat similarly, President Eisenhower genuinely expected his party chair to be the "political expert" in his delegation of administrative responsibilities.

Still, a facetious anecdote shared by Sen. Robert Dole about his tenure as party chair captures well the contemporary character of the relationship. Dole tells of receiving a telephone call from the White House, informing him that his longstanding request to see President Nixon was about to be granted. All he had to do was to turn his television set to the proper channel to receive the president's scheduled campaign address.[7]

Cabinet Meetings. Although no one has served simultaneously as party chair and as a cabinet secretary since 1947, several party chairs have made individual arrangements to attend cabinet meetings either regularly or intermittently. At these sessions, party chairs can be kept informed of the administration's public policy proposals, can assess their partisan ramifications, and can seek to present the party's perspective on them. In addition, cabinet meetings can provide the chair with opportunities to request and establish clearance procedures for political appointments. In general, while the party chair's physical presence at cabinet meetings undoubtedly affords an avenue of access to the president, the value is more symbolic than substantive.

Congressional Leadership Meetings. The inclination of some modern presidents to name incumbent legislators as party chair has introduced a new arena for interaction—the weekly congressional leadership meetings. Although none of these chairs has been a ranking member of the party congressional hierarchy, several of them (along with chairs who are not members of Congress) have requested that they be present at sessions where legislative strategy is planned and progress is monitored. Here, the presence of the party chair enables coordination of legislative activities with the party's organs of party policy and publicity and provides a forum to bring the chair's point of view directly to the president.

Headquarters Management

Another form of interaction between the White House and the national committee is the management of the national party headquarters. Ostensibly, headquarters management would appear to be the primary responsibility of the chair, but few chairs have devoted much personal attention to this task. Other responsibilities with higher priority and other institutional and professional affiliations typically conflict with that of administrator. The accepted procedure is for the chair to exercise discretion in delegating managerial authority to a chosen subordinate. The chair then remains free in varying degrees to engage in other activities.

On several occasions in recent years, the president or White House aides have deployed at party headquarters a presidential agent with managerial authority. Typically, these instances have occurred when a legislator has been named chair and by definition serves part-time. Such a situation developed during the Truman presidency with the assignment of Truman's old Missouri political assistant William Boyle to a management position at the Democratic

National Committee then headed by Sen. Howard McGrath.

In his first months in office, Nixon sought to establish an analogous arrangement at the Republican National Committee. According to journalists Rowland Evans and Robert Novak, he promised a position there to longtime associate Murray Chotiner. Their apparent understanding was that Chotiner would have responsibility for running the headquarters operation with an appropriate title under a figurehead chair. When the designated chair, Rep. Rogers Morton, refused to go along with the plan, it fell through. Subsequently, however, Nixon succeeded with a similar arrangement, using Thomas Evans at the outset of the tenure of Morton's successor, Sen. Robert Dole.[8]

Even chairs who are not members of Congress receive this treatment. While retaining Kennedy-designate John Bailey as party chair, President Lyndon Johnson sent his Texas operative Clifton Carter to the Democratic National Committee headquarters to represent the president's interests there. President Jimmy Carter originally installed fellow-Georgian Phil Wise as Chairman Ken Curtis's executive director.

Financial and Organizational Collaboration

The national party organization engages in a great deal of congenial accommodation on behalf of the White House. Routinely, the White House relies on the financial and organizational structures of the national committee to sponsor what are really White House programs. For example, the White House bills the national committee for travel and living expenses incurred by the president while attending to party leadership responsibilities. Such situations include personal campaigning, campaigning for other party candidates, and appearances at party-sponsored affairs such as fund-raisers, rallies, and the national convention. Occasionally, the national committee can be prevailed upon to carry on its payroll individuals who actually work at the White House.

The national committee staff and the White House also interact in the preparation of publications that serve as publicity for the administration. The White House staff is in a position to furnish the party headquarters with data and inside information to make the publication attractive, relevant, and substantive. Typically, the party headquarters both seeks and welcomes such assistance.

Convention Arrangements and Management

An impending national nominating convention provides the setting for a great deal of interaction between the White House and the national party organization. Although the national committee has responsibility for arranging and conducting the convention, it does so under the close supervision of the incumbent president, even when the incumbent is not a candidate for the presidential nomination.

When the party is out of power, the national committee is supposed to be neutral toward competing candidacies for the nomination. When an incumbent president is seeking the nomination, however, the party headquarters usually strongly supports that candidacy.

When the incumbent is not a candidate for the nomination, concern and interest about the party's choice abound. Typically, the retiring president's aides will monitor convention arrangements and become deeply involved in maneuverings during the proceedings. In past years, these agents have afforded the outgoing president considerable influence at the convention.

The national committee formally establishes the site of the convention, but the president's preference, if not volunteered, is routinely solicited and accepted. According to Nixon campaign aide Jeb Stuart Magruder, for personal and political reasons Nixon insisted that the 1972 Republican national convention meet in San Diego, California. The White House sent Magruder, an official at the Committee for the Reelection of the President, to Denver, Colorado, in July 1971, to monitor the meeting of the Republican National Committee's site selection committee. The committee was not inclined to choose San Diego, but the party chair, Sen. Robert Dole of Kansas, informed the members that "if the president wanted the convention in San Diego, it would just have to be in San Diego." [9] Although the site selection committee obediently chose San Diego, the convention site subsequently had to be shifted to Miami Beach, Florida. The change took place amid concerns about insufficient hotel facilities in San Diego and fears that security arrangements there would be inadequate to deal with the expected onslaught of demonstrators at the convention site protesting the Vietnam War.

Similarly, the convention date can be manipulated to the benefit of the incumbent. It is no coincidence that modern conventions expected to nominate incumbent presidents all have been scheduled relatively late in the summer, after those of the opposition party. (See Table 3.) The 1964 and 1968 Democratic national conventions occurred the week of President Lyndon Johnson's birthday. In the former instance, the convention schedule afforded time for a birthday celebration. For a unified party led by an incumbent president, a late convention builds momentum for the upcoming general election campaign.

When the president is a candidate, considerable White House input is usually evident in the preparation of the party platform. Such participation ensures that the president's policies receive party endorsement, equates the party's stance on issues with that of the president, and precludes significant divergence toward an independent position. Even when the president is not a candidate, the presidential presence is likely to hover over platform deliberations. Beyond party policy, recent presidents and White House staffs have concerned themselves with administrative details of convention management, to the point of preparing minute-by-minute scenarios.

Traditionally, the national party has convened only in connection with the nomination of the presidential ticket. In 1974, however, the out-of-power Democrats met in Kansas City for an issues conference midway through the presidential term. Four years later, with Democrat Jimmy Carter in the White House, a similar conference was held in Memphis, which provided an unprecedented opportunity for interaction between the White House and the national committee.

On this occasion, encountering substantial anti-Carter sentiment in the ranks of the delegates, the White House and presidential agents at the national party headquarters designed and controlled the agenda. They mounted a monitoring operation on the floor of the conference to ensure that the administration's positions would prevail against intraparty challenges. The effort duplicated the typical pattern of White House surveillance and supervision re-

Table 3 National Party Convention Sites, Dates, and Nominees, 1944-1988

Year	President	Democrats	Republicans
1944	Roosevelt (D)	Chicago July 19-21 Roosevelt [a]	Chicago June 26-28 Dewey
1948	Truman (D)	Philadelphia July 12-14 Truman [a]	Philadelphia June 21-25 Dewey
1952	Truman (D)	Chicago July 21-26 Stevenson	Chicago July 7-11 Eisenhower [a]
1956	Eisenhower (R)	Chicago August 13-17 Stevenson	San Francisco August 20-23 Eisenhower [a]
1960	Eisenhower (R)	Los Angeles July 11-15 Kennedy [a]	Chicago July 25-28 Nixon
1964	Johnson (D)	Atlantic City August 24-27 Johnson [a]	San Francisco July 13-16 Goldwater
1968	Johnson (D)	Chicago August 26-29 Humphrey	Miami Beach August 5-8 Nixon [a]
1972	Nixon (R)	Miami Beach July 10-13 McGovern	Miami Beach August 21-23 Nixon [a]
1976	Ford (R)	New York July 12-15 Carter [a]	Kansas City August 16-19 Ford
1980	Carter (D)	New York August 11-14 Carter	Detroit July 14-17 Reagan [a]
1984	Reagan (R)	San Francisco July 16-19 Mondale	Dallas August 20-23 Reagan [a]
1988	Reagan (R)	Atlanta July 18-21 Dukakis	New Orleans August 15-18 Bush [a]

a. Won election.

peatedly demonstrated at the nominating conventions. Neither party has held a midterm convention since 1982.

Presidential exercises of convention leadership have produced a long string of successes for presidents who wanted to be renominated. Not since Chester A. Arthur in 1884 has an incumbent president who sought his party's nomination been denied it. Indeed, most of Arthur's successors have been nominated with ease. Although both Truman and Johnson were constitutionally eligible to seek another presidential term, both chose not to in the face of growing opposition.

In 1976 and 1980, strong nomination challenges were mounted against the Republican and the Democratic incumbents, respectively. Reagan's contest against President Ford and Sen. Edward Kennedy's against President Carter suggest that post-1968 reforms in the methods of selecting convention delegates may offset partially the incumbent's traditional advantages. These reforms drastically reduced the state party organizations' control over delegate selection and increased popular participation in that process.

Customarily, an incumbent president seeking the nomination could count on the support of the state party leaders. They had been the beneficiaries of presidential favors and attention and would fear presidential reprisal should support be withheld. Thus, even an unpopular president could be quite secure in the face of a nomination challenge. Party reforms deprive modern presidents of this bulwark of potential sustenance, however, leaving them potentially more vulnerable to intraparty challengers able to capitalize on popular disenchantment.

The immediate postconvention task of selecting the party chair assumed by nonincumbent presidential nominees has less relevance for incumbents. Incumbents usually retain the current chair at least through the general election. Put differently, incumbent presidents expecting renomination have installed their choices as party chairs well in advance of the nominating convention.

Presidential Election Campaigns

Journalist Theodore H. White observed that a presidential campaign "starts with a candidate, a handful of men, a theme and a plan. By November of election year it has enlisted hundreds of thousands of volunteers, politicians, state staffs, national staffs, media specialists and has become an enterprise." [10] A key question is, what is the relationship of the national party organization to the presidential campaign?

Traditionally, that role was central. National party committees came into being in the mid-nineteenth century to provide direction to the presidential campaign. Party chairs customarily served as campaign managers. Indeed, the practice of allowing the presidential nominee to name the party chair developed to facilitate integration of the presidential campaign with the party effort.

The campaign manager and a handful of key associates would set up shop at the headquarters of the national party. The party organization provided the nominee with the potent party symbol legitimizing the candidacy. Further, it made available the personnel necessary for the labor-intensive campaign that had to be waged.

More recently, however, presidential nominees have tended instead to establish autonomous campaign organizations, headquartered separately from the national party. A number of factors account for this development. Strategic considerations can turn a campaign away from the party organizations. A nominee representing the minority party in the electorate, for example, might prefer to maintain some distance between the candidacy and the party effort in hopes of attracting broader support. Republican Richard Nixon's 1960 and 1968 campaigns took this approach.

On the Democratic side, the relative autonomy of Adlai Stevenson's 1952 campaign resulted in part from his ongoing status as governor of Illinois, necessitating the establishment of campaign headquarters in Springfield, the state capital. The Stevenson campaign also wanted to distance itself symbolically from the "mess in Washington," the home base of Democratic president Harry Truman and the national party headquarters.

Modern presidential nominees seek to appeal to an electorate that is decreasingly dependent on partisan sources and structures for political information, economic employment, and social services. As a result, the electorate appears decreasingly inclined to make durable partisan attachments. Thus, the nominees are wary and disinclined

to rely primarily on the party organization to carry them to victory.

Modern communications and transportation also have altered the character of election campaigns. Television brings a candidate into living rooms throughout the country. Jet airplanes allow an office seeker to cross the country both rapidly and comfortably. Candidates now can wage far more individualistic efforts than they could previously, and with far less need to rely on the party.

From a different standpoint, changes in the rules governing presidential nominations and elections have contributed to this shift toward more autonomous campaigns. The expansion of presidential primaries has made the coveted presidential nomination increasingly attainable through an appeal to the party electorate rather than the party organization. Indeed, recent nominating conventions have served less as decision-making bodies than as ratification conventions for the party's nominee, already chosen in the fragmented and decentralized delegate selection contests.

This development contributes to autonomy in the campaign organization, since candidates must assemble an effective campaign staff well before the nominating convention in order to run in the primaries. During the preconvention period, unless an incumbent president is seeking the nomination, the party organization is expected to be neutral toward competing candidacies, which precludes integration of the party and the campaign staffs. Yet after the convention, the tested campaign vehicle of the victor remains intact. This both complicates integration and makes it relatively unnecessary.

Finally, federal election laws enacted in the 1970s require a separate campaign organization for a candidate to qualify for public funds. Thus, the likelihood of the traditional sort of integrated campaign, conducted under the auspices of the party apparatus, is virtually nil.

All in all, no longer does the presidential campaign provide the context for interaction initiating the president-to-be's leadership relationship with the national party organization. The other traditions on which the relationship was based—political operations and patronage—also have eroded. Thus, the national party organization has become increasingly superfluous in presidential politics.

Presidential Party Leadership within the Executive

Presidential party leadership within the executive branch has undergone dramatic structural changes since the 1930s. White House aides have taken over party management responsibilities once assigned to members of the cabinet, particularly the postmaster general. Appointments once provided the president as party chief with party-building resources, but the decline in the quantity and elevation in the quality of presidential patronage have diminished drastically this party leadership consideration. Although partisanship is still a part of presidential appointments, it remains significant primarily as an indicator of policy responsiveness and has become largely divorced from party-building concerns.

The Constitution authorizes the president to act as chief executive, that is, as head of the executive branch. Party leadership augments executive authority in presidential relations with the administration and the bureaucracy.

In the context of party leadership in the executive, three conceptual distinctions should be made. First, the word *presidency* refers to the office of the president, those elements within the executive branch most directly under the control of the chief executive. Second, *administration* applies to a particular president and the surrounding team of appointed aides, advisers, and managers within the upper echelons of the executive branch. Third, the *bureaucracy* is the permanent government, the men and women who are essentially full-time governmental employees more removed from the president's direct supervision.

Party Management in the Executive Branch

The president's exercise of party leadership has long featured the establishment of organizational bases within the executive branch for oversight of party affairs. Traditionally, the president's cabinet, composed of the executive department heads, included one or more key political advisers who were deeply involved in party management.

The Post Office and Party Politics

For more than a century, the post office provided the customary haven for a political adviser and party manager. Since it was established as a cabinet office during President Andrew Jackson's administration, the position of postmaster general often went to a leading party strategist. Before the Civil War new presidents frequently named their campaign managers as postmasters general. In that position, this person's political acumen could be put to fruitful use. The primary task was to allocate the considerable resources of federal patronage available through the post office.

With the strengthening of party organization in the latter half of the nineteenth century, the postmaster generalship regularly went to a prominent party politician. After the turn of the century, it became established practice to place the national party chair in that position.

George Cortelyou (R, appointed in 1905), Frank Hitchcock (R, 1909), Will Hays (R, 1921), James Farley (D, 1933), Robert Hannegan (D, 1945), and Arthur Summerfield (R, 1953) were all incumbent party chairs who became postmasters general. Democrat Frank Walker (D, 1943) reversed the process when, while serving as postmaster general, he became the party chair in 1943. Hitchcock and Summerfield resigned their position as party chair on assuming their responsibilities at the post office; the others held the two positions simultaneously, at least for a time.

The alliance was one of convenience, and the keystone was government patronage, dispensed by the post office to recipients authorized by the party organization. This practice also gave formal representation to the party organization in the inner circles of presidential politics. Thus, President Truman could refer to Hannegan as the "political representative of the Democratic party in the cabinet of the president." [11] No party chair since Hannegan, however, has held the two offices at the same time; and no party chair since Summerfield has been named to head the post office.

Nevertheless, through the 1960s, the head of the post office continued to be associated with party politics and political operations. Lyndon Johnson named White House political aide Lawrence O'Brien postmaster general in 1965. O'Brien went on to chair the Democratic National Committee on two occasions, 1968-1969 and 1970-1972. After O'Brien resigned in 1968 to direct Sen. Robert Kennedy's presidential campaign, Johnson appointed another White House political assistant, appointments secretary Marvin Watson, a former Texas state Democratic party chair, as postmaster general. Richard Nixon's choice for that position was Winton Blount, an Alabama prominent

Courtesy of St. Louis Post-Dispatch; Harry S. Truman Library

Robert Hannegan simultaneously served as postmaster general and Democratic party chair. His good friend President Harry Truman referred to Hannegan as the "political representative of the Democratic party in the cabinet of the president."

in the growth of the Republican party in the South and a visible symbol of Nixon's southern strategy, an effort to expand his personal and partisan base in that region.

During the Nixon presidency, administrative reform changed the structure of the post office, removing it from the cabinet and reconstituting it as a government corporation, the U.S. Postal Service. This development ended the historic connection between the post office, party management, and the party chair.

Three important factors brought about this change. First, after World War II the post office had severe financial problems, which required the exercise of active and effective management at the top. The traditional assumption that the department essentially would run itself, leaving the postmaster general free to tend to partisan politics, had to be discarded. Thus began a trend toward placing business and public administration executives in this traditional sanctuary of party managers.

Second, presidents began to realize that the major justification for placing a party manager in the post office no longer applied. Even before World War II, the increasing proportion of executive branch positions under civil service protection had greatly depreciated the value of the post office as a strategic operating base for dispensing federal patronage. The civil service classification of the positions of postmasters, the basic patronage commodity, was virtually complete by 1938, although a residual degree of discretion lingered. Moreover, the Hatch Act of 1939 prohibited overtly partisan political activity of government employees. This law thereby restricted the maintenance of an ongoing political organization through a network of post office activists.

In her 1943 study of the political significance of the postmaster generalship, Dorothy G. Fowler made a prediction that became an epitaph: "Shorn of his patronage weapon, his employees forbidden to participate in party management or be assessed for campaign funds, the postmaster general may become, like his British counterpart, merely the head of a large business organization rather than the political adviser of the president." [12]

Finally, considerations of "good government" contributed to the separation of the post office from party politics. In the years immediately following World War II, influential public administration specialists decried the official coupling of the political and administrative responsibilities. The Hoover Commission officially recommended that the postmaster general "should not be an official of a political party, such as chairman of a national committee." [13]

Presidents often find it politically expedient and beneficial to appear nonpartisan. The separation of the post office from party politics provided an appropriate opportunity to do so.

The Justice Department and Party Politics

In a 1959 study, political scientist Richard Fenno observed, "If a party politician lands in the cabinet at some other position [than postmaster general], it is likely to be that of attorney general." [14]

Warren G. Harding appointed his 1920 presidential campaign manager Harry Daugherty to that position. Homer Cummings, a former chair of the Democratic National Committee, became Franklin Roosevelt's first attorney general in 1933. Soon after election in his own right in 1948, Truman moved campaign party chair Howard

McGrath over to head the Justice Department. Similarly, in 1953 Dwight Eisenhower named former GOP national chair and key campaign strategist Herbert Brownell to this position.

Subsequently, John Kennedy appointed his 1960 presidential campaign manager, brother Robert Kennedy, attorney general. Nixon did the same for his 1968 campaign manager, John Mitchell. When Mitchell resigned early in 1972 to head up Nixon's reelection effort, his successor was his deputy, Richard G. Kleindienst, an old hand in Republican presidential campaigns.

Thus, by the early 1970s, the designation of a leading campaign official as attorney general had become a standard feature of the postwar presidency. When the Watergate scandal enveloped both Mitchell and Kleindienst in criminal prosecutions that resulted in convictions, this particular recruitment pattern came under serious attack.

Presidential candidate Jimmy Carter was one of the leading critics of the modern tendency to politicize the Justice Department. Nevertheless, his choice for attorney general, Griffin B. Bell, was an old political ally, adviser, and friend. Indeed, Bell was the only figure with such a background to be named to the cabinet. In the Reagan administration, the attorney generalship went first to his California associate William French Smith. Following Smith's resignation, Edwin Meese III, an even closer political aide and adviser, took over the office.

The Justice Department always has been politically sensitive and significant. Presidents have long recognized that the office of attorney general is one that can occupy profitably the talents of a key political adviser.

Several prestigious political appointments are channelled through the Justice Department, including U.S. attorneys, assistant U.S. attorneys, and federal marshals. The department also makes important recommendations about presidential nominations of federal judges, including justices of the Supreme Court.

The increasing tendency of interest groups to resort to litigation as a means of achieving their objectives has heightened the political sensitivity of the Justice Department. The increasing extent of government regulation of the economy places the Justice Department in the midst of significant government decisions about benefits and penalties. Key political constituencies can be cultivated and managed by lending support and by exercising discretionary aspects of its law enforcement and prosecutorial powers.

It behooves a president to place a politically astute ally in this crucial post. Moreover, the position itself is a very attractive one. Compared with that of postmaster general, it is more prestigious and substantive. For a lawyer, the attorney generalship is a distinct professional as well as political honor. It is also sometimes a steppingstone to a seat on the Supreme Court.

Thus, after World War II, the attorney generalship supplanted the position of postmaster general as the office within the cabinet to be occupied by a key political adviser. Still, the attorney general is less affected by explicit party politics than was the postmaster general. The party thus lost an institutional identity within the cabinet.

White House Office

Because of the creation and growth of the White House Office, White House staff assistants today have the major responsibility for the conduct of political operations and the management of party affairs.

The White House Office was established in 1939 during Franklin Roosevelt's administration. Previous presidents had received clerical support from a handful of secretaries and personal aides, but the growing size of and demands on the federal government in the New Deal era led a 1937 presidential commission on administrative management to report that "the president needs help." [15] Congress responded by passing a governmental reorganization act creating the White House Office as part of the Executive Office of the President and authorizing the president to hire additional administrative assistants. Since then, White House staff has expanded tremendously. In 1987, near the end of the Reagan presidency, the *U.S. Government Manual* listed eighty-four titled assistants under the heading "White House Office."

These aides usually have come from the campaign organizations of incoming presidents. They typically exhibit a strong personal loyalty to the president and an organizational responsibility to the presidential office. Although recruits almost always come from the president's political party, their political experience often is limited to efforts on behalf of their candidate. Only a very few former elected officials and party warhorses appear on the rosters of the White House staff. Thus, the political interests of the president dominate the personal and organizational perspectives of the members of the White House staff.

With this enlarged staff, Truman and all subsequent presidents have chosen to set up political operations inside the White House. White House staff assistants now handle many of the political chores once assigned to the national party organization. Further, such assistants have become the principal instruments through which the president exercises party leadership.

Two ongoing practices have produced this turn of events. The first is the designation of staff assistants as the president's personal contacts with party and political leaders throughout the country, including the national party organization and the congressional party. The second is the employment of personnel and the establishment of an apparatus at the White House for handling political appointments.

Staff Liaison. As liaison, a presidential staff assistant ostensibly serves merely as a conduit in a two-way flow of advice and information, requests and demands, between the president and representatives of the political party. In speaking and acting for the president in party matters, however, a White House aide inevitably supersedes and supplants the party chair in that central linkage role.

To be sure, the president's primacy as party leader has always made the White House the focus of attention for party representatives. Still, the establishment of a sizable White House staff, sufficient and willing to meet expectations, has enhanced this tendency greatly. In the process of conveying messages, power gravitates to the conveyer, at the expense of those who once dealt with the president directly and now do so through a presidential assistant.

Every White House staff since Truman's has included at least one such figure. This modern pattern of White House staff management of president-party relations first emerged in Matthew Connelly, Truman's appointments secretary. During most of the Eisenhower years, chief of staff Sherman Adams filled this role. For Kennedy, it was Kenneth O'Donnell. Walter Jenkins and then Marvin Watson served Johnson in this crucial capacity. Nixon used

H. R. (Bob) Haldeman to direct a team of political operators. Ford relied on Donald Rumsfeld and later Richard Cheney. Hamilton Jordan was Carter's chief political agent. During the Reagan years, the White House chief of staff had overall responsibility for political operations, while subordinates Lyn Nofziger and later Edward Rollins and Mitchell Daniels were primarily in charge of Reagan's interaction with the Republican party.

In recommending the establishment of the White House office, FDR's Commission on Administrative Management envisioned presidential assistants operating with a passion for anonymity. Instead, these political operators have become very visible and powerful presidential party managers.

Personnel Management. In the White House, as in any other office, expansion in size has been accompanied by increased division of labor and specialization. Another characteristic feature of White House staff organization has been the assignment of a presidential assistant to operate an in-house personnel office managing presidential appointments. In the late 1940s, Truman administrative assistant Donald Dawson set up such an office as a clearinghouse for information on jobs available and potential candidates to fill them. In subsequent administrations, this administrative apparatus and function has been maintained and has become institutionalized.

This organizational development has placed White House aides at the center of what was once a major responsibility of the national party organization. Since partisanship continues to be a major factor in presidential appointments, this element within the White House Office also serves as a major component of presidential party management.

Partisanship and Political Appointments

Political appointments constitute a chief means by which presidents exercise leadership within the executive branch. The Constitution confers on the president a broad appointing power. Article II, section 2, provides that the president "shall nominate, and by and with the Advice and Consent of the Senate, shall appoint ... Officers of the United States, whose Appointments are not herein otherwise provided for, and which shall be established by Law." In addition, it authorizes the Congress to "vest the Appointment of such inferior Officers, as they think proper, in the President alone."

What is the significance of partisanship in presidential appointments and the influence of party in the making of those appointments? Generally, the president's primary concern in making executive appointments is policy responsiveness. Partisanship and party influence are less ends in themselves than instruments for achieving that purpose.

Development of the Spoils System

As the first president, George Washington had the initial responsibility of filling subordinate positions within the executive branch. Ostensibly, partisanship played no role in his decisions; for at the outset of his administration, political parties had yet to appear on the scene. Washington deplored even the idea of partisan division and put forward instead the criterion of fitness of character for consideration as a presidential appointee. Nevertheless, the great majority of the fit characters receiving presidential appointments during his administration turned out to be followers of the policies advocated by Alexander Hamilton.

Thus, by the time Thomas Jefferson entered the presidential office in 1801, the executive branch was filled with his partisan adversaries. For the most part, Jefferson did not so much clean house as make new and replacement appointments with partisan considerations in mind. Andrew Jackson, the seventh president, joyfully embraced what came to be called the *spoils system* (from the old Roman saying, "to the victor belong the spoils"). Under the spoils system appointive positions within the federal executive were viewed as rewards of electoral victory, to be doled out to the supporters of the winning presidential candidate. Thus, after a half-century under the Constitution, the principle of partisanship as a criterion for a presidential appointment had become well-established.

Presidents needed assistance in making the appointments available. If partisanship was to be a major expectation, who better than the party could provide that help? The emerging national party organizations of the post-Jacksonian era quickly asserted claims on the distribution of federal patronage. They had assembled and directed the campaign support essential to electoral victory, and patronage was the means by which they could reward the party faithful. Within the federal government, the post office offered a harvest of available jobs, establishing the longstanding connection between the post office and party politics detailed earlier. Presidents usually retained personal control over the high-level appointments in the executive branch, but they customarily delegated responsibility for the vast number of lower-level appointments to the party managers.

The operation of the spoils system in the mid-nineteenth century produced extensive partisanship and party control over presidential appointments. Further, it enhanced policy responsiveness within the executive branch. It also was associated, however, with allegations of incompetence and scandal. Increasingly, reformers called for its abolition in favor of a system of civil service based on merit.

Rise of the Merit Principle

The 1881 assassination of President James A. Garfield by Charles Guiteau, who was angry at not being appointed U.S. consul to Paris, led Congress in 1883 to pass the Pendleton Act, also known as the Civil Service Reform Act. This landmark legislation sought to replace partisanship with merit as the essential standard for lower-level positions within the executive branch. It established a nonpartisan Civil Service Commission with authority over certain classes of executive positions.

Initially, only a small minority, about 10 percent, of the total number of executive branch positions came under the coverage of the Civil Service Commission. The majority remained in the hands of the president and continued to be allocated through the party as spoils. Gradually, however, the number and proportion of civil service positions increased. By the turn of the century, more than 40 percent were classified. Under President Theodore Roosevelt (1901-1909), a reformer and former Civil Service commissioner, civil service covered more than 50 percent of the positions within the executive branch.

In the 1910s, classification extended to 60 and then 70 percent of the positions and hovered around 80 percent by 1930. The percentage declined to 67 percent during the presidency of Franklin Roosevelt, when the absolute numbers of federal positions increased dramatically as the federal government responded to the crises of the Great Depression and World War II. The percentage rose into the mid-eighties shortly after the war and remained relatively constant at that level for over two decades.[16] In the late 1980s it hovered at slightly more than 90 percent, a rough reversal of the percentage distribution at the outset a century earlier.

Partisan considerations dominated this expansion of civil service coverage. Under the "good government" guise of civil service reform, presidents would extend classification to large groups of their appointees, who had been awarded jobs because of their party affiliations. In turn, subsequent presidents would find their discretion in making appointments severely limited by the actions of their predecessors.

Establishment of the White House personnel offices further changed the procedures for allocating presidential appointments. Partisanship remained important, but the role of the party organization was reduced.

Critical Developments: Roosevelt to Eisenhower

Several critical developments encompassing the presidencies of Franklin Roosevelt and Dwight Eisenhower illustrate these patterns.

After Roosevelt's election in 1932, national party chairman Jim Farley took on the assignment of patronage distribution. Besieged by job seekers during the depression-ridden early days of the New Deal, Farley allocated government positions by the thousands to "deserving Democrats." According to his own testimony, he gave special favor to those members of the F.R.B.C. club (For Roosevelt Before Chicago, the site of the nominating convention). He discussed major appointments directly with the president and other high government figures, but he had considerable leeway in making the lower-level appointments. He intended to deal with applicants at national party headquarters. He soon found their numbers so great, however, that he moved to the more spacious post office building. Serving as both party chairman and postmaster general, he easily could make this shift.[17]

In making political appointments, Roosevelt and Farley benefited from New Deal legislation creating several new executive organizations to administer the expansive New Deal social and economic programs. Initially, positions in these new entities were not covered by the civil service. Thus, they could be and indeed were awarded to loyal Democrats. Presidents Roosevelt and Truman later extended civil service protection over many of the positions.

Recognizing the partisan character of the executive branch under Roosevelt, Congress passed another landmark law affecting the civil service, the Hatch Act of 1939. It prohibited partisan political activity by federal government workers. A second Hatch Act a year later extended this prohibition to state and local government employees engaged in programs supported by federal funds. Political scientist Herbert Kaufman has observed, "While the Civil Service Act sought to keep political workers out of the government service, the Hatch Acts operated to keep government workers out of the parties." [18]

Meanwhile, within the Roosevelt administration, Jim Farley's stature diminished considerably after the 1936 reelection campaign. In retirement some years later, Farley attempted to analyze the circumstances surrounding his fall from grace.

> Almost before I knew it, I was no longer called to the White House for morning bedside conferences. My phone no longer brought the familiar voice in mellifluous tones. Months dragged by between White House luncheon conferences. Soon I found I was no longer being consulted on appointments, even in my own state.... White House confidence on politics and policy went to a small band of zealots, who mocked at party loyalty and knew no devotion except unswerving obedience to their leader.[19]

Farley's fate reflects institutional as well as personal considerations. The emerging White House Office was beginning to have an influence on presidential politics, to the detriment of the traditional party organization representatives. As noted earlier, during the Truman administration, White House aide Donald Dawson set up a personnel office to serve as a clearinghouse for information on jobs available and potential candidates to fill them.

Dawson toiled in relative obscurity at the White House, while the public spotlight continued to focus on the party chair as the administration's patronage dispenser. Indeed, the party headquarters continued to play a significant patronage role. It was by no means ignored or completely supplanted by the White House personnel office. Yet an administrative structure, inside the White House and apart from the party, had begun to handle presidential appointments.

During the Eisenhower years, the changing patterns of patronage availability and allocation came sharply into focus. The 1952 presidential election returned the presidency to the Republicans for the first time in twenty years. The hopes of party regulars clamoring for jobs climbed then quickly plummeted into disillusionment as they discovered to their dismay that patronage of the variety they remembered and expected simply no longer existed. Indeed, the expansion of civil service coverage had had the effect of classifying jobs held by Democratic partisans.

Moreover, their standard-bearer was neither attuned nor sympathetic to the idea of using patronage as a tool for party building. Within the White House, Eisenhower assigned responsibilities for managing political appointments to Charles Willis, one of Chief of Staff Sherman Adams's assistants. An energetic young businessman, Willis was an amateur in politics who had cofounded and directed Citizens for Eisenhower, an amalgamation of independents and "discerning" Democrats, enthusiastically committed to the Eisenhower presidential candidacy but distinctly uncomfortable with the regular Republican party organization. The selection of Willis at the outset reflected the new president's organizational and philosophical disposition to keep presidential appointments out of the realm of party politics.

The Republican national organization, under the capable direction of party chairman Leonard Hall, sought to assert its traditional prerogatives in the appointments process. Hall was able to institute a procedure whereby the party headquarters was to be informed of any job openings and was entitled to make recommendations. For a time Willis formally routed employment applications through the Republican National Committee. When press reports publicly exposed this program a few months after its incep-

Franklin D. Roosevelt Library

National party chairman Jim Farley, right, speaks to President Franklin Roosevelt. Using new executive organizations created by New Deal legislation, these two collaborated to award jobs to loyal Democrats.

tion, however, considerable criticism ensued from proponents of a depoliticized civil service; and the Eisenhower administration quietly abandoned it.

Thus, over the years, two clear patterns developed. The first was the reduction of the political appointments available to the president. The second was the shift of influence over the appointment-making process from the national party organization to the White House. These patterns continued in the subsequent presidencies.

Diminishing Patronage Categories and Party Role

The decline in patronage has coincided with a significant alteration in the general categories of available patronage. The classification process over time [virtually] "blanketed in" the types of jobs, such as postmaster, that the political party was best able to fill from the ranks of its qualified activists. Since the New Deal era, low-level jobs for deserving partisans have been in exceedingly short supply; and the old-style patronage, associated with party chairs such as Jim Farley, is nearly obsolete.

Today, executive branch presidential patronage applies primarily to the relatively small number of political appointments to upper-level, executive positions in the departments and agencies that the president is authorized to fill. To be sure, party affiliation continues to be an important consideration in presidential appointments. Democratic presidents tend to appoint Democratic partisans; Republican presidents appoint Republicans. But the shift in primary organizational responsibility for handling presidential appointments from the national party to the White House means that patronage has become much less oriented toward party building than was true in the past.

Table 4 Partisanship and Presidential Appointments, 1961-1984

President	Number of appointees	From president's party (%)	Party affiliated (%)	Non-party (%)
Kennedy	430	63	73	27
Johnson	524	47	58	42
Nixon	737	65	73	27
Ford	293	56	64	36
Carter (1977-78)[a]	402	58	65	35
Reagan (1981-84)[a]	524	82	85	15

Sources: Roger G. Brown, "Party and Bureaucracy: From Kennedy to Reagan," *Political Science Quarterly* 97 (Summer 1982): 283; updated by Brown, in James W. Davis, *The American Presidency: A New Perspective* (New York: Harper and Row, 1987), 296.

a. Data for 1979-1980 were not comparable to data for other years and so were not included.

The party organization's role has become peripheral rather than central. Although it may be called on to make recommendations or to provide political clearances, these requests occur at the discretion of the White House. *(See Table 4.)*

Policy responsiveness has always been a primary presidential objective in presidential appointments. In years past, however, it usually went hand in hand with party building. Consider the case of a Democratic president, for example, doling out jobs to deserving partisans. The very act of placing party loyalists in positions charged with enforcing policies provided both (1) the expectation that implementation would occur according to the president's designs and (2) a significant reward for services rendered the party. Prospects of such rewards constituted important incentives for partisan involvement. Further, the holders of these positions could be expected to look out for the interests of the party from their strategic vantage points. This has become much less the case in the post-World War II era. The two have become separated.

The staffing practices developed by the Reagan White House illustrate well this altered emphasis in managing presidential appointments. Control over appointments was centralized tightly in the White House, under the supervision of personnel officer E. Pendleton James. Ideological compatibility with the president emerged as the chief standard in making appointments. Indeed, for this reason President Reagan, compared with his predecessors, was able to effect noteworthy success in ensuring responsiveness from his appointees in the executive branch.

Civil Service Classification and Policy Responsiveness

The extension of civil service classification has generated new problems for policy responsiveness. A bureaucracy designed to enhance expertise may well sacrifice accountability in the process. Modern presidents have grown increasingly frustrated with the perceived unresponsiveness of the permanent bureaucracy.

In 1978 President Carter promoted the cause of civil service reform to increase presidential control. In that year, Congress enacted the Civil Service Reform Act, which had two important features.

First, the reform act created the Senior Executive Service (SES), a group comprising mostly high-level career civil servants. From the president's perspective, this innovation was designed to increase the flexibility of the White House in dealing with the upper echelons of the bureaucracy and to increase the responsiveness of the bureaucracy to White House initiatives. The experience of Presidents Carter and Reagan with the Senior Executive Service, however, has not altered existing patterns significantly.

Second, the 1978 Civil Service Reform Act abolished the Civil Service Commission, that bipartisan body created in 1883 to oversee the establishment of the merit principle in the federal bureaucracy. Congress created the Office of Personnel Management (OPM). Headed by a single presidential appointee, OPM seeks to increase presidential direction of the civil service. Still, while the president wants a responsive bureaucracy, the concerns of the Office of Personnel Management are not specifically partisan, thus widening the breech between policy responsiveness and party building.

Presidential Party Leadership in Congress

Presidential party leadership within the executive branch augments the executive authority the Constitution provides for the president. Such constitutional authority is largely lacking when the chief executive confronts the Congress. Rather, the constitutional principle of separation of powers positions the president as an outsider in dealing with the legislature. Moreover, legislative leadership is not a constitutional responsibility. Rather, it emerges out of the presidents' ambitions and the expectations of their followers.

Presidents seeking to lead the Congress in the enactment of presidential initiatives must do so without formal command authority. Persuasion becomes the key.

With the conspicuous exception of Thomas Jefferson, and to a lesser extent Andrew Jackson, nineteenth-century presidents did not seek much in the way of legislative initiatives, nor was Congress disposed to look to the president for legislative leadership. In the first half of the twentieth century, however, such pivotal presidents as Theodore Roosevelt, Woodrow Wilson, and Franklin Roosevelt, by dint of their expansive conceptions of the presidential office and in response to new situations and demands, succeeded in altering the political environment, placing the presidency in a much more activist legislative posture. *(See "Historical Development," p. 67, in Legislative Leader chapter.)*

In the separated institutional environment, party emerges as an important unifying force. Presidents can employ their standing as party leaders to secure cooperation from party members in Congress. In theory, the idea and the organization of party can bridge the constitutionally separated institutions under the leadership of the president. Thus, from the presidential perspective, party leadership provides the foundation for legislative leadership.

This leadership is, however, extremely problematic. Its success is dependent on numerous structural and stylistic factors. Indeed, relatively few U.S. presidents have been able to unlock the party key to legislative leadership.

The Congressional Party

Political parties had no formal standing in 1787 when the Constitution organized and defined the powers of Congress. But today, we speak of the congressional party, or the party in Congress, a concept founded on the fact that virtually all members of Congress have long been elected as nominees of political parties. Collectively, the party nominees elected to Congress make up the congressional parties. In addition, the partisans in each chamber constitute separate units. Thus, today we observe four congressional parties: House Democrats, House Republicans, Senate Democrats, and Senate Republicans.

Further, partisanship provides the basis for the leadership and organization of Congress. The purpose of congressional party leaders and organizations is to heighten the significance of the party cue in congressional behavior. In each chamber, House and Senate, the members of the congressional parties constitute the party caucuses, or, as the Republicans style themselves, the party conferences. At the outset of each session of Congress, the party caucuses meet to select their party leaders.

Party Leaders

Congressional party leadership includes the constitutional leadership positions within the Congress: the Speaker of the House and the president pro tempore of the Senate. When Congress formally convenes, House members uniformly vote according to party lines for their parties' candidates for the leadership position of Speaker. The senatorial counterpart is also elected on party lines. The incumbent does not stand for reelection at the outset of each Congress, however, as does the Speaker. Rather, the incumbent remains in office so long as the party retains its majority. Thus, changes will occur with (1) the departure of the incumbent from the Senate or (2) a change in party power. Thus, the majority party in each chamber is able to elect its nominee to the constitutional leadership position.

The parties choose other leaders as well. In the House, each party caucus elects a leader. The leader of the majority party becomes the Speaker. The caucus also designates a deputy to fill the position of majority leader, and the House will confirm this action. In turn, the candidate of the minority party for Speaker becomes the minority leader. The majority and minority leaders are also called "floor leaders."

In addition, both party caucuses select party whips to assist their leaders in maintaining two-way communication with the party members, especially about party positions and expectations on pending legislation. Both parties have established whip organizations, consisting of deputy and regional whips. The whips extend the congressional party leadership well into the rank and file.

The Constitution names the vice president of the United States as the president of the Senate, or presiding officer, who votes only to break a tie. The Constitution also authorizes the designation of a president pro tempore to preside in the absence of the vice president. In the nineteenth century, vice presidents routinely attended to their presiding responsibilities. In their occasional absences, presidents pro tempore were elected ad hoc to serve until the return of the vice president.

Beginning in 1980, the position became much more stable, with the incumbent now serving until the Senate otherwise orders. Twentieth-century vice presidents have virtually abandoned their senatorial presiding duties, so opportunities for the president pro tempore have increased. Since 1945, the position of president pro tempore customarily has gone to the member of the majority party who has served the longest. Junior members of the majority typically assume much of the daily burdens of presiding.

Despite its constitutional authorization and the status of its incumbent as the senior majority party member, the position of president pro tempore has not emerged as a significant party leadership position as has the House Speakership. Rather, it is much more an honorific office.

The main party leaders in the Senate are the majority and minority leaders, chosen by the party caucuses. As in the House, each floor leader is assisted by a whip. Because of the smaller size and less formal operating procedures that differentiate the Senate from the House, however, much less elaborate whip organizations have evolved in the upper chamber.

Party Organizations

Congressional party leadership positions operate within the context of partisan organizations within each body. The caucuses have already been introduced. While traditionally, their responsibilities have been limited to presession preparation, they have occasionally maintained a presence throughout the session.

During the Jeffersonian era, the Democratic-Republican caucus reportedly met frequently during the course of congressional sessions. More recently, among House Democrats, noteworthy instances of ongoing caucus meetings occurred during the early years of the presidencies of both Woodrow Wilson and Franklin Roosevelt, and again in the mid-1970s when the Republicans Richard Nixon and Gerald Ford occupied the White House. For the House Republicans, regular meetings of the conference were a standard feature in the 1940s and 1950s.

In addition, in the twentieth century, both congressional parties have established "steering" and "policy" committees to work with the leadership on scheduling and strategy. Further, both have created ad hoc groups to recommend committee assignments. These various tasks have frequently been combined in single bodies.

The congressional parties play central roles in the committees of Congress. The party caucuses authorize procedures and ratify decisions for the assignments of party members to the committees. Further, the majority party in each chamber controls the chairs of all the committees in that chamber, with positions on all committees distributed roughly proportionally between the parties: the larger a party's majority within the chamber that term, the larger its majority on each committee. For example, the 1964 elections increased the Democratic majority in the 435-member House by 37, up 8.5 percent from 258 to 195. When the eighty-ninth Congress convened in 1965, Democratic representation on the 50-member Appropriations Committee went up 8 percent, from 30 to 34.

Within the congressional committees in the twentieth century, leadership typically has been established and maintained according to the *seniority system,* a custom whereby the position of committee chair goes to the member of the majority party with the most years of continuous service on the committee.

Additional party organizations in Congress include the diverse array of specific party interests that have proliferated in recent years. These interests typically are based on

Table 5 Presidential Support by Party, House of Representatives, 1953-1988

Year	President	Democrats (%)	Republicans (%)
1953	Eisenhower (R)	49	74
1954	Eisenhower	45	71
1955	Eisenhower	53	60
1956	Eisenhower	52	72
1957	Eisenhower	50	54
1958	Eisenhower	55	58
1959	Eisenhower	40	68
1960	Eisenhower	44	59
	Eisenhower average	49	65
1961	Kennedy (D)	73	37
1962	Kennedy	72	42
1963	Kennedy	73	32
	Kennedy average	73	37
1964	Johnson (D)	74	38
1965	Johnson	74	42
1966	Johnson	64	38
1967	Johnson	69	46
1968	Johnson	64	51
	Johnson average	77	43
1969	Nixon (R)	48	57
1970	Nixon	53	66
1971	Nixon	47	72
1972	Nixon	47	64
1973	Nixon	36	61
1974	Nixon/Ford (R)	44	57
	Nixon average	46	63
1975	Ford (R)	38	63
1976	Ford	32	63
	Ford Average	35	63
1977	Carter (D)	63	42
1978	Carter	60	36
1979	Carter	64	34
1980	Carter	63	40
	Carter average	63	38
1981	Reagan (R)	42	68
1982	Reagan	39	64
1983	Reagan	28	70
1984	Reagan	34	60
1985	Reagan	30	67
1986	Reagan	25	65
1987	Reagan	24	62
1988	Reagan	25	57
	Reagan average	31	64

Source: Congressional Quarterly Almanac (Washington, D.C.: Congressional Quarterly Inc., various issues).

the members' ideology, region, or entry "class" (the election or Congress in which the members initially took office). Examples include the Democratic Study Group, the Republican Study Committee, the California Democratic Congressional Delegation, and the Ninety-ninth New Members Caucus (Democratic).

Finally, since the Civil War, congressional parties have maintained their own campaign committees. These committees assist the election campaigns of party candidates to Congress. Thus, the congressional party as a concept embraces a wide variety of specific groups and organizations.

Congressional Party Voting and Presidential Support

Empirical research on congressional behavior shows that party is the major influence on roll call voting and that party is the foundation of presidential support in Congress. Yet other factors also affect members' voting decisions. It is therefore difficult to know exactly how much influence the parties have.

It is entirely correct to observe, for example, that Democrats tend to vote with other Democrats, and Republicans with other Republicans. Similarly, presidents receive stronger support from their partisans in Congress than from the opposition. Yet disquieting questions emerge when we try to draw conclusions from these findings. Do Democrats vote with other Democrats simply because they belong to the same party? Common policy preferences, constituency pressures, or the personal influence of other members may be the reasons; party affiliation may be merely coincidental. Similar questions surround ostensibly partisan support for presidential initiatives.

Still, these questions notwithstanding, party remains a key to presidential support in Congress. The president's challenge as party leader is to mobilize this base of support, to heighten the significance of the party cue. *(See Tables 5 and 6.)*

The President and the Congressional Party

How does the president as party leader exercise influence? Thomas Jefferson's pioneering exercise of presidential party leadership extended to designating floor leaders and even, according to contemporaneous although inadequately substantiated Federalist reports, meeting with and presiding over the caucus.

Jefferson's successors have fallen far short of these alleged accomplishments. By and large, the congressional party organizes itself and selects its leadership without regard to the president's needs and interests. It does so in keeping with the principle of separation of powers and with the institutional need to protect itself against outside, presidential domination.

No direct presidential participation in the congressional party caucuses has even been alleged in the post-Jeffersonian era. Activist presidents such as Woodrow Wilson and Franklin Roosevelt, however, have conveyed messages to the caucuses informing the members of presidential concerns.

Leadership Selection

Respectful of congressional sentiments, wary of the consequences of unsuccessful initiatives, and aware that hierarchical succession is often the norm, presidents usually are loath to intervene in congressional party leadership contests. A noteworthy exception occurred in 1937, when, following the death of Senate Majority Leader Joseph T. Robinson, President Roosevelt did not hide his clear preference that the successor be Alben W. Barkley of Kentucky rather than B. Patton (Pat) Harrison of Mississippi. Barkley won a narrow victory.

Much more typically, presidents view the party leadership contests as internal congressional matters and are content to work with the leaders thus chosen. Similarly, in the committees, the seniority system insulates leadership positions from presidential influence.

This hands-off approach can invest congressional party leadership in individuals antagonistic toward the president and presidential objectives. The death of Senate Republican majority leader Robert A. Taft in 1953, early in President Eisenhower's first term, resulted in the elevation of Republican senator William F. Knowland of California. Knowland frequently opposed Eisenhower's legislative objectives. Democratic representative John W. McCormack, who succeeded Sam Rayburn in the Speaker's chair after Rayburn's death in 1961, represented a faction in Massachusetts politics that sometimes conflicted with that of the president, John Kennedy. In each case, however, the presidents had no effective say in the determination of the congressional party.

Meetings with Congressional Party Leadership

Franklin Roosevelt and the presidents who have succeeded him have set up regular meetings with the congressional party leadership. Typically, these sessions have occurred on a weekly basis when Congress is in session. They provide regular opportunities to trace the course of the president's program in Congress, to establish priorities, and to develop and coordinate strategies and tactics.

Depending on the president's style and schedule, these sessions may take place in the early morning over coffee and doughnuts or perhaps in the late afternoon accompanied by bourbon and branch water. Should the president's party be in the minority in a congressional chamber, then the opposition party leadership may well be invited to participate in such sessions.

In addition to regular meetings with the party leadership, presidents can and do meet with committee chieftains and individual members and groups of the party rank-and-file in pursuit of their legislative objectives. The frequency with which a president does so depends very much on considerations of personal style. Lyndon Johnson did so often; Jimmy Carter, less so.

White House Legislative Liaison

The determination of the Brownlow Commission that "the president needs help" has had an institutional influence on the presidential conduct of legislative leadership. With the expansion of the White House Office, specific presidential assignments to White House aides of responsibilities for congressional relations have followed.

During the Eisenhower administration, the structure of a legislative liaison office took formal shape under Wilton B. ("Jerry") Persons, a deputy to Chief of Staff Sherman Adams. When Persons replaced Adams as chief of staff in 1958, Bryce Harlow took charge of the liaison office.

These staffers and a handful of associates had the task of establishing and maintaining a presidential presence on Capitol Hill. In a word, they became the president's official lobbyists.

In the ensuing years, this office has grown in size and stature. It has become a vital part of the president's conduct of legislative leadership. It has partisan significance in that it usually is staffed by members of the president's party and it works more closely with the leaders and members of the president's party than with the opposition.

Table 6 Presidential Support by Party, Senate, 1953-1988

Year	President	Democrats (%)	Republicans (%)
1953	Eisenhower (R)	47	67
1954	Eisenhower	40	71
1955	Eisenhower	56	72
1956	Eisenhower	39	72
1957	Eisenhower	52	69
1958	Eisenhower	45	67
1959	Eisenhower	38	72
1960	Eisenhower	42	65
	Eisenhower average	45	69
1961	Kennedy (D)	65	37
1962	Kennedy	63	40
1963	Kennedy	73	44
	Kennedy average	67	40
1964	Johnson (D)	62	45
1965	Johnson	65	48
1966	Johnson	57	43
1967	Johnson	61	53
1968	Johnson	48	47
	Johnson average	59	47
1969	Nixon (R)	47	66
1970	Nixon	45	62
1971	Nixon	41	65
1972	Nixon	44	67
1973	Nixon	37	61
1974	Nixon/Ford (R)	39	56
	Nixon average	42	63
1975	Ford (R)	47	68
1976	Ford	39	63
	Ford average	43	66
1977	Carter (D)	70	52
1978	Carter	66	41
1979	Carter	68	47
1980	Carter	62	45
	Carter average	67	46
1981	Reagan (R)	49	80
1982	Reagan	43	74
1983	Reagan	42	73
1984	Reagan	41	76
1985	Reagan	35	75
1986	Reagan	37	78
1987	Reagan	36	64
1988	Reagan	47	68
	Reagan average	41	73

Source: Congressional Quarterly Almanac (Washington, D.C.: Congressional Quarterly Inc., various issues).

Presidential Appeals

Personally, and with the assistance of legislative liaison assistants, presidents put forward a variety of appeals to their fellow partisans in encouraging them to support the president's legislative initiatives. In many respects, they merely overlap with and build upon the foundations established at the outset by Thomas Jefferson. In a study of presidential influence in Congress that casts doubt on the ultimate value of these appeals, political scientist George C. Edwards III details a number of these diverse approaches.[20]

These appeals may be purely partisan, focusing on the centrality of the measure in question to the party program, and calling for support on the basis of party loyalty. Oftentimes, this invocation itself is sufficient. Themselves elected on the party ticket, members of the president's party typically are sympathetic to rallies to the party banner that call forth their own emotional commitments to the party, its programs, and its leader.

More specific approaches aimed primarily at the partisan audience include patronage and campaign assistance. As noted earlier, the quantity of political appointments the president can bestow has declined markedly in the twentieth century, but party is an important consideration for presidents in making such appointments as remain. These can be used to entice or reward supportive members of Congress—who tend to be vitally interested in presidential appointments in their states and districts—by designating individuals recommended by the members. At the outset of the Kennedy administration, the White House staff functions of patronage distribution and legislative liaison were combined in a single office under the direction of Lawrence F. O'Brien. This ensured that the congressional party interest in patronage would be addressed.

Another service the president as party leader can provide for fellow partisans in the legislature is campaign assistance. The president can agree to campaign on behalf of members running a close race, honoring them and their constituencies with the presidential presence and establishing a credit balance for future dealings. The president also may influence the national party organization in deciding whether to offer its financial and organizational resources to a particular legislator's campaign.

Supplementing partisan appeals are those directed at members without regard to partisan affiliation. Among these bipartisan efforts are some of a more personal nature, in which presidents solicit backing as a personal favor. Lyndon Johnson could call on old congressional and senatorial colleagues of decades-long standing, pleading with them on the basis of friendship to support him on a critical issue. Ronald Reagan's background lacked congressional experience and familiarity with congressional personages. Nevertheless, he would resort to his experience as a Hollywood actor, imploring members of Congress to "win one for the Gipper."

Members of Congress are often quite susceptible to such entreaties, for they invoke the prestige of the presidential office and entail direct access to the president, either over the telephone or in person. Further, they are typically linked with an overarching national interest transcending the party one. Among recent presidents, Lyndon Johnson was particularly prone to invoke nationalistic themes in appealing for congressional support. While he clearly did so in a calculating fashion, he was also unquestionably sincere and emotional in his personal patriotism.

Similarly, presidents can use the numerous amenities at their disposal to curry favor with members of Congress and thus reinforce these personal appeals. These include visits to the White House, photo opportunities with the president, cruises down the Potomac River on the presidential yacht, flights on *Air Force One,* and the like. The president's desk in the Oval Office is filled with souvenirs bearing the presidential seal, such as cuff links, matches, ash trays, and golf balls. Visitors to the presidential retreat at Camp David are provided with windbreakers similarly labeled. Members of Congress are far from immune to such blandishments.

Conversely, presidents can make themselves available to members of Congress at the members' initiatives. Lyndon Johnson and Gerald Ford took care to return promptly telephone calls from members of Congress. Richard Nixon and Jimmy Carter were much less attentive. The accessibility of the president looms large in congressional responses to and evaluations of presidential legislative leadership.

Presidents also can resort to bargaining in pursuit of their legislative objectives. Here, presidents provide favors to members of Congress in return for legislative support. In the congressional vernacular, this is called "logrolling"—you scratch my back and I'll scratch yours.

Edwards has documented several examples. He reported that President Kennedy was attempting with little success to persuade Sen. Robert Kerr of Oklahoma, an influential member of the Finance Committee, to support an investment tax credit bill that was languishing in committee. In turn, Kerr expressed his dissatisfaction with the administration's unwillingness to back an Arkansas River project he was pushing. Kerr proposed a trade, to which Kennedy responded, "You know, Bob, I never really understood that Arkansas River bill before today." Thus, the deal was done, to the mutual satisfaction of president and senator.[21] Although the president or presidential aides occasionally may initiate bargaining, members of Congress are perhaps more likely to do so as this anecdote suggests, in response to a presidential request for help.

Presidents have at their disposal a variety of services that can be useful to members of Congress. Making these services available builds good will and potential support. Although job-related patronage has long been in decline, another brand of patronage continues to flourish—pork barrel patronage, the allocation of federal projects among the states and congressional districts. As Senator Kerr's behavior indicates, pork barrel patronage provides the president with a potential device to encourage cooperation on the part of members.

As head of the executive branch, the president is in a position to make available the resources and assistance of the executive branch on behalf of a member's special legislative interests. The president also can provide assistance to a member's constituents as an incentive for legislative support. Both presidents Kennedy and Johnson instructed their legislative liaison offices to solicit from members of Congress such opportunities to provide assistance.

All of the above are carrots offered by the president or presidential agents as incentives for support. In contrast, the president has relatively few sticks available to use if Congress chooses not to cooperate. About all the president alone can do in the way of pressure is to threaten to withhold the available incentives. This can be effective for members of Congress who are accustomed to them and reliant on them. For more independent members who are willing and able to do without presidential support, the president's threats often can be disregarded.

During the Johnson presidency, Sen. J. William Fulbright, an Arkansas Democrat, chaired the powerful Senate Foreign Relations Committee. After Fulbright began expressing reservations about the administration's Vietnam War policies, he found that his once warm relationship with the president began to cool noticeably. Indeed, where invitations to White House state dinners for visiting foreign dignitaries had once been commonplace, befitting Fulbright's leadership position, they were no longer forthcoming. Fulbright ignored the obvious slights and continued his opposition.

Alternatively, presidents can seek to pressure members of Congress through the use of outside strategies, employing and relying on interest groups and public opinion to encourage or intimidate members to support presidential initiatives. This approach is akin to a bank shot in billiards. The president appeals directly to interest groups and the public, and they in turn exert pressure on the members of Congress.

For example, a president seeking to influence members of Congress from industrial states to support a presidential program might encourage allies in the labor unions to lobby those members on behalf of the president. Alternatively, in reaching out to members from farming states, the president could deploy supporters from among agricultural interest groups.

In the television age, the president has the opportunity to go public with pleas to citizens across the nation to write their representatives and senators.

Shifting the perspective from individual members to the Congress as a whole, the Constitution does authorize a presidential veto of legislation unacceptable to the chief executive. Its utilization is thus indicative of unsuccessful legislative leadership. In this fashion, the veto stands as a dramatic negative form of legislative leadership. Interestingly, the president who resorted most often to the veto was Franklin Roosevelt, routinely acknowledged as a masterful legislative party leader. He did so on more than six hundred occasions. *(See "The Veto," p. 57, in Legislative Leader chapter.)*

Limitations on Presidential Party Leadership in Congress

For generations, political scientists have spoken with appreciation of a responsible party government model. This model contains several components. Initially, parties develop programs to which they commit themselves. Then, they nominate candidates for public office who share those programmatic commitments. Competing parties provide voters with clear policy alternatives. Voters choose between or among the competing parties and authorize one to govern. Then, the governmental representatives of the party so authorized demonstrate sufficient discipline and cohesion to enact the party's promises as public policies, thus fulfilling its commitments to the voters.

The British party system has long been viewed as an excellent working illustration of responsible parties. American parties, however, have been roundly criticized for falling well short of the mark, particularly with regard to the behavior of the party in the government.

As noted earlier, party does provide the central cue for congressional voting behavior and the primary foundation for presidential support. Still, the members of the congressional party exhibit an independence from the party program and the party leadership in both the Congress and the White House that is striking when compared with their European counterparts. Why are the party leaders and members in Congress often disinclined to respond positively to presidential leadership? The initial answers may be found in the Constitution.

Separation of Powers

The Constitution does not provide for political parties, nor does it authorize party leadership. Further, the separation of powers principle places the president outside the legislative arena. This is in distinct contrast to a parliamentary form of government, as in Great Britain or Canada, that officially combines executive and legislative authority, establishing the leader of the majority party in the legislature as the chief executive.

The presence of party competition within the context of separation of powers makes possible divided party government, again impossible under the classic parliamentary system. Should the president encounter an entire Congress or a chamber controlled by the opposition party, the limitations of party leadership are obvious. A president hardly can be expected to pursue legislative objectives primarily on partisan grounds when the party constitutes a legislative minority.

This awkward situation has confronted all of the Republican presidents in the post-World War II era. Eisenhower had to deal with Democratic majorities in both houses for six of his eight years in office. Nixon and Ford faced opposition party control throughout their presidencies. During the Reagan years, the Democrats prevailed throughout in the House and for the last two years in the Senate. Among the postwar Democratic presidents, only Truman from 1946 to 1948 had to deal with opposition party control of the Congress.

As an offshoot of separation of powers, the constitutional principle of checks and balances consciously breeds antagonism between the two separated branches. In James Madison's view, expressed in *Federalist* No. 51, protections against concentration of power, leading toward tyranny, necessitated not merely separating the executive and the legislature, but also pitting the two against each other, providing "constitutional means and personal motives to resist encroachments.... Ambition must be made to counteract ambition." [22]

Bicameralism further divides the congressional party into House and Senate bodies. Institutionally, the members of each chamber are conditioned to preserve and protect their particular prerogatives, against each other as well as the president.

Federalism

The other great organizing constitutional principle is federalism, the division of governmental power between the central government and those of the states. The federal principle inhibits the president's party leadership in Congress from several vantage points. First, it works to decentralize party organization in the United States. Party organization parallels government organization at each level: national, state, and local, separating national parties from their state and local counterparts.

Party nominating power for congressional offices clearly rests with the local party organizations. Further, the advent of the direct primary method of party nomination places control over the nominations in the hands of party voters in the states and districts, far removed from the president's party leadership. Thus, the national party and the president as party leader have minimal say over who receives party nominations for seats in the legislature. Indeed, those nominations could go even to individuals openly antagonistic toward the president and the party program.

Second, the federal principle provides for different electoral constituencies—national for the president, state and local for senators and representatives. Diverse constituencies undermine the unifying potential of party. In the heterogeneous American culture, regional variations persist. Massachusetts Democrats and Arkansas Democrats can be two distinctive breeds, as can Pennsylvania and California Republicans.

Staggered Elections

In addition, the Constitution staggers electoral terms and schedules. Presidents serve four-year terms, representatives two, and senators six. In the context of any given presidential election, all the representatives and one-third of the senators will be elected simultaneously. Two years later, however, all the representatives and another third of the senators will be elected apart from the president. These disjointed elections also undermine the unity that party can bring to the political order by partially separating presidential and congressional elections.

Moreover, the midterm congressional elections almost invariably produce a decline in the numbers of the president's party in Congress. This development weakens the influence of the president on the legislature. It undermines the base of party support and encourages the opposition.

In large measure because of these constitutional features of separation of powers, federalism, and staggered elections, political parties in the United States have not developed the discipline and responsibility demonstrated by their counterparts in parliamentary systems. Many of the limitations on party leadership by the president also hold true for the congressional party leadership. Take, for example, regional differences enhanced by the federal system. Democratic president Jimmy Carter lacked rapport with many northern liberals in the congressional party; some southern conservative Democrats viewed House Speaker Thomas P. (Tip) O'Neill with suspicion because of his Massachusetts background. Neither Carter nor O'Neill, both representing central, national party leadership, had much say over who the voters in the 435 congressional districts and the 50 states sent to Congress. Of course, should congressional party leaders be antagonistic toward the president, presidential problems intensify.

Political Culture

The political culture in the United States—that is, the widely held attitudes and beliefs about politics and the political order—is another limitation on presidential leadership in Congress. In the United States, the general public has long viewed political parties with considerable disfavor. In part, this negative view can be traced to the antiparty position of the Framers in the late eighteenth century. It was reinforced about a century later by the intellectual assault on parties brought forth by the progressive era reformers.

Further, the American political culture is an individualistic one. We expect our political representatives to look out for us and not to subordinate our needs and interests on the altar of party. Thus, we effectively discourage members of Congress from the fundamental commitment to party loyalty as a behavioral cue.

Presidential Influence on the Partisan Composition of Congress

All these specific and general limitations notwithstanding, the fact remains that members of the president's party in Congress are relatively more inclined to support presidential legislative initiatives than are the partisan opposition. Therefore, among the most potentially effective exercises of presidential party leadership are those that influence the election of fellow partisans to Congress. Presidential coattails, midterm campaigning, and party purges are three ways presidents have tried to affect the partisan composition of Congress.

Presidential Coattails

Presidential coattails is the voting phenomenon by which voters attracted to a presidential candidacy are inclined to cast their ballots for the nominees of the president's party for seats in Congress. In a classic sense, the coattails theory is usually based on the presumption that voters cast straight party votes; therefore, the more popular the presidential nominee at the head of the ticket, the more likely the election of congressional party nominees. A variation holds that presidential coattails are generated not so much by normally straight party ticket voters as by ticket splitters who, having voted for the presidential nominee of the opposition party, proceed to support congressional nominees of the president's party.

For generations, observers of presidential elections noted a generally positive relationship between the two votes, one that could not be explained purely in terms of straight party ticket voting. In other words, the popular appeal of a presidential candidate was held to increase the electoral support for the party's congressional nominees resulting in the election of more of them to Congress.

In turn, the coattails effect presumably translated into increased presidential support in Congress. Since shared party affiliation produces a predisposition to support the president, a swelling of the ranks of the congressional partisans should increase presidential support. Further, the members who have ridden into office on the president's coattails should be particularly grateful to their benefactor and thus inclined to be particularly supportive. *(See Table 7.)*

This theory of presidential coattails as an influence on Congress is, however, both riddled with holes and difficult to test. In the first place, not all presidents have "coattails." In the post-World War II presidential elections, several presidents appear to have been associated with minimal changes in the size of the congressional parties. Moreover, there is also the possibility of reverse coattails. In such an instance, the presidential nominee would run behind the congressional party nominees in their states and districts.

For example, in 1960, Democratic presidential nominee John Kennedy, a Massachusetts Catholic, ran behind the party's congressional and senatorial nominees throughout the South. Conversely, in 1976, the party's presidential nominee, Jimmy Carter of Georgia, trailed the party ticket in many northern states and districts.

The Democratic party's domination of Congress in the post-World War II era also complicates the theory of a coattails effect. The Democrats seized control of both houses of Congress in the election of 1948, when Harry Truman won by a narrow margin. They relinquished it in 1952 when Dwight Eisenhower won the presidency. Only two years later, however, the Democrats reestablished majority control and have maintained it ever since in the House. After a twenty-six year drought, the Republicans gained control of the Senate in 1980 when Ronald Reagan won the presidency. Six years later, the Democrats returned to power in the Senate, once again giving them majorities in both chambers.

Thus only Presidents Truman and Eisenhower can be associated with shifting party control of both chambers; Reagan, with shifting party control of only one. The gains and losses of the president's party in the remaining presidential elections affected the size of existing party majorities, to be sure, but not the majorities themselves.

From an empirical examination of the coattails effect in the House of Representatives, political scientist George Edwards identified specific coattails victories.[23] He concluded that "the coattail effect on congressional elections has been minimal for some time" and attributes this result primarily to decreasing competitiveness of congressional districts.[24] In other words, safe seats have become pervasive in Congress and severely reduce presidential opportunities to influence electoral outcomes. He sees the explanation for this phenomenon in the heightened congressional responsiveness to the voters.

The decline of the coattails effect hinders the president's ability to exercise party leadership in Congress. If the president is unable to carry partisan supporters into office on the strength of popular appeal at the head of the party ticket, then presidents have lost a key incentive in winning congressional support.

Midterm Campaigning

Midway through the president's term, the Constitution mandates elections for the entire House and one-third of the Senate. By campaigning for party nominees for seats in Congress, the president may influence the partisan composition of Congress.

Midterm campaigning is one of the most visible manifestations of presidential party leadership. Here the president departs from an above-partisanship stance to assume openly the mantle of party chief. Among the forms this activity can take are public speeches, general statements and gestures of support for the party ticket, appearances throughout the country on behalf of the selected party congressional nominees, mobilization and deployment of administrative personnel such as cabinet members, access to the organizational resources of the national party, and fund-raising.

As a dimension of presidential party leadership, midterm campaigning has emerged relatively recently. Political scientist Roger Brown points to President Woodrow Wilson as the inaugurator of the practice in 1918.[25] In that year, Wilson put forward an unprecedented plea to the electorate to vote Democratic to demonstrate support for and to protect the integrity of his foreign policy objectives.

More recently, the allegedly nonpolitical Dwight Eisenhower can be credited with extending presidential involvement in midterm campaigns. Indeed, his participation in the 1954 and 1958 campaigns went well beyond the precedents already established. In 1962, President John Kennedy exceeded his predecessor's pace. In the ensuing years, presidential midterm campaigning has become an important component of the expectations and responsibilities of presidential party leadership.

Thus, in 1966 when President Lyndon Johnson cut short his projected campaign activities and appearances, party figures reacted very negatively. They did so in the face of public opinion polls indicating low popularity for the president and reservations expressed by some party

Table 7 Gains and Losses in House and Senate in Presidential Election Years, 1944-1988

Presidential Election Year	Winner of Presidential Race	Party	House	Senate
1944	Roosevelt	Dem.	−50	−12
1948	Truman	Dem.	+75	+9
1952	Eisenhower	Rep.	+22	+1
1956	Eisenhower	Rep.	−3	0
1960	Kennedy	Dem.	−21	+1
1964	Johnson	Dem.	+37	+1
1968	Nixon	Rep.	+5	+7
1972	Nixon	Rep.	+12	−2
1976	Carter	Dem.	+1	+1
1980	Reagan	Rep.	+33	+12
1984	Reagan	Rep.	+14	−2
1988	Bush	Rep.	−3	−1

candidates about the possible harm of presidential campaigning. Since then, the presidential presence in midterm elections has been generally high.

These exercises of presidential party leadership cannot be associated with conspicuous success. Indeed, one of the abiding truisms of electoral politics in the United States is that the president's party loses seats in the House of Representatives at the midterm elections. The record in the Senate is less clear, but significant gains have not been the norm.

Efforts to explain this phenomenon point in a variety of directions. Although some analysts view the president as a central actor in accounting for election outcomes, others focus attention elsewhere, alternatively contending that different electorates are present in presidential and midterm elections, that economic conditions have significant influence, and that incumbency is the critical variable in election outcomes.

Whatever the explanation, midterm campaigning appears more an effort to minimize losses than to maximize gains. One of the most visible exercises of presidential party leadership therefore appears, at least on the surface, to be one of the least productive.

When one party controls the presidency and another controls at least one house of Congress, midterm campaigning responsibilities carry with them potentially severe disadvantages for presidential legislative leadership. Midterm campaigning can inflame partisan opposition, making the president's subsequent bipartisan appeals less effective. Further, some presidents have found members of the opposition party to be more consistently supportive than their own partisans. They have thus been reluctant to campaign against those members.

For this and other reasons, presidents occasionally delegate certain of their midterm campaign chores to their vice presidents. Most notably, President Eisenhower asked Nixon to campaign in 1954 and 1958, and President Nixon assigned campaign tasks to Spiro Agnew in 1970. In the 1958 and 1970 elections, a Republican president confronted a Congress controlled by Democratic majorities

The presidential placement of the vice president in the forefront of the party effort in midterm congressional campaigns can be interpreted as an attempt to fulfill party leadership responsibilities while avoiding direct personal involvement that might antagonize the leaders and members of the opposition party and impair presidential stakes in the upcoming Congress.

Party Purges

In the decentralized parties, presidents are usually far removed from the selection of party senatorial and congressional nominees. This is the task of the voters in party primaries in the states and districts. Further, one of the fundamental norms of U.S. party politics is that the party organization should be neutral toward competing candidacies for a nomination, and then it should willingly support whoever secures that nomination. Departures from this norm, when they do occur, strongly benefit incumbents against challengers.

Nevertheless, on rare occasions, presidents facing members of the party in Congress who consistently oppose them and their policy initiatives have undertaken efforts to secure the defeat of those persons in nominating contests. The most well known and widespread of these efforts occurred in 1938 when President Roosevelt openly sought the defeat of several congressional party incumbents who had voted against key New Deal legislation. According to political scientist Sidney Milkis, "In the dozen states within which the president acted against entrenched incumbents, he was successful in only two of them." [26] Thus, the blatant purge effort must be judged a failure.

In the 1970 general election, the Nixon administration undertook to purge a single Republican senator by supporting the candidacy of Conservative party nominee James L. Buckley (N.Y.) over the incumbent Republican Charles E. Goodell (N.Y.). Although President Nixon stopped short of an endorsement of Buckley, confining himself to a statement of appreciation, vice president Agnew was openly critical of Goodell as a betrayer of party interests. Aided by administration support, Buckley succeeded in his campaign to unseat Goodell.

This incident notwithstanding, presidents are unlikely to exercise party leadership by seeking the removal from Congress of antagonistic partisans. When attempted, party purges are rarely successful and therefore are not a very realistic option available to the president.

President, Party, and Judiciary

The federal judiciary consists of the Supreme Court of the United States, explicitly provided for in the Constitution, and inferior courts, established by Congress under constitutional authorization. The system of inferior courts consists of district courts and courts of appeals, or circuit courts.

The constitutional principles of separation of powers and checks and balances frame the relationship between the executive and judicial branches of the federal government. The chief presidential check is the president's responsibility for nominating federal judges. The judiciary's check on the presidency is its capacity to exercise *judicial review*, which holds the president's actions accountable to the Supreme Court's interpretation of presidential power under the Constitution.

Partisan considerations rarely surface directly in treatments of the federal judiciary. Unlike the chief executive and members of Congress, federal judges are not elected in the wake of party nominations. Rather, they are appointed.

Moreover, unlike the legislature, the judiciary is not organized along partisan lines, with majority and minority institutions. Judges do not take action as overt partisans. Indeed, the judicial role ostensibly requires a nonpartisan stance.

One should not assume, however, that partisan considerations and presidential party leadership have no relevance in the federal judiciary. They do, but in an indirect and often shrouded fashion. In the judicial arena, partisanship manifests itself perhaps most clearly in the appointment of judges.

Appointment in turn is a two-stage process consisting of nomination and confirmation. Article III of the Constitution specifically empowers the president to nominate justices of the Supreme Court. The appointment occurs by and with the advice and consent, or confirmation, of the Senate to the president's nomination. The appointment process for lower federal judges also consists of presidential nomination and senatorial confirmation.

Partisanship and Supreme Court Appointments

According to the Constitution, Congress determines the size of the Supreme Court. Over the years, the number of justices has fluctuated between five and ten. Since 1869, the number has been set at nine.

In making nominations to the Supreme Court when vacancies occur, the president normally considers several factors. Partisanship looms large among these. Certainly, the record of appointments to date indicates that presidents are strongly inclined to name persons who share their party affiliation. Political scientist Henry Abraham found that presidents do so approximately 85 percent of the time. From his examination of the 105 presidential appointees who actually served on the Court since Washington's day, he was able to identify only thirteen or fourteen instances when a president crossed partisan lines in the appointment process.[27] *(See Table 8.)*

Thus, the question is not whether partisanship is associated with presidential nominations to the Supreme Court, but why partisanship is important. Do Supreme Court nominations constitute a presidential party leadership opportunity?

The answer is a qualified yes. In the words of President Theodore Roosevelt,

> In the ordinary and low sense which we attach to the words "partisan" and "politician," a judge of the Supreme Court should be neither. But in the highest sense, in the proper sense, he is not in my judgment fitted for the position unless he is a party man, a constructive statesman constantly keeping in mind his adherence to the principles and policies under which this nation has been built up and in accordance with which it must go on.[28]

Supreme Court nominations are probably the highest form of presidential patronage. They can be used to reward persons for previous services rendered to the president and the party. Several presidents, for example, have elevated members of their cabinets to the court, with the attorney generalship in particular being a steppingstone. In the twentieth century, five attorneys general have been named to the high court: James C. McReynolds (1914), Harlan Fiske Stone (1925), Frank Murphy (1940), Robert H. Jackson (1941), and Thomas C. Clark (1949).

From a slightly different and more symbolic perspective, Supreme Court nominations provide presidents as party leaders with opportunities to reward supportive groups or to broaden the party coalition by reaching out to new groups within the electorate. Here persons appointed can be identified with larger groups of which they are a part. Consider the longstanding customs of maintaining geographical, Catholic, and Jewish seats on the Court, along with the more recent appointments of a black and a woman.

In 1967, in an era featuring dramatic advances in federal civil rights policies, President Johnson nominated noted black civil rights lawyer Thurgood Marshall to a Court seat. In 1981, with women's groups becoming increasingly visible and assertive in the political process, President Reagan named Sandra Day O'Connor to fill a Court vacancy. In each instance, the president recognized an important political constituency and achieved a historic first by choosing a member of a previously unrepresented group.

Notwithstanding presidential initiatives, these interests can and do put pressure on the president for representation on the Court. Similarly, party managers encourage the president to be attentive to party interests in making Supreme Court nominations. In 1969, with two vacancies on the Court confronting President Nixon, national party chairman Rogers Morton encouraged the president to "think Republican." He added, "That's the name of the game. This is our opportunity and we ought to take it." [29]

Party leadership considerations alone, however, are not the primary motivations underlying Supreme Court nominations. Rather, as in the executive branch, presidents first seek policy responsiveness. The stakes are much higher in appointing Supreme Court nominees because of their tenure. Executive appointees serve at the pleasure of the president, but justices, according to the Constitution, hold office during good behavior, which is tantamount to a lifetime term. Thus, presidential nominees on the Court can influence the course of public policy long after the departure of the president.

From this vantage point, partisanship takes on significance as an indicator of policy orientation. Ideological compatibility emerges as the overriding presidential expectation, with party-building considerations occupying a slot of secondary importance.

Republican president Theodore Roosevelt illustrated his endorsement of this distinction in an observation to Henry Cabot Lodge about the prospect of nominating Democrat Horace H. Lurton: "The nominal politics of the man has nothing to do with his actions on the bench. His real politics are all important." [30]

Partisan considerations can reinforce ideological ones in the senatorial confirmation process for presidential appointees. In 1969-1970, the Democrat-controlled Senate rejected two of Republican president Nixon's nominations. More recently, the return of the Democrats to majority status in the Senate in the 1986 elections set the stage for the Senate's 1987 rejection of Republican president Reagan's nominee Robert H. Bork.

Partisanship and Lower Federal Court Appointments

As of 1985, the lower federal court system comprised ninety-four U.S. district courts, with 576 judges, and thirteen U.S. courts of appeals, with 168 judges. The formal

Table 8 Nonpartisan Presidential Supreme Court Nominations

Year	President	President's Party	Nominee	Nominee's Party
1845	Tyler	Whig	Samuel Nelson	Dem.
1863	Lincoln	Rep.	Stephen J. Field	Dem.
1893	B. Harrison	Rep.	Howell E. Jackson	Dem.
1909	Taft	Rep.	Horace H. Lurton	Dem.
1910	Taft	Rep.	Edward D. White [a]	Dem.
1910	Taft	Rep.	Joseph R. Lamar	Dem.
1916	Wilson	Dem.	Louis D. Brandeis	Rep.
1922	Harding	Rep.	Pierce Butler	Dem.
1932	Hoover	Rep.	Benjamin N. Cardozo	Dem.
1939	F. Roosevelt	Dem.	Felix Frankfurter	Ind.
1941	F. Roosevelt	Dem.	Harlan F. Stone [a]	Rep.
1945	Truman	Dem.	Harold H. Burton	Rep.
1956	Eisenhower	Rep.	William J. Brennan, Jr.	Dem.
1971	Nixon	Rep.	Lewis F. Powell, Jr.	Dem.

Source: Henry J. Abraham, *The Judicial Process*, 5th ed. (New York: Oxford University Press, 1986), 68.

a. Elevated from Associate Justice to Chief Justice

appointments process for judges on lower federal courts is the same as for justices on the Supreme Court: presidential nomination and senatorial approval. The president tends to be much less involved, however, owing to the larger number of appointments. Typically, the attorney general and Justice Department associates play a critical role in the recruitment process.

The longstanding practice known as senatorial courtesy also comes into play in these judicial nominations. Under this tradition, senators of the president's party from the state in which the nominee is to serve have effective veto power over that nomination. Thus, presidents or their agents usually consult the relevant senators before making the nomination.

Further, presidents may well encourage recommendations from these senators, or the senators may volunteer candidates. In practice, senators' recommendations for district court judges carry more weight than those for the appeals courts.

Should a judicial vacancy occur in a state where the president's party is not represented in the Senate, the senatorial role remains important. The opposition senators normally are at least consulted. In this case, bipartisan consensus or perhaps allocation of nominations between the senators and the president may occur.

State and local party leaders can play significant roles in these presidential nominations. In addition, members of the state delegation in the House of Representatives who share the president's party affiliation may assume and assert influence over presidential nominations. Their participation is not institutionalized in the fashion of senatorial courtesy; there is no guarantee they will be consulted. Rather, their influence depends on such considerations as power relationships, friendships, and favors owed and claimed. State party leaders sometimes mediate disagreements within the state's senatorial delegation over judicial appointments. Alternatively, if the state delegation in the Congress does not include a member of the president's party, the state party leader may play a significant role.

Other persons and groups who may influence judicial nominations include the American Bar Association, sitting

Table 9 Federal Judicial Appointments from the President's Party, 1884-1985 (percentages)

President	Party	Percentage
Cleveland	Democratic	97.3
B. Harrison	Republican	87.9
McKinley	Republican	95.7
T. Roosevelt	Republican	95.8
Taft	Republican	82.2
Wilson	Democratic	98.6
Harding	Republican	97.7
Coolidge	Republican	94.1
Hoover	Republican	85.7
F. Roosevelt	Democratic	96.4
Truman	Democratic	93.1
Eisenhower	Republican	95.1
Kennedy	Democratic	90.9
L. Johnson	Democratic	95.2
Nixon	Republican	93.7
Ford	Republican	81.2
Carter	Democratic	94.8
Reagan (1985)	Republican	98.0

Source: Henry J. Abraham, *The Judicial Process,* 5th ed. (New York: Oxford University Press, 1986), 75.

judges, and interest groups. In these cases, partisan and party leadership considerations recede in importance.

Lower federal court judges share the president's party affiliation in even higher percentages than do Supreme Court justices—about 90 percent of the time, in Abraham's study. *(See Table 9.)* As with Supreme Court nominations, policy responsiveness remains the overriding consideration. Ideological compatibility also transcends partisanship. Party leadership considerations receive greater weight in staffing the lower federal courts, however, simply because of the vast number of positions, the key role of the senatorial party, and the pressure from state party leaders.

Because members of the Senate are more directly involved in the recruitment of lower court judges, the confirmation process itself is rarely controversial or overtly partisan. The Judiciary Committee receives the nomination, typically holds brief hearings, and then recommends the nomination to the entire Senate. On the Senate floor, lower federal court nominations ordinarily pass by voice votes.

President, Party, and the Electorate

This section examines the relations between the president and the party in the electorate. The concept of the party in the electorate refers to people who are qualified to vote and who identify with the party, its causes, and its candidates.

Party Identification in the U.S. Electorate

Party identification is a psychological attachment a person feels toward a political party. It is ascertained by self classification and manifests itself most significantly in electoral behavior, especially voting.

Survey research over the past half-century indicates that most Americans do develop partisan attachments. These attachments are relatively persistent for individual voters and, in the aggregate, are stable over time. Since the 1930s, for example, the percentage of American adults identifying with the Democratic party has fluctuated some fourteen points between 37 and 51 percent. Republican identifiers have varied about sixteen points, between 22 and 38 percent of the population.[31]

Party identification develops through the process of political socialization, the acquisition of political information and attitudes. Students of political socialization have learned that party loyalties emerge relatively early in a person's life; they are usually in place by the elementary school years. This finding points to the family as a primary agent for determining a person's party identity. Further, surveys of elementary school children indicate that while they may know little else about politics, children are fully aware of the identity of the president and generally associate the president with a political party.[32]

The president's extremely high public visibility and name recognition, and the inevitable association with the president's political party, combine to make the president's status as party leader perhaps most clear from the perspective of the party in the electorate. Here, there is no real appreciation for the conflicts, rivalries, and tensions that can beset exercises of presidential party leadership over the party organization or the congressional party. Rather, the president's party leadership is readily and uncritically acknowledged.

Partisanship and Presidential Support

Partisanship in the electorate influences evaluations of the president by providing filters or screens through which people see the chief executive. As Gallup poll surveys show, voters who identify with the president's party are inclined to be supportive, and opposition party identifiers are not so inclined. *(See Table 10.)*

In addition, evidence indicates that members of the president's party associate themselves and the president with similar policy positions. On the one hand, they tend to assign to the president their stances. On the other, they may alter theirs to conform to the president's.[33]

Forging the Link

This link between the president and the party in the electorate emerged during the presidency of Andrew Jackson. It was not a part of Thomas Jefferson's pioneering presidential party leadership. In Jefferson's day, voter eligibility was restricted by state law to white male property holders.

Moreover, the Constitution had placed presidential selection in the hands of electors, themselves chosen by methods determined by the state legislatures. At the outset, the state legislatures divided between those making the choice of electors themselves and those authorizing the popular vote to do so. More opted for the former than the latter.

Gradually, however, more democratic norms and practices began to prevail. Over the next three decades, revised state constitutions eliminated property requirements for voting, and the constitutions of the new states entering the Union omitted them. Also, the state legislatures that initially had retained control over selection of presidential electors passed that power to the voters. Thus, by the Jackson presidency, the country was more democratic than it was at the founding. A connection between president and mass party had been established.

In turn, Jackson was a popular hero who seized this opportunity unavailable to his predecessors to forge the link. In doing so, he dramatically increased the power of the president in the U.S. political system. Henceforth, the president could claim to have been chosen by the majority of the people and derive power from their sovereignty.

Twentieth-century Technology

Twentieth-century innovations in the realm of communications technology enhanced this popular connection. First radio and then television brought the president into the living rooms of partisan supporters throughout the nation, heightening the sense of identification. In this fashion, the president emerges as the embodiment of the party in the eyes of the voters.

An intriguing question arises about a president's capacity to influence and even induce party identification within the electorate. Most studies of the distribution of party loyalties point toward social class, region, religion, race, and gender as controlling factors. They see individual personalities, and issues also, as having short-term importance in explaining departures from party loyalty.

Thus, in the 1950s, millions of Americans could like Ike (Dwight Eisenhower) without abandoning their traditional Democratic loyalties. Similarly, in the 1980s, even though the Democrats continued to hold the professed allegiance of more voters than did the Republicans, Reagan could attract droves of Democratic voters in his sweeping electoral victories.

Still, fundamental realignments of party loyalties have taken place in years past and have elevated new parties into positions of dominance. Environmental factors, especially economic ones producing depressions, remain an important explanation of these phenomena. But we cannot ignore the potential contribution of presidential party leadership.

One of the major challenges of presidential party leadership becomes establishing or maintaining the party in the dominant position. By this standard, Franklin Roosevelt was eminently successful, and Dwight Eisenhower fell short.

Party identification in the electorate appears to have declined in recent years. This decline can been seen first in a weakening of the commitments of the professed party identifiers and second in the corresponding rise in split-ticket voting. Third, the number of declared independents is on the rise. This trend could undermine the significance of party and of party leadership in presidential relationships with the electorate.

Parties as Coalitions

Students of voting behavior routinely observe that individual voters can be viewed as members of groups within the population. Political parties can be described as shifting coalitions of diverse electoral interests. For example, we

Table 10 Partisanship and Public Approval of the President, 1953-1980

Year	President's party	Partisan group approval (%)		
		Democrats	Republicans	Independents
1953	Rep.	56	87	67
1954	Rep.	49	87	69
1955	Rep.	56	91	74
1956	Rep.	56	93	75
1957	Rep.	47	86	66
1958	Rep.	36	82	56
1959	Rep.	48	88	66
1960	Rep.	44	87	64
1961	Dem.	87	58	72
1962	Dem.	86	49	69
1963	Dem.	79	44	62
1964	Dem.	84	62	69
1965	Dem.	79	49	69
1966	Dem.	65	31	64
1967	Dem.	59	26	38
1968	Dem.	58	27	36
1969	Rep.	50	83	61
1970	Rep.	42	83	57
1971	Rep.	36	79	49
1972	Rep.	41	86	67
1973	Rep.	26	71	43
1974	Rep.	25	60	35
1975	Rep.	33	66	45
1976	Rep.	36	71	51
1977	Dem.	73	46	60
1978	Dem.	56	28	42
1979	Dem.	47	25	35
1980	Dem.	54	26	36

Source: Gallup poll; George C. Edwards III, *The Public Presidency* (New York: St. Martin's Press, 1983), 214.

speak of the New Deal or of the Roosevelt coalition assembled by Franklin Roosevelt under the banner of the Democratic party in the 1930s. The party embraced disparate groups such as southerners, farmers, blue-collar workers, and racial minorities, who provided the party with electoral support for years to come.

To speak of the party in the electorate is to recognize that the electorate is divided into many different groups. Parties seek to enlist the support of these groups on behalf of their nominees. In turn, appealing nominees can point voters in these groups toward their parties. In the electorate a president's personal and party leadership interests converge in an effort to maintain and expand the party's electoral coalition.

In the context of presidential campaigns, candidates make specific overtures to various groups in seeking their support. The most common approach takes the form of an issue or policy stance proposed to gain favor with the group. A candidate seeking to appeal to Jewish voters, for example, might emphasize a commitment to aid for Israel. In 1980, Ronald Reagan called the business community home to the Republican party with a strong advocacy of deregulation.

Political parties assemble platforms, or wide-ranging statements of issue positions, and present them to voters as promises in return for support. The party's presidential nominee usually has a significant role in the development of the platform. The positions that presidential nominees and incumbent presidents take inevitably are attributed to the nominating party.

Presidential Patronage

Patronage provides presidents with opportunities to develop and maintain support from interest groups. Appointments to positions in the executive and judicial branches, particularly those with high visibility, enable the president to recognize and to reward representatives of key interest groups in the electoral coalition. Also, presidents can reach out to new constituencies through an astute use of the appointing power.

As mentioned earlier, President Lyndon Johnson's 1967 nomination of Thurgood Marshall, a black, to a seat on the Supreme Court had immense symbolic value. It recognized the contribution of black voters to the electoral successes of the president and the Democratic party. Further, it demonstrated the abiding commitment of the Johnson administration to the cause of black civil rights.

Political scientist Nelson Polsby identifies "clientele representation" as one of three strategies presidents use in forming cabinets. Presidents acknowledge that many cabinet departments serve as advocates for major interests, and they appoint as departmental secretaries leaders who reflect these interests.[34] Two of President Carter's designations clearly fit this pattern. He selected Cecil Andrus, a former governor of Idaho with close ties to environmentalist groups, to head the Department of Interior. He also named Bob Bergland as secretary of agriculture. Bergland brought to the assignment a lifelong background in agricultural concerns.

Public Liaison

In addition to electoral and symbolic appeals to distinct groups, presidents since Franklin Roosevelt have made the White House a point of direct access for representatives of supportive interest groups. Previous presidents, of course, had to be attentive to the groups that composed the party coalitions. However, the modern presidency has developed an organizational machinery to work directly with a variety of interests, which evolved into the White House Office of Public Liaison.

As with any organization, the expansion of the White House Office has been accompanied by division of labor and specialization. Early on, in the Truman White House, one task of presidential assistant David Niles was to maintain relations with representatives of minority groups. Subsequent presidents built on this foundation and broadened it by designating specific aides as liaisons with specific interest groups. For example, inside the Eisenhower White House, Frederick Morrow, the first black appointed to the White House staff, served as a contact point for the black community on issues pertaining to civil rights. Through designated staff assistants, Lyndon Johnson reached out to Jews and Catholics.

During the Nixon administration, plans to organize and give more official standing to public liaison activities took shape. President Ford established the Office of Public Liaison, with a director and a staff, in the White House. The office has continued under Ford's successors, and it appears to be established firmly as part of the White House Office.

Public liaison aides play an intermediary role. On the one hand, they communicate to the president the needs and interests of the various groups. On the other, they seek to build support for the president and presidential policies within and among the groups.

In institutionalizing this liaison function in the White House Office, in one sense presidents have advanced the cause of presidential party leadership. Because of the clear identification in the public mind between president and party, the party can benefit from the president's successful efforts to call forth support from interest groups.

In another sense, however, this establishment of direct presidential communications with interest groups can work to the detriment of the political party. Historically, parties served as intermediary associations connecting the electorate with the government. The development and maintenance of direct ties between interest groups and the presidency largely bypass the party as an intermediary. To the extent that the president can assemble interest groups into a coalition of supporters, they themselves constitute a party, in a manner of speaking.

This aggregation must then be linked up in an enduring fashion with the existing party organization. The capacity to do so constitutes a measure of considerable success in presidential party leadership. Failure, in turn, intensifies separation between president and party.

FDR to Reagan, Party Leadership Portraits

Presidential style is an elusive concept. As used in this section, it refers to the distinctive behavior of the president as party leader. The presidency is an extremely personal office that takes on the character of its immediate occupant. In a study of presidential character, political scientist James David Barber focused attention on the significance of the personal dimensions of the presidency.[35]

At the same time, presidents exercise leadership within a structural framework that provides opportunities in some situations and constraints in others. An assessment of individual presidents as party leaders therefore must consider both personal and structural factors.

The background and experiences of the president, particularly as they pertain to party politics, are highly relevant. Structurally balancing these characteristics are the distribution and significance of partisanship in both the electorate and Congress during the president's tenure, along with the vitality of the party organization. Linking the two are the assistance the party is able to provide toward the achievement of the president's political objectives and the personal contributions of the president to the structure of party competition.

Political scientist Ralph Goldman has developed a useful categorization for assessing presidents as party leaders. He classifies presidents as nonpartisan, subpartisan, transpartisan, or partisan. Nonpartisans largely lack experience in party politics and try to remain above the party battle. Subpartisans tend to be seen and to act as representatives of factions within the party. Transpartisans exhibit weak party identities and cross party lines in their own political careers. Finally, partisans openly identify with their parties and engage in party management and party-building activities.[36] *(See Table 11.)*

In assessing the recent presidents, Goldman describes most of them as partisan. His exceptions are Eisenhower, whom he classifies as nonpartisan, and Carter, viewed as a subpartisan.

Political scientists Roger Brown and David Welborn have categorized presidents as party leaders another way, using two characteristics. The first is party leadership, which they define as "the encouragement and development of party organization and . . . the active solicitation of public support for a party's objectives and candidates." The second is partisanship, the presidents' attitudes toward their parties "in the affective and symbolic sense," that is emotionally and associationally. From their descriptions of presidents as either "weak" or "strong" in these two characteristics, Brown and Welborn created a four-part grid.[37]

Presidents classified as "strong" with reference to party leadership were seen as relatively attentive to the needs and interests of the party organization. For example, in making presidential appointments and relating positively to its ranking officials as enthusiastic about rallying the public to the causes of the party through midterm campaigning. "Weak" party leadership presidents were viewed as inattentive and even antagonistic toward the party organization and less willing to invest their own political capital on behalf of the party.

The "partisanship" dimension refers to the president's personal identification with the party, a function of background and experiences. "Strong" partisans have a well-established association with the party label, while their "weak" counterparts lack, in relative terms, this connection. *(See Figure 1.)*

Franklin D. Roosevelt

Franklin D. Roosevelt was a transitional figure in the history of the presidency. He presided over the emergence of the modern presidency. His actions as party leader prefigured some developments and patterns that have become standard features for his successors. Roosevelt was an enthusiastic partisan who was instrumental in remaking the Democratic party.

Roosevelt came from a distinguished New York family. His branch of Roosevelts settled in Hyde Park, where they were known as the Democratic Roosevelts. This label distinguished them from their Oyster Bay cousins, led by Theodore, who were Republican to the core.

While still in his twenties, Franklin Roosevelt entered party politics and ran successfully for a seat in the state Senate. He supported Woodrow Wilson's presidential candidacy in 1912. After Wilson was elected, he named Roosevelt assistant secretary of the navy. Roosevelt held this position until the end of the Wilson administration. The Democratic party nominated him for the vice presidency and James M. Cox for the presidency in 1920.

Unsuccessful in that quest, he retired to private life and underwent a debilitating bout with polio. He labored in behalf of fellow Democrat Al Smith in Smith's campaigns for the Democratic presidential nomination in 1924 and 1928. Following Smith's nomination in 1928, Roosevelt received the state party nomination to succeed Smith as governor. Elected in 1928 and reelected in 1930, he sought his party's presidential nomination in 1932 with a clear and longstanding identity as a Democrat.

His successful nomination campaign was spearheaded

Table 11   Types of Presidential Party Leadership

Nonpartisan	Subpartisan	Transpartisan	Partisan
Washington	J. Adams	Tyler	Jefferson
J. Q. Adams	Pierce	Fillmore	Madison
W. H. Harrison	Buchanan	Lincoln (1865)	Monroe
Taylor	Hayes	A. Johnson	Jackson
Grant	Arthur	Cleveland (1893)	Van Buren
Eisenhower	Taft	T. Roosevelt	Polk
	Harding		Garfield
	Carter		Cleveland (1885)
			B. Harrison
			McKinley
			Wilson
			Coolidge
			Hoover
			F. D. Roosevelt
			Truman
			Kennedy
			L. B. Johnson
			Nixon
			Ford
			Reagan

Source: Ralph M. Goldman, "The American President as Party Leader: A Synoptic History," in *Presidents and Their Parties: Leadership or Neglect?* ed. Robert Harmel (New York: Praeger, 1983), 21.

by party chieftain James A. Farley, who traveled the country lining up support among key party activists. For the general election campaign, he named Farley as party chair and emphasized his party affiliation. His electoral victory accompanied Democratic successes in the congressional elections.

Thus, Roosevelt entered the White House as an unabashed partisan with comfortable party majorities in Congress. Not surprisingly, he openly grasped the mantle of party leadership. The Democrats in Congress responded positively by enacting a broad social and economic program commonly called the "New Deal."

Roosevelt's relations with congressional Democrats also featured considerable conflict, however. Not only did the president fail dramatically in his effort to gain legislative approval to add justices to the Supreme Court (the "court-packing" plan), he also vetoed a record number of congressional bills.

Both inside and outside Congress, Roosevelt sought to remake the Democratic party in a modified image that would alter its structure and its ideological orientation. This effort entailed bringing new groups and forces into the Democratic electoral coalition. It also meant moving the party in a more liberal direction ideologically. This required extraordinary efforts to influence the composition of the party in office by openly campaigning against recalcitrant incumbents in congressional party primaries.

Finally, he sought to relocate control within the party away from the traditional party bosses in the states and localities, replacing them as leaders with his agents in positions of responsibility within the ranks of the federal government. It was partly this development that led to a widely publicized falling-out between Roosevelt and party chairman Farley.

Although he fell short of full achievement of these ambitious party leadership objectives, Roosevelt nonethe-

Figure 1   Strength of Partisanship and Party Leadership
in Recent Presidencies

Partisanship

		STRONG	WEAK
S T R O N G		Kennedy Ford	
W E A K		Nixon	Johnson Carter

Party Leadership

Source: Roger G. Brown and David M. Welborn, "Presidents and
Their Parties: Performance and Prospects," *Presidential Studies
Quarterly* 12 (Summer 1982): 305.

less enjoyed conspicuous success in his exercise of presidential party leadership. Further, his extraordinarily long tenure, spanning both the Great Depression and World War II, established him as the exemplar of the modern presidency. Thus, subsequent presidents are evaluated as party leaders against Roosevelt's benchmark.

Harry S Truman

On Roosevelt's death in 1945, Vice President Harry S Truman succeeded to the presidency. In his rise to the vice presidency, Truman developed an intimate association with Democratic party politics. Indeed, he began his political career in his native Missouri toiling on behalf of the Pendergast machine in the Kansas City area, renowned for its strength and its corruption. He served as county judge and received the party nomination for the United States Senate in return for his loyalty to and services in behalf of the party organization. Party loyalty marked his senatorial career, placing him in position to receive the vice-presidential nomination in 1944. He held that office less than three months before Roosevelt's death.

A vice president elevated to the presidency through a vacancy inherits certain constitutionally based roles and responsibilities. The presidential role of party leader, however, operates outside the specific constitutional framework. Thus, Truman's exercise of party leadership as an accidental president illlustrates a variation from the normal pattern whereby the party nomination initially confers leadership status that is confirmed by the victory in the general election.

Truman became party leader without the legitimacy of nomination and election. Nevertheless, he benefited from Robert Hannegan's presence in the national party chair. Hannegan was an old Missouri political ally who held that position in part because of Senator Truman's earlier recommendation. In turn, Hannegan had been instrumental in

pushing for Truman's selection as Roosevelt's vice-presidential running mate in 1944.

Thus, the relationship between the president and the party organization began on a positive note. Following Hannegan's departure, Truman did not hesitate to exercise his presidential prerogative in recommending a successor to the national committee. His choice, Sen. J. Howard McGrath of Rhode Island, quickly received committee approval.

Truman began his presidential tenure with Democratic party majorities in both houses of Congress. The foreign and defense policy tasks of concluding World War II and preparing for peace in the postwar world precluded, however, any major domestic policy initiatives at the outset. In the 1946 midterm congressional elections, the Republicans won majorities in both houses. The president pursued a combative strategy in dealing with the Republican congressional leadership for the next two years of his presidency.

In 1948, Truman won an upset victory over his Republican challenger, Gov. Thomas E. Dewey of New York. The Democrats also regained control of Congress and maintained it for the duration of Truman's presidency. During these years, Truman sought without noteworthy success to secure the enactment of his domestic policy agenda, the Fair Deal.

One major problem Truman faced in his party relations was the developing strains in the Democratic party coalition. A major controversy over the party's commitment to civil rights split the 1948 national convention, resulting in a walkout by several southern delegations and the subsequent formation of the Dixiecrat party for the general election. The party also experienced ideological conflict that led to the departure of a portion of its left wing that year under the banner of former vice president Henry Wallace and the Progressive party.

In sum, Truman followed Roosevelt in openly and enthusiastically embracing partisanship. He was a partisan Democrat to the core, fully comfortable with the mantle of party leadership in spite of the extraordinary conditions surrounding his accession. Yet his presidential party leadership did not demonstrate the transformational character of his predecessor's.

Dwight D. Eisenhower

Dwight D. Eisenhower entered national politics at the presidential level following his distinguished military career. He lacked any background or experience in party politics. Courted by representatives of both major parties, he cast his lot with the Republicans when they had not won a presidential election in more than two decades and when they held the allegiance of a distinct minority of the electorate.

Eisenhower's presidential candidacy attracted an abundance of enthusiastic amateurs under the organizational umbrella Citizens for Eisenhower. In the years to come, the president labored without noteworthy success to integrate this element into the regular party organization. In that effort, he encountered resistance from both amateurs and party regulars.

As president, he exhibited a leadership style that political scientist Fred Greenstein has characterized as "hidden hand." [38] He self-consciously and systematically sought to obscure his political activities. While all presidents are aware of the political benefits to be derived from a nonpolitical posture, Eisenhower appreciated this reality more than most.

He was acutely aware of his lack of formal authority over the Republican party. This is clearly evident in his comments at two press conferences about midway through his tenure. In the first, weeks away from his 1956 reelection victory, he observed:

> Now, let's remember, there are no national parties in the United States. There are forty-eight state parties, then they are the ones that determine the people that belong to those parties.
>
> There is nothing I can do to say that one is not a Republican. The most I can say is that in many things they do not agree with me. We have got to remember that these are state organizations, and there is nothing I can do to say so-and-so is a Republican and so-and-so is not a Republican.[39]

In the second statement, less than six months into his second term, he noted: "He, the president, is the leader not of the, you might say, hierarchy of control in any political party. What he is is the leader who translates the platform into a legislative program in collaboration with his own executive departments and with the legislative leaders."[40]

He regularly bemoaned his inability to move the party in the direction of the "modern Republicanism" he espoused. In turn, party activists often viewed him as inattentive to their interests. Certainly, he demonstrated little concern with or enthusiasm for the exercise of patronage power as a party-building device.

His administrative style featured extensive delegation of authority, and he tended to view "politics" as the special province of the party chair. Thus, the party chairs who served during his presidency found themselves generally more within the presidential circle than has been typical since World War II. His 1956 reelection campaign, under the general direction of party chairman Leonard Hall, featured extensive integration with the national party effort.

In Congress, the Republican party gained a majority of the seats in both houses in the 1952 elections that brought Eisenhower to the White House. The party lost control of Congress in the midterm 1954 elections, however, and remained in the minority for the remainder of his presidency. This development forced Eisenhower to look beyond the party ranks in seeking support for his policy initiatives and further muted his partisanship.

Thus, for Eisenhower, personal and structural factors combined to diminish the emphasis on presidential partisanship in comparison with the Roosevelt and Truman years. He was not personally comfortable with its exercise. Neither did the political climate encourage it. Indeed, Eisenhower perceived political benefits in denying it. Further, such efforts as he made to reshape the Republican party and make it over as a majority party failed. Still, he remained a revered and unifying figure in the eyes of most of his fellow Republicans.

John F. Kennedy

In contrast with his predecessor, John F. Kennedy ardently embraced partisanship. His family was closely identified with the Democratic party, and successful congressional and senatorial contests under the party banner had preceded his race for the presidency. In the early days of his presidential candidacy, he proclaimed his leadership responsibilities in the party arena.

No president, it seems to me, can escape politics. He has not only been chosen by the nation—he has been chosen by his party. And if he insists that he is "president of all the people" and should, therefore, offend none of them—if he blurs the issues and differences between the parties—if he neglects the party machinery and avoids his party's leadership—then he has not only weakened the political party ... he has dealt a blow to the democratic process itself.[41]

Kennedy installed his long-time political ally, Connecticut party chairman John Bailey, in the national chair. There, Bailey lacked direct access to the president. White House appointments secretary Kenneth P. O'Donnell provided primary liaison between the party organization and the president.

In Congress, Democratic majorities controlled both chambers during the Kennedy administration, but a large portion of the party and committee leadership consisted of southern conservatives, who were not especially keen on his policy initiatives. As a result, the Kennedy administration had failed to achieve noteworthy legislative successes at the time of the president's assassination.

As party leader, President Kennedy reverted to the Roosevelt-Truman pattern of unabashed partisanship in his rhetoric. His substantive accomplishments in this realm were not particularly noteworthy. Any evaluation of his presidency must take into account, however, his short tenure in office.

Lyndon B. Johnson

Although clearly identified as a Democrat, Lyndon B. Johnson sought consensus throughout his political career. He came to Washington from a background in the one-party politics of his native Texas, where party organization was notoriously weak. In his rise to the presidency he served consecutively as congressional assistant, New Deal bureaucrat, congressman, senator, and vice president.

On assuming the presidency following the assassination of John Kennedy, Johnson inherited the party management team assembled by his predecessor. He retained them, in the interest of party unity and also because he needed their expertise in his upcoming quest for a presidential term on his own. Still, he felt he could not fully trust the Kennedy loyalists to act in his behalf.

Johnson interspersed his own group of trusted associates amid the Kennedy holdovers. In the realm of party relations, the main responsibilities initially were assigned to Walter Jenkins at the White House and Clifton Carter, who went to the national committee as the president's untitled representative. Subsequently, Marvin Watson took over the White House end, and John Criswell succeeded Carter at the national headquarters. Having established this structure, Johnson generally was inattentive and occasionally even antagonistic toward the needs and interests of the party organization.

In Johnson's 1964 campaign for president, his agents supervised the convention proceedings closely. The national party headquarters, however, was much less visible within the campaign organization than its counterpart had been during President Eisenhower's 1956 reelection campaign. After the Republicans nominated Barry Goldwater, a strong ideological conservative, Johnson was able to draw support from disaffected Republicans. In doing so, he blurred his own partisanship and undertook a nonpartisan effort. The result was a landslide victory of historic proportions.

The 1964 elections also brought impressive Democratic majorities to both houses of Congress, giving Johnson a strengthened partisan base on which to seek the enactment of his party's legislative program. He was much more successful than his predecessor not only because of the improved arithmetic, but also because of his considerable skill as a legislative leader. He clearly appealed to party loyalty and unity, but he also worked closely and cooperatively with the opposition leadership, particularly on civil rights legislation, to offset southern Democratic opposition and to promote national unity.

As his term wore on, Johnson faced increasing opposition within the ranks of his own party to both his domestic initiatives and his foreign policies. The Vietnam War was especially divisive. At the beginning of the 1968 presidential campaign season, Sen. Eugene McCarthy of Minnesota announced his challenge to Johnson's expected renomination. McCarthy's impressive early showing in the New Hampshire primary encouraged Sen. Robert F. Kennedy of New York to join the race. In a dramatic nationally televised address on March 31, 1968, President Johnson announced that he would neither seek nor accept the party's presidential nomination. For the remainder of his term, Johnson affected a nonpartisan stance, although his agents were very visible at that summer's Democratic national convention.

President Johnson never appeared fully comfortable in his role as party leader. His consensus style did not allow the exclusion of significant elements of Congress or the electorate from his domain.

During his retirement years, the vehement opposition he had engendered within the ranks of the party lingered, precluding his assumption of a role as party elder statesman. Indeed, at the 1972 national convention, he received none of the accolades customarily accorded a former nominee and president. He died in 1973.

Richard Nixon

Richard Nixon began his campaign for the White House in 1968 with a well-deserved reputation as a slashing Republican partisan. He had earned this designation during his years as a member of the U.S. House and Senate from 1946 through 1952. He reinforced it as Eisenhower's vice president from 1953 to 1961. As vice president he assumed many of the responsibilities of party leadership with which Eisenhower was uncomfortable. He gained the enduring gratitude of the Republican activists for his extensive party-building efforts. His scathing attacks on Democratic personalities and programs simultaneously generated emotional public support and antagonism. In his successful 1968 presidential campaign, however, Nixon labored to appear above partisanship and called for a lowering of voices and an end to divisiveness.

In the Oval Office, President Nixon frequently disappointed party regulars with his general disregard and occasional animosity toward the party organization. He assembled a team of personal loyalists in the White House who demonstrated a low regard for the needs and interests of the party organization. Three national party chairmen—Rep. Rogers Morton, Sen. Robert Dole, and George Bush—found themselves largely excluded from the conduct of presidential party leadership.

In Congress, Nixon encountered Democratic party majorities in both houses. This reality forced on him a nominal posture of bipartisanship, although the opposition Democrats were not inclined to support his policy initiatives.

When the time came to organize his 1972 reelection effort, Nixon chose virtually to ignore the Republican National Committee in favor of the Committee to Re-elect the President, a personal electoral vehicle. The presidential effort went forward with little attention to the needs of other Republicans on the party ticket. In seeking reelection, Nixon did give rhetorical support to the concept of a "new American majority" that would realign the party coalitions.

In June 1972, agents of the president's campaign organization were arrested on charges of breaking and entering the headquarters of the Democratic National Committee at the Watergate office building. The scandal that ensued, known as "Watergate," had little effect on the election. President Nixon won an overwhelming victory.

Eventually, however, Watergate and related scandals drove the president from office. By the time he resigned on August 9, 1974, he had lost the support of large numbers of party activists and officeholders whom he had treated so cavalierly throughout his presidency. Further, the Republican party inevitably was tainted by the scandal. Like his predecessor Lyndon Johnson, Nixon was viewed as a pariah in party circles in the years immediately following his departure.

As president, Nixon backed away from the extreme partisanship that had characterized his political career. Indeed, his attitudes and behavior toward the Republican party were surprisingly hostile. In part, this shift can be attributed to his conception of the presidential office as above the party battle. Moreover, his position as a minority party president mitigated against emphasis on partisanship. This was true both for Congress and the electorate. Thus, Nixon's party leadership experience was unsatisfactory in several respects.

Gerald R. Ford

Gerald R. Ford became president on August 9, 1974. His background was in Congress, where he had toiled from 1949 until 1973 in behalf of the Republican party. He served as minority leader from 1965 until his elevation to the vice presidency in 1973.

The unique circumstances that produced his accession, and his struggle to maintain his incumbency in the face of vigorous nomination and general election challenges that dominated his tenure, elevated the significance of party leadership considerations. Ford was not only the first president to come to office via the resignation of his predecessor; he was also the first person to become vice president through the procedures of the Twenty-fifth Amendment—nomination by the president and confirmation by majority vote of both houses of Congress.

In his interaction with the national party organization, Ford was unlike any of his "accidental" predecessors in that he had come to both the vice presidency and the presidency under the procedures of the Twenty-fifth Amendment. In no way had the national party legitimized his incumbency.

In certain respects, the pattern of Ford's dealings with the national party organization did not differ significantly from Nixon's. A vacancy in the party chair occurred when Ford sent George Bush to head the U.S. Liaison Office in China. The incumbent vice chair, Mary Louise Smith, received the president's blessing as Bush's successor. She became the first woman to chair the Republican National Committee. Meanwhile, White House political advisers provided liaison with the party headquarters.

The initial expectation that Ford might be a caretaker president and not seek the 1976 presidential nomination for himself, and the subsequent prospect and presence of a serious nomination challenge from Ronald Reagan, produced an unusual relationship between the party chair and the president. Although Smith publicly supported Ford, she did not overtly forestall or hinder the Reagan challenge in a manner comparable to previous party chairs favoring incumbent presidents.

Ford's postnomination choice of Sen. Robert Dole as his vice-presidential running mate signaled his intention to assume an above-the-battle, presidential stance in the upcoming general election campaign. A former party chair, Dole spiritedly took on the tasks of partisan attacks on the Democratic opposition.

Ford's dealings with the Democratic-controlled Congress were more congenial (if no less partisan) than Nixon's had been during the latter years of his presidency. During Ford's long years of service in the House of Representatives, he had established comfortable social and working relationships with the Democratic party leaders in the Congress. Executive-legislative relations during his presidency, however, suffered not only from conflicts over policy and ideology but also from the legislators' desires to assert themselves against a presidency weakened by the ravages of Vietnam and Watergate.

As party leader, President Ford openly and willingly embraced his party. He asserted his presidential prerogatives in party affairs despite his unique status as an accidental president. He strove with some success to restore the party's credibility in the aftermath of Watergate. As is true of John Kennedy, his brief tenure as president makes evaluation inconclusive.

Jimmy Carter

In 1976, former Georgia governor Jimmy Carter came out of obscurity to win the Democratic presidential nomination and then to defeat President Ford in the general election. He assumed the reins of party leadership as an outsider unfamiliar with national party politics.

In his dealings with the national party organization, he followed closely in the pattern of his recent predecessors. After receiving the party nomination, he retained the incumbent party chair, Robert Strauss, for the duration of the campaign while keeping intact and relying on his personal campaign organization for the conduct of the general election campaign. After the election, he brought Strauss into the administration and designated former Maine governor Ken Curtis as the party chair.

Meanwhile, political operations were controlled by the White House. Indeed, the national committee became so outraged by the unwillingness of the White House to address the needs and interests of the party organization, especially in the realm of patronage, that it formally rebuked the president for his neglect.

One year into his presidency, Carter attempted to make amends. He replaced Curtis as party chair with

Lyndon B. Johnson Library

One of the most influential presidential lobbyists was Lyndon B. Johnson, shown here with Senate Majority Leader Mike Mansfield, left, and Minority Leader Everett McKinley Dirksen.

Texas politico John C. White and pledged increased accommodation and sensitivity in the future. For the remainder of his presidency, the national committee operation supported the president without incidents. This support was an important factor in the president's successful effort to thwart a major challenge to his renomination mounted by Massachusetts senator Edward M. Kennedy.

In dealing with the Congress, Carter had the benefit of comfortable party majorities in both houses. Still, he achieved little success for his legislative initiatives. His difficulties stemmed from several sources. First, his electoral victory had been narrow, and he had run behind Democratic senatorial and congressional victors in most districts and states. Thus, he could not claim that his coattails had secured the positions of many legislators. Second, his ideological leanings were moderate, placing him at odds with many of his fellow partisans of a more liberal bent. As an outsider, he was unfamiliar with the norms and procedures of the Congress. Finally, he appeared uncomfortable with expectations of many legislators that presidents seeking their support shower them with personal attention and engage in lengthy bargaining sessions.

President Carter was never comfortable with the cloak of party leadership. His approach to presidential leadership was more administrative and technical than political. His antiestablishment campaign placed him at odds with both the party organization and the congressional party.

Ronald Reagan

Ronald Reagan came to Republican party politics relatively late in life. After a lengthy career as a Hollywood actor, during most of which he claimed a Democratic party affiliation, he gradually shifted allegiance during the 1950s. In 1960, he openly supported Nixon's presidential candidacy; and in 1964, he was highly visible in behalf of Barry Goldwater. By this time, he clearly identified with the ideological conservatives of the Republican party's right wing and served as one of that faction's chief spokespersons.

Reagan successfully sought the Republican nomination for the governorship of California in 1966, and he went on to win in the general election. In 1968, he conducted a very tentative campaign for the GOP presidential nomination that failed to ignite. He won reelection as governor in 1970, retiring at the end of his second term in 1974. In 1976, he challenged incumbent president Gerald Ford for the party's presidential nomination and came close to success. In 1980, he won a comfortable nomination victory, followed by his election in November over President Jimmy Carter.

Although late blooming, Reagan's Republican party loyalty had become extremely strong over the previous two decades. He willingly accepted the responsibilities of party leadership. Structurally, the relationship between the Reagan White House and the Republican National Committee developed along the lines of his presidential predecessors, with White House aides assuming responsibility for political operations, including party liaison. Rumors of White House dissatisfaction with his performance accompanied the resignation of Richard Richards as national party chair after two years in office.

Nevertheless, the spirit of the relationship between the party chair and the White House was much more positive than it had been during the Johnson, Nixon, and Carter presidencies. Cooperation and good will prevailed as President Reagan provided strong support and encouragement for the party-building efforts undertaken by the national headquarters.

In dealing with the Congress, Reagan benefited from the 1980 senatorial elections that placed the Republican party in a majority position for the first time in a quarter-century. He worked closely and cooperatively with the congressional party leadership in pursuit of economic policy objectives.

His relations with the House of Representatives, still controlled by the Democrats, were more antagonistic. He tried to expand the boundaries of his secure party base by enlisting the support of conservative House Democrats. In that respect, he emphasized ideology over partisanship.

In 1984, Reagan won a massive reelection victory over Democratic challenger Walter F. Mondale. The party majorities in the House and Senate remained stable. In 1986, however, the Democrats recaptured control of the Senate, preventing the president from relying primarily on the party symbol in pursuing his policy objectives there. Increasingly, he resorted to threats of presidential vetoes in congressional relations.

Reagan's record of party leadership may be regarded as among the most successful in the modern era. He was a committed partisan who established and maintained congenial relations with the congressional party and the party organization.

Moreover, his electoral successes attracted new groups of voters to the Republican ranks. Whether they stay in this camp remains to be seen. Nevertheless, he restored a positive aura to the presidential role of party leader following a sequence of negative experiences.

As this review has indicated, the experiences of the modern presidents as party leaders have differed in numerous and significant ways, yet some common features also have emerged. The variations appear to be threefold. They pertain first to the presidents' personal orientations toward partisanship, generally positive or negative; second to the tone of president-party relations, relatively congenial or hostile; and third to the political circumstances confronted by the incumbents, either favorable or unfavorable for the exercise of party leadership.

These factors can either inform and reinforce one another or diverge for particular presidents.

Among modern presidents, Roosevelt, Truman, Kennedy, Ford and Reagan viewed partisanship in generally positive fashions. Eisenhower, Johnson, Nixon, and Carter were less affirmatively disposed. Party relations were relatively congenial for presidents Roosevelt, Truman, Eisenhower, Kennedy, and Reagan, while they were more hostile for presidents Johnson, Nixon, and Carter.

Political circumstances relate primarily to party competition in the electorate and in the government. Since the Great Depression, the Democratic party has consistently claimed more professed loyalists than its Republican opposition, measured by public opinion surveys and voter registration totals.

Further, the Democratic party has controlled Congress the great majority of the time. The only exceptions were 1947-1949, 1953-1955, and 1981-1987. On the first two occasions, the GOP held both houses; on the third, only the Senate came under Republican domination. Thus, in general, for the time period considered, Democratic presidents would appear to be better positioned to exercise party leadership in the political arena than their Republican counterparts.

Roosevelt, Eisenhower, Johnson, Nixon (1972), and Reagan all won comfortable, if not landslide, electoral victories. Truman, Kennedy, Nixon (1968), and Carter had much narrower winning margins. Ford was an unelected president throughout his brief tenure. The general expectation is that a generous margin of electoral victory should enhance the prospects for presidential party leadership.

Taking these factors together, Roosevelt more clearly combined personal partisan commitment, positive party relations, and a favorable political context for the exercise of presidential party leadership. Truman, Kennedy, Ford, and Reagan generally shared his positive orientations and congenial relations amid less favorable political circumstances.

Alternatively, while Eisenhower's party relations were relatively congenial, he lacked partisan commitment and confronted a political setting that inhibited party leadership. Johnson, Nixon and Carter faced very different political circumstances—Johnson's positive and the others less so. All not only appeared personally uncomfortable with party leadership, they also experienced and contributed to generally antagonistic relations with the parties they nominally led.

Party Leadership and Presidential Power

This section addresses the relationship of party leadership to presidential power by examining the relationship between party chief and other presidential roles.

In a constitutional sense, party leadership conveys no power. The president derives no legal power from it, and within the party, the president lacks command authority. Rather, party leadership operates within the domains of bargaining and negotiation.

Party leadership ordinarily is intertwined with other leadership roles and responsibilities. The reason other elements in the party—elected and appointed public officials, party organization officials and activists, and party supporters in the electorate—look to the president for leadership has less to do with party power per se than with power coming from other sources, such as the Constitution and the laws, or public support.

The exercise of party leadership often enables the president to perform successfully in other roles. Policy responsiveness is an important presidential expectation in making executive appointments. Although partisanship is not an absolute requirement for policy responsiveness, it serves as a convenient indicator. Presidents' effectiveness as chief executive turns in part on their success as party leader.

Similarly, by acting as party leader the president can be an effective legislative leader, another presidential role that has no constitutional authority. The party connection can unite the separated executive and legislative branches under presidential leadership. In a divided party government, however, where opposing parties control the White House and Congress, presidential party leadership turns into an obstacle rather than an opportunity.

Party leadership is relevant to the president's powers and responsibilities as chief economic manager because the general public identifies the president with the party. The president's success in the economic arena can influence the electoral fortunes of the party's nominees, including the president.

Further, presidential approaches to economic management can reflect ideological positions associated with the party. For example, the more ideologically conservative Republican presidents have tended to view monetary policy as more appropriate than fiscal policy. The more liberal Democratic presidents have tended to prefer fiscal to monetary policy.

Presidential party leadership has less obvious relevance for the president's responsibilities in the diplomatic and military arenas of foreign affairs. The United States has a long heritage of foreign policy bipartisanship. Nevertheless, the electoral and ideological considerations mentioned above can come into play here also, along with those elements of partisanship associated with political appointments.

The presidential role of chief of state surely has the least relevance for party leadership. In symbolizing the nation undivided, the president ostensibly puts partisanship aside. The problem here is that presidential roles cannot simply be discarded like hats. The basic contradiction between these two roles produces tension for the president and confusion throughout the political system.

President Nixon's attempts to deal with allegations concerning his involvement in the Watergate scandal while pursuing his ongoing presidential responsibilities illustrate this situation. In his January 1974 State of the Union message, he bemoaned that "One year of Watergate is enough," and he asserted that in responding to congressional demands, he would never do "anything that weakens the office of the president of the United States or impairs the ability of the presidents of the future to make the great decisions that are so essential to this nation and to the world." [42]

A few weeks later, during a March 19 question-and-answer session before the National Association of Broadcasters, the president urged the House Judiciary Committee considering the issue of presidential impeachment to resolve the question quickly, asserting that "dragging out Watergate drags down America." [43]

The paradoxes of the president's role as party chief will remain unresolved. The president of all the people is the champion of a specific part and the antagonist of another. Yet, in acknowledging the divisiveness inherent in presidential party leadership, we also must credit it with providing the means for presidential leadership in other roles. Without embodying specific powers, it nevertheless enhances the president's power position in the political order.

Notes

1. Woodrow Wilson, *Constitutional Government in the United States* (New York: Columbia University Press, 1980), 67.
2. James MacGregor Burns, *Leadership* (New York: Harper and Row, 1978), 4.
3. Frank J. Sorauf, *Party Politics in America* (Boston: Little, Brown, 1968), 11-12.
4. This section draws on Harold F. Bass, Jr., "Thomas Jefferson's Presidential Party Leadership" (Paper presented at the 1987 annual meeting of the American Political Science Association, Chicago, September 3-6, 1987).
5. Robert V. Remini, "The Emergence of Political Parties and Their Effect on the Presidency," in *Power and the Presidency,* ed. Philip C. Dolce and George H. Skau (New York: Scribner's, 1976), 30-32.
6. This section draws on Harold F. Bass, Jr., "The President and the National Party Organization," in *Presidents and Their Parties: Leadership or Neglect?* ed. Robert Harmel (New York: Praeger, 1983), 59-89.
7. Theodore H. White, *The Making of the President 1972* (New York: Atheneum, 1973), 61.
8. Rowland Evans and Robert Novak, *Nixon in the White House: The Frustration of Power* (New York: New American Library, 1968) 71-74, 364.
9. Jeb S. Magruder, *An American Life: One Man's Road to Watergate* (New York: Atheneum, 1975), 178.
10. Theodore H. White, *Breach of Faith: The Fall of Richard Nixon* (New York: Atheneum, 1975), 97.
11. Harry S Truman, "The President's News Conference of October 31, 1945," *Public Papers of the Presidents of the United States, Harry S Truman, 1945* (Washington, D.C.: Government Printing Office, 1953), 456.
12. Dorothy G. Fowler, *The Cabinet Politician: The Postmaster General, 1829-1909* (New York: Columbia University Press, 1943), 302.
13. Hoover Commission, *Report on Organization of the Executive Branch of Government* (New York: McGraw-Hill, 1949), 224-225.
14. Richard Fenno, *The President's Cabinet: An Analysis in the Period from Wilson to Eisenhower* (Cambridge: Harvard University Press, 1959), 70.

15. President's Committee on Administrative Management, *Administrative Management of the Government of the United States* (Washington, D.C.: Government Printing Office, 1937), 5.

16. Herbert Kaufman, "The Growth of the Federal Personnel System," in *The Federal Government Service*, 2d ed., ed. Wallace S. Sayre (Englewood Cliffs, N.J.: Prentice-Hall, 1965), 40-53.

17. James A. Farley, *Behind the Ballot: The Personal History of a Politician* (New York: Harcourt, Brace, 1938), 223-238.

18. Kaufman, "Growth of the Federal Personnel System," 55.

19. James A. Farley, *Jim Farley's Story: The Roosevelt Years* (New York: Whittlesey House, 1948), 68.

20. George C. Edwards III, *Presidential Influence in Congress* (San Francisco: Freeman, 1980), 125-188 passim.

21. Ibid., 129, citing Harry McPherson, *A Political Education* (Boston: Little, Brown, 1972), 197; and Russell D. Renka, "Legislative Leadership and Marginal Vote-Gaining Strategies in the Kennedy and Johnson Presidencies" (Paper delivered at the annual meeting of the Southwestern Political Science Association, Houston, Texas, April, 1978, 26-27).

22. James Madison, *Federalist No. 51*, in *The Federalist Papers*, Alexander Hamilton, James Madison, and John Jay (New York: Bantam, 1982), 262.

23. George C. Edwards III, *The Public President: The Pursuit of Public Support* (New York: St. Martin's Press, 1983), 83-88.

24. Edwards, *Presidential Influence in Congress*, 77.

25. Roger G. Brown, "Presidents and Midterm Campaigners," in *Presidents and Their Parties*, ed. Harmel, 127.

26. Sidney M. Milkis, "Presidents and Party Purges: With Special Emphasis on the Lessons of 1938," in *Presidents and Their Parties*, ed. Harmel, 167.

27. Henry J. Abraham, *The Judicial Process: An Introductory Analysis of the Courts of the United States, England, and France*, 5th ed. (New York: Oxford University Press, 1986), 68.

28. Walter F. Murphy and C. Herman Pritchett, *Courts, Judges, and Politics: An Introduction to the Judicial Process*, 4th ed. (New York: Random House, 1986), 150; citing Henry Cabot Lodge, *Selections from the Correspondence of Theodore Roosevelt and Henry Cabot Lodge, 1894-1918* (New York: Scribner's, 1925), vol. 1, 517-519.

29. Abraham, *The Judicial Process*, 74; citing *New York Times*, May 17, 1969, 1.

30. Ibid., 76; citing Lodge, *Correspondence of Theodore Roosevelt and Henry Cabot Lodge*, vol. 2, 228.

31. William H. Flanigan and Nancy H. Zingale, *Political Behavior of the American Electorate*, 4th ed. (Boston: Allyn and Bacon, 1979), 54; Frank J. Sorauf and Paul Allen Beck, *Party Politics in America*, 6th ed. (Glenwood, Ill.: Scott, Foresman, 1988), 167.

32. See Fred I. Greenstein, *Children and Politics* (New Haven: Yale University Press, 1965); Robert D. Hess and Judith V. Torney, *The Development of Political Attitudes in Children* (Chicago: Aldine, 1967).

33. Edwards, *The Public Presidency*, 213.

34. Nelson W. Polsby, "Presidential Cabinet Making: Lessons for the Political System," *Political Science Quarterly* 93 (Spring 1978): 19.

35. James David Barber, *The Presidential Character: Predicting Performance in the White House*, 2d ed. (New York: Prentice-Hall, 1977).

36. Ralph M. Goldman, "The American President as Party Leader: A Synoptic History," in *Presidents and Their Parties*, ed. Harmel, 20-22; Goldman, "Titular Leadership of Presidential Parties," in *The Presidency*, ed. Aaron Wildavsky (Boston: Little, Brown, 1969), 384-410.

37. Roger G. Brown and David M. Welborn, "Presidents and Their Parties: Performance and Prospects," *Presidential Studies Quarterly* 12 (Summer 1982): 304-305.

38. Fred I. Greenstein, *The Hidden Hand Presidency: Eisenhower as Leader* (New York: Basic Books, 1982).

39. Dwight D. Eisenhower, "The President's Press Conference of October 11, 1956," *Public Papers of the Presidents, Dwight D. Eisenhower, 1956*, (Washington, D.C.: Government Printing Office, 1956), 891.

40. Ibid., 1957, "The President's News Conference of June 5, 1957," 435.

41. *New York Times*, January 15, 1960, 14.

42. Congressional Quarterly, *Watergate: Chronology of a Crisis*, vol. 2 (Washington, Congressional Quarterly, 1974), 228.

43. Ibid., 286.

Selected Bibliography

Brown, Roger G. "Party and Bureaucracy: From Kennedy to Reagan." *Political Science Quarterly* 97 (Summer 1982): 279-294.

———. "The Presidency and the Political Parties." In *The Presidency and the Political System*, ed. Michael Nelson. Washington, D.C.: CQ Press, 1985.

———, and David M. Welborn. "Presidents and Their Parties: Performance and Prospects." *Presidential Studies Quarterly* 12 (Summer 1982): 302-316.

Cotter, Cornelius P. "Eisenhower as Party Leader." *Political Science Quarterly* 98 (Summer 1983): 255-284.

Cronin, Thomas E. "The Presidency and the Parties." In *Party Renewal in America*, ed. Gerald M. Pomper. New York: Praeger, 1980.

Goldman, Ralph M. "Titular Leadership of Presidential Parties." In *The Presidency*, ed. Aaron Wildavsky. Boston: Little, Brown, 1969.

Harmel, Robert, ed. *Presidents and Their Parties: Leadership or Neglect?* New York: Praeger, 1983.

Kessell, John H. *Presidential Parties*. Homewood, Ill.: Dorsey, 1984.

Ketchum, Ralph. *Presidents above Party: The First American Presidency, 1789-1829*. Chapel Hill: University of North Carolina Press, 1984.

Milkis, Sidney M. "The Presidency and the Political Parties." In *The Presidency and the Political System*, ed. Michael Nelson. 2d ed. Washington, D.C.: CQ Press, 1988.

Odegard, Peter H. "Presidential Leadership and Party Responsibility. *Annals of the American Academy of Political and Social Science* 307 (September 1956): 66-81.

Parker, Joseph, and Edward N. Kearny. "The President and Political Parties." In *Dimensions of the Modern Presidency*, ed. Edward N. Kearny. St. Louis: Forum Press, 1981.

Ranney, Austin. "The President and His Party." In *Both Ends of the Avenue: The Presidency, the Executive Branch, and Congress in the 1980s*, ed. Anthony King. Washington, D.C.: American Enterprise Institute, 1983.

Seligman, Lester. "The Presidential Office and the President as Party Leader (with a Postscript on the Kennedy-Nixon Era)." In *Parties and Elections in an Antiparty Age*, ed. Jeff Fishel. Bloomington: Indiana University Press, 1978.

Chief Economist

The authors of the Constitution clearly intended Congress to be the branch of government most concerned with the economic affairs of the nation. Article I, section 8, of the Constitution grants Congress numerous economic powers, including the authority to:

> lay and collect taxes, duties, imposts and excises, to pay the debts and provide for the common defense and general welfare of the United States ...; borrow money on the credit of the United States ...; regulate commerce with foreign nations, and among the several states ...; and coin money, regulate the value thereof, and of foreign coin....

In contrast, the Constitution grants the president no specific economic powers. Nevertheless, the Framers expected presidents to have significant influence over the economy. They would, after all, oversee the implementation of Congress's spending and taxing decisions, suggest economic legislation in their State of the Union address and other communications to Congress, negotiate commercial treaties with foreign nations, and have the power to veto legislation on economic matters.

Presidential economic power, however, has developed beyond these constitutional powers. Presidents have effectively used their visibility and their prerogatives over the execution of policy to promote their own economic programs. In addition, as management of the economy has grown more complex during the twentieth century, Congress has given presidents greater economic power through statutes.

Because the American people associate the presidency—the nation's most powerful and identifiable political office—with the performance of the federal government, they have come to expect presidents to produce economic prosperity for the United States just as presidents are expected to enforce its laws and ensure its security. As political scientist Clinton Rossiter observed near the end of the Eisenhower administration:

> The people of this country are no longer content to let disaster fall upon them unopposed. They now expect their government, under the direct leadership of the President, to prevent a depression or panic and not simply wait until one has developed before putting it to rout. Thus the President has a new function which is still taking shape, that of Manager of Prosperity.[1]

By Daniel C. Diller and Dean J. Peterson

Limitations on Presidential Power over the Economy

Despite the expectations of the American public and the president's pivotal role in economic policy making, the president's ability to influence economic conditions does not measure up to presidential responsibility for them. All presidents would like to be able to adjust the economy from a central switch in the White House, but no absolutely reliable controls exist.

When unemployment, inflation, and budget deficits rise, presidents receive most of the blame. Herbert C. Hoover, Gerald R. Ford, and Jimmy Carter lost their reelection bids, in part because of the poor economic conditions that prevailed during their presidencies. The president's party also may suffer in midterm congressional elections if the economy is in a recession.

Presidents themselves are partially responsible for high public expectations of their economic management. As candidates, future presidents usually have overestimated their ability to improve the economy.[2] Presidential candidates never promise just to "prevent economic decline" or "do the best they can." To get elected, presidents must promise to produce economic growth with low inflation, and balanced budgets, even if their predecessors have left them with serious economic problems that cannot be quickly or easily corrected.

This relationship between presidential popularity and the economy, however, also may work to a president's advantage. Presidents are quick to take credit for economic growth, price stability, and low unemployment. Presidential candidate Ronald Reagan capitalized on poor economic conditions in 1980 by asking voters, "Are you better off now than you were four years ago?" Voters responded "no" and elected Reagan to succeed Jimmy Carter. Four years later, however, when the economy was in the midst of a strong expansion after the recession of 1981-1982, Reagan repeated the question, and the American people reelected him in a landslide.

Four factors combine to limit the president's control over the U.S. economy. First, the chief executive must share power with other individuals and government bodies. As the enumeration of congressional economic powers shows, Congress has the constitutional authority to frus-

Economic Terms

Classical economic theory: a body of theory developed during the late eighteenth and early nineteenth centuries maintaining that economies naturally tend to achieve full employment and that government intervention in economic matters should be limited.

Contractionary policy: restrictive fiscal or monetary policy designed to decrease demand thereby reducing inflation.

Expansionary policy: stimulative fiscal or monetary policy designed to increase demand thereby decreasing unemployment and promoting economic growth.

Federal Reserve System: the central bank of the United States; oversees the nation's banking system and controls monetary policy.

Fiscal policy: the manipulation of government spending and tax rates for the purpose of altering the levels of unemployment, inflation, and economic growth.

Gross national product: the value of goods and services produced by an economy in a given year; the principal measure of economic growth.

Inflation: a sustained increase in prices.

Keynesian theory: the body of economic theory developed by British economist John Maynard Keynes that advocates government intervention in the economy to stimulate or dampen demand as a way to deal with high unemployment or inflation.

Laissez faire: an approach to economic policy that advocates a limited government role in the economy in favor of a reliance upon free-market forces.

Monetarism: an approach to economic policy making that emphasizes the role of the money supply in determining inflation, unemployment, and economic growth.

Monetary policy: the manipulation of the money supply for the purpose of altering the levels of unemployment, inflation, and economic growth.

Price stability: the absence of inflation.

Protectionism: an attempt by a government to protect the domestic markets of its industries from foreign competition by erecting trade barriers.

Recession: a prolonged downturn in the economy during which investment, incomes, and employment all decline.

Stabilization policy: monetary and fiscal policies designed to smooth undesirable fluctuations in inflation, unemployment, and the rate of economic growth.

Stagflation: simultaneous high inflation and unemployment.

Supply-side theory: an economic theory that focuses on the role played by incentives in achieving economic growth; supply-siders generally favor lower tax rates and government efforts to stimulate investments.

Tariff: a tax on imports or exports.

Trade barriers: protectionist devices such as tariffs or import quotas that make it more difficult for foreign companies to sell their goods and services in a given country.

Trade deficit: condition when a nation's imports exceed its exports.

---

trate virtually any presidential economic initiative. Most important, the president cannot levy taxes or appropriate money without the consent of Congress.

Executive branch organizations also cut into presidential economic power. The independent Federal Reserve Board, which sets monetary policy, is not obliged to cooperate with the president. *(See "Monetary Policy," p. 266, in this chapter.)* Spending and taxing policies adopted by presidents to achieve one economic result may be undercut by the monetary policies of the Federal Reserve Board designed to achieve a conflicting result. The president's own economic advisers also can check presidential power by unenthusiastically implementing the chief executive's directives or refusing to join a policy consensus.

Each economic advisory organization has a different mission that disposes it to concentrate on a particular economic problem rather than the entire economic situation. The Office of Management and Budget (OMB) looks to trim the budget; the president's Council of Economic Advisers (CEA) focuses on lowering unemployment and inflation and promoting economic expansion; the Treasury Department oversees the national debt and develops international monetary policy; and the heads of other departments and agencies seek to protect funding for projects within their jurisdictions. These missions often conflict,

making agreement on policy goals difficult and creating rivalries within an administration.

A second factor limiting presidential control of the economy is the highly complex and theoretical nature of the science of economics. Presidents with little formal training in economics may feel overwhelmed, as did Warren Harding who once confided to an associate:

I don't know what to do or where to turn on this taxation matter. Somewhere there must be a book that tells all about it, where I could go to straighten it out in my mind. But I don't know where the book is, and maybe I couldn't read it if I found it. There must be a man in the country somewhere who could weigh both sides and know the truth. Probably he is in some college or other. But I don't know where to find him, I don't know who he is and I don't know how to get him.[3]

Even if presidents do trust the judgment of their economic advisers, there is little consensus among economists about which economic theory or theories should guide economic policy.

A third factor limiting presidential economic control is the imprecision of economic information. When presidents attempt to adjust the economy, they assume that they have accurate and timely information about how the economy is performing. Economic statistics and indicators do not, however, measure the immediate conditions of the economy, but rather the conditions that prevailed between one and four months ago, depending on the particular economic statistic. Consequently, presidents who take action on the basis of incoming economic information may be reacting to a problem that no longer exists or is much worse than believed. In such cases presidential economic policies may destabilize the economy. A president's attempts to manage the economy, therefore, are only as good as the information upon which they are based.

When government figures indicate that unemployment is rising and consumer demand is falling the president may wish to enact spending increases or a tax cut. If, however, the unemployment figures are misleading or the estimate of consumer demand is outdated, such antirecession measures could cause an inflationary spiral. In 1977 President Carter was forced to abandon his tax rebate proposal and initiate an anti-inflation program because the economy had already begun to pull out of the recession he had intended to correct.[4]

Similarly, an anti-inflation strategy based on inaccurate information can deepen a recession. At the beginning of 1980 the inflation rate reached 18 percent. Although many economists had predicted that a recession would occur during the first half of that year, mixed economic indicators suggested that the economy was still expanding. In March Carter and his advisers decided to impose credit controls designed to lower inflation. Later in the year, however, as more complete economic statistics about the first quarter became available, it was apparent that the recession predicted by economists was already under way when Carter initiated his anti-inflationary policies. The second quarter saw the sharpest decline in gross national product (GNP) in a single three-month period since World War II. Unemployment rose from 6.3 percent in March to 7.5 percent in June. Economic statistics had provided Carter with an incomplete economic picture that induced him to take measures that exacerbated the economy's troubles.[5]

Finally, presidential control over the economy is limited by forces outside the reach of the federal government. The economic policies of state and local governments may undercut those of the federal government; international factors such as the price of oil or foreign trade policies may exacerbate U.S. economic problems; bad weather may limit agricultural production; public expectations may make certain economic options such as large cuts in Social Security and Medicare politically impossible; and large corporations may make business decisions that adversely affect unemployment, inflation, the trade deficit, and other economic problems. A president making all the right decisions will not, therefore, necessarily produce a thriving economy; nor will an economically inexperienced or inept president inevitably bring on a national economic disaster or even a recession.

Yet in spite of these limitations, no single force has more influence over the U.S. economy than the president. As chief executive the president oversees the government's economic and regulatory functions and appoints cabinet and Federal Reserve Board members who make many economic decisions; as chief legislator the president proposes spending, tax, and other economic-related legislation and can use the veto to influence what legislation becomes law; as commander in chief the president oversees the multibillion-dollar purchases of the Defense Department; as chief diplomat the president negotiates with foreign governments about trade and currency issues; and as chief of state the president affects the morale, attitudes, and expectations of the American people.

Early Presidential Economic Management

From the beginning of the Republic presidents understood that promoting the nation's prosperity was as much a part of their job as ensuring its security and enforcing its laws. Presidents did not, however, attempt to affect the performance of the economy through spending and taxing decisions until the Great Depression of the 1930s. Before then, the classical theory of economics, associated with the writings of Adam Smith, the eighteenth-century British economist, prevailed. This theory held that a laissez-faire approach to government economic activity—one that allowed farmers, merchants, and manufacturers to operate unencumbered by government intervention and regulation—would result in the most prosperous economic conditions. Consequently, if the economy were running smoothly, the president's economic responsibilities were limited primarily to executing the spending and revenue measures passed by Congress, promoting a balanced budget, and working with business leaders and foreign governments to expand industrial development and trade.

The U.S. economy did not always run smoothly, however. As it became increasingly industrialized in the late nineteenth and early twentieth centuries, fluctuations in employment became more frequent and severe. The growth of industry also created new demands on the nation's financial system and forced the government to protect consumers and workers from the power of monopolies. Society came to believe that government should work to prevent crises and create a stable and fair business environment. Consequently, presidents in the late nineteenth and early twentieth centuries occasionally abandoned their laissez-faire stance and proposed or supported solutions to obvious economic problems. The public increasingly looked to the president, the symbol of government and the leader of the party, for economic innovation and direction. By the time the Great Depression struck, laissez-faire attitudes toward the executive's economic role had already given way to more activist conceptions of governmental and presidential power.

Financial Foundations of the New Nation

George Washington ensured that economic affairs would have a central place in his administration when he appointed Alexander Hamilton, his closest adviser, as secretary of the Treasury. Hamilton often worked independently of Washington, who seldom intervened in his treasury secretary's unfinished projects. Hamilton recognized that the international reputation of the United States and its ability to command respect among its own citizens—many of whom felt stronger loyalties to their home state than to the new federal government—depended on the government's financial stability and the vibrancy of the American economy. Hamilton, therefore, aggressively promoted the interests of merchants and manufacturers and tried to create an atmosphere of confidence through measures that included the assumption of state debts by the national government and the establishment of a national bank.

Debt Assumption

Both the federal government and the states had gone heavily into debt to finance the Revolutionary War. Congress and the states had borrowed money from virtually anyone who would lend it. The United States owed money to the French government, Dutch bankers, state treasuries, and individual holders of bonds and promissory notes. A comprehensive plan was needed that would allow the government to pay back the debts without imposing burdensome taxes on its citizens, establish good international credit, and reconcile the competing interests of its domestic creditors.

Ten days after Hamilton assumed the office of secretary of the Treasury, the House of Representatives asked him to draft a plan for the "adequate support of the public credit." Hamilton used this simple mandate to construct an ambitious plan to resolve the debt situation and bring fiscal stability to the federal government.[6]

The scope and intricacy of Hamilton's plan surprised Congress when he presented it to that body on January 14, 1790. It called for federal assumption of the $25 million in debts incurred by the states during the Revolutionary War and refunding of the national debt through various bonds and securities. Existing tariffs, which Congress eventually continued at Hamilton's urging, would provide the primary source of revenues to gradually retire the debt.

The most politically divisive aspect of the debt question was how and to what degree the federal government would assume the debts of states. Predictably, the states that had paid their wartime debts, including Virginia, Maryland, North Carolina, and Georgia were against having the federal government take over the financial burden of the states with a large debt, while the latter, including Massachusetts, Connecticut, and South Carolina, pressed for full assumption.

Division over the assumption question initially led to rejection of Hamilton's plan by a slim margin in both houses of Congress. With Thomas Jefferson's help, however, a compromise was reached whereby the debt assumption bill was linked to a measure moving the capital from New York to Philadelphia for ten years and then to what would become Washington, D.C. This act placated a few southern members of Congress who changed their votes, and the bill was passed. President Washington signed it on August 4, 1790.[7]

Establishment of the National Bank

In addition to the assumption of debts by the federal government the other component of Hamilton's plan to bring financial credibility and stability to the new nation was the establishment of a national bank. Hamilton outlined his bank proposal to Congress in December 1790. He asked Congress to charter a national bank to assist in the financial operations of the United States. It was to be run primarily by private directors and funded by private capital. Of the bank's original $10 million capitalization, only $2 million were to come from the Treasury, while the rest would be provided by individual investors.

Opponents and supporters of the bank saw that it would provide the president with added power over the economy and would serve as a symbol of the preeminence of the federal government. Many of the bank's detractors opposed it because they feared granting more influence to the federal government. Others, including James Madison, argued that the bank was unconstitutional since the Constitution did not explicitly give the government the power to charter a bank.[8] Legislators in favor of the bill prevailed, however, and the legislation passed both houses by February 1791.

George Washington solicited the opinions of his cabinet on whether to sign the bill. Two members of his cabinet, Secretary of State Thomas Jefferson and Attorney General Edmund Randolph concurred with Madison, their fellow Virginian. They saw the bank as a violation of the yet unratified Tenth Amendment which, in their view, prohibited the federal government from exercising authority not granted to it by the Constitution.[9]

Washington, who conceived of the president's veto as a tool to prevent the passage of unconstitutional legislation, was concerned about these charges against the bank. Although he favored the establishment of the bank as a practical step toward a stronger U.S. economy he was prepared to veto the bill if he became convinced of its unconstitutionality. On February 16, 1791, he asked Hamilton for an assessment of the objections of Madison, Jefferson, and Randolph. Hamilton responded with his "Defense of the Constitutionality of an Act to Establish a Bank." The paper artfully refuted the Virginians' claim that the bank would be unconstitutional by emphasizing the necessity of a broad interpretation of the government's economic powers. On February 25, Washington signed the bill chartering the bank.[10]

The First Bank of the United States functioned well for 20 years, but Congress refused to recharter it in 1811 by one vote. Because the bank was the brainchild of Federalist Alexander Hamilton, many members of the Democratic-Republican Party, which dominated U.S. politics in the early nineteenth century, tended to be against renewing its charter. Some party members agreed with Democratic-Republican Party leaders Thomas Jefferson and James Madison that the bank was unconstitutional. This inherent opposition to the bank, combined with the lobbying efforts of commercial banks that competed for business with the national bank, led to its demise.[11]

Development of Presidential Involvement in the Economy

The election of Thomas Jefferson in 1800 ushered in an economic era in the United States that was dominated by agrarian interests. Jefferson and his successors, most notably Andrew Jackson, rejected the Hamiltonian economic approach of concentrating the federal government's activities on the promotion and protection of industry and business.[12] Most economic regulatory activity and responsibility for internal improvements that benefited commerce, such as the construction of roads, bridges, and railroads, were left to the states. Even central banking came to be considered outside the government's proper domain. After refusing to recharter the national bank in 1811, Congress chartered the Second Bank of the United States in 1816 after experiencing difficulties with national finance during the War of 1812. Andrew Jackson, however, vetoed the bill that would have rechartered the second bank of the United States and its charter expired in 1836. The United States went without a central bank until 1914 when the

Federal Reserve System was established.[13]

Nevertheless, the federal government did not entirely abandon business promotion. It maintained tariffs to protect industries from foreign competition, provided systems of money and patents, and in 1817 gave U.S. ships a monopoly on East Coast trade. Yet until the Civil War, the United States remained essentially an agrarian society with the proponents of agrarianism dominating national politics.[14]

The Civil War brought greater industrialization and the political division of northern and southern agrarian interests. The Republican presidents of the second half of the nineteenth century were generally conservative men who favored federal promotion of business affairs, but not federal regulation. These presidents in cooperation with Congress aided manufacturing and commercial interests by raising protective tariffs to new highs, giving land to railroads, and continuing to rely on regressive taxes.[15]

As the American business community grew, however, the need for regulation became more apparent. By the 1880s the power of major corporations had begun to alarm many members of the public. State governments no longer were adequate to control companies that operated in many states and functioned as monopolies. The federal government gradually responded to growing demands for regulation.

In the 1890s Congress passed the Sherman Antitrust Act and other laws which gave the president and the executive branch the power to break up monopolies and otherwise regulate business activity. Presidents Theodore Roosevelt and William Howard Taft sharply increased government prosecutions of antitrust cases and expanded other regulation activities, setting the stage for further economic reforms that would widen presidential authority over the economy.

Establishment of Income Tax

During the eighteenth and nineteenth centuries the federal government had financed its activities through excise taxes, sales of the vast national lands that stretched to the Pacific, and most importantly, tariffs. Tariffs were simple to administer but were not always an adequate source of income. In wartime, when the government required increased revenue, tariff receipts would fall as trade with other countries was disrupted.[16]

During the Civil War, Congress had levied a tax on incomes to help make up the gap between peacetime revenue sources and wartime expenses. The tax expired in 1872, and there was no attempt to revive it until 1894 when Congress levied a 2 percent tax on personal incomes over $3,000. In 1895, however, the Supreme Court declared income tax unconstitutional in *Pollock v. Farmers' Loan & Trust Co.* The Court held that an income tax was an example of a direct tax that violated Section 9, Clause 4 of the Constitution which prohibited direct taxes unless each state paid a share in proportion to its population.

With the support of President Taft this obstacle was overcome on February 23, 1913, when the 16th Amendment was ratified. It stated: "The Congress shall have power to lay and collect taxes on incomes from whatever source derived, without apportionment among the several states, and without regard to any census or enumeration." Although Congress passed a 1 percent income tax in 1913, the power of income tax as a source of revenue was not demonstrated until World War I when an expanded income tax

generated the revenues necessary for U.S. participation in the war.

Thereafter income taxes grew in importance. In 1915 custom duties and excise taxes provided eighty-five percent of federal revenues. By 1930 income taxes were providing over half of the funds coming into the treasury, while the share from customs and excises had fallen below thirty percent.[17]

Although the 16th amendment had given Congress the power to levy income taxes, the amendment greatly expanded presidential power by providing a source of revenue that could finance presidential foreign policy and domestic initiatives. As political scientist Emmet J. Hughes noted, the income tax was "ready for lavish use by future Presidents to meet future needs or crises. And without such a reservoir of funds, there hardly could have followed any grand dreams of Presidential programs in the realms of welfare, education, health, housing, and transport."[18] The tax also enhanced the president's ability to make fiscal policy. Increasing and decreasing income taxes would become one of the methods most commonly used by presidents and Congress to combat inflation and recession.

Budget and Accounting Act of 1921

During the eighteenth and nineteenth centuries presidents had no formal responsibility to submit a budget to Congress or even conduct a comprehensive review of executive branch spending proposals. Executive departments and agencies submitted budget requests directly to Congress in a "Book of Estimates." A number of presidents, such as John Quincy Adams, Van Buren, Tyler, Polk, Buchanan, Grant, and Cleveland did insist on revising budget estimates, but the budgeting process continued to be dominated by Congress and individual executive departments and agencies.[19]

During the budget process, there was no means by which Congress could balance expenditures with revenues or evaluate alternative spending programs. As a result, the overlapping or extravagant spending proposals submitted by executive departments and agencies could not be weeded out of the budget. Moreover, the lack of central coordination made the use of the budget as an instrument of fiscal policy impossible.[20]

With the 1921 Budget and Accounting Act, Congress sought to reform the financial machinery of the executive branch. The nation had incurred a series of budget deficits before and during World War I that created a debt problem and led Congress to set up new procedures and organizations to provide more central coordination of the budget process.[21] The 1921 act established two important offices—the Bureau of the Budget (which became the Office of Management and Budget in 1970) and the General Accounting Office. The former was created to centralize fiscal management of the executive branch directly under the president; the latter was designed to strengthen congressional oversight of spending.

The act ended the practice of allowing executive departments and agencies to address their annual budget proposals directly to Congress. The Budget Bureau, originally a subdivision of the Treasury Department, but later placed under the direct control of the president, became a central clearinghouse for all budget requests. The Budget Bureau evaluated these requests, adjusted them to fit the president's goals, and consolidated them into a single executive branch budget for the consideration of Congress.

Consequently, the Budget Act of 1921 transformed budget making from a random and fragmented process over which presidents had little control into a tool through which presidents could advance their social, economic, and defense priorities.

Presidential Economic Stabilization Policy

Every president has been concerned with the U.S. economy, but close presidential supervision of its performance is a relatively recent historical development. Before the Great Depression of the 1930s, Americans generally believed that extensive government intervention in the economy was counterproductive. The human suffering of the depression, however, convinced the American public and its leaders that the government should intervene to relieve and prevent periods of economic trauma. Moreover, by the time World War II ended, a national consensus had developed that the government, and especially the president, should use every means available to produce the best economic conditions possible even if the economy were not depressed. The president had become not just a guardian against economic disaster, but an economic manager whose popularity usually depended on a strong and stable economy.

Post-depression presidents have attempted to create the best economic conditions possible through their *stabilization policies*. The U.S. economy, like all capitalist economies, experiences cyclical patterns of expansion and contraction in which the levels of inflation, unemployment, and economic growth vary. During contractionary periods businesses lose sales, investment decreases, unemployment grows, and prices tend to increase at a slower rate or even fall. During expansionary periods consumers spend more, investment increases, unemployment declines, and prices tend to increase at a faster rate. The objective of stabilization policy is to smooth out the natural swings in the economy so unemployment does not become too severe during contractionary periods and inflation does not get out of control during expansionary periods. Ideally, an administration should achieve these goals while maintaining a steady rate of economic growth and balancing the federal budget, or at least running manageable deficits that can be corrected during periods of prosperity.

The tools presidents use to stabilize the economy are *fiscal policy* and *monetary policy*. Fiscal policy refers to the government's taxing and spending decisions. Presidents make fiscal policy in cooperation with Congress, which passes spending and tax bills. Monetary policy refers to decisions about the supply of money. Although presidents do not have legal control over monetary policy, which is determined by the independent Federal Reserve Board, they do exercise much informal influence over it.

As the history of stabilization policy shows, it has been one of the most frustrating aspects of the president's job. No single economic theory has explained the behavior of the economy or held the key to prosperity for long. As theories have been tested in the laboratory of national economic stabilization policy, their limitations have surfaced. Few national leaders or economists would call themselves pure *Keynesians, monetarists, or supply-siders*. Economists who once stridently espoused a single theory have been forced to add broad qualifications to their insights and incorporate other theories into their economic thought. As a result, presidents have been left without a clear economic orthodoxy.

The New Deal and the Emergence of Keynesian Theory

Before the Great Depression most economists believed that the president could best contribute to the health of the economy by working for a balanced federal budget and not overregulating business activity. Deficit spending by the federal government was regarded as an imprudent and irresponsible practice that eroded business confidence in the monetary system and produced inflation.[22]

This conservative economic orthodoxy handcuffed President Herbert Hoover when the stock market crashed and the depression began to unfold in 1929. All of Hoover's efforts to turn the economy around proved ineffectual, and by 1933 unemployment had reached a staggering 25 percent. Like presidents before him, Hoover believed in the conventional wisdom that public debt could undermine the economic health of the nation just as private debt could undermine a person's financial well-being. He therefore was suspicious of deficit spending programs that would have reduced the severity of the depression. Nevertheless, in his search for an answer to the country's economic troubles Hoover did try a variety of measures, including a tax reduction, intended to put more money into the hands of the public. He quickly gave up on this approach, however, when it appeared not to be working and returned to a conservative strategy of cutting expenditures in an effort to balance the budget.[23] This policy, combined with the Federal Reserve Board's failure to expand the money supply, deepened the depression.[24] In fact, many modern economists believe the depression would have been limited to a severe recession had the president and the Federal Reserve Board not exacerbated the problem.

While campaigning for the presidency in 1932 Franklin D. Roosevelt did not advocate revolutionary fiscal policies. Like Hoover before him, he promised to cut expenditures and balance the budget. Indeed, during the campaign he had attacked Hoover for failing to achieve a balanced budget.

Roosevelt, however, was a pragmatic leader who believed that the government should take emergency measures to fight the depression. Once in office he initiated "New Deal" policies, which created government construction and relief programs that threw the federal budget into deficit. The deficit spending, however, was not a fiscal strategy designed to stimulate the economy but a byproduct of the president's decision to spend the money necessary to reduce the suffering of the poor, the elderly, and the unemployed and to begin putting Americans back to work.[25] Most New Deal initiatives were to be phased out as economic conditions improved, and indeed some were terminated within a few years. Other programs, however, including Social Security and federal credit assistance to home buyers, small businesses, and farmers, became permanent government activities.

While the United States and the world struggled through the depression, the theories of the British economist John Maynard Keynes became widely known. Keynes outlined his theories in *The General Theory of Employment, Interest and Money*, published in 1936. Keynes's thought focused on unemployment. He argued that recessions occurred when industrial, consumer, or government demand for goods and services fell. This caused unsold inventories to mount, industries to scale back their operations, and unemployment to rise.

Keynes posited that the government could counteract a recession by cutting taxes or increasing its expenditures. Lower taxes would put more money into the hands of consumers, thereby stimulating demand for goods and services. Tax cuts given to industry would create new jobs by boosting firms' investment in their productive facilities. Greater government expenditures would create jobs and prime the economy through a "multiplier effect." According to Keynes, each dollar spent by the government could stimulate private economic transactions equaling much more than the original dollar. Keynes's recession remedy of having the government put money into the hands of its citizens contradicted the conservative economic goal of balancing the budget. It nevertheless quickly gained a following among economists.

In May 1937, after the U.S. economy had achieved a partial recovery, a new recession confronted Roosevelt. This recession was caused in part by the Federal Reserve Board, which had again contracted the money supply in its concern to prevent inflation.[26] The president initially ignored the advice of converted Keynesians in his administration and attempted to cut spending in an effort to balance the budget. Roosevelt's strategy deepened the recession and solidified a consensus among his advisers in favor of government spending designed to stimulate demand. By April 1938 the president himself was convinced that greater government expenditures were needed to combat the depression. Roosevelt continued to pay lip service to a balanced budget, but he worked to increase expenditures and accepted growing budget deficits as a necessary evil in a difficult economic period.[27] Unemployment gradually declined from its 1933 high of 25 percent to under 15 percent in 1940.

World War II ultimately brought massive government expenditures financed by borrowing that woke the U.S. economy from the nightmare of the 1930s. The war effort required a total mobilization of the U.S. productive resources, which ended unemployment.[28] In 1944 unemployment stood at just 1.2 percent. Most economists saw the economic results of New Deal and wartime expenditures as a validation of Keynesian theory.

Keynesianism as Orthodox Theory

By Franklin Roosevelt's last term in office Keynesianism had become the dominant economic theory both in policy-making and in academic circles. Some conservative economists and politicians clung to theories about balancing the budget, but even they recognized that Keynes had provided a good explanation of the economic conditions during the depression and World War II.

Following the war, Congress debated the role government should play in the economy given the success of Keynesian policies. Many members of Congress believed that since Keynesian economic theory had provided the federal government with a tool through which it seemingly could hold down the level of joblessness, the government should be obliged to use that tool to promote full employment. In 1945 the Full Employment Bill was introduced into the Senate. It mandated that full employment should

Table 1 Inflation and Unemployment, 1929-1987 (percent)

Year	Inflation, all items [a]	Unemployment
1929	0.0	3.2
1933	−5.1	24.9
1939	−1.4	17.2
1940	1.0	14.6
1941	5.0	9.9
1942	10.7	4.7
1943	6.1	1.9
1944	1.7	1.2
1945	2.3	1.9
1946	8.5	3.9
1947	14.4	3.9
1948	7.8	3.8
1949	−1.0	5.9
1950	1.0	5.3
1951	7.9	3.3
1952	2.2	3.0
1953	0.8	2.9
1954	0.5	5.5
1955	−0.4	4.4
1956	1.5	4.1
1957	3.6	4.3
1958	2.7	6.8
1959	0.8	5.5
1960	1.6	5.5
1961	1.0	6.7
1962	1.1	5.5
1963	1.2	5.7
1964	1.3	5.2
1965	1.7	4.5
1966	2.9	3.8
1967	2.9	3.8
1968	4.2	3.6
1969	5.4	3.5
1970	5.9	4.9
1971	4.3	5.9
1972	3.3	5.6
1973	6.2	4.9
1974	11.0	5.6
1975	9.1	8.5
1976	5.8	7.7
1977	6.5	7.1
1978	7.7	6.1
1979	11.3	5.8
1980	13.5	7.1
1981	10.4	7.6
1982	6.1	9.7
1983	3.2	9.6
1984	4.3	7.5
1985	3.6	7.2
1986	1.9	7.0
1987	3.7	6.2

Sources: Labor Department, Council of Economic Advisers.

a. Pecentage change in consumer price index year to year.

be a national goal and the government should run budget deficits when necessary to provide the investment and expenditures required to achieve it.

The bill alarmed many business leaders and economic conservatives, however, who saw the law as a first step toward budget deficits, inflation, and excessive regulation of the economy. Despite President Harry S Truman's support for the Full Employment Act, the House promoted a more modest version, which eventually was passed by both chambers.[29]

The final version of the act was called the Employment Act of 1946. It stated that the government should work for "maximum employment, production and purchasing power," rather than "full" employment, and references to budget deficits as the tool that would be used to achieve high employment were deleted. A statement also was added that measures taken to implement the act must be consistent with the free enterprise system. Economist Herbert Stein wrote of the revision of the bill:

> Given the experience of the 1930s, it was inconceivable that the government would fail to commit itself to maintaining high employment.... But the form that commitment took in the United States, as embodied in the Employment Act of 1946, could hardly have been more satisfactory to conservatives. That is, after a major national discussion the Congress rejected an overly ambitious, inflationary definition of the goal, rejected exclusive reliance on deficit financing as the means, and reaffirmed its devotion to the free enterprise system.[30]

Although the original Full Employment Act had been watered down, the Employment Act of 1946 nevertheless demonstrated the new national consensus that government leaders should deeply involve themselves in the management of the economy. Beyond stating the government's responsibility to work for low unemployment, the act reinforced the president's role as the public official primarily responsible for managing the economy. Although the legislation did not provide presidents with new economic powers, it did require them to report annually to Congress on the state of the economy, and created the Council of Economic Advisers, which gave presidents an economic advisory body answerable only to them.[31] These measures encouraged Congress, the business community, and the American public to continue to look to presidents for economic leadership as they had done during the depression.

Despite the demise of the original Full Employment Bill, Keynesian theory continued to gain adherents. The strong postwar economy convinced people that the structure of the economy was sound and major economic reforms were unnecessary to prevent a return to depression. What was needed was steering between the problems of inflation and unemployment. Keynesian theory implicitly held that there was an inverse relationship between inflation and unemployment. Presidents could expect higher inflation when they attempted to reduce unemployment by stimulating demand through spending increases or tax cuts. Conversely, tax increases and budget cuts would reduce demand, bringing price stability at the cost of greater unemployment. Until the 1970s this trade-off between inflation and unemployment governed presidential stabilization policy. Presidents and their economic advisers generally believed that if inflation or unemployment became severe, they could use Keynesian fiscal policies to reestablish a balance.

Truman Administration

When Harry Truman succeeded to the presidency following Franklin Roosevelt's death in April 1945, the U.S. economy was booming. Federal expenditures had grown from just $8.8 billion in 1939 to $92.7 billion in 1945, and unemployment was virtually nonexistent. Many Americans feared that the economic sluggishness of the 1930s would return when the war ended, but the years following the war saw continued expansion and a relatively smooth transition from a wartime to a peacetime footing. Many women and elderly workers who had entered the work force during the war because labor was in short supply retired when the war ended, thus making room in the work force for returning soldiers. The influx of GIs also created greater demand for housing and consumer goods that partially offset the decrease in demand caused by reduced government spending for defense.

Inflation was a more serious problem. Although Truman had enthusiastically supported the original version of the Employment Act, which mandated measures to achieve full employment, as president he followed a pragmatic course that often made fighting inflation the highest economic priority. After the war, inflation was fueled by consumers who demanded goods that had been in short supply during the conflict. Moreover, wartime controls had held the prices of many goods below their true value. As these price controls were lifted in 1946 and 1947, prices inevitably rose dramatically to correct the artificial imbalance. Inflation, which had been just 2.3 percent in 1945, rose to 8.5 percent in 1946 and 14.4 percent in 1947. Truman, who had vetoed one price control removal bill but reluctantly signed a second in July 1946, urged labor groups to resist price and wage hikes and sent an anti-inflation program to Congress in October 1947 that included consumer credit controls, rent controls, price ceilings on selected products and controls over the allocation of some scarce commodities. The Republican Congress put off most of the program until the following year and then enacted only a part of it.[32] Inflation, however, peaked in 1947, falling to 7.8 percent in 1948 and then disappearing entirely in 1949 while the economy endured a recession.

In 1947 and 1948 Congress tried to force a tax cut on the president, which, it maintained, would reverse the tax and spend policies of Truman and of Roosevelt before him. Truman vetoed three such bills on the grounds that they would lead to budget deficits and greater inflation. Congress, however, overrode the last of Truman's vetoes in April 1948. The tax cut was timely, since the economy fell into a mild recession later in the year. The extra money in the hands of consumers stimulated demand, thereby reducing the recession's severity.

The Korean War, which began on June 24, 1950, when North Korea invaded South Korea, rekindled inflationary pressures that had eased after the post-World War II price acceleration. Growing military expenditures on the war effort stimulated industrial demand. Demand for consumer goods also increased as consumers bought many items in anticipation of wartime shortages. In 1951 inflation shot back up to 7.8 percent. Congress reluctantly granted part of Truman's tax increase request and agreed to wage, price, and credit controls, which succeeded in holding inflation below 1 percent during 1952 and 1953.

Eisenhower Administration

In spite of the prominence of Keynesian thought among economists, President Dwight D. Eisenhower entered office skeptical of its utility. He emphasized the traditional conservative economic priorities of balancing the federal budget, limiting government interference in the economy, and, most important, fighting inflation.[33] During Eisenhower's eight years in office, he produced three budget surpluses—a significant achievement given that since 1961 only the 1969 budget has been in surplus.

Throughout his presidency, Eisenhower was willing to accept higher rates of unemployment than his Keynesian critics thought necessary. In response to a recession in 1953 and early 1954, the administration did accept some minor tax increases and sped up government expenditures. Although the administration took credit for helping the recovery with "speedy and massive actions," the modest antirecession measures of 1954 were an exception to Eisenhower's rule of nonintervention.[34]

During his second term Eisenhower pursued an antiinflationary strategy in defiance not only of his critics but also of several of his own advisers who urged him to support a tax cut. Unemployment averaged a post-depression high of 6.8 percent during the 1958 recession, but Eisenhower remained true to his noninterventionist principles. Moreover, he vetoed a number of spending bills during his last two years in office in pursuit of a balanced budget and low inflation.[35] As a result unemployment averaged 5.5 percent in 1959 and 1960 when it could have been significantly lower.

When signs of a recession appeared in the spring of 1960, Eisenhower's vice president, Richard Nixon, who was running for president that year, advocated following CEA chairman Arthur Burns's advice to increase defense expenditures and loosen credit. Eisenhower, however, sided with other administration economic advisers who rejected the proposal because they did not believe the recession, if there was one, would be of sufficient magnitude to warrant government intervention.[36] Nixon undoubtedly lost votes because of the economic slump.

Although Eisenhower's stiff resistance to antirecession measures appears old-fashioned by today's standards, he was successful in holding down consumer prices, which never climbed more than 4 percent in any year of his presidency.

Kennedy Administration

With the election of John F. Kennedy to the presidency in 1960, Democrats believed they could change the economic goals of the nation. During the Eisenhower years price stability and balanced budgets had been the highest economic priorities. In contrast, Kennedy and his advisers were determined to achieve full employment and sustained economic expansion through fiscal stimulation. They hoped to be able not just to correct the swings of the business cycle but to stimulate the economy to greater growth and productivity. They were motivated by their desire to alleviate poverty and to improve medical care, education, and other social services and by their concern over the apparent rapid growth of the Soviet economy and its military expenditures.

Kennedy also came into office with a more aggressive attitude toward the president's role in ensuring the nation's prosperity than his predecessor. Whereas Eisenhower believed that the U.S. economy would perform best if it were left alone and was willing to accept a significant degree of unemployment, Kennedy believed the economy never would create jobs for everyone without government stimulation. He and his advisers were confident they could direct the economy to greater prosperity. For the first time the Keynesian views of professional economists were fully applied to the political situation.[37]

In the opening months of Kennedy's term, the economy was pulling itself out of the recession that had begun in 1960. Since the budget was in deficit and inflation was a concern, Kennedy hoped that he would not have to use fiscal stimulation to achieve his employment and expansion goals. By early 1962, however, the economy had begun to slow. Kennedy agreed with his advisers that the economy should be stimulated through increased government spending. They believed such a policy would help low-income people and be less controversial than a tax cut at a time when budget deficits persisted. Congress, however, resisted Kennedy's spending plans. Kennedy responded in late 1962 by proposing a tax cut.

The president and his economic advisers attempted to sell the tax cut by promoting the concept of the "full employment budget." The administration argued that although the government was currently running budget deficits, the greater tax revenues produced by an economy operating at full employment would result in budget surpluses. Therefore, if a tax cut could produce full employment and sustained economic expansion, it would increase government revenues rather than decrease them.[38] Kennedy lobbied Congress to pass the tax cut during 1963, but before he could persuade lawmakers to pass it, he was assassinated in November.

Johnson Administration

Following Kennedy's death, President Lyndon B. Johnson delivered an emotional speech to Congress on November 27, 1963. He asked lawmakers to honor Kennedy by passing his civil rights bill and asserted: "No act of ours could more fittingly continue the work of President Kennedy than the early passage of the tax bill for which he fought all this long year." Johnson used his legendary lobbying skills and Congress's feelings for the slain president to push the tax cut through Congress quickly. Johnson signed the Revenue Act of 1964 on February 26. It was the largest tax cut in U.S. history up to that time. The act reduced personal income taxes for 1964 and 1965 by about 20 percent and corporate taxes by 4 percent.[39]

The 1964 tax cut was a milestone in the history of U.S. stabilization policy. It was the first time the president and Congress had intentionally stimulated the economy through a tax cut while the economy was expanding. Unemployment fell from 5.7 percent in 1963 to 4.5 percent in 1965. Despite the reduction in tax rates, revenue rose beyond what inflation and normal economic growth would have been expected to produce had the tax cut not been enacted.[40] The impressive results of the tax cut generated enthusiasm and confidence among President Johnson's economic advisers. They believed they could "fine tune" the economy through Keynesian stabilization policies.

The Vietnam War, however, forced Johnson to reconsider his economic priorities. By 1966 expenditures on the war and "Great Society" social programs had caused a growing budget deficit and rising inflation. Johnson's advisers urged him to correct the overstimulation of the economy caused by the deficit spending through an excise tax or increase in income taxes. Congress, however, showed no enthusiasm for a tax hike, and Johnson feared that higher taxes would erode public support for the Vietnam War.[41] Consequently, Johnson did not push for an income tax increase, and the task of fighting inflation was left to the Federal Reserve Board's monetary policy.

The following year, however, Johnson recognized that he had to slow inflation and reduce the deficit. He pro-

On January 26, 1964, President Lyndon Johnson signs the Revenue Act of 1964 in the presence of congressional leaders. To that point, it was the largest tax cut in history.

UPI/Bettmann Newsphotos

posed new taxes, but Congress did not react to Johnson's 1967 tax hike proposal until the summer of 1968. In that year inflation had risen to 4.2 percent from just 1.7 percent in 1965, and the deficit had expanded to $25.2 billion from only $1.6 billion in 1965. This deficit disappeared in 1969, when Johnson's 10 percent tax increase and Johnson's successor's efforts to cut government spending led to the first budget surplus since 1960. This belated fiscal restraint failed, however, to eliminate the long-term inflationary pressures that had been built into the economy or the rising unemployment that was left for Johnson's successor, Richard Nixon, to combat.

Retreat from Keynesianism and the Emergence of Monetarism

Walter Heller, who served as chairman of the Council of Economic Advisers under Kennedy, declared in 1967 that "Economics has come of age in the 1960s."[42] Heller and many of his colleagues believed that the combination of Keynesian economic theory, computer technology, and enlightened leaders had made it possible for the government successfully to promote prosperity through stabilization policy. The economic conditions of the the mid-1960s with its low unemployment and inflation demonstrated that Heller's optimism was not unfounded.[43] Yet his remark contrasts sharply with the loss of confidence by economists during the 1970s that the economy could be fine tuned.

The main problem with applying Keynesian theory to the management of the economy was that the political process made the Keynesian solution to inflation—cutting spending and raising taxes—difficult to enact. Politicians were predictably unwilling to adopt measures to control inflation because high taxes and cuts in government programs were unpopular with their constituents. Even if an

administration were willing to propose a tax increase to combat inflation, it would seldom be able to persuade Congress to risk a recession, especially in election years.[44] Keynesian theory, therefore, offered presidents a politically practicable response only to recession. Some other means had to be found to control inflation.

The theory to which many national leaders turned was *monetarism*. The monetarists, led by economist Milton Friedman, argue that inflation occurs when the money supply is allowed to grow faster than the economy, because a greater number of dollars is available to chase the goods and services produced. The best way to control inflation, the monetarists believe, is to reduce the amount of money in circulation.

Economists had acknowledged since the late 1950s that monetary policy had a role in stablizing the economy. The political problems involved in reducing inflation through fiscal policy during the late 1960s, however, gave monetarism a new attractiveness. The appointees of the Federal Reserve Board who were responsible for regulating the money supply could cool down the economy without having to worry, as members of Congress and the president did, that their actions would cost them the next election. The solution to inflation would, therefore, be removed from the political atmosphere that made the Keynesian response unusable. When inflation was under control, the Federal Reserve Board carefully could relax its tight monetary policy to allow for greater economic growth.

The inflation dilemma became particularly acute in the 1970s when rising prices seemed beyond the control of presidents and Congress. Not only did national leaders find it difficult to muster the political will to fight inflation, when they did cut government spending and raise taxes, inflation did not fall as expected. The inverse relationship between inflation and unemployment (increases in one had been accompanied by decreases in the other) implicit in Keynesian policies appeared to have disintegrated. Policy makers could no longer be confident that tolerance for a period of higher unemployment would result in lower inflation. Nor could acceptance of higher inflation be relied upon to bring decreased unemloyment. The prevailing conditions of high inflation and unemployment, which came to be known as *stagflation*, defied Keynesian logic and caused presidents to lean heavily on monetary policy.

Nixon Administration

Richard Nixon entered office intending to fight inflation through small spending cuts coordinated with a tight monetary policy. He hoped his incremental stategy would reduce inflation while holding unemployment near 4 percent.[45] Nixon submitted a budget to Congress for fiscal 1970 that would have yielded a small budget surplus. Congress did trim some spending but refused to go along with Nixon's cuts, many of which targeted social programs. The relationship between Nixon and the Democratic Congress became increasingly confrontational as the president vetoed a number of appropriations bills and resorted to impounding appropriated funds.[46] *(See "Impoundment Powers," p. 31, in Chief Executive chapter.)*

Despite Nixon's budget cutting efforts and the Federal Reserve Board's tight monetary policy, inflation continued to rise. By 1970 inflation had reached 6 percent. Moreover, the increase in inflation was not accompanied by a corresponding decrease in unemployment, which had risen from 3.6 percent in 1968 to 4.9 percent in 1970. The worsening unemployment situation was exacerbated by the deescalation of the Vietnam War, which brought hundreds of thousands of troops back into the civilian work force.

Congress responded to the bleak economic conditions by passing the Economic Stabilization Act of 1970. Under this act, Congress gave the president the authority to combat inflation through wage and price controls. Nixon signed the act but renounced the use of such controls, saying on June 17, 1970: "I will not take this nation down the road of wage and price controls, however politically expedient they may seem." Nixon objected to wage and price controls because he believed they were an incursion on the rights of Americans and would only postpone a burst of inflation.

In 1971, with his reelection bid less than two years away, Nixon was unwilling to fight inflation by allowing a recession as Eisenhower might have done. Early that year he had abandoned his attempts to achieve a balanced budget and had initiated stimulative fiscal policies to combat rising unemployment that averaged 5.9 percent for the year. Nixon, like John Kennedy, justified deficit spending by arguing that the budget would be balanced if the economy were operating at full employment and output. Nixon admitted to an interviewer in January 1971, "I am now a Keynesian in economics." [47]

Inflation, however, was the more troubling economic problem. The president received pressure from Congress, the public, and even prominent leaders of his party to take dramatic action against inflation. On August 15, 1971, President Nixon announced that, owing to the economic crisis, he was using the authority granted to him by Congress to impose a wage and price control policy.

His "New Economic Policy" had several phases. Phase I froze wages, prices, and rents for ninety days. Phase II created a pay board and price commission that acted to limit inflation to 3 percent and wage increases to 5.5 percent per year. In January 1973 Phase III relaxed the controls, and in July of that year Phase IV replaced controls with commitments from businesses to limit price increases for a year. In April 1974 all wage and price control activity ended when Congress refused to extend President Nixon's wage and price control authority.[48]

Initially the controls were successful and popular. Consumer prices rose 4.3 percent in 1971 but just 3.3 percent in 1972. Unemployment fell from 5.9 percent in 1971 to 5.6 percent in 1972 and 4.9 percent in 1973. The brightening economic picture helped Nixon easily win a second term as president in the November 1972 elections.

As Nixon had feared, however, the problems with wage and price controls began to surface during his second term. Shortages of some goods occurred when many manufacturers began exporting a greater share of their products overseas where prices were higher. In addition, the numerous exemptions from the controls program that had been granted to various industries caused economic distortions. For example, grain prices had been exempted from controls while meat prices remained fixed. Consequently, high feed costs forced many meat producers to slaughter their stock causing immediate meat shortages and meat price increases later in the decade.

UPI/Bettmann Newsphotos

In January 1974, cars line up at gas stations, causing traffic jams in Chicago, left, and across the country. In October 1973, the Arab oil-producing states had imposed an embargo on the United States for its support of Israel during the Yom Kippur War.

More important, the wage and price controls proved to be only a temporary remedy for inflation. In 1972 the growing number of exemptions weakened the controls, and the consumer price index began rising again in the second half of the year. Then in October 1973 the economy received a severe shock when the Arab oil-producing states imposed an embargo on the United States for its support of Israel during the Yom Kippur War of 1973. The price of a barrel of oil rose from under $3 in early 1973 to between $10 and $14 in 1974. Rising oil prices, a poor 1973 harvest, and the phasing out of price controls begun in 1973 and completed in 1974 led to a dramatic jump in inflation. Prices increased 6.2 percent in 1973 and a painful 11.0 percent in 1974. That year the Nixon administration attempted to fight inflation with more restrictive fiscal and monetary policies, but the Watergate scandal made any cooperation with Congress difficult. On August 9, Nixon resigned to avoid impeachment for his part in the Watergate affair.

Ford Administration

Like Richard Nixon, Gerald Ford assumed the presidency intending to fight inflation through a policy of moderate fiscal restraint supported by a tight monetary policy. The inflationary effects of the 1973 Arab oil embargo and the removal of the wage and price freeze remained strong after Ford took office. He asked Congress for a 5 percent tax surcharge on corporations and the upperclass and for selected spending cuts and deferrals.

A minor part of Ford's economic program, however, received the most attention. He encouraged Americans to fight inflation voluntarily by saving more, conserving energy, increasing charitable contributions, and resisting price and wage increases. The voluntary measures were to be symbolized by "WIN" buttons, which stood for "Whip Inflation Now." The buttons were ridiculed as a symbol of the ineffectuality of the administration's policies.[49]

Ford, however, was forced to abandon his anti-inflationary strategy in early 1975. Statistics showed that the economy had fallen into a deep recession in 1974 before he took office, partly as a result of the sharp rise in oil prices, which forced businesses to cut back their operations. Unemployment reached 9 percent late in the year.

He responded in January by asking Congress for a $16 billion tax cut and new investment tax credits for business to stimulate the economy. Congress and the president compromised with a $23 billion tax cut bill that favored the lower class. The tax cut, however, was enacted in March 1975 when the recession began to ease. Consequently, by the time the benefits of the cut reached Americans the economy was already growing.[50]

Despite the persistently high rates of inflation, many Democrats in Congress pressed the president to make low unemployment the nation's first economic priority. During the rest of 1975 and early 1976 Ford battled Congress over economic policy, repeatedly vetoing spending measures he considered inflationary. Nevertheless, Ford compromised on several appropriations bills, which, coupled with large unemployment compensation and welfare payments caused by the recession, increased federal deficits to new highs of $53 billion in 1975 and $74 billion in 1976.

In early 1976 inflation leveled off, and the economy appeared to be improving just in time for Ford's reelection bid. Inflation had fallen from 11 percent in 1974 to 9 percent in 1975 and just 5.8 percent in 1976. Meanwhile, unemployment averaged 7.7 percent in 1976, which was an encouraging improvement after 8.5 percent in 1975. The country, however, voted for Jimmy Carter to replace Ford in the White House, as the incumbent could not overcome the recent tough economic times and the legacy of Richard Nixon.

Carter Administration

Jimmy Carter took over an economy that had improved slightly during the last year of the Ford administration. The Federal Reserve Board's tight monetary policies had brought down inflation to 5.8 percent for 1976, and Carter entered office intending to work on lowering unemployment.

Despite this slight economic improvement, Carter was taking over the economy in an era that would be.dominated by forces outside his control. During the late 1960s and 1970s, several factors had combined to produce an increasingly difficult economic environment where astute stabilization policy could not necessarily be relied upon to produce prosperity. The inflationary pressures built up during the Vietnam War had not yet dissipated. In addition, OPEC engineered the second major oil price hike of the decade in 1979. Oil prices increased from under $15 a barrel in 1979 to almost $40 a barrel in 1981. Also, the growth of regulation during the 1970s in areas such as environmental protection, job safety, and consumer protection increased the cost of producing goods and contributed to inflation. Simultaneous with these inflationary pressures the economy was also experiencing a continued decline in productivity relative to foreign competitors that had begun in the 1960s. Finally, the maturation of federal benefit programs had decreased the controllable portion of the budget that could be cut from year to year, nearly ensuring budget deficits in the absence of a tax increase or substantial spending cuts.[51] Although Carter was not responsible for the underlying economic conditions he faced as president, his policies did little to help the situation.

Carter entered office hoping to focus his economic policy on reducing unemployment. He proposed a stimulative program that included a $50 tax rebate. Carter withdrew the rebate proposal when economic statistics showed that unexpectedly strong economic growth threatened to spark a renewed surge of inflation, but much of the rest of his plan, including increased spending for jobs programs and public works, was enacted. Until late 1979, Carter gave priority to reducing unemployment. From 1977 to 1979 he encouraged a stimulative monetary policy that brought the biggest expansion of the money supply of any three-year period since World War II.[52] As a result, the economy continued the expansion that had begun in late 1975.

During this period, however, the public became increasingly concerned about inflation. Consumer prices had risen 7.7 percent in 1978, up from 5.8 percent in 1976. The OPEC price hike of 1979 triggered a jump in inflation, which rose 11.5 percent for the year. Carter recognized that inflation had become the nation's foremost economic problem.

One of Carter's most fateful economic decisions was the appointment of Paul Volcker as chairman of the Federal Reserve Board in 1979 after William Miller had resigned. On October 6, 1979, Volcker indicated that he would use monetary policy vigorously to fight inflation. Although in the long run, Volcker's contractions of the money supply were effective in bringing down inflation, the consumer price index did not respond to the tight monetary policy in 1979 and 1980. Consequently, interest rates soared without an accompanying drop in inflation. In 1979, prices increased 13.5 percent, real per capita income declined 0.7 percent, and the prime lending rate of banks stood at a whopping 15.25 percent. Carter complemented Volcker's tough stand with fiscal restraint designed to combat inflation and lower the budget deficit. Just as the demands of economic management had induced a conservative Richard Nixon to adopt the very liberal tool of wage and price controls, Carter had abandoned his liberal goal of achieving low levels of unemployment and had adopted the traditionally conservative strategy of fighting inflation with monetary and fiscal policy while pursuing a balanced budget.[53]

For the first time since presidents began submitting an annual economic report thirty years before, Carter's 1980 report forecasted a recession. In the second quarter of that year the recession came as predicted, while double-digit inflation remained. During that year, Republican presidential nominee Ronald Reagan attacked Carter for producing a "misery index" (the combined total of the inflation and unemployment rates) over 20. In August 1980 a CBS News/*New York Times* poll found that only 19 percent of those polled approved of Carter's "handling of the economy."[54] With the public convinced of the president's inability to manage economic affairs, Reagan defeated Carter in a landslide.

Supply-side Theory

During the late 1970s, a theory outside mainstream economics began to gain influential supporters. *Supply-side economic theory* was based on the premise that economic growth and low unemployment could best be achieved by promoting investment and productivity. Supply-side theorists advocated using tax policy to encourage individuals and businesses to invest more and be more productive. The supply-siders asserted that income tax rates affect people's choice between work and leisure and between saving and consumption. The more individuals are taxed, the less incentive they have to work and save. Similarly, the more businesses are taxed, the less money they have to invest in new plants and equipment that would raise their productivity.

By cutting taxes the theorists believed the government could increase personal and corporate productivity and investment thereby increasing the amount of goods and services produced. Thus, whereas Keynesian economic strategists sought to promote economic growth by stimulating demand for goods and services, a strategy that often led to inflation, supply-siders focused on increasing the supply of goods and services. Since supply-siders claimed to be able to stimulate the economy without increasing inflation, their theory seemed to provide a promising solution to the economic condition that plagued the 1970s—simultaneous high inflation and unemployment.

Supply-side theory was also attractive because many of its advocates asserted that tax cuts would not create larger budget deficits. They predicted that the expansion of the economy brought on by a supply-side strategy would generate enough revenue to decrease deficits even though tax rates were lower. This principle was illustrated by the Laffer Curve, developed by Arthur B. Laffer of the University of Southern California. Laffer posited that government revenues rise as tax rates rise until they reach a point at which the increases in revenue brought by higher rates are less than the loss of revenue caused by the public's reduced incentive to work. Laffer and his adherents challenged the assumptions of most professional economists by arguing that the tax rates in force under the Carter administration were above this optimal level. Therefore, they believed tax revenues could be increased not by raising rates, which would intensify the disincentives to produce, but by lowering the rates so that they would be closer to the optimal rate of taxation.[55]

Ironically, in 1963 President Kennedy also had argued that his proposed tax cut would ultimately result in greater revenue. Kennedy's reasoning was based on Keynesian theory rather than supply-side theory, and his tax cut occurred when economic conditions were very different from the late 1970s, but some supply-siders pointed to the increase in tax revenue following Kennedy's tax cut as evidence of the validity of the Laffer Curve.[56]

Although few professional economists supported a supply-side approach to the economic problems of the late 1970s, the theory was adopted by several members of Congress. Its most visible proponent in government was Rep. Jack F. Kemp (R-N.Y.), who with the cooperation of Sen. William V. Roth, Jr., (R-Del.), had constructed an income tax reduction plan in 1977 based on supply-side theory. With the nomination in 1980 of Ronald Reagan as the Republican presidential candidate, however, supply-side theory was thrust into the political limelight. Reagan had become a believer in supply-side economic theory, including Laffer's controversial assertions about deficit reduction, during the late 1970s as he prepared to run for the Republican presidential nomination. Reagan had been defeated for the nomination in 1976 by incumbent Gerald Ford in part because he had advocated an austere policy of budget cuts with tax relief being conditioned on the success of deficit reduction.[57] Supply-side theory gave Reagan a justification for moving away from painful economic prescriptions without abandoning his conservative philosophies about balancing the budget.

Reagan campaigned on his plan to cut taxes while balancing the budget through domestic budget cuts and increases in revenue, which he hoped would be produced by the tax cut. Reagan's plan held out the promise of achieving general prosperity without increased budget deficits and inflation. During Reagan's campaign for the nomination his Republican opponent and eventual vice president, George Bush, reflected the skepticism of many economists and politicians when he labeled Reagan's supply-side strategy "voodoo economics." The American public, however, elected Reagan in a landslide over incumbent Jimmy Carter, setting the stage for a test of supply-side theory.

Reagan Tax Cut

Ronald Reagan's first economic policy priority was passing the largest spending and tax cuts in U.S. history. His landslide victory enabled him to claim a mandate for his plan to cut personal income taxes by 30 percent, introduce new tax incentives for businesses, and sharply cut nondefense expenditures. Opponents of Reagan's strategy warned that it could be inflationary if the public did not save an adequate percentage of their tax savings.

Some Democrats in Congress also attacked the plan as a disguised attempt to lighten the tax burden of the wealthy while cutting back on government aid to the poor, another feature of Reagan's economic program. Reagan and his advisers admitted that their tax cut was structured to benefit upper-income individuals most but argued that these were precisely the people who would be best able to invest their tax break, thus fueling the economic expansion for everyone. Reagan's critics called this reasoning a return to a predepression, Republican, "trickle down" strategy in which benefits for the rich were justified on the grounds that the poor eventually would benefit from a stronger economy.

Although many Americans perceived Reagan's taxing and spending strategy as inequitable, a strong majority of Americans supported it, and his congressional allies were able to push most of the plan through Congress despite the solid Democratic majority in the House. The president signed the Economic Recovery Tax Act of 1981 in August. It reduced individual tax rates 25 percent—5 percent less than Reagan had wanted—over thirty-three months. In addition, the bill indexed the tax system for the first time ever to keep inflation from forcing taxpayers into higher brackets as their incomes kept pace with prices. Reagan was also successful in pushing $35 billion in 1982 nondefense spending cuts through Congress.

Budget Dilemma

Reagan had hoped that his tax cut would create an economic boom that would bring increases in tax revenues. These increased revenues along with reduced domestic spending would reduce the federal budget deficit until the budget was balanced. In 1980, while running for the presidency, Reagan had attacked Carter and the Democratic-controlled Congress for their deficit spending and promised to balance the budget by 1983.[58] By late 1981, however, economic statistics showed that the country was entering a recession. This recession, the deepest since the depression, lasted through 1982. It widened the budget deficit because tax revenues were depressed by declining industrial output and personal income, while government spending on unemployment insurance and welfare increased.

In addition, after the initial wave of spending cuts, Reagan's budget cutting lost momentum as the administration and Congress refused to make major concessions to the priorities of the other. In November 1981, after less than a year in office, Reagan conceded that he probably could not balance the budget in one term. In 1982, despite his position against taxes, Reagan agreed to a tax increase that reduced the 1981 tax cut by about a quarter, with most of the restored revenue coming out of corporate tax reductions.[59]

When the economy recovered from the recession in 1983, the budget deficit, contrary to the administration's predictions, continued to grow. In 1983 the deficit reached $195 billion. Against the recommendation of several advisers, including CEA chairman Martin Feldstein and budget director David Stockman, Reagan refused to consider a further tax increase as a remedy to the deficit. He maintained that higher taxes would threaten economic growth and would not substantially reduce the budget deficit because Congress would find a way to spend most of the additional revenue.[60] Reagan's firm stand against raising taxes was popular with the public, but it ignored the growing deficit problem.

In addition, the president fought against cuts in defense spending. Reagan had charged that Carter had allowed the nation's defenses to deteriorate while the Soviet Union continued to pursue a massive military buildup. According to Reagan, the growing Soviet advantage in military capability threatened the security of the United States and its allies. During the early 1980s public support for a military buildup and tensions between the United States and the Soviet Union led Congress to accept many of Reagan's defense spending proposals. Military expenditures rose from 5.0 percent of GNP in 1980 to 6.2 percent in 1987.

However necessary increased defense spending was to U.S. national security, the president and Congress were unable to spend more on defense without deepening the deficit problem. They did not have the political will to cut Social Security and other popular entitlements to offset the increase in defense spending; nor had Reagan's supply-side tax cutting strategy proven to be a realistic cure for the growth of the federal deficit.

Economic Recovery

The recovery of 1983 became a sustained period of economic growth accompanied by low inflation that lasted through Reagan's second term, with unemployment falling below 6 percent in 1988. Reagan proudly pointed to the growth as a vindication of his policies. Many economists, however, believed that Reagan took too much credit for the expansion. The collapse of the oil cartel of the Organization of Petroleum Exporting Countries (OPEC) in the early 1980s produced falling oil prices that helped reduce inflation and spur economic growth; the restrictive monetary policies of Federal Reserve Board chairman Paul Volcker, a Carter appointee, had wrung inflation out of the economy by 1982, setting up a period when the president could concentrate on stimulating the economy with little worry that significant inflation would return; the Reagan administration's tolerance of a high dollar had contributed to the development of a large trade deficit, which exceeded $100 billion by 1984; and the Reagan administration's unprecedented tax cut pumped money into the American economy and created jobs—but at the expense of creating an intractable debt problem. Ironically, Ronald Reagan, who had repudiated Keynesian economics had presided over a period in which prosperity was achieved in part through peacetime deficit spending by the government, the classic Keynesian prescription for combating a recession.[61]

Unprecedented budget deficits loomed over the otherwise prosperous economic conditions of the mid-1980s. The budget deficit widened sharply from $79 billion in 1981 to $221 billion in 1986. Annual payments to finance the national debt had risen from $69 billion to $136 billion during the same period.

By 1985 the enormous budget deficit led legislators to pass the Gramm-Rudman-Hollings Deficit Reduction Act with the support of President Reagan. (See "Presidents and the Budget," p. 260, in this chapter.) It was intended to force spending cuts aimed at balancing the budget by 1991. Despite cuts in defense spending and other deficit reduction measures, however, the budget deficit was still $150 billion in 1987. Over the course of the Reagan administration the national debt had nearly tripled from $914.3 billion in 1980 to a projected $2.825 trillion in 1989. Cutting the deficit was widely regarded as the most pressing and difficult problem facing the incoming administration of George Bush.

Fiscal Policy

Fiscal policy is the body of spending and taxing decisions made by the government in pursuit of economic stabilization. The government can choose to combat unemployment and stagnant economic growth by stimulating the economy through tax cuts or increased spending. It can choose to fight inflation by contracting the economy through tax increases or reduced spending. Although Congress must pass legislation approving every taxation and spending decision, presidents and their advisers initiate most fiscal policy proposals and greatly influence congressional deliberations. Congress, however, rarely has rubber-stamped presidential fiscal policies. Consequently, any president hoping to exercise control over fiscal policy must persuade Congress to accept the substance of the executive branch initiatives.

The Politics of Fiscal Policy

Fiscal policy is not made by a group of economists in Washington who gather information, weigh all their options, consider the long-term and short-term needs of the country, and decide on a policy they believe will produce the best economic outcome. Rather, it is produced through an unwieldy political process of negotiation and compromise between the legislative and executive branches.

When presidents formulate economic policy, they must consider not only what is theoretically optimal but also what is politically feasible. A president's fiscal policies depend as much on the chief executive's ability to present them to the American people and bargain with Congress as on the ability of the president's economic team to understand the economic situation and formulate effective fiscal responses. The most insightful fiscal strategies are meaningless if they are objectionable to major interest groups or if a president is unable to sell them to Congress. In addition, presidents must consider the effects of their fiscal policies on their own reelection chances and the fate of their party at the polls.

Election Cycle

The performance of the economy during a president's term affects the incumbent's chances for reelection as much as any other issue. In times of peace many Americans will "vote their pocket books," by basing their vote on whether the American economy has given them the opportunity to meet their own economic expectations. Moreover, an economy that improves during the year before an election can erase voters' memories of a longer period of economic stagnation or inflation.

Even second-term or newly elected presidents who are not immediately concerned with their own reelection chances understand that economic conditions will affect the outcome of midterm elections, which will determine the strength of their party in Congress. Since the entire House and one-third of the Senate face an election every other year, significant turnover in congressional membership is possible. If an administration loses too many congressional allies its programs may be threatened, and the president's reelection chances in two years may be weakened. Fiscal

policy, therefore, is never completely free from the influence of electoral politics and in an election year may be dominated by it.

The connection between economic conditions and the political success of presidents is a powerful incentive for an incumbent administration to try to create short-term improvements in the economy before an election. Economist Edward R. Tufte has identified several economic trends that correspond to the U.S. election cycle. His studies of the economy from 1948 to 1976 have shown that the unemployment rate on presidential election days tends to be significantly lower than twelve to eighteen months before and after an election.[62]

The elections that occurred during Eisenhower's presidency are notable exceptions to this trend. Eisenhower believed that Americans were more concerned with achieving a balanced budget and low inflation than low unemployment and economic growth. He therefore opposed short-term stimulations of the economy for political purposes. The Republican losses in Congress in 1954 and 1958 and John Kennedy's victory over Richard Nixon in 1960, all of which occurred during economic slumps, provide evidence that Eisenhower may have been wrong.[63] After his 1960 defeat, Nixon wrote:

> The bottom of the 1960 dip did come in October and the economy started to move up in November—after it was too late to affect the election returns. In October, usually a month of rising employment, the jobless roles increased by 452,000. All the speeches, television broadcasts, and precinct work in the world could not counteract that one hard fact.[64]

Tufte also found that increases in Social Security payments—the most direct way to put more money into the hands of voters—usually were enacted with the president's approval in even-numbered years during the ten months preceding an election. Since increases in payroll taxes required to pay for the higher Social Security payments start at the beginning of a year for administrative reasons, the price of Social Security increases was not felt by taxpayers until after the election.[65] In 1975, however, Social Security benefits were indexed so recipients receive annual cost-of-living increases to offset inflation, thereby weakening the justification for politically motivated benefit increases.

In addition to stimulative fiscal policies and increased transfer payments, other presidential economic policies have been affected by electoral politics. Lyndon Johnson did not press Congress for a tax hike in 1966 partly because he did not wish to focus attention on the growing costs of the Vietnam War before the midterm congressional elections.[66] Despite Nixon's personal distaste for severe government economic intervention, he imposed wage and price controls on the nation in August 1971 because the deteriorating economic situation threatened his upcoming 1972 reelection bid.[67]

Presidential efforts to manipulate the economy for political purposes are seldom in the best interests of the nation's long-term economic health. Although some politicians may argue that election year economic stimulations are attentive political responses to the desires of voters, the public pays a price for these short-term boosts. Presidents and Congresses do not always have the political will to take away pre-election benefits and tax cuts after the election. Consequently, electoral pressures on economic policy contribute to budget deficits and inflation. Even when the president and law-makers do agree on measures to offset their election year generosity, there is evidence that short-term decreases in unemployment brought about by election year tax cuts and spending hikes may be more transitory than the increases in inflation that usually accompany them.[68]

Beyond the inflationary and budgetary costs of pandering to voters' short-term economic desires, this practice makes coherent economic policy making difficult. Tufte has concluded:

> The electoral-economic cycle breeds a lurching, stop-and-go economy the world over. Governments fool around with transfer payments, making an election-year prank out of the social security system and the payroll tax. There is a bias toward policies with immediate, highly visible benefits and deferred, hidden costs—myopic policies for myopic voters.[69]

Legislative Requirement

In addition to the distortions caused by electoral politics, fiscal policy is complicated by the requirement that it be enacted through the legislative process. Having 535 members of Congress examine, debate, and vote on a fiscal policy proposal ensures that the American people, through their elected representatives, will have a say over the government's taxing and spending decisions. This democratic necessity reduces, however, the effectiveness of fiscal policy as a presidential economic stabilization tool.

Even when no election is imminent, the legislative process required to enact fiscal policy may take so long that by the time the policy takes effect it may be irrelevant or counterproductive to the needs of the economy. This "lag" between the time a policy is needed and the time it can be enacted is a major weakness of fiscal policy.[70] Taxing and spending legislation usually takes months and may take more than a year to weave its way through committees and emerge in a form acceptable to a majority of both houses of Congress. Consequently, fiscal policy is often unresponsive to the most recent economic information. The democratic process guarantees that legislation will get a fair hearing, but in the case of fiscal policy, the fair hearing may render the legislation irrelevant.

Fiscal policy is also weakened by the narrow economic focus of many members of Congress. Individual senators and representatives are seldom held responsible for a general economic decline by their constituents. If they are members of the same party as the president, they may suffer from an antiparty vote when the economy is performing badly, but usually they are judged according to how well they serve the interests of their district or state. Although many members of Congress do have a national perspective on some economic issues, few will put the economic interests of the nation ahead of the local economic interests of their constituency. Fiscal legislation that costs jobs in a particular district will almost always be opposed by that district's representative. Thus, the American democratic political system encourages a narrow focus by members of Congress that contributes to the difficulty of making rational fiscal policy.

Interest Groups

Presidents are chosen by a national electorate and therefore do not have to worry about promoting prosperity in a particular state or congressional district as members of Congress do. Nevertheless, presidents are not immune to the pressures interest groups can exert on taxing and spending decisions. Labor unions, trade associations, business and agricultural interests, the financial community, ethnic groups, senior citizens organizations, and many other interest groups seek to affect fiscal policy.[71] These groups have political clout because they are able to offer campaign contributions, to mobilize blocs of voters, and to publicize their opinions in an effort to support candidates who work for causes important to their members. They can also use the same tools to seek the defeat of candidates whom they consider hostile to their interests.

No single decision to yield to the requests of an interest group is likely to undermine a president's fiscal policy, but if the president gives in to too many groups, the cumulative effect may inflate the president's budget. President Carter faced this problem when he was beset by groups who expected a Democratic president to deliver policies favorable to their interests. Organized labor, farmers, and a variety of groups advocating traditional Democratic social policies lobbied the White House to address their budgetary concerns. Carter was forced to compromise with many of these groups whose support was crucial to his presidency. As a result many budget items received more funds than Carter had intended. This failure to restrain spending contributed to the budget deficit and inflation.[72]

Despite their susceptibility to interest group pressures, presidents are in the best position to rise above politics and provide impartial economic leadership. This is because the American people ultimately will hold them responsible if the economy falters during their presidency. The support of certain interest groups will mean little to a president's popularity and chances for reelection if the public is unsatisfied with the current levels of inflation and unemployment and other economic factors.

Presidents and the Budget

The budget is the most important annual document produced by the Executive Office of the Presidency. It not only spells out the funding decisions of the president and his advisers, it is an important fiscal policy tool that can be used to influence the levels of inflation, unemployment, and economic growth. Moreover, as Gerald R. Ford has said, "The budget reflects the President's sense of priorities. It reflects his best judgment of how we must choose among competing interests."[73] It is therefore a document that affects presidential political and social programs as much as it affects fiscal policy.

As previously noted, the president had little effect on the budget-making process until Congress enacted the 1921 Budget and Accounting Act, which required the chief executive to submit a comprehensive executive budget to Congress. Since then presidents have exercised varying influence on the budget, depending on their relationship with Congress and their interest in budget details. Some presidents such as Jimmy Carter and Gerald Ford have chosen to immerse themselves in budget management. Others such as Richard Nixon and Ronald Reagan showed interest only in broad budgetary decisions that could not be easily delegated to someone else.[74]

Regardless of their interest in the budget, presidents are ultimately responsible for the executive branch's spending proposals and can greatly influence Congress's consideration of them. The political, social, and economic priorities of presidents provide guidelines to OMB officials and others involved in constructing the budget. Presidents also must arbitrate disputes between agencies and hear last-minute appeals from agency heads who feel a cherished program has been shortchanged.[75]

Since the late 1960s, the budget-making process has been a struggle to limit budget deficits despite erratic economic growth and dramatic increases in funding for entitlements, social programs, and defense. The American people consistently indicate in surveys that they believe government spending should be reduced. They also predictably say they do not want higher taxes. Yet this desire for less government spending is not accompanied by a willingness to sacrifice funding for specific programs. The public believes the government spends too much in only a few policy areas such as foreign aid, welfare, and space exploration.[76] Thus the budget is one of the most persistent political dilemmas facing presidents. They must try to reduce overall spending (or convince the electorate that they are trying to reduce it) while funding the programs that the American public has come to expect.

Presidential Impoundment of Appropriations

The Constitution did not spell out whether presidents were required to promptly spend funds appropriated by Congress or whether they could make independent judgments on the timing and even the necessity of putting appropriated funds to use. Many presidents during the nineteenth century took advantage of this constitutional ambiguity to impound appropriated funds they believed unnecessary or wasteful. In effect, the impoundment "power" gave presidents a second veto over appropriations since they could withhold funds Congress intended to be spent.

After World War II presidents increasingly used impoundments as a fiscal policy tool. Presidents Truman, Eisenhower, and Kennedy all clashed with Congress over their withholding of appropriations for defense projects. In 1966 Lyndon Johnson impounded $5.3 billion in domestic appropriations to slow inflationary trends brought on by the Vietnam War.

Presidential impoundments reached their zenith under Richard Nixon, who impounded billions of dollars of appropriations during the first five years of his presidency. He argued that he was withholding funds only as a financial management technique designed to slow inflation. Democratic leaders in Congress, however, charged that Nixon used impoundments to overturn Congress's spending decisions and further his own social goals. The conflict between Nixon and Congress over impoundments led to the passage of an act that restricted presidential use of impoundments.

Congressional Budget and Impoundment Control Act of 1974

The 1974 Congressional Budget and Impoundment Control Act created new procedures designed to prevent a president from impounding appropriations against the will of Congress. Under the act presidents must notify Congress when they decide to permanently impound appropriated funds. Congress has forty-five days in which to signal its disapproval of these permanent impoundments, known as rescissions, by a majority vote of both houses. After forty-five days, if Congress has not acted, presidents may make their proposed rescissions.[77] The law also allows presidents to defer spending appropriated funds by notifying Congress they are doing so. The funds can be held until Congress passes an act directing the president to spend the funds.

The rules governing impoundments, however, were only a small part of the Congressional Budget and Impoundment Control Act. It was an attempt by Congress to revitalize the entire budget process and link congressional deliberations on spending and revenue legislation. The act created a timetable designed to force action on the budget, moved the start of the fiscal year from July 1 to the following October 1 to give Congress more time to consider budgetary details, and established measures intended to aid Congress in evaluating the budget as a whole rather than as a group of unconnected spending bills. The act created the House and Senate Budget committees to centralize congressional budget making and the Congressional Budget Office to provide Congress with an expert staff to analyze the budget.[78]

Although many members of Congress lauded the new process, it did not achieve its two primary goals: bringing more order to the budget process and reducing the federal deficit. Deficits continued to grow after 1974, and Congress struggled, often unsuccessfully, to meet the budgetary deadlines set down in the act.[79]

The potential of the 1974 Budget Act as an executive tool, however, was not realized until 1981. At that time Ronald Reagan used the process to push his dramatic fiscal program of increased defense spending, decreased domestic spending, and a large tax cut through Congress. The new centralized budget-making process in Congress allowed him to negotiate with congressional leaders on the substance of his entire budget plan rather than being forced to bargain on a dozen or more appropriations bills, each of which might have been opposed by a different congressional bloc. To get his budget approved, Reagan used his public popularity to build a conservative coalition in the House of Representatives despite the Democratic majority.

Political scientist Louis Fisher explained why the new process favored the president:

> Whereas the politics of incrementalism under the old process had operated as a brake on radical changes, the Budget Act of 1974 strengthened Reagan's hand by requiring Congress to vote on an overall budget policy.... Although the administration did not get everything it wanted, the omnibus measure was more of an advantage to the executive branch than to Congress. By packaging all the cuts in a single bill, the White House was able to build a majority for final passage. Members could announce that they objected to specific cuts but supported the bill "on balance."[80]

After Reagan's dramatic 1981 budget victory, however, Congress regrouped and became more resistant to his domestic budget-cutting proposals.

Federal Budget Deficits

Budget deficits are not a phenomenon unique to the 1970s and 1980s. The federal government often has been forced to run deficits during wars and other national emergencies, including the depression. Yet not until the 1970s did budget deficits become a persistent peacetime economic problem. Between 1792 and 1946 the federal government had produced 93 budget surpluses and 61 budget deficits. From 1947 to 1969, a period during which two wars

Table 2 U.S. Federal Debt, Interest Payments, and
Budget Deficits, 1971-1987 (billions of dollars)

Fiscal year	Total federal debt	Budget deficit	Interest payments
1971	409.5	−23.0	14.8
1972	437.3	−23.4	15.5
1973	468.4	−14.9	17.3
1974	486.2	−6.1	21.4
1975	544.1	−53.2	23.2
1976	631.9	−73.7	26.7
1977	709.1	−53.6	29.9
1978	780.4	−59.2	35.4
1979	833.8	−40.2	42.6
1980	914.3	−73.8	52.5
1981	1,003.9	−78.9	68.7
1982	1,147.0	−127.9	85.0
1983	1,381.9	−207.7	89.8
1984	1,576.7	−185.3	111.1
1985	1,827.5	−212.3	129.4
1986	2,130.0	−221.2	136.0
1987	2,355.3	−150.4	138.6

Source: Office of Management and Budget, 1988.

were fought, the government produced 8 surpluses and 15 deficits; but since 1970 the budget has been in deficit every year.[81]

The size of deficits since the Vietnam War has been especially troubling. In the past, periods of deficit spending were followed by years of surplus or at least balanced budgets. From 1975 to 1988, however, budget deficits have exceeded $45 billion every year except 1979, despite the absence of a war or significant military conflict. Moreover, the deficit widened dramatically under Ronald Reagan, surpassing $200 billion in 1983, 1985, and 1986. These deficits alarmed most economists and common citizens and forced the president and Congress to search for ways to get the budget under control.

Large budget deficits have several negative effects on the economy. First, they limit the government's flexibility to fight a recession through tax cuts and deficit spending because the president and Congress must be concerned about exacerbating the debt problem. Since tax revenues fall during a recession and unemployment insurance and welfare payments rise, the budget would be under further strain precisely when deficit spending would be needed to pull the economy out of recession.

Second, large deficits reduce the amount of funds available for achieving the nation's social and defense goals because interest must be paid on the national debt. As larger budget deficits have pushed the national debt toward $3 trillion, interest payments have taken up an increasing share of the federal budget. In 1987 interest payments on the federal debt totaled $138.6 billion, or almost 14 percent of federal goverment spending. This was more money than the government spent on any other budget category except defense and Social Security and came close to equaling the deficit itself.

Third, large budgets can threaten the economy by "crowding out" corporate and private borrowers from the credit market. Because the government must borrow heavily to finance its deficit, it competes with businesses and individuals also seeking to borrow funds. This in-

creased competition forces interest rates higher causing loans to become more expensive. As a result, businesses can afford to purchase less plant and equipment to expand and modernize their operations, and fewer consumers can afford to finance purchases of expensive items such as houses and cars. The resulting reduction in demand may threaten economic growth.

Finally, budget deficits of the 1980s have become so large that domestic savings no longer can provide enough capital to service the debt. Consequently the government must borrow from foreign sources to make up the difference. This makes the United States dependent on foreign investors and raises the small possibility of a "stabilization crisis," which can occur if foreign investors lose confidence in the dollar and liquidate their U.S. investments. Such a crisis could cause the dollar to plummet and interest rates and inflation to rapidly accelerate.[82]

The Uncontrollable Budget

Presidents hoping to limit budget deficits must face the fiscal difficulties brought by the spending items that are reqired from year to year by existing law. These are known as uncontrollable or mandatory budgetary items. Although the term "uncontrollable" is somewhat misleading since these programs can be changed by an act of Congress, it does accurately describe the lack of power presidents have over these items in any given year.

Before the depression, most of the federal budget was devoted to the costs of running the government and, in times of war, the costs of defense. With the establishment of Social Security in the 1930s, however, the government began making large-scale payments directly to people who qualified for them. These transfer payment programs, which now include Medicare, Medicaid, welfare, job training assistance, student loan guarantees, food stamps, subsidized school lunches, unemployment compensation, and federal retirement benefits are intended to alleviate suffering and poverty, promote the health and advancement of individuals, and provide a safety net for those members of society who cannot provide for themselves because of economic recession, poverty, old age, or physical infirmity. Some of these transfer payment programs, such as welfare and unemployment insurance, also act as automatic economic stabilizers, since they increase the amount of money in the hands of the public when the economy goes into recession.[83]

These payments have consciously been expanded by Congress and several presidents, most notably Franklin Roosevelt and Lyndon Johnson, in an effort to use the wealth generated by the U.S. economy to promote social welfare and care for the less fortunate. Many federal transfer payment programs were established or substantially enlarged during the 1960s when the strong American economy seemed capable of providing funds for virtually any worthy purpose. This goal has become an accepted role of the government from which there appears to be no retreat. Even Ronald Reagan, who denounced the growth of the federal government and advocated deep cuts in domestic spending, did not propose dramatic reductions in funds for established entitlement programs such as Social Security that make up society's "safety net."

Transfer payments pose a special problem for presidents and their advisers who must be concerned with balancing the budget because the payments are not based on a yearly congressional appropriation or the government's ability to pay for them in a given year. They continue from year to year unless a law is passed that supersedes the measure which created them. Moreover, in 1974 Congress established cost-of-living increases for Social Security payments, thereby ensuring that these benefits would not be reduced by the eroding effects of inflation.[84]

Predictably, presidents and Congress have seldom been willing to assume the political risk of significantly reducing entitlement programs, subsidies, and other payments as the capacity of the government to pay for them has fallen. The growth of transfer payments has been accompanied by an increase in the activities of interest groups who attempt to protect these payments from cutbacks. Lobbyist organizations representing senior citizens, veterans, farmers, and other groups can pressure the president or a member of Congress to protect benefits to their constituents by offering or withholding campaign contributions, threatening them with negative publicity, and mobilizing blocs of voters that can make or break their candidacies. The activities of these lobbyists and the negative public reaction to cuts in transfer payments received by tens of millions of Americans have made large sections of the budget politically untouchable.

Consequently, the ability of presidents to propose significant cuts in the budget from year to year has been reduced as federal transfer payments have claimed a greater portion of the budget. In 1962 transfer payments stood at $29.5 billion, or less than one-third of the budget. By fiscal year 1983 they had reached $362 billion, or almost half of the budget.

In addition to transfer payments, other items in the budget are also outside the control of the president and Congress. Interest payments on the national debt are determined by the size of the debt and prevailing interest rates and must be subtracted from the incoming revenue. Also, the federal government is obligated to pay for items that it has ordered in previous years. For example, large weapon systems such as a new fighter plane or nuclear missile must be paid for over a span of years. Consequently, funds committed in the past to such items cannot be cut from a current budget without breaking contracts and wasting the funds spent on the items in past years. Expenditures for many other items in the budget, such as defense and the costs of operating the government, can be trimmed but not eliminated entirely.

Presidents seeking to reduce government spending, therefore, can search for cuts in only a fraction of the budget. The Office of Management and Budget estimated that in 1967 59 percent of the budget was uncontrollable. During the 1980s uncontrollable spending has climbed above 75 percent. According to political scientists Kim Hill and John Plumlee, this trend has diminished presidential budgetary power: "Presidential budgetary discretion has been significantly eroded.... The President in fact must propose and defend a budget much of which is determined elsewhere and in prior years." [85]

Gramm-Rudman-Hollings Deficit Reduction Act

In response to popular concern about growing budget deficits, Congress passed in 1985 the Gramm-Rudman-Hollings Deficit Reduction Act with President Reagan's approval. The bill was an acknowledgment that Congress and the president needed to be forced to make the tough budget-cutting decisions necessary to reduce the deficit. The legislation required $36-billion decreases in the deficit for five years. To ensure that these budget cuts were made, the law mandated "across the board" cuts known as "sequesters" to meet the deficit reduction targets if the projected deficit for a fiscal year exceeded the targeted amount by more than 10 billion dollars. The authors of the bill reasoned that since nobody would want these indiscriminate cuts—half of which were to come from defense and half from domestic spending—to occur, Congress and the president would meet the deficit reduction targets through normal budget procedures.

Critics of Gramm-Rudman-Hollings charged that it reduced the government's flexibility and encouraged the use of accounting techniques that would disguise rather

UPI/Bettmann Newsphotos

Congress responded to growing budget deficits by passing a landmark deficit reductions act in 1985. Sponsored by Senators Warren Rudman, Phil Gramm, and Ernest Hollings, the law required "across the board" cuts if deficit reduction targets were not met.

than lower the budget deficit. Some critics also claimed that the bill was unconstitutional because the president and Congress would be abdicating their budget-making responsibilities if the automatic cuts were used. The Supreme Court objected to a more limited and technical aspect of the law. The Court ruled on July 7, 1986, that because the law assigned to the comptroller general the final responsibility for determining the size of the budget cuts and for executing the automatic cuts, the bill was unconstitutional; only the president and the executive branch are empowered to execute the laws. The comptroller general heads the General Accounting Office, considered part of the legislative branch.[86] Congress responded to the Court's ruling in September 1987 by passing an amendment that gave the Office of Management and Budget—an executive branch agency—the final authority to determine the magnitude of cuts necessary to meet the deficit reduction goals. The amendment also substantially eased the deficit reduction targets, which were recognized as unrealistic. Under the revised Gramm-Rudman-Hollings the federal budget did not have to be balanced until 1993.

Apart from the law's constitutional problems, many critics of the plan doubted that the deep cuts mandated by the law would be carried out. In 1987 Congress and the president reached their deficit reduction target after an extended period of negotiation. The adopted 1988 and 1989 budgets were within minimum Gramm-Rudman-Hollings guidelines, but depended on optimistic OMB forecasts of economic growth. Meeting the targets for 1990 and subsequent years, however, appeared to be difficult without a tax increase, which President-elect George Bush had promised not to accept, or substantial cuts in Social Security and Medicare, which were opposed by a solid block in Congress. This increased the possibility that the government might be forced to accept automatic spending cuts or again amend the Gramm-Rudman-Hollings law.[87]

Balanced Budget Amendment Proposals

The sharp growth of federal budget deficits during the 1970s and 1980s convinced many government officials and common citizens that the only way to control deficit spending was through a balanced budget amendment. Such an amendment was seen by its supporters as the best way to ensure that the president and Congress would only spend what revenues they took in, since they would be required to do so by the highest law of the land. Under the pressure provided by the amendment Congress and the president would be more capable of making the politically difficult budgeting decisions necessary to balance the budget.

Critics of a balanced budget amendment argued that the amendment would be hard to enforce. Would the president and Congress be penalized for failing to balance the budget? If so, critics asked, who would be responsible for enforcing such penalties? In addition, since the precise amount of spending and revenues for the following year is affected by the size of transfer payments, tax revenues, and other variables unknown to budget makers, a balanced budget amendment would depend on highly imprecise forecasts of spending and revenues that would be subject to dispute.[88] For example, the budget forecasts of the Congressional Budget Office, a congressional agency, routinely differ from the estimates of the president's Office of Management and Budget. A balanced budget amendment would require one set of budget estimates that is recognized as official.

Perhaps the most important criticism of the balanced budget amendment, however, was its effect on fiscal policy as a stabilization tool. If the government did live up to budget-balancing requirements, it would no longer be able to use fiscal policy to stabilize the economy. Since tax receipts fall and transfer payments rise during a recession, balancing the budget would require additional spending cuts or higher taxes that would likely deepen the recession. During expansionary periods budget balancing would risk spurring inflation, because tax revenues would rise, requiring the government to spend more or cut taxes to dispose of the surplus.[89]

The balanced budget amendment found a strong proponent in Ronald Reagan. He advocated its passage during his campaign in 1980 and during the early days of his presidency. Some observers believed the amendment had a chance to become part of the Constitution since it was supported by a popular president. When Ronald Reagan entered office in 1981 thirty-two states already had voted in favor of a constitutional convention to consider a balanced budget amendment. In 1982 the Senate voted 69-31, two votes more than the necessary two-thirds majority, for a constitutional amendment that would have required a balanced budget. The same year, the House voted 236-187 for a similar amendment, falling 46 votes short of the necessary two-thirds. By 1983 growing skepticism that current budget deficits could be quickly reduced deflated the balanced budget amendment movement. Even the president's budget projections did not envision achieving a balanced budget within five years. Consequently, an amendment that would force the government to balance the budget when no acceptable means existed for doing so in the near future was unrealistic.[90] Ronald Reagan continued to pay lip service to the concept of a balanced budget amendment, but it became an idea to be reconsidered in the future when budget deficits were under control.

Line-Item Veto

Another proposal designed to control the federal government's deficit spending is to give the president a line-item veto. Currently, presidents only may sign an appropriations bill or veto it. A line-item veto would give presidents the third option of vetoing specific spending items within a bill while approving the balance of the legislation. Proponents of such a veto argue that it could be used by presidents to guard against wasteful and unnecessary spending items that become law only because they are attached to worthy appropriations bills.

Although many presidents have supported a line-item veto, Ronald Reagan was a particularly vocal advocate of the device. He repeatedly called on Congress in major speeches to enact legislation giving him and future presidents this power. In his last State of the Union address in 1988, Reagan asked Congress to

help ensure our future of prosperity by giving the President a tool that—though I will not get to use it—is one I know future presidents of either party must have. Give the president the same authority that forty-three governors use in their states, the right to reach into massive appropriations bills, pare away the waste, and enforce budget discipline. Let's approve the line item veto.

As described by President Reagan, the line-item veto appeared to be a simple and effective way to control government spending. In reality, although it might help presidents make some cuts in the budget, it is a highly controversial tool that could have several negative effects. If the president were armed with the line-item veto, Congress would be tempted to pass many pork barrel spending items to satisfy their constituents while relying on the president to make the politically difficult choices about which items to cut. Even if the president were to veto a substantial number of these items, the budget might still contain more fat than if Congress had not been given a way out of its legislative responsibilities. The line-item veto also might make budgetary restraint more difficult because a president would be able to threaten a member of Congress with a line-item veto of a program that would benefit that member's state or district unless that member agreed to vote for a bill supported by the administration. Even if the line-item veto did result in less budget waste, it could cause a dramatic shift of legislative power to the president that would violate traditional American principles of separated powers.[91]

Some opponents of a line-item veto have also argued that its supporters have overestimated its effectiveness in reducing budget deficits. A line-item veto would have no effect on entitlements, interest payments on the national debt, and other parts of the budget that cannot be controlled from year to year. Moreover, contrary to popular perceptions, few spending bills contain significant line items that could be cut with a line-item veto. Spending details are often found in the reports of congressional committees and agency budget justification documents, while the legislation funding the activities of a particular unit of an agency or department only mentions the lump sum allocated to it.[92] Given these limitations, the line-item veto is not the answer to huge deficits. At best it would allow the president to make minor cuts in the controllable budget.

Tax Policy

Traditionally, presidents have exerted less influence over tax policy than over spending matters. Whereas presidents are required to submit an executive budget to Congress outlining their spending proposals each year, tax laws do not require the executive to make major annual revisions. In addition, legislators, especially members of the powerful House Ways and Means Committee, have historically regarded tax policy as a special province of Congress.

Nevertheless, presidential influence over tax policy is significant and has grown since World War II. This increase in influence has been furthered by the growth in presidential responsibility for economic policy in general.[93] As Congress and the nation have become used to looking to the president for economic initiatives, the chief executive has taken over much of the burden of proposing and campaigning for changes in the tax code.

In addition to proposing tax legislation, presidents influence tax policy by standing ready to veto tax bills passed by Congress that they believe are unfair, excessive, or harmful to the economy. Presidents after World War II rarely have had to veto tax bills, since the threat to veto them usually has been enough to stop congressional tax initiatives opposed by the president. Ronald Reagan's success at preventing tax increases during his second term despite huge budget deficits demonstrates the president's power over tax policy. Presidents may not be able to get their tax measures passed by Congress, but they will usually be able to stop or at least force the modification of any tax bill they do not like.

Congress, however, has similar power to negate the president's tax proposals. Political scientist John Witte has written: "Although the earlier notion that presidents should set only general revenue targets has been replaced by more detailed, almost annual tax proposals, the majority of the tax agenda is still set by Congress. Furthermore, there is no doubt that when presidential requests run counter to legislative momentum or the short-term mood of Congress, they can and are summarily dismissed by congressional actions." [94]

Within the executive branch, the Treasury Department has primary responsibility for tax policy. Its Office of the Tax Legislative Council drafts tax legislation and reviews tax regulations. The Office of Tax Analysis estimates the effect tax changes have on revenues. In addition, the Treasury Department's Internal Revenue Service is responsible for collecting taxes and enforcing the tax laws passed by Congress.[95] Other officials in the administration, particularly the director of the Office of Management and Budget, also are involved in formulating tax strategies.

Although tax policy and expenditure policy are the two components of fiscal policy, they are rarely coordinated. When formulating the budget, presidents and lawmakers generally have anticipated revenue to be the amount of funds current taxes will produce. Tax cuts and increases only occasionally have been direct responses to expected revenue shortfalls.[96]

All presidents face the dilemma of taxation. While taxes are unpopular, the operation of the government requires revenue. The American public has come to expect many government services, but they also expect that their taxes will be kept to a minimum. Consequently, presidents must back taxes that will raise sufficient revenue to run the government while avoiding responsibility for any tax increases.

Partly because of the political dangers inherent in this dilemma and partly because of the complicated and tedious nature of tax policy, few presidents have placed tax changes or reforms at the top of their domestic policy. Presidents Kennedy and Reagan were two exceptions. Both pressed Congress for major tax cuts to stimulate the economy. Kennedy's tax cut, enacted in 1964 after his death, was smaller than Reagan's, but more successful in promoting economic growth.[97] The growing budget deficit forced Reagan to reclaim part of his 1981 tax cut through "revenue enhancers" enacted in 1982.

Reagan also supported the bipartisan Tax Reform Act of 1986. It was a sweeping attempt to simplify the tax code and eliminate loopholes without increasing or decreasing tax revenues. The bill reduced the number of tax brackets from fourteen to just two. It cut the top individual tax rate from 50 to 28 percent and taxed 85 percent of taxpayers at the bottom rate of 15 percent. President Reagan hailed the law as "the best anti-poverty bill, the best pro-family measure, and the best job-creation program ever to come out of the Congress of the United States." The bill received a favorable reception from the American public although many taxpayers did not believe paying their federal income taxes had been made any easier. In addition government figures indicated in 1988 that the revised tax codes had produced less revenue than the old tax codes would have yielded.

Using tax policy as a tool of fiscal policy is complicated by the government's need for revenue. Although some tax cuts have generated greater revenues, most notably the Kennedy tax cut of 1964, tax cuts usually result in less revenue and higher deficits than would have resulted had they not been enacted. The supply-side economic theory that cutting tax rates would result in higher revenues became popular in the early 1980s, but the budget deficits that followed Ronald Reagan's 1981 tax cut diminished public and professional enthusiasm for this concept. *(See "Supply-side Theory," p. 257, in this chapter.)* A tax cut meant to stimulate the economy may succeed, but policy makers risk higher budget deficits. Conversely, raising taxes may increase revenues in the short term but also contract the economy, resulting in higher unemployment.

Tax cuts are a popular fiscal policy tool because they directly increase net personal income. Tax cuts have often been used successfully to stimulate the economy. The unpopularity of tax increases, however, has made them difficult to enact with the speed that is necessary if they are to be an effective fiscal policy tool. Political scientist Godfrey Hodgson has written of Lyndon Johnson's experience with this problem:

> Even a timely shift in the direction of tax policy for macroeconomic reasons is generally beyond the capacity of...congressional procedures. Lyndon Johnson found this to his cost in 1965-68, when he tried to raise tax revenues to pay for the Vietnam War. His inability to do so may have cost him the presidency. Certainly it spelled the end for his great society programs and gave a sharp new impetus to the inflation combined with economic stagnation that has troubled the economy ever since.[98]

The wave of antitax sentiment that hit the United States during the late 1970s and 1980s further diminished the relevancy of anti-inflationary tax measures. Presidential candidates during this period who did advocate a tax increase, such as 1984 Democratic nominee Walter Mondale and 1988 Democratic contender Bruce Babbitt, were praised by many observers for their realism but fared poorly with voters. Mondale won only thirteen electoral votes in his election battle with Reagan, and Babbitt bowed out of the 1988 Democratic nomination race after receiving meager support in the early primaries.

One proposal that has been offered by proponents of a more efficient fiscal policy process is giving the president the authority to manipulate tax rates to stabilize the economy the way the Federal Reserve Board can manipulate the supply of money. This reform would require a constitutional amendment, since it would shift much taxation power from the Congress to the president.

Under such an amendment the president would be empowered to make small adjustments in personal and corporate income tax rates to stimulate or contract the economy. These adjustments would not require the approval of Congress but would be subject to congressional review and veto. The change in tax rates could have a limited duration, and their size could be constrained to a certain percentage of existing rates, such as 5 or 10 percent. This authority would provide the president with a way to act swiftly to stabilize the economy without having to depend on the time-consuming legislative process that often delivers tax measures too late to be effective as stabilization tools. The danger of such an amendment, however, is that it would disrupt the balance of economic power between the president and Congress and make fiscal policy less democratic.[99] Since Congress would object vigorously to the transfer of power inherent in the amendment and the public would probably fear that it would lead to higher taxes, it is highly unlikely that such an amendment could ever be ratified.

Monetary Policy

Monetary policy, like fiscal policy, is a tool with which the government attempts to stabilize the economy. It is based on the relationship of the supply of money in circulation to the performance of the economy. Since changes in the rate of growth of the money supply profoundly affect unemployment, inflation, and interest rates, the government can regulate economic activity by controlling the supply of money. Increasing the rate of growth of the money supply will stimulate the economy; decreasing it will contract the economy and combat inflation.

The Mechanics of Monetary Policy

In contrast to fiscal policy, which is made through a slow public process of conflict and compromise between the president, Congress, and executive departments, monetary policy is determined within the Federal Reserve System, known as the "Fed." The Fed consists of twelve regional banks, several advisory bodies, and a Board of Governors. The members of the Board of Governors, who are appointed by the president, are responsible for setting monetary policy and overseeing the operations of the Federal Reserve System.

Between 1836 when the charter of the Second Bank of the United States was allowed to expire, and 1914, the United States did not have a central bank. The nation had experienced several banking panics between 1873 and 1907 that prompted Congress to establish the National Monetary Commission to study the American banking system and its problems. In 1912 the commission recommended that the country needed a central bank to regulate credit conditions and provide stability to the banking system of the United States. With these goals in mind, Congress passed the Federal Reserve Act in 1914, which created the Fed.[100] Unlike the First and Second Banks of the United States, Congress gave the Federal Reserve System a permanent charter to avoid the type of political fight that prevented the first two national banks from being rechartered. The Federal Reserve Act does not mention a stabilization policy role for the Federal Reserve System. This role evolved gradually after the Great Depression until stabilization of the economy through monetary policy became its primary function.

The Fed studies the economy and constructs economic forecasts that it uses to determine its monetary policy. Like fiscal policy, the goals of monetary policy include low inflation, low unemployment, and strong economic growth. Fighting inflation, however, has traditionally been the Fed's first priority.

Managing the Money Supply

The Fed has several means through which it can change the rate of growth of the supply of money. First, it can require commercial banks to keep a greater or smaller proportion of deposits on reserve. If this reserve requirement is lowered, banks have more money to lend, and the money supply grows faster. If the reserve requirement is raised, banks have fewer funds to loan, and the growth of the supply of money slows. Second, the Fed can slow or accelerate the growth of the money supply by decreasing or increasing the rate at which banks may borrow funds from the Federal Reserve System. When this rate, known as the *discount rate,* increases, banks can afford to borrow less from the Fed and therefore will have less money to loan. A lower discount rate will put more money in the hands of banks by making it cheaper for them to borrow from the Fed. Finally, the Fed can alter the growth of the money supply by buying and selling U.S. securities. This process, known as *open market operations,* is by far the most commonly used method for affecting the money supply. When the Fed buys securities, it pumps money into the banking system. Selling securities to banks brings money into the Fed that banks could have loaned, thereby slowing the growth of the money supply.[101]

The Fed's manipulations of the money supply affect the performance of the economy through their impact on interest rates. If the Fed increases the money supply, interest rates fall because banks have more funds available to loan. The lower interest rates induce firms to borrow more money to invest in the expansion and modernization of their operations. This increase in investment causes the economy to expand. Consumers also find borrowing cheaper, so they are able to finance the purchase of expensive items such as homes and cars more easily. If the Fed slows the growth of the money supply, banks have fewer funds to loan, and the competition for these limited funds forces interest rates up. Firms and consumers respond to more expensive rates of interest by borrowing less money for investment and purchases, so the economy contracts.

Monetary Policy as a Stabilization Tool

Monetary policy is an attractive policy tool because it is less constrained by politics than is fiscal policy. Since the monetary policy-making structure created by Congress was intended to be nonpolitical, politicians usually have tried to avoid the appearance of interfering in the Fed's business. In addition, the complexity of monetary policy discourages many potential critics from looking over the Fed's shoulder. Monetary policy also has a less visible and immediate effect on the economic welfare of the American public than a major spending or tax decision and therefore will draw less public protest.[102]

Monetary policy's primary role in stabilization policy has been to fight inflation. Monetary policy has two advantages over fiscal policy as an inflation-fighting tool. First, the time required to decide on and execute a strategy is much shorter for monetary policy than for fiscal policy. After an economic problem has been recognized, the Fed can reach a monetary policy decision within days. In contrast, the president may not be able to develop a fiscal policy program and secure congressional approval for many months, if at all. Although monetary policy, once implemented, takes longer to affect the economy than fiscal policy, this delay is usually shorter than the delay caused by the fiscal policy process.[103] Second, the Fed's relative insulation from politics makes its fight against inflation simpler than the president's. Fiscal policy remedies for inflation—tax increases and expenditure cuts—are seldom popular with voters. Since the members of the Fed are not elected, they do not have to worry that growing unemployment or declining economic growth brought on by anti-inflationary monetary policy may anger constituents or cause them to lose an election.[104]

Despite these advantages, monetary policy, like fiscal policy, has its limitations. Although a tight monetary policy can be used to control inflation when the economy is growing too fast, during a period of stagflation when both unemployment and inflation are rising, restrictive monetary policies are likely to deepen the recession.[105] The restrictive monetary policies of Fed Chairman Paul Volcker during the late 1970s and early 1980s succeeded in dramatically lowering inflation, but they also contributed to the severe recession of 1981-1982. Although Volcker deserves much credit for making the tough policy choices necessary to relieve the high inflation that had plagued the U.S. economy since the Vietnam War, the Fed can become too concerned with inflation. The Fed's relative political independence and banking orientation may dispose it to emphasize low inflation at the expense of other economic goals. Specifically, the Fed may at times tolerate unacceptably high unemployment in its pursuit of low inflation.[106]

Presidential Influence over Monetary Policy

The Federal Reserve System is relatively free of formal congressional or executive control. Although there are other independent agencies, none serves such an important and politically sensitive function as formulating monetary policy. The Fed ultimately is answerable to Congress, but the only formal power Congress has over the Fed is the authority to restrict or revise the Fed's powers through legislation. Congress can neither pass judgment on nor veto Fed policies. Since the Fed is self-financing, Congress also cannot gain leverage by threatening to withhold appropriations.

The Fed's independent control of monetary policy is a potent restriction on presidential control of the economy. Except for their power to appoint Federal Reserve Board officials, presidents have no formal means through which they can influence monetary policy. Yet presidents will receive most of the blame or the praise for changes in the economy brought on by monetary policy. Given this situation, presidents naturally try to exert as much informal influence over Fed decisions as possible.

Presidential influence over Fed policy is derived primarily from the president's status as the nation's chief economic manager. Board members recognize a practical need to coordinate fiscal and monetary policy and, despite some prominent exceptions, have usually cooperated with presidential efforts to do so. The Fed also has been mindful that the president is the elected representative of the people who, theoretically, embodies the policy directions preferred by the American electorate.

Although the independence of the Fed is a restraint on presidential control of the economy, it does enable presidents to rely on the Board of Governors to make politically unpopular economic decisions that take some public pressure off the White House. For example, in 1965 President Johnson's advisers urged him to propose a tax increase to cool down the economy, which was beginning to produce inflation. Johnson, however, refused to propose higher taxes, thus forcing the Fed to bear the responsibility for fighting inflation. When the Fed raised the discount rate, Johnson told reporters, "The Federal Reserve Board is an independent agency. Its decision was an independent action. I regret, as do most Americans, any action that raises the cost of credit, particularly for homes, schools, hospitals, and factories." As political scientist Richard Pious has noted, "Had Johnson fought for the politically unpopular

Economic Advisers...

As presidential economic responsibilities increased during the twentieth century, the fulfillment of those responsibilities became increasingly institutionalized. Congress created new organizations, and presidents expanded existing organizations to increase the executive branch's capacity to analyze, coordinate, and manage the American economy and economic relations with other countries. Although White House political advisers and virtually all cabinet secretaries have some influence on economic policy, three executive branch units dominate economic policy making. These are the Treasury Department, the Council of Economic Advisers, and the Office of Management and Budget. The leaders of these three units function as the president's chief economic advisers and meet frequently with one another to coordinate economic policy. Recent presidents have established working groups beneath the three leaders with representatives from various departments to develop and analyze economic policies.

Department of the Treasury

The Treasury Department, one of the original cabinet departments created in 1789 by an act of Congress, was the first executive branch unit to be responsible for advising the president on economic policy and has remained an important participant in economic policy making throughout U.S. history. The department has a variety of economic responsibilities, including collecting taxes and customs, managing the nation's currency and debt, developing tax legislation, and working with foreign governments to adjust the value of the dollar relative to other currencies. Because the Treasury oversees the financing of the debt, the department traditionally has advocated taxes that will bring balanced budgets and monetary policies that yield low interest rates.

The Treasury secretary's position as head of a large cabinet department lends status to the post relative to other top presidential economic advisers. The Treasury secretary's influence on presidential economic decision making, however, may be constrained in some administrations by the time the secretary spends overseeing the many operational responsibilities of the department. As the world's economies have become more interdependent, the Treasury secretary's international economic policy activities have become increasingly important. James A. Baker III, Treasury secretary during Ronald Reagan's second term, spent much of his time formulating exchange rate policies and developing a plan to reschedule Latin American debt payments to the United States.

Council of Economic Advisers

The Council of Economic Advisers (CEA) is a three-member body appointed by the president and subject to Senate confirmation. It is headed by a chair who oversees the operations of the council's small staff, reports to the president, and represents the CEA before the rest of the executive branch and Congress.

The primary function of the CEA is to provide the president with expert economic advice and analysis. The Employment Act of 1946, which established the CEA as a unit in the Executive Office of the President, states that each member of the council "shall be a person who, as a result of his training, experience and attainments is ex-

but necessary tax increase, there would have been no need to blame the board for its action." [107]

Presidential Appointment of Board Members

The most obvious source of influence presidents have over monetary policy is their power to appoint the members of the Fed's Board of Governors. The Federal Reserve Board of Governors consists of a chair appointed by the president to a four-year term with the approval of the Senate and six members appointed to fourteen-year terms, also subject to Senate confirmation. The members' terms are staggered so that one of their terms expires at the end of January in each even-numbered year. Barring deaths or resignations by board members, a president will appoint two members and a chair during a four-year term.

The chair's term, which is renewable, does not coincide with the president's term. Consequently, during the first part of their time in office first-term presidents must work with a chair appointed by their predecessor. These appointment rules are designed to ensure the independence of the Fed's Board of Governors and to prevent any president from dominating its policies by packing the board with administration supporters. The expectations of the financial and scholarly communities that presidents will appoint board members with high academic credentials and relatively nonpartisan backgrounds also serve as a check against overly political appointments.

The chances that the Fed will cooperate with the president, however, are increased greatly if the Fed chair is a recent appointee of the incumbent president. In 1977, President Carter's expansionary fiscal policy was countered by the anti-inflationary monetary policy of Fed chair Arthur Burns, the conservative appointee of Richard Nixon. When Burns's term expired in 1978, Carter replaced him with G. William Miller, a Carter associate who worked closely with the president's economic team. [108]

Coordination of Fiscal and Monetary Policy

Although the organization of the Fed is designed to insulate it from outside influence, monetary policy is most effective when it is coordinated with the administration's fiscal policy. Both tools are seeking to promote economic stability and prosperity, but the effects of one may cancel, blunt, or distort the intended effects of the other if the president and the Fed do not cooperate. For example, the president may ask Congress to stimulate the economy by spending more than the government receives in revenues.

... to the President

ceptionally qualified to analyze and interpret economic developments, to appraise programs and activities of the government ... and to formulate and recommend national economic policy." Because the council does not represent a large bureaucratic body and has no responsibilities in operating the government other than preparing the president's annual economic report, Congress hoped that the CEA would have the time and independence to provide presidents with long-term, nonpartisan advice on economic policy and professional analysis of economic conditions. Traditionally, the CEA has been most concerned with promoting growth and managing the trade-off between inflation and unemployment.

The CEA's influence depends entirely on the president. If the president values its advice and involves it in decision making, the CEA can have considerable power because its three members and small staff of professional economists usually possess the greatest amount of economic expertise within an administration. Because of this expertise, however, CEA members can be vulnerable to charges from other economic advisers that they approach the realities of economic policy making from a perspective that is too theoretical. CEA members must, therefore, be careful to pay adequate attention to the president's political needs if they wish to retain their influence.

Office of Management and Budget

In 1921 Congress created the Bureau of the Budget to coordinate and modify the budget estimates of the executive departments. It was originally located within the Treasury Department but was placed under the newly created Executive Office of the President in 1939. In 1970 Richard Nixon expanded its staff and duties and renamed it the Office of Management and Budget (OMB).

OMB's primary function is to formulate an executive branch budget for the president that considers how much revenue the government is likely to raise through taxes and how much each federal agency and program should receive. OMB, therefore, continually analyzes the merits of budget requests and makes recommendations to the president on what funding should be cut, preserved, or expanded. The office is also responsible for budget forecasts that estimate the size of the budget deficit or surplus. The institutional bias of OMB has been to limit spending. This tendency is a result of OMB's role as the central budgetary control within the administration that must pare down the budget requests of department and agency heads who usually will seek as much funding as is politically possible for their unit.

The post of budget director has become highly politicized since the Nixon administration. Budget directors frequently testify before Congress and are involved in shaping and promoting the president's social agenda through their budget recommendations. David Stockman, budget director under Ronald Reagan from 1981 to 1985, epitomized the budget director's new role. President Reagan gave him a broad mandate to cut items from the budget in pursuit of smaller budget deficits. In the first six months of the Reagan administration he became not only the dominant presidential adviser on the budget within the administration, but also a symbol of Reagan's domestic budget cuts and social agenda that emphasized a more limited role for the federal government.

This requires the government to borrow funds, which increases competition for loans, thereby driving up interest rates. The higher interest rates, however, may offset the stimulative effects of the government's spending increases unless the Federal Reserve Board accommodates the president's fiscal policy by increasing the money supply.

The Fed has sometimes "leaned against the wind" to counter administration policies it considered wrong. In 1957, the Fed kept a tight reign on the money supply while the Eisenhower administration was pursuing a moderately expansionary fiscal policy. Similarly, the Fed fought inflation during the late 1960s while spending on the Vietnam War and Lyndon Johnson's Great Society social programs stimulated the economy.

The Fed may even use public pressure to attempt to change administration policies. In 1977 Fed chairman Arthur Burns testified against Jimmy Carter's tax cut proposals, raising the possibility that if the tax cuts were passed, the Fed would use monetary policy to offset their stimulative effect.[109] Fed chairman Alan Greenspan warned the incoming Bush administration through testimony before Congress on January 24, 1989, that the Fed would not tolerate an acceleration of inflation. George Bush and his economic advisers had placed a high priority on continued strong economic growth, but Greenspan indicated the Fed might slow growth in the near future to combat inflation, saying, "The Federal Reserve policy at this juncture might be well advised to err more on the side of restrictiveness than stimulus."

Presidents, therefore, generally try to coordinate their fiscal policies with the Fed to produce the best economic results and limit political friction between economic policy makers. Coordination is accomplished through informal meetings between the Fed chair and the president's top economic advisers. The Fed chair, the Treasury secretary, the budget director, and the chair of the CEA—a group known as the "quadriad"—usually will meet at least once a month to discuss coordination of fiscal and monetary policy. Any agreements forged out of these discussions, however, are nonbinding, and the Fed may pursue a monetary policy at odds with the administration's goals.

Proponents of greater executive control over monetary policy have proposed several reforms. The most radical would be to place the Federal Reserve under executive control and allow presidents and their advisers to set monetary policy in addition to performing their other economic functions. This reform would result in the greatest degree of coordination possible between fiscal and monetary policy, since the incumbent administration would be making both. It would, however, allow presidents to use monetary policy for political purposes. For example, presidents could quietly stimulate the economy through monetary policy in an election year to improve their chances of being re-elected.

A more modest reform that has been considered by Congress but never passed is to make the term of the Fed chair coincide with the president's term of office. This would improve coordination since the president would presumably enter office with a like-minded Fed chair. The chair, however, would retain independent control over monetary policy.[110]

International Economic Policy

The president's international economic powers have become increasingly important as nations have become more economically interdependent. Because of high volumes of trade, integrated financial markets, multinational corporations, and other factors that bind the world's economies, prosperous conditions in the United States cannot be sustained if other large economies, especially those of Western Europe and Japan, are ailing. Specific economic problems in other countries can be transferred to and from the U.S. economy. For example, inflation caused by one economic power's expansionary conditions can contribute to inflation in other countries because consumers faced with domestic inflation may increase their purchases of less expensive imports. This increased demand for foreign goods puts pressure on prices outside the inflationary country that contributes to worldwide inflation. Similarly, a recession in one country can contribute to slower economic growth in other countries because consumers in the country experiencing a recession will have to cut back on their purchases of imports.

Because of this shared economic destiny between industrial nations, presidents must function not just as national economic managers, but also as international economic coordinators. They dispatch the U.S. trade representative to international negotiations aimed at reducing trade barriers, oversee the Treasury Department's negotiations with other finance ministries about the value of major currencies, and announce U.S. economic policies to the international community.

Since 1975 presidents also have attended annual economic summits where the leaders of the major industrial nations have met to confer on broad issues of economic policy. These meetings, which are attended by the leaders of the United States, Japan, West Germany, France, Great Britain, Italy, and Canada (known collectively as the Group of Seven or G-7) have greatly increased international economic coordination. The summits have focused attention on the international component of economic policy, forced politicians to develop a better understanding of international economic issues, created a justification for frequent meetings between finance ministers and other economic officials, and provided a forum where economic matters can be discussed in the broader context of allied relations. Because the annual meetings compel the G-7 leaders to face one another, they have had a positive influence on free trade. The leader of a country that has erected protectionist trade barriers or taken other measures contrary to the interests of the group must justify those measures to the other leaders and face their collective pressure to reverse the action.

Trade Policy

President Ronald Reagan noted in his 1983 State of the Union address that "one out of every five jobs in our country depends on trade. We export over 20 percent of our industrial production, and 40 percent of our farmland produces for export." Given the importance of trade to the U.S. economy, one of the most important international economic goals of presidents has been to maximize U.S. access to foreign markets.

Because the Constitution gives Congress the power "to regulate Commerce with foreign Nations," the rules governing foreign trade are set by legislation. Since the depression, however, trade legislation has contained broad grants of power to the president to implement the laws through international negotiations and the implementation of tariffs and other trade barriers designed to force other countries to open up their markets to American products.

Congress has granted the executive broad trade powers because only the president has the authority to negotiate with foreign governments. Therefore, when Congress adopted the strategy of pursuing mutual reductions in tariffs through international negotiations in 1934, it had to turn to the president to carry out those negotiations. In addition, Congress wanted to isolate U.S. trade policy from pressures for protectionism from specific industries. Since individual members of Congress have to be concerned with the economic conditions in their states and districts, protectionist sentiments have tended to be stronger in Congress than in the executive branch. If a single industry such as agriculture or steel predominates in a congressional district, that district's representative often will be disposed to support protectionist measures for that industry. Political scientist Erwin Hargrove explained that by delegating power to the president Congress is able to respond to the local interests of its constituents without undermining the free trade position of the nation:

> Congress would rather not have responsibility for setting specific tariff levels because the flood of demands for individual industrial areas would be far too intense. Therefore, it has allowed the Executive to set such levels within parameters set by Congress. This permits members of Congress to make their requests in behalf of constituency interests and still permit the President to do what is needed for a national position on international trade.[111]

Throughout much of its history the U.S. economy has benefited from trade surpluses. In 1981, however, the U.S. trade position began to decline rapidly as U.S. exports failed to keep pace with imports. The following year the U.S. current account, a measure of the net flow of goods and services traded with other countries, dropped into deficit. By 1987 the current account deficit reached $154 billion. The large current account deficit cost the U.S. economy good jobs because Americans were buying so many products manufactured overseas. In addition, because the U.S. had to borrow to finance the trade imbalance, the current account deficit was increasing the U.S. dependence on foreign credit and adding to the debts of the nation.

These problems focused public attention on the trade deficit and increased pressure on Congress to pass legislation to protect American industries from foreign competition. In response to the mounting U.S. trade deficit, Congress enacted the Omnibus Trade Act in 1988, which mandated retaliatory responses to unfair foreign trade practices. President Reagan's firm support of free trade prevented Congress from enacting a more protectionist trade bill, but the persistence of the current account deficit, which improved to only about $140 billion in 1988 despite a decrease in the value of the dollar, sustained protectionist sentiments in Congress and among the American people. *(See box, 1988 Omnibus Trade Act, p. 272.)*

Protectionism

The primary question that trade policy must decide is whether to pursue free trade or whether to erect barriers that protect U.S. industries but ultimately risk reducing the overall flow of trade. Few economists or politicians would argue that the ideal trade environment for enhancing international prosperity is one in which nations can trade goods and services without trade barriers such as tariffs, import quotas, embargoes, and strict licensing procedures for importing goods. Yet even the most ardent free trade advocates recognize that the threat of protectionism is the most effective negotiating tool the government has to convince other nations to end their unfair trading practices. Appeals for protection from specific industries often have diverted national policy from the ideal of free trade. Nevertheless, since 1934, even when Congress has enacted bills to protect specific industries or to pry open foreign markets, policy makers have maintained the consensus that the U.S. economy will benefit from free trade.

Throughout U.S. history, tariffs have been a contentious political issue. The nation's first Treasury secretary, Alexander Hamilton, supported high tariffs, which he hoped would nurture the infant industries of the Northeast. Although the tariffs enacted during the Federalist era were not swept away when Thomas Jefferson took power in 1800, the pro-agrarian Democratic-Republicans favored trade policies that enhanced the ability of farmers to sell their products overseas.

During most of the nineteenth century the industrial and commercial interests of the North contended with the agricultural interests of the South over national tariff policy. Because the South was dependent on foreign markets for its agricultural products, it opposed tariffs that could trigger a retaliatory response from its foreign customers. In addition, tariffs raised the price of many goods the South needed to buy from foreign countries. The intersectional tensions over trade policy led to the nullification crisis in South Carolina in 1832. After Congress passed a high-tariff bill in 1832, the South Carolina state legislature passed an ordinance declaring the tariff void in that state. President Andrew Jackson, determined to assert federal authority, threatened to enforce the law in South Carolina with federal troops. Hostilities were averted when Jackson and South Carolina leaders accepted a compromise tariff. Tensions caused by the tariff issue remained, however, and eventually contributed to the secession of southern states in 1861 that brought on the Civil War.

For the rest of the nineteenth century, tariffs remained high as American industries desirous of protection grew and the protariff Republican party dominated national politics. Average U.S. tariff rates generally ranged from 35 to 50 percent of the cost of imports subject to tariffs. With the election of President Wilson in 1913, tariff policy was reversed. That year, with President Wilson's strong support, Congress enacted the Underwood-Simmons Tariff Act, which sharply cut tariffs. Wilson saw tariff reduction as a way to help American consumers, limit the influence of powerful probusiness lobbyists, and stimulate competition.

Table 3 Current Account Surplus or Deficit, 1950-1987 (billions of dollars)

Year	Current account surplus or deficit (−) [a]
1950	−1.8
1951	0.9
1952	0.6
1953	−1.3
1954	0.2
1955	0.4
1956	2.7
1957	4.8
1958	0.8
1959	−1.3
1960	2.8
1961	3.8
1962	3.4
1963	4.4
1964	6.8
1965	5.4
1966	3.0
1967	2.6
1968	0.6
1969	0.4
1970	2.3
1971	−1.4
1972	−5.8
1973	7.1
1974	2.0
1975	18.1
1976	4.2
1977	−14.5
1978	−15.4
1979	−1.0
1980	1.9
1981	6.3
1982	−8.7
1983	−46.2
1984	−107.0
1985	−116.4
1986	−141.4
1987	−154.0

Sources: Office of Management and Budget, Commerce Department, Treasury Department, 1988.

a. Net total of U.S. international trade in merchandise, services, and investments.

America's participation in World War I rekindled "America first" sentiments in the United States that led to a return of high tariffs. The Tariff Act of 1921 and the Fordney-McCumber Act of 1922, both supported by Republican president Warren Harding, returned tariffs roughly to their pre-1913 levels.

When the depression struck in 1929, the governments of the major industrialized nations reacted by erecting trade barriers to protect their domestic industries. In 1930 Congress passed the Smoot-Hawley Act, which established the highest tariffs the United States had ever erected. The trade war of the early 1930s strangled trade between nations until it was a small fraction of what it had been. Protectionist measures left the world to dig out of the depression without the benefits of international trade.[112]

1988 Omnibus Trade Act

On August 23, 1988, President Reagan signed the Omnibus Trade and Competitiveness Act of 1988. The act signaled Congress's determination to take a more activist role in trade policy and mandated a limited but significant change in the staunchly free trade policies of the Reagan administration.

Sentiment in Congress for an overhaul of trade legislation developed during the early 1980s as trade deficits grew and the Reagan administration refused to intervene in currency markets to push the dollar lower or take a discernibly tougher position toward other nations' unfair trade practices. In 1985, members of Congress began work on the trade bill, which proceeded slowly because of other economic priorities, the bill's broad scope, and administration resistance to some of its proposed provisions. Although the act evolved considerably from its inception, its major intent from the beginning was to increase the use of retaliatory trade measures and give Congress more control over trade policy. By strengthening the retaliatory measures already a part of U.S. trade law, Congress hoped to pry open foreign markets to ailing domestic industries by using the threat of restricting access to U.S. markets.

In 1987 both chambers passed separate trade bills with many protectionist features. Lawmakers realized, however, that they had to make the bill acceptable to the Reagan administration or their efforts would be nullified by a presidential veto they would have little hope of overriding. Negotiations between the two houses and the administration to produce a single bill resulted in a trade bill that was much less protectionist than its earlier versions. In particular, a highly publicized proposal by Rep. Richard Gephardt that would have required cuts in U.S. imports from countries that had trade surpluses with the United States and refused to moderate unfair trade practices was abandoned. Congress also gave the administration a five-year extension of the president's authority to negotiate trade agreements, a power delegated to the executive branch almost continuously since the 1930s.

Despite compromises made by Congress, President Reagan vetoed the bill on May 24, 1988, citing provisions requiring advanced notice of plant closings and restrictions on Alaskan oil exports. Congress passed an identical trade bill, minus the provisions cited by the president in July. The bill became law when President Reagan signed it in August.

The act's most significant provisions for U.S. trade were its mandating of retaliatory steps against violations of trade agreements or other "unjustifiable" trade practices by foreign countries and its shifting of much authority over trade policy from the president to the U.S. trade representative, a cabinet-level official appointed by the president who has functioned as the main U.S. negotiator at trade talks. Congress transferred the authority to decide whether a foreign trade practice was unfair and how to respond from the president to the trade representative.

Since the trade representative would still be a member of the president's administration, however, it was unlikely that the trade representative would seriously diverge from administration policy. In addition, although Congress required the trade representative to retaliate against unfair trade practices, the president retained the authority to block retaliation by issuing a waiver on one of several grounds. These included an agreement by the foreign government in question to stop its unfair practice or a determination by the president that the retaliatory measure could harm U.S. national security.

Nevertheless, Congress hoped that the shift of power would make retaliation more likely because the trade representative, who is required to testify before Congress and consult with legislators on trade matters, would be more accountable to Congress and more likely to implement tough responses to unfair trading practices. Ultimately, the direction of U.S. trade policy depended less on who possessed authority to develop it than on how voters saw foreign trade practices affecting the trade deficit and the domestic economy. If the American public came to perceive that foreign governments were to blame for U.S. economic problems, the pressures for retaliation and protectionism would be difficult for even the most strident advocates of free trade in Congress and the executive branch to resist.

International Trade Negotiations

As with many other areas of economic policy, the depression forced Congress and the president to reconsider the country's position on trade. Franklin Roosevelt proposed to stimulate trade and thereby the depressed American economy by negotiating mutual reductions in tariffs with U.S. trading partners. With the enthusiastic support of his secretary of state, Cordell Hull, Roosevelt asked the Democrat-controlled Congress to delegate him the authority to reduce U.S. tariffs up to 50 percent in return for equal tariff concessions by other nations. Despite nearly unanimous Republican opposition, Congress passed the Trade Agreements Act of 1934, which delegated this power to the president. Armed with new authority the Roosevelt administration negotiated bilateral agreements with many nations that cut tariffs and increased the flow of trade. The increased access to foreign markets that resulted helped stimulate the U.S. economy. After the initial success of Roosevelt's negotiations, congressional grants of authority to the president to negotiate mutual tariff reductions became a regular feature of U.S. trade policy.

After World War II, President Truman sought to establish more sweeping arrangements to reduce international protectionism. At the urging of the United States, 23 nations signed the General Agreement on Tariffs and Trade (GATT) in 1947. Since then most noncommunist nations have signed the agreement. Under GATT, mutilateral negotiations aimed at reducing trade barriers were to be held at regular intervals. The signatories also agreed to the "most-favored-nation" principle, which committed each nation to apply tariff rates equally to all the other GATT participants. In addition, the agreement prohibited certain restrictive trade practices such as import quotas and set up procedures to mediate trade disputes and implement sanctions against violators of the agreement.

Since 1947 GATT signatories have held eight multinational trade negotiation rounds. The first five rounds produced small but significant tariff reductions. In 1962 Congress passed the Trade Expansion Act with the strong support of the Kennedy administration. The act gave the president the broad authority to reduce or eliminate U.S. import duties in return for similar trade concessions from other countries. The sixth round of GATT, known as the "Kennedy Round," resulted in sharp mutual cuts in tariffs. Fifty-three nations agreed to cuts in tariffs on industrial products averaging more than 35 percent.[113] When the round ended in 1967, however, many industries in the United States and in other countries lobbied against further cuts in tariffs because they feared increased foreign competition.

Following the end of the Kennedy Round in 1967, dozens of bills with protectionist provisions were introduced in Congress. Few were passed, but the apex of trade barrier reduction clearly had been reached. Congress did not renew the president's authority to participate in multilateral trade negotiations, which had expired in 1967, until it passed the Trade Act of 1974 after the next GATT round was already under way.[114] Although this act extended the president's authority to negotiate reductions of trade barriers, it placed more restrictions on the president's power and reflected the growing pressures from U.S. domestic industries to retaliate against foreign unfair trading practices. The seventh round of GATT (Tokyo Round) and the present Uruguay Round have been far less successful in reducing tariff barriers than the Kennedy Round, although they have made some progress on eliminating nontariff barriers.

International Monetary Relations

When one nation imports goods from another, it usually must pay for those goods with the seller's currency. Consequently, the buyer must purchase the seller's currency at the prevailing exchange rate. Exchange rates affect a country's ability to export its goods because the higher its currency is valued on international markets, the more expensive its goods will be for foreign buyers. Since a dollar that is worth less relative to foreign currencies will make U.S. goods cheaper for foreigners to buy, intervention to lower the value of the dollar is the primary tool presidents have used to fight trade deficits.

Bretton Woods Agreement

After World War II the United States led the world in setting up an international monetary system that established stable exchange rates conducive to free trade. Forty-four nations signed an agreement at Bretton Woods, New Hampshire, in 1944 that made gold the standard by which currencies were valued. The Bretton Woods agreement established the International Monetary Fund (IMF) to oversee adjustments in exchange rates and the World Bank to provide loans for postwar reconstruction. The intention of the United States was to build a predictable international currency system that would prevent destabilizing fluctuations in exchange rates and deliberate currency devaluations that could threaten free trade.

Each member of the IMF was required to declare a "par" value for its currency in relation to the U.S. dollar, which was pegged to gold at $35 dollars per troy ounce. Official exchange rates of the world's currencies were not allowed to fluctuate more than 1 percent from their par value. Because the United States held most of the world's gold reserves and the U.S. dollar's value was backed by the government's pledge to convert dollars into gold, nations used the dollar as an international trading currency and as a reserve of wealth just like gold. In effect, the United States functioned as banker to the world.[115]

The Bretton Woods arrangement functioned well during the 1940s, 1950s, and early 1960s. The stability it produced brought an enormous increase in world trade and the resurgence of economies devastated by World War II. By the mid-1960s, however, the dollar's role as an international reserve currency was causing the United States economic problems. Because other nations wanted to hold dollars to trade and back up their own currencies, dollars flowed overseas but failed to return. The result was a growing U.S. balance-of-payments deficit that weakened international confidence in the dollar and led many foreign investors to exchange their dollars for gold. U.S. gold reserves fell from more than $23 billion in 1949 to just $10 billion in 1971.

In response to this problem, on August 15, 1971, Richard Nixon stunned the world by announcing that the U.S. Treasury would no longer convert dollars into gold. The dollar's value would be allowed to "float" to a level determined by international currency markets. Since other currencies depended on the dollar, they, too, would have to float. The dollar, which had been overvalued, declined against other currencies, making U.S. goods cheaper overseas.[116]

Nixon's decision ushered in a new era of international monetary relations that required a higher degree of coordination between governments. Although several countries proposed plans to salvage the Bretton Woods system, by 1973 all major currencies were floating. Nations found that currency values could not be left entirely to market forces because the markets produced sharp fluctuations in exchange rates as investors shifted large amounts of money from currency to currency in search of higher earnings. Moreover, the market forces did not always push exchange rates in the direction that was needed to prevent trade imbalances. Thus, between 1981 and 1985, despite a growing U.S. trade deficit that would have been slowed by a weaker dollar, the dollar's value increased as foreign investors converted their money to dollars to take advantage of the high interest rates, low inflation, and political stability to be found in the United States.

Managing the Value of the Dollar

Under the post-Bretton Woods system of floating exchange rates, governments may attempt to adjust the value of their currency through intervention in the currency markets. The United States and other governments intervene in currency markets through their central banks. If U.S. policy makers decide that the value of the dollar is too high they can lower its value by selling dollars on the open

In June 1988 in Toronto, President Reagan attended his eighth economic summit. Next to him, clockwise, are Canadian prime minister Mulroney; French president Mitterrand; West German chancellor Kohl; Italian premier de Mita; ECC president Delors; Japanese premier Takeshita; and British prime minister Thatcher.

Bill Fitz-Patrick, The White House

market. Conversely, a weak dollar can be strengthened by having the central bank shrink the supply by buying dollars on the open market.

Technically, the president has no role in intervention. It is the U.S. central bank—the Federal Reserve System—which makes the currency transactions that affect the value of the dollar. Yet it is difficult for even the Fed with its massive reserves to alter the value of the dollar without cooperation from the central banks of the other industrialized powers. Consequently, coordination of exchange rate policies between the major industrialized countries is necessary to control currency values effectively. The president, as chief economic manager and the official charged with negotiating with foreign countries, must oversee this coordination.

Negotiations with other nations on currency levels are usually led by the Treasury secretary and attended by representatives of the Federal Reserve Board of Governors. Currency levels are also frequently discussed by the president and the leaders of the G-7 nations at their annual economic summits. Negotiations between governments often have resulted in informal agreements to take concerted action to adjust exchange rates. In January 1989, for example, the major industrial nations agreed to slow the rise of the dollar, which was being pushed up near a previously agreed upon secret limit by rising interest rates in the United States that were attracting foreign capital. At the same time, West Germany wanted its currency to be held up because of fears in that country that a weaker mark would lead to inflation by increasing the costs of imports. The world's major central banks responded by buying marks with dollars, thereby holding down the dollar's rise and propping up the mark.[117]

The importance of currency intervention was illustrated dramatically in the early 1980s. The strong dollar had encouraged American consumers to buy foreign goods and made American goods too expensive overseas to compete with comparable foreign products, thus contributing to the growing U.S. trade deficit. During Ronald Reagan's first term the administration largely had ignored the dollar's value. The president maintained early in his term that

the strong dollar was a sign that his policies had restored international confidence in the U.S. economy.[118] Perhaps this was true, but with the current account deficit jumping from $46 billion in 1983 to $107 billion in 1984 the Reagan administration concluded that it had to act to bring down the value of the dollar. It therefore announced in January 1985, shortly after James Baker had taken over as Treasury secretary, that the U.S. would intervene in the currency markets to bring down the value of the dollar. U.S. intervention, sometimes with the cooperation of other central banks, succeeded in dramatically lowering the value of the dollar from the peak reached in February 1985. Although the lower dollar did not produce a reduction in the U.S. current account deficit until 1988, the U.S. trade problem would have been much worse without intervention.

Notes

1. Clinton Rossiter, *The American Presidency* (New York: Harcourt Brace, 1956), 21.
2. Harold M. Barger, *The Impossible Presidency: Illusions and Realities of Executive Power* (Glenview, Ill.: Scott, Foresman, 1984), 320.
3. Francis Russell, *The Shadow of Blooming Grove* (New York: McGraw-Hill, 1968), 559.
4. Richard Pious, *The American Presidency* (New York: Basic Books, 1979), 305.
5. Rudiger Dornbusch and Stanley Fischer, eds., *Macroeconomics*, 4th ed. (New York: McGraw-Hill, 1987), 450-451.
6. Michael P. Riccards, *A Republic, If You Can Keep It: The Foundation of the American Presidency, 1700-1800* (New York: Greenwood Press, 1987), 90.
7. Ibid., 91-97.
8. Jonathan Hughes, *American Economic History*, 2d ed. (Glenview, Ill.: Scott, Foresman, 1987), 195.
9. Riccards, *A Republic, If You Can Keep It*, 100-101.
10. Ibid., 101.
11. Hughes, *American Economic History*, 199.
12. James E. Anderson, *Politics and the Economy* (Boston: Little, Brown, 1966), 9.
13. Hughes, *American Economic History*, 195.

14. Anderson, *Politics and the Economy*, 9-10.
15. Ibid., 11-12.
16. Arthur M. Johnson, *The American Economy* (New York: Free Press, 1974), 52.
17. John F. Witte, "The President vs. Congress on Tax Policy," in *The President and Economic Policy*, ed. James P. Pfiffner (Philadelphia: Institute for the Study of Human Issues, 1986), 166.
18. Emmet John Hughes, *The Living Presidency* (Baltimore: Penguin Books, 1974), 216-217.
19. Louis Fisher, *The Politics of Shared Power: Congress and the Executive*, 2d ed. (Washington, D.C.: CQ Press, 1987), 192.
20. Anderson, *Politics and the Economy*, 123.
21. George C. Edwards III and Stephen J. Wayne, *Presidential Leadership, Politics and Policy Making* (New York: St. Martin's Press, 1985), 262.
22. Richard A. Watson and Norman C. Thomas, *The Politics of the Presidency*, 2d ed. (Washington, D.C.: CQ Press, 1988), 400.
23. Herbert Stein, *Presidential Economics* (New York: Simon and Schuster, 1984), 32-33.
24. Anthony S. Campagna, *U.S. National Economic Policy 1917-1985* (New York: Praeger, 1987), 101.
25. Pious, *The American Presidency*, 295.
26. Campagna, *U.S. National Economic Policy*, 131.
27. Ibid., 141.
28. Watson and Thomas, *Politics of the Presidency*, 405.
29. Campagna, *U.S. National Economic Policy*, 196.
30. Stein, *Presidential Economics*, 77.
31. Dorothy Buckton James, *The Contemporary Presidency*, 2d ed. (Indianapolis: Bobbs-Merrill, 1974), 94.
32. Campagna, *U.S. National Economic Policy*, 210-211.
33. Charles E. Jacob, "Macroeconomic Policy Choices of Postwar Presidents," in *The President and Economic Policy*, 65.
34. Campagna, *U.S. National Economic Policy*, 238-243.
35. Jacob, "Macroeconomic Policy Choices," 67.
36. Richard Nixon, *Six Crises* (New York: Doubleday, 1962), 309-310.
37. Jacob, "Macroeconomic Policy Choices," 67.
38. Stein, *Presidential Economics*, 102-106.
39. Campagna, *U.S. National Economic Policy*, 306-307.
40. Stein, *Presidential Economics*, 112.
41. Watson and Thomas, *Politics of the Presidency*, 405.
42. Pious, *The American Presidency*, 297.
43. Jacob, "Macroeconomic Policy Choices," 69.
44. James, *The Contemporary Presidency*, 96.
45. Campagna, *U.S. National Economic Policy*, 351.
46. James, *The Contemporary Presidency*, 103.
47. Ibid., 106.
48. Watson and Thomas, *Politics of the Presidency*, 407.
49. Stein, *Presidential Economics*, 213-214.
50. Campagna, *U.S. National Economic Policy*, 401-402.
51. Jacob, "Macroeconomic Policy Choices," 75.
52. Stein, *Presidential Economics*, 218.
53. Ibid., 231-232.
54. Jacob, "Macroeconomic Policy Choices," 74.
55. Campagna, *U.S. National Economic Policy*, 485-488.
56. Ibid., 486.
57. Stein, *Presidential Economics*, 255-256.
58. Mary H. Cooper, "Federal Budget Deficit," *Editorial Research Reports*, January 20, 1984, 50.
59. James P. Pfiffner, "The Crisis of Confidence in U.S. Economic Policy," in *The President and Economic Policy*, 10.
60. Cooper, "Federal Budget Deficit," 50-51.
61. The U.S. current account, the net total of international transactions including merchandise, services, and investments, plunged from a $6-billion surplus in 1981 to a $107-billion deficit in 1984. Despite the Reagan administration's support for a lower dollar in 1985, which improved trade figures by raising the cost of imports for Americans and making U.S. exports cheaper for foreign consumers, the current account deficit reached $154 billion in 1987 and had improved only to

about $140 billion in 1988.
62. Edward R. Tufte, *Political Control of the Economy* (Princeton, N.J.: Princeton University Press, 1978), 19-21.
63. Tufte, *Political Control of the Economy*, 7-9.
64. Nixon, *Six Crises*, 310-311.
65. Tufte, *Political Control of the Economy*, 29-33.
66. Watson and Thomas, *Politics of the Presidency*, 405.
67. James, *The Contemporary Presidency*, 106.
68. William R. Keech, "Elections and Macroeconomic Policy Optimization," *American Journal of Political Science* 24 (1980): 345-367.
69. Tufte, *Political Control of the Economy*, 143.
70. Dornbusch and Fischer, *Macroeconomics*, 442-443.
71. Watson and Thomas, *Politics of the Presidency*, 413-416.
72. Erwin C. Hargrove and Michael Nelson, *Presidents, Politics and Policy* (Baltimore: Johns Hopkins University Press, 1984), 190.
73. Kim Quaile Hill and John Patrick Plumlee, "Presidential Success in Budgetary Policymaking: A Longitudinal Analysis," *Presidential Studies Quarterly* 12 (Spring 1982): 174.
74. Edwards and Wayne, *Presidential Leadership*, 268.
75. Hill and Plumlee, "Presidential Success in Budgetary Policymaking," 175.
76. Pfiffner, "The Crisis of Confidence in U.S. Economic Policy," 2.
77. Joseph A. Pechman, *Federal Tax Policy* (Washington, D.C.: Brookings, 1983), 56-57.
78. Pious, *The American Presidency*, 322-324.
79. Fisher, *The Politics of Shared Power*, 199-201.
80. Ibid., 204-205.
81. Cooper, "Federal Budget Deficit," 48-52.
82. Ibid., 56.
83. Anderson, *Politics and the Economy*, 113.
84. Edwards and Wayne, *Presidential Leadership*, 263.
85. Hill and Plumlee, "Presidential Success in Budgetary Policymaking," 179.
86. Donald L. Robinson, *"To the Best of My Ability"* (New York: Norton, 1987), 210-211.
87. David Rapp,"Is Anyone Really Trying to Balance the Budget?" *Congressional Quarterly Weekly Report*, November 26, 1988, 3387.
88. Campagna, *U.S. National Economic Policy*, 471.
89. Ibid., 472.
90. Stein, *Presidential Economics*, 311-312.
91. Fisher, *The Politics of Shared Power*, 213.
92. Ibid., 212-213.
93. Witte, "The President vs. Congress on Tax Policy," 180.
94. Ibid., 180.
95. Pechman, *Federal Tax Policy*, 39.
96. Paul Peretz, "The Politics of Fiscal and Monetary Policy," in *The Politics of American Economic Policy Making*, ed. Paul Peretz (Armonk, N.Y.: Sharpe, 1987), 145.
97. Peretz, "Politics of Fiscal and Monetary Policy," 145-146.
98. Godfrey Hodgson, *All Things to All Men* (New York: Simon and Schuster, 1980), 227.
99. Neil H. Jacoby, "The President, the Constitution, and the Economist in Economic Stabilization," *History of Political Economy* 3 (Fall 1971): 411-412.
100. William J. Baumol and Alan S. Blinder, *Economics, Principles and Policy* (New York: Harcourt Brace Jovanovich, 1979), 218.
101. Alberta Sbragia, "Monetary Policy and Monetary Theory: The Poverty of Choice," in *The President and Economic Policy*, 222.
102. Peretz, "Politics of Fiscal and Monetary Policy," 149.
103. Dornbusch and Fischer, *Macroeconomics*, 439-446.
104. Peretz, "Politics of Fiscal and Monetary Policy," 149.
105. Edwards and Wayne, *Presidential Leadership*, 279.
106. Peretz, "Politics of Fiscal and Monetary Policy," 148.
107. Pious, *The American Presidency*, 315.
108. Michael Bradley, *Economics* (Glenview, Ill.: Scott, Foresman, 1980), 576-577.
109. Pious, *The American Presidency*, 313.

110. Jonas Prager, *Fundamentals of Money, Banking and Financial Institutions* (New York: Harper and Row, 1982), 297.
111. Erwin C. Hargrove, *The Power of the Modern Presidency* (Philadelphia: Temple University Press, 1974), 159.
112. Miroslav Nincic, *United States Foreign Policy, Choices and Trade-offs* (Washington, D.C.: CQ Press, 1988), 334-335.
113. I.M. Destler, *Making Foreign Economic Policy* (Washington, D.C.: Brookings, 1980), 134.
114. Charles W. Kegley and Eugene R. Wittkopf, *American Foreign Policy, Pattern and Process* (New York: St. Martin's Press, 1979), 146-147.
115. Nincic, *United States Foreign Policy*, 337-338.
116. James, *The Contemporary Presidency*, 117-118.
117. Walter S. Mossberg, "Dollar Selling Aimed at Curbing Its Rise," *Wall Street Journal*, January 12, 1989, A2.
118. Mary H. Cooper, "Dollar Diplomacy," *Editorial Research Reports*, March 13, 1987, 118.

Selected Bibliography

Anderson, James E. *Politics and the Economy*. Boston: Little, Brown, 1966.

Barger, Harold M. *The Impossible Presidency: Illusions and Realities of Executive Power*. Glenview, Ill: Scott, Foresman, 1984.

Campagna, Anthony S. *U.S. National Economic Policy 1917-1985*. New York: Praeger, 1987.

Dornbusch, Rudiger, and Stanley Fischer, eds. *Macroeconomics*. 4th ed. New York: McGraw-Hill, 1987.

Fisher, Louis. *The Politics of Shared Power: Congress and the Executive*. 2d ed. Washington, D.C.: CQ Press, 1987.

Hughes, Jonathan. *American Economic History*. 2d ed. Glenview, Ill.: Scott, Foresman, 1987.

Pechman, Joseph A. *Federal Tax Policy*. Washington, D.C.: Brookings, 1983.

Peretz, Paul, ed. *The Politics of American Economic Policy Making*. Armonk, N.Y.: Sharpe, 1987.

Pfiffner, James P., ed. *The President and Economic Policy*. Philadelphia: Institute for the Study of Human Issues, 1986.

Pious, Richard. *The American Presidency*. New York: Basic Books, 1979.

Stein, Herbert. *Presidential Economics*. New York: Simon and Schuster, 1984.

Tufte, Edward R. *Political Control of the Economy*. Princeton, New Jersey: Princeton University Press, 1978.

Watson, Richard A., and Norman C. Thomas. *The Politics of the Presidency*. 2d ed. Washington, D.C.: CQ Press, 1988.

Index